POWER

ESSENTIAL WORKS OF
FOUCAULT
1954–1984

PAUL RABINOW
SERIES EDITOR

Ethics
Edited by Paul Rabinow

Aesthetics, Method, and Epistemology
Edited by James D. Faubion

Power
Edited by James D. Faubion

MICHEL FOUCAULT

POWER

Edited by
JAMES D. FAUBION

Translated by
ROBERT HURLEY AND OTHERS

ESSENTIAL WORKS OF
FOUCAULT
1954–1984

THE NEW PRESS
NEW YORK

© 1994 by Editions Gallimard.
Compilation, introduction, and new translations © 2000 by The New Press.

No part of this book may be reproduced, in any form, without written permission from the publisher. The "Note on Terms and Translations" section beginning on page xlii is an extension of this page.

Published in the United States by The New Press, New York, 2000
Distributed by W.W. Norton & Company, Inc., New York

LIBRARY OF CONGRESS CATALOGING-IN-PUBLICATION DATA

Foucault, Michel.
   [Selections. English. 1997]
   The essential works of Foucault, 1954–1984 / Paul
Rabinow, series editor.
     p. cm.
   Includes bibliographical references and index.
   Contents: 1. Ethics— 2. Aesthetics, method, and
epistemology— 3. Power.
   ISBN 1–56584–257–X (hc.)
   1. Philosophy, French—20th century. I. Rabinow,
Paul. II. Title.
B2430.F722E5 2000
 194—dc21   96–31819

Selections from *Dits et écrits, 1954–1984*, ed. Daniel Defert and François Ewald, with the assistance of Jacques Lagrange (Paris: Editions Gallimard, 1994).

The New Press is grateful for support of this publication from the French Ministry of Culture.

The New Press was established in 1990 as a not-for-profit alternative to the large, commercial publishing houses currently dominating the book publishing industry. The New Press operates in the public interest rather than for private gain, and is committed to publishing, in innovative ways, works of educational, cultural, and community value that are often deemed insufficiently profitable.

www.thenewpress.com

Book design by Paul Carlos
Printed in the United States of America

9 8 7 6 5 4 3

CONTENTS

Series preface by *Paul Rabinow*
vii

Acknowledgments
ix

Introduction by *Colin Gordon*
xi

Note on Terms and Translations
xlii

Truth and Juridical Forms
1

The Politics of Health in the Eighteenth Century
90

Preface to *Anti-Oedipus*
106

Truth and Power
111

The Birth of Social Medicine
134

Lives of Infamous Men
157

About the Concept of the "Dangerous Individual" in
Nineteenth-century Legal Psychiatry
176

Governmentality
201

Questions of Method
223

Interview with Michel Foucault
239

"Omnes et Singulatim": Toward a Critique of Political Reason
298

The Subject and Power
326

Space, Knowledge, and Power
349

Contents

The Risks of Security
365

What Is Called "Punishing"?
382

Interview with *Actes*
394

The Political Technology of Individuals
403

Pompidou's Two Deaths
418

Summoned to Court
423

Letter to Certain Leaders of the Left
426

The Proper Use of Criminals
429

Lemon and Milk
435

Open Letter to Mehdi Bazargan
439

For an Ethic of Discomfort
443

Useless to Revolt?
449

So Is It Important to Think?
454

Against Replacement Penalties
459

To Punish Is the Most Difficult Thing There Is
462

The Moral and Social Experience of the Poles Can No Longer
Be Obliterated
465

Confronting Governments: Human Rights
474

Index
477

Michel Foucault provides a splendid definition of work: "That which is susceptible of introducing a significant difference in the field of knowledge, at the cost of a certain difficulty for the author and the reader, with, however, the eventual recompense of a certain pleasure, that is to say of access to another figure of truth."[1] Diverse factors shape the emergence, articulation, and circulation of a work and its effects. Foucault gave us intellectual tools to understand these phenomena. In Michel Foucault's *Essential Works*, we use these very tools to understand his own work. Though he intended his books to be the core of his intellectual production, he is also well known for having made strategic use of a number of genres—the book and the article to be sure, but also the lecture and the interview. Indeed, few modern thinkers have used such a wide array of forms in so skillful a fashion, making them an integral component in the development and presentation of their work. In this light, our aim in this series is to assemble a compelling and representative collection of Foucault's written and spoken words outside those included in his books.

Foucault died on June 25, 1984, at age fifty-seven, of AIDS, just days after receiving the first reviews of the second and third volumes of *The History of Sexuality*, in the hospital. A year previous to his death, when he was showing no signs of illness, he had written a letter indicating that he wanted no posthumous publications; through the course of complex negotiations between those legally responsible to him, intellectually engaged with him, and emotionally close to him, it was decided that this letter constituted his will. He left behind, as far as we know, no cache of unpublished texts; we must conclude, then, that his papers were "in order." Ten years later, Editions Gallimard published *Dits et écrits*, well over three thousand pages of texts, organized chronologically. The editors, Daniel Defert and François Ewald, sought to collect all of Foucault's published texts (prefaces, introductions, presentations, interviews, articles, interventions, lectures, and so on) not included in his books. We have made a selection, eliminating overlapping or repetition of different versions of similar materials. Likewise, a number of the lectures and courses will in time be published separately in English.

What we have included in this and the previous two volumes are the writings that seemed to us central to the evolution of Foucault's thought. We have organized them thematically. Selecting from this corpus was a formidable responsibility that proved to be a challenge and a pleasure. Many of these texts were previously unavailable in English. In broad lines, the organization of the series follows one proposed by Foucault himself when he wrote: "My objective has been to create a history of the different modes by which, in our culture, human beings are made subjects. My work has dealt with three modes of objectification which transform human beings into subjects."[2] In Volume One, following his course summaries from the Collège de France, which provide a powerful synoptic view of his many unfinished projects, the texts address "the way a human being turns him- or herself into a subject."[3] Volume Two is organized around Foucault's analysis of "the modes of inquiry which try to give themselves the status of the sciences."[4] Science, for Foucault, was a domain of practices constitutive of experience as well as of knowledge. Consequently, this volume treats the diverse modes of representations, of signs, and of discourse. Finally, Volume Three contains texts treating "the objectivizing of the subject in dividing pratices,"[5] or, more generally, power relations.

Paul Rabinow

NOTES

1 Foucault, "Des Travaux," in *Dits et écrits* (Paris: Gallimard, 1994), vol. 4, p. 367.

2 Foucault, "The Subject and Power," in *Michel Foucault: Beyond Structuralism and Hermeneutics*, 2d ed., Hubert Dreyfus and Paul Rabinow (Chicago: University of Chicago Press, 1983), p. 208.

3 Ibid.

4 Ibid.

5 Ibid.

ACKNOWLEDGMENTS

I would like to thank Zeynep Gursel for her role in editing this volume. Thanks, too, to Mia Fuller for her help with the translations and for her bibliographical sleuthing. Paul Rabinow and I offer special thanks to Colin Gordon, who selected the texts for the volume and provided us with a draft of the introduction. Mr. Gordon was to have served as editor, but was unable to complete the project. I have accordingly emended the manuscript, and we have jointly revised Mr. Gordon's introductory essay for publication here.

—JDF

INTRODUCTION

———

Foucault did not characterize himself as a political theorist or philosopher and wrote no text intended to sum up his political thought. As Isaiah Berlin correctly observed, Foucault was not a Left intellectual at all, if by that one means a thinker with a political manifesto to put forward. Foucault was, however, a person whose work contains a powerful, original, and coherent body of political ideas, which it is well worth trying to see in full and as a whole, for he was a courageous, ingenious, and creative political actor and thinker. This volume assembles Foucault's own writings and interviews on the questions of power and the political from the last twelve years of his life, when he became, in France and sometimes beyond, an increasingly influential figure as a thinker with a public voice—what in France is called an "intellectual." "Power" was not the rubric of a separate compartment in Foucault's work, so it is preferable by far to read this volume in company with *Essential Works of Foucault, 1954–1984* volumes I and II, *Ethics* and *Aesthetics, Method, and Epistemology*. Later on we will try to sketch the intrinsic links between Foucault's thinking about these other axes of concern.

The pieces collected here fall into an interesting variety of categories. There are interviews where Foucault is explaining a recent book (see pp. 429, 435, and 443)—and, sometimes, as in the extended discussion with Trombadori (see pp. 239), answering to a critical inquisition on a much longer passage of his career. These papers stand as small but strategic connecting blocks within the

edifice of Foucault's research—the paper on the "Dangerous Individual," for example, and the Tanner lectures (see pp. 298) setting out the notions of "pastoral power" and "governmental
rationality." The four Brazilian lectures from 1974 on ("Truth and
Juridical Forms," published here in English for the first time) fill
a different kind of gap by providing a Nietzschean prologue and
variant working draft for the book *Discipline and Punish*, published in France a year later. The 1976 interview with two Italian
friends, "Truth and Power," and the 1982 papers on "The Subject
and Power," published by two American friends, are successive,
classic statements—the latter certainly definitive—of Foucault's
whole interest in the topic of power and his view of how power
can be studied. There are debates, like the discussion with the
group of historians in "Questions of Method," where critical
thrusts are parried or sidestepped but, more importantly, where
positions are cogently argued on the way intellectual and ethico-
political ends and responsibilities can, and should, connect with
one another. Another group of discussion-interviews features exchanges of ideas about what is to be done in some problem areas
of public policy touched on in his critical and investigative writings, such as penal justice or the reform of the welfare state (see
pp. 365, 394, 459, and 462).

One thread running through these discussions is a series of statements on the role of intellectuals—what Foucault thinks they may
or should not do, what should and should not be expected from
them. He considers how the public function and the utterance of
expert or thinker may be connected at the deepest or most universal level, at least within the Western tradition, to the vocation of
philosophy and the public role of the "truth-teller" (the theme explored in some of his last lectures, entitled "The Courage of
Truth"), to the problems of power (including the power of truth)
and to what he views as the persistent idea in Western culture of a
necessary linkage between the "manifestation of truth" and the "exercise of sovereignty." In some of these pieces Foucault discusses,
in immediate and practical terms, how intellectuals and citizens
should deal with the holders of governmental power (see pp. 394,
443, 454, and 474).

Last but not least, we have included a series of some of Foucault's shortest (and potentially most ephemeral) writings, the writing of the intellectual in action: letters, manifestos, or newspaper articles published to intervene in or address a live political issue—such as the right to abortion, the death penalty and judicial scandal, revolts and liberties in Spain, Poland, and Iran, a political extradition, law-and-order policy, the boat people. Some contextual information, compiled by Foucault's excellent French editors, François Ewald and Daniel Defert, has been included to set the contemporary and local background of some of these interventions. It is never easy to predict how far such writings will retain their original force across distances of time and space. Moreover, anyone who cares for Foucault and his work must feel some diffidence about the risks of any hagiographic commentary that glamorizes or attributes exemplary status to the intellectual role as he practiced it. But the issues Foucault wrote about are still quite recognizable and relevant. Some of the stereotyped views of Foucault still current in the English-speaking academic world have portrayed him as a thinker incapable of coherent practical action or viable moral utterance. The comprehensive curriculum vitae documented in *Dits et écrits* clearly shows the opposite to be the case. It is a matter of history that the Socialist government elected in 1981 abolished the death penalty, liberalized the law of political asylum, and introduced reforms to penal justice and the rule of law. Foucault was, by general consent, one of the voices within France over the previous decade that seemed to have most effectively stirred the Left politicians' reforming will around these subjects.

One of the most arresting of these documents to reread today is "Letter to Certain Leaders of the Left," written in 1978. This concerns the West German lawyer Klaus Croissant, who defended the members of the Baader-Meinhof left-wing terrorist organization. On being charged by the West German authorities with complicity with his own defendants, Croissant sought asylum in France. The conservative French government, with minimal procedural delay, extradited Croissant to the West German police, and proceeded to prosecute the private French citizens who had sheltered the fugitive lawyer in France. Foucault asked the (unnamed) French politicians of the Left—principally, no doubt, François Mitterrand—to declare their position, as a would-be government, on this affair.

His article emphasized, with feeling, the fundamental value and sanctity of actions of private solidarity and moral comfort to political fugitives.

THE EMERGENCE OF POWER

Foucault's work in the seventies was an innovation, and perhaps the most real and important one of its time. It was, perhaps, so innovative that its contribution could be accepted and used only within a Left transformed and renewed beyond recognition. In the short term, political events seemed to take a different turn. The period around 1977–80 in France was one in which the politico-intellectual space formed by the Communist Party, its Maoist, anarchist, and Trotskyist rivals, and their respective cadres, fellow travelers, dissidents, and renegades, passed through a process of rapid contraction, not to say implosion. Although Foucault did not like to play the role of ideological traffic policeman, he was one of the most prominent thinkers to make clear during this period the view that Left values do not prohibit one from being anticommunist or compel one to desire revolution.

Discipline and Punish brought Nietzsche to the aid of Marx; what *Capital* had done for the study of relations of production, it proposed to do for relations of power—duly recognizing, of course, the profoundly material interconnection of the two factors. In his analysis of trends of penal-reform thought in England and France in the late eighteenth century, Foucault is explicit about the economic interests driving the pursuit of more efficient policing and penal policies, for example, in the London docks. What, however, was controversial about an analysis suggesting that techniques of power such as discipline and supervision have, as techniques, their distinct existence as historical factors was the readily available inference that the same techniques of power may be made to serve more than one political or social interest. The fateful point in Foucault's analysis of the origin of the modern penitentiary prison is the quote from Jeremy Bentham, remarking that his model Panopticon prison would work equally well to control its prisoners regardless of who occupied the darkened supervisory space of its central control tower. The relevance of the point to the history of communist states and parties did not need further spelling out to be grasped by Foucault's readers. Yet Foucault's main point was not about the nature of communist power but, rather, about the presence in modern history of a repertoire of techniques of power which do not bear the distinctive emblem of the regime—socialist, communist, fascist—that uses them. From legislation against dangerous minorities to concentration camps, Foucault points out that the liberal, democratic West has generally been in the vanguard of technical invention, and its experts—for example in criminology—have not uncommonly shared their expertise with other regimes concerned with the same problems. One of the messages of Foucault's book is, therefore, that the apparent neutrality and political invisibility of techniques of power is what makes them so dangerous.

In nineteenth-century France, he argues, bourgeoisie and police used a "divide and rule" tactic against the urban masses, cultivating and heightening the gap between the respectable proletarianized "plebs," who had passed through the training school of factory discipline, and the lumpen category of the criminal, marginal, and precarious fringes of the reserve army. Prisons and police, Foucault argued, worked deliberately to create a well-defined criminal subclass that could be drawn upon when needed for strike-breaking or counterrevolutionary violence. Encouraged by Marx and Engels, the working class came to value the regime of the factory as its training school as a disciplined political force, while taking correspondingly less interest in the fate of the lumpen marginals and the problems of penal justice. In the France of the early seventies, Foucault evidently saw as consequences of this historical legacy the marked lack of sympathy of the old communist Left for some of the causes and struggles in which he then found himself actively involved.

Foucault was interested in the possibility of gaining, helped by historical analysis, new and more effective political ways of seeing. These new ways of seeing concerned, in particular, the relations of power and knowledge, and their respective relation to "the subject." He said in 1975: "I have been trying to make visible the constant articulation I think there is of power on knowledge and of knowledge on power. We should not be content to say that power has a need for a certain discovery, a certain form of knowledge, but we should add that the exercise of power creates and causes to emerge new objects of knowledge and accumulates new bodies of information. . . . The exercise of power perpetually creates knowledge and, conversely, knowledge constantly induces effects of power."¹ The knowledges that Foucault particularly studied within this scenario were the theories and disciplines that, in French parlance, had come to be grouped over the past two centuries under the heading of the "human sciences"—knowledges such as psychology, sociology, psychiatry, psychoanalysis, and criminology, together with some aspects of medicine. In *Discipline and Punish* and *The History of Sexuality* Volume One, as earlier in *Madness and Civilization* and *The Birth of the Clinic*, he was intent to show how closely the emergence of these forms of knowledge was enmeshed in the problems and practices of power, the social government and management of individuals. Early in his work, Foucault had pointed out that the idea of a scientific knowledge of the person as an individual is a relatively recent modern project. Here, he set out to show how in recent Western history the knowable individual has been the individual caught in relations of power, as that creature who is to be trained, corrected, supervised, controlled.

This analysis was not without a perceptible and astringent critical edge. Foucault wrote as an admirer and continuer of Nietzsche's genealogy of morals, tracing the mundane and ignoble historical origins of Western ideas and values. Foucault's project was certainly not the discrediting or devaluation of science in general. Indeed one of his aims was to break with a Marxist theory of ideology that denounced those forms of false bourgeois knowledge designed to mask the realities of exploitation in capitalist society (while, conversely, identifying the true path of Marxist science with the just cause of the proletariat). Foucault was interested in the role of knowledges as useful and necessary to the exercise of power because they were practically serviceable, not because they were false. He had developed for this purpose an analysis of "discourses," identifiable collections of utterances governed by rules of construction and evaluation which determine within some thematic area what may be said, by whom, in what context, and with what effect.

In *Discipline and Punish*, Foucault draws from this kind of analysis some caustic conclusions about our ways of existing and knowing ourselves as individuals. The dignity and gravity of our self-concern as human "subjects," knowing and knowable beings, coexists with and is rooted in a less noble aspect of our modern condition as individuals whose conduct and normality is subject to constant and pervasive supervision.

Foucault's work subverts and challenges a certain modern version of enlightenment, made up of morally and intellectually validated schemes of social improvement, therapy and order, which operate by identifying and correcting various forms of individual deviation from a norm. From the viewpoint of a contemporary culture where the right to deviate is being vigorously asserted by a set of new social constituencies, his analysis casts a new and sometimes cold light on a series of modern alliances between moralization, science, and power. It is, in a way that is characteristic and perhaps paradigmatic of its time, an exercise in extending our capacity for suspicion, or at least for vigilance and doubt.

Foucault wanted to generate doubt and discomfort, and to help stimulate a wider process of reflection and action leading to other and more tolerable ways of thinking and acting. Not surprisingly, especially in the period of his growing international celebrity following the publication of *Discipline and Punish*, all this generated considerable controversy and criticism, some of it acrimonious and polemical. One section of international academia is content to this day to assert that Foucault considered truth to be no more than an effect of power, that his thought is a wholesale and nihilistic rejection of the values of the Enlightenment, that he and his work are incapable of contributing to any form of rational and morally responsible action. Readers can find in this volume Foucault's own responses to such charges, and reach their own conclusions, but I will provide a few basic clarifications here. Foucault convincingly disavows any general intention through his analyses of discrediting or invalidating science in general, or any specific science: the implication of psychiatry, for example, in institutions and practices of power "in no way impugns the scientific validity or the therapeutic effectiveness of psychiatry; it does not endorse psychiatry, but neither does it invalidate it."[2] Some of his work in the sixties is about the definition of the successive thresholds of scientificity which a discourse or domain of knowledge may pass through in the course of its historical development. For a large part of his work, Foucault is demonstrably in close intellectual proximity to the kind of history and philosophy of science practiced in France by his predecessor and mentor Georges Canguilhem. Foucault is not a relativist or a solipsist, but he does not believe that knowledge confers ultimate acquaintance with reality, or that means of verification used to determine truth are available to us in forms which we know to be definitive. Truth, Foucault says, is "a thing of this world"—meaning that truth exists or is given and recognized only in worldly forms, through actual experiences and modes of verification; and meaning also that truth is a serious matter and a serious force in our world, and that there is work for us to do in investigating the presence and effects of truth in the history of our societies.

From time to time, as we have seen, Foucault found it necessary to disavow any direct attempt through his work to refute or discredit currently existing forms of knowledge or disciplines such as psychiatry or criminology, whose historical origins are touched on in *Madness and Civilization* and *Discipline and Punish*. He does on occasion express a clear opinion that the human sciences are not, and are probably not capable of becoming, sciences in the same epistemological sense as the physical sciences, and *The Order of Things* contains a famous speculation that the human sciences as we know them could disappear. Even here, though, it is important to realize that Foucault is not using scientificity as a judicial category. The human sciences are not to be condemned because they are not sciences like physics, and their possible disappearance is not predicated on the emergence of a more genuinely scientific alternative. Foucault insists that a historical analysis of its origins has no forensic bearing on the evaluation of a form of knowledge. Commenting on the irate reactions of some psychiatrists or criminologists to his book, he remarks that a physicist might be intrigued if a historian were able to demonstrate the implication of his science's beginnings in some odious or sordid episode of human history but would by no means feel thereby threatened in terms of the scientific value or status of his own work.

One of the key clarifying points Foucault makes is that what is most interesting about links between power and knowledge is not the detection of false or spurious knowledge at work in human affairs but, rather, the role of knowledges that are valued and effective because of their reliable instrumental efficacy. Foucault often uses the French word *savoir*—a term for knowledge with connotations of "know-how" (a way to make a problem tractable or a material manageable)—for this middle sort of knowledges, which may fall short of rigorous scientificity but command some degree of ratification within a social group and confer some recognized instrumental benefit. The reason the combining of power and knowledge in society is a redoubtable thing is not that power is apt to promote and exploit spurious knowledges (as the Marxist theory of ideology has argued) but, rather, that the rational exercise of power tends to make the fullest use of knowledges capable of the maximum instrumental efficacy. What is wrong or alarming about the use of power is not, for Foucault, primarily or especially the fact that a wrong or false knowledge is being used. Conversely, power and the use of knowledge by power are not guaranteed to be safe, legitimate, or salutory because (as an optimistic rationalist tradition extending from the Enlightenment to Marxism has inclined some to hope) the knowledge that guides or instrumentalizes the exercise of power is valid and scientific. Nothing, including the exercise of power, is evil in itself—but everything is dangerous. To be able to detect and diagnose real dangers, we need to avoid equally the twin seductions of paranoia and universal suspicion, on the one hand, and the compulsive quest for foundationalist certainties and guarantees, on the other—both of which serve to impede or dispense us from the rational and responsible work of careful and specific investigation.

THE PRODUCTIVITY OF POWER

The two ideas that came to guide Foucault's own investigation were those of the *productivity of power* (power relations are integral to the modern social productive apparatus, and linked to active programs for the fabricated part of the collective substance of society itself) and the *constitution of subjectivity through power relations* (the individual impact of power relations does not limit itself to pure repression but also comprises the intention to teach, to mold conduct, to instill forms of self-awareness and identities). In addition to contesting the neo-Marxian idea, current at the time, that (bourgeois, capitalist) power is maintained partly through the propagation of pseudo-knowledges or ideologies, Foucault also wanted to challenge the neo-Freudian idea that power acts like a lawgiver that forbids and represses.

For some, this seems to lend itself to the objection that Foucault so far exaggerates the effectiveness or success of the panoptic schemes of society's would-be programmers as to produce a dystopian vision of modern society in which aspirations for progress are either hopeless or discredited. Foucault's answer was already implicit in the closing words of *Discipline and Punish*: "In this central and centralized humanity . . . we must hear the rumble of battle." Awakening ourselves to the real world of power relations is awakening ourselves to a world of endemic struggle. The history of power is also a memory of struggles and therefore, potentially at least, a reawakening to refusals and new struggles—not least by showing how contingent and arbitrary the given conditions of the present are which we so readily take for granted.

Much could be, and has been, written about the method of inquiry Foucault practiced since *Discipline and Punish*. One can identify some of the features of this method which Foucault himself felt were important. One key point is the emphasis on the *mobility* of the objects analyzed: specific kinds of human practice that change over time and the events that punctuate and shape their history. A second feature is the *multiplicity* of objects, domains, layers, and strata involved in the network of cause and determination Foucault tries to trace—as well as the absence of a privileged or fundamental causal factor. A third important feature of the power–knowledge frame of analysis was the *intentionality* and *reversibility* of the social realities that power–knowledge relations contribute to producing and shaping: these realities, as Foucault put it, always contain in themselves a certain necessary ingredient of thought—thought that analysis can show to be contingent and contestable. Foucault was always at pains to say that resistance is an endemic fact in the world of power relations. Yet, for some readers' tastes, he did not give the right answers about who or what resists power, and why. Although he was passionately exercised by the question, he may have thought it had no single, definitive answer, because the answer is everywhere: There is always something in the social body, and in each person, which evades or wrestles with others' attempt to act on our own ways of acting. Foucault annoyed some political commentators with his Nietzschean refusal to say, in general terms, what principle legitimates a just resistance—here as elsewhere, he was an antifoundationalist. But we may guess he did not entirely agree with Tocqueville who, reflecting on "the source of this passion for political liberty," concluded that the question must in some sense necessarily remain unanswered: "Do not ask me to analyse this sublime taste: it is one which can only be experienced." Foucault's need to understand, for instance, what motivated a dissident in the Soviet bloc to risk his or her life in a nonviolent act of refusal was, as we will try to show, a powerful motive of his later political and ethical investigations.

THE HYPOTHESIS OF WAR

The question Foucault set out to explore in his 1976 lectures at the Collège de France was, indeed, characteristic of the political conjuncture of the period and the intentions of his preceding work to contribute to it. It was the testing of the validity of what might be called the "hypothesis of war"—the idea that the notion of war or struggle could serve as the tool par excellence of political analysis. These remarkable and astonishingly rich and original lectures are due to appear shortly in a complete English-language edition (following earlier editions in Italy and France) and cannot be adequately summarized here.[5]

The course began with two lectures (subsequently well-known, through publication in Italian and English) in which Foucault defined his current positions in methodology, critized the dominance in political theory of juridical notions of legitimation, political justice, and rights, and rehearsed in sympathetic terms the heuristic idea, already developed in *Discipline and Punish*, that politics can be regarded as war continued by other means.

In the event, the continuation and conclusion of the course did not quite provide the philosophical celebration of a Nietzschean-Leftist militant ideal that the opening lectures might have led one to expect (or fear). Foucault's way of showing the "hypothesis of war" at work was to do a genealogy of its proponents, starting from the English and French authors of the seventeenth and eighteenth centuries (notably John Lilburne, Henri Comte de Boulainvilliers, and Abbé de Mably) who produced militant rewritings of national history focused on interpretations of historical conquests (Roman, Frankish, and Norman) and the historical wrongs committed and suffered in and following these warlike episodes by the ancestors of the social classes and estates of the contemporary nation. Characteristic of these authors was the denunciation of the false legal titles to sovereignty claimed by the victors, and the call for a final battle to throw off the yoke of conquest. Foucault succeeds in tracing a strand of influence from these writers, by way of the ideas of the French Revolution, down to the French historians of class struggle who influenced Marx, but also down to nineteenth-century theories of racial struggle. By their conclusion, then, the lectures not only provided the promised historical celebration of militant thought but also exposed the limitations and immense dangers of that style of thought through its implication for the history of revolutionary class warfare and state racism. As Foucault makes it into the object of a historical analysis (albeit one couched as a "eulogy" [*éloge*]) the idea of a militant critique that exposes power relations in their nakedness and uncovers as their actual basis the arbitrariness of a primal act of usurpation becomes problematic as to both its reliability and its consequences. *Discipline and Punish* contains a line of argument in which one might sense a faint trace of Lilburne or Boulainvilliers, to the effect (crudely summarized) that progressive Western societies have ostensibly operated for two centuries on principles of liberty and the rule of law, while effectively operating on a basis of coercive *dressage* and disciplinary order. Foucault continued for several years to develop in both analytical and polemical modes his concern—especially during the continuing period of conservative government in France up to 1981—that the coupling of "law" and "order" in current governmental practice and policy was incoherent and uncontrolled, and therefore both unworkable and dangerous. For a polemical statement, see the *Le Monde* piece "Lemon and Milk;" for a historical analysis, see "About the Concept of the 'Dangerous Individual' in Nineteenth-century Legal Psychiatry."

On the other hand, though, beginning around the time of the socialist–communist Left's defeat in parliamentary elections in 1978, Foucault's work carries a message to a constituency on the Left that an oppositional discourse of pure denunciation was likely to prove neither analytically effective nor electorally convincing.

GOVERNMENTALITY

Foucault's lectures at the Collège de France in 1978 and 1979, one of which, "Governmentality," is reproduced here (together with some later American lectures—"Omnes et Singulatim" and "The Political Technology of Individuals"—which recapitulate much of this material), were in part an immediate response to a contemporary political fact, namely, the striking simultaneous ascendancy in Western Europe in the governments of Helmut Schmidt and Valéry Giscard d'Estaing of the discourse and doctrine of economic neoliberalism. After a period around 1970 when conservatives had diagnosed symptoms of a "crisis of governability" in the discrediting of elected politicians and the expansion of civil disobedience and protest, and following the impacts on Western economies of the two oil price "shocks" of 1973 and 1976, these governments appeared in a striking fashion to have reconquered a kind of pedagogical ascendancy and a claim to lead, confronting their citizens with the realities and disciplines of the market and tutoring them in the duties of economic enterprise.

Three ideas or shifts of thought come together in these lectures. First, Foucault shifts the focus of his own work from specialized practices and knowledges of the individual person, such as psychiatry, medicine, and punishment, to the exercise of political sovereignty by the state over an entire population. Second, he addresses *government* itself as a practice—or a succession of practices—animated, justified, and enabled by a specific rationality (or, rather, by a succession of different rationalities). In the context of modern Europe, this leads him to particularly attentive analyses of liberalism and neoliberalism. Lastly, he advises his audience that socialism historically lacks a distinctive concept and rationale for the activity of governing, a fact that places it at a damaging disadvantage in confronting its contemporary political adversary. A Left that cannot show it knows how to govern or has a clear conception of what governing is will not be likely to achieve power.

Foucault's thinking about "governmentality" was advanced by an important intellectual friendship with his contemporary and fellow professor at the Collège de France, Paul Veyne. Veyne, a historical sociologist of classical antiquity, had recently published *Le Pain et le Cirque*, a study of the practice of public benefactions in Hellenic and Roman society. Veyne's key idea was that, even if comparative analyses show that human societies manifest a certain number of shared, universal structures and behaviors, the meaning of some of these seeming universals is an extremely variable, contingent, and local construction, which it is a task of empirical and historical analysis and interpretation to reconstruct in its various constitutive aspects—the identity and role of the actor, the perceived content of the activity, its intended goal, and the human or other material objects on which it is conceived to work and act.

Foucault had been working, in the footsteps of Nietzsche, on just such a differentiating, decomposing, periodizing form of analysis of such apparently timeless and universal practices as the management of the insane, or the practice of punishment. At this point in his career, he was (as he publicly acknowledged) stimulated and encouraged by Veyne's work to address in a similar way the historical meanings of the "macro" practice of government. Veyne, in turn, credited Foucault with an important contribution to the methodology of his own profession, in an essay called *"Foucault révolutionne l'histoire."*[4] Veyne's essay stresses, in particular, the anthropological variability Foucault discerns between the way different historical practices of government identify their human objects—a flock to be herded or tended, the inhabitants of a territorial possession, a human population, or a civil society. Applied in this field, this type of analysis has the same effect as elsewhere—it increases our awareness of the role of construction and the constructed in governmental landscapes and institutions, and of the way in which habit leads us to accept these constructions as facts of nature or universal categories.

The new way of analyzing power which Foucault had proposed in *Discipline and Punish* and *La Volonté de savoir* was described and framed as a "microphysics"—a study of the forms and means of power focused on individuals and the details of their behavior and conduct. As a choice of method this was, in large part, a function of the material and questions examined, and therefore not—a caveat Foucault was often obliged to repeat—a universal recipe prescribed for every form of political analysis. Foucault was interested here in showing that power "comes from below," that is, that global and hierarchical structures of domination within a society depend on and operate through more local, low-level, "capillary" circuits

of power relationship.[5] Another methodological principle was a refusal to treat "power" as a substantive entity, institution, or possession, independent of the set of relationships in which it is exercised.
This did not mean that Foucault regarded the forms of sovereign
political power operating on a global social scale as derivative or
in some sense illusory phenomena. In *La Volonté de savoir*, for instance, continuing earlier discussions of this theme in *Madness and
Civilization* and *Birth of the Clinic*, he discusses the developing concern in early modern Europe for coordinating the government of
individuals with the government of a human collectivity understood
as a *population*; part of the privileged role of the theme of sexuality
in the knowledge–power of modern societies, he argues, is as a
junction point between individual regulation of conduct and questions of demographics.

Often in his books Foucault makes connections between criticism and transformation at the level of political institutions and
innovation and reform within local practices of regulation and normalization—the different effect of the French Revolution on public
health and the government of the insane, for example, and the linkage of late eighteenth-century criticisms of despotic government to
proposals for more effective forms of penal justice and social assistance. Foucault's sure and confident touch in tracing this kind of
connection set a new standard for an important area of historical
inquiry, thoroughly informed by research but with a sharpness of
focus and a range of synthesis seldom previously found in professional historiography. Introducing into his work the theme of governmental rationalities was partly a matter of providing himself
with a fully satisfactory way of drawing together the levels of "mi-
cro" and "macro" analyses of power. The "microphysical" emphasis
of the seventies books was, in part, an argument for the primacy of
analyses of practice over analyses of institutions—explaining the
origin of the prison, for example, on the basis of analysis of the
changing meaning assigned to the practice of punishing. Analyzing
governmental practices and their rationalities, he argued, could
provide similar gains in empirical understanding, beyond a political
analysis focused only on the study of state institutions. But this was
not the only innovative feature of these analyses.

We can see some of the latter more clearly after considering one
of the major new texts translated in this volume, dating from a few

years earlier. In his 1974 lectures in Brazil, "Truth and Juridical Forms," Foucault gives an introduction to his work of that period on power and knowledge through a commentary on a passage in Nietzsche, and on Sophocles' *Oedipus Rex*. He draws on the work of his mentor Georges Dumézil on the social structure of early Indo-European societies to interpret the drama of Oedipus as enacting the fall of a certain model of political power—the rule of the early Greek "tyrant," which Foucault considers a Western offshoot of the Assyrian model of kingship in which knowledge (wisdom, expertise) and the function of political rule are conceived as an indivisible unity. Sophocles' drama, like the philosophy of Plato, is a rebuttal of the claim of the ruler to an intrinsic and proprietary form of knowledge. Greek philosophy asserts the autonomy of truth from power, and affirms the permanent possibility of an external, critical challenge to power in the name of truth.

Foucault never defines his own position as subversive of philosophy. But he does position himself in this discussion within the heritage of Nietzsche presented as the thinker who transforms Western philosophy by rejecting its founding disjunction of power and knowledge as a myth. Foucault does not mean by this, as some of his critics have chosen to suppose, that power cannot be criticized, or that there are no intrinsic criteria for establishing claims to know; he is saying, rather, that the actual forms of Western politics and Western rationality have both, from the time of the Greeks to our own present, incorporated features not dreamed of (or at any rate only intermittently perceived and investigated) in the pre-Nietzschean canon of Western philosophy.

Some of these features are directly addressed in Foucault's 1978–79 lectures on the forms of rationality intrinsic to Western practices of government. One of these is the concept of pastoral power. Plato's dialogues consider but discard the conception of political rule (known to Greek culture as a concept of older Eastern monarchies) as an individualized care for the ruled, like the care of the shepherd for his flock. Such an individualized care, Plato writes in *Statesman*, exceeds the capability of the mortal sovereign. The "shepherd game" of pastoral care remains incompatible, in Greek political thought, with the "city game" of the polis and the free citizen. Foucault thinks it is the special accomplishment of the West, through the penetration of the pastoral ecclesiastical government of the Church into secular political culture, to have merged or hybridized these two traditions. Key topics of Foucault's analyses here (afterward summarized in the Stanford lectures "*Omnes et Singulatim*: Toward a Critique of Political Reason") are the doctrines of government in early modern Europe of *raison d'état* and the *Polizeistaat* or "police state." *Raison d'état* has in Foucault's interpretation something of the character of the expertise of the Greek tyrant: it is the reason that is intrinsic to the state and the practices of governing, not derived from the transcendent rule of wisdom or justice, and not assimilated to the conventions of custom or tradition which legitimate sovereign rule. The *Polizeiwissenschaft* (science of police), elaborated especially in the new German territorial states in the period following the Thirty Years' War, is reason of state translated into a program of exhaustive, detailed knowledge and regulation of a population of individual subjects. It amounts to a secularized pastoral (equipped, in some of its proposed forms, with a secular version of the Christian confessional), but where the care of the individual's life and happiness is attuned to maximizing the health and strength of the state. This is government with the motto *omnes et singulatim*—of all and of each. It represents the modern, biopolitical and "daemonic" fusion of pastoral and polis. As Foucault puts it, it is a power that both individualizes and totalizes.

It is very easy to see the historical and thematic continuity of some of this discussion with the chapters in *Discipline and Punish* in which Foucault traces the genesis of techniques of discipline and exhaustive surveillance (such as the police regulations for plague-infested cities) later found in their fullest elaboration in penitentiaries and other closed carceral spaces of the nineteenth century. One of the more provocative implications of that book was that carceral order might be the underside, or the unacknowledged truth, of liberal societies characterized by individual rights, constitutional government, and the rule of law. One of the most interesting elements of Foucault's lectures on governmental rationality is his recognition of the original and durable impact of liberalism, considered precisely as an innovation in the history of governmental rationality.

Foucault in fact takes the meaning of liberalism in governmental thought to be the equivalent of a Kantian critique. Liberalism is a critique of state reason, a doctrine of limitation, designed to mature

and educate government by displaying to it the intrinsic limits of
its power to know. Liberalism advocates an "economic government"—a government, in other words, that economizes on the use
of resources and effort to achieve its ends, and, more particularly,
accepts that to govern well is to govern less. It makes a kind of
Copernican revolution in political knowledge: the state ceases to be
either the natural subject or the natural object of political knowledge; the knowledge necessary to guide its actions, to be imparted
to it (from however close range) by the discipline of political economy will concern the intrinsic regularities and processes of an objective, social, and economic reality distinct from and independent
of the state.

Investigating the adventures of modern government as liberal
constitutional governments addressed in the context of an emerging industrial society and the agendas of social order and security
deriving from the era of the police states, Foucault and his co-
researchers were able to weave together the "microphysical" and
"macrophysical" strands of power–knowledge analysis with remarkable success and effect, providing a greatly enriched framework for the contemporary history and problems of Western
democratic societies. While Foucault's concerns led him in other
directions after 1979, this genre of investigation, although as yet
apparently limited in its influence on mainstream political theory
and history, has produced significant and continuing results.

How did this new departure mark a difference or an advance in
terms of Foucault's thinking on politics and power? One view could
be that it led him to the true adversary or problem—government.
As he was to write in an open letter to Mehdi Bazargan: "Why, in
the expression 'Islamic government,' should one throw suspicion
first of all on the adjective 'Islamic'? The word 'government' is
enough, on its own, to awaken our vigilance" (see p. 438).

We could also say that the problematic of government seemed to
Foucault to provide a more helpful way to address the relation between power and freedom. The notion of government encapsulated
the key insight that power, understood as form of action on the
actions of others, only works where there is some freedom. Some
of the key concepts deployed by rationalities of government, he suggested—for example, the notion of "civil society," in eighteenth-
century Britain—are best understood as functioning neither as

juridical theorems nor as empirical abstractions but, rather, as inventions serving purposes of negotiation, "transactional realities." In the case at hand, "civil society" served as a bridge between what had been found to be the discordant orders of political obedience and economic interest; it was a vehicle for "the common interplay of relations of power and all those things that ceaselessly escape their grasp."[6]

For Foucault, government means "the conduct of others' conduct,"[7] perhaps the paradigmatic form of power, but also, surely, a form that had a specific interest for him, and whose distinctiveness has to do with a certain ethical component in the rationale of the activity and its intended targets: the notion of concern for a way of living or of life conduct. As Foucault was aware, Max Weber had posed the same ensemble of problems—life conduct as one of the sectors of rationalization in the history of the West; the troubling capacity of secular government to interest itself in the "soul of the citizen"; and the legacy, dating from the roots of the Reformation, of the rejection of pastoral government for its excess of prescriptions for living.[8] As Foucault had suggested in the closing pages of *The History of Sexuality* Volume One, he saw contemporary societies as the scene of a comparable historical explosion of dissenting "counterconducts."

LEGITIMATION, LAW, AND RIGHTS

Political philosophy, from Aristotle to Rawls, includes theories and doctrines about the best form of government, the form and nature of political sovereignty, the foundations of legitimate rule, political justice, and the nature and basis of rights. In his lecture of January 1976 and in *La Volonté de savoir*, Foucault formulates a sharp and resonant critique of the themes of law and rights as the established language in which much of our political culture continues to conceptualize the foundations of political sovereignty, the way power is exercised, and the terms in which it can be challenged.

He thinks this mistake is a kind of anachronism. As he had described it in earlier lectures and in the Brazil lectures of 1974 reproduced here, the medieval monarchy indeed initially consolidates its power by confiscating a monopoly in dispensing justice, in the process redefining crime itself and establishing, following an ear-

lier practice of ecclesiastical government, a new form of power–
knowledge in jurisprudence, the form of the judicial inquiry or *en-
quête*. His thesis (later restated in *Discipline and Punish*) is that,
from the early modern period, secular government has acquired
additional techniques of power–knowledge, focused around the different (originally ecclesiastical) technique of the examination, the
investigation and questioning of the individual. All Foucault's analyses in the seventies of techniques of discipline, *raison d'état*, and
the police state are linked by their characterization as procedures
and techniques of power which dispense with or bypass the credentials and processes of law. Foucault's period of intense involvement in post-1968 militant politics was directed, especially in
relation to the prison, at developing and promoting the antidisci-
plinary orientation of radical struggle. As a consequence, both in
debate with the radical liberal Noam Chomsky and with some
French Maoists, he is sometimes sharply critical of the languages
of rights or justice as ways to articulate the resistance and rejection
of actually existing forms of power. (Behind the dispute with Chomsky, Foucault is also conducting another philosophical dispute with
the grounding of the language of natural right in a human nature—
and, consequently, with the allied notion of power as the repression
of the true, original form of that nature.)

But in other senses, Foucault had long known that the law was
in some ways his enemy's enemy, and thus possibly his ally. The
history of how the institutions of psychiatric internment came to be
founded in the moment of triumph of constitutional liberalism had
been, in part, the history of a hidden defeat of law by order: the
displacement, in the eighteenth century, of forensic scruple over
the legal competence and responsibility of legal subjects by the
more summary criteria of the orderly and disorderly conduct of
social subjects. The history of the birth of the prison Foucault was
writing in the early seventies was, similarly, the story of modern
penal practice as a defeat of law, the exercise of an uncontrolled,
parajudicial power within the closed space of the penitentiary.
There is no paradox, then, in the fact that he found himself often
acting in alliance with radical lawyers and forming a relationship
of mutual respect with their new post-1968 organization, the Syndicat de la Magistrature.

By 1976, Foucault had also moderated his idea that the language of rights was of no value to political struggle. He argued, in concluding his second 1976 lecture, that one should look "toward the possibility of a new form of right, one which must indeed be anti-disciplinarian, but at the same time liberated from the principle of sovereignty." This meant that political action can be given rational form without immediate recourse to theories of the fundamental legitimation of power, but also that concepts of rights can exist and be created without requiring foundational juridical premises: they can be created and affirmed through invention and struggle.[9] We shall see below how he later elaborated his views on the creation of rights.

Foucault wanted, then, to move both the descriptive and prescriptive functions of political analysis away from the "juridico-discursive" language of legitimation. To try to put the matter as simply as possible: he does not think that all power is evil or all government unacceptable, but does think that theorems claiming to confer legitimacy on power or government are fictions; in a lecture of 1979, he expresses sympathy with the view of earlier political skeptics that "civil society is a bluff and the social contract a fairy tale." This does not mean that the subject matter of political philosophy is evacuated, for doctrines of legitimation have been and may still act as political forces in history. But his analytic quarrel with legitimation theory is that it can divert us from considering the terms in which modern government confers rationality, and thus possible acceptability, on its activity and practice. This is the main reason why he argues political analysis is still immature, having still not cut off the king's head.[10]

The deployment and application of law is, for Foucault, like everything else, not good or evil in itself, capable of acting in the framework of liberalism as an instrument for economizing and moderating the interventions of governmental power, necessary as an indispensable restraint on power in some contexts, uses, and guises; it is to be resisted as an encroaching menace in others. In his governmentality lectures, Foucault investigates the evolution, from the era of the police states through the development of parliamentary liberal government, of the ambiguous and dangerous hybridization of law with a rationality of security and with new theories of social solidarity and social defense. This historical analysis and diagnosis informs Foucault's commentary on the civil liberties

politics of seventies France, with its distinctive contemporary re-
crudescence of *raison d'état* and the police state. But at the same
time, in a way we tend not to think of as typically French, he dryly
mocked and debunked the excesses of what he called "state pho-
bia"—the image of the contemporary state as an agency of essential
evil and limitless despotism. The state, he said, does not have a
unitary essence or indeed the importance commonly ascribed to it:
what are important to study are the multiple governmental practices that are exercised through its institutions and elsewhere. (In
a lecture describing the seventeenth-century theory of *raison d'état*,
Foucault characterized it as a doctrine of the "permanent coup
d'état"—a piquant choice of phrase, because it had been the title of
a polemical book written against de Gaulle by François Mitterrand.
We know that Foucault did not share the view, common in the
French Left, of de Gaulle's government as an antidemocratic putsch
with crypto-fascistic tendencies.[11] The Left, he also suggested,
should expect to win elected power not by demonizing the state
(never a very convincing platform for a socialist party) but by showing it possessed its own conception of how to govern.

Two of Foucault's unfulfilled plans, shortly before his death,
were a book of interviews with Didier Eribon on the governmental
incompetence of the French socialist party in the twentieth century
(Daniel Defert cites Foucault as asking the question, in July 1983,
"Do the Socialists have a problematic of government, or only a
problematic of the state?"), and (jointly with his friend Robert Badinter, socialist Minister of Justice) for a new center for research on
the philosophy of law.[12] One has the impression from Foucault's
1979 lectures on German neoliberalism that he is intrigued by aspects of their conception of the role of law: these authors advocate
an activist and constructive legal policy, designed to stabilize and
secure, independent of state intervention, the artificial and autonomous market "game" of a society composed of enterprizing, self-
shaping individuals. Badinter has recorded that, in their last
discussions together, Foucault "stressed the importance of better
understanding the importance of the rule of law and its architectural function in a secular, multicultural society, transcending the
normative role to serve as the keystone in the arch of the social
edifice—supported by opposing forces while ensuring the balance
of the whole."[13]

Three key formulations can be drawn from Foucault's discussions from the early eighties of the positive problem in current politics. *Security and autonomy:* In his discussion with the trade union official Robert Bono, Foucault speaks of the need for a new flourishing of governmental inventiveness to reshape the welfare state so that older demands (and achievements) in the area of individual social security are satisfied conjointly with new demands of personal autonomy. A condition of achieving such solution, he argued, would be a reduction of the "decisional distance" between the forums making and applying social policies and those whom the policies affected. *Capacities and dominations*: At a slightly more abstract level, in one of his texts discussing Kant's "What is Enlightenment?", Foucault speaks of the problematic of maximizing capacities while minimizing domination: "How can the growth of capabilities be disconnected from the intensification of power relations?"[14] *Relational rights:* He thought that a concern felt in gay culture but with a wider social presence was the "impoverishment of the relational fabric" in society. We know, he suggested, how to demand rights for individuals or groups, but we do little to extend the rights of forming relationships. Foucault called for the creation a generalized set of rights (including adoption) for the recognition of relationships between individuals of whatever age or gender. In his discussion with Bono, he also argued the cause of another neglected, and strictly individual, right—the right to suicide.

A POLITICAL ETHIC

In a 1976 interview, Foucault described and advocated a changed way in which intellectuals might act and intervene publicly in political matters. They would no longer try to speak as what he called the "master of justice and truth," qualified to pronounce authoritatively on key public issues on the basis of a universal and global wisdom and knowledge. He thought this kind of universal intellectual was being, and needed to be, replaced by what he called the specific intellectual, the scientist or expert qualified—such as the nuclear scientist Robert Oppenheimer—to alert the public and warn of dangers in a specific problem area about which he or she knew professionally.

It is not clear that Foucault fitted his own definition of the specific

intellectual, even if the areas he intervened in politically were matters of personal experience or concern. Later on, he talked more
about the specific role of the intellectual in terms of his own activity
and ethics—not, certainly, in order to present his own choices as
exemplary, but to declare, in considered terms and often with almost epigrammatic brevity, the reasons for those choices. He
summed up his view of this role in May 1984: "The work of an
intellectual is not to form the political will of others; it is, through
the analyses he does in his own domains, to bring assumptions and
things taken for granted again into question, to shake habits, ways
of acting and thinking, to dispel the familarity of the accepted, to
take the measure of rules and institutions and, starting from that
re-problematization (where he plays his specific role as intellectual) to take part in the formation of a political will (where he has
his role to play as citizen)."[15]

In a series of lectures and short texts from 1978 to 1984, Foucault
discusses his fascination with a short article by Kant, written in
1783 for the periodical *Der Berlinische Monatsschift*, and entitled
"What is Enlightenment?" Foucault presents this text as a point of
emergence of a new kind of figure or role in our culture, the philosopher as journalist. Kant, in Foucault's reading, identifies the
Enlightenment, *Aufklärung*, as an event or process occurring in the
contemporary world which is of capital importance in the history
of thought and human history in general, consisting of a commitment by humanity to the free use of reason, liberating itself from
the state of "self-imposed tutelage," under the motto "dare to
know." Foucault relates this article to another short piece by Kant,
also intended for a public audience, commenting on the significance of the French Revolution for the prospects of human progress. Kant, writing in 1798, while positively characterizing the
Revolution as an event in which a free people adopts a mode of
government of its own choice and which excludes the possibility of
waging aggressive war, detaches the question of the eventual happy
or unhappy outcome of the French Revolution itself from what he
sees as its value as a sign of progress. The evidence of this value,
Kant says, is not the outcome of the event itself for its own protagonists but, rather, the "sympathy bordering on enthusiasm" it inspires in other, external, disinterested witnesses and observers. It
is this reaction, rather than the event by itself, that testifies unmis-

takably to a disposition in humanity toward progress which Kant judges certain, in time, to prevail.

In the course of this set of commentaries, Foucault himself subscribes quite explicitly to the aspiration and motto of Enlightenment as Kant states them, albeit without sharing Kant's confidence that humans will in fact ever attain rational maturity in the Kantian sense. He writes that "we are fortunately committed to a rationality that is unfortunately traversed by intrinsic dangers." But he also focused attention on something he finds quite interesting and distinctive in the Kantian texts, to which he evidently attaches exemplary and programmatic value, namely, the quality of philosophical interest, attentive curiosity, and concern with respect to contemporary events which Kant's articles both exemplify and thematize. He finds appearing first in Kant the notion that what is occurring in the present time is something which critically affects, implicates, or concerns our own identity as rational and reflective beings; a process which may also involve, or provoke, our own participation in the reinvention or redefinition of what we are.

Foucault was reticent about theorizing modernity. Indeed, at one point he told an interviewer he was unclear what the word "modern" (let alone "postmodern") actually means. One can identify two significant places where he does use the term. One, undoubtedly tinged with the full force of Nietzschean sarcasm, is his characterization of the investigation in *Discipline and Punish* as a "genealogy of the modern soul," the soul here in question being the form of subjectivity which Foucault presents as invented or instilled by the modern social disciplines of individualized surveillance and normalization. The second appears in the article where he moves from Kant's "What is Enlightenment?" to discuss Baudelaire's conception of the self-inventing modern personage of the artist-dandy-*flâneur*, who manifests a distinctive form of the "heroism of modern life." Foucault picks up from Baudelaire, widens, and endorses the idea that a mode of living can in itself be a valid creative product. "Why should this lamp be a work of art, and not my life?"[16]

It is clear that Foucault's point in these texts is not to advocate a culture of aestheticized narcissism: the two volumes of the *History of Sexuality* that he completed just before his death are entirely focused around the existence in classical antiquity of an "aesthetics of existence," explicitly moral in its content and motivation, which he thinks provides a possible alternative model, as a form of ethics, to the (Christian) model of morality as obedience to a code of commandments and prohibitions. His interest in the invention of a modern way of life conduct has particularly to do with the way an identity, a set of commitments and adherences, can be transformed and remade through work, encounters, and engagements with a present. He narrates the shared experiences on a postwar, noncommunist French Left, which found and then questioned its identity as a group precisely through the experiences of revulsion, concern, and divided sympathies generated by such international events as Hungary in 1956, the Algerian War, and the question of Israel and Palestine, and through the doubts and reappraisals, notably concerning the desirability of Revolution itself, these experiences characteristically prompted. "Since 1956," he said in 1977, "philosophers have no longer been able to think history by means of pre-established categories. They therefore have to resensitize themselves to events. Philosophers must become journalists."

In his *Le Monde* article "Useless to Revolt?," addressing the question whether the brutal character of the Ayatollah Khomeini's theocratic rule in Iran discredited the action of those (like himself) who reported sympathetically on the ideas of those who had campaigned to overthrow the shah, Foucault defended himself against earlier critics. The intellectual observer's duty and role, he contends, is not to weigh the justness or political prudence of others' struggles, but to pay attention to their singularity, to give a hearing to their protagonists' reasons, to the reasons why some risk death by nonviolent action to refuse a way of being governed. In one of his most notable political statements, a manifesto text in support of the Vietnamese boat people entitled "Confronting Governments: Human Rights", he affirms the universal solidarity of the governed, which grounds rights and obligations of solidarity, exercised and fulfilled in our time through new forms of governmental action. He formulated this ethical concern at the time of the declaration of martial law in Poland in 1981: "In abandoning the Poles, he wrote, "we abandon a part of ourselves."

Foucault's work suggests that the governmental relation needs to be remoralized, from both sides. He set out some ideas on this in his interview welcoming the socialist election victory in 1981. He spoke of a "logic of the Left," an agenda for political reform based

in a new respect for those who govern for the governed, the acceptance that the conduct of government must be rationally justified
to and accepted by those whom it affects, and a practice, on the side
of the governed, of participative cooperation with government,
without unconditional complicity, compliance, or subservience—
neither shoulder to shoulder, nor on bended knee, but, as he put
it, *"debout et en face,"* upright and face to face. In the event, Foucault
mostly found that the French Socialist party, after having renewed
its electoral appeal by co-opting many of the new radicalisms of the
post-1968 era, preferred once in power a more traditional role for
its loyal intellectuals, as its public advocates and defenders. He
voiced his intense irritation when the President's press attaché
complained about what was called the "silence of Left intellectuals"—characteristically retorting that the government's difficulties
were related to its distaste for dialogue with those who might help
it to perform more competently.

THE RIGHTS OF THE GOVERNED

In November 1977, as we have seen, Foucault commented publicly
on the case of the extradition from France to West Germany of
Klaus Croissant, defense lawyer of the Baader-Meinhof terrorist
group. He criticized, specifically, the suppression of due process in
the extradition hearings in support of the apparent intention of the
German state to suppress the right of free defense for its accused.
He does not condone the Baader-Meinhof group's actions, or equate
their situation with that of the Eastern dissidents (he cross-refers
here to the trial of Anatoly Sharansky taking place at this time in
the Soviet Union). Instead, he discusses, in more general terms, the
right to defense, the condition of the dissident, and the law of asylum in terms of a more general *right of "the governed."* This right,
he says, "is more precise, more historically determined than the
rights of man, while it is wider than the right prescribed in administrative law and the right of the citizen." He speaks of the changing
concept of the "political" offense in the context of modern totalitarianism, and the shift from the typical nineteenth-century figure
of the political émigré, treated with prudent respect as the potential
future ruler of his country, to the "perpetual dissident"—the person
"who is in global disagreement with the system he lives in, ex-

presses this disagreement with the means available to him, and is prosecuted for doing so." The question of rights here is "not centered on the right to take power but on the right to leave, to be free, to leave, to not be persecuted—in short, on legitimate self-defense in relation to government." He speaks here of the value and desirability of extending, at any contingent opportunity, the rights of the governed, as the rights "of those who no longer want to be governed, or, in any case, not to be governed here, in this way, by these people."

A few years later, in 1981, Foucault wrote and delivered a short statement at an international conference in Geneva on the problem of piracy and the situation of the Vietnamese boat people.[17] Foucault describes the event as a meeting of private individuals with no qualification to speak out other than "a difficulty in bearing things which are taking place." Comparing this initiative to other previous one such as the Plane for El Salvador and Amnesty International, he identifies three principles that provide, in his view, their shared direction.

The first principle is the existence of an international citizenship with the right and duty to react against abuses of power committed against anyone and by anyone: "After all, we are all governed, and as such, are joined by solidarity."

The second principle is to deny governments the right, because of their claim to act in the general good, to write off human miseries due to their action or negligence as an item in a general account of profits and losses.

The third principle is to reject the division of labor, favored by governments themselves, which assigns the role of pious indignation and ineffectual talk to the governed, and that of effective action to governments. Governments, he remarks, themselves often show a marked preference for ineffectual talk in place of action: private initiatives such as Amnesty, Terre des Hommes, and Médecins du Monde have established the right and capacity of private individuals to intervene effectively in the world of international policy.

DISSIDENCE AS DISSENT

In the earliest of his documented commentaries on "What is Enlightenment?," a talk given to an audience of philosophers in May

1978,[18] Foucault characterizes the critical attitude as *the will not to be governed*—or, at any rate, as "the will not to be governed thus." Foucault characterizes the late medieval and early modern period of the fifteenth and sixteenth centuries as marking the expansion across secular societies of the Christian idea of pastoral government and the direction of conscience: the idea that each individual should be governed in a relationship to truth, composed of dogma, individualizing knowledge, and individual examination and confession. Foucault here characterizes the critical attitude as par excellence taking the form of the will not to be governed: "a sort of general cultural form, at once a moral and political attitude, a way of thinking, etc., which I would simply call the art of not being governed or again the art of not being governed like that, or at that price."

Foucault traces, as manifestations of this attitude, the development of modern critical domains of knowledge, challenging point by point the grounds of an unacceptable pastoral government: biblical theology, the juridical theory of natural right, and the pursuit of the means of certainty in the face of authority. If government, then, is "a social practice of subjecting individuals by mechanisms of power which lay claim to truth," critique will be "the movement by which the subject assumes the right to question truth on its effects of power, and power on its effects of truth," "the art of voluntary nonservitude, of considered nondocility." Kant defined Enlightenment in 1784 as the decision of humanity to escape a certain state of tutelage in which it was retained by external authority, a tutelage consisting in an incapacity of humanity to make use of its own understanding except under exterior guidance, and which Kant also characterized as a lack of decision and courage. At the same time, Foucault notes, the boldness of Kant's concept of *enlightenment* was balanced by the caution of his agenda for *critique*: daring to know will mean, in philosophy, understanding the limits of our capacity to know. Foucault then proceeds to locate his own power–knowledge analyses within post-Kantian critiques of the abuse or distortion of knowledge by power. Yet, in abandoning the primary concern with criteria of legitimation in favor of a descriptive inquiry into conditions of acceptability and acceptance, he recenters them back onto the agenda of enlightenment and the critical attitude, namely, "a certain decided (*décisoire*) will not to be governed."

Foucault said in one of his last interviews: nothing is more untenable than a political regime which is indifferent to truth; but nothing is more dangerous than a political system that claims to prescribe the truth. The function of 'truth telling' is not made to take the form of a law, just as it would be vain to imagine that it inhabits, as of right, the spontaneous play of communication. The task of truth telling is an endless work: respecting it in its complexity is an obligation no power can dispense with. Unless to impose the silence of servitude.[19]

COLIN GORDON

NOTES

1 From 1975 interview, "Interview on the prison: the book and its method," collected in volume 1 of *Dits et écrits*, p. 752. Cf. "The Ethics of the Concern for Self as a Practice of Freedom," interview with H. Becker et al. in *Ethics, Subjectivity, and Truth (Essential Writings, Vol. 1)* (New York: New Press 1997), p. 296: "when I talk about power relations and games of truth, I am absolutely not saying that games of truth are just concealed power relations— that would be a horrible caricature" (translation amended). For more clarification on this point, see James Faubion's introduction to volume 2 in this series.

2 "The Ethics of the Concern for Self," p. 296.

3 Foucault's own summaries of the courses may be found in volume 1 of this series.

4 Added as an appendix to the second edition of Veyne's book *Comment on écrit l'histoire*: not included in the English translation.

5 In his 1974 lectures "Truth and Juridical Forms," and also in "Lives of Infamous Men," Foucault further suggests that innovations in forms of social control—including the origins of policing—arose partly through initiatives or demands of minority religious groups and the humbler strata of society.

6 Collège de France lecture, 4 April 1979.

7 Cf. "Preface to *The History of Sexuality*, vol. 2," in volume 1 of *Essential Works*, p. 203. Translated as "guiding [their] conduct."

8 For a fuller discussion, see Colin Gordon, "The Soul of the Citizen: Max Weber and Michel Foucault on Rationality and Government," in S. Whimster and S. Lash, eds., *Max Weber, Rationality, and Modernity* (Boston: Allen and Unwin, 1987).

9 "Two Lectures: Lecture Two, 14 January 1976," *Power/Knowledge*, Colin Gordon, ed. (New York: Pantheon, 1980), p. 118.

10 See, eg., "Questions of Method," p. 238 this volume.

11 "*Phobie d'état*," *Libération* 30 June /1 July 1984. Extracted from Foucault's Collège de France lecture of 31 January 1979, omitted from republication in *Dits et écrits*.

12 Daniel Defert, "Chronologie," in *Dits et écrits*, vol. 1, p. 62–63.

13 "Au nom des mots," in Foucault, *Une Histoire de la vérité* (Paris: Syros, 1985), p. 73–75.

14 "What Is Enlightenment?" in *Essential Works*, volume 1, p. 317.

15 From "*Le souci de la vérité*" ("The Concern for [or, Care for] the Truth"), in volume IV of *Dits et écrits*, pp. 676–77.

16 From "On the Geneology of Ethics: An Overview of a Work in Progress" (*Essential Works* volume 1, p. 261).

17 "Confronting Governments: Human Rights," in this volume. For the background and influence of this text, see David Macey, *Lives of Michel Foucault.* (New York: Pantheon, 1993), pp. 437–38; for his earlier involvement in the question, ibid. p. 412–14.

18 "Qu'est-ce que la critique? Critique et *Aufklärung*," Bulletin de la Société Française de Philosophie 84.2 (April–June 1990), pp. 35–63. The text is one of those excluded from republication in *Dits et écrits*, as *"parutions posthumes non authentifiés par M. Foucault ou par les éditeurs."* (I am grateful to Dominique Seglard for pointing out this text to me.)

19 "Le souci de la vérité," interview with François Ewald (1984), *Dits et écrits*, volume 4, pp. 668–78.

NOTE ON TERMS AND TRANSLATIONS

This volume comprises essays, lectures, interviews, and position papers that Foucault wrote or gave between 1972 and 1984. Some of these are already well known in English (indeed, a few were originally published in English), but the majority are not. As we did in producing the first and second volumes of the series, we have called upon Robert Hurley to translate all the selections that remained in French. Once again, we have undertaken a careful review of the selections that have already appeared in translation, editing them for terminological consistency and conceptual accuracy. As much as possible, we have also sought to preserve the stylistic and tonal diversity of the selections, the occasions, and the audiences, all of which differ markedly from one instance to the next.

For all the complexities of Foucault's thought and usage, his "political vocabulary" largely allows of straightforward translation. One can readily gloss *pouvoir* as "power," *la gouvernementalité* as "governmentality," and so on. The difficulties that arise are for their part much the same as those that arose with the texts collected in the first and second volumes. As Colin Gordon notes in his introduction, and as I have discussed at length in my introduction to the second volume, *savoir* and *connaissance* register distinctions in French that are often blurred in English. Both denote "knowledge," but *connaissance* might often require glossing as "cognition," or "recognition," or "learning," or "expertise." Suffice it to say that when Foucault couples "knowledge" with power, as either knowledge-power or power-knowledge, he always uses *savoir*, never *connaissance*. In the earlier volumes, we often decided to translate *assujettissement* as "subjectivation," registering what we identified as a technical usage of the term in Foucault's writings on sexuality and ethics. In this volume, its gloss is virtually always the more standard "subjugation." In this case, however, as in many others, we have clarified our choices by providing the French in brackets.

*   *   *

TRUTH AND JURIDICAL FORMS*

I

What I would like to tell you in these lectures are some things that may be inexact, untrue, or erroneous, which I will present as working hypotheses, with a view to a future work. I beg your indulgence, and more than that, your malice. Indeed, I would be very pleased if at the end of each lecture you would voice some criticisms and objections so that, insofar as possible and assuming my mind is not yet too rigid, I might gradually adapt to your questions and thus at the end of these five lectures we might have done some work together or possibly made some progress.

Today, under the title "Truth and Juridical Forms," I will offer some methodological reflections to introduce a problem that may appear somewhat enigmatic to you. I will try to present what constitutes the point of convergence of three or four existing, already-explored, already-inventoried series of inquiries, which I will compare and combine in a kind of investigation. I won't say it is original, but it is at least a new departure.

The first inquiry is historical: How have domains of knowledge been formed on the basis of social practices? Let me explain the point at issue. There is a tendency that we may call, a bit ironically, "academic Marxism," which consists of trying to determine the way in which economic conditions of existence may be reflected and expressed in the consciousness of men. It seems to me that this form of analysis, traditional in university Marxism in France, exhibits a very serious defect—basically, that of assuming that the human subject, the subject of knowledge, and forms of knowledge themselves are somehow given beforehand and definitively, and that economic, social, and political conditions of existence are merely laid or imprinted on this definitely given subject.

My aim will be to show you how social practices may engender domains of knowledge that not only bring new objects, new concepts, and new techniques to light, but also give rise to totally new forms of subjects and subjects of knowledge. The subject of knowledge itself has a history; the relation of the subject to the object; or, more clearly, truth itself has a history.

Thus, I would especially like to show how a certain knowledge of man was formed in the nineteenth century, a knowledge of individuality, of the normal or abnormal, conforming or nonconforming individual, a knowledge that actually originated in social practices of control and supervision [*surveillance*]. And how, in a certain way, this knowledge was not imposed on, proposed to, or imprinted on an existing human subject of knowledge; rather, it engendered an utterly new type of subject of knowledge. The history of knowledge domains connected with social practices—excluding the primacy of a definitively given subject of knowledge—is a first line of research I suggest to you.

The second line of research is a methodological one, which might be called "discourse analysis." Here again there is, it seems to me, in a tradition that is recent but already accepted in European universities, a tendency to treat discourse as a set of linguistic facts linked together by syntactic rules of construction.

A few years ago, it was original and important to say and to show that what was done with language—poetry, literature, philosophy, discourse in general—obeyed a certain number of internal laws or regularities: the laws and regularities of language. The linguistic character of language facts was an important discovery for a certain period.

Then, it seems, the moment came to consider these facts of discourse no longer simply in their linguistic dimension, but in a sense—and here I'm taking my cue from studies done by the Anglo-Americans—as games, strategic games of action and reaction, question and answer, domination and evasion, as well as struggle. On one level, discourse is a regular set of linguistic facts, while on another level it is an ordered set of polemical and strategic facts. This analysis of discourse as a strategic and polemical game is, in my judgment, a second line of research to pursue.

Lastly, the third line of research that I proposed—and where it meets the first two, it defines the point of convergence where I will place myself—is a reworking of the theory of the subject. That theory has been profoundly modified and renewed, over the last several years, by a certain number of theories—or, even more seriously, by a certain number of practices, among which psychoanalysis is of course in the forefront. Psychoanalysis has undoubtedly been the practice and the theory that has reevaluated in the most fundamental way the somewhat sacred priority conferred on the subject, which has become established in Western thought since Descartes.

Two or three centuries ago, Western philosophy postulated, explicitly or implicitly, the subject as the foundation, as the central core of all knowledge, as that in which and on the basis of which freedom revealed itself and truth could blossom. Now, it seems to me that psychoanalysis has insistently called into question this absolute position of the subject. But while psychoanalysis has done this, elsewhere—in the field of what we may call the "theory of knowledge," or in that of epistemology, or in that of the history of the sciences, or again in that of the history of ideas—it seems to me that the theory of the subject has remained very philosophical, very Cartesian and Kantian; for, at the level of generalities where I situate myself, I don't differentiate between the Cartesian and Kantian conceptions.

Currently, when one does history—the history of ideas, of knowledge, or simply history—one sticks to this subject of knowledge, to this subject of representation as the point of origin from which knowledge is possible and truth appears. It would be interesting to try to see how a subject came to be constituted that is not definitively given, that is not the thing on the basis of which truth happens to history—rather, a subject that constitutes itself within history and is constantly established and reestablished by history. It is toward that radical critique of the human subject by history that we should direct our efforts.

A certain university or academic tradition of Marxism has not yet given up the traditional philosophical conception of the subject. In my view, what we should do is show the historical construction of a subject through a discourse understood as consisting of a set of strategies which are part of social practices.

That is the theoretical background of the problems I would like to raise.

Among the social practices whose historical analysis enables one to locate the emergence of new forms of subjectivity, it seemed to me that the most important ones are juridical practices.

The hypothesis I would like to put forward is that there are two histories of truth. The first is a kind of internal history of truth, the history of a truth that rectifies itself in terms of its own principles of regulation: it's the history of truth as it is constructed in or on the basis of the history of the sciences. On the other hand, it seems to me that there are in society (or at least in our societies) other places where truth is formed, where a certain number of games are defined—games through which one sees certain forms of subjectivity, certain object domains, certain types of knowledge come into being—and that, consequently, one can on that basis construct an external, exterior history of truth.

Judicial practices, the manner in which wrongs and responsibilities are settled between men, the mode by which, in the history of the West, society conceived and defined the way men could be judged in terms of wrongs committed, the way in which compensation for some actions and punishment for others were imposed on specific individuals—all these rules or, if you will, all these practices that were indeed governed by rules but also constantly modified through the course of history, seem to me to be one of the forms by which our society defined types of subjectivity, forms of knowledge, and, consequently, relations between man and truth which deserve to be studied.

There you have a general view of the theme I intend to develop: juridical forms and their evolution in the field of penal law as the generative locus for a given number of forms of truth. I will try to show you how certain forms of truth can be defined in terms of penal practice. For what is called the *inquiry*—the inquiry as practiced by philosophers of the fifteenth to the eighteenth century, and also by scientists, whether they were geographers, botanists, zoologists, or economists—is a rather characteristic form of truth in our societies.

Now where does one find the origin of the inquiry? One finds it in political and administrative practice, which I'm going to talk about; one also finds it in judicial practice. The inquiry made its appearance as a form of search for truth within the judicial order in the middle of the medieval era. It was in order to know exactly who did what, under what conditions, and at what moment, that the West devised complex techniques of inquiry which later were to be used in the scientific realm and in the realm of philosophical reflection.

In the same way, other forms of analysis were invented in the nineteenth century, from the starting point of juridical, judicial, and penal problems—rather curious and particular forms of analysis that I shall call *examination*, in contradistinction to the inquiry. Such forms of analysis gave rise to sociology, psychology, psychopathology, criminology, and psychoanalysis. I will try to show you how, when one looks for the origin of these forms of analysis, one sees that they arose in direct conjunction with the formation of a certain number of political and social controls, during the forming of capitalist society in the late nineteenth century.

Here, then, is a broad sketch of the topic of this series of lectures. In the next one, I will talk about the birth of the inquiry in Greek thought, in something that is neither completely a myth nor entirely a tragedy—the story of Oedipus. I will speak of the Oedipus story not as a point of origin, as the moment of formulation of man's desire or forms of desire, but, on the contrary, as a rather curious episode in the history of knowledge and as a point of emergence of the inquiry. In the next lecture I will deal with the relation of conflict, the opposition that arose in the Middle Ages between the system of the *test* and the system of the inquiry. Finally, in the last two lectures, I will talk about the birth of what I shall call the examination or the sciences of examination, which are connected with the formation and stabilization of capitalist society.

For the moment I would like to pick up again, in a different way, the methodological reflections I spoke of earlier. It would have been possible, and perhaps more honest, to cite only one name, that of Nietzsche, because what I say here won't mean anything if it isn't connected to Nietzsche's work, which seems to me to be the best, the most effective, the most pertinent of the models that one can draw upon. In Nietzsche, one finds a type of discourse that

undertakes a historical analysis of the formation of the subject itself, a historical analysis of the birth of a certain type of knowledge
[*savoir*]—without ever granting the preexistence of a subject of
knowledge [*connaissance*]. What I propose to do now is to retrace
in his work the outlines that can serve as a model for us in our
analyses.

I will take as our starting point a text by Nietzsche, dated 1873,
which was published only after his death. The text says: "In some
remote corner of the universe, bathed in the fires of innumerable
solar systems, there once was a planet where clever animals invented knowledge. That was the grandest and most mendacious
minute of 'universal history.' "[1]

In this extremely rich and difficult text, I will leave aside several
things, including—and above all—the famous phrase "that was the
most mendacious minute." Firstly and gladly, I will consider the
insolent and cavalier manner in which Nietzsche says that knowledge was invented on a star at a particular moment. I speak of
insolence in this text of Nietzsche's because we have to remember
that in 1873, one is if not in the middle of Kantianism then at least
in the middle of neo-Kantianism; the idea that time and space are
not forms of knowledge, but more like primitive rocks onto which
knowledge attaches itself, is absolutely unthinkable for the period.

That's where I would like to focus my attention, dwelling first on
the term "invention" itself. Nietzsche states that at a particular point
in time and a particular place in the universe, intelligent animals
invented knowledge. The word he employs, "invention"—the
German term is *Erfindung*—recurs often in these texts, and always
with a polemical meaning and intention. When he speaks of invention, Nietzsche always has an opposite word in mind, the word "origin" [*Ursprung*]. When he says "invention," it's in order not to say
"origin"; when he says *Erfindung*, it's in order not to say *Ursprung*.

We have a number of proofs of this, and I will present two or
three of them. For example, in a passage that comes, I believe, from
The Gay Science where he speaks of Schopenhauer, criticizing his
analysis of religion, Nietzsche says that Schopenhauer made the
mistake of looking for the origin—*Ursprung*—of religion in a metaphysical sentiment present in all men and containing the latent
core, the true and essential model of all religion. Nietzsche says
this is a completely false history of religion, because to suppose that

religion originates in a metaphysical sentiment signifies, purely and simply, that religion was already given, at least in an implicit state, enveloped in that metaphysical sentiment. But history is not that, says Nietzsche, that is not the way history was made—things didn't happen like that. Religion has no origin, it has no *Ursprung*, it was invented, there was an *Erfindung* of religion. At a particular moment in the past, something happened that made religion appear. Religion was made; it did not exist before. Between the great continuity of the *Ursprung* described by Schopenhauer and the great break that characterizes Nietzsche's *Erfindung*, there is a fundamental opposition.

Speaking of poetry, still in *The Gay Science*, Nietzsche declares that there are those who look for the origin, the *Ursprung*, of poetry, when in fact there is no *Ursprung* of poetry, there is only an invention of poetry.[2] Somebody had the rather curious idea of using a certain number of rhythmic or musical properties of language to speak, to impose his words, to establish by means of those words a certain relation of power over others. Poetry, too, was invented or made.

There is also the famous passage at the end of the first discourse of *The Genealogy of Morals* where Nietzsche refers to a sort of great factory in which the ideal is produced.[3] The ideal has no origin: it too was invented, manufactured, produced by a series of mechanisms, of little mechanisms.

For Nietzsche, invention, *Erfindung*, is on the one hand a break, on the other something with a small beginning, one that is low, mean, unavowable. This is the crucial point of the *Erfindung*. It was by obscure power relations that poetry was invented. It was also by pure and obscure power relations that religion was invented. We see the meanness, then, of all these small beginnings as compared with the solemnity of their origin as conceived by philosophers. The historian should not be afraid of the meanness of things, for it was out of the sequence of mean and little things that, finally, great things were formed. Good historical method requires us to counterpose the meticulous and unavowable meanness of these fabrications and inventions, to the solemnity of origins.

Knowledge was invented, then. To say that it was invented is to say that it has no origin. More precisely, it is to say, however paradoxical this may be, that knowledge is absolutely not inscribed in human nature. Knowledge doesn't constitute man's oldest instinct; and, conversely, in human behavior, the human appetite, the human instinct, there is no such thing as the seed of knowledge. As a matter of fact, Nietzsche says, knowledge does have a connection with the instincts, but it cannot be present in them, and cannot even be one instinct among the others. Knowledge is simply the outcome of the interplay, the encounter, the junction, the struggle, and the compromise between the instincts. Something is produced because the instincts meet, fight one another, and at the end of their battles finally reach a compromise. That something is knowledge.

Consequently, for Nietzsche knowledge is not of the same nature as the instincts, it is not like a refinement of the instincts. Knowledge does indeed have instincts as its foundation, basis, and starting point, but its basis is the instincts in their confrontation, of which knowledge is only the surface outcome. Knowledge is like a luminescence, a spreading light, but one that is produced by mechanisms or realities that are of completely different natures. Knowledge is a result of the instincts; it is like a stroke of luck, or like the outcome of a protracted compromise. It is also, Nietzsche says, like "a spark between two swords," but not a thing made of their metal.

Knowledge—a surface effect, something prefigured in human nature—plays its game in the presence of the instincts, above them, among them; it curbs them, it expresses a certain state of tension or appeasement between the instincts. But knowledge cannot be deduced analytically, according to a kind of natural derivation. It cannot be deduced in a necessary way from the instincts themselves. Knowledge doesn't really form part of human nature. Conflict, combat, the outcome of the combat, and, consequently, risk and chance are what gives rise to knowledge. Knowledge is not instinctive, it is counterinstinctive; just as it is not natural, but counternatural.

That is the first meaning that can be given to the idea that knowledge is an invention and has no origin. But the other sense that could be given to Nietzsche's assertion is that knowledge, beyond merely *not* being bound up with human nature, *not* being derived from human nature, isn't even closely connected to the world to be known. According to Nietzsche, there is no resemblance, no prior affinity between knowledge and the things that need to be known.

In more strictly Kantian terms, one should say the conditions of experience and the conditions of the object of experience are completely heterogeneous.

That is the great break with the prior tradition of Western philosophy, for Kant himself had been the first to say explicitly that the conditions of experience and those of the object of experience were identical. Nietzsche thinks, on the contrary, that between knowledge and the world to be known there is as much difference as between knowledge and human nature. So one has a human nature, a world, and something called knowledge between the two, without any affinity, resemblance, or even natural tie between them.

Nietzsche says repeatedly that knowledge has no affinity with the world to be known. I will cite just one passage from *The Gay Science*, aphorism 109: "The total character of the world is chaos for all eternity—in the sense not of a lack of necessity but of a lack of order, arrangement, form, beauty, wisdom."⁴ The world absolutely does not seek to imitate man; it knows no law. Let us guard against saying that there are laws in nature. Knowledge must struggle against a world without order, without connectedness, without form, without beauty, without wisdom, without harmony, and without law. That is the world that knowledge deals with. There is nothing in knowledge that enables it, by any right whatever, to know this world. It is not natural for nature to be known. Thus, between the instincts and knowledge, one finds not a continuity but, rather, a relation of struggle, domination, servitude, settlement. In the same way, there can be no relation of natural continuity between knowledge and the things that knowledge must know. There can only be a relation of violence, domination, power, and force, a relation of violation. Knowledge can only be a violation of the things to be known, and not a perception, a recognition, an identification of or with those things.

It seems to me that in this analysis by Nietzsche there is a very important double break with the tradition of Western philosophy, something we should learn from. The first break is between knowledge and things. What is it, really, in Western philosophy that certifies that things to be known and knowledge itself are in a relation of continuity? What assurance is there that knowledge has the ability to truly know the things of the world instead of being indefinite error, illusion, and arbitrariness? What in Western philosophy guarantees that, if not God? Of course, from Descartes, to go back no further than that, and still even in Kant, God is the principle that ensures a harmony between knowledge and the things to be known. To demonstrate that knowledge was really based in the things of the world, Descartes had to affirm the existence of God.

If there is no relation between knowledge and the things to be known, if the relation between knowledge and known things is arbitrary, if it is a relation of power and violence, the existence of God at the center of the system of knowledge is no longer indispensable. As a matter of fact, in the same passage from *The Gay Science* where he speaks of the absence of order, connectedness, form, and beauty in the world, Nietzsche asks, "When will all these shadows of God cease to darken our minds? When will we complete our de-deification of nature?"5

Second, I would say that if it is true that between knowledge and the instincts—all that constitutes, that makes up the human animal—there is only discontinuity, relations of domination and servitude, power relations, then it's not God that disappears but the subject in its unity and its sovereignty.

When we retrace the philosophical tradition starting from Descartes, to go no further back than that, we see that the unity of the subject was ensured by the unbroken continuity running from desire to knowledge [*connaissance*], from the instincts to knowledge [*savoir*], from the body to truth. All of that ensured the subject's existence. If, on the one hand, it is true that there are mechanisms of instinct, the play of desire, the affrontment between the mechanisms of the body and the will, and on the other hand, at a completely different level of nature, there is knowledge, then we don't need the postulate of the unity of the human subject. We can grant the existence of subjects, or we can grant that the subject doesn't exist. In this respect, then, the text by Nietzsche I have cited seems to present a break with the oldest and most firmly established tradition of Western philosophy.

Now, when Nietzsche says that knowledge is the result of the instincts, but that it is not an instinct and is not directly derived from the instincts, what does he mean exactly? And how does he conceive of that curious mechanism by which the instincts, without having any natural relation with knowledge, can, merely by their activity, produce, invent a knowledge that has nothing to do with them? That is the second series of problems I would like to address.

There is a passage in *The Gay Science*, aphorism 333, which can be considered one of the closest analyses Nietzsche conducted of that manufacture, of that invention of knowledge. In this long text titled "The Meaning of Knowing," Nietzsche takes up a text by Spinoza in which the latter sets *intelligere*, to understand, against *ridere* [to laugh], *lugere* [to lament], and *detestari* [to detest].[6] Spinoza said that if we wish to understand things, if we really wish to understand them in their nature, their essence, and hence their truth, we must take care not to laugh at them, lament them, or detest them. Only when those passions are calmed can we finally understand. Nietzsche says that not only is this not true, but it is exactly the opposite that occurs. *Intelligere*, to understand, is nothing more than a certain game, or more exactly, the outcome of a certain game, of a certain compromise or settlement between *ridere, lugere*, and *detestari*. Nietzsche says that we understand only because behind all that there is the interplay and struggle of those three instincts, of those three mechanisms, or those three passions that are expressed by laughter, lament, and detestation.

Several points need to be considered here. First, we should note that these three passions, or these three drives—laughing, lamenting, detesting—are all ways not of getting close to the object or identifying with it but, on the contrary, of keeping the object at a distance, differentiating oneself from it or marking one's separation from it, protecting oneself from it through laughter, devalorizing it through complaint, removing it and possibly destroying it through hatred. Consequently, all these drives, which are at the root of knowledge and which produce it, have in common a distancing of the object, a will to remove oneself from it and to remove it at the same time—a will, finally, to destroy it. Behind knowledge there is a will, no doubt obscure, not to bring the object near to oneself or identify with it but, on the contrary, to get away from it and destroy it—a radical malice of knowledge.

We thus arrive at a second important idea: These drives—laughing, lamenting, detesting—can all be categorized as bad relations. Behind knowledge, at the root of knowledge, Nietzsche does not posit a kind of affection, drive, or passion that makes us love the object to be known; rather, there are drives that would place us in a position of hatred, contempt, or fear before things that are threatening and presumptuous.

If these three drives—laughing, lamenting, hating—manage to produce knowledge, this is not, according to Nietzsche, because they have subsided, as in Spinoza, or made peace, or because they have attained a unity. On the contrary, it's because they have tried, as Nietzsche says, to harm one another, it's because they're in a state of war—in a momentary stabilization of this state of war, they reach a kind of state, a kind of hiatus, in which knowledge will finally appear as the "spark between two swords."

So in knowledge there is not a congruence with the object, a relation of assimilation, but, rather, a relation of distance and domination; there is not something like happiness and love but hatred and hostility; there is not a unification but a precarious system of power. The great themes traditionally present in Western philosophy are thoroughly called into question in the Nietzsche text I've cited.

Western philosophy—and this time it isn't necessary to limit the reference to Descartes, one can go back to Plato—has always characterized knowledge by logocentrism, by resemblance, by congruence, by bliss, by unity. All these great themes are now called into question. One understands, then, why Nietzsche mentions Spinoza, because of all the Western philosophers Spinoza carried this conception of knowledge as congruence, bliss, and unity the farthest. At the center, at the root of knowledge, Nietzsche places something like hatred, struggle, power relations.

So one can see why Nietzsche declares that it is the philosopher who is the most likely to be wrong about the nature of knowledge, since he always thinks of it in the form of congruence, love, unity, and pacification. Thus, if we seek to ascertain what knowledge is, we must not look to the form of life, of existence, of asceticism that characterize the philosopher. If we truly wish to know knowledge, to know what it is, to apprehend it at its root, in its manufacture, we must look not to philosophers but to politicians—we need to understand what the relations of struggle and power are. One can understand what knowledge consists of only by examining these relations of struggle and power, the manner in which things and men hate one another, fight one another, and try to dominate one another, to exercise power relations over one another.

So one can understand how this type of analysis can give us an effective introduction to a political history of knowledge, the facts of knowledge and the subject of knowledge.

At this point I would like to reply to a possible objection: "All that is very fine, but it isn't in Nietzsche. Your own ravings, your obsession with finding power relations everywhere, with bringing this political dimension even into the history of knowledge or into the history of truth has made you believe that Nietzsche said that."

I will say two things in reply. First, I chose this passage from Nietzsche in terms of my own interests, not with the purpose of showing that this was *the* Nietzschean conception of knowledge— for there are innumerable passages in Nietzsche on the subject that are rather contradictory—but only to show that there are in Nietzsche a certain number of elements that afford us a model for a historical analysis of what I would call the politics of truth. It's a model that one does find in Nietzsche, and I even think that in his work it constitutes one of the most important models for understanding some of the seemingly contradictory elements of his conception of knowledge.

Indeed, if one grants that this is what Nietzsche means by the discovery of knowledge, if all these relations are behind knowledge, which, in a certain sense, is only their outcome, then it becomes possible to understand certain difficult passages in Nietzsche.

First, there are those places where Nietzsche asserts that there is no knowledge in itself. Once again, we need to think of Kant, we need to compare the two philosophers and note all their differences. What the Kantian critique questioned was the possibility of a knowledge of the in-itself, a knowledge of a truth or a reality in itself. In *On the Genealogy of Morals*, Nietzsche says: "Henceforth, dear philosophers, let us be on guard against . . . the snares of such contradictory concepts as 'pure reason', 'absolute spirit', 'knowledge in itself'."[7] Or again, in *The Will to Power*, Nietzsche states that there is no being in itself, just as there cannot be any knowledge in itself.[8] And when he says this, he has in mind something completely different from what Kant understood by knowledge in itself. Nietzsche means that there is not a nature of knowledge, an essence of knowledge, of the universal conditions of knowledge; rather, that knowledge is always the historical and circumstantial result of conditions outside the domain of knowledge. In reality, knowledge is an event that falls under the category of activity.

Knowledge is not a faculty or a universal structure. Even when it uses a certain number of elements that may pass for universals, knowledge will only belong to the order of results, events, effects.

The series of texts in which Nietzsche asserts that knowledge has a perspectival character can also be understood in this way. When he says that knowledge is always a perspective, he doesn't mean (in what would be a blend of Kantianism and empiricism) that, in man, knowledge is bounded by a certain number of conditions, of limits derived from human nature, the human body, or the structure of knowledge itself. When Nietzsche speaks of the perspectival character of knowledge, he is pointing to the fact that there is knowledge only in the form of a certain number of actions that are different from one another and multifarious in their essence—actions by which the human being violently takes hold of a certain number of things, reacts to a certain number of situations, and subjects them to relations of force. This means that knowledge is always a certain strategic relation in which man is placed. This strategic relation is what will define the effect of knowledge; that's why it would be completely contradictory to imagine a knowledge that was not by nature partial, oblique, and perspectival. The perspectival character of knowledge derives not from human nature but always from the polemical and strategic character of knowledge. One can speak of the perspectival character of knowledge because there is a battle, and knowledge is the result of this battle.

It is for that reason that in Nietzsche we find the constantly recurring idea that knowledge is at the same time the most generalizing and the most particular of things. Knowledge simplifies, passes over differences, lumps things together, without any justification in regard to truth. It follows that knowledge is always a misconstruction [*méconnaissance*]. Moreover, it is always something that is aimed, maliciously, insidiously, and aggressively, at individuals, things, situations. There is knowledge only insofar as something like a single combat, a tête-à-tête, a duel is set up, contrived, between man and what he knows. There is always something in knowledge that is analogous to the duel and accounts for the fact that it is always singular. That is the contradictory character of knowledge, as it is defined in the Nietzsche texts that seem to contradict one another—generalizing and always singular.

So that is how, through Nietzsche's text, one can restore, not a general theory of knowledge but a model that enables us to tackle the object of these lectures: the problem of the formation of a certain number of domains of knowledge on the basis of the relations of force and the political relations in society.

Now I'll go back to my starting point. In a certain academic conception of Marxism or a certain conception of Marxism that was imposed on the university, there is always the underlying idea that relations of force, economic conditions, and social relations are given to individuals beforehand but at the same time are imposed on a subject of knowledge that remains identical, except in relation to ideologies construed as errors.

We thus arrive at the very important and at the same time cumbersome notion of ideology. In traditional Marxist analyses, ideology is a sort of negative element through which the fact is conveyed that the subject's relation to truth, or simply the knowledge relation, is clouded, obscured, violated by conditions of existence, social relations, or the political forms imposed on the subject of knowledge from the outside. Ideology is the mark, the stigma of these political or economic conditions of existence on a subject of knowledge who rightfully should be open to truth.

What I intend to show in these lectures is how, in actual fact, the political and economic conditions of existence are not a veil or an obstacle for the subject of knowledge but the means by which subjects of knowledge are formed, and hence are truth relations. There cannot be particular types of subjects of knowledge, orders of truth, or domains of knowledge except on the basis of political conditions that are the very ground on which the subject, the domains of knowledge, and the relations with truth are formed. Only by shedding these grand themes of the subject of knowledge—imputed to be at once originary and absolute—and perhaps by using the Nietzschean model, will we be able to do a history of truth.

I will present some sketches of that history starting from judicial practices that gave rise to models of truth which still circulate in our society, are still imposed on it, and operate not only in the political domain and in the domain of everyday behavior, but even in the realm of science. Even in science one finds models of truth whose formation derives from political structures that are not imposed on the subject of knowledge from the outside but, rather, are themselves constitutive of the subject of knowledge.

II

Today I would like to speak to you about the story of Oedipus, a subject that has lost much of its appeal over the past year. Since Freud, the Oedipus story has been regarded as the oldest fable of our desire and our unconscious. However, since last year's publication of the book by Gilles Deleuze and Félix Guattari, *Anti-Oedipus*, the reference to Oedipus plays an entirely different role.[9]

Deleuze and Guattari try to show that the Oedipal father–mother–son triangle does not reveal an atemporal truth or a deeply historical truth of our desire. They try to show that this famous Oedipal triangle constitutes, for the analysts who manipulate it within the treatment, a certain way of containing desire, of making sure that it is not invested in and does not spread into the world around us, into the historical world, that desire stays in the family and unfolds like a little, almost bourgeois drama between the father, the mother, and the son.

In this conception, then, Oedipus is not a truth of nature, but an instrument of limitation and constraint that psychoanalysts, starting with Freud, use to contain desire and insert it within a family structure defined by our society at a particular moment. In other words, Oedipus, according to Deleuze and Guattari, is not the secret content of our unconscious, but the form of constraint which psychoanalysis, through the cure, tries to impose on our desire and our unconscious. Oedipus is an instrument of power, a certain manner by which medical and psychoanalytic power is brought to bear on desire and the unconscious.

I admit that a problem such as this is very appealing to me, and that I am also tempted to look behind what is claimed to be the Oedipus story for something unrelated to the indeterminate, endlessly repeated story of our desire and our unconscious, but related to the history of a power, a political power.

I'll digress long enough to point out that everything that I'm trying to say, everything that Deleuze and Guattari have shown with much more depth in *Anti-Oedipus*, is part of a group of studies that, contrary to what the newspapers say, are not concerned with what is traditionally called "structure." Neither Deleuze, nor Jean-François Lyotard, nor Guattari, nor I ever do structural analyses; we are absolutely not "structuralists." If I were asked what I do and what others do better, I would say that we don't study structures; indulging in wordplay, I would say that we study dynasties. Playing on the Greek words *dunamis dunasteia*, I would say that we try to bring to light what has remained until now the most hidden, the most occulted, the most deeply invested experience in the history of our culture—power relations. Curiously, the economic structures of our society are better known, more thoroughly inventoried, more clearly defined than the structures of political power. In this series of lectures I would like to show how the political relations have been established and deeply implanted in our culture, giving rise to a series of phenomena that can be explained only if they are related not to economic structures, to the economic relations of production, but to the power relations that permeate the whole fabric of our existence.

I want to show how the tragedy of Oedipus, the one we can read in Sophocles[10]—I'll leave aside the problem of the mythical background to which it is linked—is representative and in a sense the founding instance of a definite type of relation between power and knowledge [*savoir*], between political power and knowledge [*connaissance*], from which our civilization is not yet emancipated. It seems to me that there really is an Oedipus complex in our civilization. But it does not involve our unconscious and our desire, nor the relations between desire and the unconscious. If there is an Oedipus complex, it operates not at the individual level but at the collective level; not in connection with desire and the unconscious but in connection with power and knowledge. That is the "complex" I want to analyze.

The first evidence we have of the search for truth in Greek judicial procedure dates back to the *Iliad*. It appears in the story of the dispute between Antilochus and Menelaus during the games organized to mark the death of Patroclus.[11] Among these games there is a chariot race that is run, as usual, in an out-and-back circuit, going around a post that has to be passed as closely as possible. The games' organizers have placed a man there to make sure the rules of the race are followed; Homer, without naming him personally, says this man is a witness, *histor*, one who is there to see.

The race unfolds and the men in the lead at the turn are Antilochus and Menelaus. An infringement occurs and, when Antilochus
arrives first, Menelaus lodges a protest and says to the judge, or to
the jury who must award the prize, that Antilochus committed a
foul. Protest, dispute—how is the truth to be established? Curiously,
in this text by Homer the parties involved do not call upon the person who saw, the famous witness who was near the turning post
and who should attest to what happened. He's not called to testify,
not asked a single question. There is only a dispute between the
adversaries Menelaus and Antilochus. It develops in the following
way: After Menelaus' accusation "You committed a foul," and Antilochus' defense "I didn't commit any foul," Menelaus delivers a
challenge: "Come, lay your right hand on your horse's forehead,
grasp your whip with your left hand and swear by Zeus that you
didn't commit any foul." At that moment, Antilochus, faced with this
challenge, which is a test, declines to swear an oath and thereby
acknowledges that he committed the foul.[12]

This is a peculiar way to produce truth, to establish juridical
truth—not through the testimony of a witness but through a sort of
testing game, a challenge hurled by one adversary at another. If by
chance he had accepted the risk, if he had actually sworn, the responsibility for what would happen, the final uncovering of the
truth would immediately devolve upon the gods. And it would be
Zeus who, by punishing the one who uttered the false oath if that
were the case, would have manifested the truth with his thunder-
bolt.

Here we have the old and very archaic practice of the test of
truth, where the latter is established judicially not by an investigation, a witness, an inquiry, or an inquisition but, rather, by a
testing game. The test is a feature of archaic Greek society. We will
meet it again in the early Middle Ages.

It is evident that when Oedipus and the whole city of Thebes are
seeking the truth this is not the model they use. Centuries have
gone by. It is interesting, however, to note that we do encounter in
Sophocles' tragedy one or two remnants of the practice of establishing the truth by means of the test. First, in the scene between
Creon and Oedipus—when Oedipus criticizes his brother-in-law for
having distorted the Delphic oracle's response, telling him, "You
invented all that simply to take my power, to replace me." Creon

replies, without trying to establish the truth through witnesses, "Well then, let's swear an oath. And I will swear that I didn't plot against you in any way." This is said in the presence of Jocasta, who accepts the game, who is the game's referee as it were. Creon replies to Oedipus according the old formula of the dispute between warriors.[15]

We could say that we find this system of challenge and test throughout the entire play. When he learns that the plague afflicting Thebes is due to the curse of the gods in response to corruption and murder, Oedipus vows to banish the person who committed the crime, not knowing of course that he himself committed it. He is thus implicated by his own oath, in the same way that during rivalries between archaic warriors the adversaries included themselves in their oaths of promise and malediction. These remnants of the old tradition reappear at times over the entire length of the play. In reality, though, the whole Oedipus tragedy is based on a completely different mechanism. It is this mechanism for establishing the truth I would like to focus on.

It seems to me that initially this truth mechanism follows a rule, a kind of pure form, that we might call the "rule of halves." The discovery of the truth proceeds in *Oedipus* by the fitting together and interlocking of halves. Oedipus sends a person to consult the god of Delphi, Apollo the King. Examined in detail, Apollo's answer is given in two parts. Apollo begins by saying, "The land has been defiled." In a sense, a half is missing from this reply: there is a defilement, but who did the defiling and what was defiled? So a second question must be posed, and Oedipus forces Creon to give a second reply, by asking what caused the defilement. The second half appears: What caused the defilement was a murder. But whoever says murder is saying two things, who murdered and who was murdered. Apollo is asked, "Who was murdered?" The answer is Laius, the former king. He is then asked, "Who killed him?" At this moment King Apollo refuses to answer, and, as Oedipus says, the gods cannot be compelled to disclose the truth. So there remains a missing half. The murder-half corresponded to the defilement; this was the first half: the one who was murdered. But the second half, the name of the killer, is lacking.

To learn the name of the killer, it will be necessary to appeal to something, to someone, since the will of the gods cannot be forced.

That other, Apollo's double, his human double, his mortal shadow, is the prophet Tiresias, who, like Apollo, is someone divine, *theios mantis*, the divine diviner. He is very close to Apollo—he's also called king, *anax*—but he is mortal, whereas Apollo is immortal; and above all he is blind, he's immersed in darkness, whereas Apollo is the Sun god. He's the dark half of the divine truth, the double the light god projects as a shadow on the surface of earth. It is this half that will be interrogated. And Tiresias replies to Oedipus by saying, "You're the one who killed Laius."

Consequently, we can say that as early as the second scene of *Oedipus* everything has been said and enacted. We have the truth, since Oedipus is clearly identified by the combination of the replies of Apollo, on the one hand, and the reply of Tiresias, on the other. The set of halves is complete: defilement, murder; the murder victim, the murderer. It's all there, but in the quite peculiar form of prophecy, prediction, prescription. The prophet Tiresias does not exactly say to Oedipus, "You're the killer." He says: "You promised to banish the killer; I command you to fulfill your vow and expel yourself." In the same way, Apollo had not exactly said: "There is corruption and that is why the city is immersed in plague." Apollo said: "If you want the plague to end you must cleanse yourself of the corruption." All this was said in the form of the future, of prescription, of prediction; nothing refers to the actuality of the present, there is no pointing of the finger.

We have the whole truth, but in the prescriptive and prophetic form characteristic of both the oracle and the prophet. Though this truth is in a sense complete, total—everything has been said—it lacks something which is in the dimension of the present, of actuality, the naming of someone. Missing is the evidence of what really came to pass. Curiously, this old story is formulated by the prophet and by the god entirely in the form of the future. Now we need the present and the evidence of the past—the present evidence of what actually happened.

This sequel, past and present, of this prescription and forecast is given by the rest of the play. This too is given through a strange game of halves. First, it is necessary to establish who killed Laius. That is achieved in the course of the play by the coupling of two statements. The first is given spontaneously and inadvertently by Jocasta, when she says: "Listen now, it wasn't you, Oedipus, who killed Laius, contrary to what the prophet says. The best proof of this is that Laius was killed by several men at a place where three roads come together." This statement will be answered by the anxiety, the near-certainty already, of Oedipus: "Kill a man at a crossroads—that's exactly what I did; I remember that when I got to Thebes I killed someone at a place where three roads meet." Thus, through the joining of these two complementary halves, Jocasta's recollection and Oedipus' recollection, we have that almost complete truth, the truth about the murder of Laius. Almost complete, because a small piece is still missing—whether he was killed by one man or by several is a matter that the play actually leaves unresolved.

But that is just the half involving the story of Oedipus, for Oedipus is not just the person who killed King Laius, but also the one who killed his own father then married his own mother. This second half of the story is still lacking after the joining of Jocasta's and Oedipus' statements. What is lacking is precisely what gives them a kind of hope, for the god prophesied that Laius would be killed not by just anyone but by his son. Consequently, so long as it has not been proven that Oedipus is the son of Laius, the prophecy will not have come true. This second half is necessary in order for the whole prediction to be established, in the last part of the play, by the coupling of two different evidential statements. The first will be that of the slave who comes from Corinth to announce to Oedipus that Polybus is dead. Oedipus does not shed any tears over his father's death, but rejoices, saying: "So! But at least I didn't kill him, contrary to what the prophecy said." And the slave answers: "Polybus was not your father."

We thus have a new element: Oedipus is not the son of Polybus. It is then that the last slave comes into the play, the one who had fled after the calamity, who had buried himself in the depths of Cithaeron, who had hidden the truth in his hut, the shepherd who is summoned to be questioned about what had happened and who says: "It's true. Long ago I gave this messenger a child who came from Jocasta's palace and who was said to be her son."

We see that the final certainty is still lacking, for Jocasta is not present to attest that it was she who gave the child to the slave. But, except for that little difficulty, the cycle is now complete. We know that Oedipus was Laius' and Jocasta's son, that he was given to Polybus, that it was he who, thinking he was the son of Polybus and returning to Thebes—which he didn't know was his native land—to escape the prophecy, killed King Laius, his real father, at a place where three roads crossed. The cycle is closed. It was closed by a series of nested halves that fit together. As if this whole long and complex story of the child who is at once exiled and in flight from a prophecy, exiled because of the prophecy, had been broken in two, and then each fragment again broken in two, and all these fragments parceled out among different hands. It took this meeting of the god and his prophet, of Jocasta and Oedipus, of the slave from Corinth and the slave from Cithaeron for all these halves and these halves of halves to match up, align themselves, and fit together to form the whole pattern of the story.

This figure of the broken and rejoined parts, which is truly impressive in Sophocles' *Oedipus*, is not just rhetorical—it is also religious and political. It is the famous technique of the *sumbolon*, the Greek symbol. It is an instrument of power and its exercise whereby a person who holds some secret or power breaks some ceramic object in half, keeping one part and entrusting the other to an individual who is to carry the message or certify its authenticity. By fitting these two parts together it is possible to verify the authenticity of the message, that is, the continuity of the power exercised. Power manifests itself, completes its cycle, maintains its unity by means of this little game of separate fragments of the same whole, a unique object whose overall configuration is the manifest form of power. The Oedipus story is the fragmentation of that token, the possession of which, complete and reunified, authenticates the holding of power and the orders given by it. The messengers whom it sends and who must return will authenticate their connection to power by the fact that each of them has a fragment of the token and can fit it to the other fragments. This is the juridical, political, and religious technique of what the Greeks call *sumbolon*, the sumbol.

The story of Oedipus, as it is enacted in Sophocles' tragedy, conforms to this *sumbolon*, which is not a rhetorical form but a religious, political, quasi-magical form of the exercise of power.

If we now look not at the form of this mechanism, the game of halves which break apart and eventually fit back together, but at the effect produced by these mutual alignments, we see a number of things. First, there is a sort of displacement as the halves are brought together. The first set of halves which fit together is that of Apollo the king and Tiresias the prophet—the level of prophecies or of the gods. The next series of complementary halves is formed by Oedipus and Jocasta. Their two statements occur in the middle of the play; this is the level of the royalty, the rulers. Finally, the last pair of statements that intervene, the last half that completes the story, is supplied not by the gods or the royalty but by the servants and the slaves. The most humble slave of Polybus and, decisively, the most hidden herdsman of the forest of Cithaera pronounce the final truth and provide the final piece of evidence.

We thus have a curious result. What had been said in terms of prophecy at the beginning of the play will be said again in the form of statements by two shepherds. And just as the play moves from the gods to the slaves, the mechanisms of truth-telling and the form in which truth is told change as well. When the god and the seer speak, truth is expressed in the form of prescription and prophecy, through the eternal and omnipotent gaze of the sun god and the gaze of the soothsayer who, though blind, sees past, present, and future. It is this sort of magico-religious gaze that, at the beginning of the play, illuminates a truth that Oedipus and the Chorus don't want to accept. At the humblest level there is again a gaze—for, if the two slaves can testify, it's because they have seen. The first saw Jocasta place a child in his hands to be taken into the forest and abandoned; the second saw his fellow slave hand this child over to him and recalls having carried the child to Polybus' palace. It's still a matter of the gaze—no longer the great eternal, illuminating, dazzling, flashing gaze of the god and his prophet, but that of those persons who saw and remember having seen with their own human eyes. It is the gaze of the witness. It is the gaze that Homer made no reference to when he spoke of the conflict and formal dispute between Antilochus and Menelaus.

So we can say that the entire *Oedipus* play is a way of shifting the enunciation of the truth from a prophetic and prescriptive type of discourse to a retrospective one that is no longer characterized by prophecy but, rather, by evidence. This was also a way of shifting the luminescence or, rather, the light of the truth of the prophetic and divine luminescence to the more empirical and everyday gaze of the shepherds. There is a correspondence between the shepherds and the gods. They say the same thing, they see the same thing, but not with same language or with the same eyes. All through the tragedy, we see that same truth presented and formulated in two different ways, with different words in a different discourse, with another gaze. But these gazes communicate with one another. The shepherds correspond exactly to the gods, and it can even be said that the shepherds symbolize them—what the shepherds say is essentially what the gods have already said, but in a different way.

Here we have one of the basic features of the Oedipus tragedy: the communication between the shepherds and the gods, between the recollection of men and the divine prophecies. This correspondence defines the tragedy and establishes a symbolic world in which the memory and the discourse of men are like an empirical margin around the great prophecy of the gods.

This is one of the points on which we should dwell in order to understand this mechanism of the progress of truth in *Oedipus*. On one side there are the gods, on the other, the shepherds; between the two there is the level of the royalty, or more exactly, the level of Oedipus. What is his level of knowledge? What does his gaze signify?

On that subject, certain things need correcting. When the play is analyzed, it's often said that Oedipus is the one who didn't know anything, who was blind, whose eyes were clouded and whose memory was blocked, because he never mentioned and appeared to have forgotten his own actions in killing the king at the triple crossroad. Oedipus, the man of forgetfulness, the man of non-knowledge, the man of the unconscious for Freud. We're aware of all the wordplay that has been made with the name Oedipus.[14] But let's not forget that this wordplay is multifarious, or that the Greeks themselves had already noted that in *Oidipous* we have the word *oida* which means both "to have seen" and "to know." I would like to show that Oedipus, in this mechanism of the *sumbolon*—of communicating halves, of the interplay of responses between the shepherds and the gods—is not the one who didn't know but, rather, the one who knew too much. He is the one who joined his knowledge and his power in a certain reprehensible way, and whom the *Oedipus* story was meant to expel finally from history.

The very title of Sophocles' tragedy is interesting. *Oedipus* is *Oedipus the King, Oidipous turannos*. It's difficult to translate the word *turannos*—the translation doesn't capture the exact signification of the word. Oedipus is the man of power, the man who exercises a certain power. And it is characteristic that the title of Sophocles' play is not *Oedipus the Incestuous*, or *Oedipus, the Killer of His Father*, but *Oedipus the King*. What does the kingship of Oedipus mean?

We may note the importance of the thematic of power throughout the play. What is always in question, essentially, is the power of Oedipus, and that is why he feels threatened.

In the entire tragedy, Oedipus will never say that he is innocent, that he may have done something but it was not of his own accord, that when he killed that man he didn't know it was Laius. That defense at the level of innocence and unconsciousness is never ventured by Sophocles' protagonist in *Oedipus the King*.

It's only in *Oedipus at Colonus* that we will see a blind and wretched Oedipus wailing throughout the play, saying: "I couldn't help it, the gods caught me in a trap that I didn't know about."[15] In *Oedipus the King*, he does not at all defend himself in terms of his innocence. His only problem is power—can he stay in power? It is this power that is at stake from the beginning of the play to the end.

In the first scene, the inhabitants appeal to Oedipus for help against the plague insofar as he is the supreme ruler. "You have the power, you must cure us of the plague." And he answers by saying: "Curing you of the plague would be to my great benefit, for this plague that assails you, also assails me in my sovereignty and my royalty." Oedipus will look for the solution to the problem as one interested in preserving his own kingship. And when he begins to feel threatened by the responses that spring up around him, when the oracle points to him and the prophet says more clearly that he is the culprit, Oedipus, not answering in terms of innocence, says to Tiresias: "You want my power. You have hatched a plot against me to deprive me of my power."[16] He is not afraid of the idea that he may have killed the father or the king. What frightens him is the thought of losing his own power.

During the great dispute with Creon, he says to him: "You have brought an oracle from Delphi, but you have falsified that oracle, because, son of Laius, you claim a power that was given to me."[17] Here again, Oedipus feels threatened by Creon at the level of power and not at the level of his innocence and his culpability. What's at issue in all these confrontations of the play's beginning is power.

And when, at the end of the play, the truth will be uncovered, when the slave from Corinth says to Oedipus, "Don't worry, you're not the son of Polybus,"[18] Oedipus will not consider that, not being Polybus' son, he could be the son of someone else and possibly of Laius. He says: "You say that to make me ashamed, to make the people think that I'm the son of a slave; but even if I'm the son of a slave that will not prevent me from exercising power; I am a king like any other."[19] Once more, it's a question of power. It's as the chief officer of the law, as the sovereign that Oedipus will then summon the last witness, the slave from Cithaeron. It's as the sovereign that, threatening the latter with torture, he will extract the truth from him. And when the truth is extracted, when it is known who Oedipus was and what he did—killing of the father, incest with the mother—what do the people of Thebes say? "We were calling you our king." This means that the people of Thebes, while acknowledging Oedipus as the man who was their king, by using the imperfect—"were calling"—now declare him to be stripped of the kingship.

What is in question is Oedipus' fall from power. The proof is that when Oedipus surrenders power to Creon, the last lines of the play are still about power. The final words addressed to Oedipus, before he is taken inside the palace, are pronounced by the new king, Creon: "Don't try to be the master anymore."[20] The word used is *kratein*, which means that Oedipus must no longer command. Creon adds *akratēsas*, a word that means "after having reached the zenith of power" but is also a play on words where the α has a privative meaning "no longer possessing power"; *akratēsas* signifies at the same time "you who rose to the top and who no longer have the power."

After that, the people speak, hailing Oedipus for the last time, "You who were *kratistos*," that is, "You who were at the zenith of power." Now, the Thebans' first greeting to Oedipus was *"o kratunōn Oidipous,"* meaning "Oedipus, the all-powerful!" The entire tragedy has unfolded between these two greetings. It's the tragedy of political power and power-holding. But what is this power that Oedipus had? What characterizes it? Its characteristics are present in Greek thought, Greek history, and Greek philosophy of that period. Oedipus is called *basileus anax*, the first among men, the one who has the *krateia*, the one who holds the power, and he is even called *turannos*. "Tyrant" shouldn't be understood here in its strict sense, given that Polybus, Laius, and all the others were also called *turannos*.

A certain number of characteristics of this power appear in the tragedy of Oedipus. Oedipus has the power; but he has obtained it through a series of episodes, adventures that have made him, at the start, the most wretched of men—outcast child, lost soul, vagabond—and then the most powerful of men. He's known an erratic destiny. He's experienced misery and glory. He's been to the highest point, when he was believed to be the son of Polybus, and to the lowest point, when he became an individual wandering from city to city. Later, he again reaches the top. "The years that have grown along with me," he says, "have sometimes lowered me, sometimes lifted me up."

This alternation of destiny is a characteristic trait of two types of figure: the legendary figure of the epic hero who has lost his citizenship and his country but who regains his glory after a certain number of trials; and the historical figure of the Greek tyrant from the end of the sixth to the beginning of the fifth century. The tyrant being the one who, after having several adventures and having reached the apex of power, was always under the threat of losing it. As described in the Greek texts of that period, the changeableness of fate is characteristic of the figure of the tyrant.

Oedipus is the one who, after having experienced misery, experienced glory; the one who became a king after being a hero. But he becomes the king because he has healed the city by killing the divine Singer, the Bitch who was devouring those who could not solve her riddles. He had healed the city, had enabled it to raise itself up, as he says, to breathe again when it had lost its breath. To designate this healing of the city, Oedipus employs the expression *orthōsan*, "to raise up," *anorthōsan polin*; "to raise up the city." We find this same expression in Solon. Solon, who was not exactly a tyrant but, rather, the Lawgiver, prided himself on having raised up the Athenian city-state at the end of the sixth century. This is also a characteristic of all the tyrants who rose to power in Greece during the seventh and sixth centuries. Not only did they experience ups and downs but they also had the role of lifting the cities up by means of a just economic distribution—like Cypselus at Corinth, or through just laws, like Solon at Athens. So these are two basic characteristics of the Greek tyrant as they are presented in the texts of the time of Sophocles or even ones prior to that.

We also find in *Oedipus* a series of negative characteristics of tyranny. Oedipus is reproached with several things in his exchanges with Tiresias and Creon and even with the people. Creon, for example, tells him, "You're wrong; you identify with this city where you were not born, you imagine that you belong to this city and that it belongs to you; I belong to this city as well, it's not yours alone."[21] Now, if we look at the stories of Herodotus, for example, telling about the old Greek tyrants, in particular about Cypselus of Corinth, we'll see that they're about someone who thought he owned the city.[22] Cypselus said that Zeus had given the city to him and he had given it in turn to the citizens. One finds exactly the same thing in the tragedy of Sophocles.

In the same way, Oedipus is the one who attaches no importance to the laws and who replaces them with his whims and his orders. He says this in so many words. When Creon reproaches him for wanting to banish him, saying that this decision was not just, Oedipus answers, "No matter if it's just or not, it will have to be obeyed all the same."[23] His wish will be the law of the city. It's for this reason that, when his fall begins, the Chorus of the people will reproach Oedipus with having shown contempt for *dikē*, for justice. So in Oedipus we have no trouble recognizing a figure that is clearly defined, highlighted, catalogued, characterized by Greek thought of the fifth century—the tyrant.

This tyrant figure is characterized not only by power but also by a certain type of knowledge. The Greek tyrant was not just the person who took power: he was the person who took power because he possessed or emphasized the fact of possessing a certain knowledge that was superior in its efficacy to that of others. That is precisely the case with Oedipus. Oedipus is the person who succeeded in solving by means of his thought, his knowledge, the famous riddle of the Sphinx. And just as Solon was in fact able to give Athens just laws and restore the city to health because he was *sophos*, wise, so Oedipus was also able to solve the riddle of the Sphinx because he was *sophos*.

What is this knowledge Oedipus possesses? What are its characteristics? Oedipus' knowledge is characterized the whole length of the play. Oedipus says repeatedly that he has defeated the others, he has solved the riddle of the Sphinx, has cured the city by means of what he calls *gnōmē*, his knowledge or his *tekhnē*. Other times, he describes himself as the one who has found, *ēurēka*, to indicate his mode of knowledge. This is the word that Oedipus uses most often to designate what he did in the past and is trying to do now. Oedipus solved the riddle of the Sphinx because he "found." If he is to save Thebes again, he will again have to find, *euriskein*. What does *euriskein* signify? That "finding" activity is characterized initially in the play as a thing done by oneself. Oedipus stresses that constantly: "When I solved the riddle of the Sphinx, I didn't call upon anyone," he says to the people and to the prophet. He tells the people: "You wouldn't have been able to help me in any way to solve the riddle of the Sphinx. You couldn't do anything against the divine Singer." And he says to Tiresias: "What kind of a prophet are you anyway? You weren't even able to rescue Thebes from the Sphinx. When everyone was plunged into terror, I delivered Thebes all by myself; I didn't learn anything from anyone, I didn't use any messenger, I came in person." Finding is something done by oneself. Finding is also what one does when one opens one's eyes. And Oedipus is the one who says repeatedly: "I asked questions, and since no one was able to inform me, I opened my eyes and ears, and I saw." The verb *oida*, which means at the same time "to know" and "to see," is frequently employed by Oedipus. *Oidipous* is the one who is capable of that activity of knowing and seeing. He is the man of seeing, the man of the gaze, and he will be that to the end.

If Oedipus falls into a trap, it's precisely because, in his determination to know, he has forced the testimony and the recollection of the persons who saw: he pressed the search until the slave who had witnessed everything and who knew the truth, was ferreted out of the depths of Cithaeron. Oedipus' knowledge is the kind that comes from experience. It is also that solitary knowledge, that firsthand acquaintance, of the man who, all by himself, without relying on what is said, wishes to see with his own eyes. It is the autocratic knowledge of the tyrant who can govern the city through his own abilities. The metaphor of that which governs, that which commands, is frequently employed by Oedipus to indicate what he does. Oedipus is the captain, the one who at the prow of the ship opens his eyes to see. And precisely because he opens his eyes to what is happening, he finds the accident, the unexpected, fortune, *tukhē*.

Because he was that man of the autocratic gaze, open to things, Oedipus fell into the trap.

What I would like to show is that in Sophocles' play Oedipus basically represents a certain type of what I would call knowledge-and-power, power-and-knowledge. It's because he exercises a certain tyrannical and solitary power, aloof from both the oracle of the gods—which he doesn't want to hear—and what the people say and want, that, in his craving to govern by discovering for himself, he finds, in the last instance, the evidence of those who have seen.

We thus see how the game of halves could function, and how, at the end of the play, Oedipus is a superfluous figure. He is superfluous in that this tyrannical power, this knowledge of one who wants to see with his own eyes without listening either to the gods or to men enables an exact match-up of what the gods had said and what the people knew. Without meaning to, Oedipus succeeds in establishing the junction between the prophecy of the gods and the memory of men. Oedipal knowledge, the excess of power and the excess of knowledge were such that he became unnecessary: the circle closed on him or, rather, the two fragments of the tessera were fit together—and Oedipus, in his solitary power, became unnecessary. Once the two fragments were conjoined, the image of Oedipus became monstrous. With his tyrannical power, Oedipus could do too much; with his solitary knowledge, he knew too much. In that state of excess, he was also his mother's husband and his sons' brother. Oedipus is the man of excess, the man who has too much of everything—in his power, his knowledge, his family, his sexuality. Oedipus, the double man, was excessive with regard to the symbolic transparency of what the shepherds knew and what the gods had said.

The tragedy of Oedipus is rather close, then, to what will be, a few years later, Platonic philosophy. It should be said that for Plato the knowledge of slaves, the empirical recollection of what has been seen, will be devalorized in favor of a deeper, essential memory that is the recollection of what was seen in intelligible heaven. But the important thing is what will be fundamentally devalorized, discredited, both in Sophocles' tragedy and in Plato's *Republic*: the theme or, rather, the figure, form, of a political knowledge both privileged and exclusive. What is targeted by Sophocles' tragedy and Plato's philosophy, when they are placed in a historical dimension, what is aimed at behind Oedipus *sophos*—Oedipus the wise man, the knowing tyrant, the man of *tekhnē*, of *gnōmē*—is the famous sophist, the professional of political power and knowledge, who actually existed in the Athenian society of Sophocles' era. But, behind him, the real object of Plato and Sophocles is another category of figure, of which the sophist was in a sense the little representative, the continuation, and the historical end—the figure of the tyrant. In the seventh and sixth centuries, the tyrant was the man of power and knowledge, the one who ruled both by the power he exercised and by the knowledge he possessed. Ultimately, what was aimed at behind all these figures, without it being present in Plato's text or in that of Sophocles, was the great historical personage that actually existed, though he had been absorbed into a legendary context—the famous Assyrian king.

In European societies of the Mediterranean East, at the end of the second millennium and the beginning of the first, political power always implied the possession of a certain type of knowledge. By the fact of holding power, the king and those around him held a knowledge that could not and must not be communicated to the other social groups. Knowledge and power were exactly reciprocal, correlative, superimposed. There couldn't be any knowledge without power; and there couldn't be any political power without the possession of a certain special knowledge.

This is the form of power-knowledge that Georges Dumézil, in his studies concerning the three functions, has isolated, showing that the first function was that of a magical and religious political power.[24] Knowledge of the gods, knowledge of the action that can be brought to bear on us by the gods—that whole magico-religious knowledge is present in the political function.

What occurred at the origin of Greek society, at the origin of the Greek age of the fifth century, at the origin of our civilization, was the dismantling of that great unity of a political power that was, at the same time, a knowledge—the dismantling of that unity of a magico-religious power which existed in the great Assyrian empires; which the Greek tyrants, impregnated with Oriental civilization, tried to restore for their own purposes; and which the sophists of the sixth and fifth centuries still used as they could, in the form of lessons paid for in cash. We witness that long decomposition during the five or six centuries of archaic Greece. And when classical Greece appeared—Sophocles represents its starting date, its sunrise—what had to disappear for this society to exist was the union of power and knowledge. From this time onward, the man of power would be the man of ignorance. In the end, what befell Oedipus was that, knowing too much, he didn't know anything. From then on, Oedipus would function as the man of power, the blind ruler who didn't know, and who didn't know because he could do too much.

So, whereas power was taxed with ignorance, inattention, obliviousness, obscurity, there would be, on one side, the seer and the philosopher in communication with the truth, the eternal truths of the gods or of the mind, and, on the other, the people, holding none of the power, who bore the memory or could still give evidence of the truth. Thus, beyond a power that had become monumentally blind like Oedipus, there were the shepherds who remembered and the prophets who spoke the truth.

The West would be dominated by the great myth according to which truth never belongs to political power: political power is blind—the real knowledge is that which one possesses when one is in contact with the gods or when one remembers things, when one looks at the great eternal Sun or one opens one's eyes to what came to pass. With Plato there began a great Western myth: that there is an antinomy between knowledge and power. If there is knowledge, it must renounce power. Where knowledge and science are found in their pure truth, there can no longer be any political power.

This great myth needs to be dispelled. It is this myth which Nietzsche began to demolish by showing, in the numerous texts already cited, that, behind all knowledge [*savoir*], behind all attainment of knowledge [*connaissance*], what is involved is a struggle for power. Political power is not absent from knowledge, it is woven together with it.

III

In the preceding lecture I referred to two forms or types of judicial settlement, litigation, contest, or dispute that were present in Greek civilization. The first, rather archaic form is found in Homer. Two warriors came face to face to determine who was wrong and who was right, who had violated the other's rights. The task of resolving that question comes down to a rule-governed dispute, the challenge between the two warriors. One would challenge the other, "Can you swear before the gods that you didn't do what I am accusing you of?" In a procedure like this there was no judge, judgment, inquiry, or testimony to determine who spoke the truth. The responsibility for deciding—not who spoke the truth, but who was right—was entrusted to the fight, the challenge, the risk that each one would run.

The second form is the one that unfolds throughout *Oedipus the King*. To solve a problem that, in a sense, is also a problem of contestation, a criminal issue—who killed King Laius?—there appears a new figure, absent from the old Homeric procedure, the shepherd. Though a man of no importance, a slave holed up in his hut, the shepherd saw what he saw, and because he possesses that little fragment of a recollection, because in his discourse he bears the evidence of what he saw, he can challenge and overthrow the pride of the king or the presumptuousness of the tyrant. The witness, the humble witness, solely by the action of the truth he saw and he utters, can single-handedly defeat the most powerful of men. *Oedipus the King* is a kind of compendium of the history of Greek law. Several of Sophocles' plays, such as *Antigone* and *Electra*, are a kind of theatrical ritualization of the history of law. This dramatization of the history of Greek law offers us a summary of one of the great conquests of Athenian democracy: the story of the process through which the people took possession of the right to judge, of the right to tell the truth, to set the truth against their own masters, to judge those who governed them.

That great conquest of Greek democracy, that right to bear witness, to oppose truth to power, was established in a long process born and instituted in a definitive way in Athens throughout the fifth century. That right to set a powerless truth against a truthless power gave rise to a series of major cultural forms that were characteristic of Greek society.

First, there was the elaboration of what we may call the rational forms of proof and demonstration: how to produce truth, under what conditions, what forms to observe, what rules to apply. Those forms are philosophy, rational systems, scientific systems. Second, and in relation to the previous forms, an art of persuading developed, an art of convincing people of the truth of what is said, of winning the victory for truth or, what is more, by means of truth. Here we have the problem of Greek rhetoric. Third, there was the development of a new type of knowledge—knowledge gained through witnessing, through recollection, through inquiry. A knowledge by inquiry which historians such as Herodotus, a short time before Sophocles, naturalists, botanists, geographers, Greek travelers, would develop and Aristotle would totalize and make encyclopedic.

In Greece there was, then, a sort of great revolution which, through a series of political struggles and contestations, resulted in the elaboration of a specific form of judicial, juridical discovery of truth. The latter constituted the mold, the model on the basis of which a series of other knowledges—philosophical, rhetorical, and empirical—were able to develop and to characterize Greek thought.

Quite curiously, the history of the birth of the inquiry remained forgotten and was lost, having been taken up again, in other forms, several centuries later, in the Middle Ages.

In the European Middle Ages, one sees a kind of second birth of the inquiry which was slower and more obscure than the first, but had much more success. The Greek method of inquiry had remained stationary, had not achieved the founding of a rational knowledge capable of indefinite development. By contrast, the inquiry that arose in the Middle Ages would acquire extraordinary dimensions. Its destiny would be practically coextensive with the particular destiny of so-called "European" or "Western" culture.

The old law that settled disputes between individuals in Germanic societies, at the time when these came into contact with the Roman Empire, was in a sense very close in some of its forms to archaic Greek law. It was a law in which the system of inquiry did not exist; disputes between individuals were settled by the testing game.

Ancient Germanic law during the period when Tacitus began to analyze that odd civilization extending to the gates of the Empire can be characterized, schematically, in the following way.

In the first place, there was no public legal action; that is, there was no one—representing society, the group, authority, or the holder of power—charged with bringing accusations against individuals. For a penal type of trial to take place, there had to be a wrong, or at least someone claiming he had suffered a wrong or presenting himself as a victim, and this self-declared victim had to name his adversary. The victim could be the person directly offended or someone who belonged to his family and was handling the relative's suit. What characterized a penal action was always a kind of duel, an opposition between individuals, families, or groups; there was no intervention by any representative of authority. It was a matter of a complaint made by one individual to another, involving only these two parties, the defendant and the accuser. We only know of two rather curious cases in which there was a sort of public action—treason and homosexuality. The community then intervened, considering itself as being injured, and collectively demanded reparation from the individual. Consequently, the first condition for a penal action in the old Germanic law was the existence of two personages, never three.

The second condition was that, once the penal action was introduced—once any individual declared himself to be a victim and called for reparation from the other party—the judicial settlement would ensue as a kind of continuation of the clash between the individuals. A kind of private, individual war developed, and the penal procedure was merely the ritualization of that conflict between individuals. Germanic law did not assume an opposition between war and justice, or an identity between justice and peace; on the contrary, it assumed that law was a special, regulated way of conducting war between individuals and controlling acts of revenge. Law was thus a regulated way of making war. For example, when someone was killed, one of his close relatives could make use of the judicial practice of revenge, which meant not renouncing the possibility of killing someone, normally the murderer. Entering the domain of law meant killing the killer, but killing him according to certain rules, certain forms. If the killer had committed the crime in such-and-such manner, it would be necessary to kill him by cutting him to pieces or by cutting his head off and placing it on a stake at the entrance to his house. These acts would ritualize the gesture of revenge and characterize it as judicial revenge. Law, then, was the ritual form of war.

The third condition was that, while it was true that there was no opposition between law and war, it was nonetheless possible to reach an agreement—that is, to break off those regulated hostilities.

Ancient Germanic law always offered the possibility, throughout that long series of reciprocal and ritual acts of revenge, to arrive at an understanding, a compromise. The series of vengeful actions could be broken with a pact. In that event, the two adversaries would appeal to an arbiter who, in harmony with them and with their mutual consent, would set a sum of money that would constitute the compensation—not compensation for a transgression [*faute*], for there was no transgression but only a wrong [*tort*] and a vengeance. In this procedure of Germanic law, one of the two adversaries would buy back the right to have peace, to escape the possible revenge of his adversary. He would redeem his own life, and not the blood that he had spilled, by thus bringing an end to the war. The cessation of the ritual war was the third act or the final act of the judicial drama in ancient Germanic law.

The system that regulated conflicts and disputes in the Germanic societies of that era was therefore entirely governed by struggle and compromise, involving a test of strength that could end with an economic settlement. It depended on a procedure that did not allow for the intervention of a third individual who would stand between the two others as a neutral party seeking the truth, trying to determine which of the two had told the truth. A procedure of inquiry, a search for the truth, never intervened in this type of system. This was how the old Germanic law was constituted, before the invasion of the Roman Empire.

I won't linger over the long series of vicissitudes that brought this Germanic law into rivalry, competition, and at times collusion with Roman law. Between the fifth and sixth centuries of our age, there was a series of penetrations and conflicts between those two systems of law. Every time a state would begin to take form on the ruins of the Roman Empire, every time a state structure began to emerge, Roman law, the old law of the state, would then be reinvigorated. Thus, in the Merovingian reigns, and above all during the epoch of the Carolingian Empire, Roman law overshadowed Germanic law in a certain way. Moreover, every time there was a disintegration of those embryonic forms, those first lineaments of a state, the old Germanic law would reappear. When the Carolingian Empire collapsed in the tenth century, Germanic law triumphed, and Roman law fell into oblivion for several centuries, slowly reappearing only at the end of the twelfth century and in the course of the thirteenth century. Hence feudal law was essentially of the Germanic type. It doesn't present any of the elements of the inquiry procedures, the truth-establishment procedures of Greek societies or the Roman Empire.

In feudal law, disputes between two individuals were settled by the system of the test. When an individual came forward with a claim, a contestation, accusing another of having killed or robbed, the dispute between the two would be resolved through a series of tests accepted by both individuals and by which both were bound. This system was a way of proving not the truth, but the strength, the weight, the importance of the one who spoke.

First of all there were social tests, tests of an individual's social importance. In the old law of eleventh-century Burgundy, when a person was accused of murder, he could completely establish his innocence by gathering about him twelve witnesses who swore that he had not committed the murder. The oath was not based, for example, on the fact that they had seen the alleged victim alive, or on an alibi for the alleged murderer. To take an oath, to testify that an individual had not killed, one had to be a relative of the accused. One had to have social relations of kinship with him, which would vouch not for his innocence but for his social importance. This showed the solidarity that a particular individual could obtain, his weight, his influence, the importance of the group to which he belonged and of the persons ready to support him in a battle or a conflict. The proof of his innocence, the proof that he had not committed the act in question was by no means what the evidence of witnesses delivered.

Second, there were tests of a verbal type. When an individual was accused of something—robbery or murder—he had to reply to that accusation with a certain number of formulas, affirming that he had not committed any murder or robbery. By uttering these formulas, he could fail or succeed. In certain cases, a person would utter the formula and lose—not for having told a falsehood, or because it was proved that he had lied, but, rather, for not having uttered the formula in the correct way. A grammatical error, a word alteration would invalidate the formula, regardless of the truth of what one asserted. That only a verbal game was involved at the level of the test is confirmed by the fact that in the case of a minor, a woman, or a priest, the accused could be replaced by another person. This other person, who later in the history of law would become the attorney, would utter the formulas in place of the accused. If he made a mistake in uttering them, the person on whose behalf he spoke would lose the case.

Third, there were the old magico-religious tests of the oath. The accused would be asked to take an oath and if he declined or hesitated he would lose the case.

Finally, there were the famous corporal, physical tests called ordeals, which consisted in subjecting a person to a sort of game, a struggle with his own body, to find out whether he would pass or fail. For example, in the time of the Carolingian Empire, there was a famous test imposed on individuals accused of murder, in certain areas of northern France. The accused was required to walk on coals and two days later if he still had scars he would lose the case. There were yet other tests such as the ordeal by water, which consisted in tying a person's right hand to his left foot and throwing him into the water. If he didn't drown he would lose the case, because the water didn't accept him as it should; and if he drowned he had won the case, seeing that the water had not rejected him. All these confrontations of the individual or his body with the natural elements were a symbolic transposition of the struggle of individuals among themselves, the semantics of which would need to be studied. Basically, it was always a matter of combat, of deciding who was the stronger. In old Germanic law, the trial was nothing more than the regulated, ritualized continuation of war.

I could have offered more convincing examples, such as the fights between two opponents during a trial, physical fights, the famous judgments of God. When two individuals clashed over property ownership, or because of a killing, it was always possible, if they agreed, for them to fight, so long as they obeyed certain rules— length of the fight, type of weapons—in front of an audience present only to ensure that what occurred was consistent with the rules. The winner of the combat would win the case, without being given the possibility of telling the truth, or rather, without being asked to prove the truth of his claim.

In the system of the feudal judicial test, it was a matter not of truth-seeking but of a kind of game with a binary structure. The individual accepted the test or declined it. If he declined, if he didn't want to try the test, he would lose the case in advance. If the test took place he would win or be defeated: there was no other possibility. The binary form is the first characteristic of the test.

The second characteristic is that the test always ended with a victory or a defeat. There was always someone who won and someone who lost, the stronger and the weaker, a favorable outcome or an unfavorable outcome. There was never anything like a judgment [*sentence*] of the sort that would come into practice at the end of the twelfth century and beginning of the thirteenth. Judgment consisted in a declaration by a third party that, a certain person having told the truth is judged to be right, another having told a lie is judged to be wrong. Consequently, judgment did not exist in feudal law; the separation of truth and untruth between individuals played no role in it—there existed only victory or defeat.

The third characteristic is that this test was, in a certain way, automatic. The presence of a third party was not necessary in order to distinguish the two adversaries. It was the balance of forces, luck, vigor, physical resistance, and mental agility that would distinguish the individuals, according to a mechanism that developed automatically. Authority intervened only as a witness to the regularity of the procedure. When the judicial tests took place, someone was there who bore the name of judge—the political sovereign or someone appointed with the mutual consent of the two adversaries— simply to verify that the fight went by the rules. The judge attested not to the truth but to the regularity of the procedure.

The fourth characteristic is that in this mechanism the test did not serve to name, to identify the one who had told the truth; rather, it established that the stronger individual was, at the same time, the one who was right. The judicial test was a way of ritualizing war or of transposing it symbolically. It was a way of giving it a certain number of secondary, theatrical forms, so that the stronger would be designated thereby as the one who was right. The test was a mechanical executor [*opérateur*] of the law, a commutator of force into law, a sort of gearing that enabled the shift from force to law. It didn't have an apophantic function, it didn't have the function of designating or manifesting or discovering the truth. It was a legal device, and not a truth device or an apophantic device. That is how the test operated in old feudal law.

This system of judicial practices disappeared at the end of the twelfth century and in the course of the thirteenth. During the en-

tire second half of the Middle Ages, one would witness the transformation of those old practices and the invention of new forms of
judicial practice and procedure—forms that were absolutely essential for the history of Europe and for the history of the whole world,
inasmuch as Europe violently imposed its dominion on the entire
surface of the earth. What was invented in this reformulation of law
was something that involved not so much the contents of knowledge as its forms and conditions of possibility. What was invented
in law during this period was a particular way of knowing, a condition of possibility of knowledge whose destiny was to be crucial
in the Western world. That mode of knowledge was the inquiry,
which appeared for the first time in Greece and which, after the
fall of the Roman Empire, remained hidden for several centuries.
However, the inquiry that reappeared in the twelfth and thirteenth
centuries was of a somewhat different type than the one we saw
exemplified in *Oedipus*.

Why did the old judicial form, some of whose basic features I
have presented to you, disappear during that era? We may say,
schematically, that one of the fundamental traits of Western feudal
society was that a relatively small segment of the circulation of
goods was carried out by commerce. It was handled through mechanisms of inheritance or testamentary transmission, and above all
through warlike, military, extrajudicial, or judicial contestation.
One of the most important means of ensuring the circulation of
goods in the early Middle Ages was war, rapine, occupation of a
piece of land, a castle, a town. There was a moving border between
law and war, seeing that law was a certain way of continuing war.
For example, someone in command of an armed force would occupy an estate, a forest, any kind of property, and then assert his
right; thus began a long dispute at the end of which the one who
possessed no armed force and wanted to recover his land obtained
the invader's departure only by means of a payment. This stood on
the border between the judicial and the bellicose, and it was one
of the most frequent ways for someone to become rich. In early
feudalism, the circulation and exchange of goods, impoverishment
and enrichment were brought about in most cases through this
mechanism.

It is interesting, moreover, to compare feudal society in Europe
and the so-called primitive societies currently studied by ethnolo-

gists. In these, the exchange of goods occurs through contestation and rivalry enacted above all in the form of prestige, at the level of displays and signs. In a feudal society, the circulation of goods also took place in the form of rivalry and contestation, but rivalry and contestation that were belligerent rather than prestige-driven. In so-called primitive societies, things of value are exchanged in competitive levies because they are not just goods but also signs. In feudal societies, things of value were exchanged not only because they were goods and signs, but because they were goods, signs, and weapons. Wealth was the means by which both violence and law were brought to bear on the life and death of others. Throughout the Middle Ages war, judicial litigation, and the circulation of goods were part of one great fluctuating process.

So a dual tendency characterized feudal society. First, there was a concentration of arms in the hands of the most powerful, who tended to prevent their use by the less powerful. To defeat someone was to deprive him of his weapons; the result was a concentration of armed power that, in feudal states, gave more force to the most powerful and finally to the most powerful of all, the monarch. Second and at the same time, there were judicial actions and contests that were a way of causing goods to circulate. We can thus understand why the most powerful sought to control judicial disputes, preventing them from developing spontaneously between individuals, and why they tried to take hold of the judicial and litigious circulation of goods—which implied the concentration of arms and of the judicial power that was forming during that period—in the hands of the same individuals.

The existence of executive, legislative, and judicial power is thought to be a rather old idea in constitutional law. The truth is that it's a recent idea, which dates approximately from Montesquieu. But what interests us here is to see how something like a judicial power took form. In the early Middle Ages, there was no judicial power. Settlements were reached between individuals. People asked the most powerful figure, or the one exercising sovereignty, not to see that justice was done but to verify the regularity of the procedure, as a function of his political, magical, and religious powers. There was no autonomous judicial power, and no judicial power in the hands of the holder of military and political power. Insofar as judicial contest ensured the circulation of goods, the right to regulate and control that judicial contest was usurped by the richest and most powerful because it was a means of accumulating wealth.

The accumulation of wealth and armed power and the concentration of judicial power in the hands of a few were one and the same process operating in the early Middle Ages, reaching its maturity at the time of the formation of the first great medieval monarchy, in the middle and at the end of the twelfth century. At that time, things appeared that were completely new relative to feudal society, the Carolingian Empire, and the old rules of Roman law.

First: A mode of proceeding [*une justice*] that is no longer a contestation between individuals and a voluntary acceptance by those individuals of a certain number of rules of settlement but, rather, one imposed from above on individuals, adversaries, and parties. Thereafter individuals would no longer have the right to resolve their own disputes, whether regularly or irregularly; they would have to submit to a power external to them, imposing itself as a judicial political power.

Second: There appeared a totally new figure, without precedent in Roman law—the prosecutor. That curious personage, who appeared in Europe around the twelfth century, would present himself as the representative of the sovereign, the king, or the master. When there was a crime, an offense, or a dispute between individuals, he would appear as a power that was injured by the mere fact that an offense or a crime had occurred. The prosecutor would make common cause with the victim; he would be behind the one instituting an action, saying: "If it is true that that man did injury to another, I can affirm, as the representative of the sovereign, that his sovereignty, his power, the order that he ensures, and the law that he established have also been injured by that individual. Thus, I too stand against him." In this way, the sovereign and political authority stood in for and gradually replaced the victim. This utterly new phenomenon would enable political power to take control of the judicial procedures. The prosecutor, therefore, appeared as the representative of the sovereign, who was injured by the offense.

Third: An absolutely new concept appeared—the infraction. So long as the judicial drama unfolded between two individuals, the victim and the accused, it was only a matter of the wrong that one individual had done to another. The question was whether there had been a wrong committed and who was right. From the moment that the sovereign, or his representative, the prosecutor, said, "I too was injured by the offense," the wrong was not just an offense of one individual against another, but also an individual's offense against the state, against the sovereign as the state's representative; not an attack upon an individual but an attack against the law of the state itself. Thus, in the concept of crime the old concept of wrong was to be replaced by that of infraction. The infraction was not a wrong committed by one individual against another, it was an offense or injury done by an individual to order, to the state, to the law, to society, to sovereignty, to the sovereign. The infraction is one of the great inventions of medieval thought. We thus see how state power appropriated the entire judicial procedure, the entire mechanism of interindividual settlement of disputes in the early Middle Ages.

Fourth: There is one more discovery still, a last invention just as diabolical as that of the prosecutor and the infraction. The state, or rather, the sovereign (since we cannot speak of a state existing during that period), was not only the injured party but also the one that demanded the compensation. When an individual lost a trial, he was declared guilty and still owed a compensation to his victim. But the compensation was absolutely not that of ancient feudal law or ancient Germanic law: it was no longer a matter of buying back one's peace by settling accounts with one's adversary. The guilty party was required not just to compensate for the offense he had committed against another individual but also to compensate for the offense he had committed against the sovereign, the state, the law. In this way there appeared, along with the mechanism of fines, the great mechanism of confiscations. These confiscations of property were one of the chief means for the great emerging monarchies to enrich and enlarge their holdings. The Western monarchies were founded on the appropriation of the judicial system, which enabled them to apply these mechanisms of confiscation. That is the political background of this transformation.

Now we need to explain the establishment of the judgment [*sentence*], to explain how one reached the end of a process in which one of the principal figures was the prosecutor. If the main victim of an infraction was the king, if the prosecutor was the primary plaintiff, it is understandable that judicial settlement could no longer be obtained through the mechanisms of the test. The king or his representative, the prosecutor, could not risk their own lives or their own possessions every time a crime was committed. The accused and the prosecutor did not confront each other on even ground, as in a clash between two individuals; it was necessary to find a new mechanism that was no longer that of the test, of the struggle between two adversaries, to determine whether someone was guilty or not. The warlike model could no longer be applied.

What model was to be adopted? This was one of the great moments of the history of the West. There were two models for solving the problem. One was a model indigenous to the judicial institution. In feudal law itself, in ancient Germanic law, there was a circumstance in which the collectivity as a whole could intervene, accuse someone, and obtain his conviction: this was the flagrant offense, where an individual was surprised in the very act of committing the crime. In that instance, the persons who surprised him had the right to bring him before the sovereign, the holder of a political authority, and say, "We saw him doing such-and-such thing and so he must be punished or made to pay a compensation." Thus, in the very sphere of law, there was a model of collective intervention and authoritative judgment for the settlement of a judicial suit. It applied to the flagrant offense, when the crime was discovered as it was taking place. Obviously that model couldn't be used when the individual was not caught in the act, which was usually the case. The problem, then, was to determine under what conditions the model of the flagrant offense could be generalized and used in the new legal system that was emerging, completely controlled by political sovereignty and by the representatives of the political sovereign.

The authorities preferred to use a second, extrajudicial model, which was in turn subdivided in two or, rather, during that period, had a double existence, a double usage. This was the inquiry model, which had existed in the time of the Carolingian Empire. When the representatives of the sovereign had to resolve a problem of law, of power, or a question of taxes, morals, ground rent, or ownership, they initiated something that was perfectly ritualized and regular—the *inquisitio*, the inquiry. The representative of power would summon the persons regarded as being knowledgeable about morals, law, or property titles. He would assemble these persons, making them swear to tell the truth, to tell what they knew, what they had seen or what they had learned from having heard it said. Then, left to themselves, these persons would deliberate; at the end of this deliberation they would be asked for the solution to the problem. This was a model of administrative management, which the officials of the Carolingian Empire routinely applied. It was still employed, after the breakup of the empire, by William the Conqueror in England. In 1066, the Norman conquerors occupied England; they seized the Anglo-Saxon properties and entered into litigation with the indigenous population and each other over the possession of those properties. To establish order, to integrate the new Norman population into the ancient Anglo-Saxon population, William the Conqueror carried out an enormous inquiry concerning the status of properties, the status of taxes, the system of ground rent, and so on. This was the famous *Domesday Book*, the only comprehensive example that we have of those inquiries that were an old administrative practice of the Carolingian emperors.

This procedure of administrative inquiry had several important characteristics:

1. Political power was the essential personage.

2. Power was exercised first of all by posing questions, by interrogating; it did not know the truth and sought to discover it.

3. In order to determine the truth, power appealed to the notables, to the persons fit to know, given their position, their age, their wealth, their notability, etc.

4. Contrary to what one sees at the end of *Oedipus the King*, the king consults the notables without forcing them to tell the truth through the use of violence, pressure, or torture. They are asked to meet voluntarily and give their collective opinion; they are allowed to say collectively what they deem to be the truth.

We thus have a type of truth-establishment closely tied to the administrative management of the first great state form known in the West. Yet these inquiry procedures were forgotten during the tenth and eleventh centuries in early feudal Europe, and would have been completely forgotten had not the Church used them in the management of its own possessions. This analysis must be complicated a little, though: if the Church made new use of the Carolingian method of inquiry, it was because the Church had already employed it before the Carolingian Empire, for reasons that were more spiritual than administrative.

So there was an inquiry practice in the Church of the early Middle Ages, in the Merovingian and Carolingian Church. That method was called *visitatio*; it consisted in the visit the bishop was officially required to make in traveling through his diocese, and it was later adopted by the great monastic orders. On arriving at an appointed place, the bishop would first initiate the *inquisitio generalis*, the general inquisition, by questioning all those who should know—the notables, the elders, the most learned, the most virtuous—about what had happened in his absence, especially if there had been transgressions, crimes, and so on. If this inquiry met with an affirmative response, the bishop would pass to a second stage, the *inquisitio specialis*, the special inquisition, which consisted in trying to find out who had done what, in determining who was really the author and what was the nature of the act. There is a third and last point: the offender's confession could interrupt the inquisition at any stage, in its general or special form. The person who had committed the crime could present himself and declare publicly: "Yes, a crime was committed. It consisted in this. I am its author."

This spiritual, essentially religious form of the ecclesiastical inquiry continued to exist down through the Middle Ages, acquiring administrative and economic functions. When the Church came to be Europe's only coherent economico-political body, in the tenth, eleventh, and twelfth centuries, the ecclesiastical inquisition was at the same time a spiritual inquiry concerning sins, transgressions, and crimes committed, and an administrative inquiry concerning the way in which the Church's assets were managed and the profits gathered, accumulated, distributed, and so on. This religious and administrative model of the inquiry subsisted up to the twelfth century, when the state that was forming—or, rather, the person of the sovereign that was emerging as the source of all power—appropriated judicial procedures. Those judicial procedures could no longer function according to the system of the test. In what way, then, was the prosecutor to establish whether someone was guilty or not? This model—spiritual and administrative, religious and political—this method for managing, overseeing, and controlling souls was found in the Church: the inquiry understood as a gaze focused as much on possessions and riches as on hearts, acts, and intentions. It was this model that was taken up and adapted in judicial procedure. The king's prosecutor would do the same thing that the visiting ecclesiastics did in the parishes, dioceses, and communities. He would seek to establish through an *inquisitio*, through an inquiry, whether there had been a crime, what crime it was, and who had committed it.

The hypothesis that I'd like to put forward is that the inquiry had a dual origin: an administrative origin, connected to the emergence of the state during the Carolingian period, and a religious, ecclesiastical origin that remained present during the Middle Ages. It was this inquiry procedure that the king's prosecutor—the developing monarchical judicial system—used to deal with the case of the flagrant offense I spoke of earlier. The problem was how to generalize the flagrant offense procedure to cover crimes that were not of the domain, the field of actuality. How could the king's prosecutor bring the guilty person before a judicial authority if he didn't know who the guilty person was, since there had not been any flagrant offense. The inquiry was to be the substitute for the flagrant offense procedure: if one managed to assemble persons who could affirm under oath that they had seen, that they knew, that they were well informed—if it was possible to establish through them that something had actually taken place—then one would have, by means of the inquiry via these persons who knew, the indirect equivalent of the flagrant offense. And one could treat gestures, actions, offenses, crimes that were no longer in the field of actuality, as if they were discovered in flagrante delicto. This was a new way of extending actuality, of transferring it from one time period to another and of offering it to the gaze, to knowledge, as if it were still present. This integration of the inquiry procedure, reactualizing what had transpired, making it present, tangible, immediate, and true, as if one had witnessed it, constituted a major discovery.

We can draw some conclusions from this analysis.

First: It is customary to contrast the old tests of barbarian law with the new rational inquiry procedure. I called attention above to the different ways in which people tried to establish who was right in the early Middle Ages. We have the impression that those were crude, archaic, irrational systems. People are still impressed by the fact that it was necessary to await the twelfth century to arrive finally at a rational system of truth-establishment, with the inquiry procedure. I don't believe, however, that the latter was simply the result of a kind of progress of rationality. The inquiry was not arrived at by rationalizing judicial procedures. The use of that procedure in the judicial domain was made not only possible but necessary by a whole political transformation, a new political structure. In medieval Europe, the inquiry was primarily a governmental process, an administrative technique, a management method—in other words, it was a particular way of exercising power. It would be a mistake to see the inquiry as the natural result of reason acting upon itself, developing itself, making its own progress, or to see it as the effect of a knowledge [*connaissance*], of a subject of knowledge engaged in self-transformation.

No history constructed in terms of a progress of reason, of a refinement of knowledge, can account for the acquisition of the rationality of the inquiry. Its emergence was a complex political phenomenon. Analysis of the political transformations of medieval society is necessary in order to explain how, why, and when this type of truth-establishment, based on completely different juridical procedures, appeared. No reference to a subject of knowledge and its internal history would account for the phenomenon. Only an analysis of the games of political force, of power relations, can explain the appearance of the inquiry.

Second: The inquiry derived from a certain type of power relation, from a way of exercising power. It was brought into law from the Church and, therefore, was permeated with religious categories. In the conception of the early Middle Ages, the essential notion was the wrong [*tort*], something having occurred between two individuals; there was no transgression [*faute*] or infraction. Transgression, sin, and moral culpability did not play any role whatever. The problem was to know if there had been an offense, who had done it, and if the one claiming to have sustained it was capable of enduring the test he proposed to his adversary. There was no fault, culpability, or any connection with sin. But when the inquiry was introduced into judicial practice, it brought the important notion of infraction with it. When one individual wronged another, there was always, a fortiori, a wrong done against sovereignty, against the law, against power. Further, given all the religious implications and connotations of the inquiry, the wrong would be a moral, almost religious transgression, or one with a religious connotation. Thus, around the twelfth century, one saw a conjoining of lawbreaking and religious transgression. Doing injury to the sovereign and committing a sin were two things that began to merge, and they were to be closely joined in Classical law. We are not yet entirely free of that conjunction.

Third: The inquiry that appeared in the twelfth century, as a result of this transformation in political structures and power relations, completely reorganized all the judicial practices of the Middle Ages, the Classical age, and even those of the modern era (or they all reorganized themselves around it). More generally, judicial inquiry spread into many other areas of social and economic practice and domains of knowledge. From the thirteenth century onward, based on the model of the judicial inquiries conducted by the king's prosecutor, a series of new forms of inquiry procedure was propagated.

Some of these were mainly administrative or economic. Through inquiries about population, wealth, money, and resources, royal agents were able to establish, secure, and increase royal power. In this way, a whole economic knowledge, a knowledge of the economic administration of states, was accumulated at the end of the Middle Ages and in the seventeenth and eighteenth centuries. This was the period when a regular form of administration of states, of transmission and continuity of political power, was born, along with sciences such as economics, statistics, and so on.

These inquiry techniques also spread into areas not directly connected to the domains of exercise of power: fields of knowledge or learning [*connaissance*] in the traditional sense of the word.

Beginning in the fourteenth and fifteenth centuries there appeared types of inquiry that sought to establish truth on the basis of a certain number of carefully collected items of testimony in fields such as geography, astronomy, and the study of climates. In particular, there appeared a technique of voyage—as a political, power-exercising venture and a curiosity-driven, knowledge-acquiring venture—that ultimately led to the discovery of America.

All the great inquiries that dominated the end of the Middle Ages were essentially the unfolding and dissemination of that first form, that matrix originating in the twelfth century. Even domains such as medicine, botany, and zoology were, starting in the sixteenth and seventeenth centuries, vectors of this process. The whole great cultural movement that, from the twelfth century, prepared the way for the Renaissance can be defined in large part as that of the development, the flowering of the inquiry as a general form of knowledge.

While the inquiry developed as a general form of knowledge within which the Renaissance would blossom, the test tended to disappear. We find only the ingredients, the remnants of the latter in the notorious form of torture, but already mingled with the concern for obtaining a confession, a test of verification. One could write an entire history of torture, as situated between the procedures of the test and the inquiry. The test tended to disappear from judicial practice; it also disappeared from the domains of knowledge. One might suggest two examples.

First, consider alchemy. Alchemy was a knowledge that had the test for its model. It was not a matter of doing an inquiry to find out what happens, to discover the truth. What was involved, essentially, was a encounter between two forces: that of the alchemist, who wanted to know, and that of nature, which guarded its secrets; that of darkness and that of light, that of good and evil, that of Satan and that of God. The alchemist engaged in a kind of struggle in which he was both the spectator—the one who would see the outcome of the combat—and one of the combatants, given that he could win or lose. We can say that alchemy was a chemical, naturalistic form of the test. That alchemical knowledge was essentially a test is confirmed by the fact that it was absolutely not transmitted, not accumulated, as a result of inquiries enabling one to arrive at the truth. Alchemical knowledge was transmitted only in the form of secret or public rules and procedures: this is how to go about it, that is what should be done, those are the principles to respect, the entreaties to make, the texts to read, the codes that must be present. Alchemy essentially constituted a corpus of rules, of procedures. Alchemy's disappearance, the fact that a new type of knowledge was constituted that was completely outside its domain resulted from the fact that this new knowledge took the inquiry matrix as its model. No inquiry-based knowledge—naturalistic, botanical, mineralogical, philological knowledge—had any connection with alchemical knowledge, which conformed to the judicial model of the test.

Second, the crisis of the medieval university at the end of the Middle Ages can also be analyzed in terms of an opposition between the test and the inquiry. In the medieval university, knowledge was manifested, transmitted, and authenticated through well-defined rituals, the most famous and best known of which was the *disputatio*, the dispute. This was a confrontation between two adversaries who used the verbal weapon, rhetorical procedures, and demonstrations based essentially on the appeal to authority. One appealed not to witnesses of truth, but to witnesses of strength. In the *disputatio*, the more authors one of the participants had on his side, the more evidence of authority, strength, and gravity he could invoke, the greater were his chances of winning. The *disputatio* was a form of proof, of display of knowledge, of authentication of knowledge that conformed to the general scheme of the test. Medieval knowledge—especially the encyclopedic knowledge of the Renaissance, such as that of Pico della Mirandola, which would come up against the medieval form of the university—was to be precisely a knowledge of the inquiry type. To have seen, to have read the texts, to know what was actually said; to be acquainted both with what was said and with the natural phenomena about which something was said; to verify what the authors had said through observations of nature; to make use of authors no longer as authority but as witness—all this would constitute one of the great revolutions in the form of knowledge transmission. The disappearance of alchemy and of the *disputatio*—or, rather, the fact that the latter was relegated to completely ossified academic forms, and that from the sixteenth century on it did not show any current vigor or any efficacy as one of the forms of real authentication of knowledge—was one of the numerous signs of the conflict between the inquiry and the test, as well as of the inquiry's triumph over the test at the end of the Middle Ages.

In conclusion, we might say that the inquiry is absolutely not a content but, rather, a form of knowledge—a form of knowledge situated at the junction of a type of power and a certain number of knowledge contents [*contenus de connaissance*]. Those wishing to establish a relation between what is known and the political, social, or economic forms that serve as a context for that knowledge need to trace that relation by way of consciousness or the subject of knowledge. It seems to me that the real junction between the economico-political processes and the conflicts of knowledge might be found in those forms which are, at the same time, modes of power exercise and modes of knowledge acquisition and transmission. The inquiry is precisely a political form—a form of power management and exercise that, through the judicial institution, became, in Western culture, a way of authenticating truth, of acquiring and transmitting things that would be regarded as true. The inquiry is a form of knowledge-power. Analysis of such forms should lead us to a stricter analysis of the relations between knowledge conflicts and economico-political determinants.

IV

In the previous lecture, I tried to show the mechanisms and the effects of the appropriation of the penal justice system by the state in the Middle Ages. Now I would like us to place ourselves at the end of the eighteenth and the beginning of the nineteenth century, during the founding of what I will try to analyze in this lecture and the next one under the name the "disciplinary society." Contemporary society deserves the name "disciplinary society" for reasons that I will explain. I would like to show what forms of penal practice characterize that society; what power relations underlie those penal practices; what forms of knowledge [*savoir*], types of knowledge [*connaissance*], and types of knowledge subject [*sujet de connaissance*] emerged, appearing on the basis of—and in the space of—the disciplinary society that contemporary society is.

The formation of disciplinary society can be characterized by the appearance, at the end of the eighteenth and the beginning of the nineteenth century, of two contradictory facts or, rather, one fact with two aspects, two seemingly contradictory sides: the reform or reorganization of the judicial and penal systems in the different countries of Europe and the world. That transformation doesn't manifest the same forms, the same amplitude, or the same chronology in different countries.

In England, for example, forms of justice remained relatively stable, while the content of the laws, the set of penally sanctioned acts, was radically altered. In the eighteenth century, there were in England 315 acts that could lead a person to the gallows, to the scaffold—315 crimes punished by death. This made the eighteenth-century English penal code, penal law, penal system one of the most savage and bloody that the history of civilizations has known. This situation was profoundly changed at the beginning of the nineteenth century, without a comparably deep change occurring in judicial forms and institutions. In France, on the other hand, very deep changes in judicial institutions took place, without a change in the content of the penal law.

What did these transformations of the penal systems consist in? In a theoretical reworking of penal law. This can be found in Cesare de Beccaria, Jeremy Bentham, J. P. Brissot de Warville, and in the legislators who were the authors of the first and second French Penal Code of the revolutionary period.

The basic principle of the theoretical system of penal law, defined by those authors, was that the crime, in the penal sense of the term (or, more technically, the infraction), must not have any relation with moral or religious transgression. The transgression is a violation of natural law, of religious law, of moral law. The crime, or the penal infraction, is a breach of civil law, explicitly established within a society by the legislative function of political power. For there to be an infraction, there must be a political authority and a law, and that law must have been actually formulated. There cannot be any infraction before the law exists. According to those theorists, only acts expressly defined as sanctioned by the law can be punished.

A second principle is that, in order to be good laws, those positive laws formulated by political authority within a society cannot be simple transcriptions of natural, religious, or moral law. A penal law must simply represent what is useful for society. The law defines as reprehensible that which is harmful to society, thus defining, by negation, what is useful to it.

The third principle is deduced naturally from the first two: There must be a clear and simple definition of crime. A crime is not something related to sin and transgression; it is something that harms society; it is a social injury, a trouble, a disturbance for the whole of society.

Consequently, there is also a new definition of the criminal: the criminal is the social enemy. We find that very clearly stated in all the theorists and also in Rousseau, who declares that the criminal is an individual who has broken the social contract. The criminal is an internal enemy. This idea of the criminal as an internal enemy, as an individual in society who has broken the theoretically postulated pact, is a new and crucial definition in the history of the theory of crime and punishment.

If a crime is a social injury, if the criminal is society's enemy, how should criminal law treat that criminal or react to that crime? If a crime is a disturbance for society, if a crime no longer has any connection with transgression, with natural, divine, or religious law, it is clear that penal law cannot prescribe a revenge, the redemption of a transgression. Penal law must only enable a reparation of the disturbance that was caused to society. Penal law must be made in such a way that the harm caused by the individual to society is obliterated. If that is not possible, then it is essential that the harm not be recommenced by the individual in question or by another. Penal law must repair the harm, or prevent similar harms being done to the social body.

For those theorists, four possible types of punishment follow from these premises. First, there is the punishment expressed in the declaration: "You have broken the social compact; you no longer belong to the social body; you have deliberately placed yourself outside the space of legality; we will expel you from the social space in which that legality functions." Basically, this is the idea, often encountered in those authors (Beccaria, Bentham, et al.), that the ideal punishment would be simply to expel, exile, banish, or deport. It's the idea of deportation.

The second possibility is a sort of exclusion in place. Its mechanism is not physical deportation, transfer outside the social space, but isolation within the moral, psychological, public space constituted by public opinion. It's the idea of punishment as scandal, shame, and humiliation of the one who has committed an infraction. His offense is publicized; his person is exhibited in public; a reaction of aversion, contempt, and condemnation is induced in the public. That was the penalty; Beccaria and others invented mechanisms for provoking shame and humiliation.

The third kind of penalty was compensation for social damage—

forced labor. It consisted in forcing persons to perform an activity that was useful to the state or to society, so that the damage that was caused would be compensated. We thus have a theory of forced labor.

Finally, the fourth option was the penalty ensuring that the harm would not be done again, making sure that neither the individual in question nor any others would any longer be inclined to cause society the same harm they had previously done—by making them feel repugnance for the crime they had committed. The ideal penalty, perfectly suited for obtaining that result, was retaliation. The killer should be killed, the thief's possessions should be confiscated, and—in the opinion of certain theorists of the eighteenth century—the rapist should undergo something similar to his crime.

So there was a batch of proposed penalties: deportation, forced labor, shame, public scandal, and retaliation—proposals actually presented not just by pure theorists such as Beccaria but also by legislators such as Brissot and Ferdinand Louis Felix Le Peletier de Saint-Fargeau, who helped draft the first Revolutionary Penal Code. Such people were already rather far along in the organization of a penal regime centered on the penal infraction and on the violation of a law representative of public utility. Everything stems from that project, even the array of penalties and the way in which they are applied.

We thus have these proposals, texts, and even decrees adopted by legislatures. But if we examine what really occurred, how penal institutions functioned a short time later, around 1820, at the time of the Restoration in France and the Holy Alliance in Europe, we note that the system of penalties adopted by the emerging and developing industrial societies was completely different from what had been planned a few years earlier. Not that the practice contradicted the theory, but it soon turned away from the theoretical principles we find in Beccaria and in Bentham.

Let's look again at the system of penalties. Deportation disappeared rather quickly; forced labor was in general a purely symbolic penalty in its compensatory function; the mechanisms of scandal never managed to be put into practice; the penalty of retaliation quickly disappeared, denounced as too archaic for a developed society.

These extremely precise proposals for punishment were replaced by a rather curious penalty that Beccaria had spoken of slightingly and Brissot had mentioned in a decidedly marginal way. I am referring to imprisonment, the prison.

Prison was not part of the theoretical plan for penal reform in the eighteenth century. It appeared at the beginning of the nineteenth century, as a de facto institution, almost without theoretical justification.

Not only was imprisonment—a penalty whose use became general in the nineteenth century—not called for in the eighteenth-century program, but penal legislation was to undergo a tremendous shift of emphasis in relation to the tenets of the preceding theory. Indeed, from the start of the nineteenth century and increasingly rapidly throughout the century, the direction of penal legislation was to veer away from what one might call the principle of social utility; it no longer focused on what was socially useful but, rather, targeted the individual. As an example, we can cite the great reforms of penal legislation in France and other European countries between 1825 and 1850–60, involving the definition of what we call mitigating circumstances, enabling the strict application of the law, as it is found in the Code, to be modified by the judge or jury's stipulation, depending on the individual being tried. The principle of a universal law representing only social interests was considerably strained by the use of mitigating circumstances, which were to have greater and greater importance. Moreover, the penal regime that developed in the nineteenth century aimed less and less to define in an abstract and general way what was harmful to society, to remove individuals harmful to society or prevent them from reoffending. In the nineteenth century, penal justice aimed, in an increasingly insistent way, not so much at the general defense of society as the control and psychological and moral reform of the attitudes and behavior of individuals. It was a form of penal regime totally different from the one planned in the eighteenth century: for Beccaria, the great penal principle was that there should be no punishment without an explicit law and an explicit behavior violating that law. So long as there was no law and no explicit infraction, there could be no punishment—that was Beccaria's fundamental principle.

The entire penal regime of the nineteenth century became a control not so much over what individuals did—was it lawful or unlawful?—as over what they might do, what they were capable of doing, what they were liable to do, what they were imminently about to do.

Thus, toward the end of the nineteenth century the great idea of criminology and penal theory was the scandalous idea, in terms of penal theory, of *dangerousness*. The idea of *dangerousness* meant that the individual must be considered by society at the level of his potentialities, and not at the level of his actions; not at the level of the actual violations of an actual law, but *at the level of the behavioral potentialities they represented.*

The last major point that penal theory questioned more forcefully than Beccaria had was that, to ensure the control of individuals—which was no longer a penal reaction to what they had done but, rather, a control of their future behavior while this was still taking form—the penal institution could no longer be completely in the hands of an autonomous power, the judiciary.

We thus come to question the great separation made (or at least formulated) by Montesquieu between judicial, executive, and legislative powers. The control of individuals, this sort of punitive penal control of individuals at the level of their potentialities, could not be performed by the judiciary itself; it was to be done by a series of authorities other than the judiciary, such as the police and a whole network of institutions of surveillance and correction—the police for surveillance, the psychological, psychiatric, criminological, medical, and pedagogical institutions for correction. In this way, in the nineteenth century, there developed around the judicial institution—to enable it to assume the function of controlling individuals at the level of their *dangerousness*—a vast series of institutions that would enclose individuals in their bounds throughout their existence: pedagogic institutions such as the school, psychological or psychiatric institutions such as the hospital, the asylum, the police, and so on. This whole network of nonjudicial power was designed to fulfill one of the functions that the justice system assumed at this time: no longer punishing individuals' infractions, but correcting their potentialities.

We thus enter the age of what I would call social orthopedics. I'm talking about a form of power, a type of society that I term "disciplinary society," in contrast to the penal societies known hitherto. This is the age of social control. Among the theorists I cited earlier, there was one who in a sense foresaw and presented a kind of diagram of this society of supervision [*surveillance*], of this great social orthopedics—I'm thinking of Jeremy Bentham. I hope historians of philosophy will forgive me for saying this, but I believe that Bentham is more important for our society than Kant or Hegel. All our societies should pay homage to him. It was he who programmed, defined, and described in the most exact manner the forms of power in which we live, and who presented a marvelous and celebrated little model of this society of generalized orthopedics—the famous Panopticon,[25] a form of architecture that makes possible a mind-over-mind-type of power; a sort of institution that serves equally well, it would seem, for schools, hospitals, prisons, reformatories, poorhouses, and factories. The Panopticon is a ring-shaped building in the middle of which there is a yard with a tower at the center. The ring is divided into little cells that face the interior and exterior alike. In each of these little cells there is, depending on the purpose of the institution, a child learning to write, a worker at work, a prisoner correcting himself, a madman living his madness. In the central tower there is an observer. Since each cell faces both the inside and the outside, the observer's gaze can traverse the whole cell; there is no dimly lit space, so everything the individual does is exposed to the gaze of an observer who watches through shuttered windows or spy holes in such a way as to be able to see everything without anyone being able to see him. For Bentham, this marvelous little architectonic ruse could be used by a variety of different sorts of institutions. The Panopticon is the utopia of a society and a type of power that is basically the society we are familiar with at present, a utopia that was actually realized. This type of power can properly be given the name panopticism. We live in a society where panopticism reigns.

Panopticism is a form of power that rests not on the inquiry but on something completely different, which I will call the "examination." The inquiry was a procedure by which, in judicial practice, people tried to find out what had happened. It was a matter of reactualizing a past event through testimony presented by persons who, for one reason or another, because of their general knowledge [*savoir*], or because they were present at the event, were considered apt to know.

With panopticism, something altogether different would come

into being; there would no longer be inquiry, but supervision [*surveillance*] and examination. It was no longer a matter of reconstituting an event, but something—or, rather, someone—who needed total, uninterrupted supervision. A constant supervision of individuals by someone who exercised a power over them—schoolteacher, foreman, physician, psychiatrist, prison warden—and who, so long as he exercised power, had the possibility of both supervising and constituting a knowledge concerning those he supervised. A knowledge that now was no longer about determining whether or not something had occurred; rather, it was about whether an individual was behaving as he should, in accordance with the rule or not, and whether he was progressing or not. This new knowledge was no longer organized around the questions: "Was this done? Who did it?" It was no longer organized in terms of presence and absence, of existence and nonexistence; it was organized around the norm, in terms of what was normal or not, correct or not, in terms of what one must do or not do.

So we have, in contrast to the great knowledge of the inquiry—organized in the middle of the Middle Ages through the appropriation of the judicial system by the state, consisting in assembling the means to reactualize events through testimony—a new knowledge of a completely different type, a knowledge characterized by supervision and examination, organized around the norm, through the supervisory control of individuals throughout their existence. This examination was the basis of the power, the form of knowledge–power, that was to give rise not, as in the case of the inquiry, to the great sciences of observation, but to what we call the "human sciences"—psychiatry, psychology, sociology.

I would like now to analyze how that came about. How did we come to have, on the one hand, an elaborate penal theory that clearly programmed a certain number of things and, on the other, a real social practice that led to completely different results?

I will consider in turn two examples that are among the most important and decisive instances of this process—that of England, and that of France. I'll leave aside the example of the United States, which is just as important. I would like to show how in France, and especially in England, there existed a series of mechanisms of control: control of the population, continuous control of the behavior of individuals. These control mechanisms took form in an obscure fashion during the eighteenth century to meet a certain number of needs; as they assumed more and more importance, they were finally extended to the whole of society and superimposed on penal practice. That new theory was not able to deal with these phenomena of supervision, which arose completely apart from it; it wasn't able to program them. It could even be said that eighteenth-century penal theory ratified a judicial practice that formed in the Middle Ages, the appropriation of the justice system by the state. Beccaria thought in terms of a state-controlled judicial system.[26] Though he was a great reformer in a certain sense, he didn't see the emergence, next to and outside that state-controlled judicial system, of methods of control that would be the real content of the new penal practice.

What were these control mechanisms, where did they come from, and what needs did they meet? Let's take the example of England. Beginning in the second half of the eighteenth century, there formed, at relatively low levels of the social scale, spontaneous groups of persons who assigned themselves, without any delegation from a higher authority, the task of maintaining order and of creating new instruments for ensuring order, for their own purposes. These groups were numerous, and they proliferated during the entire eighteenth century.

First, in chronological order, there were the religious communities dissenting from Anglicanism—the Quakers, the Methodists—who took it upon themselves to organize their own police. Thus, among the Methodists, John Wesley, for example, visited the Methodist communities on inspection trips, a bit like the bishops of the early Middle Ages. All cases of disorderly conduct—drunkenness, adultery, refusal to work—were submitted to him. Quaker-inspired societies of friends functioned in a similar way. All these societies had the dual task of supervision and welfare assistance. They took on the task of helping those who didn't possess the means of subsistence, those too old to work, the sick, the mentally ill. At the same time as they offered assistance, though, they accorded themselves the possibility and right to observe the conditions in which the assistance was given: observing whether the individual who wasn't working was actually ill, whether his poverty and his misery were not due to debauchery, drunkenness, the vices. So this movement involved groups establishing their own internal supervision, one with a deeply religious origin, operation, and ideology.

Second, there were, alongside these strictly religious communities, societies related to them that kept a certain distance, a certain aloofness from them. For example, at the end of the seventeenth century, in 1692 in England, a society was founded called, in a rather characteristic way, the Society for the Reform of Manners. This was a very important society which had, in the time of William III, a hundred branches in England and, counting only those in the city of Dublin, ten in Ireland. This society, which disappeared in the eighteenth century and reappeared, under Wesley's influence, in the second half of the century, set out to reform manners: getting people to respect Sunday (we owe the exciting English Sunday largely to the action of these great societies), preventing gambling and drunkenness, curbing prostitution, adultery, cursing, blasphemy—everything that might show contempt for God. As Wesley said in his sermons, it was a matter of preventing the lowest and basest class from taking advantage of inexperienced young people and fleecing them of their money.

Toward the end of the eighteenth century, that society was surpassed in importance by another one, inspired by a bishop and certain court aristocrats, called the Proclamation Society, having obtained from the King a proclamation for the encouragement of piety and virtue. In 1802, this society changed its name and took the characteristic title of the Society for the Suppression of Vice, its goals being to ensure the observance of the Lord's Day, to prevent the circulation of licentious and obscene books, to file lawsuits against pernicious literature, and to secure the closure of gaming houses and brothels. Though this society was still essentially moral in its mission, remaining close to the religious groups, it was already somewhat secularized.

Third, we encounter, in England, other groups more interesting and more troubling—self-defense groups of a paramilitary sort. They sprang up in response to the first great social, not yet proletarian, disturbances, the great political and social movements—still with a strong religious connotation—at the end of the century, particularly those of the followers of Lord Gordon. In response to these great popular disturbances, the moneyed milieus, the aristocrats, the bourgeoisie, organized into self-defense groups. In this way a series of associations—the Military Infantry of London, the Company of Artillery—were organized spontaneously, without support, or with only lateral support, from state power. They had the function of bringing political order, penal order, or simply order, to reign in a district, a city, a region, or a county.

As a last category, there were the strictly economic societies. The great companies and great commercial firms organized police societies, private police forces, to defend their property, their stock, their wares, the ships anchored in the port of London, against riot, banditry, everyday pillage and petty thievery. These privately organized police forces patrolled the districts of London and large towns such as Liverpool.

These societies answered a demographic or social need; they were a response to urbanization, to the great movement of populations from the country to the towns. They were also a response—and we'll return to this subject—to a major economic transformation, a new form of accumulation of wealth, for when wealth began to accumulate in the form of stocks, of warehoused goods, of machines, it became necessary to have it guarded and protected. And they were a response, finally, to a new political situation, to new forms of popular revolt that, from an essentially peasant origin in the sixteenth and seventeenth centuries, now became great urban, popular, and, later, proletarian revolts.

It is interesting to observe the evolution of these voluntary associations in England in the eighteenth century. There is a threefold shift during the course of their history.

Let's consider the first shift. At the start, these groups were almost popular, formed from the petty bourgeoisie. The Quakers and the Methodists of the end of the seventeenth and the beginning of the eighteenth century who organized themselves to try to suppress vice, to reform manners, were lower-middle-class citizens, grouped together for the obvious purpose of establishing order among themselves and around them. But this desire to establish order was basically a way of escaping from political power, because the latter possessed a formidable, terrifying, and sanguinary instrument—penal legislation. Indeed, for more than three hundred kinds of offense one could be hung. This meant that it was very easy for authority, for the aristocracy, for those who controlled the judicial apparatus, to bring terrible pressures to bear on the popular strata. It is easy to understand how it was in the interest of the religious groups to try and escape from a judicial authority so bloodthirsty and threatening.

To escape that judicial authority, individuals organized into moral reform societies, prohibited drunkenness, prostitution, theft, everything that would enable state power to attack the group, destroy it, to use any pretext to send people to the gallows. So it was more a matter of groups for self-defense against the law than of effective surveillance organizations. This strengthening of self-organized penal processes was a way of escaping from the penal regime of the state.

Now, in the course of the eighteenth century, these groups changed their social affiliation and tended more and more to abandon their popular or petty-bourgeois recruitment. At the end of the eighteenth century, it was the aristocracy, the bishops, the richest persons who were initiated into these groups of moral self-defense, these leagues for the elimination of vice.

We thus have a social shift that indicates perfectly well how this moral reform enterprise stopped being a penal self-defense and became, on the contrary, a reinforcing of the power of penal justice itself. Alongside the dreadful penal instrument it possessed, state power was to lay claim to these instruments of pressure, of control. What was involved, in a sense, was a mechanism for bringing social control organizations under state control.

The second shift consists in the following: whereas, with the first group, it was a matter of establishing a moral order different from the law allowing individuals to escape from the law, at the end of the eighteenth century these groups—now controlled, prompted by aristocrats and rich persons—aimed essentially at obtaining from political power new laws that would ratify the moral effort. We thus have a shift from the moral toward the penal.

Third, we may say that, from that moment, this moral control was exerted by the upper classes, the holders of power, over the lower, poorer strata, the popular strata. It thus became an instrument of power for the wealthy over the poor, for the exploiting over the exploited, which conferred a new political and social polarity on these agencies of control. I will cite a text, dated 1804, from the end of this evolution I'm trying to trace, written by a bishop named

Watson, who preached before the Society for the Suppression of Vice: "The laws are good, but unfortunately they are broken by the lower classes. Undoubtedly the upper classes do not take them very much into consideration, either. But this fact would not have any importance if the upper classes did not serve as an example to the lower classes."[27] Impossible to be any clearer: the laws are good, good for the poor; unfortunately, the poor escape from the laws, which is really deplorable. The rich also escape from the laws, but that has no importance, for the laws were not made for them. However, the consequence is that the poor follow the example of the rich in not observing the laws. So Bishop Watson says to the rich: "I ask you to follow these laws that were not made for you, for in that way there will be at least the possibility of controlling and supervising the poorer classes."

In this gradual state takeover—in this transfer of the points of control from the hands of petty-bourgeois groups trying to escape from state power to those of the social group actually holding power—in this whole evolution, we can observe how a morality with a religious origin was brought into and disseminated in a state-appropriated penal system that, by definition, turned a blind eye to morals and vowed to cut the ties with morality and religion. Religious ideology, arisen and nurtured in the little Quaker and Methodist groups in England at the end of the seventeenth century, now sprang up at the other pole, at the other extremity of the social scale, on the side of power, as an instrument of a control exerted from the top on the bottom. Self-defense in the seventeenth century, an instrument of power at the beginning of the nineteenth century. This is the process that we can observe in England.

In France, a rather different process occurred. This is explained by the fact that France, a country of absolute monarchy, possessed a powerful state apparatus, which eighteenth-century England had already lost, having been shaken in part by the bourgeois revolution of the seventeenth century. England had freed itself of that absolute monarchy, rushing through that stage in which France remained caught for a hundred and fifty years.

This powerful monarchic state apparatus in France relied on a two-pronged instrument: a classic judicial instrument—the *parlements* [high courts—TRANS.], the courts—and a parajudicial instrument, the police, which France had the privilege of inventing. A police that comprised the intendants, the mounted police corps, the police lieutenants; that was equipped with architectural instruments like the Bastille, Bicêtre, the great prisons; that also had its institutional aspects, such as the curious *lettres de cachet*.

The *lettre de cachet* was not a law or a decree but an order from the king that concerned a person individually, compelling him to do something. One could even force someone to marry through a *lettre de cachet*. In most cases, though, it was an instrument of punishment.

One could exile someone by means of a *lettre de cachet*, strip him of certain functions, imprison him. It was one of the major instruments of power of the absolute monarchy. The *lettres de cachet* have been much studied in France, and it has become common to class them as something dreadful, an instrument of royal despotism crashing down on someone like a lightning bolt, able to imprison him for the rest of his days. We need to be more cautious and say that the *lettres de cachet* didn't function only in that manner. Just as we have seen that the moral reform societies were a way of escaping the law, we can likewise observe a rather curious game in the case of the *lettres de cachet*.

When one examines the *lettres de cachet* sent by the king in rather large numbers, one notes that in most cases he was not the one who made the decision to send them. He did so in certain instances, for affairs of state; but most of these letters—tens of thousands of *lettres de cachet* sent by the monarchy—were actually solicited by various individuals: husbands outraged by their wives, fathers dissatisfied with their children, families wanting to get rid of an individual, religious communities disturbed by someone, parishes unhappy with their priests. All these individuals or small groups would request a *lettre de cachet* from the king's intendant; the latter would then investigate to see if the request was justified. When this was the case, he would write to the king's minister in charge of such matters, asking him to send a *lettre de cachet* authorizing the arrest of someone's cheating wife, or prodigal son, or prostitute daughter, or the misbehaving village priest. So the *lettre de cachet* presented itself—in its aspect as terrible instrument of royal despotism—as a kind of counterpower, a power that came from below, enabling groups, communities, families, or individuals to exercise power over someone. They were instruments of a control that was voluntary in a sense, a control from below which society and the community exercised on itself. Hence, the *lettre de cachet* was a way of regulating the everyday morality of social life, a way for the group or groups—family, religious, parochial, regional, and local— to provide for their own police control and ensure their own order. Looking at the behaviors that prompted the request for a *lettre de cachet* and were sanctioned by it, we can distinguish three categories.

First, the category of what could be called immoral conduct: debauchery, adultery, sodomy, drunkenness. Such conduct prompted a request from families and communities for a *lettre de cachet* that was accepted immediately. So the object here was moral repression. A second class of *lettres de cachet* was issued to sanction religious behavior judged dangerous and dissident. This was a way that witches could be arrested, long after the time when they could be burned at the stake.

Third, in the eighteenth century it is interesting to note that *lettres de cachet* were used fairly often in labor conflicts. When employers, bosses, or foremen were not satisfied with their apprentices or their workers in the guilds, they could get rid of them by expelling them or, in rarer cases, by soliciting a *lettre de cachet*.

The first real strike in the history of France was that of the clockmakers in 1724. The clockmaker bosses reacted against it by singling out those whom they considered to be the leaders and wrote to the king requesting a *lettre de cachet*, which was sent at once. Some time later, though, the king's minister wanted to rescind it and free the striking workers. It was the clockmakers guild itself which then asked the king not to free the workers and to keep the *lettres de cachet* in force.

We see, then, how these social controls, relating here not to morality or religion but to labor problems, were exerted from below and through the intermediary of the system of *lettres de cachet* on the emerging working population.

In cases where the *lettre de cachet* was punitive, it resulted in the imprisonment of the individual. It's interesting to note that imprisonment was not a legal sanction in the penal system of the seventeenth and the eighteenth centuries. The jurists were perfectly clear in that regard: they declared that when the law punished someone, the punishment would be death—burning at the stake, quartering, branding, banishment, or paying a fine. Imprisonment was not a penalty.

Imprisonment, which would become the major penalty of the nineteenth century, had its origin precisely in that parajudicial practice of the *lettre de cachet*, of the use of royal power for the self-regulation of groups. When a *lettre de cachet* was sent against someone, that someone wasn't hung or branded or fined: he was put in prison for an unspecified period of time. The *lettre de cachet* rarely said that someone must remain in prison for six months or one year, for example. Generally speaking, it determined that someone must remain locked up until further notice, and the further notice came only when the person who had requested the *lettre de cachet* affirmed that the imprisoned individual had corrected himself. This idea of imprisoning for correction, of keeping a person prisoner until he corrected himself—this paradoxical, bizarre idea, without any foundation or justification at the level of human behavior—had its origin precisely in that practice.

There also appeared the idea of a penalty that was not meant to be a response to an infraction but had the function of correcting individuals at the level of their behavior, their attitudes, their dispositions, the danger they represented—at the level of their supposed potentialities. This form of penalty applied to individuals' potentialities, this penal regime that sought to correct them through hard labor or confinement, did not in truth belong to the sphere of law, did not originate in the juridical theory of crime, did not derive from the great reformers such as Beccaria. This idea of a penal sanction that sought to correct by imprisoning was a police idea, born parallel to the judicial system, outside it, in a practice of social control or in a system of exchanges between group demands and the exercise of power.

After these two analyses, I would like to draw some provisional conclusions that I will try to use in the next lecture.

The terms of the problem are the following: How was a theory of penal law, which ought to have led to one kind of legislation, in fact blurred and overlaid by a completely different penal practice, which then acquired its own theoretical elaboration during the nineteenth century when the theory of penalties, of criminology was reworked? How was Beccaria's great lesson forgotten, relegated and finally buried by a completely different penal practice based on individuals—on their behavior and their potentialities—and designed to correct them?

It seems to me that the origin of this development lies in a field of practice outside the penal domain. In England, it was those social groupings which, to evade the penal law, acquired instruments of control that were eventually appropriated by the central power. In France, where the structure of political power was different, the state instruments devised in the seventeenth century to control the aristocracy, the bourgeoisie, and rioters were reused by social groups from the bottom up.

So the question arises of the reason for this movement, for these groups of control; what was the motivating factor? We have seen what needs they met at the beginning; but why did they take this trajectory, why did they undergo this shift, why did power or those who held it take up these control mechanisms situated at the lowest level of the population?

To answer these questions we need to take an important phenomenon into consideration—the new form of economic production. At the origin of the process I have tried to analyze, there was the new material form of wealth. In reality, what emerged in England at the end of the eighteenth century (much more than in France, moreover) was the fact that wealth was invested more and more in capital that was no longer monetary. The wealth of the sixteenth and seventeenth centuries was essentially constituted by land fortunes, by cash money, or, to a certain extent, by bills of exchange, which individuals could trade. In the eighteenth century, there appeared a form of wealth invested in a new type of materiality that was no longer monetary; instead, it was invested in goods, stocks, raw materials, workshops, products to be shipped. And the birth of capitalism, or the transformation and acceleration of the establishment of capitalism, would be expressed in this new mode of material investment of wealth. The point is that this wealth consisting of stocks of goods, raw materials, imported objects, machines, and workshops was vulnerable to theft. That whole population of poor people, unemployed workers, people looking for work now had a kind of direct, physical contact with fortune, with wealth. In England, at the end of the eighteenth century, theft from ships, pillaging of warehouses and stocks, and larceny in the workshops became common. Not surprisingly, then, the great problem of power in England during this period was to set up control mechanisms that would make it possible to protect this new material form of wealth. So we can understand why the creator of the police in England, Patrick Colquhoun, was someone who began as a merchant and was then commissioned by a shipping company to organize a system for overseeing goods stored in the London docks. The London police was born of the need to protect the docks, wharves, warehouses, and stocks. This was the first reason, much stronger in England than in France, for the sense of the absolute necessity of this control. In other words, it's the reason why this control, which had an almost popular function at the social base, was reappropriated from the top at a given moment.

The second reason is that, both in France and in England, land ownership also changed forms, with the multiplication of small properties, the division and delimitation of properties. The fact that from then on there were no longer any great empty or nearly uncultivated spaces, nor any common lands on which everyone might live, meant that property would be divided, fragmented, enclosed, and every property owner would be exposed to depredations.

And, especially among the French, there would be that perpetual idée fixe of peasant pillage, pillage of the land, the idea of those vagabonds and farm laborers, often out of work, impoverished, living from hand to mouth, stealing horses, fruit, vegetables. One of the great problems of the French Revolution was to bring an end to this type of peasant plunder. The great political revolts of the second part of the French Revolution in the Vendée and in Provence were in a way the political result of a malaise on the part of the small peasantry, agricultural workers who no longer found, in this new system of property division, the means of existence they had had under the regime of the large agricultural estates.

So it was this new spatial and social distribution of industrial and agricultural wealth which demanded new social controls at the end of the eighteenth century.

These new systems of social control that were now established by power, by the industrial class, by the class of owners, were adapted from controls that had popular or semipopular origins and were then given authoritarian, state-manufactured versions.

In my view, this story is at the origin of disciplinary society. I will try to explain in the next lecture how this movement—which I have only sketched out for the eighteenth century—was institutionalized, becoming a form of political relation internal to society in the nineteenth century.

                                    V

In the last lecture, I attempted to define something that I called "panopticism." Panopticism is one of the characteristic traits of our society. It's a type of power that is applied to individuals in the form of continuous individual supervision, in the form of control, punishment, and compensation, and in the form of correction, that is, the molding and transformation of individuals in terms of certain norms. This threefold aspect of panopticism—supervision, control, correction—seems to be a fundamental and characteristic dimension of the power relations that exist in our society.

In a society like feudal society, one doesn't find anything similar to panopticism. That doesn't mean that in a society of a feudal type or in the European societies of the seventeenth century, there weren't any agencies of social control, punishment, and compensation. Yet the way these were distributed was completely different from the way they came to be established at the end of the eighteenth century and the beginning of the nineteenth. Today we live in a society programmed basically by Bentham, a panoptic society, a society where panopticism reigns.

I'll try to show in this lecture that the appearance of panopticism involves a kind of paradox. At the very time it appeared—or, more exactly, in the years immediately preceding its appearance—we see a certain theory of penal law, of punishment, taking form, with Beccaria as its most important representative, a theory essentially based on a strict legalism. That theory of punishment subordinated the punishment, the possibility of punishing, to the existence of an explicit law, to the explicit establishment that a breach of this law had taken place, and finally to a punishment that would compensate for or, to the extent possible, prevent the injury done to society by the offense. That legalistic theory, a truly social, almost collectivist, theory, is completely antithetical to panopticism. In panopticism, the supervision of individuals is carried out not at the level of what one does but of what one is, not at the level of what one does but of what one might do. With this system, supervision tends increasingly to individualize the author of the act, while ceasing to take account of the juridical nature, the penal qualification of the act itself. Panopticism stood in opposition, then, to the legalistic theory developed during the preceding period.

Now, it is important to note here the essential historical fact that this legalistic theory was duplicated in a first phase—and subsequently covered over and totally obscured—by panopticism, which had formed apart from or alongside it. It is the birth of panopticism—formed and driven by a force of displacement operating, from the seventeenth through to the nineteenth century, across the entire social space—it is this subsumption of popular control mechanisms by central power that characterizes the process from the seventeenth century on and explains how, at the start of the nineteenth century, there dawns an age of panopticism, a system that was to spread over the whole practice, and, to a certain degree, the whole theory of penal law.

To justify these arguments I'm presenting, I would like to cite some authorities. People at the beginning of the nineteenth century, or at least some of them, did not fail to notice the appearance of what I've been calling—somewhat arbitrarily but, at any rate, in homage to Bentham—"panopticism." As a matter of fact, several persons thought about and were very intrigued by what was occurring in their time, by the organization of penal institutions or the ethic of the state. There is one author, quite important in those years, a professor at the University of Berlin and a colleague of Hegel's, who wrote and published in 1830 a great treatise in several volumes titled *Lessons on the Prisons*.[28] This man, named Nicolaus Heinrich Julius, whom I recommend that you read, and who offered a course on prisons at Berlin for several years, is an extraordinary figure who at certain moments spoke in an almost Hegelian voice.

In his *Lessons on the Prisons*, there is a passage that says: "Modern architects are discovering a form that was not previously known." Referring to Greek civilization, he says:

Formerly, architects were mainly concerned with solving the problem of how to make the spectacle of an event, an action, of a single individual accessible to the greatest possible number of people. This was the case with religious sacrifice, a unique event in which the greatest possible number of people must participate; it was also the case with theater, which derives, moreover, from sacrifice; and with circus games, orations, and speeches. Now, this problem, present in Greek society insofar as it was a community that participated in dramatic events that formed its unity—religious sacrifices, theater, or political speeches—continued to dominate Western civilization up to the modern period. The problem of churches is still exactly the same. Everyone must be present or must serve as spectators in the case of the sacrifice of mass or as an audience for the priest's sermon. Currently, the fundamental problem confronting modern architecture is the opposite. What is wanted is to arrange that the greatest possible number of persons is offered as a spectacle to a single individual charged with their surveillance.[29]

In writing that, Julius was thinking of Bentham's Panopticon, and, more generally, of the architecture of prisons and, to a certain extent, of hospitals and schools. He was referring to the problems of an architecture not of spectacle, like that of Greece, but of surveillance—one that would allow a single gaze to scan the greatest number of faces, bodies, attitudes, in the greatest possible number of cells. "Now," says Julius, "the appearance of this architectural problem is correlative with the disappearance of a society that lived in the form of a spiritual and religious community and the emergence of a state-controlled society. The state presents itself as a certain spatial and social arrangement of individuals, in which all are subjected to a single surveillance." In concluding his statement concerning these two types of architecture, Julius declares that "more is involved than a simple problem of architecture . . . this difference is decisive in the history of the human mind."[30]

Julius was not the only person in his time to notice this phenomenon of an inversion of spectacle into surveillance or of the birth of a society of panopticism. One finds similar analyses of the same type in many contemporary texts. I will cite only one of those, written by Jean-Baptiste Treilhard, Councillor of State, Jurist of the Empire, a text that forms the introduction to his *Code of Criminal Procedure* of 1808. In this text, Treilhard states: "The *Code of Criminal Procedure* I present to you constitutes a real innovation not only in the history of justice, of judicial practice, but in that of human societies. With this code, we give the prosecutor, who represents state power or social power facing the defendants, a completely new role."[51] And Treilhard uses a metaphor. The prosecutor must not have as his only function that of prosecuting individuals who have committed offenses; his main, primary function must be that of supervising individuals even before the infraction has been committed. The prosecutor is not just the agent of law who acts when the law is violated; the prosecutor is, above all, a gaze, an eye constantly trained on the population. The eye of the prosecutor must transmit information to the eye of the attorney general, who in turn transmits it to the great eye of surveillance, which at the time was the minister of police. The latter transmits information to the eye of the one who is at the highest point of society, the emperor—who, as it happens, then used the symbol of an eye. The emperor is the universal eye observing the entire expanse of society, an eye assisted by a series of gazes, arrayed in the form of a pyramid starting from the imperial eye, and watching over the whole society. For Treilhard, for the jurists of the empire, for those who founded French penal law—which, unfortunately, has had a good deal of influence worldwide—this great pyramid of gazes constituted the new form of the judicial process.

I won't analyze here all the institutions in which these characteristics of panopticism, which are peculiar to modern, industrial, capitalist society, are manifested. I would simply like to take hold of this panopticism, this surveillance, at the base, at the place where it appears perhaps less clearly, where it is farthest away from the center of decision-making, from the power of the state—to show how this panopticism exists, at the simplest level and in the daily operation of institutions that envelop the lives and bodies of individuals: the panopticism, then, of individual existence.

What did this panopticism consist in and, above all, what purpose did it serve? Let me give you a riddle to solve. I'll present the prescribed routine of an institution that actually existed during the years 1840–45 in France—that is, at the beginning of the period I am analyzing. I'll describe the routine without saying whether it's a factory, a prison, a psychiatric hospital, a convent, a school, or a barracks, and you will guess which institution I have in mind. It was an institution in which there were four hundred people who weren't married and who had to get up every morning at 5 o'clock; at 5:50 they had to have finished washing and dressing, made their bed, and had their coffee; at 6 the compulsory work began, lasting until 8:15 in the evening, with a one-hour break for lunch; at 8:15, dinner and group prayer; retirement to the dormitories was at 9 o'clock on the hour. Sunday was a special day. Article 5 of this institution's rulebook said: "We want to preserve the spirit which Sunday should have, that is, devote it to religious observances and to rest. However, since boredom would soon make Sunday more tiring than the other days of the week, various exercises will need to be done so that one might spend this day in a cheerful, Christian manner." In the morning, there were religious exercises, followed by reading and writing exercises, and then recreation, finally, during the last hours before noon; in the afternoon, there was catechism, vespers, and walks if the weather wasn't too cold. If it was cold, there was reading together. The religious exercises and mass were not observed in the church nearby, because that would have allowed the residents of this establishment to come in contact with the outside world; thus, to prevent the church itself from being the place or pretext of a contact with the outside world, religious services were held in a chapel constructed inside the establishment. "The parish church," the rulebook explained, "could be a point of contact with the world and that is why a chapel was constructed inside the establishment." The faithful from outside were not allowed to enter. The inmates could leave the establishment only during the Sunday walks, but always under the supervision of the religious staff. That staff supervised the walks and the dormitories, and was in charge of the security and operation of the workshops. So the religious personnel had control not only of work and morality but of the economic enterprise. The residents received no wages but, rather, a payment, a lump sum set at 40–80 francs per year, which was given to them only upon leaving. In the event that a person of the opposite sex needed to come into the establishment for material or economic reasons, that person must be chosen with the greatest care and must remain there for a very short time. Silence was enjoined on them on pain of expulsion. In a general way, the two organizational principles, according to the regulations, were: the residents must never be alone in the dormitory, the cafeteria, or the yard; and any mingling with the outside world must be avoided, as one and the same spirit must prevail in the establishment.

What sort of institution was this? Basically the question has no importance, for it could have been any of them: an institution for men or women, for young people or adults, a prison, a boarding school, an academy, or a reformatory. It's not a hospital, because there's a lot of talk about work. And it's not a barracks, either, because work is done inside. It could be a psychiatric hospital, or even a licensed brothel. In reality, it was simply a factory—a women's factory in the Rhône area, employing four hundred workers.

Someone might say that this is a caricatural, comical example, a kind of utopia. Prison factories, convent factories, wageless factories where the worker's time is fully bought, once and for all, at a yearly price collected only at the exit gate. It must be an employer's dream or what the capitalist's desire has always produced at the level of fantasy, a limit case that never had any real historical existence. I will answer by saying: on the contrary, this employer's dream, this industrial panopticon, actually existed, and on a large scale at the beginning of the nineteenth century. In a single region of France, in the southeast, there were forty thousand women textile workers working under this regimen, which at that time was a substantial number. The same type of institution also existed in other areas and other countries—Switzerland in particular, and England. As a matter of fact, that was how Owen got the idea of his reforms. In the United States, there was a whole complex of textile factories organized on the model of these prison factories, boarding factories, convent factories.

So we're talking about a phenomenon that had, in this period, a very large economic and demographic extent. So we can say not only was all this the dream of employers, but it was an employer's dream come true. Actually, there are two sorts of utopia: proletarian socialist utopias, which have the property of never being realized, and capitalist utopias, which often have the unfortunate tendency to be realized. The utopia I'm speaking of, that of the prison factory, was actually realized. And it was realized not only in industry but also in a series of institutions that materialized during the same era. Institutions that essentially followed the same principles and the same operational models; institutions of a pedagogical type such as schools, orphanages, training centers; correctional institutions like prisons, reformatories, houses of correction for young adults; institutions that were correctional and therapeutic at once, such as hospitals, psychiatric hospitals, everything that Americans call "asylums" and that an American historian has analyzed in a recent book.[32] In that book, he tried to show how those buildings and institutions which spread across Western society appeared in the United States. That history is beginning to be written for the United States; it needs to be done for other countries as well, attempting above all to take the measure of its importance, to quantify its political and economic scope and impact.

One must go further still. Not only were there industrial institutions and a series of other institutions alongside them, but what happened was that those industrial institutions were, in a certain sense, perfected. Effort was immediately concentrated directly on building them; they were a direct concern of capitalism. Yet very quickly they were found not to be viable or manageable by capitalism. The economic cost of these institutions immediately proved too heavy, and the rigid structure of these prison factories soon caused many of them to collapse. Ultimately, they all disappeared. Indeed, as soon as there was a production crisis and it was necessary to discharge a certain number of workers, to readjust production, as soon as the growth rhythm of production accelerated, those enormous firms, with a fixed number of workers and equipment set up on a permanent basis, revealed themselves to be utterly unserviceable. The preferred option was to phase out those institutions, while preserving, in a certain way, some of the functions they served. Lateral or marginal techniques were organized to ensure, in the industrial world, the functions—confining, segregating, and containing of the working class—initially served by these rigid, fanciful, somewhat utopian institutions. Measures were taken, therefore—such as the creation of workers' housing estates, savings banks, relief funds—a series of means for attaching the working population, the developing proletariat, to the very body of the production apparatus.

The question that would need answering is the following: What aim was sought through this institution of internment in its two forms—the compact, hard form found at the beginning of the nineteenth century and even afterward in institutions such as schools, psychiatric hospitals, reformatories, and prisons, and the milder, more diffuse form of confinement manifested in institutions such as the workers town, the savings bank, the relief fund?

After a cursory look, one might say that this confinement was a direct legacy of two currents or tendencies we find in the eighteenth century. On the one hand, the French technique of confinement, and, on the other, the English type of control procedure. In the previous lecture, I tried to show how, in England, social surveillance originated in the control exercised within the religious group by the group itself, especially in dissenting groups; and how, in France, the surveillance and social control were exerted by the state apparatus—strongly infiltrated by private interests, it should be said—whose principal sanction was confinement in prisons or in other institutions of reclusion. Consequently, one might say that reclusion in the nineteenth century was a combination of moral and social control as conceived in England, and the properly French and state-administered institution of reclusion in a place, a building, an institution, an architecture.

However, the phenomenon that appeared in the nineteenth century is an innovation both with respect to the English mode of control and with respect to the French reclusion. In the English system of the eighteenth century, control was exerted by the group on an individual, or individuals, belonging to that group. At least in its initial phase, this was the situation at the end of the seventeenth and the beginning of the eighteenth century. The Quakers and the Methodists always exercised control over those belonging to their own groups or over those who were in the social and economic space of the group itself. It wasn't until later that the controlling agency shifted toward the top and to the state. The fact that an individual belonged to the group was what made him liable to supervision by his own group. Already in the institutions that formed in the nineteenth century, it was not as a member of a group that an individual was placed under supervision; on the contrary, it was precisely because he was an individual that he was placed in an institution, that institution being what constituted the group, the collectivity to be supervised. It was as an individual that one entered school; it was as an individual that one entered the hospital or prison. The prison, the hospital, the school, and the workshop were not forms of supervision of the group itself. It was the structure of supervision which, drawing individuals to it, taking hold of them individually, incorporating them, would constitute them secondarily as a group. We can see how, in the relation between this supervision and the group, there was a major difference between these two moments.

With regard to the French model, confinement in the nineteenth century was also rather different from what it was in France in the eighteenth century. In the former period, when someone was confined, it was always an individual who was marginalized with respect to the family, the social group, the local community to which he belonged—someone who didn't act according to the rule and had become marginal through his behavior, his disorder, the irregularity of his life. Confinement responded to this de facto marginalization with a kind of second-degree marginalization in the form of punishment. It was as if the individual was told, "Since you separated yourself from your group, we are going to separate you definitively or temporarily from society." So, at that time in France, there was an exclusionary confinement.

In the age we're concerned with, the aim of all these institutions—factories, schools, psychiatric hospitals, hospitals, prisons—is not to exclude but, rather, to attach individuals. The factory doesn't exclude individuals: it attaches them to a production apparatus. The school doesn't exclude individuals, even in confining them: it fastens them to an apparatus of knowledge transmission. The psychiatric hospital doesn't exclude individuals: it attaches them to an apparatus of correction, to an apparatus of normalization of individuals. The same is true of the reformatory or the prison: even if the effects of these institutions are the individual's exclusion, their primary aim is to insert individuals into an apparatus of normalization of people. The factory, the school, the prison, or the hospitals have the object of binding the individual to a process of production, training [*formation*], or correction of the producers. It's a matter of guaranteeing production, or the producers, in terms of a particular norm.

This means that we can draw a contrast between the confinement of the eighteenth century, which excluded individuals from the social circle, and the confinement that appeared in the nineteenth century, which had the function of attaching individuals to the producer's apparatuses of production, training, reform, or correction. What this involved, then, was an inclusion through exclusion. That is why I distinguish confinement from sequestration: the confinement of the eighteenth century, whose essential function was to exclude marginal individuals or reinforce marginality, and the sequestration of the nineteenth century, which aimed at inclusion and normalization.

There is, finally, a third set of differences from the eighteenth century, which gives an original configuration to the reclusion of the nineteenth century. In eighteenth-century England, there was a method of control that, at the start, was clearly independent of the state and even in opposition to it—a sort of defense reaction of religious groups against state domination, by means of which they managed their own control. In France, on the other hand, there was an apparatus that was very state-controlled, at least in its form and its instruments, seeing that it consisted essentially in the institution of the *lettres de cachet*. So there was an absolutely extra-statist formula in England and an absolutely statist formula in France. In the nineteenth century, there appeared something new that was much milder and richer: a series of institutions—schools, factories . . . — about which it is difficult to say whether they were plainly statist or extrastatist, whether they were part of the state apparatus or not. In actual fact, depending on the institutions, the countries, and the circumstances, some of these institutions were controlled directly by the state apparatus. In France, for example, there was conflict before the basic educational institutions could be brought under state control—a political issue was made of it. But at the level where I place myself, the question is not significant; it doesn't seem to me that this difference is very important. At bottom, what is new and interesting is that the state and what was not state-determined merged together, interlaced, inside these institutions. Instead of statist or non-statist, we should say that there exists an institutional network of sequestration, which is intrastatist. The difference between a state apparatus and what is not a state apparatus does not seem important for analyzing the functions of this general apparatus of sequestration, of this network of sequestration within which our existence is imprisoned.

What purpose is served by this network and these institutions? We can characterize their function in the following way: first of all, these institutions—pedagogical, medical, penal, or industrial—have the very curious property of involving control over, responsibility for, all or nearly all of individuals' time. They are institutions that, in a certain way, take charge of the whole temporal dimension of individuals' lives.

In this regard, I think one can distinguish modern society from feudal society. In feudal society and in many societies that ethnologists call "primitive," the control of individuals is based on local insertion, on the fact that they belong to a particular place. Feudal power was exercised over men insofar as they belonged to a manor. Local geographic inscription was a means of exercising power. Power was inscribed in men through their localization. In contrast, the modern society that formed at the beginning of the nineteenth century was basically indifferent or relatively indifferent to individuals' spatial ties: it was not interested in the spatial control of individuals insofar as they belonged to an estate, a locale, but only insofar as it needed people to place their time at its disposal. People's time had to be offered to the production apparatus; the production apparatus had to be able to use people's living time, their time of existence. The control was exerted for that reason and in that form. Two things were necessary for industrial society to take shape. First, individuals' time must be put on the market, offered to those wishing to buy it, and buy it in exchange for a wage; and, second, their time must be transformed into labor time. That is why we find the problem of, and the techniques of, maximum extraction of time in a whole series of institutions.

In the example I referred to, we saw this phenomenon in its compact form, its pure state. The workers' entire living time, from morning to night and night to morning, was bought once and for all, at the cost of a recompense, by an institution. We encounter the same phenomenon in other institutions, in closed pedagogical institutions that would open little by little in the course of the century, reformatories, orphanages, and prisons. In addition, a number of diffuse forms take place, especially from the moment it was realized that those prison factories were unmanageable, that one had to go back to a type of labor in which people would come in the morning, work, and stop working in the evening. We see a subsequent proliferation of institutions in which people's time, though it was not really extracted in its entirety, was controlled so that it became labor time.

During the nineteenth century, a series of measures aimed at eliminating holidays and reducing time off were to be adopted. A very subtle technique for controlling the workers' savings was perfected in the course of the century. On the one hand, in order for the market economy to have the necessary flexibility, the employers must be able to lay off workers when the circumstances required it; but, on the other hand, in order for the workers to be able to start working again after an obligatory period of unemployment, without dying of hunger in the interval, it was necessary for them to have reserves and savings—hence the rise in wages that we clearly see begin in England in the 1840s and in France in the 1850s. But when the workers had money, they were not to spend their savings before their time of unemployment came around. They mustn't use their savings whenever they wished, for staging a strike or having a good time—thus the need to control the worker's savings became apparent. Hence the creation, in the 1820s and especially the 1840s and 1850s, of savings banks and relief funds, which made it possible to channel workers' savings and control how they were used. In this way, the worker's time—not just the time of his working day but his whole lifespan—could actually be used in the best way by the production apparatus. Thus, in the form of institutions apparently created for protection and security, a mechanism was established by means of which the entire time of human existence was put at the disposal of the labor market and the demands of labor. This extraction of the whole quantity of time was the first function of these institutions of subjugation. It would also be possible to show how this general control of time was exercised in the developed countries by the mechanism of consumption and advertising.

The second function of these institutions of subjugation was that of controlling not the time of individuals but simply their bodies. There is something very odd about these institutions: it lies in the fact that while they were all apparently specialized—factories designed for production, hospitals, psychiatric or not, designed for healing, schools for teaching, prisons for punishment—the operation of these institutions implied a general discipline of existence that went far beyond their seemingly precise ends. It is very curious to observe, for example, how immorality (sexual immorality) constituted, for the factory owners at the beginning of the nineteenth century, a considerable problem. And this was not related simply to concerns about the birthrate, which resisted control, at least at the level of demographic impact; the reason was that the employers couldn't bear the idea of working-class debauchery—in other words, working-class sexuality. One may also wonder why, in the hospitals, psychiatric or not—which were designed for healing— sexual behavior, sexual activity, was forbidden. A certain number of reasons having to do with hygiene can be adduced; yet these are marginal in comparison with a kind of general, fundamental, and universal decision according to which a hospital, psychiatric or not, should take responsibility not only for the particular function it exercised over individuals but also for their existence as a whole. Why is it that in schools people weren't just taught to read, but also obliged to wash? There is a sort of polymorphism at work here, a polyvalence, an indiscretion or nondiscretion, a syncretism of that function of control of existence.

But if one closely analyzes the reasons for which individuals' entire existence was controlled by these institutions, one sees that, at bottom, it was not just a matter of appropriating, extracting the maximum quantity of time but also of controlling, shaping, valorizing the individual's body according to a particular system. If one were to do a history of the social control of the body, one could show that, up through the eighteenth century, the individual body was essentially the inscription surface for tortures and punishments; the body was made to be tortured and punished. Already in the control authorities that appeared from the nineteenth century onward, the body acquired a completely different signification; it was no longer something to be tortured but something to be molded, reformed, corrected, something that must acquire aptitudes, receive a certain number of qualities, become qualified as a body capable of working. In this way, we see the second function of subjugation clearly emerging. The first function is to extract time, by transforming people's time, their living time, into labor time. Its second function consists in converting people's bodies into labor power. The function of transforming the body into labor power corresponds to the function of transforming time into labor time.

The third function of these institutions of subjugation consists in the creation of a new and peculiar type of power. What is the form of power that is exercised in these institutions? A polymorphous, polyvalent power. First, in a certain number of cases there is an economic power. In the case of a factory, the economic power offers a wage in exchange for a period of labor in a production apparatus belonging to the factory owner. There is also an economic power of another type: the fee-paying character of the treatment in certain hospital institutions. But, second, in all these institutions there is not only an economic power but also a political power: the persons who direct these institutions claim the right to give orders, establish rules, take measures, expel certain individuals, admit others. Third, that same economic and political power is also a judicial power: in these institutions, one does not give orders but one makes decisions; one not only has charge of functions such as production and training but one also has the right to punish and reward; one has the power to bring individuals before the judging authorities. The micropower that functions inside these institutions is, at the same time, a judicial power. This fact is surprising, for example, in the case of the prisons, where individuals are sent because they were judged by a court of law, but where their existence is placed under the observation of a kind of microcourt, a permanent petty tribunal constituted by the guards and the prison warden, which, from morning to night, will punish them according to their behavior. The school system is based on a kind of judicial power as well. One is constantly punishing and rewarding, evaluating and classifying, saying who's the best, who's not so good. There is, then, a judicial power within the school which simulates—in a rather arbitrary fashion, if one doesn't consider its general function—the judicial model of power. Why must one punish and reward in order to teach something to someone? That system seems self-evident, but if we think about it we see that this self-evidence melts away. If we read Nietzsche, we see that one can imagine a system of knowledge transmission that doesn't remain within an apparatus of judicial, political, and economic power.

Finally, there is a fourth characteristic of power—a power that, in a sense, traverses and drives those other powers. I'm thinking of an epistemological power—that is, a power to extract a knowledge from individuals and to extract a knowledge *about* those individuals who are subjected to observation and already controlled by those different powers. This occurs, then, in two different ways. In an institution like the factory, for example, the worker's labor and the

worker's knowledge about his own labor, the technical improve-
ments—the little inventions and discoveries, the microadaptations
he's able to implement in the course of his labor—are immediately
recorded, thus extracted from his practice, accumulated by the
power exercised over him through supervision. In this way, the
worker's labor is gradually absorbed into a certain technical knowledge of production which will enable a strengthening of control. So
we see how there forms a knowledge that's extracted from the individuals themselves and derived from their own behavior.

There is, moreover, a second knowledge formed from this situation—a knowledge about individuals that stems from the observation and classification of those individuals, from the recording
and analysis of their actions, from their comparison. Thus, we see
the emergence, alongside that technical knowledge characteristic
of all institutions of sequestration, an observational knowledge, a
clinical knowledge, as it were, like that of psychiatry, psychology,
and criminology. Thus, the individuals over whom power is exercised are either those from whom the knowledge they themselves
form will be extracted, retranscribed, and accumulated according
to new norms, or else objects of a knowledge that will also make
possible new forms of control. In this way, for example, a psychiatric knowledge was born and developed up to Freud, who was the
first to break with it. Psychiatric knowledge was formed on the basis
of an observation practiced exclusively by physicians who held
power within a closed institutional field constituted by the asylum
and the psychiatric hospital. In the same way, pedagogical methods
were formed out of the child's own adaptations to school tasks, adaptations that were observed and extracted to become operational
directives for institutions and forms of power brought to bear on
the child.

With this third function of sequestering institutions that operate
through these interactions of power and knowledge—a multiform
power and a knowledge that intermesh and operate simultaneously
in these institutions—we have the transformation of time-power
and labor-power and their integration in production. This conversion of living time into labor power and labor power into productive
force is made possible through the action of a series of institutions,
an action that defines them, in a schematic and global sense, as
institutions of sequestration. It seems that when we examine these

institutions of sequestration closely, we always find, whatever their point of insertion, their particular point of application, a general scheme, a great mechanism of transformation: How can men's time and their bodies, their lives, be made into something that is productive force? It is that set of mechanisms which is ensured by sequestration.

To finish, I will present, a little abruptly, some conclusions. First, it seems to me that on the basis of this analysis one can explain the emergence of the prison, an institution that, as I've already said, is rather enigmatic. How, starting from a theory of penal law such as that of Beccaria, did one end up with something as paradoxical as imprisonment? How was an institution as paradoxical and as full of disadvantages as the prison able to impose itself on a penal law that was, in appearance, the product of a rigorous rationality? How was a correctional prison project able to impose itself on Beccaria's legalistic rationality? It seems to me that if imprisonment prevailed in this way, it was because, at bottom, it was only the concentrated, exemplary, symbolic form of all these institutions of sequestration created in the nineteenth century. The prison is isomorphic with all of this. In the great social panopticism, whose function is precisely that of transforming people's lives into productive force, the prison serves a function much more symbolic and exemplary than truly economic, penal, or corrective. The prison is the reverse image of society, an image turned into a threat. The prison conveys two messages: "This is what society is. You can't criticize me since I only do what you do every day at the factory and the school. So I am innocent. I'm only the expression of a social consensus." That is what we find in penal theory and criminology: prison is not so unlike what happens every day. At the same time, though, prison conveys a different message: "The best proof that you're not in prison is that I exist as a special institution, separated from the others, meant only for those who have committed a violation of the law."

Thus, prison acquits itself of being prison by dint of resembling all the rest, and acquits all the other institutions of being prisons by presenting itself as being applicable only to those who have committed a violation. It's precisely this ambiguity in the position of the prison that seems to me to explain its incredible success, its nearly self-evident character, the ease with which it was accepted;

whereas as soon as it appeared, as soon as the great penal prisons were developed, from 1817 to 1830, everyone was aware of its drawbacks as well as its sinister and dangerous character. That is why prison was able to find a place and continues to play its role in the pyramid of social panopticisms.

The second conclusion is more controversial. Someone said that man's concrete essence is labor. Actually, this idea was put forward by several people. We find it in Hegel, in the post-Hegelians, and also in Marx, the Marx of a certain period, as Althusser would say. Since I'm interested not in authors but in the function of statements, it makes little difference who said it or exactly when it was said. What I would like to show is that, in point of fact, labor is absolutely not man's concrete essence or man's existence in its concrete form. In order for men to be brought into labor, tied to labor, an operation is necessary, or a complex series of operations, by which men are effectively—not analytically but synthetically—bound to the production apparatus for which they labor. It takes this operation, or this synthesis effected by a political power, for man's essence to appear as being labor.

So I don't think we can simply accept the traditional Marxist analysis, which assumes that, labor being man's concrete essence, the capitalist system is what transforms that labor into profit, into hyperprofit [*sur-profit*] or surplus value. The fact is, capitalism penetrates much more deeply into our existence. That system, as it was established in the nineteenth century, was obliged to elaborate a set of political techniques, techniques of power, by which man was tied to something like labor—a set of techniques by which people's bodies and their time would become labor power and labor time so as to be effectively used and thereby transformed into hyperprofit. But in order for there to be hyperprofit, there had to be an infrapower [*sous-pouvoir*]. A web of microscopic, capillary political power had to be established at the level of man's very existence, attaching men to the production apparatus, while making them into agents of production, into workers. This binding of man to labor was synthetic, political; it was a linkage brought about by power. There is no hyperprofit without an infrapower. I speak of "infrapower," for what's involved is the power I described earlier, and not the one traditionally called "political power." I'm referring not to a state apparatus, or to the class in power, but to the whole set of little powers, of little institutions situated at the lowest level. What I meant to do was analyze this infrapower as a condition of possibility of hyperprofit.

The last conclusion is that this infrapower, a prior condition of hyperprofit, in establishing itself, in beginning to function, gave rise to a series of knowledges—a knowledge of the individual, of normalization, a corrective knowledge—that proliferated in these institutions of infrapower, causing the so-called human sciences, and man as an object of science, to appear.

So we see how the destruction of hyperprofit necessarily entails challenging and attacking infrapower, how this challenge is necessarily connected with the questioning of the human sciences and of man considered as the fundamental, privileged object of this type of knowledge. We also see, if my analysis is correct, that we cannot situate the human sciences at the level of an ideology that is purely and simply the reflection and expression, in human consciousness, of the relations of production. If what I have said is true, it cannot be said that these forms of knowledge [*savoirs*] and these forms of power, operating over and above productive relations, merely express those relations or enable them to be reproduced. Those forms and knowledge and power are more deeply rooted, not just in human existence but in relations of production. That is the case because, in order for the relations of production that characterize capitalist societies to exist, there must be, in addition to a certain number of economic determinations, those power relations and forms of operation of knowledge. Power and knowledge are thus deeply rooted—they are not just superimposed on the relations of production but, rather, are very deeply rooted in what constitutes them. Consequently, we see how the definition of what is called "ideology" needs to be revised. The inquiry and the examination are precisely those forms of power–knowledge that came to function at the level of the appropriation of wealth in feudal society, and at the level of capitalist production and hyperprofit. It is at that basic level that forms of power–knowledge like the inquiry or the examination are situated.

NOTES

* The following five lectures were delivered at the Pontifical Catholic University of Rio de Janeiro in May 1973. [eds.]

1 Friedrich Nietzsche, "On Truth and the Lie in an Extra-moral Sense," trans. Walter Kaufmann, in *The Portable Nietzsche* (New York: Penguin, 1976), p. 42.

2 Nietzsche, *The Gay Science*, "On the Origin of Religions," trans. Walter Kaufmann (New York: Vintage, 1974), pp. 296–97.

3 Nietzsche, *On the Genealogy of Morals*, trans. Walter Kaufmann and R. J. Hollingdale (New York: Vintage, 1989), pp. 46–47: "Would anyone like to take a look into the secret of how *ideals are made* on earth? . . . This workshop where *ideals are manufactured*—It seems to me it stinks of so many lies."

4 Nietzsche, *Gay Science*, p. 168.

5 Ibid.

6 Nietzsche, *Gay Science* no. 333, p. 261.

7 Nietzsche, *Genealogy of Morals*, Third Essay, sec. 12, "What is the Meaning of Ascetic Ideals?" p. 119.

8 Nietzsche, *La Volonté de puissance* (1885–88; trans. G. Bianquis), vol. 1, bk. 1: *Critique des valeurs supérieures, rapportées á la vie*, no. 175, p. 92. [There is no English translation of this edition of *The Will to Power*—TRANS.]

9 Gilles Deleuze and Félix Guattari, *Anti-Oedipus*, trans. Robert Hurley, Mark Seem, and Helen Lane (New York: Viking, 1977).

10 Sophocles, *Oedipus the King*, trans. Robert Fagles, in *The Three Theban Plays* (New York: Penguin, 1984).

11 Homer, *The Iliad*, bk. 23: 262–652, trans. Robert Fagles (New York: Penguin, 1990), pp. 567–79.

12 Ibid., 581–85, p. 577. [Here and in his discussion of the Oedipus play, Foucault paraphrases instead of quoting—TRANS.]

13 Sophocles, *Oedipus the King*, 642–48, p. 196.

14 "Oedipus" derives from the Greek "to swell" (*oideo*) and "foot" (*pous*); thus, Oedipus is "the swollen-footed." But Foucault focuses on other etymological possibilities in his own remarks.

15 Sophocles, *Oedipus the King*, 399–400, p. 182.

16 Ibid., 1016–1018, p. 218.

17 Ibid., 1202, p. 233.

18 Ibid., 1522–23, p. 250.

19 Ibid., 629–30, p. 195.

20 Ibid., 1675–77, p. 250.

21 Ibid., 705, p. 195.

22 Herodotus, *The Histories*, trans. A. de Sélincourt and J. Marincola (New York: Penguin, 1972), bk. 5, sec. 92, pp. 312–14. Cypselus reigned over Corinth 657–27 B.C.

23 Sophocles, *Oedipus the King*, 627–28, p. 195.

24 Georges Dumézil, *Jupiter, Mars, Quirinus: essai sur la conception indo-européenne de la société et sur les origines de Rome* (Paris: Gallimard, 1941); *Mythe et épopée*, vol. 1: *L'Idéologie des trois fonctions dans les épopées des peuples indo-européens* (Paris: Gallimard, 1968).

25 Jeremy Bentham, *Panopticon, Works*, vol. 4, ed. Bowring [1838–43] (New York: Russel and Russel, 1971).

26 Cesare de Beccaria, *Dei Delitti e delle Pene* (Milan, 1764).

27 R. Watson (Bishop of Llandaff), *A Sermon Preached Before the Society for the Suppression of Vice, in the Parish Church of St. George*, May 3, 1804 (London: Printed for the Society for the Suppression of Vice, 1804). In 1802, the Society for the Suppression of Vice and the Teaching of Religion replaced the Society for the Proclamation Against Vice and Immorality, founded in 1787 to support George III's proclamation.

28 N. H. Julius, *Vorlesungen über die Gefängnisskunde* (Berlin: Stuhr, 1828). French trans., *Leçons sur les prisons, présentées en forme de cours au public de Berlin en l'année 1827*, trans. Lagarmitte (Paris: F. G. Levrault, 1831).

29 Julius, *Leçons sur les prisons*, vol. 1, pp. 384–86.

30 Ibid., p. 384.

31 Jean-Baptiste Treilhard, *Exposé des motifs des lois composant le Code d'instruction criminel* (Paris: Hacquart, 1808), p. 2.

32 Erving Goffman, *Asylums* (New York: Doubleday, 1961).

THE POLITICS OF HEALTH IN THE EIGHTEENTH CENTURY

T o begin with, two preliminary remarks:

First: It is, no doubt, not very fruitful to look for a relation of anteriority or dependence between the two terms of, on the one hand, a private, "liberal" medicine that was subject to the mechanisms of individual initiative and to the laws of the market, and, on the other, a medical politics drawing support from structures of power and concerning itself with the health of a collectivity. It is somewhat mythical to suppose that Western medicine originated as a collective practice, endowed by magico-religious institutions with its social character and gradually dismantled through the subsequent organization of private clienteles.[1] But it is equally inadequate to posit, at the historical threshold of modern medicine, the existence of a singular, private, individual medical relation, "clinical" in its economic functioning and epistemological form, and to imagine that a series of corrections, adjustments, and constraints gradually came to socialize this relation, causing it, to some extent, to be taken charge of by the collectivity.

What the eighteenth century shows, in any case, is a double-sided process. The development of a medical market in the form of private clienteles, the extension of a network of personnel offering qualified medical attention, the growth of individual and family demand for health care, the emergence of a clinical medicine strongly centered on individual examination, diagnosis, and therapy, the explicitly moral and scientific (and secretly economic) exaltation of "private consultation"—in short, the progressive emplacement of what was to become the great medical edifice of the nineteenth century: these things cannot be divorced from the concurrent organization of a politics of health, the consideration of disease as a political and economic problem for social collectivities which they must seek to resolve as a matter of overall policy. "Private" and "socialized" medicine, in their reciprocal support and opposition, both derive from a common global strategy. No doubt, there is no society that does not practice some kind of "noso-politics": the eighteenth century didn't invent it. But it prescribed new rules, and above all transposed the practice onto an explicit, concerted level of analysis such as had been previously unknown. At this point, the age entered is one not so much of social medicine as of a considered noso-politics.

Second: The center of initiative, organization, and control for this politics should not be located only in the apparatuses of the state. In fact, there were a number of distinct health policies, and various different methods for taking charge of medical problems: those of religious groups (the considerable importance, for example, of the Quakers and the various dissenting movements in England); those of charitable and benevolent associations, ranging from the parish *bureaux* to the philanthropic societies, which operated rather like organs of the surveillance of one class over those others which, precisely because they are less able to defend themselves, are sources of collective danger; those of the learned societies, the eighteenth-century academies and the early nineteenth-century statistics societies, which endeavor to organize a global, quantifiable knowledge of morbid phenomena. Health and sickness, as characteristics of a group, a population, are problematized in the eighteenth century through the initiatives of multiple social instances, in relation to which the state itself plays various different roles. On occasion, it intervenes directly: a policy of free distributions of medicines is pursued in France on a varying scale from Louis XIV to Louis XVI. From time to time it also establishes bodies for purposes of consultation and information (the Prussian Sanitary Collegium dates from 1685; the Royal Society of Medicine is founded in France in 1776). Sometimes the state's projects for authoritarian medical organization are thwarted: the Code of Health elaborated by Mai and accepted by the Elector Palatine in 1800 was never put into effect. Occasionally, the state is also the object of solicitations, which it resists.

Thus the eighteenth-century problematization of noso-politics correlates not with a uniform trend of state intervention in the practice of medicine but, rather, with the emergence at a multitude of sites in the social body of health and disease as problems requiring some form or other of collective control measures. Rather than being the product of a vertical initiative coming from above, noso-politics in the eighteenth century figures as a problem with a number of different origins and orientations, being the problem of the health of all as a priority for all, the state of health of a population as a general objective of policy.

The most striking trait of this noso-politics, concern with which extends throughout French, and indeed European society in the eighteenth century, certainly consists in the displacement of health problems relative to problems of assistance. Schematically, one can say that up to the end of the seventeenth century, institutions for assistance to the poor serve as the collective means of dealing with disease. Certainly, there are exceptions to this: the regulations for times of epidemic, measures taken in plague towns, and the quarantines enforced in certain large ports all constituted forms of authoritarian medicalization not organically linked to techniques of assistance. But outside these limit cases, medicine understood and practiced as a "service" operated simply as one of the components of "assistance." It was addressed to the category, so important despite the vagueness of its boundaries, of the "sick poor." In economic terms, this medical service was provided mainly thanks to charitable foundations. Institutionally, it was exercised within the framework of lay and religious organizations devoted to a number of ends: distribution of food and clothing, care for abandoned children, projects of elementary education and moral proselytism, provision of workshops and workrooms, and in some cases the surveillance of "unstable" or "troublesome" elements (in the cities, the hospital *bureaux* had a jurisdiction over vagabonds and beggars, and the parish *bureaux* and charitable societies also very explicitly adopted the role of denouncing "bad subjects"). From a technical point of view, the role of therapeutics in the working of

the hospitals in the Classical age was limited in extent when compared with the scale of provision of material assistance or with the
administrative structure. Sickness is only one among a range of
factors—including infirmity, old age, inability to find work, and des-
titution—that compose the figure of the "needy pauper" who
deserves hospitalization.

The first phenomenon in the eighteenth century we should note
is the progressive dislocation of these mixed and polyvalent procedures of assistance. This dismantling is carried out or, rather, is
called for (since it only begins to become effective late in the century) as the upshot of a general reexamination of modes of investment and capitalization. The system of "foundations," which
immobilize substantial sums of money and whose revenues serve
to support the idle and thus allow them to remain outside the circuits of production, is criticized by economists and administrators.
The process of dismemberment is also carried out as a result of a
finer grid of observation of the population and the distinctions this
observation aims to draw between the different categories of un-
fortunates to which charity confusedly addresses itself. In this process of the gradual attenuation of traditional social statuses, the
"pauper" is one of the first to be effaced, giving way to a whole
series of functional discriminations (the good poor and the bad
poor, the willfully idle and the involuntarily unemployed, those who
can do some kind of work and those who cannot). An analysis of
idleness—and its conditions and effects—tends to replace the
somewhat global charitable sacralization of "the poor." This analysis has as its practical objective at best to make poverty useful by
fixing it to the apparatus of production, at worst to lighten as much
as possible the burden it imposes on the rest of society. The problem is to set the "able-bodied" poor to work and transform them
into a useful labor force; but it is also to assure the self-financing
by the poor themselves of the cost of their sickness and temporary
or permanent incapacitation, and further to make profitable in the
short or long term the education of orphans and foundlings. Thus,
a complete utilitarian decomposition of poverty is marked out, and
the specific problem of the sickness of the poor begins to figure in
the relationship of the imperatives of labor to the needs of production.

But one must also note another process more general than the first, and more than its simple elaboration: this is the emergence of the health and physical well-being of the population in general as one of the essential objectives of political power. Here it is not a matter of offering support to a particularly fragile, troubled, and troublesome margin of the population but of how to raise the level of health of the social body as a whole. Different power apparatuses are called upon to take charge of "bodies," not simply so as to exact blood service from them or levy dues but to help and if necessary constrain them to ensure their own good health. The imperative of health—at once the duty of each and the objective of all.

Taking a longer perspective, one could say that from the heart of the Middle Ages power traditionally exercised two great functions, that of war and peace. It exercised them through the hard-won monopoly of arms, and that of the arbitration of lawsuits and punishments of crimes, which it ensured through its control of judicial functions. *Pax et justitia.* To these functions were added—from the end of the Middle Ages—those of the maintenance of order and the organization of enrichment. Now, in the eighteenth century we find a further function emerging, that of the disposition of society as a milieu of physical well-being, health, and optimal longevity. The exercise of these three latter functions—order, enrichment, and health—is assured less through a single apparatus than by an ensemble of multiple regulations and institutions which in the eighteenth century take the generic name of "police." Down to the end of the ancien régime, the term "police" does not signify (at least not exclusively) the institution of police in the modern sense; "police" is the ensemble of mechanisms serving to ensure order, the properly channeled growth of wealth, and the conditions of preservation of health "in general." N. De Lamare's *Treatise* on police, the great charter of police functions in the Classical period, is significant in this respect. The eleven headings under which it classifies police activities can readily be distinguished in terms of three main sets of aims: economic regulation (the circulation of commodities, manufacturing processes, the obligations of tradespeople both to one another and to their clientele), measures of public order (surveillance of dangerous individuals, expulsion of vagabonds and, if necessary, beggars, and the pursuit of criminals), and general rules of hygiene (checks on the quality of foodstuffs sold, the water supply, and the cleanliness of streets).

At the point when the mixed procedures of police are being broken down into these elements and the problem of sickness among the poor is identified in its economic specificity, the health and physical well-being of populations comes to figure as a political objective that the "police" of the social body must ensure along with those of economic regulation and the needs of order. The sudden importance assumed by medicine in the eighteenth century originates at the point of intersection of a new, "analytical" economy of assistance with the emergence of a general "police" of health. The new noso-politics inscribes the specific question of the sickness of the poor within the general problem of the health of populations, and makes the shift from the narrow context of charitable aid to the more general form of a "medical police," imposing its constraints and dispensing its services. The texts of Th. Rau (the *Medizinische Polizei Ordnung* of 1764), and above all the great work of J. P. Frank, *System einer medizinische Polizei*, give this transformation its most coherent expression.

What is the basis for this transformation? Broadly, one can say it has to do with the preservation, upkeep, and conservation of the "labor force." No doubt, though, the problem is a wider one. It arguably concerns the economico-political effects of the accumulation of men. The great eighteenth-century demographic upswing in Western Europe, the necessity for coordinating and integrating it into the apparatus of production, and the urgency of controlling it with finer and more adequate power mechanisms cause "population," with its numerical variables of space and chronology, longevity and health, to emerge not only as a problem but as an object of surveillance, analysis, intervention, modifications, and so on. The project of a technology of population begins to be sketched: demographic estimates, the calculation of the pyramid of ages, different life expectancies and levels of mortality, studies of the reciprocal relations of growth of wealth and growth of population, various measures of incitement to marriage and procreation, the development of forms of education and professional training. Within this set of problems, the "body"—the body of individuals and the body of populations—appears as the bearer of new variables, not merely as between the scarce and the numerous, the submissive and the restive, rich and poor, healthy and sick, strong and weak, but also as between the more or less utilizable, more or less amenable to profitable investment, those with greater or lesser prospects of survival, death and illness, and with more or less capacity for being usefully trained. The biological traits of a population become relevant factors for economic management, and it becomes necessary to organize around them an apparatus that will ensure not only their subjection [*asujettissement*] but the constant increase of their utility.

This enables us to understand the main characteristics of eighteenth-century noso-politics as follows:

(1) *The privilege of the child and the medicalization of the family.* The problem of "children" (that is, of their number at birth and the relation of births to mortalities) is now joined by the problem of "childhood" (that is, of survival to adulthood, the physical and economic conditions for this survival, the necessary and sufficient amount of investment for the period of child development to become useful—in brief, the organization of this "phase" perceived as being both specific and finalized). It is no longer just a matter of producing an optimum number of children, but one of the correct management of this age of life.

New and highly detailed rules serve to codify relations between adults and children. The relations of filial submission and the system of signs these entail certainly persist, with few changes. But they are to be henceforth invested by a whole series of obligations imposed on parents and children alike: obligations of a physical kind (care, contact, hygiene, cleanliness, attentive proximity), suckling of children by their mothers, clean clothing, physical exercise to ensure the proper development of the organism—the permanent and exacting corporal relation between adults and their children. The family is no longer to be just a system of relations inscribed in a social status, a kinship system, a mechanism for the transmission of property; it is to become a dense, saturated, permanent, continuous physical environment that envelops, maintains, and develops the child's body. Hence, it assumes a material figure defined within a narrower compass; it organizes itself as the child's immediate environment, tending increasingly to become its basic framework for survival and growth. This leads to an effect of tightening, or at least intensification, of the elements and relations constituting the restricted family (the group of parents and children). It also leads to a certain inversion of axes: the conjugal bond serves no longer only, nor even perhaps primarily, to establish the junction of two lines of descent, but also to organize the matrix of the new adult individual. No doubt, it still serves to give rise to two lineages and hence to produce a descent; but it serves also to produce—under the best possible conditions—a human being who will live to the state of adulthood. The new "conjugality" lies, rather, in the link between parents and children. The family, seen as a narrow, localized pedagogical apparatus, consolidates itself within the interior of the great traditional family-as-alliance. And at the same time health—and principally the health of children—becomes one of the family's most demanding objectives. The rectangle of parents and children must become a sort of homeostasis of health. At all events, from the eighteenth century onward the healthy, clean, fit body, a purified, cleansed, aerated domestic space, the medically optimal siting of individuals, places, beds, and utensils, and the interplay of the "caring" and the "cared for" figure among the family's essential laws. And from this period the family becomes the most constant agent of medicalization. From the second half of the eighteenth century, the family is the target for a great enterprise of medical acculturation. The first wave of this offensive bears on care of children, especially babies. Among the principal texts are Audrey's *L'Orthopédie* (1749), Vandermonde's *Essai sur la manière de perfectionner l'espèce humaine* (1756), Cadogan's *An Essay upon Nursing, and the Management of Children, from Their Birth to Three Years of Age* (1748; French trans., 1752), des Essartz's *Traité de l'éducation corporelle en bas age* (1760), Ballexserd's *Dissertation sur l'éducation physique des enfants* (1762), Raulin's *De la Conservation des enfants* (1768), Nicolas' *Le Cri de la nature en faveur des enfants nouveau-nés* (1775), Daignan's *Tableau des sociétés de la vie humaine* (1786), Saucerotte's *De la Conservation des enfants* (year IV), W. Buchan's *Advice to Mothers on the Subject of Their Own Health; and on the Means of Promoting the Health, Strength and Beauty of Their Offspring* (1803; French trans., 1804), J. A. Millot's *Le Nestor français* (1807), Laplace-Chanvre's *Dissertation sur quelques points de l'éducation physique et morale des enfants* (1813), Leretz's *Hygiène des enfants* (1814), and Prévost-Leygonie's *Essai sur l'éducation phy-*

sique des enfants (1813). This literature gains even further in extension in the nineteenth century with the appearance of a whole series
of journals that address themselves directly to the lower classes.

The long campaign of inoculation and vaccination has its place
in this movement to organize around the child a system of medical
care for which the family is to bear the moral responsibility and at
least part of the economic cost. Via different routes, the policy for
orphans follows an analogous strategy. Special institutions are
opened: the Foundling Hospital, the Enfants Trouvés in Paris; but
there is also a system organized for placing children with nurses
or in families where they can make themselves useful by taking at
least a minimal part in domestic life, and where, moreover, they
will find a more favorable milieu of development at less cost than
in a hospital where they would be barracked until adolescence.

The medical politics outlined in the eighteenth century in all European countries has as its first effect the organization of the family
or, rather, the family–children complex, as the first and most important instance for the medicalization of individuals. The family is
assigned a linking role between general objectives regarding the
good health of the social body and individuals' desire or need for
care. This enables a "private" ethic of good health as the reciprocal
duty of parents and children to be articulated onto a collective system of hygiene and scientific technics of cure made available to
individual and family demand by a professional corps of doctors
qualified and, as it were, recommended by the state. The rights and
duties of individuals respecting their health and that of others, the
market where supply and demand for medical care meet, authoritarian interventions of power in the order of hygiene and illness
accompanied at the same time by the institutionalizing and protection of the private doctor–patient relation—all these features in
their multiplicity and coherence characterize the global functioning
of the politics of health in the nineteenth century. Yet they cannot
be properly understood if one abstracts them from this central element formed in the eighteenth century, the medicalized and medicalizing family.

(2) *The privilege of hygiene and the function of medicine as an instance of social control.* The old notion of the regime, understood at
once as a rule of life and a form of preventive medicine, tends to
become enlarged into that of the collective "regime" of a population

in general, with the disappearance of the great epidemic tempests, the reduction of the death rate, and the extension of the average lifespan and life expectancy for every age group as its triple objective. This program of hygiene as a regime of health for populations entails a certain number of authoritarian medical interventions and controls.

First of all, control of the urban space in general: it is this space that constitutes perhaps the most dangerous environment for the population. The disposition of various quarters, their humidity and exposure, the ventilation of the city as a whole, its sewage and drainage systems, the siting of abattoirs and cemeteries, the density of population—all these are decisive factors for the mortality and morbidity of the inhabitants. The city with its principal spatial variables appears as a medicalizable object. Whereas the medical topographies of regions analyze climatic and geological conditions outside human control, and can only recommend measures of correction and compensation, the urban topographies outline, in negative at least, the general principles of a concerted urban policy. During the eighteenth century the idea of the pathogenic city inspires a whole mythology and very real states of popular panic (the Charnel House of the Innocents in Paris was one of these high places of fear); it also gave rise to a medical discourse on urban morbidity and the placing under surveillance of a whole range of urban developments, constructions, and institutions.[2]

In a more precise and localized fashion, the needs of hygiene demand an authoritarian medical intervention in what are regarded as the privileged breeding grounds of disease: prisons, ships, harbor installations, the *hôpitaux généraux* where vagabonds, beggars, and invalids mingle together; the hospitals themselves—whose medical staffing is usually inadequate—aggravate or complicate the diseases of their patients, to say nothing of their diffusing of pathological germs into the outside world. Thus, priority areas of medicalization in the urban environment are isolated and are destined to constitute so many points for the exercise and application of an intensified medical power. Doctors will, moreover, have the task of teaching individuals the basic rules of hygiene, which they must respect for the sake of their own health and that of others: hygiene of food and habitat, exhortations to seek treatment in case of illness.

Medicine, as a general technique of health even more than as a service to the sick or an art of cures, assumes an increasingly important place in the administrative system and the machinery of power, a role constantly widened and strengthened throughout the eighteenth century. The doctor wins a footing within the different instances of social power. The administration acts as a point of support and sometimes a point of departure for the great medical inquiries into the health of populations; and, conversely, doctors devote an increasing amount of their activity to tasks, both general and administrative, assigned to them by power. A "medico-administrative" knowledge begins to develop concerning society, its health and sickness, its conditions of life, housing and habits; this serves as the basic core for the "social economy" and sociology of the nineteenth century. And there is likewise constituted a politico-medical hold on a population hedged in by a whole series of prescriptions relating not only to disease but to general forms of existence and behavior (food and drink, sexuality and fecundity, clothing and the layout of living space).

A number of phenomena dating from the eighteenth century testify to this hygienist interpretation of political and medical questions and the "surplus of power" it bestows on the doctor: the increasing presence of doctors in the academies and learned societies, the very substantial medical participation in the production of the Encyclopedias, their presence as counselors to representatives of power, the organization of medical societies officially charged with a certain number of administrative responsibilities and qualified to adopt or recommend authoritarian measures, the frequent role of doctors as programmers of a well-ordered society (the doctor as social or political reformer is a frequent figure in the second half of the eighteenth century), and the superabundance of doctors in the Revolutionary Assemblies. The doctor becomes the great adviser and expert, if not in the art of governing at least in that of observing, correcting, and improving the social "body" and maintaining it in a permanent state of health. And it is the doctor's function as hygienist rather than his prestige as a therapist that assures him this politically privileged position in the eighteenth century, prior to his accumulation of economic and social privileges in the nineteenth century.

* * *

The challenge to the hospital institution in the eighteenth century can be understood on the basis of these three major phenomena: the emergence of "population" with its biomedical variables of longevity and health; the organization of the narrowly parental family as a relay in a process of medicalization for which it acts both as the permanent source and the ultimate instrument; and the interlacing of medical and administrative instances in organizing the control of collective hygiene.

The point is that, in relation to these new problems, the hospital appears as an obsolete structure in many respects. A fragment of space closed in on itself, a place of internment of men and diseases, its ceremonious but inept architecture multiplying the ills in its interior without preventing their outward diffusion, the hospital is more the seat of death for the cities where it is sited than a therapeutic agent for the population as a whole. Not only the difficulty of admission and the stringent conditions imposed on those seeking to enter, but also the incessant disorder of comings and goings, inefficient medical surveillance, and the difficulty of effective treatment cause the hospital to be regarded as an inadequate instrument from the moment the population in general is specified as the object of medicalization and the overall improvement in its level of health as the objective. The hospital is perceived as an area of darkness within the urban space that medicine is called upon to purify. And it acts as a dead weight on the economy since it provides a mode of assistance that can never make possible the diminution of poverty, but at best the survival of certain paupers—and hence their increase in number, the prolongation of their sicknesses, the consolidation of their ill-health with all the consequent effects of contagion.

Hence there is the idea, which spreads during the eighteenth century, of a replacement of the hospital by three principal mechanisms. The first of these is the organization of a domestic form of "hospitalization." No doubt, this has its risks where epidemics are concerned, but it has economic advantages in that the cost to society of the patient's upkeep is far less as he is fed and cared for at home in the normal manner. The cost to the social body is hardly more than the loss represented by his forced idleness, and then only where he had actually been working. The method also offers medical advantages, in that the family—given a little advice—can attend to the patient's needs in a constant and adjustable manner impossible under hospital administration: each family will be enabled to function as a small, temporary, individual, and inexpensive hospital. But such a procedure requires the replacement of the hospital to be backed by a medical corps dispersed throughout the social body and able to offer treatment either free or as cheaply as possible. A medical staffing of the population, provided it is permanent, flexible, and easy to make use of, should render unnecessary a good many of the traditional hospitals. Finally, it is possible to envisage the care, consultation, and distribution of medicaments already offered by certain hospitals to outpatients being extended to a general basis, without the need to hold or intern the patients: this is the method of the dispensaries that aim to retain the technical advantages of hospitalization without its medical and economic drawbacks.

These three methods gave rise, especially in the latter half of the eighteenth century, to a whole series of projects and programs. They inspired a number of experiments. In 1769, the Red Lion Square dispensary for poor children was opened in London. Thirty years later almost every district of the city had its dispensary, and the annual number of those receiving free treatment there was estimated at nearly 50,000. In France it seems that the main effort was toward the improvement, extension, and more or less homogeneous distribution of medical personnel in town and country. The reform of medical and surgical studies (in 1772 and 1784), the requirement of doctors to practice in boroughs and small towns before being admitted to certain of the large cities, the work of investigation and coordination performed by the Royal Society of Medicine, the increasing part occupied by control of health and hygiene in the responsibilities of the Intendants, the development of free distribution of medication under the authority of doctors designated by the administration, all these measures are related to a health policy resting on the extensive presence of medical personnel in the social body. At the extreme point of these criticisms of the hospital and this project for its replacement, one finds under the Revolution a marked tendency toward "dehospitalization"; this tendency is already perceptible in the reports of the *Comité de mendicité*, with the project to establish a doctor or surgeon in each rural district to care for the indigent, supervise children under assistance, and practice inoculation. It becomes more clearly formulated under the Convention, with the proposal for three doctors in each district to provide the main health care for the whole population. However, the disappearance of the hospital was never more than the vanishing point of a utopian perspective. The real work lay in the effort to elaborate a complex system of functions in which the hospital comes to have a specialized role relative to the family (now considered as the primary instance of health), to the extensive and continuous network of medical personnel, and to the administrative control of the population. It is within this complex framework of policies that the reform of the hospitals is attempted.

The first problem concerns the spatial adaptation of the hospital, and in particular its adaptation to the urban space in which it is located. A series of discussions and conflicts arise between different schemes of implantation, respectively advocating massive hospitals capable of accommodating a sizable population, uniting and thus rendering more coherent the various forms of treatment—or, alternatively, smaller hospitals where patients will receive better attention and the risks of contagion will be less grave. There was another, connected problem: Should hospitals be sited outside the cities, where ventilation is better and there is no risk of hospital miasmas being diffused among the population?—a solution which in general was linked to the planning of large architectural installations; or should a multiplicity of small hospitals be built at scattered points where they can most easily be reached by the population that will use them? a solution that often involves the coupling of hospital and dispensary. In either case, the hospital is intended to become a functional element in an urban space where its effects must be subject to measurement and control.

It is also necessary to organize the internal space of the hospital so as to make it medically efficacious, a place no longer of assistance but of therapeutic action. The hospital must function as a "curing machine." First, in a negative way: all the factors that make the hospital dangerous for its occupants must be suppressed, solving the problem of the circulation of air (which must be constantly renewed without its miasmas or mephitic qualities being carried from one patient to another), and solving as well the problem of the changing, transport, and laundering of bed linen. Second, in a positive way, the space of the hospital must be organized according to a concerted therapeutic strategy, through the uninterrupted presence and hierarchical prerogatives of doctors, through systems of observation, notation, and record-taking. These make it possible to fix the knowledge of different cases, to follow their particular evolution, and also to globalize the data that bear on the long-term life of a whole population, and, finally, the substitution of better-adapted medical and pharmaceutical cures for the somewhat indiscriminate curative regimes that formed the essential part of traditional nursing. The hospital tends toward becoming an essential element in medical technology, not simply as a place for curing, but as an instrument which, for a certain number of serious cases, makes curing possible.

Consequently, it becomes necessary in the hospital to articulate medical knowledge with therapeutic efficiency. In the eighteenth century, specialized hospitals emerge. If there existed certain establishments previously reserved for madmen or venereal patients, this was less for the sake of any specialized treatment than as a measure of exclusion or out of fear. The new "unifunctional" hospital, on the other hand, comes to be organized only from the moment when hospitalization becomes the basis, and sometimes the condition, for a more or less complex therapeutic approach. The Middlesex Hospital, intended for the treatment of smallpox and the practice of vaccination, was opened in London in 1745, the London Fever Hospital dates from 1802, and the Royal Ophthalmic Hospital from 1804. The first Maternity Hospital was opened in London in 1749. In Paris, the Enfants Malades was founded in 1802. One sees the gradual constitution of a hospital system whose therapeutic function is strongly emphasized—designed, on the one hand, to cover with sufficient continuity the urban or rural space whose population it has charge of, and, on the other, to articulate itself with medical knowledge and its classifications and techniques.

Finally, the hospital must serve as the supporting structure for the permanent staffing of the population by medical personnel. Both for economic and medical reasons, it must be possible to make the passage from treatment at home to a hospital regime. By their visiting rounds, country and city doctors must lighten the burden of the hospitals and prevent their overcrowding; in return the hospital must be accessible to patients on the advice and at the request of their doctors. Moreover, the hospital as a place of accumulation and development of knowledge must provide for the training of doctors for private practice. At the end of the eighteenth century, clinical teaching in the hospital—the first rudiments of which appear in Holland with Sylvius and then Boerhaave, at Vienna with Van Swieten, and at Edinburgh through the linking of the School of Medicine with the Edinburgh Infirmary—becomes the general principle around which the reorganization of medical studies is undertaken. The hospital, a therapeutic instrument for the patients who occupy it, contributes at the same time, through its clinical teaching and the quality of the medical knowledge acquired there, to the improvement of the population's health as a whole.

The return of the hospitals, and more particularly the projects for their architectural, institutional, and technical reorganization, owed its importance in the eighteenth century to this set of problems relating to urban space, the mass of the population with its biological characteristics, the close-knit family cell and the bodies of individuals. It is in the history of these materialities, which are at once political and economic, that the "physical" process of transformation of the hospitals is inscribed.

NOTES

1   Cf. George Rosen, *A History of Public Health* (New York: MD Publications, 1958).

2   Cf., for example, J. P. L. Morel, *Dissertation sur les causes qui contribuent le plus à rendre cachectique et rachitique la constitution d'un grand nombre d'enfants de la ville de Lille* [A dissertation on the causes which most contribute to rendering the constitution of a great number of children in the city of Lille cachectic and rachitic], 1812.

During the years 1945–65 (I am referring to Europe), there
was a certain way of thinking correctly, a certain style of political
discourse, a certain ethics of the intellectual. One had to be on familiar terms with Marx and not let one's dreams stray too far from
Freud. And one had to treat sign-systems—the signifier—with the
greatest respect. These were the three requirements that made the
strange occupation of writing and speaking a measure of truth
about oneself and one's time acceptable.

Then came the five brief, impassioned, jubilant, enigmatic years.
At the gates of our world, there was Vietnam, of course, and the
first major blow to the powers that be. But here, inside our walls,
what exactly was taking place? An amalgam of revolutionary and
antirepressive politics? A war fought on two fronts—against social
exploitation and psychic repression? A surge of libido modulated by
the class struggle? Perhaps. At any rate, it is this familiar, dualistic
interpretation that has laid claim to the events of those years. The
dream that cast its spell, between World War I and fascism, over
the dreamiest parts of Europe—the Germany of Wilhelm Reich, and
the France of the Surrealists—had returned and set fire to reality
itself: Marx and Freud in the same incandescent light.

But is that really what happened? Had the utopian project of the
thirties been resumed, this time on the scale of historical practice?
Or was there, on the contrary, a movement toward political struggles that no longer conformed to the model that Marxist tradition

had prescribed? Toward an experience and a technology of desire that was no longer Freudian? It is true that the old banners were raised, but the combat shifted and spread into new zones.

Anti-Oedipus shows first of all how much ground has been covered. But it does much more than that. It wastes no time in discrediting the old idols, even though it does have a great deal of fun with Freud. Most important, it motivates us to go further.

It would be a mistake to read *Anti-Oedipus* as *the* new theoretical reference (you know, that much-heralded theory that finally encompasses everything, that finally totalizes and reassures, the one we are told we "need so badly" in our age of dispersion and specialization where "hope" is lacking). One must not look for a "philosophy" amid the extraordinary profusion of new notions and surprise concepts: *Anti-Oedipus* is not a flashy Hegel. I think that *Anti-Oedipus* can best be read as an "art," in the sense that is conveyed by the term "erotic art," for example. Informed by the seemingly abstract notions of multiplicities, flows, arrangements, and connections, the analysis of the relationship of desire to reality and to the capitalist "machine" yields answers to concrete questions. Questions that are less concerned with *why* this or that than with *how* to proceed. How does one introduce desire into thought, into discourse, into action? How can and must desire deploy its forces within the political domain and grow more intense in the process of overturning the established order? *Ars erotica, ars theoretica, ars politica.*

Whence the three adversaries confronted by *Anti-Oedipus*. Three adversaries who do not have the same strength, who represent varying degrees of danger, and whom the book combats in different ways:

1. The political ascetics, the sad militants, the terrorists of theory, those who would preserve the pure order of politics and political discourse. Bureaucrats of the revolution and civil servants of Truth.

2. The poor technicians of desire—psychoanalysts and semiologists of every sign and symptom—who would reduce

the multiplicity of desire to the binary law of structure and lack.

3. Last but not least, the major enemy, the strategic adversary is fascism (whereas *Anti-Oedipus'* opposition to the others is more of a tactical engagement). And not only historical fascism, the fascism of Hitler and Mussolini—which was able to mobilize and use the desire of the masses so effectively—but also the fascism in us all, in our heads and in our everyday behavior, the fascism that causes us to love power, to desire the very thing that dominates and exploits us.

I would say that *Anti-Oedipus* (may its authors forgive me) is a book of ethics, the first book of ethics to be written in France in quite a long time (perhaps that explains why its success was not limited to a particular "readership": being anti-oedipal has become a lifestyle, a way of thinking and living). How does one keep from being fascist, even (especially) when one believes oneself to be a revolutionary militant? How do we rid our speech and our acts, our hearts and our pleasures, of fascism? How do we ferret out the fascism that is ingrained in our behavior? The Christian moralists sought out the traces of the flesh lodged deep within the soul. Deleuze and Guattari, for their part, pursue the slightest traces of fascism in the body.

Paying a modest tribute to Saint Francis de Sales,[1] one might say that *Anti-Oedipus* is an *Introduction to the Nonfascist Life*.

This art of living counter to all forms of fascism, whether already present or impending, carries with it a certain number of essential principles that I would summarize as follows if I were to make this great book into a manual or guide to everyday life:

• Free political action from all unitary and totalizing paranoia.

• Develop action, thought, and desires by proliferation, juxtaposition, and disjunction, and not by subdivision and pyramidal hierarchization.

- Withdraw allegiance from the old categories of the Negative (law, limit, castration, lack, lacuna), which Western thought has so long held sacred as a form of power and an access to reality. Prefer what is positive and multiple, difference over uniformity, flows over unities, mobile arrangements over systems. Believe that what is productive is not sedentary but nomadic.

- Do not think that one has to be sad in order to be militant, even though the thing one is fighting is abominable. It is the connection of desire to reality (and not its retreat into the forms of representation) that possesses revolutionary force.

- Do not use thought to ground a political practice in Truth, nor political action to discredit, as mere speculation, a line of thought. Use political practice as an intensifier of thought, and analysis as a multiplier of the forms and domains for the intervention of political action.

- Do not demand of politics that it restore the "rights" of the individual, as philosophy has defined them. The individual is the product of power. What is needed is to "de-individualize" by means of multiplication and displacement, diverse combinations. The group must not be the organic bond uniting hierarchized individuals, but a constant generator of de-individualization.

- Do not become enamored of power.

It could even be said that Deleuze and Guattari care so little for power that they have tried to neutralize the effects of power linked to their own discourse. Hence the games and snares scattered throughout the book, rendering its translation a feat of real prowess. But these are not the familiar traps of rhetoric: the latter work to sway the reader without his being aware of the manipulation, and ultimately win him over against his will. The traps of *Anti-Oedipus* are those of humor—so many invitations to let oneself be put out, to take one's leave of the text and slam the door shut. The book often leads one to believe it is all fun and games, when something essential is taking place, something of extreme seriousness:

the tracking down of all varieties of fascism, from the enormous ones that surround and crush us to the petty ones that constitute the tyrannical bitterness of our everyday lives.

NOTE

* This essay first appeared in French in 1976. [eds.]

1 A seventeenth-century priest and Bishop of Geneva, known for his *Introduction to the Devout Life.*

————

Q: *Could you briefly outline the route that led you from your work on madness in the Classical age to the study of criminality and delinquency?*

A: When I was studying during the early fifties, one of the great problems that arose was that of the political status of science and the ideological functions it could serve. It wasn't exactly the Lysenko business that dominated everything, but I believe that around that sordid affair—which had long remained buried and carefully hidden—a whole number of interesting questions were provoked. These can all be summed up in two words: power and knowledge. I believe I wrote *Madness and Civilization* to some extent within the horizon of these questions. For me, it was a matter of saying this: If, concerning a science like theoretical physics or organic chemistry, one poses the problem of its relations with the political and economic structures of society, isn't one posing an excessively complicated question? Doesn't this set the threshold of possible explanations impossibly high? But, on the other hand, if one takes a form of knowledge [*savoir*] like psychiatry, won't the question be much easier to resolve, since the epistemological profile of psychiatry is a low one and psychiatric practice is linked with a whole range of institutions, economic requirements, and political issues of social regulation? Couldn't the interweaving of effects of power and knowledge be grasped with greater certainty in the case of a science as "dubious" as psychiatry? It was this same question which I wanted to pose concerning medicine in *The Birth of the Clinic*:

medicine certainly has a much more solid scientific armature than psychiatry, but it too is profoundly enmeshed in social structures. What rather threw me at the time was the fact that the question I was posing totally failed to interest those to whom I addressed it. They regarded it as a problem that was politically unimportant and epistemologically vulgar.

I think there were three reasons for this. The first is that, for Marxist intellectuals in France (and there they were playing the role prescribed for them by the PCF), the problem consisted in gaining for themselves the recognition of the university institutions and establishment. Consequently, they found it necessary to pose the same theoretical questions as the academic establishment, to deal with the same problems and topics: "We may be Marxists, but for all that we are not strangers to your preoccupations, rather, we are the only ones able to provide new solutions for your old concerns." Marxism sought to win acceptance as a renewal of the liberal university tradition—just as, more broadly, during the same period the communists presented themselves as the only people capable of taking over and reinvigorating the nationalist tradition. Hence, in the field we are concerned with here, it followed that they wanted to take up the "noblest," most academic problems in the history of the sciences: mathematics and physics, in short the themes valorized by Pierre Maurice Marie Duhem, Edmund Husserl, and Alexandre Koyré. Medicine and psychiatry didn't seem to them to be very noble or serious matters, nor to stand on the same level as the great forms of classical rationalism.

The second reason is that post-Stalinist Stalinism, by excluding from Marxist discourse everything that wasn't a frightened repetition of the already said, would not permit the broaching of uncharted domains. There were no ready-made concepts, no approved terms of vocabulary available for questions like the power-effects of psychiatry or the political function of medicine, whereas on the contrary innumerable exchanges between Marxists and academics, from Marx via Engels and Lenin down to the present, had nourished a whole tradition of discourse on "science," in the nineteenth-century sense of that term. The price Marxists paid for their fidelity to the old positivism was a radical deafness to a whole series of questions posed by science.

Finally, there is perhaps a third reason, but I can't be absolutely sure that it played a part. I wonder nevertheless whether, among intellectuals in or close to the PCF, there wasn't a refusal to pose the problem of internment, of the political use of psychiatry, and, in more general sense, of the disciplinary grid of society. No doubt, little was then known in 1955–60 of the real extent of the Gulag, but I believe that many sensed it, in any case many had a feeling that it was better not to talk about those things—it was a danger zone, marked by warning signs. Of course, it's difficult in retrospect to judge people's degree of awareness. But, in any case, you well know how easily the Party leadership—which knew everything, of course—could circulate instructions preventing people from speaking about this or that, or precluding this or that line of research. At any rate, if the question of Pavlovian psychiatry did get discussed among a few doctors close to the PCF, psychiatric politics and psychiatry as politics were hardly considered to be respectable topics.

What I myself tried to do in this domain was met with a great silence among the French intellectual Left. And it was only around 1968, and in spite of the Marxist tradition and the PCF, that all these questions came to assume their political significance, with a sharpness I had never envisaged, showing how timid and hesitant those early books of mine had still been. Without the political opening created during those years, I would surely never have had the courage to take up these problems again and pursue my research in the direction of penal theory, prisons, and disciplines.

Q: *So there is a certain "discontinuity" in your theoretical trajectory. Incidentally, what do you think today about this concept of discontinuity, on the basis of which you have been all too rapidly and readily labeled as a "structuralist" historian?*

A: This business about discontinuity has always rather bewildered me. In the new edition of the *Petit Larousse* it says: "Foucault: a philosopher who founds his theory of history on discontinuity." That leaves me flabbergasted. No doubt, I didn't make myself sufficiently clear in *The Order of Things*, though I said a good deal there about this question. It seemed to me that in certain empirical forms of knowledge like biology, political economy, psychiatry, medicine, and so on, the rhythm of transformation doesn't follow the smooth, continuist schemas of development which are normally accepted. The great biological image of a progressive maturation of science still underpins a good many historical analyses; it does not seem to me to be pertinent to history. In a science like medicine, for example, up to the end of the eighteenth century one has a certain type of discourse whose gradual transformation, within a period of twenty-five or thirty years, broke not only with the "true" propositions it had hitherto been possible to formulate but also, more profoundly, with the ways of speaking and seeing, the whole ensemble of practices which served as supports for medical knowledge. These are not simply new discoveries, there is a whole new "regime" in discourse and forms of knowledge. And all this happens in the space of a few years. This is something that is undeniable, once one has looked at the texts with sufficient attention. My problem was not at all to say 'Voilà, long live discontinuity, we are in the discontinuous and a good thing too," but to pose the question "How is it that at certain moments and in certain orders of knowledge, there are these sudden take-offs, these hastenings of evolution, these transformations which fail to correspond to the calm, continuist image that is normally accredited?" But the important thing here is not that such changes can be rapid and extensive or, rather, it is that this extent and rapidity are only the sign of something else—a modification in the rules of formation of statements which are accepted as scientifically true. Thus, it is not a change of content (refutation of old errors, recovery of old truths), nor is it a change of theoretical form (renewal of a paradigm, modification of systematic ensembles). It is a question of what *governs* statements, and the way in which they *govern* each other so as to constitute a set of propositions that are scientifically acceptable and, hence, capable of being verified or falsified by scientific procedures. In short, there is a problem of the regime, the politics of the scientific statement. At this level, it's not so much a matter of knowing what external power imposes itself on science as of what effects of power circulate among scientific statements, what constitutes, as it were, their internal regime of power, and how and why at certain moments that regime undergoes a global modification.

It was these different regimes that I tried to identify and describe in *The Order of Things*, all the while making it clear that I wasn't trying for the moment to explain them, and that it would be necessary to try and do this in a subsequent work. But what was lacking here was this problem of the "discursive regime," of the effects of power peculiar to the play of statements. I confused this too much with systematicity, theoretical form, or something like a paradigm. This same central problem of power, which at that time I had not yet properly isolated, emerges in two very different aspects at the point of junction of *Madness and Civilization* and *The Order of Things.*

Q: *We need, then, to locate the notion of discontinuity in its proper context. And perhaps there is another concept that is both more difficult and more central to your thought, the concept of an event. For, in relation to the event, a whole generation was long trapped in an impasse, in that following the works of ethnologists — some of them great ethnologists — a dichotomy was established between structures (the* thinkable) *and the event considered as the site of the irrational, the unthinkable, that which does not and cannot enter into the mechanism and play of analysis, at least in the form which this took in structuralism. In a recent discussion published in the journal* L'Homme, *three eminent anthropologists posed this question once again about the concept of event, and said: The event is what always escapes our rational grasp, the domain of "absolute contingency"; we are thinkers who analyze structures, history is no concern of ours, what could we be expected to have to say about it, and so forth. This opposition, then, between event and structure is the site and the product of a certain anthropology. I would say this has had devastating effects among historians who have finally reached the point of trying to dismiss the event and the "événementiel" as an inferior order of history dealing with trivial facts, chance occurrences, and so on. Whereas it is a fact that there are nodal problems in history which are neither a matter of trivial circumstances nor of those beautiful structures that are so orderly, intelligible, and transparent to analysis. For instance, the "great internment" you described in* Madness and Civilization *perhaps represents one of these nodes which elude the dichotomy of structure and event. Could you elaborate from our present standpoint on this renewal and reformulation of the concept of event?*

A: One can agree that structuralism formed the most systematic effort to evacuate the concept of the event, not only from ethnology but from a whole series of other sciences and in the extreme case from history. In that sense, I don't see who could be more of an antistructuralist than myself. But the important thing is to avoid trying to do for the event what was previously done with the concept of structure. It's not a matter of locating everything on one level, that of the event, but of realizing that there are actually a whole order of levels of different types of events differing in amplitude, chronological breadth, and capacity to produce effects.

The problem is at once to distinguish among events, to differentiate the networks and levels to which they belong, and to reconstitute the lines along which they are connected and engender one another. From this follows a refusal of analyses couched in terms of the symbolic field or the domain of signifying structures, and a recourse to analyses in terms of the genealogy of relations of force, strategic developments, and tactics. Here I believe one's point of reference should not be to the great model of language [*langue*] and signs but, rather, to that of war and battle. The history that bears and determines us has the form of a war rather than that of a language—relations of power, not relations of meaning. History has no "meaning," though this is not to say that it is absurd or incoherent. On the contrary, it is intelligible and should be susceptible of analysis down to the smallest detail—but this in accordance with the intelligibility of struggles, of strategies and tactics. Neither the dialectic, as the logic of contradictions, nor semiotics, as the structure of communication, can account for the intrinsic intelligibility of conflicts. "Dialectic" is a way of evading the always open and hazardous reality of conflict by reducing it to a Hegelian skeleton, and "semiology" is a way of avoiding its violent, bloody, and lethal character by reducing it to the calm Platonic form of language and dialogue.

Q: *In the context of this problem of discursivity, I think one can be confident in saying that you were the first person to pose the question of power regarding discourse, and that at a time when analyses in terms of the concept or object of the "text," along with the accompanying methodology of semiology, structuralism, and so on, were the prevailing fashion. Posing for discourse the question of power means basically to ask whom discourse serves. It isn't so much a matter of analyzing discourse into its unsaid, its implicit meaning, because (as you have often repeated) discourses are transparent, they need no interpretation, no one to assign them a meaning. If one reads "texts" in a certain way, one perceives that they speak clearly to us and require no further supplementary sense or interpretation. This question of power that you have addressed to discourse naturally has particular effects and implications in relation to methodology and contemporary historical researches. Could you briefly situate within your work this question you have posed—if indeed it's true that you have posed it?*

A: I don't think I was the first to pose the question. On the contrary, I'm struck by the difficulty I had in formulating it. When I think back now, I ask myself what else it was that I was talking about in *Madness and Civilization* or *The Birth of the Clinic*, but power? Yet I'm perfectly aware that I scarcely ever used the word and never had such a field of analyses at my disposal. I can say that this was an incapacity linked undoubtedly with the political situation in which we found ourselves. It is hard to see where, either on the Right or the Left, this problem of power could then have been posed. On the Right, it was posed only in terms of constitution, sovereignty, and so on, that is, in juridical terms; on the Marxist side, it was posed only in terms of the state apparatus. The way power was exercised—concretely, and in detail—with its specificity, its techniques and tactics, was something that no one attempted to ascertain; they contented themselves with denouncing it in a polemical and global fashion as it existed among the "other," in the adversary camp. Where Soviet socialist power was in question, its opponents called it totalitarianism; power in Western capitalism was denounced by the Marxists as class domination; but the mechanics of power in themselves were never analyzed. This task could only begin after 1968, that is to say, on the basis of daily struggles at grass-roots level, among those whose fight was located in the fine meshes of the web of power. This was where the concrete nature of power became visible, along with the prospect that these analyses of power would prove fruitful in accounting for all that had hitherto remained outside the field of political analysis. To put it very simply, psychiatric internment, the mental normalization of individuals, and penal institutions have no doubt a fairly limited importance if one is only looking for their economic significance. On the other hand, they are undoubtedly essential to the general functioning of the wheels of power. So long as the posing of the question of power was kept subordinate to the economic instance and the system of interests this served, there was a tendency to regard these problems as of small importance.

Q: *So a certain kind of Marxism and a certain kind of phenomenol-*
ogy constituted an objective obstacle to the formulation of this prob-
lematic?
A: Yes, if you like, to the extent that it's true that, in our student
days, people of my generation were brought up on these two forms
of analysis, one in terms of the constituent subject, the other in
terms of the economic in the last instance, ideology and the play of
superstructures and infrastructures.

Q: *Still within this methodological context, how would you situate*
the genealogical approach? As a questioning of the conditions of pos-
sibility, modalities, and constitution of the "objects" and domains you
have successively analyzed, what makes it necessary?
A: I wanted to see how these problems of constitution could be
resolved within a historical framework, instead of referring them
back to a constituent object (madness, criminality, or whatever).
But this historical contextualization needed to be something more
than the simple relativization of the phenomenological subject. I
don't believe the problem can be solved by historicizing the subject
as posited by the phenomenologists, fabricating a subject that
evolves through the course of history. One has to dispense with the
constituent subject, to get rid of the subject itself, that's to say, to
arrive at an analysis that can account for the constitution of the
subject within a historical framework. And this is what I would call
genealogy, that is, a form of history that can account for the constitution of knowledges, discourses, domains of objects, and so on,
without having to make reference to a subject that is either transcendental in relation to the field of events or runs in its empty
sameness throughout the course of history.

Q: *Marxist phenomenology and a certain kind of Marxism have*
clearly acted as a screen and an obstacle; there are two further con-
cepts that continue today to act as a screen and an obstacle—ideology,
on the one hand, and repression, on the other.
    All history comes to be thought of within these categories, which
serve to assign a meaning to such diverse phenomena as normaliza-
tion, sexuality, and power. And, regardless of whether these two con-
cepts are explicitly utilized, in the end one always comes back, on the
one hand, to ideology—where it is easy to make the reference back to
Marx—and, on the other, to repression, which is a concept often and

readily employed by Freud throughout the course of his career. Hence, I would like to put forward the following suggestion: Behind these concepts and among those who (properly or improperly) employ them, there is a kind of nostalgia. Behind the concept of ideology lies the nostalgia for a quasi-transparent form of knowledge, free from all error and illusion, and behind the concept of repression is the longing for a form of power innocent of all coercion, discipline, and normalization. On the one hand, a power without a bludgeon, and, on the other, knowledge without deception. You have called these two concepts, ideology and repression, negative, "psychological," insufficiently analytical. This is particularly the case in Discipline and Punish *where, even if there isn't an extended discussion of these concepts, there is nevertheless a kind of analysis that allows one to go beyond the traditional forms of explanation and intelligibility, which in the last (and not only the last) instance rest on the concepts of ideology and repression. Could you perhaps use this occasion to specify more explicitly your thoughts on these matters? With* Discipline and Punish, *a kind of positive history seems to be emerging, free of all the negativity and psychologism implicit in those two universal skeleton keys.*

A: The notion of ideology appears to me to be difficult to make use of, for three reasons. The first is that, like it or not, it always stands in virtual opposition to something else that is supposed to count as truth. Now, I believe that the problem does not consist in drawing the line between that which, in a discourse, falls under the category of scientificity or truth, and that which comes under some other category; rather, it consists in seeing historically how effects of truth are produced within discourses that, in themselves, are neither true nor false. The second drawback is that the concept of ideology refers, I think necessarily, to something of the order of a subject. Thirdly, ideology stands in a secondary position relative to something that functions as its infrastructure, as its material, economic determinant, and so on. For these three reasons, I think that this is a notion that cannot be used without circumspection.

The notion of repression is a more insidious one, or, in any event, I myself have had much more trouble in freeing myself of it insofar as it does indeed appear to correspond so well with a whole range of phenomena that belong among the effects of power. When I wrote *Madness and Civilization*, I made at least an implicit use of this notion of repression. I think indeed that I was positing the existence of a sort of living, voluble, and anxious madness that the mechanisms of power and psychiatry were supposed to have come to repress and reduce to silence. But it seems to me now that the notion of repression is quite inadequate for capturing what is precisely the productive aspect of power. In defining the effects of power as repression, one adopts a purely juridical conception of such power, one identifies power with a law that says no—power is taken, above all, as carrying the force of a prohibition. Now, I believe that this is a wholly negative, narrow, skeletal conception of power, one that has been curiously widespread. If power were never anything but repressive, if it never did anything but to say no, do you really think one would be brought to obey it? What makes power hold good, what makes it accepted, is simply the fact that it doesn't only weigh on us as a force that says no; it also traverses and produces things, it induces pleasure, forms knowledge, produces discourse. It needs to be considered as a productive network that runs through the whole social body, much more than as a negative instance whose function is repression. In *Discipline and Punish*, what I wanted to show was how, from the seventeenth and eighteenth centuries onward, there was a veritable technological take-off in the productivity of power. Not only did the monarchies of the Classical period develop great state apparatuses (the army, the police, and fiscal administration) but, above all, in this period what one might call a new "economy" of power was established, that is to say, procedures that allowed the effects of power to circulate in a manner at once continuous, uninterrupted, adapted, and "individualized" throughout the entire social body. These new techniques are both much more efficient and much less wasteful (less costly economically, less risky in their results, less open to loopholes and resistances) than the techniques previously employed, which were based on a mixture of more or less forced tolerances (from recognized privileges to endemic criminality) and costly ostentation (spectacular and discontinuous interventions of power, the most violent form of which was the "exemplary," because exceptional, punishment).

Q: *Repression is a concept used, above all, in relation to sexuality. It was held that bourgeois society represses sexuality, stifles sexual desire, and so forth. And when one considers for example the campaign launched against masturbation in the eighteenth century, or the medical discourse on homosexuality in the second half of the nineteenth century, or discourse on sexuality in general, one does seem to be faced with a discourse of repression. In reality, though, this discourse serves to make possible a whole series of interventions, tactical and positive interventions of surveillance, circulation, control, and so forth, which seem to have been intimately linked with techniques that give the appearance of repression or are at least liable to be interpreted as such. I believe the crusade against masturbation is a typical example of this.*

A: Certainly. It is customary to say that bourgeois society repressed infantile sexuality to the point where it refused even to speak of it or acknowledge its existence. It was necessary to wait until Freud for the discovery at last to be made that children have a sexuality. Now, if you read all the books on pedagogy and child medicine—all the manuals for parents that were published in the eighteenth century—you find that children's sex is spoken of constantly and in every possible context. One might argue that the purpose of these discourses was precisely to prevent children from having a sexuality. But their *effect* was to din it into parents' heads that their children's sex constituted a fundamental problem in terms of their parental educational responsibilities, and to din it into children's heads that their relationship with their own body and their own sex was to be a fundamental problem as far as *they* were concerned; and this had the consequence of sexually exciting the bodies of children while at the same time fixing the parental gaze and vigilance on the peril of infantile sexuality. The result was a sexualizing of the infantile body, a sexualizing of the bodily relationship between parent and child, a sexualizing of the familial domain. "Sexuality" is far more one of the positive products of power than power was ever repressive of sex. I believe that it is precisely these positive mechanisms that need to be investigated, and here one must free oneself of the juridical schematism of all previous characterizations of the nature of power. Hence, a historical problem arises, namely that of discovering why the West has insisted for so long on seeing the power it exercises as juridical and negative rather than as technical and positive.

Q: *Perhaps this is because it has always been thought that power is mediated through the forms prescribed in the great juridical and philosophical theories, and that there is a fundamental, immutable gulf between those who exercise power and those who undergo it.*

A: I wonder if this isn't bound up with the institution of monarchy. This developed during the Middle Ages against the backdrop of the previously endemic struggles between feudal power agencies. The monarchy presented itself as a referee, a power capable of putting an end to war, violence, and pillage and saying no to these struggles and private feuds. It made itself acceptable by allocating itself a juridical and negative function, albeit one whose limits it naturally began at once to overstep. Sovereign, law, and prohibition formed a system of representation of power which was extended during the subsequent era by the theories of right: political theory has never ceased to be obsessed with the person of the sovereign. Such theories still continue today to busy themselves with the problem of sovereignty. What we need, however, is a political philosophy that isn't erected around the problem of sovereignty or, therefore, around the problems of law and prohibition. We need to cut off the king's head. In political theory that has still to be done.

Q: *The king's head still hasn't been cut off, yet already people are trying to replace it with discipline, that vast system instituted in the seventeenth century comprising the functions of surveillance, normalization, and control, and, a little later, those of punishment, correction, education, and so on. One wonders where this system comes from, why it emerges and what its use is. And today there is rather a tendency to attribute a subject to it, a great, molar, totalitarian subject, namely the modern state, constituted in the sixteenth and seventeenth centuries and bringing with it (according to the classical theories) the professional army, the police, and the administrative bureaucracy.*

A: To pose the problem in terms of the state means to continue posing it in terms of sovereign and sovereignty, that is to say, in terms of law. If one describes all these phenomena of power as dependent on the state apparatus, this means grasping them as essentially repressive: the army as a power of death, police and justice as punitive instances, and so on. I don't want to say that the state isn't important; what I want to say is that relations of power, and hence the analysis that must be made of them, necessarily extend beyond the limits of the state—in two senses. First of all, because the state, for all the omnipotence of its apparatuses, is far from being able to occupy the whole field of actual power relations; and, further, because the state can only operate on the basis of other, already-existing power relations. The state is superstructural in relation to a whole series of power networks that invest the body, sexuality, the family, kinship, knowledge, technology, and so forth. True, these networks stand in a conditioning–conditioned relationship to a kind of "metapower" structured essentially around a certain number of great prohibition functions; but this metapower with its prohibitions can only take hold and secure its footing where it is rooted in a whole series of multiple and indefinite power relations that supply the necessary basis for the great negative forms of power. That is just what I was trying to make apparent in my book.

Q: *Doesn't this open up the possibility of overcoming the dualism of political struggles that eternally feed on the opposition between the state, on the one hand, and revolution, on the other? Doesn't it indicate a wider field of conflicts than that where the adversary is the state?*
A: I would say that the state consists in the codification of a whole number of power relations that render its functioning possible, and that revolution is a different type of codification of the same relations. This implies that there are many different kinds of revolution, roughly speaking, as many kinds as there are possible subversive recodifications of power relations—and, further, that one can perfectly well conceive of revolutions that leave essentially untouched the power relations that form the basis for the functioning of the state.

Q: *You have said about power as an object of research that one has to invert Clausewitz's formula so as to arrive at the idea that politics is the continuation of war by other means. Does the military model seem to you on the basis of your most recent researches to be the best one for describing power; is war here simply a metaphorical model, or is it the literal, regular, everyday mode of operation of power?*
A: This is the problem I now find myself confronting. As soon as one endeavors to detach power with its techniques and procedures from the form of law within which it has been theoretically confined up until now, one is driven to ask this basic question: Isn't power simply a form of warlike domination? Shouldn't one

therefore conceive of all problems of power in terms of relations of war? Isn't power a sort of generalized war that, at particular moments, assumes the forms of peace and the state? Peace would then be a form of war, and the state a means of waging it.

A whole range of problems emerge here. Who wages war against whom? Is it between two classes, or more? Is it a war of all against all? What is the role of the army and military institutions in this civil society where permanent war is waged? What is the relevance of concepts of tactics and strategy for analyzing structures and political processes? What is the essence and mode of transformation of power relations? All these questions need to be explored. In any case, it's astonishing to see how easily and self-evidently people talk of warlike relations of power or of class struggle without ever making it clear whether some form of war is meant, and if so what form.

Q: *We have already talked about this disciplinary power whose effects, rules, and mode of constitution you describe in* Discipline and Punish. *One might ask here, why surveillance? What is the use of surveillance? Now, there is a phenomenon that emerges during the eighteenth century, namely the discovery of population as an object of scientific investigation; people begin to inquire into birth rates, death rates, and changes in population, and to say for the first time that it is impossible to govern a state without knowing its population. M. Moheau for example, who was one of the first to organize this kind of research on an administrative basis, seems to see its goal as lying in the problems of political control of a population. Does this disciplinary power then act alone and of itself, or rather, doesn't it draw support from something more general, namely, this fixed conception of a population that reproduces itself in the proper way, composed of people who marry in the proper way and behave in the proper way, according to precisely determined norms? One would then have, on the one hand, a sort of global, molar body, the body of the population, together with a whole series of discourses concerning it, and then, on the other hand, down below, the small bodies, the docile, individual bodies, the microbodies of discipline. Even if you are only perhaps at the beginning of your researches here, could you say how you see the nature of the relationships—if any—engendered between these different bodies: the molar body of the population and the microbodies of individuals?*

A: Your question is exactly on target. I find it difficult to reply because I am working on this problem right now. I believe one must keep in view the fact that, along with all the fundamental technical inventions and discoveries of the seventeenth and eighteenth centuries, a new technology of the exercise of power also emerged which was probably even more important than the constitutional reforms and new forms of government established at the end of the eighteenth century. In the camp of the Left, one often hears people saying that power is that which abstracts, which negates the body, represses, suppresses, and so forth. I would say instead that what I find most striking about these new technologies of power introduced since the seventeenth and eighteenth centuries is their concrete and precise character, their grasp of a multiple and differentiated reality. In feudal societies, power functioned essentially through signs and levies. Signs of loyalty to the feudal lords, rituals, ceremonies, and so forth, and levies in the form of taxes, pillage, hunting, war, and so on. In the seventeenth and eighteenth centuries, a form of power comes into being that begins to exercise itself through social production and social service. It becomes a matter of obtaining productive service from individuals in their concrete lives. And, in consequence, a real and effective "incorporation" of power was necessary, in the sense that power had to be able to gain access to the bodies of individuals, to their acts, attitudes, and modes of everyday behavior. Hence the significance of methods such as school discipline, which succeeded in making children's bodies the object of highly complex systems of manipulation and conditioning. At the same time, though, these new techniques of power needed to grapple with the phenomena of population, in short to undertake the administration, control, and direction of the accumulation of men (the economic system that promotes the accumulation of capital and the system of power that ordains the accumulation of men are, from the seventeenth century on, correlated and inseparable phenomena): hence there arise the problems of demography, public health, hygiene, housing conditions, longevity, and fertility. And I believe that the political significance of the problem of sex is due to the fact that sex is located at the point of intersection of the discipline of the body and the control of the population.

Q: *Finally, a question you have been asked before: The work you do,*
these preoccupations of yours, the results you arrive at, what use can
one finally make of all this in everyday political struggles? You have
spoken previously of local struggles as the specific site of confrontation
with power, outside and beyond all such global, general instances as
parties or classes. What does this imply about the role of intellectuals?
If one isn't an "organic" intellectual acting as the spokesman for a
global organization, if one doesn't purport to function as the bringer,
the master of truth, what position is the intellectual to assume?

A: For a long period, the "left" intellectual spoke, and was acknowledged the right of speaking, in the capacity of master of truth
and justice.[1] He was heard, or purported to make himself heard, as
the spokesman of the universal. To be an intellectual meant something like being the consciousness/conscience of us all. I think we
have here an idea transposed from Marxism, from a faded Marxism
indeed. Just as the proletariat, by the necessity of its historical situation, is the bearer of the universal (but its immediate, unreflected
bearer, barely conscious of itself as such), so the intellectual,
through his moral, theoretical, and political choice, aspires to be
the bearer of this universality in its conscious, elaborated form. The
intellectual is thus taken as the clear, individual figure of a universality whose obscure, collective form is embodied in the proletariat.

Some years have now passed since the intellectual was called
upon to play this role. A new mode of the "connection between
theory and practice" has been established. Intellectuals have become used to working not in the modality of the "universal," the
"exemplary," the "just-and-true-for-all," but within specific sectors,
at the precise points where their own conditions of life or work
situate them (housing, the hospital, the asylum, the laboratory, the
university, family and sexual relations). This has undoubtedly given
them a much more immediate and concrete awareness of struggles.
And they have met here with problems that are specific, "nonuniv-
ersal," and often different from those of the proletariat or the
masses. And yet I believe intellectuals have actually been drawn
closer to the proletariat and the masses, for two reasons. First, because it has been a question of real, material, everyday struggles;
and second, because they have often been confronted, albeit in a
different form, by the same adversary as the proletariat, namely,
the multinational corporations, the judicial and police apparatuses,

the property speculators, and so on. This is what I would call the "specific" intellectual as opposed to the "universal" intellectual.

This new configuration has a further political significance. It makes it possible if not to integrate them at least to rearticulate categories that were previously kept separate. The intellectual par excellence used to be the writer: as a universal consciousness, a free subject, he was counterposed to those intellectuals who were merely *competent instances* in the service of the state or capital—technicians, magistrates, teachers. Since the time when each individual's specific activity began to serve as the basis for politicization, the threshold of *writing*, as the sacralizing mark of the intellectual, has disappeared. And it has become possible to develop lateral connections across different forms of knowledge and from one focus of politicization to another. Magistrates and psychiatrists, doctors and social workers, laboratory technicians and sociologists have become able to participate—both within their own fields and through mutual exchange and support—in a global process of politicization of intellectuals. This process explains how, even as the writer tends to disappear as a figurehead, the university and the academic emerge if not as principal elements then at least as "exchangers," privileged points of intersection. If the universities and education have become politically ultrasensitive areas, this is no doubt the reason why. And what is called the "crisis of the universities" should be interpreted not as a loss of power but, on the contrary, as a multiplication and reinforcement of their power effects as centers in a polymorphous ensemble of intellectuals who virtually all pass through and relate themselves to the academic system. The whole relentless theorization of writing we saw in the sixties was doubtless only a swan song. Through it, the writer was fighting for the preservation of his political privilege. But the fact that it was precisely a matter of theory, that he needed scientific credentials (founded in linguistics, semiology, psychoanalysis), that this theory took its references from the direction of Saussure, or Chomsky, and so on, and that it gave rise to such mediocre literary products—all this proves that the activity of the writer was no longer at the focus of things.

It seems to me that this figure of the "specific" intellectual has emerged since World War II. Perhaps it was the atomic scientist (in a word or, rather, a name: Oppenheimer) who acted as the point of transition between the universal and the specific intellectual. It's because he had a direct and localized relation to scientific knowledge and institutions that the atomic scientist could make his intervention; but, since the nuclear threat affected the whole human race and the fate of the world, his discourse could at the same time be the discourse of the universal. Under the rubric of this protest, which concerned the entire world, the atomic expert brought into play his specific position in the order of knowledge. And for the first time, I think, the intellectual was hounded by political powers, no longer on account of a general discourse he conducted but because of the knowledge at his disposal: it was at this level that he constituted a political threat. I am only speaking here of Western intellectuals. What happened in the Soviet Union is analogous with this on a number of points, but different on many others. There is certainly a whole study that needs to be made of scientific dissidence in the West and the socialist countries since 1945.

It is possible to suppose that the "universal" intellectual, as he functioned in the nineteenth and early twentieth centuries, was in fact derived from a quite specific historical figure—the man of justice, the man of law, who counterposes to power, despotism, and the abuses and arrogance of wealth the universality of justice and the equity of an ideal law. The great political struggles of the eighteenth century were fought over law, right, the constitution, the just in reason and law, that which can and must apply universally. What we call today "the intellectual" (I mean the intellectual in the political not the sociological sense of the word, in other words, the person who uses his knowledge, his competence, and his relation to truth in the field of political struggles) was, I think, an offspring of the jurist, or at any rate of the man who invoked the universality of a just law, if necessary against the legal professions themselves (Voltaire, in France, is the prototype of such intellectuals). The "universal" intellectual derives from the jurist or notable, and finds his fullest manifestation in the writer, the bearer of values and significations in which all can recognize themselves. The "specific" intellectual derives from quite another figure, not the jurist or notable, but the savant or expert. I said just now that it's with the atomic scientists that this latter figure comes to the forefront. In fact, it was preparing in the wings for some time before and was even present on at least a corner of the stage from about the end of the nineteenth century. No doubt it's with Darwin or, rather, with the post-Darwinian evolutionists that this figure begins to appear clearly. The stormy relationship between evolutionism and the socialists, as well as the highly ambiguous effects of evolutionism (on sociology, criminology, psychiatry, and eugenics, for example) mark the important moment when the savant begins to intervene in contemporary political struggles in the name of a "local" scientific truth—however important the latter may be. Historically, Darwin represents this point of inflection in the history of the Western intellectual. (Zola is very significant from this point of view: he is the type of the "universal" intellectual, bearer of law and militant of equity, but he ballasts his discourse with a whole invocation of nosology and evolutionism, which he believes to be scientific, though he grasps them very poorly in any case, and whose political effects on his own discourse are very equivocal.) If one were to study this closely, one would have to follow how the physicists, at the turn of the century, reentered the field of political debate. The debates between the theorists of socialism and the theorists of relativity are of capital importance in this history.

At all events, biology and physics were to a privileged degree the zones of formation of this new personage, the specific intellectual. The extension of technico-scientific structures in the economic and strategic domain was what gave him his real importance. The figure in which the functions and prestige of this new intellectual are concentrated is no longer that of the "writer of genius" but that of the "absolute savant," no longer he who bears the values of all, opposes the unjust sovereign or his ministers and makes his cry resound even beyond the grave. It is, rather, he who, along with a handful of others, has at his disposal—whether in the service of the state or against it—powers that can either benefit or irrevocably destroy life. He is no longer the rhapsodist of the eternal but the strategist of life and death. Meanwhile, we are at present experiencing the disappearance of the figure of the "great writer."

Now let's come back to more precise details. We accept, alongside the development of technico-scientific structures in contemporary society, the importance gained by the specific intellectual in recent decades, as well as the acceleration of this process since around 1960. Now, the "specific" intellectual encounters certain obstacles and faces certain dangers. The danger of remaining at the level of conjunctural struggles, pressing demands restricted to particular sectors. The risk of letting himself be manipulated by the political parties or trade union apparatuses that control these local struggles. Above all, the risk of being unable to develop these struggles for lack of a global strategy or outside support—the risk, too, of not being followed, or only by very limited groups. In France, we can see at the moment an example of this. The struggle around the prisons, the penal system, and the police-judicial system, because it has developed "in solitary," among social workers and ex-prisoners, has tended increasingly to separate itself from the forces that would have enabled it to grow. It has allowed itself to be penetrated by a whole naive, archaic ideology that makes the criminal at once into the innocent victim and the pure rebel—society's scapegoat—and the young wolf of future revolutions. This return to anarchist themes of the late nineteenth century was possible only because of a failure of integration of current strategies. And the result has been a deep split between this campaign with its monotonous, lyrical little chant, heard only among a few small groups, and the masses who have good reason not to accept it as valid political currency, but who also—thanks to the studiously cultivated fear of criminals—tolerate the maintenance or, rather, the reinforcement of the judicial and police apparatuses.

It seems to me that we are now at a point where the function of the specific intellectual needs to be reconsidered. Reconsidered but not abandoned, despite the nostalgia of some for the great "universal" intellectuals and the desire for a new philosophy, a new worldview. Suffice it to consider the important results that have been achieved in psychiatry: they prove that these local, specific struggles haven't been a mistake and haven't led to a dead end. One may even say that the role of the specific intellectual must become more and more important in proportion to the political responsibilities which he is obliged willy-nilly to accept, as a nuclear scientist, computer expert, pharmacologist, and so on. It would be a dangerous error to discount him politically in his specific relation to a local form of power, either on the grounds that this is a specialist matter that doesn't concern the masses (which is doubly wrong: they are already aware of it, and in any case implicated in it), or that the specific intellectual serves the interests of state or capital (which is true, but at the same time shows the strategic position he occupies);

or, again, on the grounds that he propagates a scientific ideology (which isn't always true, and is anyway certainly a secondary matter compared with the fundamental point: the effects proper to true discourses).

The important thing here, I believe, is that truth isn't outside power or lacking in power: contrary to a myth whose history and functions would repay further study, truth isn't the reward of free spirits, the child of protracted solitude, nor the privilege of those who have succeeded in liberating themselves. Truth is a thing of this world: it is produced only by virtue of multiple forms of constraint. And it induces regular effects of power. Each society has its regime of truth, its "general politics" of truth—that is, the types of discourse it accepts and makes function as true; the mechanisms and instances that enable one to distinguish true and false statements; the means by which each is sanctioned; the techniques and procedures accorded value in the acquisition of truth; the status of those who are charged with saying what counts as true.

In societies like ours, the "political economy" of truth is characterized by five important traits. "Truth" is centered on the form of scientific discourse and the institutions that produce it; it is subject to constant economic and political incitement (the demand for truth, as much for economic production as for political power); it is the object, under diverse forms, of immense diffusion and consumption (circulating through apparatuses of education and information whose extent is relatively broad in the social body, notwithstanding certain strict limitations); it is produced and transmitted under the control, dominant if not exclusive, of a few great political and economic apparatuses (university, army, writing, media); finally, it is the issue of a whole political debate and social confrontation ("ideological" struggles).

It seems to me that what must now be taken into account in the intellectual is not the "bearer of universal values." Rather, it's the person occupying a specific position—but whose specificity is linked, in a society like ours, to the general functioning of an apparatus of truth. In other words, the intellectual has a threefold specificity: that of his class position (whether as petty-bourgeois in the service of capitalism or "organic" intellectual of the proletariat); that of his conditions of life and work, linked to his condition as an intellectual (his field of research, his place in a laboratory, the political and economic demands to which he submits or against which he rebels, in the university, the hospital, and so on); finally, the specificity of the politics of truth in our societies. And it's with this last factor that his position can take on a general significance, and that his local, specific struggle can have effects and implications that are not simply professional or sectoral. The intellectual can operate and struggle at the general level of that regime of truth so essential to the structure and functioning of our society. There is a battle "for truth," or at least "around truth"—it being understood once again that by truth I mean not "the ensemble of truths to be discovered and accepted" but, rather, "the ensemble of rules according to which the true and the false are separated and specific effects of power attached to the true," it being understood also that it's not a matter of a battle "on behalf" of the truth but of a battle about the status of truth and the economic and political role it plays. It is necessary to think of the political problems of intellectuals not in terms of "science" and "ideology" but in terms of "truth" and "power." And thus the question of the professionalization of intellectuals and the division between intellectual and manual labor can be envisaged in a new way.

All this must seem very confused and uncertain. Uncertain indeed, and what I am saying here is, above all, to be taken as a hypothesis. In order for it to be a little less confused, however, I would like to put forward a few "propositions"—not firm assertions but simply suggestions to be further tested and evaluated.

"Truth" is to be understood as a system of ordered procedures for the production, regulation, distribution, circulation, and operation of statements.

"Truth" is linked in a circular relation with systems of power that produce and sustain it, and to effects of power which it induces and which extend it—a "regime" of truth.

This regime is not merely ideological or superstructural; it was a condition of the formation and development of capitalism. And it's this same regime which, subject to certain modifications, operates in the socialist countries (I leave open here the question of China, about which I know little).

The essential political problem for the intellectual is not to criticize the ideological contents supposedly linked to science, or to ensure that his own scientific practice is accompanied by a correct ideology, but that of ascertaining the possibility of constituting a new politics of truth. The problem is not changing people's consciousnesses—or what's in their heads—but the political, economic, institutional regime of the production of truth.

It's not a matter of emancipating truth from every system of power (which would be a chimera, for truth is already power) but of detaching the power of truth from the forms of hegemony, social, economic, and cultural, within which it operates at the present time.

The political question, to sum up, is not error, illusion, alienated consciousness, or ideology; it is truth itself. Hence the importance of Nietzsche.

NOTES

* The interview was conducted in June 1976; published in Alessandro Fontana and Pasquale Pasquino, eds., *Microfisica del potere: interventi politici*, trans. C. Lazzeri. Turin: Einaudi, 1977, pp. 3–28. [eds.]

1 Foucault's response to this final question was given in writing.

In my first lecture, I tried to demonstrate that the basic problem did not lie in the opposition of antimedicine to medicine but, rather, in the development of the medical system and the model followed for the "take-off" in medicine and sanitation that occurred in the West from the eighteenth century onward. I emphasized three points that I consider important.

First: Biohistory—that is, the effect of medical intervention at the biological level, the imprint left on human history, one may assume, by the strong medical intervention that began in the eighteenth century. It is clear that humanity did not remain immune to medicalization. This points to a first field of study that has not really been cultivated yet, though it is well marked out.

We know that various infectious diseases disappeared from the West even before the introduction of the twentieth century's great chemical therapy. The plague—or the set of diseases given that name by chroniclers, historians, and doctors—faded away in the course of the eighteenth and nineteenth centuries, without our really knowing either the reasons for, or the mechanisms of, that phenomenon, which deserves to be studied.

Another notorious case, that of tuberculosis: compared with 700 patients who died of tuberculosis in 1812, only 350 suffered the same fate in 1882, when Koch discovered the bacillus that was to make him famous; and when chemical therapy was introduced in 1945, the number had shrunk to 50. How and for what reason did this retreat of the disease come about? What were the mechanisms that intervened at the level of biohistory? There is no doubt that the change of socio-economic conditions, the organism's phenomena of adaptation and resistance, the weakening of the bacillus itself, as well as the measures of hygiene and isolation played an important role. Knowledge concerning this subject is far from complete, but it would be interesting to study the evolution of relations between humanity, the bacillary or viral field, and the interventions of hygiene, medicine, and the different therapeutic techniques.

In France a group of historians—including Emmanuel Le Roy Ladurie and Jean-Pierre Peter[1]—has begun to analyze these phenomena. Using conscription statistics from the nineteenth century, they have examined certain somatic developments of the human species.

Second: Medicalization—that is, the fact that starting in the eighteenth century human existence, human behavior, and the human body were brought into an increasingly dense and important network of medicalization that allowed fewer and fewer things to escape.

Medical research, more and more penetrating and meticulous, and the development of health institutions would also merit being studied. That is what we are trying to do at the Collège de France. Some of us are studying the growth of hospitalization and its mechanisms from the eighteenth century to the beginning of the nineteenth century, while others are focusing on hospitals and are planning to carry out a study of the habitat and all that surrounds it: the roads system, transport routes, and mass infrastructure [*équipements collectifs*] that ensure the functioning of everyday life, especially in urban environments.

Third: The economy of health—that is, the integration and improvement of health, health services, and health consumption in the economic development of privileged societies. This a difficult and complex problem whose antecedents are not very well known. In France, there exists a group devoting itself to this task, the Centre d'Etudes et de Recherches du Bien-être (CEREBRE), which includes Alain Letourmy, Serge Karenty, and Charles Dupuy. It is mainly studying the problems of health consumption over the last thirty years.

THE HISTORY OF MEDICALIZATION

Given that I am mainly concerned with retracing the history of medicalization, I will proceed by analyzing some of the aspects of the medicalization of societies and the population starting in the nineteenth century, taking the French example as my reference since I am more familiar with it. Concretely, I will refer to the birth of social medicine.

It is often remarked that certain criticisms of current medical practice hold that ancient—Greek and Egyptian—medicine or the forms of medicine of primitive societies are social, collective medicines that are not centered on the individual. My ignorance in ethnology and Egyptology prevents me from having an opinion about the issue; but from what I know of Greek history, the idea leaves me puzzled and I don't see how Greek medicine can be characterized as collective or social.

But these are not important problems. The question is whether the modern—that is, scientific—medicine born at the end of the eighteenth century between Giambattista Morgagni and Xavier Bichat, with the introduction of pathological anatomy, is or is not individual. Can we affirm, as some people do, that modern medicine is individual because it has worked its way into market relations? That modern medicine, being linked to a capitalist economy, is an individual or individualistic medicine amenable only to the market relation joining the doctor to the patient, and that it is impervious to the global, collective dimension of society?

One could show that this is not the case. Modern medicine is a social medicine whose basis is a certain technology of the social body; medicine is a social practice, and only one of its aspects is individualistic and valorizes the relations between the doctor and the patient.

In this connection, I would like to refer you to the work of Varn L. Bullough, *The Development of Medicine as a Profession: The Contribution of the Medieval University to Modern Medicine*,[2] in which the individualistic character of medieval medicine becomes evident while the collective dimension of medical activity is shown to be extremely inconspicuous and limited.

What I maintain is that, with capitalism, we did not go from a collective medicine to a private medicine. Exactly the opposite occurred: capitalism, which developed from the end of the eighteenth century to the beginning of the nineteenth century, started by socializing a first object, the body, as a factor of productive force, of labor power. Society's control over individuals was accomplished not only through consciousness or ideology but also in the body and with the body. For capitalist society, it was biopolitics, the biological, the somatic, the corporal, that mattered more than anything else. The body is a biopolitical reality; medicine is a biopolitical strategy.

How was this socialization brought about? I would like to explain my position in terms of certain generally accepted hypotheses. There is no doubt that the human body was politically and socially recognized as a labor force. Yet it seems to be characteristic of the development of social medicine, or of Western medicine itself, that medical power did not concern itself at the start with the human body as labor power. Medicine was not interested in the proletarian's body, the human body, as an instrument of labor. That was not the case before the second half of the nineteenth century, when the problem of the body, health, and the level of productive force of individuals was raised.

The three stages of the formation of social medicine could be reconstructed in this way: first, state medicine, then urban medicine, and, finally, labor force medicine.

STATE MEDICINE

"State medicine" developed primarily in Germany, at the beginning of the eighteenth century. Thinking of this specific problem, one is reminded of Marx's statement that economics was English, politics French, and philosophy German. But, as a matter of fact, it was in Germany in the seventeenth century—long before France and England—that what can be called the science of the state was formed. The concept of *Staatswissenschaft* is a product of Germany. Under the term "science of the state," we can group together two aspects that appeared in that country during that era. First, a field of study [*un savoir*] whose object was the state—not only the natural resources of a society or the living conditions of its population but also the general operation of the political machine. Research concerning the resources and the functioning of states constituted an eighteenth-century German discipline. And second, the expression also denotes the methods by which the state produces and accumulates the knowledge that enable it to guarantee its operation.

The state, as an object of study, as an instrument and locus of acquisition of a specific body of knowledge, developed more rapidly in Germany than in France and England. It isn't easy to determine the reasons for this phenomenon, and historians have not yet given much attention to this question nor to the problem of the birth of a science of the state or of a state-oriented science in Germany. In my opinion, this is explained by the fact that Germany was converted to a unitary state only in the nineteenth century, after having been a mere juxtaposition of quasi-states, pseudo-states, small entities that fell short of "statehood." But it so happened that, as states were forming, state-centered technologies [*savoirs étatiques*] and interest in the very functioning of the state were developing. The small size of the states, their close proximity, their perpetual conflicts and confrontations, the always-unbalanced and changeable relation of force, obliged them to weigh and compare themselves against the others, to imitate their methods and try to replace force with other types of relations.

Large states like France or England, on the other hand, managed to function relatively well, equipped with powerful machines such as the army or the police. In Germany the smallness of the states made this discursive consciousness of the state-directed functioning of society necessary and possible.

There is another explanation for this evolution of the science of the state: the slow development or stagnation of the German economy in the eighteenth century, after the Thirty Years' War and the great treaties of France and Austria.

After the first burst of development in Germany during the Renaissance, a limited form of bourgeoisie appeared, a bourgeoisie whose economic advance was blocked in the seventeenth century, preventing it from finding an occupation and making a living in commerce and the nascent manufacture and industry. So it sought refuge in service to the sovereigns, forming a corps of functionaries available for the state machine the princes wanted to construct in order to alter the force relations with their neighbors.

This economically inactive bourgeoisie lined up beside sovereigns confronted with a situation of continuous struggle, and of-

fered them its men, its competence, its wealth, and so on, for the
organization of states. In this way, the modern concept of the state,
with its apparatus, its civil servants, its knowledge, was to develop
in Germany long before in other, politically more powerful countries such as France, or economically more developed ones such as
England.

The modern state appeared where there was neither political
power nor economic development. It was precisely for these negative reasons that Prussia, economically less developed and politically more unstable, was that first modern state, born in the heart
of Europe. While France and England clung to the old structures,
Prussia became the first modern state.

The only purpose of these historical remarks on the birth, in the
eighteenth century, of a science of the state and of reflection concerning the state, is to try to explain why and how state medicine
was able to appear first in Germany.

At the end of the sixteenth century and the beginning of the seventeenth century, in a political, economic, and scientific climate
characteristic of the epoch dominated by mercantilism, all the
nations of Europe began to take an interest in the health of their
populations. Mercantilism was not simply an economic theory,
then, but also a political practice that aimed at regulating international monetary currents, the corresponding flows of goods, and the
productive activity of the population. Mercantilist policy was based
essentially on the growth of production and of the active population—the overall object being to establish commercial exchanges
that would enable Europe to achieve the greatest possible monetary
influence and, thereby, to finance the maintenance of armies and
of the whole apparatus that endows a state with real strength in its
relations with others.

With this in view, France, England, and Austria began to evaluate
the active strength of their populations. Thus, birth and death rate
statistics appeared in France and, in England, the great census sur-
veys that began in the seventeenth century. But at the time, in both
France and England, the only health interest shown by the state
had to do with drawing up of tables of birthrate and mortality,
which were true indications of the population's health and growth,
without any organized intervention to raise the level of health.

In Germany, on the other hand, a medical practice developed

that was actually devoted to the improvement of public health. Frank and Daniel, for example, proposed, between 1750 and 1770, a program aimed in that direction; it was what was called for the first time a state "medical police." The concept of *Medizinischepolizei*, medical police, which appeared in 1764, implied much more than a simple mortality and birth census.

Programmed in Germany in the middle of the seventeenth century and set up at the end of that century and the beginning of the next, the medical police consisted of:

- A system of observation of sickness, based on information gathered from the hospitals and doctors of different towns and regions, and, at the state level, recording of the different epidemic and endemic phenomena that were observed.

- Another very important aspect that should be noted: the standardization of medical practice and medical knowledge. Up to that point, authority in the matter of medical education and the awarding of diplomas had been left in the hands of the university and, more particularly, the medical guild. Then there emerged the idea of a standardization of medical instruction and, more specifically, of a public supervision of training programs and the granting of degrees. Medicine and doctors were thus the first object of standardization. This concept began by being applied to the doctor before being applied to the patient. The doctor was the first standardized individual in Germany. This movement, which spread to all of Europe, should be studied by anyone interested in the history of the sciences. In Germany, the phenomenon affected doctors, but in France, for example, standardization of activities at the state level concerned the military industry at the start: the production of cannons and rifles was standardized first, in the middle of the eighteenth century, to ensure that any type of rifle could be used by any soldier, any cannon could be repaired in any repair shop, and so on. After standardizing cannons, France went on to "normalize" its professors. The first *écoles normales* designed to offer all professors the same type of training and, consequently, the same level of competence, were created in about 1775 and were institutionalized in 1790–91. France standardized its cannons and its professors; Germany standardized its doctors.

- An administrative organization for overseeing the activity of doctors. In Prussia and the other states of Germany, at the level of the ministry or the central administration, a special office was assigned the task of collecting the data the doctors conveyed; observing how medical investigations were carried out; verifying which treatments were administered; describing the reactions after the appearance of an epidemic disease, and so on; and, finally, issuing directives based on these centralized data. All of this presupposed, of course, a subordination of medical practice to a higher administrative authority.

- The creation of medical officers, appointed by the government, who would take responsibility for a region. They derived their power from the authority they possessed or from the exercise of the authority conferred on them by their knowledge.

Such was the plan adopted by Prussia at the beginning of the nineteenth century, a sort of pyramid going from the district doctor responsible for a population of 6,000 to 10,000 inhabitants, to officers in charge of a much larger region whose population comprised between 35,000 and 50,000 inhabitants. This was when the doctor appeared as a health administrator.

The organization of a state medical knowledge, the standardization of the medical profession, the subordination of doctors to a general administration, and, finally, the incorporation of the different doctors into a state-controlled medical organization produced a series of completely new phenomena that characterized what could be called a "state medicine."

This state medicine, which appeared somewhat precociously, since it existed before the creation of the great scientific medicine of Morgagni and Bichat, did not have the objective of forming a labor force adapted to the needs of the industries that were then developing. It was not the workers' bodies that interested this public health administration but the bodies of individuals insofar as they combined to constitute the state. It was a matter not of labor power but of the strength of the state in those conflicts that set it against its neighbors—economic conflicts, no doubt, but also political ones. Thus, medicine was obliged to perfect and develop that state strength, and this concern on the part of state medicine implied a certain economico-political solidarity. It would be a mistake, therefore, to try to link it to an immediate interest in obtaining a vigorous and available reserve of labor power.

The example of Germany is also important because it shows how, paradoxically, modern medicine appeared at statism's zenith. After these projects were introduced—for the most part at the end of the eighteenth century and the beginning of the nineteenth, after state medicine was established in Germany—no state ventured to propose a medicine that was as clearly bureaucratized, collectivized, and "statized." Consequently, there was no gradual transformation of an increasingly state-administered and socialized medicine. In a very different way, the great clinical medicine of the nineteenth century was immediately preceded by an extremely statized medicine. The other systems of social medicine in the eighteenth and nineteenth centuries were scaled-down variations of this state-dominated administrative model introduced in Germany in those years.

That is a first series of phenomena to which I wish to refer. It has not drawn the attention of historians of medicine, but it was very closely analyzed by George Rosen in his studies on the relationships between cameralism, mercantilism, and the concept of medical police. In 1953 he published in the *Bulletin of the History of Medicine* an article devoted to this problem, titled "Cameralism and the Concept of Medical Police."[3] He also studied it later in his book, *A History of Public Health*.[4]

URBAN MEDICINE

The second form of the development of social medicine is represented by the example of France, where at the end of the eighteenth century a social medicine appeared, seemingly not based on the state structure, as in Germany, but on an entirely different phenomenon—urbanization. Social medicine developed in France in conjunction with the expansion of urban structures.

To find out why and how such a phenomenon occurred, let us do a bit of history. We have to imagine a large French city between 1750 and 1780 as a jumbled multitude of heterogeneous territories and rival powers. Paris, for example, did not form a territorial unit, a region where a single authority was exercised; rather, it was made up of a set of seignorial authorities held by the laity, the Church, the religious communities, and the guilds, authorities with their own autonomy and jurisdiction. And representatives of the state existed as well: the representatives of the crown, the chief of police, the representatives of the high judicial court.

In the second half of the eighteenth century, the problem of the unification of urban authority was raised. At this time, the need was felt—at least in the large conglomerates—to unify the city, to organize the urban corporate body in a coherent and homogeneous way, to govern it by a single, well-regulated authority.

Different factors played a part in this. In the first place, there were undoubtedly economic considerations. As the city was transformed into an important market hub that centralized commercial activities—not only at the regional but also at the national and even international level—the multiplicity of jurisdictions and authorities became more intolerable for the budding industry. The fact that the city was not only a market center but also a place of production made it necessary to resort to homogeneous and coherent mechanisms of regulation.

The second reason was political. The development of cities, the appearance of a poor, laboring population that was transformed during the nineteenth century into a proletariat, was bound to increase the tensions inside the cities. The coexistence of different small groups—guilds, professions, associations, and so on—that were mutually opposed but balanced and neutralized one another, began to reduce down to a sort of confrontation between rich and poor, commoners and bourgeoisie; this resulted in more frequent urban disturbances and insurrections involving more and more people. Although the so-called subsistence revolts—that is, the fact that on the occasion of a price hike or wage cut, the poorest people, no longer able to feed themselves, would pillage the silos, markets, and granaries—were not an entirely new phenomenon in the eighteenth century, they became more and more violent and led to the great disturbances during the time of the French Revolution.

In summary, we may affirm that in Europe, up through the seventeenth century, the major social threat came from the countryside. Poor peasants, who paid more and more taxes, would grab their sickles and set out to storm the castles and towns. The revolts of the seventeenth century were peasant revolts, subsequent to which the cities were unified. In contrast, at the end of the eighteenth century, peasant revolts started to disappear thanks to the raising of the peasants' standard of living—but urban conflicts became more frequent with the formation of an underclass [*plèbe*] undergoing proletarianization. Hence the need for a real political authority capable of dealing with the problem of this urban population.

It was during this period that a feeling of fear, of anxiety, about cities emerged and grew. For example, in reference to cities, the late eighteenth-century philosopher Pierre Jean George Cabanis said that whenever men came together their morals changed for the worse; whenever they came together in closed places their morals and their health deteriorated. So there arose what could be called an urban fear, a fear of the city, a very characteristic uneasiness: a fear of the workshops and factories being constructed, the crowding together of the population, the excessive height of the buildings, the urban epidemics, the rumors that invaded the city; a fear of the sinks and pits on which were constructed houses that threatened to collapse at any moment.

The life of the big eighteenth-century cities, especially Paris, provoked a series of panics. One might mention here the example of the Cemetery of the Innocents, in the center of Paris, into which the cadavers of those who lacked the resources or the social stature to buy or to merit an individual grave were thrown, one on top of the other. Urban panic was characteristic of the politico-sanitary anxiety, the uneasiness that appeared as the urban machine developed. Measures had to be taken to control these medical and political phenomena, which caused the population of the cities to experience such intense anxiety.

At this moment a new mechanism intervened, one that, though it could be predicted, does not enter into the usual scheme of historians of medicine. What was the reaction of the bourgeois class that, while not exercising power, held back by the traditional authorities, laid claim to it? A well-known but rarely employed model of intervention was appealed to—the model of the quarantine.

Since the end of the Middle Ages, there was, not just in France but in all European countries, what would now be called an "emergency plan." It was to be applied when the plague or another serious epidemic disease appeared in a city.

1. All people must stay in their dwelling in order to be localized in a single place. Every family in its home and, if possible, every person in his or her own room. Everyone was to stay put.

2. The city was to be divided into four districts placed under the responsibility of a specially designated person. This district head supervised inspectors whose job it was to patrol all the streets by day or stand watch to verify that no one left his house. So this amounted to a generalized system of surveillance that compartmentalized and controlled the city.

3. These street or district monitors were supposed to present to the mayor a detailed daily report on everything they had observed. Thus, not only was a generalized system of surveillance employed but also a centralized system of information.

4. The inspectors were to check on all the cities' dwellings every day. In all the streets they walked through, they asked every inhabitant to show himself at the window in order to verify that he still lived there and to note this down in the register. The fact that a person did not appear at the window meant that he was sick, that he had contracted the plague and consequently needed to be transported to a special infirmary, outside the city. Thus, an exhaustive record of the number of living and dead would be compiled, with daily updating.

5. A house by house disinfection, with the help of perfumes and incense, would be carried out.

The quarantine plan represented the politico-medical ideal of a good sanitary organization of eighteenth-century cities. There were basically two great models of medical organization in Western history: one that was engendered by leprosy, the other by the plague.

In the Middle Ages, when a leprosy case was discovered he was immediately expelled from the common space, the city, exiled to a gloomy, ambiguous place where his illness would blend with that of others. The mechanism of expulsion was that of purification of the urban environment. In that era, medicalizing an individual meant separating him and, in this way, purifying the others. It was a medicine of exclusion. At the beginning of the seventeenth century, even the internment of individuals who were demented, misshapen, and so on, was still mandated by this concept.

In contrast, there was another great politico-medical system established, not against leprosy but against the plague. In this case, medicine did not exclude the afflicted person or remove him to a dismal and turbid region. Medicine's political power consisted in distributing individuals side by side, isolating them, individualizing them, observing them one by one, monitoring their state of health, checking to see whether they were still alive or had died, and, in this way, maintaining society in a compartmentalized space that was closely watched and controlled by means of a painstaking record of all the events that occurred.

So there was a medical schema of reaction against leprosy—that of a religious type of exclusion, and of purification of the city. There was also the one motivated by the plague, a strategy that did not practice internment and relocation outside the urban center; rather, it depended on a meticulous analysis of the city, on a continuous recording. The religious model was replaced, therefore, by the military model. It was military inspection, basically, that served as a model for this politico-medical organization.

Urban medicine, in the second half of the eighteenth century, with its methods of observation, hospitalization, and so on, was nothing but an improvement on the politico-medical schema of the quarantine that appeared at the end of the Middle Ages, that is, in the sixteenth and seventeenth centuries. Public hygiene was a refined variation of the quarantine, the beginnings of the great urban medicine that appeared in the second half of the eighteenth century and developed especially in France from that time on.

The main objectives of urban medicine were the following:

First: Study the accumulation and piling-up of refuse that might cause illnesses in the urban space, the places that generated and propagated epidemic or endemic phenomena. Graveyards were the main concern here. Thus, protests against cemeteries appeared between 1740 and 1750. The first great removals to the city's periphery began around 1750. It was during this period that the individualized cemetery came into existence, that is, the individual coffin and the tomb reserved for the members of a family, where each of their names was inscribed.

It is often thought that, in modern society, the cult of the dead comes to us from Christianity. I don't share that opinion. There is nothing in Christian theology that urges respect for the corpse as such. The omnipotent Christian god can raise the dead even when they have been mixed together in the ossuary.

The individualization of the corpse, the coffin, and the grave appeared at the end of the eighteenth century not for the theologico-religious reasons having to do with respect for dead bodies but, rather, for politico-sanitary reasons having to do with respect for living ones. To protect the living from the harmful influence of the dead, the latter must be just as well indexed as the former—even better, if possible.

Thus, in the outskirts of the cities, at the end of the eighteenth century, what appeared was a veritable army of dead people, as perfectly aligned as a regiment being passed in review. It was necessary therefore to monitor, analyze, and reduce this constant threat which the dead represented. So they were transported to the country and placed side by side in the great flatlands that surrounded the cities.

This was not a Christian idea but a medical and political one. The best proof of this is that when the notion of moving the Cemetery of the Innocents in Paris was conceived, Antoine-François de Fourcroy, one of the greatest chemists of the end of the eighteenth century, was consulted about combating its influence. It was he who asked that it be moved; it was he who, in studying the relations between the living organism and the ambient air, took charge of that first medical and urban policing sanctioned by the banishment of the cemeteries.

Another example is furnished by the case of the slaughterhouses, also located in the center of Paris. It was decided, after consultation with the Academy of Sciences, to install them on the city's western fringe, at La Villette.

Medicine's first objective consisted therefore in analyzing the zones of congestion, disorder, and danger within the urban precincts.

Second: Urban medicine had a new objective—controlling circulation. Not the circulation of individuals but of things and elements, mainly water and air.

It was an old eighteenth-century belief that air had a direct influence on the organism because it carried miasmas; or because its excess chilliness, hotness, dryness, or wetness would be transmitted to the organism; and, finally, because the air exerted a direct pressure on the body through mechanical action. The air was considered to be one of the great pathogenic factors.

But how to maintain air quality in a city? How to obtain healthy air when the latter was blocked and kept from circulating between the walls, houses, enclosures, and so on? Thus, the need arose to open up the avenues of the urban space in order to preserve the health of the population. The opinion of commissions from the Academy of Sciences, doctors, chemists, and so on, was also solicited in an effort to find the best methods for ventilating the city. One of the best-known cases was demolition. Due to overcrowding and the high price of land during the Middle Ages, some houses were built on the gradients. So it was thought that these houses were preventing air circulation above the streams and retaining the humid air on the slopes: they were systematically torn down. In addition, calculations were performed showing the number of deaths avoided thanks to the demolition of three houses built on the Pont-Neuf—four hundred persons per year, twenty thousand in fifty years, and so on.

In this way, aeration corridors and air currents were organized, the same as had been done with water. In Paris, in 1767, the architect Moreau had the precocious idea of organizing the banks and islands of the Seine so that the river current itself would cleanse the city of its miasmas.

Thus, the second objective of urban medicine was the establishment and control of a good circulation of water and air.

Third: Another major goal of urban medicine was the organization of what could be called distributions and sequences. Where to place the different elements necessary to the shared life of the city? The problem of the respective position of the fountains and sewers, the pumps and river washhouses was raised. How to prevent the infiltration of dirty water into the drinking water fountains? How to keep the population's clean water supply from being mixed with the waste water from the nearby washhouses?

In the second half of the eighteenth century, this organization was thought to be the cause of the main urban epidemic diseases. This led to the first hydrographic plan of Paris, in 1742. It was the first survey of the places where water that wasn't contaminated by the sewers could be drawn, and the first attempt at defining a policy for river life. When the French Revolution broke out in 1789, Paris had already been carefully studied by an urban medical police that had established directives for bringing about a veritable sanitary organization of the city.

And yet, up to the end of the eighteenth century, there had not been any conflict between medicine and the other forms of authority such as private property, for example. Official policy relating to private property, to the private dwelling, was not sketched out before the eighteenth century, except for one of its aspects—the subsurface. Underground spaces belonging to the house owner remained subject to certain rules concerning their use and the construction of tunnels.

This was the problem of subsurface ownership that was raised in the eighteenth century with the advent of mining technology. When the capability for digging deep mines developed, the problem of their ownership appeared. In the middle of the eighteenth century, a binding legislation relating to the subsoil was formulated: it provided that the state and the king were the sole owners of the subsoil, and not disposers of the ground. In this way, the Paris subsoil was controlled by the authorities, whereas the surface was not, at least as concerned private property. Public spaces, such as places of circulation, cemeteries, ossuaries, and slaughterhouses, were controlled starting in the eighteenth century, which was not the case with private property before the nineteenth century.

Medicalization of the city in the eighteenth century is important for several reasons:

First: Through urban social medicine, the medical profession came directly in contact with other related sciences, mainly chemistry. Since that period of confusion during which Paracelsus and Vahelmont tried to establish the relationships between medicine and chemistry, nothing more had been learned on the subject. It was precisely the analysis of water, of air currents, of the conditions of life and respiration which brought medicine and chemistry into contact. Fourcroy and Antoine-Laurent Lavosier became interested in the problem of the organism in connection with control of the urban air.

The entry of medical practice into a corpus of physico-chemical science was brought about through urbanization. Scientific medicine did not grow out of private, individualized medicine, nor was it inspired by greater interest in the individual. The introduction of medicine into the general functioning of scientific discourse and knowledge occurred through medicine's socialization, the establishment of a collective, social, urban medicine. It is by all this that the importance of urban medicine is measured.

Second: Urban medicine is not really a medicine of man, the body, and the organism but a medicine of things—air, water, decompositions, fermentations. It is a medicine of the living conditions of the existential milieu.

Although the term "environment" did not appear, this medicine of things already outlined the concept, and the naturalists of the end of the eighteenth century, such as Cuvier, would develop it. The relationship between the organism and the environment was established simultaneously in the field of natural sciences and of medicine via urban medicine. The progression was not from analysis of the organism to analysis of the environment. Medicine went from analysis of the environment to that of the effects of the environment on the organism and, finally, to analysis of the organism itself. The organization of urban medicine was important for the formation of scientific medicine.

Third: With urban medicine there appeared, shortly before the French Revolution, the notion of salubrity. One of the decisions made by the Constituent Assembly between 1790 and 1791 was, for example, the creation of salubrity committees in the departments and main cities.

It should be pointed out that salubrity did not mean the same thing as health; rather, it referred to the state of the environment and those factors of it which made the improvement of health possible. Salubrity was the material and social basis capable of ensuring the best possible health for individuals. In connection with this, the concept of public health [*hygiène publique*] appeared, as a technique for controlling and modifying those elements of the environment which might promote that health or, on the contrary, harm it.

Salubrity and insalubrity designated the state of things and of the environment insofar as they affected health: public health was the politico-scientific control of that environment.

Thus, the concept of salubrity appeared at the beginning of the French Revolution. The concept of public health was to be, in nineteenth-century France, the one that brought together the essential components of social medicine. One of the major journals of this period, the *Annales d'hygiène publique et de médecine légale*, which began to appear in 1829, would become the organ of French social medicine.

This medicine remained far removed from state medicine of the sort that could be found in Germany; it was much closer to small communities, such as towns and districts. At the same time, it could not count on any specific instrument of power. The problem of private property, a sacred principle, kept this medicine from being endowed with a strong authority. But while *Staatsmedizin* surpassed it in the authority at its disposal, there is no doubt that its keenness of observation and its scientific character were superior.

A large part of nineteenth-century scientific medicine originated in the experience of this urban medicine which developed at the end of the eighteenth century.

LABOR FORCE MEDICINE

The third direction of social medicine can be examined through the English example. Poor people's medicine, labor force or worker's medicine, was not the first but the last objective of social medicine. First the state, then the city, and finally poor people and workers were the object of medicalization.

What characterized French urban medicine was respect for the private sphere and the rule of not having to regard the poor, the underclass, or the people as an element that threatened public health. Consequently, the poor or the workers were not thought of in the same way as cemeteries, ossuaries, slaughterhouses, and so on.

Why didn't the problem of the poor as a source of medical danger arise in the course of the eighteenth century? There are several reasons for this. One is quantitative in nature: the number of poor people in the cities was not large enough for poverty to represent a real danger. But there was a more important reason: urban activity depended on the poor. A city's poor people accomplished a certain number of tasks: they delivered the mail, collected the garbage, picked up old furniture, used clothing, redistributed or resold scrap materials, and so on. They thus formed part of urban life. In this era, the houses didn't have numbers and there was no postal service either. No one knew the city and all its nooks better than the poor; they carried out a series of basic functions such as water hauling or refuse disposal.

Insofar as the poor formed part of the urban system, like the sewers or pipes, they performed an indisputable function and could not be considered as a danger. At the level where they were placed, they were useful. But starting in the second third of the nineteenth century, the problem of poverty was raised in terms of menace, of danger. The reasons are diverse:

1. Political reasons, first of all: during the French Revolution and in England during the great social unrest of the beginning of the nineteenth century, the destitute population transformed itself into a political force capable of revolting or at least of participating in revolts.

2. In the nineteenth century, means were found for partly replacing the services offered by the underclass, such as the setting up of a postal service and a transport system. These reforms were at the origin of a wave of popular disturbances launched against these systems, which deprived the most needy of bread and of the very possibility of living.

3. With the cholera epidemic of 1832, which began in Paris, then spread throughout Europe, a set of political and health fears occasioned by the proletarian or plebeian population crystallized.

It was in this period that the decision was first made to divide the urban space into rich areas and poor areas. The feeling was that cohabitation between rich and poor in an undifferentiated urban environment constituted a health and political hazard for the city. The establishment of rich districts and poor districts dates from this time. Political authority thus began to intervene in property and private dwelling rights. This was the time of the great reshaping, under the Second Empire, of the urban zone of Paris.

These are the reasons for which, up until the nineteenth century, the urban population was not regarded as a medical danger.

In England—where industrial development was being experienced, and where, consequently, the formation of a proletariat was faster and more extensive—a new form of social medicine appeared. This doesn't mean that state medicine projects of the German type did not exist as well. For example, in about 1840, John Chadwick was largely inspired by German methods in formulating his plans. Moreover, in 1846 Rumsay wrote a work titled *Health and Sickness of Town Populations*[5] which reflects the content of French urban medicine.

It was essentially the Poor Law[6] that made English medicine a social medicine insofar as this law implied a medical control of the destitute. Since the poor benefited from the welfare system, it became obligatory to subject them to various medical controls.

With the Poor Law, an important factor in the history of social medicine made an ambiguous appearance: the idea of a tax-supported welfare, of a medical intervention that would constitute a means of helping the poorest individuals to meet their health needs, something that poverty placed beyond their hope. At the same time, it made it possible to maintain a control by which the wealthy classes, or their government representatives, would guarantee the health of the needy classes and, consequently, protect the privileged population. In this way, an officially sanctioned sanitary cordon between the rich and the poor was set in place within the cities. To that end, the latter were offered the possibility of receiving free or low-cost treatment. Thus, the wealthy freed themselves of the risk of being victims of epidemic phenomena issuing from the disadvantaged class.

The transposition of the major problem of that period's bourgeoisie is clearly visible in the medical legislation: At what cost? Under what conditions? How to guarantee its political security? The medical legislation contained in the Poor Law was consistent with that process. But that law—and the protection assistance, together with the control assistance it entailed—was only the first component of a complex system whose other components appeared later, around 1870, with the great founders of English social medicine.

Chief among them was John Simon, who completed the medical legislation with an official service organizing not medical treatment but medical control of the population. I am referring to the systems of the Health Service, the Health Offices, which appeared in England in 1875, and were estimated to number a thousand toward the end of the nineteenth century. Their functions were the following:

- Control of vaccination, obliging the different elements of the population to be immunized.

- Organizing the record of epidemics and diseases capable of turning into an epidemic, making the reporting of dangerous illnesses mandatory.

- Localization of unhealthy places and, if necessary, destruction of those seedbeds of insalubrity.

The Health Service developed out of the same thinking that produced the Poor Law. The Poor Law provided for a medical service expressly intended for the poor. The Health Service, on the other hand, was characterized by protection of the entire population without distinction, and by the fact that it was comprised of doctors offering nonindividualized care extending to the whole population, preventive measures to be taken, and, just like French urban medicine, objects, places, social environment, and so on.

However, analysis of the Health Service's operation shows that it was a means of completing at the collective level the same controls that were guaranteed by the Poor Law. Intervention in unhealthy places, verification of vaccinations, and disease records were really aimed at controlling the needy social classes.

It was precisely for these reasons that, in the second half of the nineteenth century, English medical control administered by the Health Offices provoked violent popular reactions and resistances, small-scale antimedical insurrections. R. M. Macleod drew attention to these cases of medical resistance in a series of articles published by the journal *Public Law* in 1967.[7] I think it would be interesting to analyze how this medicine, organized in the form of a control of the needy population, incurred such reactions—not only in England but in various countries of the world. For example, it is curious to observe that the dissident religious groups, so numerous in the English-speaking Protestant countries, had the primary goal during the seventeenth and eighteenth centuries of opposing state religion and interference by the state in religious affairs, whereas those groups which reappeared in the course of the nineteenth century were concerned with combating medicalization, with asserting the right to life, the right to get sick, to care for oneself and to die in the manner one wished. This desire to escape from compulsory medicalization was one of the characteristics of these numerous apparently religious groups that were intensely active at the end of the nineteenth century, as they still are today.

In Catholic countries the situation was different. What meaning would the pilgrimage to Lourdes have, from the end of the nineteenth century to our time, for the millions of poor pilgrims who arrive there every year, if not that of being a sort of muddled resistance to the obligatory medicalization of their bodies and their illnesses?

Instead of seeing in these religious practices a present-day residue of archaic beliefs, shouldn't they be seen as the contemporary form of a political struggle against politically authoritarian medicine, the socialization of medicine, the medical control that presses mainly on the poor population? The strength of these continuing practices resides in the fact that they constitute a reaction against this poor people's medicine, in the service of a class, English social medicine being an example.

In a general way, we may affirm that, in contrast to German state medicine of the eighteenth century, there appeared in the nineteenth century—above all, in England—a medicine that consisted mainly in a control of the health and the bodies of the needy classes, to make them more fit for labor and less dangerous to the wealthy classes.

Unlike urban medicine and especially state medicine, this English approach to medicine was to have a future. The English system of Simon and his successors enabled three things to be established: medical assistance of the poor, control of the health of the labor force, and a general surveying of public health, whereby the wealthy classes would be protected from the greatest dangers. Further—and this is where its originality lies—it enabled the creation of three superimposed and coexisting medical systems: a welfare medicine designed for the poorest people; an administrative medicine responsible for general problems such as vaccination, epidemics, and so on; and a private medicine benefiting those who could afford it.

The German system of state medicine was burdensome, and French urban medicine was a general plan of control without any specific instrument of authority; but the English system made possible the organization of a medicine with different features and forms of authority—depending on whether it was a question of welfare, administrative, or private medicine—and the establishment of well-defined sectors that allowed a fairly complete medical survey to be constituted in the last years of the nineteenth century. With the Beveridge Plan[8] and the medical systems of today's richest and most industrialized countries, it is always a matter of bringing these three sectors of medicine into play, although they are linked together in different ways.

NOTES

* This is the second of two lectures that Foucault delivered at the State University of Rio de Janerio in October of 1974, both of them on the emergence of what is now known as "public health." The first lecture, titled "Crisis of Medicine or Crisis of Anti-medicine?," was published in a Portuguese translation in 1976. This essay appeared in Portuguese in 1977. [eds.]

1 Emmanuel Le Roy Ladurie, Jean-Pierre Peter, Paul Dumont, *Anthropologie du conscrit français d'après les comptes numériques et sommaires du recrutement de l'armée (1819–1826)*, (Paris: Mouton "Civilisations et Sociétés" no. 28, 1972).

2 Varn L. Bullough, *The Development of Medicine as a Profession: The Contribution of the Medieval University to Modern Medicine* (New York: Hafner, 1965).

3 George Rosen, "Cameralism and the Concept of Medical Police," *Bulletin of the History of Medicine* 27 (1953), pp. 21–42.

4 Rosen, *A History of Public Health* (New York: MD Publications, 1958).

5 TK Rumsay, *Health and Sickness of Town Populations* (London: William Ridgway, 1846).

6 A law instituted in the nineteenth century stipulating assistance for the poor at public expense. [eds.]

7 R. M. Macleod, "Law, Medicine and Public Opinion: The Resistance to Compulsory Health Legislation. 1870–1907," in *Public Law: The Constitutional and Administrative Law of the Commonwealth* (London) no. 2 (Summer 1967), pt. 1, pp. 107–128; no. 3 (Autumn 1967), pt. 2, pp. 189–211.

8 The Beveridge Plan was instituted in Great Britain in 1942. Its measures were designed to ensure that every British citizen would enjoy adequate health and medical care. [eds.]

This is not a book of history. The selection found here was guided by nothing more substantial than my taste, my pleasure, an emotion, laughter, surprise, a certain dread, or some other feeling whose intensity I might have trouble justifying, now that the first moment of discovery has passed.

It's an anthology of existences. Lives of a few lines or a few pages, nameless misfortunes and adventures gathered into a handful of words. Brief lives, encountered by chance in books and documents. *Exempla*, but unlike those collected by the sages in the course of their reading, they are examples that convey not so much lessons to ponder as brief effects whose force fades almost at once. The term "news" would fit them rather well, I think, because of the double reference it suggests: to the rapid pace of the narrative and to the reality of the events that are related. For the things said in these texts are so compressed that one isn't sure whether the intensity that sparks through them is due more to the vividness of the words or to the jostling violence of the facts they tell. Singular lives, transformed into strange poems through who knows what twists of fate—that is what I decided to gather into a kind of herbarium.

As I recall, the idea came to me one day when I was reading, at the Bibliothèque Nationale, a record of internment written at the very beginning of the eighteenth century. If I'm not mistaken, it occurred to me as I read these two notices:

Mathurin Milan, placed in the hospital of Charenton, 31 August 1707:
"His madness was always to hide from his family, to lead an obscure
life in the country, to have actions at law, to lend usuriously and
without security, to lead his feeble mind down unknown paths, and
to believe himself capable of the greatest employments."

Jean Antoine Touzard, placed in the castle of Bicêtre, 21 April 1701:
"Seditious apostate friar, capable of the greatest crimes, sodomite,
atheist if that were possible; this individual is a veritable monster of
abomination whom it would be better to stifle than to leave at large."

It would be hard to say exactly what I felt when I read these fragments and many others that were similar. No doubt, one of these
impressions that are called "physical," as if there could be any other
kind. I admit that these "short stories," suddenly emerging from two
and a half centuries of silence, stirred more fibers within me than
what is ordinarily called "literature," without my being able to say
even now if I was more moved by the beauty of that Classical style,
draped in a few sentences around characters that were plainly
wretched, or by the excesses, the blend of dark stubbornness and
rascality, of these lives whose disarray and relentless energy one
senses beneath the stone-smooth words.

A long time ago I made use of documents like these for a book.
If I did so back then, it was doubtless because of the resonance I
still experience today when I happen to encounter these lowly lives
reduced to ashes in the few sentences that struck them down. The
dream would have been to restore their intensity in an analysis.
Lacking the necessary talent, I brooded over the analysis alone. I
considered the texts in their dryness, trying to determine their reason for being, what institutions or what political practice they referred to, seeking to understand why it had suddenly been so
important in a society like ours to "stifle" (as one stifles a cry,
smothers a fire, or strangles an animal) a scandalous monk or a
peculiar and inconsequential usurer. I looked for the reason why
people were so zealous to prevent the feebleminded from walking
down unknown paths. But the first intensities that had motivated
me remained excluded. And since there was a good chance that
they wouldn't enter into the order of reasons at all, seeing that my

discourse was incapable of conveying them in the necessary way, wouldn't it be better to leave them in the very form that had caused me to first feel them?

Whence the idea of this collection, done more or less as the occasion arose. A collection compiled without haste and without a clear purpose. For a long time I thought of presenting it in a systematic order, with a few rudiments of explanation, and in such a way that it would exhibit a minimum of historical significance. I decided against this, for reasons that I will come back to later. I resolved simply to assemble a certain number of texts, for the intensity they seem to me to have. I have appended a few preliminary remarks to them, and I have distributed them so as to preserve, as best I could, the effect of each.

So this book will not answer the purpose of historians, even less than it will others'. A mood-based and purely subjective book? I would say rather—but it may come to the same thing—that it's a rule- and game-based book, the book of a little obsession that found its system. I think that the poem of the oddball usurer or that of the sodomite monk served as a model throughout. It was in order to recapture something like those flash existences, those poem-lives, that I laid down a certain number of simple rules for myself:

- The persons included must have actually existed.

- These existences must have been both obscure and ill-fated.

- They must have been recounted in a few pages or, better, a few sentences, as brief as possible.

- These tales must not just constitute strange or pathetic anecdotes; but, in one way or another (because they were complaints, denunciations, orders, or reports), they must have truly formed part of the minuscule history of these existences, of their misfortune, their wildness, or their dubious madness.

- And for us still, the shock of these words must give rise to a certain effect of beauty mixed with dread.

But I should say a little more about these rules that may appear arbitrary.

* * *

I wanted it always to be a matter of real existences: that one might be able to give them a place and a date; that behind these names that no longer say anything, behind these quick words which may well have been false, mendacious, unjust, exaggerated, there were men who lived and died, with sufferings, meannesses, jealousies, vociferations. So I excluded everything in the way of imagination or literature: none of the dark heroes that the latter have invented appeared as intense to me as these cobblers, these army deserters, these garment-sellers, these scriveners, these vagabond monks, all of them rabid, scandalous, or pitiful. And this was owing, no doubt, to the mere fact that they are known to have lived. I likewise ruled out all the texts that might be memoirs, recollections, tableaus, all those recounting a slice of reality but keeping the distance of observation, of memory, of curiosity, or of amusement. I was determined that these texts always be in a relation or, rather, in the greatest possible number of relations with reality: not only that they refer to it, but they be operative within it; that they form part of the dramaturgy of the real; that they constitute the instrument of a retaliation, the weapon of a hatred, an episode in a battle, the gesticulation of a despair or a jealousy, an entreaty or an order. I didn't try to bring together texts that would be more faithful to reality than others, that would merit inclusion for their representative value, but, rather, texts that played a part in the reality they speak of—and that, in return, whatever their inaccuracy, their exaggeration, or their hypocrisy, are traversed by it: fragments of discourse trailing the fragments of a reality they are part of. One won't see a collection of verbal portraits here, but traps, weapons, cries, gestures, attitudes, ruses, intrigues for which words were the instruments. Real lives were "enacted" [*"jouées"*] in these few sentences: by this I don't mean that they were represented but that their liberty, their misfortune, often their death, in any case their fate, were actually decided therein, at least in part. These discourses really crossed lives; existences were actually risked and lost in these words.

Another requirement of mine was that these personages themselves be obscure; that nothing would have prepared them for any notoriety; that they would not have been endowed with any of the established and recognized nobilities—those of birth, fortune, saintliness, heroism, or genius; that they would have belonged to those

billions of existences destined to pass away without a trace; that in
their misfortunes, their passions, in those loves and hatreds there
would be something gray and ordinary in comparison with what is
usually deemed worthy of being recounted; that, nevertheless, they
be propelled by a violence, an energy, an excess expressed in the
malice, vileness, baseness, obstinacy, or ill-fortune this gave them
in the eyes of their fellows—and in proportion to its very medioc-
rity, a sort of appalling or pitiful grandeur. I had gone in search of
these sorts of particles endowed with an energy all the greater for
their being small and difficult to discern.

But in order for some part of them to reach us, a beam of light
had to illuminate them, for a moment at least. A light coming from
elsewhere. What snatched them from the darkness in which they
could, perhaps should, have remained was the encounter with
power; without that collision, it's very unlikely that any word would
be there to recall their fleeting trajectory. The power that watched
these lives, that pursued them, that lent its attention, if only for a
moment, to their complaints and their little racket, and marked
them with its claw was what gave rise to the few words about them
that remain for us—either because someone decided to appeal to
it in order to denounce, complain, solicit, entreat, or because he
chose to intervene and in a few words to judge and decide. All those
lives destined to pass beneath any discourse and disappear without
ever having been told were able to leave traces—brief, incisive,
often enigmatic—only at the point of their instantaneous contact
with power. So that it is doubtless impossible to ever grasp them
again in themselves, as they might have been "in a free state"; they
can no longer be separated out from the declamations, the tactical
biases, the obligatory lies that power games and power relations
presuppose.

I will be told: "That's so like you, always with the same inability
to cross the line, to pass to the other side, to listen and convey the
language that comes from elsewhere or from below; always the
same choice, on the side of power, of what it says or causes to be
said. Why not go listen to these lives where they speak in their own
voice?" But, first of all, would anything at all remain of what they
were in their violence or in their singular misfortune had they not,
at a given moment, met up with power and provoked its forces? Is
it not one of the fundamental traits of our society, after all, that

destiny takes the form of a relation with power, of a struggle with or against it? Indeed, the most intense point of a life, the point where its energy is concentrated, is where it comes up against power, struggles with it, attempts to use its forces and to evade its traps. The brief and strident words that went back and forth between power and the most inessential existences doubtless constitute, for the latter, the only monument they have ever been granted: it is what gives them, for the passage through time, the bit of brilliance, the brief flash that carries them to us.

In short, I wanted to assemble a few rudiments for a legend of obscure men, out of the discourses that, in sorrow or in rage, they exchanged with power.

A "legend" because, as in all legends, there is a certain ambiguity between the fictional and the real—but it occurs for opposite reasons. Whatever its kernel of reality, the legendary is nothing else, finally, but the sum of what is said about it. It is indifferent to the existence or nonexistence of the persons whose glory it transmits. If they existed, the legend covers them with so many wonders, embellishing them with so many impossibilities, that it's almost as if they had never lived. And if they are purely imaginary, the legend reports so many insistent tales about them that they take on the historical thickness of someone who existed. In the texts that follow, the existence of these men and women comes down to exactly what was said about them: nothing subsists of what they were or what they did, other than what is found in a few sentences. Here it is rarity and not prolixity that makes reality equivalent to fiction. Having been nothing in history, having played no appreciable role in events or among important people, having left no identifiable trace around them, they don't have and never will have any existence outside the precarious domicile of these words. And through those texts which tell about them, they come down to us bearing no more of the markings of reality than if they had come from *La Légende dorée* or from an adventure novel.[1] This purely verbal existence, which makes these forlorn or villainous individuals into quasi-fictional beings, is due to their nearly complete disappearance, and to that luck or mischance which resulted in the survival, through the peradventure of rediscovered documents, of a scarce few words that speak of them or that are pronounced by them. A dark but, above all, a dry legend, reduced to what was said one day and preserved down to our day by improbable encounters.

That is another trait of this dark legend. It has not been trans-mitted like one that was gilded by some deep necessity, following continuous paths. By nature, it is bereft of any tradition; disconti-nuities, effacement, oblivion, convergences, reappearances: this is the only way it can reach us. Chance carries it from the beginning. It first required a combination of circumstances that, contrary to all expectations, focused the attention of power and the outburst of its anger on the most obscure individual, on his mediocre life, on his (after all, rather ordinary) faults: a stroke of misfortune that caused the vigilance of officials or of institutions, aimed no doubt at sup-pressing all disorder, to pick on this person rather than that, this scandalous monk, this beaten woman, this inveterate and furious drunkard, this quarrelsome merchant, and not so many others who were making just as much of a ruckus. And then it had to be just this document, among so many others scattered and lost, which came down to us and be rediscovered and read. So that between these people of no importance and us who have no more impor-tance than they, there is no necessary connection. Nothing made it likely for them to emerge from the shadows, they instead of others, with their lives and their sorrows. We may amuse ourselves, if we wish, by seeing a revenge in this: the chance that enabled these absolutely undistinguished people to emerge from their place amid the dead multitudes, to gesticulate again, to manifest their rage, their affliction, or their invincible determination to err—perhaps it makes up for the bad luck that brought power's lightning bolt down upon them, in spite of their modesty and anonymity.

Lives that are as though they hadn't been, that survive only from the clash with a power that wished only to annihilate them or at least to obliterate them, lives that come back to us only through the effect of multiple accidents—these are the infamies that I wanted to assemble here in the form of a few remains. There exists a false infamy, the kind with which those men of terror or scandal, Gilles de Rais, Guillery or Cartouche, Sade and Lacenaire,[2] are blessed. Apparently infamous, because of the abominable memories they have left, the misdeeds attributed to them, the respectful horror they have inspired, they are actually men of glorious legend, even if the reasons for that renown are the opposite of those that constitute or ought to constitute the greatness of men. Their infamy is only a modality of the universal *fama*. But the apostate friar, the feeble minds lost on unknown paths, those are infamous in the strict sense: they no longer exist except through the terrible words that were destined to render them forever unworthy of the memory of men. And chance determined that these words, these words alone, would subsist. The return of these lives to reality occurs in the very form in which they were driven out of the world. Useless to look for another face for them, or to suspect a different greatness in them; they are no longer anything but that which was meant to crush them—neither more nor less. Such is infamy in the strict sense, the infamy that, being unmixed with ambiguous scandal or unspoken admiration, has nothing to do with any sort of glory.

In comparison with infamy's great collection, which would gather its traces from everywhere and all times, I'm well aware that the selection here is paltry, narrow, a bit monotonous. It comprises documents that all date approximately from the same hundred years, 1660–1760, and come from the same source: archives of confinement, of the police, of petitions to the King, and of *lettres de cachet*. Let us suppose that this may be a first volume and that *Lives of Infamous Men* will be extended to other times and other places.

I chose this period and this type of texts because of an old familiarity. But if the taste I've had for them for years has not diminished, and if I come back to them now, it's because I suspect they manifest a beginning, or at any rate an important event, in which political mechanisms and discursive effects intersected.

These texts from the seventeenth and eighteenth centuries (especially when compared with the flatness of later administrative and police documents) display a brilliance, reveal a splendor of phrasing, a vehemence that belies, in our judgment at least, the pettiness of the affair or the rather shameful meanness of intent. The most pitiful lives are described with the imprecations or emphasis that would seem to suit the most tragic. A comical effect, no doubt: there is something ludicrous in summoning all the power of words, and through them the supreme power of heaven and earth, around insignificant disorders or such ordinary woes. "Unable to bear the weight of the most excessive sorrow, the clerk Duschene ventures, with a humble and respectful confidence, to throw himself at the feet of Your Majesty to implore his justice against the cruelest of all women. . . . What hope must not rise in the breast of this unfortunate one who, reduced to the last extremity, today appeals to Your Majesty after having exhausted all the ways of gentleness, remonstrance, and consideration to bring back to her duty a wife who lacks all sentiment of religion, honor, probity, and even humanity? Such is, Sire, the state of this poor wretch who dares to voice his plaintive appeal to the ears of Your Majesty." Or that abandoned wetnurse who asks for the arrest of her husband on behalf of her four children "who may have nothing to expect from their father but a terrible example of the effects of disorder. Your justice, my Lord, will surely spare them such a degrading lesson, will prevent opprobrium and infamy for me and my family, by rendering incapable of doing any injury to society a bad citizen who will not fail to bring it harm." We may laugh at this, but it should be kept in mind that to this rhetoric, grandiloquent only because of the smallness of the things to which it is applied, power responds in terms that appear no less excessive—with the difference that its words convey the fulguration of its decisions—and their solemnity may be warranted, if not by the importance of what they punish, then by the harshness of the penalty they impose. If some caster of horoscopes is locked up, this is because "there are few crimes she has not committed, and none of which she is not capable. So there is as much charity as justice in immediately ridding the public of so dangerous a woman, who has robbed it, duped it, and scandalized it with impunity for so many years." And about a young addlebrain, a bad son and a ne'er-do-well: "He is a monster of libertinage and impiety. . . . Practices all the vices: knavish, disobedient, impetuous, violent, capable of deliberate attacks on the life of his own father . . . always in the company of the worst prostitutes. Nothing that is said about his knaveries and profligacies makes any impression on his heart; he responds only with a scoundrel's smile that communicates his callousness and gives no reason to think he is anything short of incurable." With the least peccadillo, one is always in the abominable, or at least in the discourse of invective and execration. These loose women and these unruly children do not pale next to Nero or Rodogune. The discourse of power in the Classical age, like the discourses addressed to it, produces monsters. Why this emphatic theater of the quotidian?

Christianity had in large part organized power's hold on the ordinary preoccupations of life: an obligation to run the minuscule
everyday world regularly through the mill of language, revealing
the common faults, the imperceptible failings even, and down to
the murky interplay of thoughts, intentions, and desires; a ritual of
confession in which the one speaking is at the same the one spoken
about; an effacement of the thing said by its very utterance, but also
with an augmentation of the confession itself, which must remain
secret, and not leave any other trace behind it but repentance and
acts of contrition. The Christian West invented that astonishing
constraint, which it imposed on everyone, to tell everything in order
to efface everything, to express even the most minor faults in an
unbroken, relentless, exhaustive murmur which nothing must
elude, but which must not outlive itself even for a moment. For
hundreds of millions of men and over a period of centuries, evil
had to be confessed in the first person, in an obligatory and ephemeral whisper.

But, from the end of the seventeenth century, this mechanism
was encircled and outreached by another one whose operation was
very different. An administrative and no longer a religious apparatus; a recording mechanism instead of a pardoning mechanism.
The objective was the same, however, at least in part: to bring the
quotidian into discourse, to survey the tiny universe of irregularities
and unimportant disorders. In this system, though, confession does
not play the eminent role that Christianity had reserved for it. For
this social mapping and control, long-standing procedures are used,
but ones that had been localized up to then: the denunciation, the
complaint, the inquiry, the report, spying, the interrogation. And
everything that is said in this way is noted down in writing, is accumulated, is gathered into dossiers and archives. The single, instantaneous, and traceless voice of the penitential confession that
effaced evil as it effaced itself would now be supplanted by multiple
voices, which were to be deposited in an enormous documentary
mass and thus constitute, through time, a sort of constantly growing
record of all the world's woes. The minuscule trouble of misery and
transgression is no longer sent to heaven through the scarcely au-
dible confidence of the confession: it accumulates on earth in the
form of written traces. An entirely different type of relations is established between power, discourse, and the quotidian, an alto-

gether different way of governing the latter and of formulating it. For ordinary life, a new mise-en-scène is born.

We are familiar with its first instruments, archaic but already complex: they are the petitions, the *lettres de cachet* or king's orders, the various internments, the police reports and decisions. I won't go back over these things, which are already well known; I'll just recall certain aspects that may account for the strange intensity, and for a kind of beauty that sometimes emanates from these hastily drawn images in which unfortunate men assume, for us who perceive them from such a great distance, the guise of infamy. The *lettre de cachet*, internment, the generalized presence of the police— all that usually evokes only the despotism of an absolute monarchy. But one cannot help but see that this "arbitrariness" was a kind of public service. Except in the rarest of cases, the "king's orders" did not strike without warning, crashing down from above as signs of the monarch's anger. More often than not, they were requested against someone by his entourage—his father and mother, one of his relatives, his family, his sons or daughters, his neighbors, the local priest on occasion, or some notable. They were solicited for some obscure family trouble, as if it involved a great crime meriting the sovereign's wrath: rejected or abused spouses, a squandered fortune, conflicts of interest, disobedient young people, knavery or carousing, and all the little disorders of conduct. The *lettre de cachet* that was presented as the express and particular will of the king to have one of his subjects confined, outside the channels of regular justice, was nothing more than the response to such petitions coming from below. But it was not freely granted to anyone requesting it: an inquiry must precede it, for the purpose of substantiating the claims made in the petition. It needed to establish whether the debauchery or drunken spree, the violence or the libertinage, called for an internment, and under what conditions and for how long— a job for the police, who would collect statements by witnesses, information from spies, and all the haze of doubtful rumor that forms around each individual.

The system of *lettre de cachet* and internment was only a rather brief episode, lasting for little more than a century and limited to France. But it is nonetheless important in the history of power mechanisms. It did not bring about the uninvited intrusion of royal arbitrariness in the most everyday dimension of life. It ensured, rather, the distribution of that power through complex circuits and a whole interplay of petitions and responses. An absolutist abuse? Maybe so, yet not in the sense that the absolute monarch purely and simply abused his own power; rather, in the sense that each individual could avail himself, for his own ends and against others, of absolute power in its enormity—a sort of placing of the mechanisms of sovereignty at one's disposal, an opportunity to divert its effects to one's own benefit, for anyone clever enough to capture them. A certain number of consequences followed from this: political sovereignty penetrated into the most elementary dimension of the social body; the resources of an absolutist political power, beyond the traditional weapons of authority and submission, could be brought into play between subject and subject, sometimes the most humble of them, between family members and between neighbors, and in relations of interests, of profession, of rivalry, of love and hate. Providing one knew how to play the game, every individual could become for the other a terrible and lawless monarch: *homo homini rex*. A whole political network became interwoven with the fabric of everyday life. But it was still necessary, at least for a moment, to appropriate this power, channel it, capture it, and bend it in the direction one wanted; if one meant to take advantage of it, it was necessary to "seduce" it. It became both an object of covetousness and an object of seduction; it was desirable, then, precisely insofar as it was dreadful. The intervention of a limitless political power in everyday relations thus became not only acceptable and familiar but deeply condoned—not without becoming, from that very fact, the theme of a generalized fear. We should not be surprised at this inclination which, little by little, opened up the relations of appurtenance or dependence that traditionally connect the family to administrative and political controls. Nor should we be surprised that the king's boundless power, thus operating in the midst of passions, rages, miseries, and mischiefs, was able to become—despite or perhaps even because of its utility—an object of execration. Those who resorted to the *lettres de cachet* and the king who granted them were caught in the trap of their complicity: the first lost more and more of their traditional prerogatives to an administrative authority. As for the king, he became detestable from having meddled on a daily basis in so many hatreds and intrigues. As I recall, it was the Duke de Chaulieu who said, in the *Mémoires de deux jeunes mariées*, that by cutting off the king's head, the French Revolution decapitated all family men.[3]

For the moment, I would like to single out one element from all the foregoing: with this apparatus comprising petitions, *lettres de cachets*, internment, and police, there would issue an endless number of discourses that would pervade daily life and take charge of the minuscule ills of insignificant lives, but in a completely different manner from the confession. Neighborhood disputes, the quarrels of parents and children, misunderstandings between couples, the excesses of wine and sex, public altercations, and many secret passions would all be caught in the nets of power which stretched through rather complex circuits. There was a kind of immense and omnipresent call for the processing of these disturbances and these petty sufferings into discourse. An unending hum began to be heard, the sound of the discourse that delivered individual variations of behavior, shames, and secrets into the grip of power. The commonplace ceased to belong to silence, to the passing rumor or the fleeting confession. All those ingredients of the ordinary, the unimportant detail, obscurity, unexceptional days, community life, could and must be told—better still, written down. They became describable and transcribable, precisely insofar as they were traversed by the mechanisms of a political power. For a long time, only the actions of great men had merited being told without mockery: only blood, birth, and exploit gave a right to history. And if it sometimes happened that the lowliest men acceded to a kind of glory, this was by virtue of some extraordinary fact—the distinction of a saintliness or the enormity of a crime. There was never a thought that there might be, in the everyday run of things, something like a secret to raise, that the inessential might be, in a certain way, important, until the blank gaze of power came to rest on these minuscule commotions.

The birth, consequently, of an immense possibility for discourse. A certain knowledge of the quotidian had a part at least in its origin, together with a grid of intelligibility that the West undertook to extend over our actions, our ways of being and of behaving. But the birth in question depended also on the real and virtual omnipresence of the monarch; one had to imagine him sufficiently near to all those miseries, sufficiently attentive to the least of those disorders, before one could attempt to invoke him: he had to seem endowed with a kind of physical ubiquity himself. In its first form, this discourse concerning the quotidian was turned entirely toward the king; it was addressed to him; it had to slip into the great ceremonious rituals of power; it had to adopt their form and take on their signs. The commonplace could be told, described, observed, categorized, and indexed only within a power relation that was haunted by the figure of the king—by his real power or by the specter of his might. Hence the peculiar form of that discourse: it required a decorative, imprecatory, or supplicating language. All those little everyday squabbles had to be told with the emphasis of rare events worthy of royal attention; these inconsequential affairs had to be dressed up in grand rhetoric. In subsequent periods, neither the dreary reports of police administration nor the case histories of medicine or psychiatry would ever recapture such effects of language. At times, a sumptuous verbal edifice for relating an obscure piece of meanness or a minor intrigue; at others, a few brief sentences that strike down a poor wretch and plunge him back into his darkness; or the long tale of sorrows recounted in the form of supplication and humility. The political discourse of banality could not be anything but solemn.

But these texts also manifested another effect of incongruity. It often happened that the petitions for internment were lodged by illiterate or semiliterate persons of humble circumstance; they themselves, with their meager skills, or an underqualified scribe in their place, would compose as best they could the formulas or turns of phrase they believed to be required when one addressed the king or high officials, and they would stir in words that were awkward and violent, loutish expressions by which they hoped no doubt to give their petitions more force and truthfulness. In this way, crude, clumsy, and jarring expressions would suddenly appear in the midst of solemn and disjointed sentences, alongside nonsensical words; the obligatory and ritualistic language would be interspersed with outbursts of impatience, anger, rage, passion, rancor, and rebellion. The rules of this stilted discourse were thus upset by a vibration, by wild intensities muscling in with their own ways of saying things. This is how the wife of Nicolas Bienfait speaks: she "takes the liberty of representing very humbly to your Lordship that said Nicolas Bienfait, coachman, is a highly debauched man who is killing her with blows, and who is selling everything having already caused the deaths of his two wives, the first of whom he killed her child in the body, the second of whom after having sold and eaten what was hers, by his bad treatment caused her to die from languishment, even trying to strangle her on the eve of her death. . . . The third, he wishes to eat her heart on the grill, not to mention many other murders he did. My Lord, I throw myself at the feet of Your Highness to beseech Your Mercy. I hope that from your goodness you will render me justice, because my life being risked at every moment, I shall not cease praying to God for the preservation of your health. . . ."

The texts that I've brought together here are homogeneous, and they may well appear monotonous. Yet they function in the element of disparity. A disparity between the things recounted and the manner of telling them; a disparity between those who complain and those who have every power over them; a disparity between the minuscule order of the problems raised and the enormity of the power brought into play; a disparity between the language of ceremony and power and that of rage or helplessness. These are texts that nod in the direction of Racine, or Bossuet, or Crébillon; but they convey a whole stock of popular turbulence, of misery, and violence, of "baseness" as it was called, that no literature in that period could have accommodated. They bring tramps, poor wretches, or simply mediocre individuals onto a strange stage where they strike poses, speechify, and declaim, where they drape themselves in the bits of cloth they need if they wish to draw attention in the theater of power. At times they remind one of a poor troupe of jugglers and clowns who deck themselves out in makeshift scraps of old finery to play before an audience of aristocrats who will make fun of them. Except that they are staking their whole life on the performance: they are playing before powerful men who can decide their fate. Characters out of Céline, trying to make themselves heard at Versailles.

One day, all this incongruity would be swept away. Power exercised at the level of everyday life would no longer be that of a near and distant, omnipotent, and capricious monarch, the source of all justice and an object of every sort of enticement, both a political principle and a magical authority; it would be made up of a fine, differentiated, continuous network, in which the various institutions of the judiciary, the police, medicine, and psychiatry would operate hand in hand. And the discourse that would then take form would no longer have that old artificial and clumsy theatricality: it would develop in a language that would claim to be that of observation and neutrality. The commonplace would be analyzed through the efficient but colorless categories of administration, journalism, and science—unless one goes a little further to seek out its splendors in the domain of literature. In the seventeenth and eighteenth centuries, we are still in the rough and barbarous age when all these mediations don't exist: the body of the *misérables* is brought into almost direct contact with that of the king, their agitation with his ceremonies. There, not even a shared language but, rather, a clash between the cries and the rituals, between the disorders to be told and the rigor of the forms that must be followed. Whence, for us who look from afar at that first upsurge of the everyday into the code of the political, the strange fulgurations that appear, something gaudy and intense that will later be lost, when these things and these men will be made into "matters," into incidents or cases.

An important moment, this one, when a society lent words, turns of phrase, and sentences, language rituals to the anonymous mass of people so that they might speak of themselves—speak publicly and on the triple condition that their discourse be uttered and put in circulation within a well-defined apparatus of power; that it reveal the hitherto barely perceptible lower depths of social existence, and through the access provided by that diminutive war of passions and interests, it offer power the possibility of a sovereign intervention. Dionysius' ear was a small, rudimentary machine by comparison. How light power would be, and easy to dismantle no doubt, if all it did was to observe, spy, detect, prohibit, and punish; but it incites, provokes, produces. It is not simply eye and ear: it makes people act and speak.

This machinery was doubtless important for the constitution of new knowledges [*savoirs*]. It was not unconnected, moreover, with a whole new regime of literature. I don't mean to say that the *lettre de cachet* was at the point of origin of new literary forms; rather, that at the turn of the seventeenth and eighteenth centuries relations of discourse, power, everyday life, and truth were knotted together in a new way, one in which literature was also entangled.

The fable, in the proper sense of the word, is that which deserves to be told. For a long time in Western society, everyday life could accede to discourse only if it was traversed and transfigured by the legendary: it had to be drawn out of itself by heroism, the exploit, adventures, Providence and grace, or occasionally the heinous crime. It needed to be marked with a touch of impossibility—only then did it become expressible. What made it inaccessible enabled it to function as lesson and example. The more extraordinary the tale, the more capable it was of casting a spell or of persuading. In this game of the "exemplary fabulous," indifference to truth and untruth was therefore fundamental. If someone happened to describe the shabby side of reality, this was mainly to produce a comical effect: the mere fact of talking about it made people laugh.

Starting in the seventeenth century, the West saw the emergence of a whole "fable" of obscure life, from which the fabulous was banished. The impossible or the ridiculous ceased to be the condition under which the ordinary could be recounted. An art of language was born whose task was no longer to tell of the improbable but to bring into view that which doesn't, which can't and mustn't, appear—to tell the last and most tenuous degrees of the real. Just as an apparatus was being installed for forcing people to tell the "insignificant" [*"l'infime"*]—that which isn't told, which doesn't merit any glory, therefore, the "infamous"—a new imperative was forming that would constitute what could be called the "immanent ethic" of Western literary discourse. Its ceremonial functions would gradually fade; it would no longer have the task of manifesting in a tangible way the all too visible radiance of force, grace, heroism, and might but, rather, of searching for the things hardest to perceive—the most hidden, hardest to tell and to show, and lastly most forbidden and scandalous. A kind of injunction to ferret out the most nocturnal and most quotidian elements of existence (even if this sometimes meant discovering the solemn figures of fate) would mark out the course that literature would follow from the seventeenth century onward, from the time it began to be literature in the modern sense of the word. More than a specific form, more than an essential connection with form, it was this constraint—I was about to say "principle"—that characterized literature and carried its immense movement all the way to us: an obligation to tell the most common of secrets. Literature does not epitomize this great policy, this great discursive ethic by itself; and, certainly, there is more to literature than that; but that is where it has its locus and its conditions of existence.

Whence its dual relation to truth and to power. Whereas the fabulous could function only in a suspension between true and false, literature based itself, rather, on a decision of nontruth: it explicitly presented itself as artifice while promising to produce effects of truth that were recognizable as such. The importance that was given, in the Classical period, to naturalness and imitation was doubtless one of the first ways of formulating this functioning of literature "in truth." Fiction thus replaced fable, the novel broke free of the fantastical and was able to develop only by freeing itself from it ever more completely. Hence, literature belongs to the great system of constraint by which the West obliged the quotidian to enter into discourse. But literature occupies a special place within that system: determined to seek out the quotidian beneath the quotidian itself, to cross boundaries, to ruthlessly or insidiously bring our secrets out in the open, to displace rules and codes, to compel the unmentionable to be told, it will thus tend to place itself outside the law, or at least to take on the burden of scandal, transgression, or revolt. More than any other form of language, it remains the discourse of "infamy": it has the duty of saying what is most resistant to being said—the worst, the most secret, the most insufferable, the shameless. The fascination that psychoanalysis and literature have exerted on each other for years is significant in this connection. But it should not be forgotten that this singular position of literature is only the effect of a certain system [*dispositif*] of power that traverses the economy of discourses and strategies of truth in the West.

I began by saying that these texts might be read as so many "short stories." That was saying too much, no doubt; none of them will ever measure up to the least tale by Chekhov, Maupassant, or James. Neither "quasi-" nor "subliterature," they are not even the first sketch of a genre; they are the action, in disorder, noise, and pain, of power on lives, and the discourse that comes of it. *Manon Lescaut* tells one of the stories that are presented here.[4]

NOTES

* This essay is the introduction to an anthology of the prison archives of the Hôpital général and the Bastille, part of a series that Foucault compiled and presented under the collective

title *Parallel Lives* (Gallimard). The series includes the memoir of Herculine Barbin and the still untranslated *Le Désordre des familles* (*The Disorder of Families*), a volume of "poison pen letters" that Foucault compiled with the historian Arlette Farge. [eds.]

1   This is the name given to the collection of lives of saints that was compiled in the eighteenth century by the Dominican Jacques de Voragine, *La Légende dorée* (Paris: Garnier-Flammarion nos. 132–133, 1967), 2 vols. [eds.]

2   Gilles de Rais was the original Bluebeard (he killed six of his wives, and was discovered by his seventh); Cartouche was a famous highwayman; Sade is the Marquis de, after whom "sadism" is named; Lacenaire was a serial murderer condemned to death during Louis-Bonaparte's tenure (1840s), and also the author of a notorious memoir of his exploits. [eds.]

3   This is an allusion to remarks by the Duke de Chaulieu, reported in the *Lettre de Mademoiselle de Chaulieu à Madame de L 'Estorade*, in Honoré de Balzac, *Mémoires de deux jeunes mariées* (Paris: Librairie nouvelle, 1856), p. 59: "En coupant la tête à Louis XVI, la Révolution a coupé la tête à tous les pères de famille." [eds.]

4   A. F. Prévost, *Les Aventures du chevalier Des Grieux et de Manon Lescaut* (Amsterdam, 1733).

I would like to begin by relating a brief exchange which took place the other day in the Paris criminal courts. A man who was accused of five rapes and six attempted rapes, between February and June 1975, was being tried. The accused hardly spoke at all. Questions from the presiding judge:

"Have you tried to reflect upon your case?"

Silence.

"Why, at twenty-two years of age, do such violent urges overtake you? You must make an effort to analyze yourself. You are the one who has the keys to your own actions. Explain yourself."

Silence.

"Why would you do it again?"

Silence.

Then a juror took over and cried out, "For heaven's sake, defend yourself!"

Such a dialogue or, rather, such an interrogatory monologue, is not in the least exceptional. It could doubtlessly be heard in many courts in many countries. But, seen in another light, it can only arouse the amazement of the historian. Here we have a judicial system designed to establish misdemeanors, to determine who committed them, and to sanction these acts by imposing the penalties prescribed by the law. In this case, we have facts that have been established, an individual who admits to them—one who, consequently, accepts the punishment he will receive. All should be for the best in the best of all possible judicial worlds. The legislators, the authors of the legal codes in the late eighteenth and early nine-teenth centuries, could not have dreamed of a clearer situation. And yet it happens that the machinery jams, the gears seize up. Why? Because the accused remains silent. Remains silent about what? About the facts? About circumstances? About the way in which they occurred? About the immediate cause of the events? Not at all. The accused evades a question that is essential in the eyes of a modern tribunal but would have had a strange ring to it 150 years ago: "Who are you?"

And the dialogue I just quoted shows that it is not enough for the accused to say in reply to that question, "I am the author of the crimes before you, period. Judge since you must, condemn if you will." Much more is expected of him. Beyond admission, there must be confession, self-examination, explanation of oneself, revelation of what one is. The penal machine can no longer function simply with a law, a violation, and a responsible party—it needs something else, supplementary material. The magistrates and the jurors, the lawyers too, and the department of the public prosecutor cannot really play their roles unless they are provided with another type of discourse, the one given by the accused about himself, or the one he makes possible for others, through his confessions, memories, intimate disclosures, and so on. If it happens that this discourse is missing, the presiding judge is relentless, the jury is upset. They urge, they push the accused, he does not play the game. He is not unlike those condemned persons who have to be carried to the guil-lotine or the electric chair because they drag their feet. They really ought to walk a little by themselves, if indeed they want to be ex-ecuted. They really ought to speak a little about themselves, if they want to be judged. The following argument used recently by a French lawyer in the case of the kidnapping and murder of a child clearly indicates that the judicial stage cannot do without this added element, that no judgment, no condemnation is possible without it being provided, in one way or another.

For a number of reasons, this case created a great stir, not only because of the seriousness of the crime but also because the ques-tion of the retention or the abolition of the death penalty was at stake in the case. In his plea, which was directed against the death penalty more than in favor of the accused, the lawyer stressed the point that very little was known about him, and that the nature of the man had only barely been glimpsed at in the interrogations and in the psychiatric examinations. And he made this amazing remark (I quote approximately): "Can one condemn to death a person one does not know?"

This is probably no more than one illustration of a well-known fact, which could be called the "law of the third element," or the "Garofalo principle," since Garofalo was the one who formulated it with complete clarity: "Criminal law knew only two terms, the offense and the penalty. The new criminology recognizes three, the crime, the criminal and the means of repression." In large part, the evolution—if not of the penal systems then at least of the day-to-day penal practice of many countries—is determined by the gradual emergence in the course of the nineteenth century of this additional character. At first a pale phantom, used to adjust the penalty determined by the judge for the crime, this character becomes gradually more substantial, more solid, and more real, until finally it is the crime that seems nothing but a shadow hovering about the criminal, a shadow that must be drawn aside in order to reveal the only thing that is now of importance, the criminal.

Legal justice today has at least as much to do with criminals as with crimes. Or, more precisely, though for a long time the criminal had been no more than the person to whom a crime could be attributed and who could therefore be punished, today the crime tends to be no more than the event that signals the existence of a dangerous element—that is, more or less dangerous—in the social body.

From the very beginning of this development, resorting to the criminal over and above the crime was justified by a double concern: to introduce more rationality into penal practice, and to adjust the general provisions of laws and legal codes more closely to social reality. Probably, it was not realized, at least at first, that to add the notion of psychological symptomatology of a danger to the notion of legal imputability of a crime was not only to enter an extremely obscure labyrinth but also to come slowly out of a legal system that had gradually developed since its birth during the medieval inquisition. It could be said that hardly had the great eighteenth-century legal reformers completed the systematic codification of the results of the preceding evolution, hardly had they developed all its possibilities, when a new crisis began to appear in the rules and regulations of legal punishment. "What must be punished, and how?" That was the question to which, it was believed, a rational answer had finally been found. And now a further question arose to confuse the issue: "Whom do you think you are punishing?"

In this development, psychiatry and psychiatrists, as well as the notion of "danger," played a permanent role. I would like to draw attention to two stages in what one might call the "psychiatrization" of criminal danger.

The intervention of psychiatry in the field of law occurred in the beginning of the nineteenth century, in connection with a series of cases that took place between 1800 and 1835 whose pattern was about the same.

Case reported by Metzger: A retired officer who lives a solitary life becomes attached to his landlady's child. One day, "with absolutely no motive, in the absence of any passion, such as anger, pride, or vengeance," he attacks the child and hits him twice with a hammer, though not fatally.

Sélestat case: In Alsace, during the extremely hard winter of 1817, when famine threatens, a peasant woman takes advantage of her husband's being away at work to kill their little daughter, cuts off her leg, and cooks it in the soup.

In Paris in 1827, Henriette Cornier, a servant, goes to the neighbor of her employers and insists that the neighbor leave her daughter with her for a time. The neighbor hesitates, agrees; when she returns for the child, Henriette Cornier has just killed her and has cut off her head, which she has thrown out the window.

In Vienna, Catherine Ziegler kills her illegitimate child. On the stand, she explains that her act was the result of an irresistible force. She is acquitted on grounds of insanity. She is released from prison. But she declares that it would be better if she were kept there, for she will do it again. Ten months later, she gives birth to a child, which she kills immediately, and she declares at the trial that she became pregnant for the sole purpose of killing her child. She is condemned to death and executed.

In Scotland, a certain John Howison enters a house where he kills an old woman whom he hardly knows, leaves without stealing anything, and does not go into hiding. Arrested, he denies the fact against all evidence; but the defense argues that it is the crime of a madman since it is a crime without material motive. Howison is executed, and his comment to an official at the execution, that he felt like killing him, was considered in retrospect as supplementary evidence of madness.

In New England, out in the open fields, Abraham Prescott kills his foster mother, with whom he had always gotten along very well. He goes home and breaks into tears in front of his foster father, who questions him. Prescott willingly confesses his crime. He explains later that he was overcome by a sudden and acute toothache, and that he remembers nothing. The inquiry will establish that he had already attacked his foster parents during the night, an act that had been believed to be the result of a fit of sleepwalking. Prescott is condemned to death, but the jury also recommends a commutation. He is nevertheless executed.

The psychiatrists of the period, Metzger, Hoffbauer, Esquirol and Georget, William Ellis and Andrew Combe refer tirelessly to these cases and to others of the same type.

Out of all the crimes committed, why did these particular ones seem important? Why were they at issue in the discussions between doctors and jurists? First, it must be noted that they present a picture very different from what had hitherto constituted the jurisprudence of criminal insanity. In general terms, until the end of the eighteenth century, the question of insanity was raised under penal law only in cases where it was also raised in the civil code or in canon law, that is when it appeared either in the form of *dementia* and of imbecility, or in the form of *furor*. In both cases, whether it was a matter of a permanent state or a passing outburst, insanity manifested itself through numerous signs that were easy enough to recognize, to the extent that it was debated whether a doctor was really necessary to authenticate it. The important thing is that criminal psychiatry did not develop from a subtle redefining of the traditional question of *dementia* (for example, by discussing its gradual evolution, its global or partial character, its relationship to congenital disabilities of individuals), nor through a closer analysis of the symptomatology of *furor* (its remissions, it recurrences, its rhythm). All these problems, along with the discussions that had gone on for years, were replaced by a new problem, that of crimes that are not preceded, accompanied, nor followed by any of the traditional, recognized, visible symptoms of insanity. It is stressed in each case that there was no previous history, no earlier disturbance in thought or behavior, no delirium; neither was there any agitation, nor visible disorder as in *furor*. Indeed, the crime would arise out of a state one might call the zero degree of insanity.

The second common feature is too obvious to be dealt with at any length. The crimes in question are not minor offenses but serious crimes, almost all murders, sometimes accompanied by strange cruelties (cannibalism in the case of the woman from Selestat). It is important to note that the psychiatrization of delinquency occurred in a sense "from above." This is also a departure from the fundamental tendency of previous jurisprudence. The more serious the crime, the less usual it was to raise the question of insanity (for a long period, it was not taken into consideration in cases involving sacrilege or lèse majesté). That there is a considerable area of overlap between insanity and illegality was readily admitted in the case of minor offenses—little acts of violence, vagrancy—and these were dealt with, at least in some countries (such as France), by the ambiguous measure of internment. But it was not through the ill-defined zone of day-to-day disorders that psychiatry was able to penetrate penal justice in full force. Rather, it was by tackling the great criminal event of the most violent and rarest sort.

Another common feature of these great murders is that they take place in a domestic setting. They are family crimes, household crimes, and, at most, neighborhood crimes—parents who kill their progeny, children who kill their parents or guardians, servants who kill their employers' or their neighbors' child, and so on. As we can see, these are crimes that bring together partners from different generations. The child–adult or adolescent–adult couple is almost always present. In those days, such relationships of age, of place, of kinship were held to be at the same time the most sacred and the most natural, and also the most innocent. Of all relationships, they were the ones that ought to have been the least charged with material motive or passion. Rather than crimes against society and its rules, they are crimes against nature, against those laws perceived to be inscribed directly on the human heart and to link families and generations. At the beginning of the nineteenth century, the form of crime about which it appeared that the question of insanity could properly be raised was thus the crime against nature. The individual in whom insanity and criminality met in such a way as to cause specialists to raise the question of their relationship was not the man of the little everyday disorder, the pale silhouette moving about on the edges of law and normality but, rather, the great monster. Criminal psychiatry first proclaimed itself a pathology of the monstrous.

Finally, all these crimes were committed without reason—I mean without profit, without passion, without motive, not even based on disordered illusions. In all the cases I have mentioned, the psychiatrists justify their intervention by insisting that there existed between the two actors in the drama no relationship that would help to make the crime intelligible. In the case of Henriette Cornier, who had decapitated her neighbor's daughter, it was carefully established that she had not been the father's mistress, and that she had not acted out of vengeance. In the case of the woman from Sélestat who had boiled her daughter's thigh, an important element of the discussion had been, "Was there or was there not famine at the time? Was the accused poor or not, starving or not?" The public prosecutor had said, "If she had been rich, she could have been considered deranged, but she was poverty-stricken; she was hungry; to cook the leg with the cabbage was interested behavior; she was therefore not insane."

At the time when the new psychiatry was being established, and when the principles of penal reform were being applied nearly everywhere in Europe and in North America, the great and monstrous murder, without reason, without preliminaries, the sudden eruption of the unnatural in nature, was the singular and paradoxical form taken by criminal insanity or pathological crime. I say paradoxical because there was an attempt to grasp a type of derangement that manifested itself only in the moment and in the guise of the crime, a derangement that would have no symptom other than the crime itself and could disappear once the crime had been committed. And, conversely, it entailed identifying crimes whose reason, whose author—whose "legally responsible agent" so to speak—is that part of the subject beyond his responsibility; that is, the insanity that hides in him, which he cannot even control because he is frequently not even aware of it. Nineteenth-century psychiatry invented an entirely fictitious entity, a crime that is insanity, a crime that is nothing but insanity, an insanity that is nothing but a crime. For more than half a century, this entity was called "homicidal monomania." I do not intend to go over the theoretical background of the notion or to follow up the innumerable discussions it prompted between men of the law and doctors, lawyers and magistrates. I simply want to underline this strange fact: psychiatrists have tried very stubbornly to take their place in the legal machinery. They justified their right to intervene not by searching out the thousand little visible signs of madness that may accompany the most ordinary crimes but by insisting—a preposterous stance—that there were kinds of insanity which manifested themselves only in outrageous crimes and in no other way. And I would also like to underline the fact that, in spite of all their reservations about accepting this notion of monomania, when the magistrates of the time finally accepted the psychiatric analysis of crime, they did so on the basis of this same notion, so foreign and so unacceptable to them.

Why was the great fiction of homicidal mania the key notion in the protohistory of criminal psychiatry? The first set of questions to be asked is probably the following: At the beginning of the nineteenth century, when the task of psychiatry was to define its specificity in the field of medicine and to assure that its scientific character was recognized among other medical practices—at the point, that is, when psychiatry was establishing itself as a medical specialization (previously it had been an aspect rather than a field of medicine)—why then did it want to meddle in an area where so far it had intervened very discretely? Why did doctors want so badly to describe as insane, and thus to claim, people whose status as mere criminals had up to that point been unquestioned? Why can they be found in so many countries, denouncing the medical ignorance of judges and jurors, requesting pardons or the commutation of punishment for certain convicts, demanding the right to be heard as experts by the tribunals, publishing hundreds of reports and studies to show that this criminal or that one was a madman? Why this crusade in favor of the "pathologification" of crime and under the banner, no less, of homicidal mania? This is all the more paradoxical in that, shortly before, at the end of the eighteenth century, the very first students of insanity (especially Philippe Pinel) protested against the practice followed in many detention centers of mixing delinquents and the mentally ill. Why would one want to renew a kinship one had taken such trouble to break down?

It is not enough to invoke some sort of imperialism on the part of psychiatrists seeking a new domain for themselves, or even the internal dynamics of medical knowledge attempting to rationalize the confused area where madness and crime mix. Crime, then, became an important issue for psychiatrists, because what was involved was less a field of knowledge to be conquered than a modality of power to be secured and justified. If psychiatry became so important in the nineteenth century, it was not simply because it applied a new medical rationality to mental or behavioral disorders; it was also because it functioned as a sort of public hygiene.

In the eighteenth century, the development of demography, of urban structures, of the problem of industrial labor, had raised in biological and medical terms the question of human "populations," with their conditions of existence, of habitation, of nutrition, with their birth and mortality rates, with their pathological phenomena (epidemics, endemic diseases, infant mortality). The social "body" ceased to be a simple juridico-political metaphor (like the one in the *Leviathan*) and became, instead, a biological reality and a field for medical intervention. The doctor must therefore be the technician of this social body, and medicine a public hygiene. At the turn of the nineteenth century, psychiatry became an autonomous discipline and assumed such prestige precisely because it had been able to develop within the framework of a medical discipline conceived of as a reaction to the dangers inherent in the social body. The alienists of the period may well have had endless discussions about the organic or psychic origin of mental illnesses; they may well have proposed physical or psychic therapies. Nonetheless, through all their differences, they were all conscious that they were treating a social "danger," either because insanity seemed to them to be linked to living conditions (overpopulation, overcrowding, urban life, alcoholism, debauchery), or because it was perceived as a source of danger for oneself, for others, for one's contemporaries, and also for one's descendants through heredity. Nineteenth-century psychiatry was a medical science as much for the societal body as for the individual soul.

One can see why it was important for psychiatry to prove the existence of something as extravagant as homicidal mania. One can see why for half a century there were continuous attempts to make that notion work, in spite of its meager scientific justification. Indeed, if it exists, homicidal mania shows:

First, that in some of its pure, extreme, intense manifestations, insanity is entirely crime, nothing but crime—that is, at least at the ultimate boundaries of insanity, there is crime.

Second, that insanity can produce not just behavioral disorders but absolute crime, the crime that transgresses all the laws of nature and of society.

And third, that even though this insanity may be extraordinarily intense, it remains invisible until it explodes; that for this reason no one can forecast it, unless he has considerable experience and a trained eye. In short, only a specialist can spot monomania. The contradiction is more apparent than real when the alienists eventually define monomania as an illness that manifests itself only in crime while, at the same time, they reserve the right to know how to determine its premonitory signs, its predisposing conditions.

So homicidal mania is the danger of insanity in its most harmful form: a maximum of consequences, a minimum of warning. The most effects and fewest signs. Homicidal mania thus necessitates the intervention of a medical eye, which must take into account not only the obvious manifestations of madness but also the barely perceptible traces, appearing randomly where they are the least expected, and foretelling the worst explosions. Such an interest in the great crimes "without reason," I think, indicates on the part of psychiatry not a desire to take over criminality but a desire to justify its functions—the control of the dangers hidden in human behavior. What is at stake in this great issue of homicidal mania is the function of psychiatry. It must not be forgotten that, in most Western countries, psychiatry was then striving to establish its right to impose upon the mentally ill a therapeutic confinement. After all, it had to be shown that madness, by its nature, and even in its most discrete manifestations, was haunted by the absolute danger, death. The functioning of modern psychiatry is linked to this kinship between madness and death, which was not scientifically established but, rather, symbolically represented in the figure of homicidal mania.

However, there is another question to be asked, this time from the point of view of the judges and the judicial apparatus. Why indeed did they accept if not the notion of monomania then at least the problems it entailed? It will probably be said that the great majority of magistrates refused to recognize this notion which made it possible to transform a criminal into a madman whose only illness was to commit crimes. With a great deal of tenacity—and, one might add, with a certain degree of good sense—they did everything they could to dismiss this notion the doctors proposed to them and lawyers used spontaneously to defend their clients. And yet, through this controversy about monstrous crimes, about crimes "without reason," the idea of a possible kinship between madness and delinquency became acclimatized even within the judicial institution. Why was this accomplished, and relatively easily at that? In other words, why did the penal institution, which had been able to do without medical intervention for so many centuries, which had been able to judge and condemn without the problem of madness being raised except in a few obvious cases, why did this penal institution so willingly have recourse to medical knowledge from the 1820s on? For there is no mistaking the fact that English, German, Italian, and French judges of the time quite often refused to accept the conclusions of the doctors. They rejected many of the notions the doctors proposed to them. After all, the doctors did not take them by force. They themselves solicited—following the laws, the rules, the jurisprudence that vary from country to country—the duly formulated advice of psychiatrists, and they solicited it especially in connection with those famous crimes "without reason." Why? Was it because the new codes written and applied at the beginning of the nineteenth century took into account psychiatric expertise or gave a new emphasis to the problem of pathological irresponsibility? Not at all. Surprisingly enough, these new laws hardly modified the previous situation. Most of the codes based on the Napoleonic model incorporated the old principle that the state of mental disorder is incompatible with legal responsibility and thus is immune from the usual legal consequences. Most of the codes also incorporate the traditional notions of *dementia* and *furor* used in the older legal systems. Neither the great theoreticians Cesare de Beccaria and Jeremy Bentham, nor those who actually wrote up the new penal laws, tried to elaborate upon these traditional notions, or to establish new relationships between punishment and criminal medicine, except to affirm in a very general way that penal justice must cure this illness of societies, that is, crime. It was not "from above," by way of legal codes or theoretical principles, that psychiatric medicine penetrated the penal system. Rather, it was "from below," through the mechanics of punishment and through the interpretation given to them. Among all the new techniques for controlling and transforming individuals, punishment had become a system of procedures designed to reform lawbreakers. The terrifying example of torture or exile by banishment could no longer suffice in a society in which exercise of power implied a reasoned technology applied to individuals. The forms of punishment to which all the late eighteenth-century reformers and all the early nineteenth-century legislators rallied—that is, imprisonment, forced labor, constant surveillance, partial or total isolation, moral reform—all this implies that punishment bears on the criminal himself rather than on the crime, that is, on what makes him a criminal, on his reasons, his motives, his inner will, his tendencies, his instincts. In the older systems, the horror of the punishment had to reflect the enormity of the crime; henceforth, the attempt was made to adapt the modalities of punishment to the nature of the criminal.

In these circumstances, one sees why the great unmotivated crimes posed a difficult problem for the judges. In the past, to impose a punishment for a crime one had only to find the author of the crime, and it was enough that he had no excuse and that he had not been in a state of *furor* or *dementia*. But how can one punish someone whose reasons are unknown, who keeps silent before his judges, except to admit the facts and to agree that he had been perfectly conscious of what he was doing? What is to be done when a woman like Henriette Cornier appears in court, a woman who has killed a child whom she hardly knew, the daughter of people whom she could neither have hated nor loved, who decapitates the girl but is unable to give the slightest explanation, who does not try for a moment to hide her crime, and who had nonetheless prepared for her act, had chosen the moment, had procured a knife, had eagerly sought an opportunity to be alone for a moment with her victim? Thus, in a person who had given no sign of madness, there arises an act at once voluntary, conscious, and reasoned—that is, all that is necessary for a condemnation according to the terms of the law—and yet nothing, no reason, no motive, no evil tendencies that would have made it possible to determine what should be punished in the guilty woman. It is clear that there should be a condemnation, but it is hard to understand why there should be a

punishment, except of course for the external but insufficient reason of setting an example. Now that the reason for the crime had
become the reason for the punishment, how could one punish if
the crime was without reason? In order to punish, one needs to
know the nature of the guilty person, his obduracy, the degree of
his evilness, what his interests or his leanings are. But if one has
nothing more than the crime, on the one hand, and the author, on
the other, pure and simple judicial responsibility formally author-
izes punishment but does not allow one to make sense of it.

One can see why these great unmotivated crimes, which the psychiatrists had good reason to emphasize, were also, but for very
different reasons, such important problems for the judicial apparatus. The public prosecutors obstinately referred to the law: no
dementia, no *furor*, no recognized evidence of derangement; on the
contrary, perfectly organized acts; therefore, the law must be applied. But no matter how hard they tried, they could not avoid the
question of motivation, for they knew very well that from now on,
in practice, the judges would link punishment, at least in part, to
the determination of motives. Perhaps Henriette Cornier had been
the mistress of the girl's father, and sought revenge; perhaps,
having had to abandon her own children, she was jealous of the
happy family living near her. All the indictments prove that in order
for the punitive mechanism to work, the reality of an offense and
a person to whom it can be attributed are not sufficient: the motive
must also be established, that is, a psychologically intelligible link
between the act and the author. The Sélestat case, in which a can-
nibalistic woman was executed because she *could* have been hungry, seems to me to be very significant.

The doctors who were normally called in only to certify cases of
dementia or of *furor* began now to be called upon as "specialists in
motivation"; they had to evaluate not only the subject's reason but
also the rationality of the act, the whole system of relationships that
link the act to the interests, the plans, the character, the inclina-
tions, and the habits of the subject. And even though the judges
were often reluctant to accept the diagnosis of monomania so rel-
ished by the doctors, they were obliged to entertain willingly the
set of problems raised by the notion—that is, in slightly more modern terms, the integration of the act into the global behavior of the
subject. The more clearly visible this integration, the more clearly

punishable the subject. The less obvious the integration, the more it seems as if the act has erupted in the subject, like a sudden and irrepressible mechanism, and the less punishable the responsible party appears. And justice will then agree that it cannot proceed with the case, since the subject is insane, and will commit him to psychiatric confinement.

Several conclusions can be drawn from this:

First: The intervention of psychiatric medicine in the penal system starting in the nineteenth century is neither the consequence nor the simple development of the traditional theory of the irresponsibility of those suffering from *dementia* or *furor*.

Second: It is due to the regulating of two phenomena arising necessarily—one from the functioning of medicine as a public hygiene, the other from the functioning of legal punishment as a technique for transforming the individual.

Third: These two new demands are both bound up with the transformation of the mechanism of power through which the control of the social body has been attempted in industrial societies since the eighteenth century. In spite of their common origin, though, the reasons for the intervention of medicine in the criminal field and the reasons for the recourse of penal justice to psychiatry are essentially different.

Fourth: The monstrous crime, both antinatural and irrational, is the meeting point of the medical demonstration that insanity is ultimately always dangerous, and of the court's inability to determine the punishment of a crime without having determined the motives for the crime. The bizarre symptomatology of homicidal mania was delineated at the point of convergence of these two mechanisms.

Fifth: In this way, the theme of the dangerous man is inscribed in the institutions of psychiatry as well as of justice. Increasingly in the nineteenth and twentieth centuries, penal practice and then penal theory will tend to make of the dangerous individual the principal target of punitive intervention. Increasingly, nineteenth-century psychiatry will also tend to seek out pathological stigmata that may mark dangerous individuals: moral insanity, instinctive insanity, and degeneration. This theme of the dangerous individual will give rise, on the one hand, to the anthropology of criminal man as in the Italian school, and, on the other, to the theory of social defense first represented by the Belgian school.

Sixth: Another important consequence is that there will be a considerable transformation of the old notion of penal responsibility. This notion, at least in certain aspects, was still close to civil law. It was necessary, for instance, in order to impute a violation to someone, that he be free, conscious, unafflicted by *dementia*, untouched by any crisis of *furor*. Now, however, responsibility would be limited no longer only to this form of consciousness but also to the intelligibility of the act with reference to the conduct, the character, the antecedents of the individual. The more psychologically determined an act is found to be, the more its author can be considered legally responsible. The more the act is, so to speak, gratuitous and undetermined, the more it will tend to be excused. A paradox, then: the legal freedom of a subject is proven by the fact that his act is seen to be necessary, determined; his lack of responsibility proven by the fact that his act is seen to be unnecessary. With this untenable paradox of monomania and of the monstrous act, psychiatry and penal justice entered a phase of uncertainty from which we have yet to emerge; the play between penal responsibility and psychological determinism has become the cross of legal and medical thought.

I would now like to turn to another moment that was particularly fertile for the relationship between psychiatry and penal law: the last years of the nineteenth century and the first few of the twentieth from the first congress on Criminal Anthropology (1885) to A. Prinz's publication of his *Social Defense* (1910).

Between the period I was recalling previously and the one I would like to speak about now, what happened? First of all, within the discipline of psychiatry in the strict sense of the term, the notion of monomania was abandoned, not without some hesitations and reversions, shortly before 1870. Abandoned for two reasons. First, because the essentially negative idea of a partial insanity, bearing on only one point and unleashed only at certain moments, was gradually replaced by the idea that a mental illness is not necessarily an affliction of thought or of consciousness, but that it may attack the emotions, the instincts, spontaneous behavior, leaving the forms of thought virtually intact. (What was called "moral insanity," instinctive insanity, aberration of the instincts, and finally perversion, corresponds to this elaboration, whose favored example since about the 1840s has been the deviations in sexual conduct.) But there was another reason for abandoning monomania; that is, the idea of mental illness—its evolution is complex and polymorphous—which may present one particular symptom or another at one stage or another of its development, not only at the level of the individual but also at the level of several generations; in short, the idea of degeneration.

Because of the fact that these great evolutive ramifications can be defined, it is no longer necessary to make a distinction between the great monstrous and mysterious crimes that could be ascribed to the incomprehensible violence of *insanity* and minor delinquency, which is too frequent, too familiar to necessitate a recourse to the pathological. From then on, whether one had to deal with incomprehensible massacres or minor offenses (having to do with property or sexuality), in every case one might suspect a more or less serious perturbation of instincts or the stages in an uninterruped process. Thus, there appear in the field of legal psychiatry new categories—such as necrophilia around 1840, kleptomania around 1860, exhibitionism in 1876—and also legal psychiatry's annexation of behavior like pederasty and sadism. There now exists, at least in principle, a psychiatric and criminological continuum that permits one to pose questions in medical terms at any level of the penal scale. The psychiatric question is no longer confined to some great crimes; even if it must receive a negative answer, it is to be posed across the whole range of infractions.

Now, this has important consequences for the legal theory of responsibility. In the conception of monomania, suspicions of pathology were aroused precisely when there was no reason for an act; insanity was seen as the cause of that which made no sense, and legal nonresponsibility was established in view of this inconsistency. But with this new analysis of instinct and emotions, it would be possible to provide a casual analysis for all kinds of conduct, whether delinquent or not, and whatever their degree of criminality. Hence the infinite labyrinth in which the legal and psychiatric problem of crime found itself. If an act is determined by a causal nexus, can it be considered to be free? Does it not imply responsibility? And is it necessary, in order to be able to condemn someone, that it be impossible to reconstruct the causal intelligibility of his act?

Now, as background for this new way of posing the problem, I must mention several transformations that were, at least in part, the conditions of its being possible. First, the intensive development of the police network, which led to a new mapping and closer surveillance of urban space and also to a much more systematic and efficient prosecution of minor delinquency. It must be added that social conflicts, class struggles and political confrontations, armed revolts—from the machine-smashers of the beginning of the century to the anarchists of the last few years of the century, including the violent strikes, the revolutions of 1848, and the Commune of 1870—prompted those in power to treat political misdemeanors in the same way as ordinary crimes in order to discredit them. Little by little, an image was built up of an enemy of society who can equally well be a revolutionary or a murderer—since, after all, revolutionaries do sometimes kill. Corresponding to this, throughout the whole second half of the century there developed a "literature of criminality," and I use the word in its largest sense, including miscellaneous news items (and even popular newspapers) as well as detective novels and all the romanticized writings that developed around crime—the transformation of the criminal into a hero, perhaps, but equally the affirmation that ever-present criminality is a constant menace to the social body as a whole. The collective fear of crime, and the obsession with this danger which seems to be an inseparable part of society itself, are thus perpetually inscribed in each individual consciousness.

Referring to the 9,000 murders then recorded annually in Europe, not counting Russia, B. R. Garofalo said in the preface to the first edition of his *Criminology* (1887): "Who is the enemy who has devastated this land? It is a mysterious enemy, unknown to history; his name is: the criminal."

To this must be added another element—the continuing failure of the penitentiary system, which is very frequently reported. It was the dream of the eighteenth-century reformers, then of the philanthropists of the following period, that incarceration, provided that it be rationally directed, might serve as a true penal therapy. The result was meant to be the reform of the prisoners. It soon became clear that prison had exactly the opposite result, that it was on the whole a school for delinquency and that the more refined methods of the police system and the legal apparatus, far from ensuring better protection against crime, brought about a strengthening of the criminal milieu, through the medium of prison itself.

For all sorts of reasons, a situation existed such that there was a very strong social and political demand for a reaction to, and for repression of, crime. This demand had to do with a criminality, which in its totality had to be thought of in judicial and medical terms; and yet, the key notion of the penal institution since the Middle Ages—that is, legal responsibility—seems utterly inadequate for the conceptualization of this broad and dense domain of medico-legal criminality.

This inadequacy became apparent, both at the conceptual and at the institutional level, in the conflict between the so-called school of Criminal Anthropology and the International Association of Penal Law around the 1890s. In attempting to cope with the traditional principles of criminal legislation, the Italian School (the Criminal Anthropologists) called for nothing less than a putting-aside of legality—a true "depenalization" of crime, by setting up an apparatus of an entirely different type from the one provided for by the Codes.

For the Criminal Anthropologists, this meant totally abandoning the judicial notion of responsibility, and posing as the fundamental question not the degree of freedom of the individual but the level of danger he represents for society. Moreover, it meant noting that the accused, whom the law recognized as not responsible because he was ill, insane, a victim of irresistible impulses, was precisely the most seriously and immediately dangerous. The Criminal Anthropologists emphasized that what is called "penalty" need not be a punishment but, rather, a mechanism for the defense of society; they therefore noted that the relevant difference is not between legally responsible subjects who are found guilty, and legally irresponsible subjects who are released, but between absolutely and definitively dangerous subjects and those who can cease to be dangerous provided they receive certain treatment. They concluded that there should be three main types of social reaction to crime or, rather, to the danger represented by the criminal: definitive elimination (by death or by incarceration in an institution), temporary elimination (with treatment), and more or less relative and partial elimination (sterilization and castration).

One can see the series of shifts required by the anthropological school: from the crime to the criminal; from the act as it was actually committed to the danger potentially inherent in the individual; from the modulated punishment of the guilty party to the absolute protection of others. All these shifts implied quite clearly an escape from a universe of penal law revolving around the act, its imputability to a de jure subject, the legal responsibility of the latter and a punishment proportionate to the gravity of this act as defined by law. Neither the "criminality" of an individual nor the index of his dangerousness, neither his potential or future behavior nor the protection of society at large from these possible perils—none of these are or can be juridical notions in the classical sense of the term. They can be made to function in a rational way only within a technical knowledge-system, a knowledge-system capable of characterizing a criminal individual in himself and, in a sense, beneath his acts; a knowledge-system able to measure the index of danger present in an individual; a knowledge-system that might establish the protection necessary in the face of such a danger. Hence the idea that crime ought to be the responsibility not of judges but of experts in psychiatry, criminology, psychology, and so on. Actually, that extreme conclusion was not often formulated in such an explicit and radical way, no doubt through practical prudence. But it followed implicitly from all the theses of Criminal Anthropology. And at the second meeting of this Association (1889), Pugliese expressed it straightforwardly. We must, he said, turn around the old adage "the judge is the expert of experts." Rather, it is up to the expert to be the judge of judges. "The commission of medical experts to whom the judgment ought to be referred should not limit itself to expressing its wishes: on the contrary it should render a real decision."

It can be said that a point of breakdown was being reached. Criminology, which had developed out of the old notion of monomania, maintaining a frequently stormy relationship with penal law, was in danger of being excluded from it as excessively radical. This would have led to a situation similar to the original one: a technical knowledge-system incompatible with law, besieging it from without and unable to make itself heard. As the notion of monomania could be used to overlay with madness a crime with no apparent reasons, so, to some extent, the notion of degeneration made it possible to link the most insignificant of criminals to a peril of pathological dimensions for society, and, eventually, for the whole human species. The whole field of infractions could be held together in terms of danger and thus of protection to be provided. The law had only to hold its tongue. Or to plug its ears and refuse to listen.

It is usual to say that the fundamental propositions of criminal anthropology were fairly rapidly disqualified for a number of reasons: because they were linked to a form of scientism, to a certain positivist naiveté which the very development of the sciences in the twentieth century has taken upon itself to cure; because they were related to historical and social evolutionism, which was itself quickly discredited; because they found support in a neuropsychiatric theory of degeneration that both neurology and psychoanalysis have quickly dismantled; and because they were unable to become operational within the format of penal legislation and within legal practice. The age of criminal anthropology, with its radical naivetés, seems to have disappeared with the nineteenth century; and a much more subtle psychosociology of delinquency, much more acceptable to penal law, seems to have taken up the fight.

It seems to me that, at least in its general outlines, criminal anthropology has not disappeared as completely as some people say, and that a number of its most fundamental theses—often those most foreign to traditional law—have gradually taken root in penal thought and practice. But this could not have happened solely by virtue of the truth of this psychiatric theory of crime or, rather, solely through its persuasive force. In fact, there had been a significant mutation within the law. When I say "within the law," I probably say too much, for, with a few exceptions (such as the Norwegian code, but it was written for a new state, after all), and aside from some projects left in limbo (such as the Swiss plan for a penal code), penal legislation remained pretty well unchanged. The laws relating to suspension of sentence, recidivism, or relegation were the principal modifications somewhat hesitantly made in French legislation. This is not where I see the significant mutations; rather, I see them in connection with an element at the same time theoretical and essential, namely, the notion of responsibility. And it was possible to modify this notion not so much because of the pressure of some internal shock but mainly because considerable evolution had taken place in the area of civil law during the same period. My hypothesis would be that it was civil law, not criminology, that made it possible for penal thought to change on two or three major points. It was civil law that made it possible to graft onto criminal law the essential elements of the criminological theses of the period. It may well be that, without the reformulation that occurred first in civil law, the jurists would have turned a deaf ear to the fundamental propositions of criminal anthropology, or at least would never have possessed the proper tool for integrating them into the legal system. In a way that may at first seem strange, it was civil law that made possible the articulation of the legal code and of science in penal law.

This transformation in civil law revolves around the notion of accident and legal responsibility. In a very general way, it is worth emphasizing the significance that the problem of accidents had, not only for law but also for economics and politics, especially in the second half of the nineteenth century. One could object that, since the sixteenth century, insurance plans had shown how important the idea of risk had already become. But, on the one hand, insurance dealt only with more or less individual risks and, on the other, it entirely excluded the legal responsibility of the interested party. In the nineteenth century, the development of wage-earning, of industrial techniques, of mechanization, of transportation, of urban structures, brought two important things. First, risks were incurred by third parties (the employer exposed his employees to work-related accidents; transport companies exposed not only their passengers to accidents but also people who just happened to be there). Then, these accidents could often be linked to a sort of error—but a minor error (inattention, lack of precaution, negligence)—committed, moreover, by someone who could not carry the civil responsibility for it or pay the ensuing damages. The problem was to establish in law the concept of no-fault responsibility. It was the effort of Western civil legislators and especially German jurists, influenced as they were by the demands of Bismarckian society—a society characterized not only by discipline but also by security-consciousness. In this search for a no-fault responsibility, the civil legislators emphasized a certain number of important principles:

First: This responsibility must be established not according to the series of errors committed but according to the chain of causes and effects. Responsibility is on the side of cause, rather than on the side of fault. This is what German jurists meant by *Causalhaftung*.

Second: These causes are of two orders that are not mutually exclusive: the chain of precise and individual facts, each of which has been induced by the preceding one; and the creation of risks inherent in a type of action, of equipment, of enterprise.

Third: Granted, these risks are to be reduced in the most systematic and rigorous way possible. But they will certainly never be made to disappear; none of the characteristic undertakings of modern society will be without risk. As Raymond Saleilles said, "a causal relationship linked to a purely material fact which in itself appears as hazardous fact, not in itself irregular, nor contrary to the customs of modern life, but contemptuous of that extreme caution which paralyzes action, in harmony with the activity which is imperative today and therefore defying hatreds and accepting risks, that is the law of life today, that is the common rule, and law is made to reflect this contemporary conception of the soul, in the course of its successive evolution."

Fourth: Since this no-fault liability is linked to a risk that can never entirely be eliminated, indemnity is not meant to sanction it as a sort of punishment but, rather, to repair its effects and also to tend, in an asymptotic way, toward an eventual reduction of its risks. By eliminating the element of fault within the system of liability, the civil legislators introduced into law the notion of causal probability and of risk, and they brought forward the idea of a sanction whose function would be to defend, to protect, to exert pressure on inevitable risks.

In a rather strange way, this depenalization of civil liability would constitute a model for penal law, on the basis of the fundamental propositions formulated by criminal anthropology. After all, what is a "born criminal" or a degenerate, or a criminal personality, if not someone who, according to a causal chain that is difficult to reconstruct, carries a particularly high index of criminal probability and is in himself a criminal risk? Well, just as one can determine civil liability without establishing fault—but solely by estimating the risk created and against which it is necessary to build up a defense (although it can never be eliminated)—in the same way, one can render an individual responsible under law without having to determine whether he was acting freely and, therefore, whether there was fault but, rather, by linking the act committed to the risk of criminality his very personality constitutes. He is responsible since, by his very existence, he is a creator of risk, even if he is not at fault, since he has not of his own free will chosen evil rather than good. Thus, the purpose of the sanction will not be to punish a legal subject who has voluntarily broken the law; its role will be to reduce as much as possible—either by elimination, or by exclusion or by various restrictions, or by therapeutic measures—the risk of criminality represented by the individual in question.

The general idea of the *Social Defense*, as it was put forward by Prinz at the beginning of the twentieth century, was developed by transferring to criminal justice formulations proper to the new civil law. The history of the conferences on Criminal Anthropology and conferences on penal law at the turn of the century, the chronicle of the conflicts between positivist scholars and traditional jurists, and the sudden détente that occurred at the time of Liszt, of Saleilles, of Prinz, the rapid eclipse of the Italian School after that, but also the reduction of the jurists' resistance to the psychological approach to the criminal, the establishment of a relative consensus around a criminology that would be accessible to the law, and of a system of sanctions that would take into account criminological knowledge—all of these seem indeed to indicate that at that moment the required "shunting switch" had just been found. This "switch" is the key notion of *risk* which the law assimilates through the idea of a no-fault liability, and which anthropology, or psychology, or psychiatry can assimilate through the idea of imputability without freedom. The term, henceforth central, of "dangerous being" was probably introduced by Prinz at the September 1905 session of the International Union of Penal Law.

I will not list here the innumerable legal codes, rules, and memoranda that carried into effect, in one way or another, this notion of the *dangerous state* of an individual in penal institutions throughout the world. Let me simply underline a couple of things.

First, since the great crimes without reason of the early nineteenth century, the debate did not in fact revolve so much around freedom, even though the question was always there. The real problem, the one in effect throughout, was the problem of the dangerous individual. Are there individuals who are intrinsically dangerous? By what signs can they be recognized, and how can one react to their presence? In the course of the past century, penal law did not evolve from an ethic of freedom to a science of psychic determinism; rather, it enlarged, organized, and codified the suspicion and the locating of dangerous individuals, from the rare and monstrous figure of the monomaniac to the common everyday figure of the degenerate, of the pervert, of the constitutionally unbalanced, of the immature, and so on.

It must also be noted that this transformation took place not only from medicine toward law, as through the pressure of rational knowledge on older prescriptive systems; it also operated through a perpetual mechanism of summoning and of interacting between medical or psychological knowledge and the judicial institution. It was not the latter that yielded. A set of objects and of concepts was born at their boundaries and from their interchanges.

This is the point I would like to stress, for it seems that most of the notions thus formed are operational for legal medicine or for psychiatric expertise in criminal matters. But has not something more been introduced into the law than the uncertainties of a problematic knowledge—to wit, the rudiments of another type of law? For the modern system of sanctions—most strikingly since Beccaria—gives society a claim to individuals only because of what they do. Only an act, defined by law as an infraction, can result in a sanction, modifiable of course according to the circumstances or the intentions. But by bringing increasingly to the fore not only the criminal as author of the act, but also the dangerous individual as potential source of acts, does not one give society rights over the individual based on what he is? No longer, of course, based on what he is by statute (as was the case in the societies under the Ancien Régime), but on what he is by nature, according to his constitution, character traits, or his pathological variables. A form of justice that tends to be applied to what one is—this is what is so outrageous when one thinks of the penal law of which the eighteenth-century reformers had dreamed, which was intended to sanction, in a completely egalitarian way, offenses explicitly defined beforehand by the law.

It could be objected that, in spite of this general principle, even in the nineteenth century the right to punish was applied and varied on the basis not only of what men do but also of what they are, or of what it is supposed that they are. Hardly had the great modern codes been established when attempts were made to mitigate them by legislation such as the laws dealing with extenuating circumstances, with recidivism, and with conditional release. It was a matter of taking into account the author behind the acts that had been committed. And a complete and comparative study of the legal decisions would no doubt easily show that on the penal stage the offenders were at least as present as their offenses. A form of justice applied only to what one does is probably purely utopian and not necessarily desirable. But, since the eighteenth century at least, it has constituted the guiding principle, the juridico-moral principle that governs the modern system of sanctions. There was, therefore, no question— there can still be no question—of suddenly putting it aside. Only insidiously, slowly, and, as it were, from below and fragmentally, has a system of sanctions based on what one *is* been taking shape. It has taken nearly one hundred years for the notion of "dangerous individual," which was potentially present in the monomania of the first alienists, to be accepted in judicial thought. After one hundred years, although this notion may have become a central theme in psychiatric expertise (in France, psychiatrists appointed as experts speak about the dangerousness of an individual much more than about his responsibility), the law and the codes seem reluctant to give it a place. The revision of the penal code presently under way in France has just barely succeeded in replacing the older notion of *dementia* (which made the author of an act not responsible) with the notions of discernment and control, which in effect are only another version of the same thing, hardly modernized at all. Perhaps this indicates a foreboding of the dreadful dangers inherent in authorizing the law to intervene against individuals because of what they are: a horrifying society could emerge from that.

Nonetheless, on the functional level, judges more and more need to believe that they are judging a man as he is and according to what he is. The scene I described at the beginning bears witness to this. When a man comes before his judges with nothing but his crimes, when he has nothing else to say but "this is what I have done," when he has nothing to say about himself, when he does not do the tribunal the favor of confiding to them something like the secret of his own being, then the judicial machine ceases to function.

NOTES

*This essay was first published in English in the *Journal of Law and Psychiatry* in 1978. [eds.]

GOVERNMENTALITY*

Ⅰn a previous lecture on "apparatuses of security," I tried to explain the emergence of a set of problems specific to the issue of population; on closer inspection, it turned out that we would also need to take into account the problematic of government. In short, one needed to analyze the series: security, population, government. I would now like to try to begin making an inventory of this question of government.

Throughout the Middle Ages and classical Antiquity, we find a multitude of treatises presented as "advice to the prince," concerning his proper conduct, the exercise of power, the means of securing the acceptance and respect of his subjects, the love of God and obedience to him, the application of divine law to the cities of men, and so on. But a more striking fact is that, from the middle of the sixteenth century to the end of the eighteenth, there develops and flourishes a notable series of political treatises that are no longer exactly "advice to the prince," and not yet treatises of political science, but instead are presented as works on the "art of government." Government as a general problem seems to me to explode in the sixteenth century, posed by discussions of quite diverse questions. One has, for example, the question of the government of oneself, that ritualization of the problem of personal conduct characteristic of the sixteenth century Stoic revival. There is the problem too of the government of souls and lives, the entire theme of Catholic and Protestant pastoral doctrine. There is government of children and the great problematic of pedagogy that emerges and develops during the sixteenth century. And, perhaps only as the last of these questions to be taken up, there is the government of the state by the prince. How to govern oneself, how to be governed, how to govern others, by whom the people will accept being governed, how to become the best possible governor—all these problems, in their multiplicity and intensity, seem to me to be characteristic of the sixteenth century, which lies, to put it schematically, at the crossroads of two processes: the one that, shattering the structures of feudalism, leads to the establishment of the great territorial, administrative, and colonial states; and a totally different movement that, with the Reformation and Counterreformation, raises the issue of how one must be spiritually ruled and led on this earth in order to achieve eternal salvation.

There is a double movement, then, of state centralization, on the one hand, and of dispersion and religious dissidence, on the other. It is, I believe, at the intersection of these two tendencies that the problem comes to pose itself with this peculiar intensity, of how to be ruled, how strictly, by whom, to what end, by what methods, and so on. There is a problematic of government in general.

Out of all this immense and monotonous literature on government which extends to the end of the eighteenth century, with the transformations I will try to identify in a moment, I would like to underline some points that are worthy of notice because they relate to the actual definition of what is meant by the government of the state, of what we would today call the political form of government. The simplest way to do this is to compare all of this literature with a single text that, from the sixteenth to the eighteenth century, never ceased to function as the object of explicit or implicit opposition and rejection, and relative to which the whole literature on government established its standpoint—Machiavelli's *The Prince*. It would be interesting to trace the relationship of this text to all those works that succeeded, criticized, and rebutted it.

We must first of all remember that Machiavelli's *The Prince* was not immediately made an object of execration; on the contrary, it was honored by its immediate contemporaries and immediate successors, and once again at the end of the eighteenth century (or perhaps rather at the very beginning of the nineteenth century), at the very moment when all this literature on the art of government was about to come to an end. *The Prince* reemerges at the beginning of the nineteenth century, especially in Germany, where it is translated, prefaced, and commented upon by writers such as A. W. Rehberg, H. Leo, Leopold von Ranke, and Kellerman. In Italy as well, it makes its appearance in context that is worth analyzing, one that is partly Napoleonic but also partly created by the Revolution and the problems of revolution in the United States, of how and under what conditions a ruler's sovereignty over the state can be maintained. But this is also the context in which there emerges, with Clausewitz, the problem (whose political importance was evident at the Congress of Vienna in 1815) of the relationship between politics and strategy, and the problem of relations of force and the calculation of these relations as a principle of intelligibility and rationalization in international relations; and finally, in addition, it connects with the problem of Italian and German territorial unity, since Machiavelli had been one of those who tried to define the conditions under which Italian territorial unity could be restored.

This is the context in which Machiavelli reemerges. But it is clear that, between the initial honor accorded him in the sixteenth century and his rediscovery at the start of the nineteenth, there was a whole "affair" around his work, one that was complex and took various forms: some explicit praise of Machiavelli (Naudé, Machon), numerous frontal attacks (from Catholic sources: Ambrozio Politi, *Disputationes de Libris a Christiano detestandis*; and from Protestant sources: Innocent Gentillet, *Discours sur les moyens de bien gouverner contre Nicolas Machiavel*, 1576), and also a number of implicit critiques (Guillaume de La Perrière, *Miroir Politique*, 1567; Th. Elyott, *The Governor*, 1580; P. Paruta, *Della Perfezione della Vita politica*, 1579).

This whole debate should not be viewed solely in terms of its relation to Machiavelli's text and what were felt to be its scandalous or radically unacceptable aspects. It needs to be seen in terms of something it was trying to define in its specificity, namely, an art of government. Some authors rejected the idea of a new art of government centered on the state and reason of state, which they stigmatized with the name of Machiavellianism; others rejected Machiavelli by showing that there existed an art of government that was both rational and legitimate, and of which Machiavelli's *The Prince* was only an imperfect approximation or caricature; finally, there were others who, in order to prove the legitimacy of a particular art of government, were willing to justify some at least of Machiavelli's writings (this was what Naudé did to the *Discourses on Livy*; Machon went so far as to attempt to show that nothing was more Machiavellian than the way in which, according to the Bible, God himself and his prophets had guided the Jewish people).

All these authors shared a common concern to distance themselves from a certain conception of the art of government which, once shorn of its theological foundations and religious justifications, took the sole interest of the prince as its object and principle of rationality. Let us leave aside the question of whether the interpretation of Machiavelli in these debates was accurate or not. The essential thing is that they attempted to articulate a kind of rationality that was intrinsic to the art of government, without subordinating it to the problematic of the prince and of his relationship to the principality of which he is lord and master.

Thus, the art of government is defined in a way that differentiates it from a certain capacity of the prince, which some think they can find expounded in Machiavelli's writings but others are unable to find; others still will criticize this art of government as a new form of Machiavellianism.

This politics of *The Prince*, fictitious or otherwise, from which people sought to distance themselves, was characterized by one principle: for Machiavelli, it was alleged, the prince stood in a relation of singularity and externality, and thus of transcendence, to his principality. The prince acquires his principality by inheritance or conquest, but in any case he does not form part of it, he remains external to it. The link that binds him to his principality may have been established through violence, through family heritage, or by treaty, with the complicity or the alliance of other princes; this makes no difference—the link remains, in any event, a purely synthetic one, and there is no fundamental, essential, natural, and juridical connection between the prince and his principality. As a corollary of this, given that this link is external, it will be fragile and continually under threat—from outside by the prince's enemies who seek to conquer or recapture his principality, and from within by subjects who have no a priori reason to accept his rule. Finally, this principle and its corollary lead to a conclusion, deduced as an imperative: that the objective of the exercise of power is to reinforce, strengthen, and protect the principality, but with this last understood to mean not the objective ensemble of its subjects and the territory but, rather, the prince's relation with what he owns, with the territory he has inherited or acquired, and with his subjects. This fragile link is what the art of governing or of being prince, as espoused by Machiavelli, has as its object. Consequently, the mode of analysis of Machiavelli's text will be twofold: to identify dangers (where they come from, what they consist in, their severity: which are the greater, which the slighter), and second, to develop the art of manipulating the relations of forces that will allow the prince to ensure the protection of his principality, understood as the link that binds him to his territory and his subjects.

Schematically, one can say that Machiavelli's *The Prince*, as profiled in all these implicitly or explicitly anti-Machiavellian treatises, is essentially a treatise about the prince's ability to keep his principality. And it is this savoir-faire that the anti-Machiavellian literature wants to replace with something else that's new, namely, the art of government. Having the ability to retain one's principality is not at all the same thing as possessing the art of governing. But what does this latter ability comprise? To get a view of this problem, which is still at a raw and early stage, let us consider one of the earliest texts of this great anti-Machiavellian literature—Guillaume de La Perrière's *Miroir Politique*.

This text, disappointingly thin in comparison with Machiavelli, prefigures a number of important ideas. First of all, what does La Perrière mean by "to govern" and "governor"? What definition does he give of these terms? He writes: "governor can signify monarch, emperor, king, prince, lord, magistrate, prelate, judge and the like." Like La Perrière, others who write on the art of government constantly recall that one speaks also of "governing" a household, souls, children, a province, a convent, a religious order, a family.

These points of simple vocabulary actually have important political implications: Machiavelli's prince, at least as these authors interpret him, is by definition unique in his principality and occupies a position of externality and transcendence. We have seen, however, that practices of government are, on the one hand, multifarious and concern many kinds of people—the head of a family, the superior of a convent, the teacher or tutor of a child or pupil—so that there are several forms of government among which the prince's relation to his state is only one particular mode; on the other hand, though, all these other kinds of government are internal to the state or society. It is within the state that the father will rule the family, the superior the convent, and so on. Thus, we find at once a plurality of forms of government and their immanence to the state: the multiplicity and immanence of these activities distinguish them radically from the transcendent singularity of Machiavelli's prince.

To be sure, among all these forms of government that interweave within the state and society, there remains one special and precise form: there is the question of defining the particular form of governing that can be applied to the state as a whole. Thus, seeking to produce a topology of forms of the art of government, La Mothe Le Vayer, in a text from the following century (consisting of educational writings intended for the French Dauphin), says that there are three fundamental types of government, each of which relates to a particular science or discipline: the art of self-government, connected with morality; the art of properly governing a family, which belongs to economy; and, finally, the science of ruling the state, which concerns politics. In comparison with morality and economy, politics evidently has its own specific nature, which La Mothe Le Vayer states clearly. What matters, notwithstanding this topology, is that the art of government is always characterized by the essential continuity of one type with the other, and of a second type with a third.

This means that, whereas the doctrine of the prince and the juridical theory of sovereignty are constantly attempting to draw the line between the power of the prince and any other form of power—because its task is to explain and justify this essential discontinuity between them—in the art of government the task is to establish a continuity, in both an upward and a downward direction.

Upward continuity means that a person who wishes to govern the state well must first learn how to govern himself, his goods, and his patrimony, after which he will be successful in governing the state. This ascending line characterizes the pedagogies of the prince, which are an important issue at this time, as the example of La Mothe Le Vayer shows: he wrote for the Dauphin first a treatise of morality, then a book of economics, and, finally, a political treatise. It is the pedagogical formation of the prince, then, that will assure this upward continuity. On the other hand, we also have a downward continuity in the sense that, when a state is well run, the head of the family will know how to look after his family, his goods, and his patrimony, which means that individuals will, in turn, behave as they should. This downward line, which transmits to individual behavior and the running of the family the same principles as the good government of the state, is just at this time beginning to be called "police." The prince's pedagogical formation ensures the upward continuity of the forms of government, and police the downward one. The central term of this continuity is the government of the family, termed "economy."

The art of government, as becomes apparent in this literature, is essentially concerned with answering the question of how to introduce economy—that is to say, the correct way of managing individuals, goods, and wealth within the family (which a good father is expected to do in relation to his wife, children, and servants) and of making the family fortunes prosper—how to introduce this meticulous attention of the father toward his family into the management of the state.

This, I believe, is the essential issue in the establishment of the art of government—introduction of economy into political practice. And if this is the case in the sixteenth century, it remains so in the eighteenth. In Rousseau's *Encyclopedia* article on "Political Economy," the problem is still posed in the same terms. What he says here, roughly, is that the word "economy" can only properly be used to signify the wise government of the family for the common welfare of all, and this is its actual original use; the problem, writes Rousseau, is how to introduce it, mutatis mutandis, and with all the discontinuities that we will observe below, into the general running of the state. To govern a state will mean, therefore, to apply economy, to set up an economy at the level of the entire state, which means exercising toward its inhabitants, and the wealth and behavior of each and all, a form of surveillance and control as attentive as that of the head of a family over his household and his goods.

An expression that was important in the eighteenth century captures this very well: François Quesnay speaks of good government as "economic government." This latter notion becomes tautological, given that the art of government is just the art of exercising power in the form, and according to the model, of the economy. But the reason why Quesnay speaks of "economic government" is that the word "economy," for reasons I will explain later, is in the process of acquiring a modern meaning, and it is at this moment becoming apparent that the very essence of government—that is, the art of exercising power in the form of economy—is to have as its main objective that which we are today accustomed to call "the economy."

The word "economy," which in the sixteenth century signified a form of government, comes in the eighteenth century to designate a level of reality, a field of intervention, through a series of complex processes that I regard as absolutely fundamental to our history.

The second point I should like to discuss in Guillaume de La Perrière's book consists of the following statement: "government is the right disposition of things, arranged so as to lead to a convenient end."

I would like to link this sentence with another series of observations. Government is the right disposition of things. I would like to pause over this word "things" because, if we consider what characterizes the ensemble of objects of the prince's power in Machiavelli, we will see that for Machiavelli the object and, in a sense, the target of power are two things—on the one hand, the territory, and, on the other, its inhabitants. In this respect, Machiavelli simply adapted to his particular aims a juridical principle that from the Middle Ages to the sixteenth century defined sovereignty in public law: sovereignty is exercised not on things but, above all, on a territory and consequently on the subjects who inhabit it. In this sense, we can say that the territory is the fundamental element both in Machiavellian principality and in juridical sovereignty as defined by the theoreticians and philosophers of right. Obviously enough, these territories can be fertile or infertile, the population dense or sparse, the inhabitants rich or poor, active or lazy, but all these elements are mere variables by comparison with territory itself, which is the very foundation of principality and sovereignty. On the contrary, in La Perrière's text, you will notice that the definition of government in no way refers to territory: one governs *things*. But what does this mean? I think this is not a matter of opposing things to men but, rather, of showing that what government has to do with is not territory but, rather, a sort of complex composed of men and things. The things, in this sense, with which government is to be concerned are in fact men, but men in their relations, their links, their imbrication with those things that are wealth, resources, means of subsistence, the territory with its specific qualities, climate, irrigation, fertility, and so on; men in their relation to those other things that are customs, habits, ways of acting and thinking, and so on; and finally men in their relation to those still other things that might be accidents and misfortunes such as famine, epidemics, death, and so on. The fact that government concerns things understood in this way, this imbrication of men and things, is, I believe, readily confirmed by the metaphor that is inevitably invoked in these treatises on government, namely, that of the ship. What does it mean to govern a ship? It means clearly to take charge of the sailors, but also of the boat and its cargo; to take care of a ship means also to reckon with winds, rocks, and storms; and it consists in that activity of establishing a relation between the sailors, who are to be taken care of, and the ship, which is to be taken care of, and the cargo, which is to be brought safely to port, and all those eventualities like winds, rocks, storms, and so on. This is what characterizes the government of a ship. The same goes for the running of a household. Governing a household, a family, does not essentially mean safeguarding the family property; what it concerns is the individuals who compose the family, their wealth and prosperity. It means reckoning with all the possible events that may intervene, such as births and deaths, and with all the things that can be done, such as possible alliances with other families; it is this general form of management that is characteristic of government. By comparison, the question of landed property for the family, and the question of the acquisition of sovereignty over a territory for a prince, are only relatively secondary matters. What counts essentially is this complex of men and things; property and territory are merely one of its variables.

This theme of the government of things as we find it in La Perrière can also be met with in the seventeenth and eighteenth centuries. Frederick the Great has some notable pages on it in his *Anti-Machiavel*. He says, for instance, let us compare Holland with Russia: Russia may have the largest territory of any European state, but it is mostly made up of swamps, forests, and deserts, and is inhabited by miserable groups of people totally destitute of activity and industry; if one takes Holland, on the other hand, with its tiny territory, again mostly marshland, we find that it nevertheless possesses such a population, such wealth, such commercial activity, and such a fleet as to make it an important European state, something that Russia is only just beginning to become.

To govern, then, means to govern things. Let us consider once more the sentence I quoted earlier, where La Perrière says: "government is the right disposition of things, arranged so as to lead to a convenient end." Government, that is to say, has a finality of its own, and in this respect again, I believe, it can be clearly distinguished from sovereignty. Of course, I do not mean that sovereignty is presented in philosophical and juridical texts as a pure and simple right; no jurist or, a fortiori, theologian ever said that the legitimate sovereign is purely and simply entitled to exercise his power regardless of its ends. The sovereign must always, if he is to be a good sovereign, have as his aim "the common welfare and the salvation of all." Take for instance a late seventeenth-century author. Pufendorf says: "Sovereign authority is conferred upon them [the rulers] only in order to allow them to use it to attain or conserve what is of public utility." The ruler may not have consideration for anything advantageous for himself, unless it also be so for the state. What does this common good or general salvation consist of, which the jurists talk about as being the end of sovereignty? If we look closely at the real content that jurists and theologians give to it, we can see that "the common good" refers to a state of affairs where all the subjects without exception obey the laws, accomplish the tasks expected of them, practice the trade to which they are assigned, and respect the established order insofar as this order conforms to the laws imposed by God on nature and men: in other words, "the common good" means essentially obedience to the law, either that of their earthly sovereign or that of God, the absolute sovereign. In every case, what characterizes the end of sovereignty, this common and general good, is in sum nothing other than submission to sovereignty. This means that the end of sovereignty is the exercise of sovereignty. The good is obedience to the law, hence the good for sovereignty is that people should obey it. This is an essential circularity; whatever its theoretical structure, moral justification, or practical effects, it comes very close to what Machiavelli said when he stated that the primary aim of the prince was to retain his principality. We always come back to this self-referring circularity of sovereignty or principality.

Now, with the new definition given by La Perrière, with his attempt at a definition of government, I believe we can see a new kind of finality emerging. Government is defined as a right manner of disposing things so as to lead not to the form of the common good, as the jurists' texts would have said, but to an end that is "convenient" for each of the things that are to be governed. This implies a plurality of specific aims: for instance, government will have to ensure that the greatest possible quantity of wealth is produced, that the people are provided with sufficient means of subsistence, that the population is enabled to multiply, and so on. Thus, there is a whole series of specific finalities that become the objective of government as such. In order to achieve these various finalities, things must be disposed—and this term, "dispose," is important because, with sovereignty, the instrument that allowed it to achieve its aim—that is, obedience to the laws—was the law itself: law and sovereignty were absolutely inseparable. On the contrary, with government it is a question not of imposing law on men but of disposing things: that is, of employing tactics rather than laws, and even of using laws themselves as tactics—to arrange things in such a way that, through a certain number of means, such-and-such ends may be achieved.

I believe we are at an important turning point here: whereas the end of sovereignty is internal to itself and possesses its own intrinsic instruments in the shape of its laws, the finality of government resides in the things it manages and in the pursuit of the perfection and intensification of the processes it directs; and the instruments of government, instead of being laws, now come to be a range of multiform tactics. Within the perspective of government, law is not what is important: this is a frequent theme throughout the seventeenth century, and it is made explicit in the eighteenth-century texts of the Physiocrats, which explain that it is not through law that the aims of government are to be reached.

Finally, a fourth remark, still concerning this text from La Perrière. He says that a good ruler must have patience, wisdom, and diligence. What does he mean by patience? To explain it, he gives the example of the king of bees, the bumblebee, who, he says, rules the beehive without needing a sting; through this example, God has sought to show us in a mystical way that the good governor does not have to have a sting—that is to say, a weapon of killing, a sword—in order to exercise his power; he must have patience rather than wrath, and it is not the right to kill, to employ force, that forms the essence of the figure of the governor. And what positive content accompanies this absence of sting? Wisdom and diligence. Wisdom, understood no longer in the traditional sense as knowledge of divine and human laws, of justice and equality, but, rather, as the knowledge of things, of the objectives that can and should be attained, and the disposition of things required to reach them: it is this knowledge that is to constitute the wisdom of the sovereign. As for his diligence, this is the principle that a governor should only govern in such a way that he thinks and acts as though he were in the service of those who are governed. And here, once again, La Perrière cites the example of the head of the family who rises first in the morning and goes to bed last, who concerns himself with everything in the household because he considers himself as being in its service. We can see at once how far this characterization of government differs from the idea of the prince as found in or attributed to Machiavelli. To be sure, this notion of governing, for all its novelty, is still very crude here.

This schematic presentation of the notion and theory of the art of government did not remain a purely abstract question in the sixteenth century, and it was of concern not only to political theoreticians. I think we can identify its connections with political reality. The theory of the art of government was linked, from the sixteenth century, to the whole development of the administrative apparatus of the territorial monarchies, the emergence of governmental apparatuses; it was also connected to a set of analyses and forms of knowledge that began to develop in the late sixteenth century and grew in importance during the seventeenth. These were essentially to do with knowledge of the state, in all its different elements, dimensions, and factors of power, questions that were termed precisely "statistics," meaning the science of the state. Finally, as a third vector of connections, I do not think one can fail to relate this search for an art of government to mercantilism and the Cameralists' science of police.

To put it very schematically, in the late sixteenth century and early seventeenth century, the art of government finds its first form of crystallization, organized around the theme of reason of state, understood not in the negative and pejorative sense we give to it today (as that which infringes on the principles of law, equity, and humanity in the sole interests of the state) but in a full and positive sense: the state is governed according to rational principles that are intrinsic to it and cannot be derived solely from natural or divine laws or the principles of wisdom and prudence. The state, like nature, has its own proper form of rationality, albeit of a different sort. Conversely, the art of government, instead of seeking to found itself in transcendental rules, a cosmological model, or a philosophico-moral ideal, must find the principles of its rationality in that which constitutes the specific reality of the state. In my subsequent lectures, I will be examining the elements of this first form of state rationality. But we can say here that, right until the early eighteenth century, this form of "reason of state" acted as a sort of obstacle to the development of the art of government.

This is for a number of reasons. First, there are the strictly historical ones, the series of great crises of the seventeenth century: first the Thirty Years' War with its ruin and devastation; then, in the midcentury, the peasant and urban rebellions; and finally the financial crisis, the crisis of revenues that affected all Western monarchies at the end of the century. The art of government could only spread and develop in subtlety in an age of expansion, free from the great military, political, and economic tensions that afflicted the seventeenth century from beginning to end. Massive and elementary historical causes thus blocked the propagation of the art of government. I think also that the doctrine formulated during the sixteenth century was impeded in the seventeenth by a series of other factors I might term, to use expressions I do not much care for, "mental" and "institutional" structures. The preeminence of the problem of the exercise of sovereignty—both as a theoretical question and as a principle of political organization—was the fundamental factor here so long as sovereignty remained the central question. So long as the institutions of sovereignty were the basic political institutions and the exercise of power was conceived as an exercise of sovereignty, the art of government could not be developed in a specific and autonomous way. I think we have a good example of this in mercantilism. Mercantilism might be described as the first sanctioned effort to apply this art of government at the level of political practices and knowledge of the state; in this sense one can in fact say that mercantilism represents a first threshold of

rationality in this art of government which La Perrière's text had
defined in terms more moral than real. Mercantilism is the first
rationalization of exercise of power as a practice of government;
for the first time with mercantilism we see the development of
knowledge [*savoir*] of state that can be used as a tactic of government. All this may be true, but mercantilism was blocked and arrested, I believe, precisely by the fact that it took as its essential
objective the might of the sovereign: it sought a way not so much
to increase the wealth of the country as to allow the ruler to accumulate wealth, build up his treasury, and create the army with
which he could carry out his policies. And the instruments mercantilism used were laws, decrees, regulations—that is, the traditional
weapons of sovereignty. The objective was the sovereign's might,
the instruments those of sovereignty: mercantilism sought to rein-
sert the possibilities opened up by a consciously conceived art of
government within a mental and institutional structure, that of sovereignty, which by its very nature stifled them.

Thus, throughout the seventeenth century up to the liquidation
of the themes of mercantilism at the beginning of the eighteenth,
the art of government remained in a certain sense immobilized. It
was trapped within the inordinately vast, abstract, rigid framework
of the problem and institution of sovereignty. This art of government tried, so to speak, to reconcile itself with the theory of sovereignty by attempting to derive the ruling principles of an art of
government from a renewed version of the theory of sovereignty—
and this is where those seventeenth-century jurists come into the
picture who formalize or ritualize the theory of the contract. Contract theory enables the founding contract, the mutual pledge of
ruler and subjects, to function as a sort of theoretical matrix for
deriving the general principles of an art of government. But although contract theory, with its reflection on the relationship between ruler and subjects, played a very important role in theories
of public law, in practice, as is evidenced by the case of Hobbes
(even though what Hobbes was aiming to discover was the ruling
principles of an art of government), it remained at the stage of the
formulation of general principles of public law.

On the one hand, there was this framework of sovereignty, which
was too large, too abstract, and too rigid; and, on the other, the
theory of government suffered from its reliance on a model that

was too thin, too weak, and too insubstantial, that of the family—an economy of enrichment still based on a model of the family was unlikely to be able to respond adequately to the importance of territorial possessions and royal finance.

How, then, was the art of government able to outflank these obstacles? Here again a number of general processes played their part: the demographic expansion of the eighteenth century, connected with an increasing abundance of money, which in turn was linked to the expansion of agricultural production through a series of circular processes with which the historians are familiar. If this is the general picture, then we can say more precisely that the art of government found fresh outlets through the emergence of the problem of population; or let us say, rather, that a subtle process took place, which we must seek to reconstruct in its particulars, through which the science of government, the recentering of the theme of economy on a different plane from that of the family, and the problem of population are all interconnected.

It was through the development of the science of government that the notion of economy came to be recentered onto that different plane of reality we characterize today as the "economic," and it was also through this science that it became possible to identify problems specific to the population. But, conversely, we can say as well that it was thanks to the perception of the specific problems of the population, and thanks to the isolation of that area of reality we call the economy, that the problem of government finally came to be thought, considered, and calculated outside of the juridical framework of sovereignty. And, further, that "statistics"—which in mercantilist tradition only ever worked within and for the benefit of a monarchical administration that functioned according to the form of sovereignty—now becomes the major technical factor, or one of the major technical factors, of the unfreezing [*déblocage*] of the art of government.

In what way did the problem of population make possible the unfreezing of the art of government? The perspective of population, the reality accorded to specific phenomena of population, render possible the final elimination of the model of the family and the recentering of the notion of economy. Whereas statistics had previously worked within the administrative frame and thus in terms of the functioning of sovereignty, it now gradually reveals that population has its own regularities, its own rate of deaths and diseases, its cycles of scarcity, and so on; statistics shows also that the domain of population involves a range of intrinsic, aggregate effects, phenomena that are irreducible to those of the family, such as epidemics, endemic levels of mortality, ascending spirals of labor and wealth; finally, it shows that, through its shifts, customs, activities, and so on, population has specific economic effects. Statistics, by making it possible to quantify these specific phenomena of population, also shows that this specificity is irreducible to the dimension of the family. The latter now disappears as the model of government, except for a certain number of residual themes of a religious or moral nature. On the other hand, what now emerges into prominence is the family considered as an element internal to population, and as a fundamental instrument in its government.

In other words, prior to the emergence of population, it was impossible to conceive the art of government except on the model of the family, in terms of economy conceived as the management of a family. From the moment when, on the contrary, population appears absolutely irreducible to the family, the latter becomes of secondary importance compared to population as an element internal to population: that is, no longer a model but a segment. Nevertheless, it remains a privileged segment, because whenever information is required concerning the population (sexual behavior, demography, consumption, and so on), it must be obtained through the family. But the family becomes an instrument rather than a model—the privileged instrument for the government of the population and not the chimerical model of good government. This shift from the level of the model to that of an instrument is, I believe, absolutely fundamental, and it is from the middle of the eighteenth century that the family appears in this dimension of instrumentality relative to the population, with the institution of campaigns to reduce mortality, and to promote marriages, vaccinations, and so on. Thus, what makes it possible for the theme of population to unblock the field of the art of government is this elimination of the family as model.

In the second place, population comes to appear above all else as the ultimate end of government. In contrast to sovereignty, government has as its purpose not the act of government itself, but the welfare of the population, the improvement of its condition, the increase of its wealth, longevity, health, and so on; and the means the government uses to attain these ends are themselves all, in some sense, immanent to the population; it is the population itself on which government will act either directly, through large-scale campaigns, or indirectly, through techniques that will make possible, without the full awareness of the people, the stimulation of birth rates, the directing of the flow of population into certain regions or activities, and so on. The population now represents more the end of government than the power of the sovereign; the population is the subject of needs, of aspirations, but it is also the object in the hands of the government, aware, vis-à-vis the government, of what it wants, but ignorant of what is being done to it. Interest as the consciousness of each individual who makes up the population, and interest considered as the interest of the population regardless of what the particular interests and aspirations may be of the individuals who compose it: this is the new target and the fundamental instrument of the government of population. This is the birth of a new art, or at any rate of a range of absolutely new tactics and techniques.

Finally, population is the point around which is organized what in sixteenth-century texts came to be called the "patience" of the sovereign, in the sense that the population is the object that government must take into account in all its observations and knowledge [*savoir*], in order to be able to govern effectively in a rational and conscious manner. The constitution of knowledge [*savoir*] of government is absolutely inseparable from that of a knowledge of all the processes related to population in its larger sense—that is, what we now call the economy. I said in my last lecture that the constitution of political economy depended upon the emergence, from among all the various elements of wealth, a new subject—population. The new science called "political economy" arises out of the perception of new networks of continuous and multiple relations between population, territory, and wealth; and this is accompanied by the formation of a type of intervention characteristic of government, namely, intervention in the field of economy and population. In other words, the transition that takes place in the eighteenth century from an art of government to a political science,

from a regime dominated by structures of sovereignty to one ruled
by techniques of government, turns on the theme of population,
hence also on the birth of political economy.

This is not to say that sovereignty ceases to play a role from the
moment when the art of government begins to become a political
science. On the contrary, I would say that the problem of sovereignty was never posed with greater force than at this time, because
it no longer involved—as it had in the sixteenth and seventeenth
centuries—an attempt to derive an art of government from a theory
of sovereignty; instead, given that such an art now existed and was
spreading, it involved an attempt to see what juridical and institutional form, what foundation in the law, could be given to the sovereignty that characterizes a state. It suffices to read in
chronological succession two different texts by Rousseau. In his *Encyclopedia* article on "Political Economy," we can see the way in
which Rousseau sets up the problem of the art of government by
pointing out (and the text is very characteristic from this point of
view) that the word "economy" essentially signifies the management of family property by the father, but that this model can no
longer be accepted, even if it had been valid in the past; today, says
Rousseau, we know that political economy is not the economy of
the family. And even without making explicit reference to the Physiocrats, to statistics, or to the general problem of the population,
he sees quite clearly this turning point consisting in the fact that
the economy of "political economy" has a totally new sense that
cannot be reduced to the old model of the family. He undertakes in
this article the task of giving a new definition of the art of government. Later he writes *The Social Contract*, where he poses the problem of how it is possible, using concepts such as nature, contract,
and general will, to provide a general principle of government that
allows room both for a juridical principle of sovereignty and for the
elements through which an art of government can be defined and
characterized. Consequently, sovereignty is far from being eliminated by the emergence of a new art of government, even by one
that has passed the threshold of political science; on the contrary,
the problem of sovereignty is made more acute than ever.

As for discipline, this is not eliminated either; clearly, its modes
of organization, all the institutions within which it had developed
in the seventeenth and eighteenth centuries—schools, manufacto-

ries, armies, and so on—all this can only be understood on the basis of the development of the great administrative monarchies. Nevertheless, though, discipline was never more important or more valorized than at the moment when it became important to manage a population: the managing of a population not only concerns the collective mass of phenomena, the level of its aggregate effects, but it also implies the management of population in its depths and its details. The notion of a government of population renders all the more acute the problem of the foundation of sovereignty (consider Rousseau) and all the more acute equally the necessity for the development of discipline (consider all the history of the disciplines, which I have attempted to analyze elsewhere).

Accordingly, we need to see things not in terms of the replacement of a society of sovereignty by a disciplinary society and the subsequent replacement of a disciplinary society by a society of government; in reality one has a triangle, sovereignty–discipline–government, which has as its primary target the population and as its essential mechanism the apparatuses of security. In any case, I wanted to demonstrate the deep historical link between the movement that overturns the constants of sovereignty in consequence of the problem of choices of government; the movement that brings about the emergence of population as a datum, as a field of intervention, and as an objective of governmental techniques; the process that isolates the economy as a specific sector of reality; and political economy as the science and the technique of intervention of the government in that field of reality. Three movements—government, population, political economy—that constitute from the eighteenth century onward a solid series, one that even today has assuredly not been dissolved.

In conclusion, I would like to say that, on second thought, the more exact title I would like to have given to the course of lectures I have begun this year is not the one I originally chose, "Security, Territory, and Population": what I would like to undertake is something I would term a history of "governmentality." By this word I mean three things:

1. The ensemble formed by the institutions, procedures, analyses, and reflections, the calculations and tactics that allow the exercise of this very specific albeit complex form of power,

which has as its target population, as its principal form of knowledge political economy, and as its essential technical means apparatuses of security.

2. The tendency that, over a long period and throughout the West, has steadily led toward the preeminence over all other forms (sovereignty, discipline, and so on) of this type of power—which may be termed "government"—resulting, on the one hand, in the formation of a whole series of specific governmental apparatuses, and, on the other, in the development of a whole complex of knowledges [*savoirs*].

3. The process or, rather, the result of the process through which the state of justice of the Middle Ages transformed into the administrative state during the fifteenth and sixteenth centuries and gradually becomes "governmentalized."

We all know the fascination that the love, or horror, of the state exercises today; we know how much attention is paid to the genesis of the state, its history, its advance, its power, abuses, and so on. The excessive value attributed to the problem of the state is expressed, basically, in two ways: the one form, immediate, affective, and tragic, is the lyricism of the cold monster we see confronting us. But there is a second way of overvaluing the problem of the state, one that is paradoxical because it is apparently reductionist: it is the form of analysis that consists in reducing the state to a certain number of functions, such as the development of productive forces and the reproduction of relations of production, and yet this reductionist vision of the relative importance of the state's role nevertheless invariably renders it absolutely essential as a target needing to be attacked and a privileged position needing to be occupied. But the state, no more probably today than at any other time in its history, does not have this unity, this individuality, this rigorous functionality, nor, to speak frankly, this importance. Maybe, after all, the state is no more than a composite reality and a mythicized abstraction, whose importance is a lot more limited than many of us think. Maybe what is really important for our modernity—that is, for our present—is not so much the statization [*étatisation*] of society, as the "governmentalization" of the state.

We live in the era of a "governmentality" first discovered in the eighteenth century. This governmentalization of the state is a singularly paradoxical phenomenon: if in fact the problems of governmentality and the techniques of government have become the only political issue, the only real space for political struggle and contestation, this is because the governmentalization of the state is, at the same time, what has permitted the state to survive. It is possible to suppose that if the state is what it is today, this is so precisely thanks to this governmentality, which is at once internal and external to the state—since it is the tactics of government that make possible the continual definition and redefinition of what is within the competence of the state and what is not, the public versus the private, and so on. Thus, the state can only be understood in its survival and its limits on the basis of the general tactics of governmentality.

And maybe we could even, albeit in a very global, rough, and inexact fashion, reconstitute the great forms, the great economies of power in the West in the following way. First came the state of justice, born in a territoriality of feudal type and corresponding in large part to a society of the law—customary laws and written laws—with a whole game of engagements and litigations. Second, the administrative state, born in the fifteenth and sixteenth centuries in a frontier and no longer feudal territoriality, an administrative state that corresponds to a society of regulations and disciplines. Finally, the state of government, which is no longer essentially defined by its territoriality, by the surface it occupies, but by a mass: the mass of the population, with its volume, its density, with the territory that it covers, to be sure, but only in a sense as one of its components. And this state of government, which is grounded in its population and which refers and has resort to the instrumentality of economic knowledge, would correspond to a society controlled by apparatuses of security.

There, if you like, are certain pointers [*propos*] for positioning this phenomenon—which I believe to be important—of governmentality. I will try further to show how such governmentality is born, in one part, out of an archaic model, that of the Christian pastoral, and secondly, while drawing support from a diplomatico-military model, or better, technics, and finally, thirdly, how governmentality could not have assumed the dimensions it has except thanks to a series of quite particular instruments, whose formation is precisely contemporary with the art of government, and which one could call, in the old sense of the term, that of the twelfth and thirteenth centuries, the police. The pastoral, the new diplomatico-military technics, and finally the police, I believe, were the three elements from which the phenomenon of the governmentalization of the state, so fundamental in the history of the West, could be produced.

NOTES

* This essay was presented as part of a course on "Security, Territory, and Population" (see summary in *Essential Works*, Vol. 1, pp. 67–71) that Foucault gave at the Collège de France in the 1977–78 academic year. It was first published in 1978. [eds.]

QUESTIONS OF METHOD[*]

WHY THE PRISON?

Q: *Why do you see the birth of the prison—and, in particular, this process you call "hurried substitution," which in the early years of the nineteenth century establishes the prison at the center of the new penal system—as being so important?*

Aren't you inclined to overstate the importance of the prison in penal history, given that other quite distinct modes of punishment (the death penalty, the penal colonies, deportation) remained in effect too? At the level of historical methods, you seem to scorn explanations in terms of causality or structure, and sometimes to prioritize a description of a process that is purely one of events. No doubt, it's true that the preoccupation with "social history" has invaded historians' work in an uncontrolled manner; but even if one does not accept the "social" as the only valid level of historical explanation, is it right for you to throw out social history altogether from your "interpretative diagram"?

A: I wouldn't want what I may have said or written to be seen as laying any claims to totality. I don't try to universalize what I say; conversely, what I don't say isn't meant to be thereby disqualified as being of no importance. My work takes place between unfinished abutments and anticipatory strings of dots. I like to open up a space of research, try it out, and then if it doesn't work, try again somewhere else. On many points—I am thinking especially of the relations between dialectics, genealogy, and strategy—I am still working and don't yet know whether I am going to get anywhere. What I say ought to be taken as "propositions," "game openings" where those who may be interested are invited to join in—they are not meant as dogmatic assertions that have to be taken or left en bloc. My books aren't treatises in philosophy or studies of history; at most, they are philosophical fragments put to work in a historical field of problems.

I will attempt to answer the questions that have been posed. First, about the prison. You wonder whether it was as important as I have claimed, or whether it acted as the real focus of the penal system. I don't mean to suggest that the prison was the essential core of the entire penal system; nor am I saying that it would be impossible to approach the problems of penal history—not to speak of the history of crime in general—by other routes than the history of the prison. But it seemed to me legitimate to take the prison as my object, for two reasons. First, because it had been rather neglected in previous analyses; when people had set out to study the problems of "the penal order" [*pénalité*]—a confused enough term, in any case— they usually opted to prioritize one of two directions: either the sociological problem of the criminal population, or the juridical problem of the penal system and its basis. The actual practice of punishment was scarcely studied except, in the line of the Frankfurt School, by Georg Rusche and Otto Kircheimer. There have indeed been studies of prisons as institutions, but very few of imprisonment as a general punitive practice in our societies.

My second reason for wanting to study the prison was the idea of reactivating the project of a "genealogy of morals," one that worked by tracing the lines of transformation of what one might call "moral technologies." In order to get a better understanding of what is punished and why, I wanted to ask the question *how* does one punish? This was the same procedure as I had used when dealing with madness: rather than asking *what*, in a given period, is regarded as sanity or insanity, as mental illness or normal behavior, I wanted to ask *how* these divisions are effected. It's a method that seems to me to yield—I wouldn't say the maximum of possible illumination—at least a fairly fruitful kind of intelligibility.

There was also, while I was writing this book, a contemporary issue relating to the prison and, more generally, to the numerous aspects of penal practice being brought into question. This development was noticeable not only in France but also in the United States, Britain, and Italy. Incidentally, it would be interesting to consider why all these problems about confinement, internment, the penal dressage of individuals and their distribution, classification, and objectification through forms of knowledge came to be posed so urgently at this time, well in advance of May 1968: the themes of antipsychiatry were formulated around 1958 to 1960. The connection with the matter of the concentration camps is evident—look at Bruno Bettelheim.[1] But one would need to analyze more closely what took place around 1960.

In this piece of research on the prisons, as in my other earlier work, the target of analysis wasn't "institutions," "theories," or "ideology" but *practices*—with the aim of grasping the conditions that make these acceptable at a given moment; the hypothesis being that these types of practice are not just governed by institutions, prescribed by ideologies, guided by pragmatic circumstances— whatever role these elements may actually play—but, up to a point, possess their own specific regularities, logic, strategy, self-evidence, and "reason." It is a question of analyzing a "regime of practices"—practices being understood here as places where what is said and what is done, rules imposed and reasons given, the planned and the taken-for-granted meet and interconnect.

To analyze "regimes of practices" means to analyze programs of conduct that have both prescriptive effects regarding what is to be done (effects of "jurisdiction") and codifying effects regarding what is to be known (effects of "veridiction").

So I was aiming to write a history not of the prison as an institution, but of the *practice of imprisonment*: to show its origin or, more exactly, to show how this way of doing things—ancient enough in itself—was capable of being accepted at a certain moment as a principal component of the penal system, thus coming to seem an altogether natural, self-evident, and indispensable part of it.

It's a matter of shaking this false self-evidence, of demonstrating its precariousness, of making visible not its arbitrariness but its complex interconnection with a multiplicity of historical processes, many of them of recent date. From this point of view, I can say that the history of penal imprisonment exceeded my wildest hopes. All the early nineteenth-century texts and discussions testify to the astonishment at finding the prison being used as a general means of punishment—something that had not at all been what the eighteenth-century reformers had had in mind. I did not at all take this sudden change—which was what its contemporaries recognized it as being—as marking a result at which one's analysis could stop. I took this discontinuity, this—in a sense—"phenomenal" set of mutations, as my starting point and tried, without eradicating it, to account for it. It was a matter not of digging down to a buried stratum of continuity, but of identifying the transformation that made this hurried transition possible.

As you know, no one is more of a continuist than I am: to recognize a discontinuity is never anything more than to register a problem that needs to be solved.

EVENTALIZATION

Q: *What you have just said clears up a number of things. All the same, historians have been troubled by a sort of equivocation in your analyses, a sort of oscillation between "hyperrationalism" and "infrarationality."*

A: I am trying to work in the direction of what one might call "eventalization." Even though the "event" has been for some while now a category little esteemed by historians, I wonder whether, understood in a certain sense, "eventalization" may not be a useful procedure of analysis. What do I mean by this term? First of all, a breach of self-evidence. It means making visible a *singularity* at places where there is a temptation to invoke a historical constant, an immediate anthropological trait, or an obviousness that imposes itself uniformly on all. To show that things "weren't as necessary as all that"; it wasn't as a matter of course that mad people came to be regarded as mentally ill; it wasn't self-evident that the only thing to be done with a criminal was to lock him up; it wasn't self-evident that the causes of illness were to be sought through the individual examination of bodies; and so on. A breach of self-evidence, of those self-evidences on which our knowledges, acquiescences, and practices rest: this is the first theoretico-political function of "eventalization."

Second, eventalization means rediscovering the connections, encounters, supports, blockages, plays of forces, strategies, and so on, that at a given moment establish what subsequently counts as being self-evident, universal, and necessary. In this sense, one is indeed effecting a sort of multiplication or pluralization of causes.

Does this mean that one regards the singularity one is analyzing simply as a fact to be registered, a reasonless break in an inert continuum? Clearly not, since that would amount to treating continuity as a self-sufficient reality that carries its own raison d'être within itself.

This procedure of causal multiplication means analyzing an event according to the multiple processes that constitute it. So, to analyze the practice of penal incarceration as an "event" (not as an institutional fact or ideological effect) means to determine the processes of "penalization" (that is, progressive insertion into the forms of legal punishment) of already existing practices of internment; the processes of "carceralization" of practices of penal justice (that is, the movement by which imprisonment as a form of punishment and technique of correction becomes a central component of the penal order). And these vast processes need themselves to be further broken down: the penalization of internment comprises a multiplicity of processes such as the formation of closed pedagogical spaces functioning through rewards, punishments, and so on.

As a way of lightening the weight of causality, "eventalization" thus works by constructing around the singular event analyzed as process a "polygon" or, rather, "polyhedron" of intelligibility, the number of whose faces is not given in advance and can never properly be taken as finite. One has to proceed by progressive, necessarily incomplete saturation. And one has to bear in mind that the further one breaks down the processes under analysis, the more one is enabled and indeed obliged to construct their external relations of intelligibility. (In concrete terms: the more one analyzes the process of "carceralization" of penal practice down to its smallest details, the more one is led to relate them to such practices as schooling, military discipline, and so on.) The internal analysis of processes goes hand in hand with a multiplication of analytical "salients."

This operation thus leads to an increasing polymorphism as the analysis progresses:

1. A polymorphism of the elements brought into relation: starting from the prison, one introduces the history of pedagogical practices, the formation of professional armies, British empirical philosophy, techniques of use of firearms, new methods of division of labor.

2. A polymorphism of relations described: these may concern the transposition of technical models (such as architectures of surveillance), tactics calculated in response to a particular situation (such as the growth of banditry, the disorder provoked by public tortures and executions, the defects of the practice of penal banishment), or the application of theoretical schemas (such as those representing the genesis of ideas and the formation of signs, the utilitarian conception of behavior, and so on).

3. A polymorphism of domains of reference (varying in their nature, generality, and so on), ranging from technical mutations in matters of detail to the attempted emplacement in a capitalist economy of new techniques of power designed in response to the exigencies of that economy.

Forgive this long detour, but it enables me to better reply to your question about hyper- and hyporationalisms, one that is often put to me.

It has been some time since historians lost their love of events and made "de-eventalization" their principle of historical intelligibility. The way they work is by ascribing the object they analyze to the most unitary, necessary, inevitable, and (ultimately) extrahistorical mechanism or structure available. An economic mechanism, an anthropological structure, or a demographic process that figures the climactic stage in the investigation—these are the goals of de-eventalized history. (Of course, these remarks are only intended as a crude specification of a certain broad tendency.)

Clearly, viewed from the standpoint of this style of analysis, what I am proposing is at once too much and too little. There are too many diverse kinds of relations, too many lines of analysis, yet at the same time there is too little necessary unity. A plethora of intelligibilities, a deficit of necessities.

But for me this is precisely the point at issue, both in historical analysis and in political critique. We aren't, nor do we have to put ourselves, under the sign of a unitary necessity.

THE PROBLEM OF RATIONALITIES

Q: *I would like to pause for a moment on this question of eventalization, because it lies at the center of a certain number of misunderstandings about your work. (I am not talking about the misguided portrayal of you as a "thinker of discontinuity.") Behind the identifying of breaks and the careful, detailed charting of these networks of relations that engender a reality and a history, there persists from one book to the next something amounting to one of those historical constants or anthropologico-cultural traits you were objecting to just now: this version of a general history of rationalization spanning three or four centuries, or at any rate of a history of one particular kind of rationalization as it progressively takes effect in our society. It's not by chance that your first book was a history of reason as well as of madness, and I believe that the themes of all your other books, the analysis of different techniques of isolation, the social taxonomies, and so on—all this boils down to one and the same meta-anthropological or meta-historical process of rationalization. In this sense, the "eventalization" you define here as central to your work seems to me to constitute only one of its extremes.*

A: If one calls "Weberians" those who set out to trade off [*relayer*] the Marxist analysis of the contradictions of capital for that of the irrational rationality of capitalist society, then I don't think I am a Weberian, since my basic preoccupation isn't rationality considered as an athropological invariant. I don't believe one can speak of an intrinsic notion of "rationalization" without, on the one hand, positing an absolute value inherent in reason, and, on the other, taking the risk of applying the term empirically in a completely arbitrary way. I think one must restrict one's use of this word to an instrumental and relative meaning. The ceremony of public torture isn't in itself more irrational than imprisonment in a cell; but it's irrational in terms of a type of penal practice that involves new ways of envisaging the effects to be produced by the penalty imposed, new ways of calculating its utility, justifying it, fixing its degrees and so on. One isn't assessing things in terms of an absolute against which they could be evaluated as constituting more or less perfect forms of rationality but, rather, examining how forms of rationality inscribe themselves in practices or systems of practices, and what role they play within them—because it's true that "practices" don't exist without a certain regime of rationality. But, rather than measuring this regime against a value of reason, I would prefer to analyze it according to two axes: on the one hand, that of codification/prescription (how it forms an ensemble of rules, procedures, means to an end, and so on), and, on the other, that of true or false formulation (how it determines a domain of objects about which it is possible to articulate true or false propositions).

If I have studied "practices" such as those of the sequestration of the insane, or clinical medicine, or the organization of the empirical sciences, or legal punishment, it was in order to study this interplay between a "code" that governs ways of doing things (how people are to be graded and examined, things and signs classified, individuals trained [*trier*], and so on) and a production of true discourses that served to found, justify, and provide reasons and principles for these ways of doing things. To put the matter clearly: my problem is to see how men govern (themselves and others) by the production of truth (I repeat once again that by production of truth I mean not the production of true utterances but the establishment of domains in which the practice of true and false can be made at once ordered and pertinent).

Eventalizing singular ensembles of practices, so as to make them graspable as different regimes of "jurisdiction" and "veridiction": that, to put it in exceedingly barbarous terms, is what I would like to do. You see that this is neither a history of knowledge [*connaissances*] nor an analysis of the advancing rationalities that rule our society, nor an anthropology of the codifications that, without our knowledge, rule our behavior. I would like, in short, to resituate the production of true and false at the heart of historical analysis and political critique.

Q: *It's not an accident that you speak of Max Weber. There is in your work—no doubt, in a sense you wouldn't want to accept—a sort of "ideal type" that paralyzes and mutes analysis when one tries to account for reality. Isn't this what led you to abstain from all commentary when you published the memoir of Pierre Rivère?*

A: I don't think your comparison with Max Weber is exact. Schematically, one can say that the "ideal type" is a category of historical interpretation: it's a structure of understanding for the historian who seeks to integrate, after the fact, a certain set of data—it allows him to recapture an "essence" (Calvinism, the state, the capitalist enterprise), working from general principles that are not at all present in the thought of the individuals whose concrete behavior is nevertheless to be understood on their basis.

When I try to analyze the rationalities proper of penal imprisonment, the psychiatrization of madness, or the organization of the domain of sexuality, and when I lay stress on the fact that the real functioning of institutions isn't confined to the unfolding of this rational schema in its pure form, is this an analysis in terms of "ideal types"? I don't think so, for a number of reasons.

The rational schemas of the prison, the hospital, or the asylum are not general principles that can be rediscovered only through the historian's retrospective interpretation. They are explicit *programs*; we are dealing with sets of calculated, reasoned prescriptions in terms of which institutions are meant to be recognized, spaces arranged, behaviors regulated. If they have an ideality, it is that of a programming left in abeyance, not that of a general but hidden meaning.

Of course, this programming depends on forms of rationality much more general than those they directly implement. I tried to show that the rationality envisaged in penal imprisonment wasn't the outcome of a straightforward calculation of immediate interest (internment turning out to be, in the last analysis, the simplest and cheapest solution), but that it arose out of a whole technology of human training, surveillance of behavior, individualization of the elements of a social body. "Discipline" isn't the expression of an "ideal type" (that of "disciplined man"); it's the generalization and interconnection of different techniques themselves designed in response to localized requirements (schooling, training troops to handle rifles).

These programs don't take effect in the institutions in an integral way; they are simplified, or some are chosen and not others; and things never work out as planned. But what I wanted to show is that this difference is not one between the purity of the ideal and the disorderly impurity of the real, but that in fact there are different strategies that are mutually opposed, composed, and superposed so as to produce permanent and solid effects that can perfectly well be understood in terms of their rationality, even though they don't conform to the initial programming: this is what gives the resulting apparatus its solidity and suppleness.

Programs, technologies, apparatuses—none of these is an "ideal type." I try to study the play and development of a set of diverse realities articulated onto each other; a program, the connection that explains it, the law that gives it its coercive power, and so on, are all just as much realities—albeit in a different mode—as the institutions that embody them or the behaviors that more or less faithfully conform to them.

You say to me: Nothing happens as laid down in these "programs," they are no more than dreams, utopias, a sort of imaginary production that you aren't entitled to substitute for reality. Jeremy Bentham's *Panopticon* isn't a very good description of "real life" in nineteenth-century prisons.

To this I would reply: If I had wanted to describe "real life" in the prisons, I indeed wouldn't have gone to Bentham. But the fact that this real life isn't the same thing as the theoreticians' schemes doesn't entail that these schemes are therefore utopian, imaginary, and so on. One could only think this if one had a very impoverished notion of the real. For one thing, the elaboration of these schemas corresponds to a whole series of diverse practices and strategies: the search for effective, measured, unified penal mechanisms is unquestionably a response to the disalignment of the institutions of judicial power with the new economic forms, urbanization, and so on; again, there is the attempt—very noticeable in a country like France—to reduce the autonomy and insularity of judicial practice and personnel within the overall workings of the state. There is the wish to respond to emerging new forms of criminality, and so on. For another thing, these programs induce a whole series of effects in the real (which isn't of course the same as saying that they take the place of the real): they crystallize into institutions, they inform individual behavior, they act as grids for the perception and evaluation of things. It is absolutely true that criminals stubbornly resisted the new disciplinary mechanism in the prison; it is absolutely correct that the actual functioning of the prisons, in the inherited buildings where they were established and with the governors and guards who administered them, was a witches' brew compared to the beautiful Benthamite machine. But if the prisons were seen to have failed, if criminals were perceived as incorrigible, and a whole new criminal "race" emerged into the field of vision of public opinion and "justice," if the resistance of the prisoners and the pattern of recidivism took the forms we know they did, it's precisely because this type of programming didn't just remain a utopia in the heads of a few contrivers.

These programmings of behavior, these regimes of jurisdiction and veridiction aren't abortive schemas for the creation of a reality. They are fragments of reality that induce such particular effects in the real as the distinction between true and false implicit in the ways men "direct," "govern," and "conduct" themselves and others. To grasp these effects as historical events—with what this implies for the question of truth (which is the question of philosophy itself)—this is more or less my theme. You see that this has nothing to do with the project—an admirable one in itself—of grasping a "whole society" in its "living reality."

The question I won't succeed in answering here but have been asking myself from the beginning is roughly the following: What is history, given that there is continually being produced within it a separation of true and false? By that I mean four things. First, in what sense is the production and transformation of the true/false division characteristic and decisive for our historicity? Second, in what specific ways has this relation operated in Western societies, which produce scientific knowledge whose forms are perpetually changing and whose values are posited as universal? Third, what historical knowledge is possible of a history that itself produces the true/false distinction on which such knowledge depends? Fourth, isn't the most general of political problems the problem of truth? How can one analyze the connection between ways of distinguishing true and false and ways of governing oneself and others? The search for a new foundation for each of these practices, in itself and relative to the other, the will to discover a different way of governing oneself through a different way of dividing up true and false—this is what I would call "political spirituality."

THE ANESTHETIC EFFECT

Q: *There is a question here about the way your analyses have been transmitted and received. For instance, if one talks to social workers in the prisons, one finds that the arrival of* Discipline and Punish *had an absolutely sterilizing or, rather, anesthetizing effect on them, because they felt your critique had an implacable logic that left them no possible room for initiative. You said just now, talking about eventalization, that you want to work toward breaking up existing self-evidences to show both how they are produced and how they are nevertheless always unstable. It seems to me that the second half of the picture — the aspect of instability — isn't clear.*

A: You're quite right to pose this problem of anesthesia, one that is of capital importance. It's quite true that I don't feel myself capable of effecting the "subversion of all codes," "dislocation of all orders of knowledge," "revolutionary affirmation of violence," "overturning of all contemporary culture"—these hopes and prospectuses that currently underpin all those brilliant intellectual ventures I admire all the more because the worth and previous achievements of those who undertake them guarantees an appropriate outcome. My project is far from being of comparable scope. To give some assistance in wearing away certain self-evidences and commonplaces about madness, normality, illness, crime, and punishment; to bring it about, together with many others, that certain phrases can no longer be spoken so lightly, certain acts no longer— or at least no longer so unhesitatingly—performed; to contribute to changing certain things in people's ways of perceiving and doing things; to participate in this difficult displacement of forms of sensibility and thresholds of tolerance—I hardly feel capable of attempting much more than that. If only what I have tried to say might somehow, to some degree, not remain altogether foreign to some such real effects. . . . And yet I realize how much all this can remain precarious, how easily it can all lapse back into somnolence.

But you are right, one has to be more suspicious. Perhaps what I have written has had an anaesthetic effect. But one still needs to distinguish on whom.

To judge by what the psychiatric authorities have had to say, the cohorts on the right who charge me with being against any form of power, those on the left who call me the "last bulwark of the bourgeoisie" (this isn't a pronouncement of Kanapa's—on the contrary), the worthy psychoanalyst who likened me to the Hitler of *Mein Kampf*, the number of times I've been "autopsied" and "buried" during the past fifteen years—well, I have the impression of having had an irritant rather than anesthetic effect on a good many people. The epidermises bristle with a constancy I find encouraging. A journal recently warned its readers in deliciously Pétainist style against accepting as a credo what I had had to say about sexuality ("the importance of the subject," "the personality of the author" rendered my enterprise "dangerous"). No risk of anesthesis in that direction. But I agree with you, these are trifles, amusing to note but tedious to collect. The only important problem is what happens on the ground.

We have known at least since the nineteenth century the difference between anaesthesis and paralysis. Let's talk about paralysis first. Who has been paralyzed? Do you think what I wrote on the history of psychiatry paralyzed those people who had already been concerned for some time about what was happening in psychiatric institutions? And, seeing what has been happening in and around the prisons, I don't think the effect of paralysis is very evident there, either. As far as the people in prison are concerned, things aren't doing too badly. On the other hand, it's true that certain people, such as those who work in the institutional setting of the prison—which is not quite the same as being in prison—are not likely to find advice or instructions in my books that tell them "what is to be done." But my project is precisely to bring it about that they "no longer know what to do," so that the acts, gestures, discourses that up until then had seemed to go without saying become problematic, difficult, dangerous. This effect is intentional. And then I have some news for you: for me, the problem of the prisons isn't one for the "social workers" but one for the prisoners. And on that aside, I'm not so sure what's been said over the last fifteen years has been quite so—how shall put it?—demobilizing.

But paralysis isn't the same thing as anesthesia—on the contrary. It's insofar as there's been an awakening to a whole series of problems that the difficulty of doing anything comes to be felt. Not that this effect is an end in itself. But it seems to me that "what is to be done" ought not to be determined from above by reformers, be they prophetic or legislative, but by a long work of comings and goings, of exchanges, reflections, trials, different analyses. If the social workers you are talking about don't know which way to turn, this just goes to show that they're looking and, hence, are not anesthetized or sterilized at all—on the contrary. And it's because of the need not to tie them down or immobilize them that there can be no question of trying to dictate "what is to be done." If the questions posed by the social workers you spoke of are going to assume their full amplitude, the most important thing is not to bury them under the weight of prescriptive, prophetic discourse. The necessity of reform mustn't be allowed to become a form of blackmail serving to limit, reduce, or halt the exercise of criticism. Under no circumstances should one pay attention to those who tell one: "Don't criticize, since you're not capable of carrying out a reform." That's ministerial cabinet talk. Critique doesn't have to be the premise of a deduction that concludes, "this, then, is what needs to be done." It should be an instrument for those who fight, those who resist and refuse what is. Its use should be in processes of conflict and confrontation, essays in refusal. It doesn't have to lay down the law for the law. It isn't a stage in a programming. It is a challenge directed to what is.

The problem, you see, is one for the subject who acts—the subject of action through which the real is transformed. If prisons and punitive mechanisms are transformed, it won't be because a plan of reform has found its way into the heads of the social workers; it will be when those who have a stake in that reality, all those people, have come into collision with each other and with themselves, run into dead ends, problems, and impossibilities, been through conflicts and confrontations—when critique has been played out in the real, not when reformers have realized their ideas.

Q: *This anesthetic effect has operated on the historians. If they haven't responded to your work it's because, for them, the "Foucauldean schema" was becoming as much of an encumbrance as the Marxist one. I don't know if the "effect" you produce interests you. But the explanations you have given here weren't so clear in* Discipline and Punish.

A: I really wonder whether we are using this word "anesthetize" in the same sense. These historians seemed to me more to be "anasthetized," "irritated" (in Broussais's sense of the term, of course). Irritated by what? By a schema? I don't believe so, because there is no schema. If there is an "irritation" (and I seem to recall that in a certain journal a few signs of this irritation may have been discreetly manifested), it's more because of the absence of a schema. No infra- or superstructure, no Malthusian cycle, no opposition between state and civil society: none of these schemas that have bolstered historians' operations, explicitly or implicitly, for the past hundred or hundred and fifty years.

Hence, no doubt, the sense of malaise and the questions enjoining me to situate myself within some such schema: "How do you deal with the state? What theory do you offer us of the state?" Some say I neglect its role, others that I see it everywhere, imagining it capable of minutely controlling individuals' everyday lives. Or that my descriptions leave out all reference to an infrastructure—while others say that I make an infrastructure out of sexuality. The totally contradictory nature of these objections proves that what I am doing doesn't correspond to any of these schemas.

Perhaps the reason why my work irritates people is precisely the fact that I'm not interested in constructing a new schema or in validating one that already exists. Perhaps it's because my objective isn't to propose a global principle for analyzing society. And it's here that my project has differed since the outset from that of the historians. They—rightly or wrongly, that's another question—take "society" as the general horizon of their analysis, the instance relative to which they set out to situate this or that particular object ("society, economy, civilization," as the *Annales* have it). My general theme isn't society but the discourse of true and false, by which I mean the correlative formation of domains and objects and of the verifiable, falsifiable discourses that bear on them; and it's not just their formation that interests me, but the effects in the real to which they are linked.

I realize I'm not being clear. I'll take an example. It's perfectly legitimate for the historian to ask whether sexual behaviors in a given period were supervised and controlled, and to ask which among them were heavily disapproved of. (It would of course be frivolous to suppose that one had explained a certain intensity of "repression" by the delaying of the age of marriage. Here one has scarcely even begun to outline a problem: why is it that the delay in the age of marriage takes effect thus and not otherwise?) But the problem I pose myself is a quite different one: it's a matter of how the rendering of sexual behavior into discourse comes to be transformed, what types of jurisdiction and "veridiction" it's subject to, and how the constitutive elements are formed of the domain that comes—and only at a very late stage—to be termed "sexuality" are formed. Among the numerous effects the organization of this domain has undoubtedly had, one is that of having provided historians with a category so "self-evident" that they believe they can write a history of sexuality and its repression.

The history of the "objectification" of those elements historians consider as objectively given (if I dare put it thus: of the objectification of objectivities), this is the sort of sphere I would like to traverse. A "tangle," in sum, that is difficult to sort out. This, not the presence of some easily reproducible schema, is what doubtless troubles and irritates people. Of course, this is a problem of philosophy to which the historian is entitled to remain indifferent. But if I am posing it as a problem within historical analysis, I'm not demanding that history answer it. I would just like to find out what effects the question produces within historical knowledge. Paul Veyne saw this very clearly:[3] it's a matter of the effect on historical knowledge of a nominalist critique itself arrived at by way of a historical analysis.

NOTES

* Originally titled "Round Table of 20 May 1978," this interview was published in 1980. The French editors have condensed the questions posed to Foucault by various interlocutors into those of a "collective historian." We preserve their amendation. [eds.]

1 Foucault is referring to Bettelheim's studies of concentration camp survivors; see Bettelheim, *Individual and Mass Behavior in Extreme Situations* (Indianapolis: Bobbs-Merrill, 1943) and *The Informed Heart: Autonomy in a Mass Age* (New York: The Free Press), 1960. [eds.]

2 Jean Kanapa is a leading Marxist and director of *La Nouvelle Critique*.

3 Cf. "Foucault révolutionne l'histoire," in Paul Veyne, *Comment on écrit l'histoire* (2nd ed., Paris: Seuil, 1978).

INTERVIEW WITH MICHEL FOUCAULT*

———————

Q: *The attention paid to your work, especially in the past few years, could be explained in this way, I believe: there aren't many thinking people, whatever their language or ideological viewpoint, who wouldn't acknowledge the progressive and disconcerting dissociation between words and things in the contemporary world. This suggests a direction for our discussion, aimed at a better understanding of the path you've followed in your reflections and inquiries, the shifts of field that have occurred in your analyses, the gaining of new theoretical footholds. From the exploration of fundamental forms of experience* in Madness and Civilization *to the most recent arguments put forward in the first volume of* The History of Sexuality, *it seems that you've proceeded by leaps, by shifts from one level of inquiry to another. If I wanted to draw up an account of the essential elements and points of continuity of your thought, I might begin by asking you what you see as superseded in your previous writings, in light of your recent studies on power and the will to know.*

A: Many things have been superseded, certainly. I'm perfectly aware of always being on the move in relation both to the things I'm interested in and to what I've already thought. What I think is never quite the same, because for me my books are experiences, in a sense, that I would like to be as full as possible. An experience is something that one comes out of transformed. If I had to write a book to communicate what I'm already thinking before I begin to write, I would never have the courage to begin. I write a book only

because I still don't exactly know what to think about this thing I
want so much to think about, so that the book transforms me and
transforms what I think. Each book transforms what I was thinking
when I was finishing the previous book. I am an experimenter and
not a theorist. I call a theorist someone who constructs a general
system, either deductive or analytical, and applies it to different
fields in a uniform way. That isn't my case. I'm an experimenter in
the sense that I write in order to change myself and in order not to
think the same thing as before.

Q: *In any case, the idea of a work as an experience should suggest a*
methodological reference point or at least offer the possibility of get-
ting some ideas about method from the relation between the means
you use and the results you arrive at in the research.
A: When I begin a book, not only do I not know what I'll be thinking at the end, but it's not very clear to me what method I will
employ. Each of my books is a way of carving out an object and of
fabricating a method of analysis. Once my work is finished, through
a kind of retrospective reflection on the experience I've just gone
through, I can extrapolate the method the book ought to have followed—so that I write books I would call exploratory somewhat in
alternation with books of method. Exploratory books: *Madness and*
Civilization The Birth of the Clinic, and so on. Method books: *The*
Archaeology of Knowledge. Then I wrote things like *Discipline and*
Punish, and the introduction to *The History of Sexuality*.

I also put forward some thoughts on method in articles and interviews. These tend to be reflections on a finished book that may
help me to define another possible project. They are something like
a scaffolding that serves as a link between a work that is coming
to an end and another one that's about to begin. But this is not to
state a general method that would be definitively valid for others
or for myself. What I've written is never prescriptive either for me
or for others—at most it's instrumental and tentative.

Q: *What you're saying confirms the eccentric aspect of your position*
and, in a certain sense, explains the difficulties that critics, commen-
tators, and exegetes have encountered in their attempts to systematize
your work or to assign you a precise position in contemporary phil-
osophical thought.
A: I don't regard myself as a philosopher. What I do is neither a

way of doing philosophy nor a way of discouraging others from doing philosophy. The most important authors who—I won't say shaped my thinking but enabled me to deviate from my university training—were people like Georges Bataille, Friedrich Nietzsche, Maurice Blanchot, and Pierre Klossowski, who were not philosophers in the institutional sense of the term. There were also a certain number of personal experiences, of course. What struck me and fascinated me about those authors, and what gave them their capital importance for me, was that their problem was not the construction of a system but the construction of a personal experience. At the university, by contrast, I had been trained, educated, driven to master those great philosophical machines called Hegelianism, phenomenology . . .

Q: *You speak of phenomenology, but all phenomenological thought is centered on the problem of experience and depends on it for tracing its own theoretical horizon. What sets you apart from it, then?*
A: The phenomenologist's experience is basically a certain way of bringing a reflective gaze to bear on some object of "lived experience," on the everyday in its transitory form, in order to grasp its meanings. For Nietzsche, Bataille, Blanchot, on the other hand, experience is trying to reach a certain point in life that is as close as possible to the "unlivable," to that which can't be lived through. What is required is the maximum of intensity and the maximum of impossibility at the same time. By contrast, phenomenological work consists in unfolding the field of possibilities related to everyday experience.

Moreover, phenomenology attempts to recapture the meaning of everyday experience in order to rediscover the sense in which the subject that I am is indeed responsible, in its transcendental functions, for founding that experience together with its meanings. On the other hand, in Nietzsche, Bataille, and Blanchot, experience has the function of wrenching the subject from itself, of seeing to it that the subject is no longer itself, or that it is brought to its annihilation or its dissolution. This is a project of desubjectivation.

The idea of a limit-experience that wrenches the subject from itself is what was important to me in my reading of Nietzsche, Bataille, and Blanchot, and what explains the fact that however boring, however erudite my books may be, I've always conceived of them as direct experiences aimed at pulling myself free of myself, at preventing me from being the same.

Q: *If I understand what you're saying, the three essential aspects of your intellectual attitude are: work as a constantly evolving experience, an extreme relativity of method, and a tension with regard to subjectivation. Given this set of factors, one wonders what would give credibility to the results of an inquiry, and what truth criterion might be consistent with the premises of your thinking.*

A: The problem of the truth of what I say is a very difficult one for me; in fact, it's the central problem. That's the question I still haven't answered. And yet I make use of the most conventional methods: demonstration or, at any rate, proof in historical matters, textual references, citation of authorities, drawing connections between texts and facts, suggesting schemes of intelligibility, offering different types of explanation. There is nothing original in what I do. From this standpoint, what I say in my books can be verified or invalidated in the same way as any other book of history.

In spite of that, the people who read me—particularly those who value what I do—often tell me with a laugh, "You know very well that what you say is really just fiction." I always reply, "Of course, there's no question of it being anything else but fiction."

If I had wanted, for example, to do the history of psychiatric institutions in Europe between the seventeenth and eighteenth centuries, obviously I wouldn't have written a book like *Madness and Civilization*. But my problem is not to satisfy professional historians; my problem is to construct myself, and to invite others to share an experience of what we are, not only our past but also our present, an experience of our modernity in such a way that we might come out of it transformed. Which means that at the end of a book we would establish new relationships with the subject at issue: the I who wrote the book and those who have read it would have a different relationship with madness, with its contemporary status, and its history in the modern world.

Q: *The efficacy of your discourse depends on the balance between the power of proof and the ability to connect us with an experience leading to a change of the cultural horizons against which we judge and live our present. I still don't understand what, in your view, this process has to do with the "truth criterion," as we called it earlier. That is, how are the transformations you speak of related to truth, how is it that they produce truth effects?*

A: There is a peculiar relationship between the things I've written and the effects they've produced. Look at what happened to *Madness and Civilization*: it was very well received by people such as Maurice Blanchot, Roland Barthes, and so on; it was received, in a first phase, with a bit of curiosity and a certain sympathy by psychiatrists; and completely ignored by historians, who had no interest in such things. Then, rather quickly, the psychiatrists' hostility grew to the extent that the book was judged as an attack on present-day psychiatry and a manifesto of antipsychiatry. But that was absolutely not my intention, for at least two reasons. When I wrote the book, in Poland in 1958, antipsychiatry didn't exist in Europe, and in any case it wasn't an attack on psychiatry for the very good reason that the book stops at the very start of the nineteenth century—I don't even fully examine the work of Etienne Esquirol. Despite all this, the book has continued to figure in the public mind as being an attack on contemporary psychiatry. Why? Because for me—and for those who read it and used it—the book constituted a transformation in the historical, theoretical, and moral or ethical relationship we have with madness, the mentally ill, the psychiatric institution, and the very truth of psychiatric discourse. So it's a book that functions as an experience, for its writer and reader alike, much more than as the establishment of a historical truth. For one to be able to have that experience through the book, what it says does need to be true in terms of academic, historically verifiable truth. It can't exactly be a novel. Yet the essential thing is not in the series of those true or historically verifiable findings but, rather, in the experience that the book makes possible. Now, the fact is, this experience is neither true nor false. An experience is always a fiction: it's something that one fabricates oneself, that doesn't exist before and will exist afterward. That is the difficult relationship with truth, the way in which the latter is bound up with an experience that is not bound to it and, in some degree, destroys it.

Q: *Is this difficult relationship with truth a constant that accompanies your research and can be recognized also in the works after* Madness and Civilization?

A: The same thing could be said about *Discipline and Punish*. The investigation ends at the 1830s. Yet in this case as well, readers, critical or not, perceived it as a description of contemporary society as a society of confinement. I never wrote that, though it's true that its writing was connected with a certain experience of our modernity. The book makes use of true documents, but in such a way that through them it is possible not only to arrive at an establishment of truth but also to experience something that permits a change, a transformation of the relationship we have with ourselves and with the world where, up to then, we had seen ourselves as being without problems—in short, a transformation of the relationship we have with our knowledge.

So this game of truth and fiction—or if your prefer, of verification and fabrication—will bring to light something which connects us, sometimes in a completely unconscious way, with our modernity, while at the same time causing it to appear as changed. The experience through which we grasp the intelligibility of certain mechanisms (for example, imprisonment, punishment, and so on) and the way in which we are enabled to detach ourselves from them by perceiving them differently will be, at best, one and the same thing. That is really the heart of what I do. What consequences or implications does that have? The first is that I don't depend on a continuous and systematic body of background data; the second is that I haven't written a single book that was not inspired, at least in part, by a direct personal experience. I've had a complex personal relationship with madness and with the psychiatric institution. I've also had a certain relationship with illness and death. I wrote about the birth of the clinic and the introduction of death into medical knowledge at a time when those things had a certain importance for me. The same is true of prison and sexuality, for different reasons.

A third implication: it's not at all a matter of transporting personal experiences into knowledge. In the book, the relationship with the experience should make possible a transformation, a metamorphosis, that is not just mine but can have a certain value, a certain accessibility for others, so that the experience is available for others to have.

Fourth and last: this experience must be capable of being linked in some measure to a collective practice, to a way of thinking.

That's what happened, for example, with a movement like anti-psychiatry, or with the prisoners' movement in France.

Q: *When you show or, as you say, when you open the way to a "trans-formation" capable of being connected with a "collective practice," I already perceive the outline of a methodology or a particular type of teaching. Don't you think that's the case? And if so, doesn't it seem to you that you come into contradiction with another requirement that you've indicated, namely, that of avoiding prescriptive discourse?*

A: I don't accept the word "teaching." A systematic book employing a generalizable method or offering the demonstration of a theory would convey lessons. My books don't exactly have that particular value. They are more like invitations or public gestures.

Q: *But shouldn't a collective practice be related to values, to criteria, to behaviors that would go beyond individual experience?*

A: An experience is something that one has completely alone but can fully have only to the extent that it escapes pure subjectivity and that others can also—I won't say repeat it exactly, but at least encounter it—and go through it themselves. Let's go back for a moment to the book on prisons. In a certain sense, it's a book of pure history. But the people who liked it or hated it felt that way because they had the impression that the book concerned them or concerned the purely contemporary world, or their relations with the contemporary world, in the forms in which it is accepted by everyone. They sensed that something in present-day reality was being called into question. And, as a matter of fact, I only began to write that book after having participated for several years in working groups that were thinking about and struggling against penal institutions. This was a complicated, difficult work carried out in association with prisoners, their families, prison staff, magistrates, and others.

When the book came out, different readers—in particular, correctional officers, social workers, and so on—delivered this peculiar judgment: "The book is paralyzing. It may contain some correct observations, but even so it has clear limits, because it impedes us; it prevents us from going on with our activity." My reply is that this very reaction proves that the work was successful, that it functioned just as I intended. It shows that people read it as an experience that changed them, that prevented them from always being the same or from having the same relation with things, with others, that they had before reading it. This shows that an experience is expressed in the book which is wider than mine alone. The readers have simply found themselves involved in a process that was under way— we could say, in the transformation of contemporary man with respect to the idea he has of himself. And the book worked toward that transformation. To a small degree, it was even an agent in it. That is what I mean by an experience book, as opposed to a truth book or a demonstration book.

Q: *At this point in our analysis I would like to make an observation. You speak of yourself and your research as if the latter were carried out almost independently of the historical and, above all, the cultural context in which it came to maturity. You cited Nietzsche, Bataille, and Blanchot. How did you come upon these authors? What did it mean to be an intellectual in France during your formative period, and what was the theoretical debate during that time? How did you reach the stage where you were making mature intellectual choices and settling on the main orientations of your thought?*

A: Nietzsche, Blanchot, and Bataille were the authors who enabled me to free myself from the dominant influences in my university training in the early fifties—Hegel and phenomenology. Doing philosophy in those days, and today as well in fact, mainly amounted to doing the history of philosophy—and the history of philosophy delimited, on the one hand, by Hegel's theory of systems and, on the other, by the philosophy of the subject, went on in the form of phenomenology and existentialism. Essentially, it was Hegel who was the prevailing influence. For France, this had been in a sense a recent discovery, following the work of Jean Wahl and the teaching of Jean Hyppolite. It was a Hegelianism permeated with phenomenology and existentialism, centered on the theme of the unhappy consciousness. And it was really the best thing the French university could offer as the broadest possible mode of understanding the contemporary world, which had barely emerged from the tragedy of World War II and the great upheavals that had preceded it—the Russian revolution, Nazism, and so on. While Hegelianism was presented as the way to achieve a rational understanding of the tragic as it was experienced by the generation immediately preceding ours, and still threatening for our own, it was Sartre, with his philosophy of the subject, who was in fashion outside the university. Establishing a meeting point between the academic philosophical tradition and phenomenology, Maurice Merleau-Ponty extended existential discourse into specific domains, exploring the question of the world's intelligibility, for example, the intelligibility of reality. My own choices ripened within that intellectual panorama: on the other hand, I chose not to be a historian of philosophy like my professors and, on the other, I decided to look for something completely different from existentialism. I found it in my reading of Bataille and Blanchot and, through them, of Nietzsche. What did they represent for me? First, an invitation to call into question the category of the subject, its supremacy, its foundational function. Second, the conviction that such an operation would be meaningless if it remained limited to speculation. Calling the subject in question meant that one would have to experience something leading to its actual destruction, its decomposition, its explosion, its conversion into something else.

Q: *Was an orientation of that kind conditioned only by a critical attitude toward the dominant philosophical climate, or did it also stem from a reflection on the dimensions of French reality as that looked at the end of the war? I'm thinking of the relations between politics and culture and of the way in which the new intellectual generations experienced and interpreted politics.*

A: For me, politics was the chance to have an experience in the manner of Nietzsche or Bataille. For someone who was twenty years old shortly after World War II ended, who had not been drawn into the morality of the war, what could politics in fact be when it was a matter of choosing between the America of Truman and the USSR of Stalin? Between the old SFIO[1] and Christian Democracy? To become a bourgeois intellectual, a professor, a journalist, a writer, or anything of that sort seemed repugnant. The experience of the war had shown us the urgent need of a society radically different from the one in which we were living, this society that had permitted Nazism, that had lain down in front of it, and that had gone over en masse to de Gaulle. A large sector of French youth had a reaction of total disgust toward all that. We wanted a world and a society that were not only different but that would be an alternative version of ourselves: we wanted to be completely other in a completely different world. Moreover, the Hegelianism offered to us at the university, with its model of history's unbroken intelligibility, was not enough to satisfy us. And the same was true of phenomenology and existentialism, which maintained the primacy of the subject and its fundamental value. Whereas the Nietzschean theme of discontinuity, on the other hand, the theme of an overman who would be completely different from man, and, in Bataille, the theme of limit-experiences through which the subject escapes from itself, had an essential value for us. As far as I was concerned, they afforded a kind of way out between Hegelianism and the philosophical identity of the subject.

Q: *You spoke of the "tragic experience" of World War II and of the basic impossibility of accounting for it with the speculative schemes of the philosophical tradition. Yet why do you wish to place the reflection of Jean-Paul Sartre within the limits of that incapability? Didn't he represent existentialism and didn't he also embody, especially in France, a reaction against the theoretical tradition, an attempt to re-evaluate the status of the intellectual with respect to his time?*

A: In a philosophy like that of Sartre, the subject gives meaning to the world. That point was not called back in question. The subject dispenses significations. The question was: Can it be said that the subject is the only possible form of existence? Can't there be experiences in the course of which the subject is no longer posited, in its constitutive relations, as what makes it identical with itself? Might there not be experiences in which the subject might be able to dissociate from itself, sever the relation with itself, lose its identity? Isn't that the essence of Nietzsche's experience of eternal recurrence?

Q: *Apart from the authors already mentioned, who else was writing or thinking about Nietzsche's work during that period?*

A: The discovery of Nietzsche occurred outside the university. Because of the way the Nazis had used him, Nietzsche was completely excluded from the academic syllabus. On the other hand, a continuist reading of philosophical thought was very much in fashion, an attitude toward the philosophy of history which combined Hegelianism and existentialism in a way. And, as a matter of fact, Marxist culture also shared that philosophy of history.

Q: *It's only now that you allude to Marxism and Marxist culture, as if it had been the great missing element. But I don't think one could say that.*

A: I'd like to talk about Marxist culture later on. For the moment, I'll just mention a rather curious fact. The interest in Nietzsche and Bataille was not a way of distancing ourselves from Marxism or communism—it was the only path toward what we expected from communism. Our rejection of the world in which we lived was definitely not satisfied by Hegelian philosophy. We were looking for other ways to that utterly different reality we thought was embodied by communism. That's why in 1950, without knowing Marx very well, rejecting Hegelianism and feeling uncomfortable in existentialism, I was able to join the French Communist Party. Being a "Nietzschean communist" was really untenable and even absurd. I was well aware of that.

Q: *You enrolled in the PCF. You arrived at the Communist Party after an unusual intellectual itinerary. What influence did that experience have on you and on the development of your theoretical research? What was your experience as a communist militant? How did you arrive at the decision to quit the Party?*

A: In France, the turnover of young people passing through the Communist Party was very rapid. Many entered and left without experiencing these as moments of definitive rupture. I quit after the notorious doctors' plot against Stalin, in the winter of 1952, and my decision was due to a persistent impression of malaise. Shortly before Stalin's death, the news had spread that a group of Jewish physicians had made an attempt on his life. André Wurmser held a meeting in our student cell to explain how the plot allegedly took shape. Although we weren't convinced, we tried hard to believe the story.

This also formed part of that disastrous mode or way of being in the Party: the fact of being obliged to maintain something that was radically opposed to what one could believe was also part of that exercise of dissolution of the self and the search for the entirely-other that I spoke of earlier. Stalin died. Three months later we learned that the doctors' plot had not existed. We wrote to Wurmser asking him to come explain to us what this was all about. We didn't receive any reply. You're going to tell me that this was a common practice, a little incident along the road . . . but the fact is, it was then that I left the Party.

Q: *As I see it, the story you tell is essentially the replaying of a scenario from the past, a tragic incident that also had context: the Cold War, the excesses of Stalinism, a particular relationship between ideology and politics, between the Party and its militants. In analogous and perhaps even worse situations, other individuals still didn't choose to break with the Party, they chose struggle and criticism. I don't think your solution was the best one.*

A: I realize that I'm providing all communists with arguments for reproaching me with having been a communist of the worst kind, for the worst wrong reasons, like a filthy petty-bourgeois. But I say these things because they're true and because I'm sure I was not the only one in that situation, having joined for bad reasons, that somewhat ridiculous element of conversion, asceticism, self-flagellation that is one of the important aspects of the way in which many students—still, today, in France—participate in the activity of the Communist Party. I've seen intellectuals who left the Party at the time of the Tito affair.[2] But I know others who joined at that very moment, and for that reason, because of all that happened then. And, further, as a way of answering the ones who were disillusioned and had handed back their card.

Q: *Once this brief experience in the Communist Party was over, you didn't take part in any other political activities?*

A: No, I finished my studies. During that period I saw a good deal of Louis Althusser, who was active in the PCF. As a matter of fact, it was more or less under his influence that I had joined. And when I left the Party, there was no anathema on his part; he didn't want to break off relations with me because of it.

Q: *Your ties, or at least a certain intellectual kinship with Althusser, have a more distant origin than the one that's generally imagined. I'd like to talk particularly about the fact that your name was associated several times with Althusser's in the controversy over structuralism that dominated the theoretical scene in France during the sixties. Althusser was a Marxist; you weren't, and neither were Claude Lévi-Strauss and others, but the criticism more or less grouped you all together under the term "structuralists." How do you explain that? And what was the common basis of your re-searches, if there was one?*

A: There is a point in common between all those who, over the last fifteen years, were called "structuralists" but weren't, except for Lévi-Strauss, of course: Althusser, Jacques Lacan, and myself. What was that point of convergence, in reality? It was a certain pressing desire to raise the question of the subject in a different way, to free ourselves of the fundamental postulate that French philosophy had never abandoned since Descartes, that was reinforced, even, by phenomenology. From the perspective of psychoanalysis, Lacan brought up the fact that the theory of the unconscious is not compatible with a theory of the subject (in the Cartesian but also the phenomenological sense of the term). Sartre and Georges Politzer had rejected psychoanalysis precisely by criticizing the theory of the unconscious, judging it to be incompatible with the theory of the subject. Lacan concluded instead that it was necessary to abandon the philosophy of the subject and start from an analysis of the mechanisms of the unconscious. Linguistics—the possible ways of analyzing language—and the work of Lévi-Strauss provided this new interrogation with a rational instrument; and it was based on something other than a literary or spiritual experience like those of Blanchot and Bataille. Althusser challenged the philosophy of the subject, because French Marxism was impregnated with an element of phenomenology and an element of humanism; and the theory of alienation made the human subject the theoretical instance capable of transcribing Marx's politico-economic analyses into philosophical terms. Althusser's work consisted in reexamining Marx's analyses, in asking whether they involved that conception of human nature, of the subject, of alienated man, on which the theoretical formulations of certain Marxists like Roger Garaudy, for example, were based. We know that this answer was entirely negative.

All of that is what's been called "structuralism." But in fact structuralism or the structural method in the strict sense at most served as a support or confirmation of something much more radical—the reevaluation of the theory of the subject.

Q: *You reject the structrualism definition as an inadequate label. You prefer to speak of the theme of the "decentering of the subject," refer-ring in particular to the idea of limit-experiences, to a lineage that goes from Nietzsche to Georges Bataille. And yet it's undeniable that a large part of your reflection and the maturing of your theoretical discourse result from a critical passage through the problems of epistemology and the philosophy of the sciences.*

A: That's true. The history of the sciences that I began to concern myself with is far removed from what I encountered in connection with Bataille, Blanchot, and Nietzsche. But how distant, really? When I was a student, the history of the sciences, with its theoretical debates, occupied a strategic position.

A whole aspect of phenomenology took the form of an interrogation of science, in its foundation, its rationality, its history. The great texts of Edmund Husserl, of Alexandre Koyré, formed the other face of phenomenology, opposite the more existential phenomenology of the lived-through [*le vécu*] . . . In many respects, the work of Merleau-Ponty was an attempt to recapture the two dimensions of phenomenology.

But a corresponding discourse was also coming from the Marxist camp, to the extent that Marxism, in the years following the Liberation, had acquired an important role not only in the theoretical domain but also in the daily life of students and intellectuals. Indeed, Marxism professed to be a science, or at least a general theory of the scientific character of the sciences, a sort of tribunal of reason that would enable one to distinguish what pertained to science from what pertained to ideology—in short, a general criterion of rationality for any form of knowledge. This whole mix of problems and investigations prompted people to ask questions about science and its history. To what extent could the history of science be put in question or confirm its absolute foundation in rationality? This was the question that the history of the sciences put to phenomenology. And Marxism asked itself the following question: To what degree could Marxism, by constructing a new framework for the history of society, account for the history of the sciences, for the origin and development of mathematics, of theoretical physics, and so on? This dense set of problems I've summarily described—which constituted a meeting ground for the history of the sciences, phenomenology, and Marxism—was absolutely central then; it was like a little lens in which the different problems of the period were refracted. That was where people like Louis Althusser, a bit older than me, and Jean-Toussaint Desanti, who were my professors, were important for me.

Q: *What part did the problematic around the history of the sciences play in your development?*

A: Paradoxically, more or less the same as Nietzsche, Blanchot, and Bataille. One part was asking how far the history of a science can pose a challenge to its rationality, indicate its limits, or show its linkage with external factors. What are the contingent effects that enter into a science, given that it has a history and develops in a historically determined society? Other questions followed. Can there be a rational history of science? Can a principle of intelligibility be found that explains the different vicissitudes and also, in some cases, the irrational elements that creep into the history of the sciences?

Broadly stated, these were the problems raised both in Marxism and in phenomenology. For me, though, the questions were raised in a slightly different way. It was here that reading Nietzsche was very important to me. It's not enough to do a history of rationality; one needs to do the history of truth itself. That is, instead of asking a science to what extent its history has brought it closer to the truth (or prevented it from approaching the latter), wouldn't it be necessary, rather, to tell oneself that the truth consists in a certain relationship with that discourse that knowledge maintains with itself, and ask whether that relationship itself might not be, or have, a history?

What I found striking is that for Nietzsche a rationality—that of a science, a practice, a discourse—is not measured by the truth that science, that discourse, that practice may produce. Truth itself forms part of the history of discourse and is like an effect internal to a discourse or a practice.

Q: *Nietzsche's discourse on the history of truth and on the limits of human theory undoubtedly represents a change of perspective and point of view in comparison with the conventional historical outlook, seeing that he negates its premises by proclaiming the fundamental "untruth of knowing." But I would like for you to tell me how you came to associate the analysis of the origin of science with that of limit-experiences or with experience as transformation.*

A: Might not a science be analyzed or conceived of basically as an experience, that is, as a relationship in which the subject is modified by that experience? Scientific practice, in other words, would function both as the ideal subject of science and the object of knowledge. And might not the historical root of a science lie in that reciprocal genesis of the subject and the object of knowledge? What effect of truth is produced that way? This would imply that there isn't *one* truth—which doesn't mean either that this history is irrational or that this science is illusory. Rather, it confirms the presence of a real and intelligible history, of a series of collective rational experiences conforming to a set of precise, identifiable rules and resulting in the construction of both the knowing subject and the known object.

In order to grasp this process, it seemed to me the best thing to do was to study the new, unformalized sciences that were established recently and so were closer to their origins and their immediate urgency—that type of science whose scientific character appeared with most uncertainty and which sought to understand what was the least suited to enter a field of rationality. This was the case with madness. It was a matter of understanding how, in the Western world, madness had managed to become a precise object of analysis and scientific inquiry only from the eighteenth century, whereas previously one had had medical treatises dealing, in a few short chapters, with "maladies of the mind." Here one could show that just as this object, madness, was taking form, the subject capable of understanding madness was also being constructed. Corresponding to the construction of madness as an object, there was that of a rational subject who was cognizant of madness and understood it. In *Madness and Civilization*, I sought to understand this sort of collective, plural experience that took shape between the sixteenth and the nineteenth centuries and involved an interaction between the coming into being of a rational man able to recognize and understand madness, and that of madness itself as an understandable and determinable object.

Q: *It seems that founding act marking the separation and confrontation between reason and unreason, with the consequences for the destiny of Western culture that you yourself have analyzed, appeared as an essential preliminary condition for the historical development, or the development of the history, of modern reason. Doesn't this limit-experience that opens up the possibility of history constitute itself in an atemporal dimension, outside of history itself?*

A: My work didn't consist of a kind of celebration of madness—that goes without saying. And it wasn't an irrationalist history either. Rather, I wanted to indicate how this experience—which constituted madness as an object together with the subject who knows it—couldn't be fully understood unless it was related to certain well-known historical processes: the birth of a certain normalizing society, connected with practices of confinement, with a specific economic and social context corresponding to the period of urbanization, the birth of capitalism, with the existence of a floating, scattered population, which the new requirements of the economy and the state were unable to tolerate.

So I tried to write a history, the most rational possible history, of the constitution of a knowledge [*savoir*], of a new relation of objectivity, of something that could be called the "truth of madness."

Naturally this doesn't mean that, using this new type of knowledge, people were able actually to postulate criteria that could reveal madness in its truth; no, rather, what they did was to organize an experience of the truth of madness linked to the possibility of an effective knowledge and the shaping of a subject that knowledge could be known by and know.

Q: *Let's go back for a moment. In the reconstruction of your intellectual formation, specifically in relation to epistemological problems, you never mentioned the name Gaston Bachelard. And yet it's been noted, correctly I believe, that Bachelard's rational materialism, based on the supremacy of a scientific praxis capable of constructing its own objects of analysis, represents a kind of background for the lines of research that you've developed. Don't you think that's the case?*

A: I was never directly one of Bachelard's students, but I read his books. In his reflections on discontinuity in the history of the sciences and in the idea of a labor of reason upon itself at the moment it is constituting its objects of analysis, there was a whole series of elements that I drew from and recast.

But in the domain of the philosophy of science, the individual who perhaps exerted the strongest influence on me was Georges Canguilhem, although this came much later. More than anything else, he deepened the problems of the life sciences, by trying to show how it was man as a living being that put himself in question in that experience.

By establishing the sciences of life while, at the same, forming a certain self-knowledge, the human being altered itself as a living being by taking on the character of a rational subject acquiring the power to act on itself, changing its living conditions and its own life. The human being constructed a biology that was really just the reciprocal of an inclusion of the life sciences in the general history of the human species. That is an extremely important consideration in Canguilhem, who acknowledges, I believe, a kinship with Nietzsche. And that is how, despite the paradox, and essentially around Nietzsche, one finds a kind of meeting point, expressed as kinship, between the discourse on limit-experiences, where it was a matter of the subject transforming itself, and the discourse on the transformation of the subject itself through the construction of a knowledge.

Q: *In your view, how was a relation established between limit-experiences, which in a certain way precede the constituting of reason, and knowledge [savoir], which on the contrary would define the historical limit of a cultural horizon?*
A: I use the word "*savoir*" ["knowledge"] while drawing a distinction between it and the word "*connaissance*" ["knowledge"]. I see "*savoir*" as a process by which the subject undergoes a modification through the very things that one knows [*connaît*] or, rather, in the course of the work that one does in order to know. It is what enables one both to modify the subject and to construct the object. *Connaissance* is the work that makes it possible to multiply the knowable objects, to manifest their intelligibility, to understand their rationality, while maintaining the fixity of the inquiring subject.

With the idea of archaeology, it's precisely a matter of recapturing the construction of a *connaissance*, that is, of a relation between a fixed subject and a domain of objects, in its historical roots, in this movement of *savoir* which makes the construction possible. Everything I've been concerned with up to now has to do basically with the way men in Western societies have produced these experiences—fundamental ones, no doubt—which consist in engagement in a process of acquiring knowledge of a domain of objects, while at the same time they are constituting themselves as subjects with a fixed and determinate status. For example, knowing madness while constituting oneself as a rational subject; knowing illness while constituting oneself as a living subject; or the economy, while constituting oneself as a laboring subject; or as an individual knowing oneself in a certain relationship with the law . . . So there is always this involvement of oneself within one's own *savoir*. I made an effort, in particular, to understand how man had transformed certain of these limit-experiences into objects of knowledge—madness, death, crime. That is where one reencounters some of Georges Bataille's themes, but applied to a collective history which is that of the West and its knowledge [*savoir*]. It's always a question of limit-experiences and the history of truth.

I'm imprisoned, enmeshed in that tangle of problems. What I am saying has no objective value but may shed light on the problems I've tried to pose and the sequence of things in my experience.

Q: *One last observation on the cultural components of your intellectual formation. I want us to talk about phenomenological anthropology and the attempt to associate phenomenology and psychoanalysis. One of your first pieces of writing, in 1954, is an introduction to Ludwig Binswanger's* Traum und Existenz, *in which you take up and develop an idea of dreaming or the imaginary as a primordial space that helps to constitute man . . .*

A: My reading of what was called "existential analysis" or "phenomenological psychiatry" was important for me during the time I was working in psychiatric hospitals and while I was looking for something different from the traditional schemas of psychiatric observation, a counterweight to them. There's no doubt that those superb descriptions of madness as unique and incomparable fundamental experiences were important. And I believe that Roland Laing was impressed by all that as well; for a long time, he also took existential analysis as a reference (he in a more Sartrean and I in a more Heideggerian way). But we moved on to other things. Laing developed a colossal project connected with his work as a doctor; together with David Cooper, he was the real founder of antipsychiatry, whereas I only did a critical historical analysis. But existential analysis helped us to delimit and get a better grasp on what was heavy and oppressive in the gaze and the knowledge apparatus of academic psychiatry.

Q: *To what extent, on the other hand, did you accept and assimilate the teaching of Lacan?*
A: It's certain that what I was able to garner from his works had an impact on me. But I didn't follow him closely enough to be really immersed in his teaching. I read certain books of his; but everyone knows that to understand Lacan well you not only have to read him but also listen to his public lectures, take part in his seminars, and perhaps even undergo an analysis. Starting in 1955, when Lacan delivered the essential part of his teaching, I was already out of the country.

Q: *Did you live much outside France?*
A: Yes, for several years. I worked abroad as an assistant, a lecturer in the universities of Uppsala, Warsaw, and Hamburg. That happened to be during the Algerian War, which I experienced somewhat as a foreigner. And because I observed the events like a foreigner, it was easier for me to grasp their absurdity and to see the inevitable outcome of that war very clearly. Obviously, I was against the conflict. But being abroad and not experiencing what was happening in my country directly—while the clarity came easy, I didn't have to show much courage. I didn't participate personally in one of the crucial experiences of modern France.

When I returned, I had just finished writing *Madness and Civilization*, which in a certain way echoed the direct experience I had had during those years. I can speak of Swedish society, an over-medicalized, protected society in which all social dangers were mitigated in a sense by subtle and clever mechanisms; and of Polish society, in which the mechanisms of confinement were of a completely different type . . . In the years that followed, those two types of society would become a kind of obsession for Western society. But these concerns were still abstract in a France absorbed in preoccupations of war and the problems posed by the end of an age, that of colonization. Being also a fruit of this peculiar detachment from French reality, *Madness and Civilization* was favorably and immediately received by Blanchot, Klossowski, and Barthes. Among doctors and psychiatrists the reactions were varied: a certain interest on the part of some, with a liberal or Marxist orientation, such as Lucien Bonnafé, and a total rejection by others, who were more conservative. But on the whole, as I said, my work was ignored: indifference, silence on the part of intellectuals.

Q: *What were your reactions to that attitude? A short time later*, Madness and Civilization *was recognized as a work of the first rank even by those who didn't agree with its arguments. How do you explain that near-indifference with which it was greeted initially?*
A: I admit that I was a bit surprised, but I was wrong. The French intellectual milieu had just gone through experiences of a different sort. It was dominated by debates on Marxism, science, and ideology. I believe the lack of receptiveness to *Madness and Civilization* can be explained in the following way. First of all, it was a work of historical inquiry, and at the time attention was drawn to theory, to theoretical debate; second, a domain like that of mental medicine, psychiatric medicine, was considered marginal compared with the debate that was going on; and then, after all, didn't madness and the mad represent something situated at the edges of society, a kind of outer limit? I think these were more or less the reasons for the disinterest of those with highly developed political concerns. I was surprised; I thought there would be things of interest in that book, since I tried to see how a discourse claiming to be scientific, psychiatry, was formed out of historical situations. I had tried to do a history of psychiatry on the basis of transformations in the modes of production which affected the population in such a way that problems of pauperization became prominent, but also differences between the various categories of the poor, the sick, and the mad. So, despite everything, I was convinced that all that would appeal to Marxists. And there was total silence.

Q: *What do you think was responsible for the later growth of interest in your book and the accompanying fierce polemics?*
A: One can probably now piece together how that happened. Reactions and attitudes were altered or radicalized when the events of 1968 began to take shape and then exploded. These problems of madness, of confinement, of normalizing processes in a society became the favorite item of the menu, especially in extreme-left circles. Those who wanted to distance themselves from what was brewing took my book for a target, pointing out how idealistic its analysis was, how it failed to get to the root of the problems. That's

how it came about that eight years after its publication, *Evolution psychiatrique*, a very significant group of psychiatrists in France, decided to devote an entire conference in Toulouse to the business of "excommunicating" *Madness and Civilization*. Even Bonnafé, a Marxist psychiatrist, who was one of those who had greeted my book with interest when it came out, condemned it in 1968 as an ideological book. In this convergence of polemics and with the renewed interest in certain subjects, *Madness and Civilization* gained a sort of topicality.

Q: *What effects did this fresh interest in your work have in psychiatric circles? During those years, a movement began to spread which challenged traditional psychiatry, together with a much wider prevailing cultural order.*

A: There had been, to some extent before the war and especially after the war, a movement of reassessment of psychiatric practice, a movement that originated among psychiatrists themselves. After 1945, those young psychiatrists had initiated, in their analyses, reflections and projects such that what is called "antipsychiatry" would probably have been able to emerge in France in the early fifties. If that didn't occur, it's for the following reasons in my opinion. First, many of those psychiatrists were very close to Marxism if not actually Marxists, and so they were led to focus their attention on what was happening in the USSR, and from there on Pavlov and on reflexology, on a materialist psychiatry, and a whole set of theoretical and scientific problems that obviously couldn't take them very far. At least one of them traveled to the Soviet Union to study in 1954-55, but I'm not aware that he spoke or wrote about the experience after his return. So I think—and I say this without aggressive intent—that the Marxist climate gradually led them into an impasse. Second, I believe that many were very quickly brought—because of the position of psychiatrists, most of whom were state employees—to question psychiatry from a defensive trade-union angle. Thus, those individuals who, by virtue of their abilities, their interests, and their openness to so many things, would have been able to address the problems of psychiatry, were led into impasses. Faced with the explosion of antipsychiatry in the sixties, their attitude was one of rejection, which became more and more pronounced and even took an aggressive turn. It was then that my book was blacklisted as if it had been the devil's gospel. I know that in certain milieus *Madness and Civilization* is still spoken of with extraordinary disgust.

q: *Thinking back on the polemics provoked by your writings, I would now like to recall those that followed the heated debate on structuralism in the sixties. During that period there was a tense discussion in which you were the object of some harsh remarks, for example on the part of Sartre. But I'm going to remind you of other judgments concerning your thought: Roger Garaudy spoke of "abstract structuralism"; Jean Piaget of "structureless structuralism"; Mikel Dufrenne of "neopositivism"; Henri Lefebvre of "Neo-Eliatism"*[*]; *Sylvie Le Bon of "desperate positivism"; Michel Amiot of "cultural relativism" or "historicizing skepticism"; and so on. A set of observations and a meeting of different, even opposite, terminologies that converged on a criticism of your arguments, around the period after the publication of* The Order of Things. *But this overheated atmosphere of French culture very likely depended on the broader polemic regarding structuralism. How do you view those judgments today and, more generally, what was the polemic really about?*

a: This matter of structuralism is hard to disentangle, but it would be very interesting for us to try. Let's leave aside for the moment a whole series of polemical outbursts with the theatrical, and even at times grotesque, quality of their formulations. Among the latter I would place at the head of the list the well-known phrase of Sartre's, labeling me "the last ideological rampart of the bourgeoisie." An unfortunate bourgeoisie, I must say. If it only had me for a rampart, it would have lost its grip on power a long time ago!

Yet we need to ask what there was in structuralism that was so upsetting. I regard people as being fairly rational, so when they lose control of what they're saying, there must be something seriously the matter. I've got some hypotheses. Let's start with an observation, first of all. In the mid-sixties the term "structuralist" was applied to individuals who had made studies that were completely different from each other but presented one common element: they tried to put an end to, or to circumvent, a form of philosophy, of reflection and analysis, centered essentially on an assertion of the primacy of the subject. That was the case with Marxism, obsessed at the time by the concept of alienation, with phenomenological

existentialism, focused on lived experience, and with those strains
of psychology that rejected the unconscious on behalf of authentic
human experience—experience of the self, let's say. It's true there
was that common point, and it may have caused aggravations.

But I think that behind this scuffle there was nonetheless something deeper, a history that wasn't given much thought at the time.
You see, structuralism as such hadn't been discovered by the structuralists of the sixties, obviously; and, more to the point, it wasn't
a French invention. Its real origin lies in a whole series of studies
carried out in the Soviet Union and central Europe around the
twenties. That great cultural expansion, in the fields of linguistics,
mythology, folklore, and so on, which had preceded the Russian
revolution of 1917 and had coincided with it in a certain way, had
been knocked to one side and even crushed by the great Stalinist
steamroller. Subsequently, structuralist culture came to circulate in
France through networks that were more or less underground or,
at any rate, little-known: think of Evgeni Trubetskoy's phonology,
of Vladimir Propp's influence on Georges Dumézil and Claude Lévi-
Strauss, and so on. So it seems to me that something like a historical
knowledge that was unfamiliar to us was present in the aggres-
siveness with which certain French Marxists opposed the structuralists of the sixties: structuralism had been the great cultural victim
of Stalinism, a possibility that Marxism hadn't been able to face.

Q: *I would say that you're privileging a certain cultural current in
describing it as a victim. The "Stalinist steamroller," as you call it,
didn't just shove structuralism aside, it did the same thing to a
whole series of cultural and ideological expressions and tendencies
to which the October revolution had given an impetus. I don't think
clear distinctions can be established. Even Marxism, for example,
was reduced to a doctrinaire corpus to the detriment of its flexibility,
its openings . . .*
A: But this curious fact still needs explaining: how was a phenomenon as particular, basically, as structuralism able to arouse so
many passions during the sixties? And why did people insist on
defining as structuralists a group of intellectuals who weren't structuralists, or at least who rejected that label? I remain convinced
that we won't find a satisfactory answer until we shift the center of
gravity of our analysis. At bottom, the problem of structuralism in

Western Europe was nothing but the after-effect of much more sub-stantial problems that were posed in the Eastern countries. Above all, we have to take account of the efforts on the part of many in-tellectuals in the period of destalinization—Soviets, Czechs, and so on—to acquire a degree of political autonomy and to free them-selves from the official ideologies. In this regard, they could appeal precisely to that "hidden tradition" of the twenties I spoke of, which had a double value: first, it was one the great forms of innovation the East could offer to Western culture (formalism, structuralism, and so on); second, this culture was directly or indirectly linked to the October revolution, and its main exponents were associated with it. The pattern becomes clearer: when destalinization oc-curred, these intellectuals had tried to get back their autonomy by reconnecting with that culturally prestigious tradition, which from a political standpoint could not be accused of being reactionary and Western. It was revolutionary and Eastern. Hence, the intent to re-activate those tendencies, to put them back into intellectual and artistic circulation. I think that the Soviet authorities were well aware of the danger and didn't want to risk an open confrontation, which, on the other hand, many intellectual forces were counting on.

It seems to me that what occurred in France was to some extent the inadvertent, uncalculated result of all that. The more or less Marxist circles—whether communist or influenced by Marxism—must have had the feeling that in structuralism, as it was practiced in France, there was something that sounded a bit like the death knell of traditional Marxist culture. A non-Marxist culture of the left was about to be born. Which accounts for some reactions that immediately denounced these forms of inquiry as technocratic and idealistic. The judgment of *Les Temps modernes*[4] was very similar to that of diehard Stalinists or to those handed down during the Khrushchev period about formalism and structuralism.

Q: *I think that you're going a little too far again, since a similarity of judgments is still not a convergence of cultural, let alone political, positions . . .*
A: I'd like to tell you two anecdotes. I'm not quite sure of the au-thenticity of the first one, which was told to me in 1974 or 1975 by a Czech exile. One of the greatest Western philosophers was invited

to Prague at the end of 1966 or the beginning of 1967 to give a lecture. The Czechs awaited him impatiently: he was the first great noncommunist intellectual to be invited during that period of intense cultural and social excitement that preceded the blossoming of the Prague Spring. People expected him to talk about the ways in which progressive thought in Western Europe was at odds with traditional Marxist culture. But from the start of his lecture, this philosopher assailed those groups of intellectuals, the structuralists, who were evidently in the service of capital and who tried to go against the great Marxist ideological tradition. He was probably hoping to please the Czechs with such talk, by offering them a kind of ecumenical Marxism. In reality, he was undermining what the country's intellectuals were trying to do. And at the same time, he was furnishing the Czech authorities with an exceptional weapon, by enabling them to launch an attack against structuralism, deemed to be a reactionary and bourgeois ideology even by a philosopher who was not communist. A great disappointment, as you can understand.

Now for the second anecdote—I myself was the individual involved. It was in 1967, when I was asked to give a series of lectures in Hungary. I had suggested dealing with the themes of the ongoing debate in the West concerning structuralism. The subjects I proposed were all accepted. All the lectures were to be held in the university theater. But when the time came for me to talk about structuralism, I was informed that on this occasion the lecture would be held in the rector's office: it was such a fine issue, I was told, that it wouldn't arouse much interest. I knew this was a lie. I asked my young interpreter about it, and he replied: "There are three things we can't talk about at the University: Nazism, the Horty regime, and structuralism." I was taken aback. It made me understand that the problem of structuralism was a problem of the East, and that the heated and confused debates that took place in France on this theme were only the repercussion, poorly understood by everybody, of a much more serious and harsh struggle conducted in the countries of the East.

Q: *Why do you speak of a repercussion? Didn't the theoretical debate in France have its own originality, which went beyond the question of structuralism?*

A: All that helps us to better understand the nature and intensity of the debate that developed in the West around structuralism. Several important issues were addressed: a certain way of posing theoretical problems, which were no longer focused on the subject, and analyses that were completely rational without being Marxist. It was the birth of a certain type of theoretical reflection that broke away from the great Marxist obedience. The values and the struggle that were engaged in the East were transposed to what was occurring in the West.

Q: *I don't quite get the meaning of that transposition. The renewal of interest in the structural method and its tradition in the Eastern European countries had very little to do with the antihumanist theoretical line expressed by the French structuralists . . .*

A: What happened in the East and in the West was the same type of phenomenon. This is what was at stake: how far can forms of reflection and analysis be constituted that are not irrationalist, that are not rightist, and yet are not tied to Marxist dogma? This is the problematic that was denounced, by those who feared it, with the all-embracing, confusing term "structuralism." And why did that word appear? Because the debate on structuralism was central in the Soviet Union and the countries of the East. There, too, it was a question of determining to what extent it was possible to constitute a rational, scientific, theoretical research outside the laws and the dogmatism of dialectical materialism.

That's what happened in the East and the West alike—but with the difference that in the West it wasn't a matter of structuralism in the strict sense, whereas in the Eastern countries it was precisely structuralism that was hidden and continues to be hidden. That helps to explain some condemnations . . .

Q: *But, curiously, Louis Althusser was also the object of those curses, although his research was fully identified with Marxism and even claimed to be its most faithful interpretation. Thus, Althusser was also placed among the structuralists. So how do you explain that a Marxist work like* Reading Capital *and your book* The Order of Things, *published in the middle of the sixties and with such a different orientation, became the targets of the same antistructuralist polemic?*

A: I can't exactly answer you on Althusser's behalf. As for myself, I think that basically they wanted to make me pay for *Madness and*

Civilization, attacking the other book, *The Order of Things*, in its place. *Madness and Civilization* had introduced a certain malaise: that book shifted the attention from noble domains to minor ones. Instead of talking about Marx, it analyzed little things like asylum practices. The scandal that should have broken before occurred when *The Order of Things* was published in 1966—it was spoken of as a purely formal, abstract text, things that people hadn't been able to say concerning my first work on madness. If they had really paid attention to *Madness and Civilization* and *The Birth of the Clinic*, which followed it, they would have noticed that *The Order of Things* didn't at all represent a totalizing book for me. The book occupied a certain dimension for the purpose of answering a certain number of questions. I hadn't put my whole method or all my concerns into it. Moreover, at the end of the book I reaffirm several times that the analysis has been conducted at the level of the transformations of *savoir* and *connaissance*, and that now a whole study of causality and an in-depth explanation remain to be done. If my critics had read my previous works, if they hadn't insisted on forgetting them, they would have had to recognize that in those books I was already offering certain of my explanations. It's a deeply rooted habit, at least in France: one reads a book as if it were a kind of absolute—each book must stand alone. Whereas I only write my books in a series: the first one leaves open problems on which the second depends for support while calling for a third—without there being a linear continuity between them. They are interwoven and overlapping.

Q: *So you link a book of method like* The Order of Things *to books of exploration like those on madness and clinical medicine? What led you to make the transition to a more systematic kind of survey, and then to extract the notion of "episteme," of a set of rules that govern discursive practices in a given culture or historical period?*
A: With *The Order of Things* I developed an analysis of procedures of classification, of tabulations, of coordination in the order of empirical knowledge. This was a problem I had signaled as soon as I first encountered it, when I was working on *The Birth of the Clinic*, which dealt with the problems of biology, medicine, and the natural sciences. But I had already met the problem of medical classification while working on *Madness and Civilization*, having noticed that

a similar methodology had begun to be applied in the domain of mental diseases. The question got shifted about like a pawn on a chessboard, pushed from square to square, sometimes with zigzags, sometimes with jumps, but always on the same board. That was why I decided to systematize in one text the complex pattern that had become apparent to me in my researches. This led to *The Order of Things*, a very technical book that was addressed, above all, to the technicians of the history of the sciences. I had written it after discussions with Georges Canguilhem, and I meant it essentially for researchers. But to tell the truth, those weren't the problems I was most keenly interested in. I've already spoken about limit-experiences, and that's the theme that really fascinated me—for me, madness, sexuality, and crime are more intense subjects. By contrast, *The Order of Things* was a kind of formal exercise for me.

Q: *Surely, though, you don't expect me to believe that* The Order of Things *had no importance for you: in that work, you made a considerable step forward in your thought. The field of inquiry was no longer the experience that founded madness but the criteria of the organization of culture and history . . .*

A: I don't say that as a way of detaching myself from the results I produced in that work. But *The Order of Things* is not a book that's truly mine: it's a marginal book in terms of the sort of passion that runs through the others. But, oddly enough, *The Order of Things* is the book that had the greatest success with the public. The criticism, with a few exceptions, was incredibly vehement, and people bought it more than any of my other books, even though it was the most difficult. I say this in order to point to the unhealthy relation obtaining between the consumption of a theoretical book and the criticism of such books in the French intellectual journals, a characteristic phenomenon of the sixties.

In that book, I tried to compare three scientific practices. By "scientific practice," I mean a certain way of regulating and constructing discourses that define a particular domain of objects and, at the same time, determine the place of the ideal subject that can and must know those objects. I had found it rather peculiar that three distinct domains, without any practical relation with each other— natural history, grammar, and political economy—were constituted, as far as their rules were concerned, more or less during the same period, in the middle of the seventeenth century, and underwent the same type of transformation at the end of the eighteenth century. It was a work of pure comparison between those heterogeneous practices—so there was no need to characterize, for example, the relationship that might exist between the origin of the analysis of wealth and the development of capitalism. The problem was not to ascertain how political economy was born but to find the points in common between various discursive practices: a comparative analysis of the procedures that were internal to scientific discourse. It was a problem that not many people were interested in at the time, apart from a few historians of the sciences. The question that was and remains dominant was roughly: How can a scientific type of knowledge arise from a real practice? It's still a current problem; the others appear secondary.

Q: *Yet this dominant problem of the formation of a knowledge [savoir] out of a social practice was relegated to the shadows in* The Order of Things. *It seems to me that, among the sharpest barbs hurled at the book, was the accusation of structural formalism, or of reduction of the problem of history and society to a series of discontinuities and ruptures inherent in the structure of knowledge acquisition* [du connaitre].

A: To those who will reproach me with not having addressed or faced this problem, my reply is that I wrote *Madness and Civilization* to show people that I'm not blind to it. If I didn't talk about it in *The Order of Things*, it's because I chose to deal with something else. One can debate the legitimacy of the comparisons I made between the different discursive practices, but one must bear in mind that what I did was for the purpose of bringing out a certain number of problems.

Q: *In* The Order of Things, *you reduced Marxism to an episode that was internal, finally, to the nineteenth-century episteme. In Marx, it would seem that there was no epistemological break with a whole cultural horizon. This low valuation of Marx's thought and its revolutionary significance provoked virulent critical reactions . . .*

A: Yes, there was a violent dispute over that; it was like a wound. At a time when it has become so fashionable to include Marx in among those most responsible for the gulags, I could claim credit for having been one of the first to say that. But it wouldn't be true:

I limited my analysis to Marx's economics. I never spoke of Marxism, and if I used the term it was in reference to the economic theory. As a matter of fact, I don't regard myself as having said something stupid in suggesting that Marxist economics—through its basic concepts and the general rules of its discourse—belongs to a type of discursive formation that was defined around the time of Ricardo. In any case, Marx himself said that his political economy owed its basic principles to Ricardo.

Q: *What was the purpose of that reference to Marxism, however marginal it may have been? Doesn't it seem to you that it was a somewhat overly expeditious way of stating your assessment of Marxism, in a parenthetical discussion occupying a dozen pages at most?*

A: I wanted to react against a certain hagiographic glorification of Marxist political economy due to the historical good fortune of Marxism as a political ideology, born in the nineteenth century and having its effects in the twentieth. But Marx's economic discourse comes under the rules of formation of the scientific discourses that were peculiar to the nineteenth century. It is not monstrous to say that. It's strange that people found it unbearable. There was an utter refusal on the part of traditional Marxists to accept that someone might say anything that might not give Marx the preeminent place. But they weren't the most aggressive ones at the time; I even think the Marxists most interested in questions of economic theory were not so scandalized by what I asserted. Those who were really offended were those neo-Marxists who were developing their views and who generally did that in opposition to the traditional intellectuals of the French Communist Party. This would mean those who would become the Marxist-Leninists or even the Maoists of the post-'68 years. For them, Marx was the object of a very important theoretical battle, directed against bourgeois ideology, of course, but also against the Communist Party, which they reproached for its theoretical inertia and for not being able to convey anything but dogma.

The people who couldn't forgive me and who sent me insulting letters were from that whole generation of anti-PCF Marxists, with their prevailing glorification and evaluation of Marx as the absolute threshold of scientific knowledge on the basis of which the history of the world had changed.

Q: *When you speak of Marxist-Leninists or Maoists, who are you thinking of in particular?*

A: Those who, after May '68, made hyper-Marxist speeches, who were responsible for the May movement's spreading a vocabulary borrowed from Marx, the likes of which had never been heard in France, and who would abandon everything a few years down the road. In other words, the events of May '68 were preceded by an inordinate glorification of Marx, a generalized hyper-Marxification, for which what I had written was intolerable, though it was limited to a modest observation, namely, that Marx's work is a Ricardian type of economic theory.

Q: *In any case, this rejection seems to have been the last to make itself felt among those we have been cataloguing here: the theme of structuralism, the resistances of a certain Marxist tradition, a decentering with regard to the philosophy of the subject . . .*

A: And also, if you will, the fact that basically people couldn't take too seriously someone who, on the one hand, concerned himself with madness and, on the other, reconstructed a history of the sciences in such a strange, eccentric way relative to the problems recognized as being valid and important. The convergence of this set of reasons provoked the anathema, the great excommunication of *The Order of Things* on everyone's part: *Les Temps modernes, Esprit, Le Nouvel Observateur*, the right, the left, the center—it was hammered from all sides. The book shouldn't have sold more than two hundred copies, but it sold tens of thousands.

Q: *The second half of the sixties is a crucial point in the history of European culture, because of the upheavals that were threatening. We're still far from a historical understanding of that period. Was the hyper-Marxism truly the sign of a co-optation or, rather, of a genuine renewal of Marx's discourse? What real processes were set in motion? What new values were emerging? These are open questions that have not yet been raised in the necessary terms perhaps.*

A: What happened before and after 1968 needs to be explored more thoroughly, taking your questions into account as well. Thinking back on that period, I would say that what was occurring definitely lacked its own theory, its own vocabulary. The changes were taking place in relation to a certain type of philosophy, of general reflection, even a type of culture that was roughly the culture of the first half of our century. Things were coming apart and there didn't exist any vocabulary capable of expressing that process. So, in *The Order of Things*, people may have recognized a sort of difference and, at the same time, they were revolted by the fact that they didn't recognize the vocabulary of what was occurring. What was occurring? First, the French were experiencing the end of the colonial age—and the fact that France now only had a provincial standing in the world order was not a negligible consideration for a country whose culture had revolved around national pride. Second, everything that certain people had tried to disguise about the Soviet Union was becoming more and more manifest: with Tito, destalinization, Budapest, there had been a progressive overturning of schemas and values, especially in left-wing milieus. Finally, we mustn't forget the Algerian War. In France, many of those who had fought the most radical struggle against the war were members of the French Communist Party or very close to it.

But they had not been supported in that action by the Party, which had an ambiguous attitude toward the war. And it paid dearly for that later—through a gradual loss of control over the youth, the students, leading finally to the most blatant confrontations in 1968–70. Moreover, with the Algerian War a long period came to an end in France during which it had naively been believed, on the Left, that the Communist Party, just struggles, and just causes were all synonymous. Before, even when one criticized the Party, one always ended by concluding that, in spite of everything, it was generally on the right side—the Soviet Union as well, generally speaking. But after Algeria this sort of unconditional allegiance was coming apart at the seams. It wasn't easy, obviously, to formulate this new critical position, because the appropriate vocabulary was lacking, seeing that people didn't want to adopt the one provided by the categories of the Right.

This problem still hasn't been resolved. And it's one of the reasons for which numerous questions have been confused and the theoretical debates have been bitter as well as muddled. This is what I mean to say: thinking critically about Stalinism, the policies of the Soviet Union, and the political swings of the PCF without speaking the language of the Right wasn't a very easy thing to do. And isn't that still true today?

Q: *Yes, I would say that it is. But speaking of vocabulary, when you wrote* The Archaeology of Knowledge, *after establishing the concepts of epistemes and discursive formulations, you effected a shift through the notion of the statement, the* énoncé, *as a material or institutional condition of scientific discourse. Don't you think this definite change of orientation—which still seems to define the current field of your research—is also due, in a certain way, to the climate, to the theoretical and practical upheavals of the years 1968–70?*

A: No. I had written *The Archaeology of Knowledge* before 1968, though it wasn't published until 1969. It was a work that responded to the discussions about structuralism, which seemed to me to have caused a lot of intellectual turmoil and confusion. Earlier you mentioned Piaget's criticism of me. Well, I recall that at the time a student of Piaget's sent me one of his own essays in which it was explained how there was no theory of structuralism in my work, although I had actually done a structural analysis. A few months later, Piaget in turn published a book in which I was spoken of as a theorist of structuralism who lacked an analysis of structures— exactly the opposite of what his student thought. You can see that, when even a master and his disciple aren't able to agree on the meaning of structuralism and structure, the discussion is hopelessly warped. Even the critics of my work didn't really know what they were talking about. So I tried to set out for my own part how my works all turned around a set of problems of the same type, namely, how it was possible to analyze the particular object that is constituted by discursive practices with their internal rules and their conditions of appearance. *The Archaeology of Knowledge* resulted from that.

Q: *With 1968, another theoretical current took on a new status, becoming an important reference point for youth culture. I'd like us to talk about the Frankfurt School. Theodor Adorno, Max Horkheimer, and especially Herbert Marcuse found themselves, together with their works, at the center of the students' ideological debates. The struggle against repression, antiauthoritarianism, the escape from civilization, the radical negation of the system: all these themes were tossed back and forth, with a varying degree of intellectual confusion, by the young. I'd like to hear where your thought is situated in relation to this theoretical vein, in part because, as far as I know, you've never spoken directly about the relation.*

A: It would be necessary to understand more clearly how it happened that the Frankfurt School was unknown for such a long time in France, despite the fact that many of its representatives had worked in Paris after being expelled from the German universities by Nazism.

People began to speak about it, with a certain intensity, in connection with Marcuse's thought and his "Freudo-Marxism." As for myself, I didn't know much about the Frankfurt School. I had read a few of Horkheimer's texts, which were part of a set of discussions where the issues weren't clear to me and which, I felt, displayed a kind of casualness with regard to the historical materials analyzed. I became interested in the Frankfurt School after reading an extraordinary book on the mechanisms of punishment which had been written in the United States, by Kirscheimer.[5]

I then understood that the representatives of the Frankfurt School had tried, earlier than I, to say things I had also been trying to say for years. This even explains a certain irritation that some people had expressed on seeing that people in France were doing things that were, if not identical, then at least very similar; indeed, a concern for correctness and theoretical productivity would have required that the Frankfurt School be studied much more seriously. For my part, I think that the philosophers of that school raised problems we're still laboring over today—in particular, that of the effects of power in their relation to a rationality that was defined historically and geographically, in the West, from the sixteenth century onward. The West wouldn't have been able to achieve the economic and cultural results that characterize it without the exercise of that particular form of rationality. And, in fact, how can that rationality be separated from the mechanisms, procedures, techniques, and effects of power that accompany it and for which we express our distaste by describing them as the typical form of oppression of capitalist societies—and perhaps socialist societies as well? Couldn't it be concluded that the Enlightenment's promise of attaining freedom through the exercise of reason has been turned upside down, resulting in a domination by reason itself, which increasingly usurps the place of freedom? This is a fundamental problem we're all struggling with, which many people have in common, whether they are communist are not. And as we know, this problem was isolated, pointed out by Horkheimer before all the others; and it was the Frankfurt School that questioned the reference to Marx in terms of that hypothesis. Wasn't it Horkheimer who maintained that in Marx there was the idea of a classless society that resembled an enormous factory?

Q: *You attribute a major importance to that current of thought. To what do you ascribe the anticipations, the results obtained by the Frankfurt School, as you have briefly summarized them?*
A: I think that the Frankfurt School philosophers had better opportunities in Germany, being very close to the USSR, to get to know and to analyze what was going on in the USSR. And this was in the context of an intense and dramatic political struggle, during the time when Nazism was burying the Weimar Republic, within a cultural world in which Marxism and theoretical reflection on Marx had a more than fifty-year-old tradition.

When I acknowledge the merits of the Frankfurt School philosophers, I do so with the bad conscience of someone who should have read them long before, who should have understood them much earlier. Had I read these works, there are many things I wouldn't have needed to say, and I would have avoided some mistakes. Perhaps, if I had known the philosophers of that school when I was young, I would have been so captivated by them that I wouldn't have done anything else but comment on them. One doesn't know whether to be glad or sorry about these retrospective influences, these people one discovers after the age when one would have been ready to come under their influence.

Q: *Thus far, you've only talked about what fascinates you in the Frankfurt School, but I'd like to know how and why you differentiate yourself from them. For example, a sharp criticism of French structuralism has emanated from the Frankfurt philosophers and their school. Recall, for example, the writings of Alfred Schmidt concerning Lévi-Strauss, Althusser, and you as well, referring to the three of you as "deniers of history."*
A: There definitely are some differences. Simplifying things, one could say, for the moment, that the conception of the subject adopted by the Frankfurt School was rather traditional, philosophical in nature—it was permeated with Marxist humanism. Its par-

ticular connection with certain Freudian concepts, such as the relation between alienation and repression, between liberation and an end to alienation and exploitation, is explainable in that way. I don't think that the Frankfurt School can accept that what we need to do is not to recover our lost identity, or liberate our imprisoned nature, or discover our fundamental truth; rather, it is to move toward something altogether different.

A phrase by Marx is pertinent here: man produces man. How should it be understood? In my judgment, what ought to be produced is not man as nature supposedly designed him, or as his essence ordains him to be—we need to produce something that doesn't exist yet, without being able to know what it will be.

As for the word "produce," I don't agree with those who would assume that this production of man by man occurs like the production of value, the production of wealth or of an economically useful object; it's the destruction of what we are as well as the creation of a completely different thing, a total innovation. Now, it seems to me that the idea the representatives of that school had about this production of man by man consisted basically in the need to free man of everything—in the repressive system connected with rationality or in the system of exploitation connected with a class society—that had kept him alienated from his fundamental essence.

Q: *The difference probably resides in the refusal or incapability for the philosophers of the school to conceive of the origin of man in a historico-genealogical sense instead of in metaphysical terms. The issue is the theme, or metaphor, of the death of man.*

A: When I speak of the death of man, I mean putting an end to everything that would set a rule of production, an essential goal for this production of man by man. In *The Order of Things*, I made the mistake of presenting this death as something that was under way in our era. I conflated two aspects. The first is a small-scale phenomenon: the observation that, in the different human sciences that developed—an experience in which man engaged his own subjectivity, transforming it—man had never found himself at the end of man's destinies.

If the promise of the human sciences had been to make us discover man, they had certainly not kept that promise; but, as a general cultural experience, it had been more a matter of constituting a new subjectivity through an operation that reduced the human subject to being an object of knowledge.

The second aspect that I confused with the preceding one is that, in the course of their history, men have never ceased to construct themselves, that is, to continually displace their subjectivity, to constitute themselves in an infinite, multiple series of different subjectivities that will never have an end and never bring us in the presence of something that would be "man." Men are perpetually engaged in a process that, in constituting objects, at the same displaces man, deforms, transforms, and transfigures him as a subject. In speaking of the death of man, in a confused, simplifying way, that is what I meant to say; but I will not give way on the basic point. That is where there is an incompatibility with the Frankfurt School.

Q: *How is this difference with the representatives of the Frankfurt School, which is clearly apparent in the theme of antihumanism, reflected in the respective ways of conceiving and analyzing history?*
A: The relation with history is an element that disappointed me in the Frankfurt School philosophers. It seemed to me that they weren't doing much history in the full sense, that they would refer to research carried out by others, to a history already written and authenticated by a certain number of good historians, usually of a Marxist tendency, and they would present that history as an explanatory background. Some of them claim that I deny history. Sartre says that as well, I believe. About them it could be said, rather, that they are eaters of history as others have prepared it. They consume it preprocessed. I don't mean to say that everyone should construct the history that suits him, but it's a fact that I have never been completely satisfied with the works of historians. Although I've referred to and used numerous historical studies, I've always insisted on doing my own historical analyses in the areas I was interested in.

I think that the philosophers of the Frankfurt School, on the other hand, reason this way when they make use of history: they consider that the work of the professional historian supplies them with a sort of material foundation that can explain phenomena of a different type which they have called "sociological" or "psychological" phenomena, for example. Such an attitude implies two postulates: first, what philosophers talk about is not of the same order as history that is taking place (what takes place in someone's head is a social phenomenon that doesn't belong to the same level of reality as historical events); second, once a history is admitted to have been well constructed and provided it speaks about the economy, it will have inherent explanatory value.

But this sort of reasoning is both too modest and too credulous. Too modest because, all things considered, what happens in someone's mind, or in the minds of a series of individuals, actually does belong to history: to say something is an event. The formulation of a scientific discourse is not situated above history or off to the side: it's as much a part of history as a battle or the invention of a steam engine, or an epidemic. Of course, these are not the same types of events but they *are* all events. Some doctor who said something asinine about madness belongs to history just as the battle of Waterloo does.

Moreover, whatever the importance of economic analyses, the fact of considering that an analysis based on the mutations of economic structure has an explanatory value in itself seems to me to be a naiveté—typical, it should be added, of those who aren't historians by trade. It isn't necessarily the case by any means. I'll take an example: a few years back, the question was raised, with a certain interest, as to why sexual prohibitions, directed in particular at children and masturbation, proliferated in the eighteenth century. Certain historians tried to explain the phenomenon by pointing out that in this period the age for marriage had been pushed back and that young people were forced to stay celibate for a longer time. Now, although important, this demographic fact, linked to economic causes of course, doesn't explain the prohibition. In the first place, why would one begin to masturbate the year immediately prior to marriage? Second, if one grants that this deferment of the age for marriage left great masses of young people in a state of celibacy for years, one doesn't see why the response to that fact had to be a greater repression instead of a broadening of sexual freedom. It may be that the delay of the marriage age, with all the possible links to the mode of production, must enter into an understanding of the phenomenon. But when it's a question of phenomena as complex as the production of a knowledge [*savoir*] or a discourse with its mechanisms and its internal rules, the intelligibility to be produced is much more complex. It's unlikely that one will be able to arrive at a single explanation, an explanation in terms of necessity. It would already be a lot if one managed to make a few connections between what one is trying to analyze and a whole series of related phenomena.

Q: *So, in your view, is the theoretical reflection always tied to a particular treatment of the historical materials? Thinking would be nothing else but a way of doing or interpreting history?*

A: The type of intelligibility that I try to produce cannot be reduced to the projection of a history—a socio-economic history, say—onto a cultural phenomenon so as to make it appear as the necessary and extrinsic product of that cause. There is no unilateral necessity: the cultural product is also part of the historical fabric. That's why I feel obliged to do historical analyses myself. Making me out to be someone who denies history is really ludicrous. I don't do anything *but* history. For them, to deny history is not to use that intangible, sacred, and all-explaining history they appeal to. It's obvious that, if I had wanted to, I could have cited this or that page from Albert Mathiez or some other historian. I didn't do so because I don't practice the same type of analysis. That's all there is to it. The idea that I reject history comes less from professional historians than from philosophical circles in which people aren't fully aware of the type of relation, detached and respectful at once, which such a historical analysis requires. Being unable to accept such a relation to history, they conclude that I deny history.

Q: *During May '68 in Paris, and immediately afterward, many French intellectuals participated in the student struggles. That raised the old questions of commitment, of the relation to politics, of the possibilities and limits of cultural action, in new terms. Your name doesn't appear among those intellectuals. Up to 1970 at least, you were absent from the debates that involved other figures from the French intellectual world. How did you experience May '68 and what did all that mean to you?*

A: During the month of May 1968, as in the period of the Algerian War, I wasn't in France; again, I was a little out of phase, an outsider. When I return to France, it's always with an outsider's way of seeing things, to a certain extent—and what I say isn't always what people want to hear. I remember that Marcuse asked one day, with a reproachful tone, what Foucault was doing at the time of the May barricades. Well, I was in Tunisia. And, I have to add, it was an important experience for me.

I've been lucky in my life: in Sweden, I saw a social democrat country that functioned well; in Poland, a people's democracy that functioned badly. I had a direct experience of Federal Germany during the time of its economic expansion, at the beginning of the sixties. And, finally, I lived in a third-world country, Tunisia, for two and a half years. That was an experience that greatly affected me: a little before the month of May in France, some very intense student revolts occurred there. It was in March 1968—strikes, suspensions of courses, arrests, and a general student strike. The police came into the university, clubbed many students, seriously injured several of them, and threw them into prison. Some were sentenced to eight, ten, even fourteen years behind bars—some are still in prison. Given my position as a professor and being French, I was protected in a way, protected from the local authorities, which allowed me to easily do some things and at the same time to get a precise grasp of the French government's reactions to all that. I had a direct idea of what was going on in all the universities of the world.

I was deeply impressed by those young women and men who exposed themselves to fearful risks by drafting a leaflet, distributing it, or calling for a strike. It was a real political experience for me.

Q: *So you had a direct political experience?*

A: Yes. After joining the PCF, and going through all the things that had followed during the years we spoke about earlier, all I had retained from my political experience was a degree of speculative skepticism. I don't hide that fact. In the period of the Algerian War, I had not been able to participate directly either, and if I had it would not have been at the risk of my personal safety. In Tunisia, on the other hand, I was led to support the students, to make contact with something completely different from all the droning of political institutions and discourses in Europe.

I think, for example, of what Marxism was, of the way in which it functioned for us, when we were students in 1950–52; I think of what it represented in a country like Poland, where it had become an object of total repugnance for most young people (irrespective

of their social conditions), where it was taught like the catechism.
I also remember those cold academic discussions on Marxism in
which I had participated in France at the beginning of the sixties.
In Tunisia, by contrast, everyone appealed to Marxism with a radical vehemence and intensity and with an impressive enthusiasm.
For those young people, Marxism didn't just represent a better way
of analyzing reality: at the same time, it was a kind of moral energy,
a kind of existential act that was quite remarkable. I felt a wave of
bitterness and disappointment when I thought of the gap that existed between the Tunisian students' way of being Marxist and what
I knew about the way Marxism functioned in Europe (France, Poland, or the Soviet Union).

That's what Tunisia was for me: I was compelled to join the political debate. It wasn't May '68 in France but March '68, in a country of the third world.

Q: *You attach a great importance to the existential character of certain political acts. Why is that? Maybe you have the impression that
it's the sole guarantee of authenticity? Don't you think that for the
young Tunisians there was a connection between their ideological
choice and the determination with which they acted?*
A: In today's world, what can prompt in an individual the desire,
the ability, and the possibility for an absolute sacrifice, without
there being any reason to suspect in their action the least ambition
or desire for power and profit? That was what I saw in Tunisia, the
evidence of the necessity of myth, of a spirituality, the unbearable
quality of certain situations produced by capitalism, colonialism,
and neocolonialism.

In this sort of struggle, the question of direct, existential, physical
involvement was inescapable, I would say. As for these struggles'
theoretical reference to Marxism, I believe it wasn't essential. Let
me explain. The Marxist education of the Tunisian students was
not very deep, and it didn't tend to gain any more depth. The real
debate between them, on the choices of tactics and strategy, on
what they should choose, was conducted in terms of different
interpretations of Marxism. But what it was really about was
something completely different. Political ideology or a political perception of the world was no doubt indispensable for launching the
struggle; but, on the other hand, the theory's exactness and its sci-

entific character were completely secondary questions that functioned more as an enticement than as a principle of proper and correct behavior.

Q: *Didn't you also find in France the signs of this lively and direct participation you experienced in Tunisia? What relations did you establish between the two experiences? After May, how did you decide to enter into contact with the student struggles, into a dialogue leading you to take a position, on various occasions, and to take part directly in movements like that of the* Groupe d'information sur les prisons [GIP], *concerning prison conditions, alongside intellectuals like Sartre, Jean-Marie Domenach, and Maurice Clavel?*

A: Actually, when I returned to France in November or December of 1968, I was surprised, astonished, and even disappointed, considering what I had seen in Tunisia. In spite of their violence, their passion, the struggles had not involved the same cost, the same sacrifices, by any means. There's no comparison between the barricades of the Latin Quarter and the real risk of getting, as in Tunisia, fifteen years of prison. People in France spoke of hyper-Marxism, of a proliferation of theories, of a splintering into small groups. It was exactly the opposite, the reverse, the contrary of what had intrigued me in Tunisia. That may explain the way in which I tried to approach things from that time onward, away from those endless discussions, that hyper-Marxization, that irrepressible discursivity which characterized university life, and, in particular, Vincennes in 1969. I tried to do things that required a personal, physical, and real involvement, things that would address problems in concrete, precise, and definite terms in a given situation.

It was only from that moment that necessary analyses could be proposed. Working with the GIP on the problem of the prisoners, I attempted to initiate and carry through an experience. At the same time, it also gave a kind of occasion for me to revisit what I had been concerned with in works like *Madness and Civilization* or *The Birth of the Clinic* and to reflect on what I had just experienced in Tunisia.

Q: *When you speak of May '68, you always speak in a tone that would minimize the significance of that event; you seem only to see the grotesque, ideologizing side of it. Although it's appropriate to under-*

score its limits, and especially those of the formation of small groups,
I don't think that one should underestimate the importance of this
mass movement that appeared in nearly all of Europe.

A: May '68 was extremely important, without any doubt. It's certain that without May '68 I wouldn't have afterward done the work
I did in regard to prison, delinquency, and sexuality. In the pre-
1968 climate, that wasn't possible. I didn't mean to say that May '68
had no importance for me, rather, that certain of the most visible
and superficial aspects at the end of 1968 and the beginning of 1969
were completely alien to me. What was really at stake, what really
made things change, was the same in France and Tunisia. It's just
that in France, through a kind of misinterpretation that May '68 had
made of itself, it had ended by being clouded over by the formation
of small groups, by the pulverization of Marxism into little bodies
of doctrine that anathematized each other. But in actual fact,
viewed in depth, things had changed in such a way that I felt more
at ease than in the preceding years, when I was in France in 1962
or in 1966. The things I concerned myself with began to be part of
the public domain. Problems that in the past had not found any
echo, with the exception of antipsychiatry, became current issues.
But in order to go further, to deepen my work, I first had to break
through that rigid yet fragmented crust formed by the little groups
and the endless discussions. It seemed to me that a new type of
relations and of collaboration, different from the past, between intellectuals and non-intellectuals, was now possible.

Q: *But what was the basis, the discussion and topics, for the rela-*
tions—since there was no common language in which to communi-
cate?
A: It's true that I didn't speak the vocabulary that was most in
fashion. I had taken different paths. And yet, in a certain sense,
there were points we shared: we managed to agree when it came
to concrete concerns, real problems. There are a lot of people who
take a keen interest as soon as one speaks of asylums, madness,
prisons, the city, medicine, life and death—all those aspects of existence that are very concrete and raise so many theoretical questions.

Q: *Your inaugural lecture at the Collège de France, which was pub-*
lished with the title L'Ordre du discours (The Order of Discourse),

dates from 1970. In that academic exposition, you begin to set out, in a clearer way, the relationship between knowledge and power. The question of the domination exerted by power on truth, hence the question of the will to truth, marks an important new stage in your thought. How did you come to pose the problem or, rather, frame it in those terms? And in what way do you think the thematic of power, as you developed it, came into contact with the impetus of the youth movement of 1968?

A: You're asking what my whole life was about up to then? What the deep malaise was that I had sensed in Swedish society? And the malaise I had sensed in Poland? And yet many Polish people recognized that the material living conditions were better that they were in other periods. I also wonder about the meaning of that enthusiasm for radical rebellion demonstrated by the students of Tunis.

What was it that was everywhere being called in question? The way in which power was exercised—not just state power but the power exercised by other institutions and forms of constraint, a sort of abiding oppression in everyday life. What was hard to bear and was always put in question, what produced that type of malaise, and what had not been spoken of for twelve years, was power. And not only the power of the state but the power that's exercised throughout the social body, through extremely different channels, forms, and institutions. People no longer accepted being governed in the broad sense of government. I'm talking not about state government in the sense the term has in public law but of those men who orient our daily lives either through administrative acts or through direct or indirect influences, for example, the influences of the media. In writing *Madness and Civilization* and *The Birth of the Clinic*, I meant to do a genealogical history of knowledge. But the real guiding thread was this problem of power.

Basically, I had been doing nothing except trying to retrace how a certain number of institutions, beginning to function on behalf of reason and normality, had brought their power to bear on groups of individuals, in terms of behaviors, ways of being, acting, or speaking that were constituted as abnormality, madness, illness, and so on. I had done nothing else, really, but a history of power. And who would disagree now that May '68 involved a rebellion against a whole series of forms of power that were exerted with a special intensity on certain age groups in certain social milieus? From all these experiences, mine included, there emerged one word, similar to those written with an invisible ink, ready to appear on the paper when the right reagent is applied—the word "power."

Q: *From the beginning of the seventies until now, your work on power and power relations has been given a detailed elaboration in articles, interviews, dialogues with students, young leftist activists, and intellectuals, a series of reflections that you subsequently summed up in a few pages of the book* La Volonté de savoir *[The History of Sexuality: An Introduction]. I want to ask you whether, as many people have said, we are being offered here a new principle for explaining reality or whether something else is involved.*

A: There have been some serious misunderstandings, or else I've explained myself badly. I've never claimed that power was going to explain everything. My problem was not to replace an economic explanation with an explanation in terms of power. I tried to co-ordinate, to systematize the different analyses I had done concerning power, without removing their empirical dimension, which is to say, the aspects of them that were still in their raw state.

For me, power is what needs to be explained. When I think back on the experiences I have had in contemporary societies or in historical investigations I have done, I always come up against the question of power, a question that no theoretical system—whether the philosophy of history or a general theory of society, or even a political theory—seems able to deal with. That is, those facts of power, those power mechanisms, those power relations at work in the problem of madness, of medicine, of prison, and so on. I have been trying to grapple with that bundle of empirical and poorly elucidated things which power relations consist of, taking them as something that needed explaining. But I'm still only at the beginning of my work; clearly, I haven't finished it. And that's why I don't understand what has been written about the fact that, for me, power was a kind of abstract principle that asserted itself as such, which I wasn't accounting for finally.

But no one has ever accounted for it. I advance one step at a time, examining different domains in succession, to see how a general conception of the relations between the establishment of a knowledge and the exercise of power might be formulated.

Q: *It might be said that the way in which you approach the theme of power, the extreme parceling out or limiting of questions, ultimately prevents the introduction of an aggregated dimension, so to speak, into the analysis of power, the transition to a comprehensive view within which the particular problem is located.*

A: It's a question that I'm often asked: "You bring up particular problems whose scope is limited, but you never take a position with regard to general choices."

It's true that the problems I pose are always concerned with particular and limited questions. Madness and psychiatric institutions, or even prisons, are cases in point. If we want to pose problems in a rigorous, exact way that's likely to allow serious investigations, shouldn't we look for these problems precisely in their most singular and concrete forms? It seems to me that none of the grand discourses that have been pronounced on the subject of society is convincing enough for us to rely on. Further, if we truly want to construct something new or, in any case, if we want the great systems to be opened up, finally, to the challenge of a certain number of real problems, we have to go and look for the data and questions where these are located. Moreover, I don't think an intellectual can raise real questions concerning the society in which he lives, based on nothing more than his textual, academic, scholarly research. On the contrary, one of the primary forms of collaboration with non-intellectuals consists in listening to their problems, and in working with them to formulate those problems: What do mental patients say? What is life like in a psychiatric hospital? What is the work of a hospital orderly like? How do they deal with what they experience?

Q: *Maybe I didn't explain myself well. I don't question the need to pose limited problems, even in a radical way, if that's what's called for. And I can appreciate what you're saying about intellectual work. Yet it seems to me that a certain way of addressing problems, by particularizing them, ends by eliminating the possibility of coordinating them with others in a general view of a given historical and political situation.*

A: There are essential theoretical and political reasons why it is necessary to localize problems. But this doesn't mean these are not general problems. After all, what is more general in a society than the way it defines its relation with madness, the way it conceptualizes itself as a rational entity? How does it confer power on reason, and on its own reason? How does it constitute its rationality, and how does it present the latter as reason in general? How, in the name of reason, does it establish men's power over things? After all, that is one of the most general problems that can be posed in regard to society, its functioning and its history. Or again, how is the line drawn between what is legal and what is not? The authority that is conferred on the law, the demarcations the law makes within society, and the mechanisms of constraint that enable the functioning of law are other questions that are among the most general ones that can be put to a society. I do pose problems in local terms, certainly, but I believe this enables me to bring out problems at least as general as those people are in the habit of considering as such in the proper sense. After all, isn't the domination of reason just as general as the domination of the bourgeoisie?

Q: *When I spoke of a general view, I was referring essentially to the political dimension of a problem and to its necessary articulation within a broader action or program and at the same time its connection with certain historico-political contingencies.*

A: The generality I try to elicit is not of the same type as the others. And when people reproach me with posing only local problems, they are confusing the local character of my problem-revealing analyses with a certain generality that is ordinarily posited by historians, sociologists, economists, and so on.

The problems I raise are just as general as those habitually raised by political parties or the great theoretical institutions that define the major problems of society. For example, the Communist or Socialist Parties have never put on their working agenda the analysis of the power of reason over unreason. Perhaps that is not their job. But if it isn't their problem, theirs is not necessarily mine either.

Q: *What you say is perfectly reasonable. But it seems to me that you're confirming a certain lack of openness or a resistance to opening your discourse, as I was saying, to the political dimension . . .*

A: But why is it that the great theoretico-political apparatuses that define the criteria of consensus in our society have never reacted to the problems that I raise, general as these are? When I raised the problem of madness, which is a general problem in every society, and especially important in the history of ours, why is it that the first reaction was silence, followed by an ideological condemnation? When, together with others, I tried in a practical way, working alongside people coming out of prison, with prison staff and prisoners' families, to pose the problem of prison in France, do you know how the PCF reacted? One of its local dailies, in the Paris suburbs, wondered why we, the people doing this work, hadn't yet been put in prison, and what our links with the police might be, seeing that the latter allowed us to do it.

That's why I ask how I can be criticized for not posing general problems, never taking a position concerning the great questions raised by the political parties. In reality, I do pose general problems—and I am bombarded with reproaches. And then, when it's noticed that the anathema slides off its target, or when it's recognized that the problems raised have a certain importance, I'm accused of not being capable of developing a whole series of questions in suitably general terms. But I reject the type of generality I've alluded to, whose principal effect, in any case, would be either to condemn me for the problems I raise or to exclude me from the work I do. It is I who ask them the question: Why do you refuse to address the general problems that I pose?

Q: *I'm not familiar with the episode you've related in connection with your work on the problems of the prisons. In any case, I didn't mean to refer to the question of your relations with French politics and, in particular, with the politics of the PCF. I had a more general question in mind. For every specific problem there is always the need to find solutions, even if they're provisional and transitory, in political terms. Hence the need to shift one's view from a particular analysis to an examination of real possibilities, so that there are two viewpoints between which a process of change and transformation may develop. The political function is in this balance between a local situation and a general framework.*

A: That's also an observation people have often made to me: "You never say what the concrete solutions might be for the problems you pose; you don't make any proposals. By contrast, the political parties are obliged to take a position vis-à-vis this or that situation; with your attitude, you don't help them any." I will reply that, for reasons essentially having to with my political preference in the broad sense of the term, I have absolutely no desire to play the role of a prescriber of solutions. I think that the role of the intellectual today is not to ordain, to recommend solutions, to prophesy, because in that function he can only contribute to the functioning of a particular power situation that, in my opinion, must be criticized.

I understand why the political parties prefer to have relations with intellectuals who offer solutions. In this way, they can establish relations between partners; the intellectual offers a proposal, the party criticizes it, or formulates another one. I reject the intellectual's functioning as the political party's alter ego, double, and alibi.

Q: *But don't you think that you have some role to play with your writings, your articles, your essays, and what might it be?*
A: My role is to raise questions in an effective, genuine way, and to raise them with the greatest possible rigor, with the maximum complexity and difficulty so that a solution doesn't spring from the head of some reformist intellectual or suddenly appear in the head of a party's political bureau. The problems I try to pose—those tangled things that crime, madness, and sex are, and that concern everyday life—cannot easily be resolved. Years, decades, of work and political imagination will be necessary, work at the grass roots, with the people directly affected, restoring their right to speak. Only then will we succeed, perhaps, in changing a situation that, with the terms in which it is currently laid out, only leads to impasses and blockages. I take care not to dictate how things should be. I try instead to pose problems, to make them active, to display them in such a complexity that they can silence the prophets and lawgivers, all those who speak for others or to others. In this way, it will be possible for the complexity of the problem to appear in its connection with people's lives; and, consequently, through concrete questions, difficult cases, movements of rebellion, reflections, and testimonies, the legitimacy of a common creative action can also appear. It's a matter of working through things little by little, of introducing modifications that are able if not to find solutions, at least to change the given terms of the problem.

I would like to facilitate a whole social project, a work within and upon the very body of society. I'd like to be able to participate in this work myself without delegating responsibilities to any specialist, including myself—to bring it about that, in the very workings of society, the terms of the problem are changed and the impasses are cleared. In short, to be done with spokespersons.

Q: *I want to give you a concrete example. Two or three years ago, Italian public opinion was roused by the case of a boy who had killed his father, putting an end to a tragic history of blows and humiliations he had received, along with his mother. How are we to judge a homicide, perpetrated by a minor, which in this case occurred at the culmination of a series of extraordinary abuses inflicted by the father? A perplexity among the prosecutors, a deeply divided public opinion, heated debates. Here we have an episode in which a solution must be found, a transitory solution, no doubt, to a very delicate problem. And it reveals the decisive function of balance and political choice. The child parricide was given a relatively light sentence considering the criminal code in force; and it's still being debated, of course. Aren't we obliged to take a position in situations of this kind?*

A: The Italian press asked me for statements concerning that affair, and I replied that I didn't know enough about the situation. But a similar event occurred in France: a young man of thirty, after having killed his wife, had sodomized and battered a twelve-year-old child to death with a hammer. Well, the interesting thing is that the killer had spent more than fifteen years in psychiatric institutions (from the age of ten to the age of twenty-five, approximately): society, the psychiatrists, the medical institutions had declared him mentally incompetent and placed him under guardianship, causing him to live in abominable conditions. He emerged, and two years later he committed that horrible crime. So here is someone who, declared not accountable for his actions previously, suddenly becomes accountable. But the most surprising thing in this affair is that the killer declared: "It's true, I'm accountable; you made me into a monster, and so, since I'm a monster, you should cut off my head." He was sentenced to life in prison. I happened to have worked several years in my seminar at the Collège de France on the problem of psychiatric judicial appraisals; one of the lawyers for the murderer, who had worked with me, asked me to take a position on this case in the press. I refused—I wasn't comfortable doing that. What meaning would it have had to begin prophesying or to play the fault-finder? I played my political role by bringing out

the problem in all its complexity, prompting such doubts and uncertainties that now no reformer or president of a psychiatrists'
union is capable of saying: "This is what needs to be done." The
problem is now posed in such conditions that it will nag for years,
creating a malaise. Changes will come out of it that are much more
radical than if I were asked to work on the drafting of a law that
would settle the question of psychiatric appraisals.

The problem is deeper and more complicated. It looks like a
technical question, but it's a whole problem not just of the relations
between medicine and justice, but also of the relations between law
and knowledge [*savoir*]—that is, of the way in which a scientific
knowledge can function within a system which is that of the law. A
huge problem. So I'm saying, what does it mean to reduce the dimensions of the problem by assigning this or that lawmaker—
whether he's a philosopher or a politician—the task of drafting a
new law? What matters is for this conflict between law and knowledge, so difficult to resolve, to be so effectively worked through at
the heart of society that the society would define a different relation
to law and to knowledge.

Q: *I wouldn't be so optimistic about these possible automatic workings that you foresee leading to a new equilibrium between law and
knowledge through an internal movement of civil society . . .*
A: I didn't say anything about civil society. I think that the theoretical opposition between the state and civil society, on which political theory has been laboring for a hundred and fifty years, is not
very productive. One of the reasons that prompts me to raise the
question of power by getting to the heart of it at the place where it
is exercised, without looking for its general formulations or its
foundations, is that I reject the opposition between a power-
wielding state that exercises its supremacy over a civil society deprived of such processes of power. My assumption is that the
opposition between the state and civil society is not useful.

Q: *Be that as it may, doesn't it seem to you that, basically, by evading
the political dimension in a way, your proposal may represent a kind
of diversion from the contingent and complex issues that are raised in
society but have an immediate effect in the sphere of institutions and
parties?*
A: This is an old leftist splinter-group reproach: accuse people

who aren't doing the same thing as you of creating a diversion. The problems I deal with are general problems. We live in a society in which the formation, circulation, and consumption of knowledge are something fundamental. If the accumulation of capital was one of the fundamental traits of our society, the same is true of the accumulation of knowledge. Furthermore, the exercise, production, and accumulation of knowledge cannot be dissociated from the power mechanisms with which they maintain complex relations that must be analyzed. Since the sixteenth century, people have always considered the development of the forms and contents of knowledge to be one of the greatest guarantees of liberation for humanity. That's one of the postulates of our civilization, one that has been extended throughout the world. Now, it's a fact already established by the Frankfurt School that the formation of the great systems of knowledge has also had effects and functions of enslavement and domination. Which leads one to thoroughly reexamine the postulate according to which the development of knowledge constitutes a guarantee of liberation. Is that not a general problem?

Do you think that posing this type of problem amounts to creating a distraction from the ones the political parties raise? Doubtless, they are not directly assimilable to the type of generalities formulated by the political parties, which basically accept only those coded generalities that fit into a program, that are coalescing factors for their clienteles, and that can be integrated into their electoral strategy. But it's intolerable for certain problems to be called marginal, local, or distracting just because they don't go through the filter of the generalities that are accepted and codified by political parties.

Q: *When you deal with the question of power, you seem to do so without referring directly to the distinction between the effects by which power is manifested at the level of states and that of different institutions. On this point, someone has said that for you power is faceless and omnipresent. Isn't there any difference, then, between a totalitarian regime and a democratic one?*

A: In *Discipline and Punish*, I tried to show how, in the West, a certain type of power brought to bear on individuals through education, through the shaping of their personality, was correlative with the birth not only of an ideology but also of a liberal regime. In other political and social systems—administrative monarchy, or feudalism—that kind of exercise of power on individuals would not have been possible. I always analyze precise and locally delimited phenomena, for example, the formation of disciplinary systems in eighteenth-century Europe. I don't do this as a way of saying that Western civilization is a disciplinary civilization in all its aspects. The systems of discipline are applied by certain individuals on others. I make a distinction between governors and governed. I make an effort to explain why and how these systems came into existence at a particular time, in a particular country, to satisfy certain needs. I don't speak of societies that have no geography or calendar. I really don't see how it could be objected that I don't distinguish between, for example, regimes that are totalitarian and those that aren't. In the eighteenth century, there weren't any totalitarian regimes in the modern sense.

Q: *But if your research were seen as an investigation of modernity, what lesson could be drawn from it? Since it poses and leaves unresolved the great questions of the relationship between knowledge and power in democratic and totalitarian societies alike, so there would appear to be no substantial difference established between them finally. In other words, the power mechanisms you analyze are identical, or nearly so, in every type of modern society.*

A: When this sort of objection to my work is raised, I am reminded of the psychiatrists who, after reading *Madness and Civilization*, which discussed arguments relating to the eighteenth century, said, "Foucault is attacking us." But it really wasn't my fault if they recognized themselves in what I had written. It simply proves that a certain number of things haven't changed.

When I wrote the book on prisons, obviously I wasn't alluding to the prisons of the people's democracies or of the USSR; I was talking about eighteenth-century France, between 1760 and 1840, to be quite exact. The analysis stops at 1840. But here you tell me, "You don't make any distinction between a totalitarian regime and a democratic regime!" What makes you think that? Such a reaction only proves that what I say is considered, basically, as applying to the present. You can place it in the USSR or in a Western country, as you wish; that's your business. For my part, I try to show, rather, how it's a matter of problems that are historically situated, in a given period.

That being said, I think that the techniques of power can be transposed, in the course of history, from armies to schools, and so on. Their history is relatively autonomous in relation to the economic processes that develop. Think of the techniques employed in the slave colonies in Latin America, which turn up again in nineteenth-century France or England. So there exists a relative, nonabsolute, autonomy of the techniques of power. But I've never argued that a power mechanism suffices to characterize a society.

The concentration camps? They're considered to be a British invention; but that doesn't mean, or authorize the notion, that Britain was a totalitarian country. If there is one country that was not totalitarian in the history of Europe, it is undoubtedly Britain—but Britain invented concentration camps, which have been one of the chief instruments of totalitarian regimes. This is an example of a transposition of a technique of power. But I've never said, and I'm not inclined to think, that the existence of concentration camps in both democratic and totalitarian countries shows that there are no differences between those countries.

Q: *Clear enough. But think for a moment about the political function, the repercussions of your discourse in the shaping of the public consciousness [du sens commun]. Might not the rigorous but, consequently, delimited analysis of the technologies of power possibly lead to an attitude of indifference toward the values, the great choices of the different contemporary political and social systems?*

A: There's a tendency that consists in absolving a certain political regime of everything it may do in the name of the principles from which it draws its inspiration. It was democracy or, rather, a certain liberalism that developed in the nineteenth century, that perfected extremely coercive techniques, which in a certain sense were the counterweight to an economic and social freedom accorded in other respects. Evidently, individuals could not be freed without a concomitant conditioning [*dressage*]. I don't see why it would disregard the specificity of a democracy to explain how and why the latter needed these techniques. It's possible that these techniques were appropriated by regimes of a totalitarian type, which made them function in a certain way; this doesn't imply an elimination of the difference between the two regimes. One can't speak of a difference of value if that isn't related to an analyzable difference. It doesn't make sense to say, "This is better than that," if one doesn't say what "this" and "that" consist of.

As an intellectual, I don't wish to prophesy or play the moralist, to announce that the Western countries are better than the Eastern ones, and so on. People have reached political and moral adulthood. It's up to them to choose, individually and collectively. It is important to say how a certain regime functions, what it consists in, and to prevent a whole series of manipulations and mystifications. But the choice has to be made by people themselves.

Q: *Two or three years ago, the* nouveaux philosophes *became the rage in France: a certain cultural current about which we could say, in short, that it aligned itself with a rejection of politics. What were your attitude and judgment concerning these "new philosophers"?*

A: I don't know what the *nouveaux philosophes* say. I haven't read very much by them. They are credited with the argument that things are always the same: the master [*maître*] is always the master and, whatever happens, we are trapped. I don't know if that's really their argument. In any case, it's certainly not mine. I try to conduct the most exact and differential analyses in order to indicate how things change, transform themselves, migrate. When I study power relations, I try to study their specific configurations; nothing is more foreign to me than the idea of a master who would impose his law on one. I don't accept either the notion of mastery or the universality of law. On the contrary, I'm very careful to get a grip on the actual mechanisms of the exercise of power; I do this because those who are enmeshed, involved, in these power relations can, in their actions, their resistance, their rebellion, escape them, transform them, in a word, cease being submissive. And if I don't say what needs to be done, it isn't because I believe there is nothing to be done. On the contrary, I think there are a thousand things that can be done, invented, contrived by those who, recognizing the relations of power in which they are involved, have decided to resist them or escape them. From that viewpoint, all my research rests on a postulate of absolute optimism. I don't construct my analyses in order to say, "This is the way things are, you are trapped." I say these things only insofar as I believe it enables us to transform them. Everything I do is done with the conviction that it may be of use.

Q: *Now, I would like to recall a letter you sent to* L'Unità *on December 1, 1978. In that letter you expressed, in particular, your willingness to meet and discuss a whole range of issues with Italian communist intellectuals. You suggested talking about: "the functioning of capitalist states and socialist states, the types of societies that characterize those different countries, the result of the revolutionary movements in the world, the organization of party strategies in Western Europe, the development, all over the world, of repressive apparatuses and security institutions, the difficult connection between local struggles and general issues. . . ." Such a discussion, you said, should not be polemical or designed to increase the distance between camps and interlocutors; rather, it would bring out the differences separating them and hence the dimensions of the research to be done. I would like to ask you what you were proposing, if you can spell it out.*

A: They were themes suggested as the basis of a possible discussion. It seems to me, in fact, that with the current economic crisis and the great oppositions and conflicts that are developing between rich and poor nations (between industrialized and nonindustrialized countries), one can see a developing crisis of government. By "government" I mean the set of institutions and practices, from administration to education, through which people's conduct is guided. This set of procedures, techniques, and methods that ensure the government of some people by others appears to me to be in crisis now, in both the Western and the socialist world. There too, people are more and more dissatisfied with the way in which they are governed: they have more and more problems with it and find it harder and harder to bear. I'm talking about a phenomenon that's expressed in forms of resistance, and at times rebellion, over questions of everyday life as well as great decisions such as the establishment of a nuclear industry or the fact of placing people in this or that economico-political bloc in which they do not feel at ease. I think that, in the history of the West, one can find a period similar to ours, even if things obviously are never repeated, not even tragedies repeated in the form of a farce: I mean the end of the Middle Ages. From the fifteenth to the sixteenth century, there was a whole reorganization of the government of men, that effervescence which produced Protestantism, the formation of the great nation-states, the establishment of absolute monarchies, the partitioning of territories placed under the authority of administrations, the Counterreformation, the Catholic Church's new mode of presence in the world. All that was a kind of reworking of the way in which people were governed in their individual, social, and political relations. It seems to me that we are again experiencing a crisis of government. The set of methods by which some people lead others is being challenged, if not of course by those who lead, who govern, even though they cannot help but take note of the difficulties. We are perhaps at the beginning of a great crisis of reevaluation of the problem of government.

Q: *You said that in this type of inquiry, "the tools of analysis are uncertain when they aren't absent." And the starting points from which certain analyses can be carried out, and new directions and judgments arrived at, are completely different. Moreover, you wanted an encounter that would transcend polemics.*

A: I've been the object of verbal attacks, violent at times, on the part of Italian and French communist intellectuals. Since I don't speak Italian, and since I didn't quite get the meaning of their criticisms, I've never replied. But seeing that they're now showing a willingness to abandon certain Stalinist methods in theoretical discussions, I would like to propose that we abandon the game in which someone says something and is then denounced as an ideologist of the bourgeoisie, a class enemy—so that we can begin a serious debate. If it is acknowledged, for example, that what I say about the crisis of governmental rationality raises an important problem, why couldn't we take that as a basis for a broad debate? Moreover, I think that the Italian communists are more inclined than the French communists to consider a whole series of problems connected, for example, with medicine, or with the local management of economic and social problems—concrete problems that raise the more general question of the relation between legislation and normalization, laws and norms, justice and medicine in contemporary societies. Why not talk about these things together?

Q: *Again relating to polemics, you also made it clear that you don't like or accept the type of discussion "that mimics warfare and parodies judicial procedures." Can you explain what you mean by that?*

A: Discussions on political subjects are parasitized by the model of war: a person who has different ideas is identified as a class enemy who must be fought until a final victory is won. This great theme of ideological struggle makes me smile a little, given that each individual's theoretical ties, when they are examined in their history, are tangled and fluctuating and don't have the clear definition of a border beyond which an enemy could be forced to flee. Isn't this struggle one tries to conduct against an enemy basically a way of giving a degree of seriousness to little disputes that don't have much importance? Don't intellectuals hope to give themselves, through ideological struggle, a greater political weight than they really have? Wouldn't it be more serious, instead, to do research side by side, if in rather divergent directions? If one always insists on saying that one is fighting an enemy, if a day comes when one finds oneself in a situation of actual warfare, which can always happen, will one then be tempted to actually treat him as such? That route leads directly to oppression; it is dangerous. I understand that an intellectual can manifest a desire to be taken seriously by a party or in a society by simulating warfare against an ideological opponent—but that looks dangerous to me. It would be wiser to consider that those with whom one disagrees have made a mistake, or that one hasn't understood what they were trying to do.

NOTES

*   This interview, conducted by D. Trombadori, took place at the end of 1978, and was first published in the Italian journal *Il Contributo* in 1980. [eds.]

1   SFIO: Section française d'internationale ouvrière, the "French Section of the Workers' International." [eds.]

2   Foucault alludes here to the Yugoslavian president's efforts to distance himself and his state from the mission and policies of the Stalinist Soviet Union. [eds.]

3   Neo-Eliatism refers to the Eliatic school of ancient philosophy, famous for its skeptics. [eds.]

4   In the 1960s and 1970s, *Les Temps modernes* was among the most prestigious journals of Marxist and leftist thought in France. [eds.]

5   O. Kirscheimer and G. Ruche, *Punishment and Social Structure* (New York: Columbia University Press, 1939). [eds.]

"*OMNES ET SINGULATIM*": TOWARD A CRITIQUE OF POLITICAL REASON *

I

The title sounds pretentious, I know. But the reason for that is precisely its own excuse. Since the nineteenth century, Western thought has never stopped laboring at the task of criticizing the role of reason—or the lack of reason—in political structures. It's therefore perfectly unfitting to undertake such a vast project once again. However, so many previous attempts are a warrant that every new venture will be just about as successful as the former ones—and in any case, probably just as fortunate.

Under such a banner, mine is the embarrassment of one who has only sketches and incompletable drafts to propose. Philosophy gave up trying to offset the impotence of scientific reason long ago; it no longer tries to complete its edifice.

One of the Enlightenment's tasks was to multiply reason's political powers. But the men of the nineteenth century soon started wondering whether reason wasn't getting too powerful in our societies. They began to worry about a relationship they confusedly suspected between a rationalization-prone society and certain threats to the individual and his liberties, to the species and its survival.

In other words, since Kant, the role of philosophy has been to prevent reason from going beyond the limits of what is given in experience; but from the same moment—that is, from the development of modern states and political management of society—the role of philosophy has also been to keep watch over the excessive powers of political rationality, which is rather a promising life expectancy.

Everybody is aware of such banal facts. But that they are banal does not mean they don't exist. What we have to do with banal facts is to discover, to try to discover, which specific and perhaps original problems are connected with them.

The relationship between rationalization and the excesses of political power is evident. And we should not need to wait for bureaucracy or concentration camps to recognize the existence of such relations. But the problem is what to do with such an evident fact.

Shall we "try" reason? To my mind, nothing would be more sterile. First, because the field has nothing to do with guilt or innocence. Second, because it's senseless to refer to "reason" as the contrary entity to nonreason. Last, because such a trial would trap us into playing the arbitrary and boring part of either the rationalist or the irrationalist.

Shall we investigate this kind of rationalism that seems to be specific to our modern culture and originates in Enlightenment? I think that that was the way of some of the members of the Frankfurt School. My purpose is not to begin a discussion of their works—they are most important and valuable. I would suggest another way of investigating the links between rationalization and power:

1. It may be wise not to take as a whole the rationalization of society or of culture, but to analyze this process in several fields, each of them grounded in a fundamental experience: madness, illness, death, crime, sexuality, and so on.

2. I think that the word "rationalization" is a dangerous one. The main problem when people try to rationalize something is not to investigate whether or not they conform to principles of rationality but to discover which kind of rationality they are using.

3. Even if the Enlightenment has been a very important phase in our history, and in the development of political technology,

I think we have to refer to much more remote processes if we want to understand how we have been trapped in our own history.

This was my modus operandi in my previous work—to analyze the relations between experiences like madness, death, crime, sexuality, and several technologies of power. What I am working on now is the problem of individuality—or, I should say, self-identity in relation to the problem of "individualizing power."

Everyone knows that in European societies political power has evolved toward more and more centralized forms. Historians have been studying this organization of the state, with its administration and bureaucracy, for dozens of years.

I'd like to suggest in these two lectures the possibility of analyzing another kind of transformation in such power relationships. This transformation is, perhaps, less celebrated. But I think that it is also important, mainly for modern societies. Apparently, this evolution seems antagonistic to the evolution toward a centralized state. What I mean in fact is the development of power techniques oriented toward individuals and intended to rule them in a continuous and permanent way. If the state is the political form of a centralized and centralizing power, let us call pastorship the individualizing power.

My purpose this evening is to outline the origin of this pastoral modality of power, or at least some aspects of its ancient history. And in the next lecture, I'll try to show how this pastorship happened to combine with its opposite, the state.

The idea of the deity, or the king, or the leader, as a shepherd followed by a flock of sheep wasn't familiar to the Greeks and Romans. There were exceptions, I know—early ones in Homeric literature, later ones in certain texts of the Lower Empire. I'll come back to them later. Roughly speaking, we can say that the metaphor of the flock didn't occur in great Greek or Roman political literature.

This is not the case in ancient Oriental societies—Egypt, Assyria, Judaea. Pharaoh was an Egyptian shepherd. Indeed, he ritually received the herdsman's crook on his coronation day; and the term "shepherd of men" was one of the Babylonian monarch's titles. But

God was also a shepherd leading men to their grazing ground and ensuring them food. An Egyptian hymn invoked Ra this way: "O Ra that keepest watch when all men sleep, Thou who seekest what is good for thy cattle . . ." The association between God and king is easily made, since both assume the same role: the flock they watch over is the same; the shepherd-king is entrusted with the great divine shepherd's creatures. An Assyrian invocation to the king ran like this: "Illustrious companion of pastures, Thou who carest for thy land and feedest it, shepherd of all abundance."

But, as we know, it was the Hebrews who developed and intensified the pastoral theme—with nevertheless a highly peculiar characteristic: God, and God only, is his people's shepherd. With just one positive exception: David, as the founder of the monarchy, is the only one to be referred to as a shepherd. God gave him the task of assembling a flock.

There are negative exceptions, too. Wicked kings are consistently compared to bad shepherds; they disperse the flock, let it die of thirst, shear it solely for profit's sake. Yahweh is the one and only true shepherd. He guides his own people in person, aided only by his prophets. As the Psalms say: "Like a flock / hast Thou led Thy people, by Moses' and by Aaron's hand." Of course, I can treat neither the historical problems pertaining to the origin of this comparison nor its evolution throughout Jewish thought. I just want to show a few themes typical of pastoral power. I'd like to point out the contrast with Greek political thought, and to show how important these themes became in Christian thought and institutions later on.

1. The shepherd wields power over a flock rather than over a land. It's probably much more complex than that, but, broadly speaking, the relation between the deity, the land, and men differs from that of the Greeks. Their gods owned the land, and this primary possession determined the relationship between men and gods. On the contrary, it's the Shepherd-God's relationship with his flock that is primary and fundamental here. God gives, or promises, his flock a land.

2. The shepherd gathers together, guides, and leads his flock. The idea that the political leader was to quiet any hostilities

within the city and make unity reign over conflict is undoubtedly present in Greek thought. But what the shepherd gathers
together is dispersed individuals. They gather together on
hearing his voice: "I'll whistle and will gather them together."
Conversely, the shepherd only has to disappear for the flock
to be scattered. In other words, the shepherd's immediate
presence and direct action cause the flock to exist. Once the
good Greek lawgiver, like Solon, has resolved any conflicts,
what he leaves behind him is a strong city with laws enabling
it to endure without him.

3. The shepherd's role is to ensure the salvation of his flock. The
Greeks said also that the deity saved the city; they never
stopped declaring that the competent leader is a helmsman
warding his ship away from the rocks. But the way the shepherd saves his flock is quite different. It's not only a matter of
saving them all, all together, when danger comes nigh. It's a
matter of constant, individualized, and final kindness. Constant kindness, for the shepherd ensures his flock's food; every
day he attends to their thirst and hunger. The Greek god was
asked to provide a fruitful land and abundant crops. He wasn't
asked to foster a flock day by day. And individualized kindness,
too, for the shepherd sees that all the sheep, each and every
one of them, is fed and saved. Later Hebrew literature, especially, laid the emphasis on such individually kindly power: a
rabbinical commentary on Exodus explains why Yahweh
chose Moses to shepherd his people: he had left his flock to
go and search for one lost sheep.

Last and not least, it's final kindness. The shepherd has a
target for his flock. It must either be led to good grazing
ground or brought back to the fold.

4. Yet another difference lies in the idea that wielding power is
a "duty." The Greek leader, naturally, had to make decisions
in the interest of all; he would have been a bad leader had he
preferred his personal interest. But his duty was a glorious
one: even if in war he had to give up his life, such a sacrifice
was offset by something extremely precious—immortality. He
never lost. By way of contrast, shepherdly kindness is much
closer to "devotedness." Everything the shepherd does is

geared to the good of his flock. That's his constant concern. When they sleep, *he* keeps watch.

The theme of keeping watch is important. It brings out two aspects of the shepherd's devotedness. First, he acts, he works, he puts himself out, for those he nourishes and who are asleep. Second, he watches over them. He pays attention to them all and scans each one of them. He's got to know his flock as a whole, and in detail. Not only must he know where good pastures are, the seasons' laws, and the order of things; he must also know each one's particular needs. Once again, a rabbinical commentary on Exodus describes Moses' qualities as a shepherd in this way: he would send each sheep in turn to graze—first, the youngest, for them to browse on the tenderest sward; then the older ones; and last the oldest, who were capable of browsing on the roughest grass. The shepherd's power implies individual attention paid to each member of the flock.

These are just themes that Hebraic texts associate with the metaphors of the Shepherd-God and his flock of people. In no way do I claim that that is effectively how political power was wielded in Hebrew society before the fall of Jerusalem. I do not even claim that such a conception of political power is in any way coherent.

They're just themes. Paradoxical, even contradictory, ones. Christianity was to give them considerable importance, both in the Middle Ages and in modern times. Among all the societies in history, ours—I mean, those that came into being at the end of Antiquity on the Western side of the European continent—have perhaps been the most aggressive and the most conquering; they have been capable of the most stupefying violence, against themselves as well as against others. They invented a great many different political forms. They profoundly altered their legal structures several times. It must be kept in mind that they alone evolved a strange technology of power treating the vast majority of men as a flock with a few as shepherds. Thus, they established between them a series of complex, continuous, and paradoxical relationships.

This is undoubtedly something singular in the course of history. Clearly, the development of "pastoral technology" in the management of men profoundly disrupted the structures of ancient society.

*   *   *

So as to better explain the importance of this disruption, I'd like to briefly return to what I was saying about the Greeks. I can see the objections liable to be made.

One is that the Homeric poems use the shepherd metaphor to refer to the kings. In the *Iliad* and the *Odyssey*, the expression poimēn laon crops up several times. It qualifies the leaders, highlighting the grandeur of their power. Moreover, it's a ritual title, common in even late Indo-European literature. In *Beowulf,* the king is still regarded as a shepherd. But there is nothing really surprising in the fact that the same title, as in the Assyrian texts, is to be found in archaic epic poems.

The problem arises, rather, as to Greek thought: there is at least one category of texts where references to shepherd models are made—the Pythagorean ones. The metaphor of the herdsman appears in the *Fragments* of Archytas, quoted by Stobeus. The word nomos (the law) is connected with the word nomeus (shepherd): the shepherd shares out, the law apportions. Then Zeus is called Nomios and Nemeios because he gives his sheep food. And, finally, the magistrate must be philanthrōpos, that is, devoid of selfishness. He must be full of zeal and solicitude, like a shepherd.

B. Grube, the German editor of Archytas' *Fragments*, says that this proves a Hebrew influence unique in Greek literature. Other commentators, such as Armand Delatte, say that the comparison between gods, magistrates, and shepherds was common in Greece; it is therefore not to be dwelt upon.

I shall restrict myself to political literature. The results of the inquiry are clear: the political metaphor of the shepherd occurs neither in Isocrates, nor in Demosthenes, nor in Aristotle. This is rather surprising when one reflects that in his *Areopagiticus*, Isocrates insists on the magistrates' duties; he stresses the need for them to be devoted and to show concern for young people. Yet not a word as to any shepherd.

By contrast, Plato often speaks of the shepherd-magistrate. He mentions the idea in *Critias, The Republic*, and *Laws*. He thrashes it out in *The Statesman*. In the former, the shepherd theme is rather subordinate. Sometimes, those happy days when mankind was governed directly by the gods and grazed on abundant pastures are evoked (*Critias*). Sometimes, the magistrates' necessary virtue—as contrasted with Thrasymachos' vice, is what is insisted upon (*The Republic*). And sometimes, the problem is to define the subordinate magistrates' role: indeed, they, just as the watchdogs, have to obey "those at the top of the scale" (*Laws*).

But in *The Statesman*, pastoral power is the central problem and it is treated at length. Can the city's decision-maker, can the commander, be defined as a sort of shepherd?

Plato's analysis is well known. To solve this question he uses the division method. A distinction is drawn between the man who conveys orders to inanimate things (for example, the architect) and the man who gives orders to animals; between the man who gives orders to isolated animals (like a yoke of oxen) and he who gives orders to flocks; and he who gives orders to animal flocks, and he who commands human flocks. And there we have the political leader—a shepherd of men.

But this first division remains unsatisfactory. It has to be pushed further. The method of opposing *men* to all the other animals isn't a good one. And so the dialogue starts all over again. A whole series of distinctions is established: between wild animals and tame ones; those which live in water and those which live on land; those with horns and those without; between cleft- and plain-hoofed animals; between those capable and incapable of mutual reproduction. And the dialogue wanders astray with these never-ending subdivisions.

So, what do the initial development of the dialogue and its subsequent failure show? That the division method can prove nothing at all when it isn't managed correctly. It also shows that the idea of analyzing political power as the relationship between a shepherd and his animals was probably a rather controversial one at the time. Indeed, it's the first assumption to cross the interlocutors' minds when seeking to discover the essence of the politician. Was it a commonplace at the time? Or, rather, was Plato discussing one of the Pythagorean themes? The absence of the shepherd metaphor in other contemporary political texts seems to tip the scale toward the second hypothesis. But we can probably leave the discussion open.

My personal inquiry bears upon how Plato impugns the theme in the rest of the dialogue. He does so first by means of methodological arguments, then by means of the celebrated myth of the world revolving around its spindle.

The methodological arguments are extremely interesting. Whether the king is a sort of shepherd or not can be told not by deciding which different species can form a flock but, rather, by analyzing what the shepherd does.

What is characteristic of his task? First, the shepherd is alone at the head of his flock. Second, his job is to supply his cattle with food; to care for them when they are sick; to play them music to get them together, and guide them; to arrange their intercourse with a view to the finest offspring. So we *do* find the typical shepherd metaphor themes of Oriental texts.

And what's the king's task in regard to all this? Like the shepherd, he is alone at the head of the city. But, for the rest, who provides mankind with food? The king? No. The farmer, the baker do. Who looks after men when they are sick? The king? No. The physician. And who guides them with music? The gymnasiarch—not the king. And so, many citizens could quite legitimately claim the title "shepherd of men." Just as the human flock's shepherd has many rivals, so has the politician. Consequently, if we want to find out what the politician really and essentially is, we must sift it out from "the surrounding flood," thereby demonstrating in what ways he *isn't* a shepherd.

Plato therefore resorts to the myth of the world revolving around its axis in two successive and contrary motions.

In a first phase, each animal species belonged to a flock led by a Genius-shepherd. The human flock was led by the deity itself. It could lavishly avail itself of the fruits of the earth; it needed no abode; and, after Death, men came back to life. A crucial sentence adds: "The deity being their shepherd, mankind needed no political constitution."

In a second phase, the world turned in the opposite direction. The gods were no longer men's shepherds; men had to look after themselves, for they had been given fire. What would the politician's role then be? Would *he* become the shepherd in the gods' stead? Not at all. His job was to weave a strong fabric for the city. Being a politician didn't mean feeding, nursing, and breeding offspring but, rather, binding: binding different virtues; binding contrary temperaments (either impetuous or moderate), using the "shuttle" of popular opinion. The royal art of ruling consisted in gathering lives together "into a community based upon concord and friendship," and so he wove "the finest of fabrics." The entire population, "slaves and free men alike, were mantled in its folds."

The Statesman therefore seems to be classical Antiquity's most systematic reflection on the theme of the pastorate that was later to become so important in the Christian West. That we are discussing it seems to prove that a perhaps initially Oriental theme was important enough in Plato's day to deserve investigation, but I stress the fact that it was impugned.

Not impugned entirely, however. Plato did admit that the physician, the farmer, the gymnasiarch, and the pedagogue acted as shepherds. But he refused to get them involved with the politician's activity. He said so explicitly: How would the politician ever find the time to come and sit by each person, feed him, give him concerts, and care for him when sick? Only a god in a golden age could ever act like that; or again, like a physician or pedagogue, be responsible for the lives and development of a few individuals. But, situated between the two—the gods and the swains—the men who hold political power are not to be shepherds. Their task doesn't consist in fostering the life of a group of individuals. It consists in forming and assuring the city's unity. In short, the political problem is that of the relation between the one and the many in the framework of the city and its citizens. The pastoral problem concerns the lives of individuals.

All this seems very remote, perhaps. The reason for my insisting on these ancient texts is that they show us how early this problem—or rather, this series of problems—arose. They span the entirety of Western history. They are still quite important for contemporary society. They deal with the relations between political power at work within the state as a legal framework of unity, and a power we can call "pastoral," whose role is to constantly ensure, sustain, and improve the lives of each and every one.

The well-known "welfare state problem" does not only bring the needs or the new governmental techniques of today's world to light. It must be recognized for what it is: one of the extremely numerous reappearances of the tricky adjustment between political power wielded over legal subjects and pastoral power wielded over live individuals.

Obviously, I have no intention whatsoever of recounting the evolution of pastoral power throughout Christianity. The immense problems this would raise can easily be imagined: from doctrinal problems, such as Christ's denomination as "the good shepherd," right up to institutional ones such as parochial organization or the way pastoral responsibilities were shared between priests and bishops.

All I want to do is bring to light two or three aspects I regard as important for the evolution of pastorship, that is, the technology of power.

First of all, let us examine the theoretical elaboration of the theme in ancient Christian literature: Chyrsostom, Cyprian, Ambrose, Jerome, and, for monastic life, Cassian or Benedict. The Hebrew themes are considerably altered in at least four ways:

1. First, with regard to responsibility. We saw that the shepherd was to assume responsibility for the destiny of the whole flock and of each and every sheep. In the Christian conception, the shepherd must render an account—not only of each sheep, but of all their actions, all the good or evil they are liable to do, all that happens to them.

   Moreover, between each sheep and its shepherd Christianity conceives a complex exchange and circulation of sins and merits. The sheep's sin is also imputable to the shepherd. He'll have to render an account of it at the Final Judgment. Conversely, by helping his flock to find salvation, the shepherd will also find his own. But by saving his sheep, he lays himself open to getting lost; so if he wants to save himself, he must run the risk of losing himself for others. If he does get lost, it is the flock that will incur the greatest danger. But let's leave all these paradoxes aside. My aim was just to underline the force and complexity of the moral ties binding the shepherd to each member of his flock. And what I especially wanted to underline was that such ties not only concerned individuals' lives but the details of their actions as well.

2. The second important alteration concerns the problem of obedience. In the Hebrew conception, God being a shepherd, the flock following him complies to his will, to his law.

   Christianity, on the other hand, conceived the shepherd-sheep relationship as one of individual and complete dependence. This is undoubtedly one of the points at which Christian pastorship radically diverged from Greek thought. If a Greek had to obey, he did so because it was the law, or the will of the city. If he did happen to follow the will of someone in particular (a physician, an orator, a pedagogue), then that person had rationally persuaded him to do so. And it had to be for a strictly determined aim: to be cured, to acquire a skill, to make the best choice.

In Christianity, the tie with the shepherd is an individual one. It is personal submission to him. His will is done, not because it is consistent with the law, and not just as far as it is consistent with it, but, principally, because it is his *will*. In Cassian's *Cenobitical Institutions*, there are many edifying anecdotes in which the monk finds salvation by carrying out the absurdest of his superior's orders. Obedience is a virtue. This means that it is not, as for the Greeks, a provisional means to an end but, rather, an end in itself. It is a permanent state; the sheep must permanently submit to their pastors—*subditi*. As Saint Benedict says, monks do not live according to their own free will; their wish is to be under the abbot's command—*ambulantes alieno judicio et imperio*. Greek Christianity named this state of obedience apatheia. The evolution of the word's meaning is significant. In Greek philosophy, apatheia denotes the control that the individual, thanks to the exercise of reason, can exert over his passions. In Christian thought, pathos is willpower exerted over oneself, for oneself. Apatheia delivers us from such willfulness.

3. Christian pastorship implies a peculiar type of knowledge between the pastor and each of his sheep.

This knowledge is particular. It individualizes. It isn't enough to know the state of the flock. That of each sheep must also be known. The theme existed long before there was Christian pastorship, but it was considerably amplified in three different ways. The shepherd must be informed as to the material needs of each member of the flock and provide for them when necessary. He must know what is going on, what each of them does—his public sins. Last but not least, he must know what goes on in the soul of each one, that is, his secret sins, his progress on the road to sanctity.

In order to ensure this individual knowledge, Christianity appropriated two essential instruments at work in the Hellenistic world—self-examination and the guidance of conscience. It took them over, but not without altering them considerably.

It is well known that self-examination was widespread among the Pythagoreans, the Stoics, and the Epicureans as a means of daily taking stock of the good or evil performed in regard to one's duties. One's progress on the way to perfection, (that is, self-mastery) and the domination of one's passions could thus be measured. The guidance of conscience was also predominant in certain cultured circles, but as advice given—and sometimes paid for—in particularly difficult circumstances: in mourning, or when one was suffering a setback.

Christian pastorship closely associated these two practices. On one hand, conscience-guiding constituted a constant bind: the sheep didn't let itself be led only to come through any rough passage victoriously, it let itself be led every second. Being guided was a state and you were fatally lost if you tried to escape it. The ever-quoted phrase runs like this: He who suffers not guidance withers away like a dead leaf. As for self-examination, its aim was not to close self-awareness in upon itself but, rather, to enable it to open up entirely to its director—to unveil to him the depths of the soul.

There are a great many first-century ascetic and monastic texts concerning the link between guidance and self-examination which show how crucial these techniques were for Christianity and how complex they had already become. What I would like to emphasize is that they delineate the emergence of a very strange phenomenon in Greco-Roman civilization, that is, the organization of a link between total obedience, knowledge of oneself, and confession to someone else.

4. There is another transformation—maybe the most important. All those Christian techniques of examination, confession, guidance, obedience, have an aim: to get individuals to work

at their own "mortification" in this world. Mortification is not death, of course, but it is a renunciation of this world and of oneself, a kind of everyday death—a death that is supposed to provide life in another world. This is not the first time we see the shepherd theme associated with death; but here it is different than in the Greek idea of political power. It is not a sacrifice for the city: Christian mortification is a kind of relation of oneself to oneself. It is a part, a constitutive part of Christian self-identity.

We can say that Christian pastorship has introduced a game that neither the Greeks nor the Hebrews imagined. It is a strange game whose elements are life, death, truth, obedience, individuals, self-identity—a game that seems to have nothing to do with the game of the city surviving through the sacrifice of the citizens. Our societies proved to be really demonic since they happened to combine those two games—the city-citizen game and the shepherd-flock game—in what we call the modern states.

As you may notice, what I have been trying to do this evening is not to solve a problem but to suggest a way to approach a problem. This problem is similar to those I have been working on since my first book about insanity and mental illness. As I told you previously, this problem deals with the relations between experiences (like madness, illness, transgression of laws, sexuality, self-identity), knowledge (like psychiatry, medicine, criminology, sexology, psychology), and power (such as the power wielded in psychiatric and penal institutions, and in all other institutions that deal with individual control).

Our civilization has developed the most complex system of knowledge, the most sophisticated structures of power. What has this kind of knowledge, this type of power made of us? In what way are those fundamental experiences of madness, suffering, death, crime, desire, individuality connected—even if we are not aware of it—with knowledge and power? I am sure I'll never get the answer; but that does not mean that we don't have to ask the question.

II

I have tried to show how primitive Christianity shaped the idea of a pastoral influence continuously exerting itself on individuals and through the demonstration of their particular truth. And I have tried to show how this idea of pastoral power was foreign to Greek thought despite a certain number of borrowings such as practical self-examination and the guidance of conscience.

I would like at this time, leaping across many centuries, to describe another episode that has been in itself particularly important in the history of this government of individuals by their own verity.

This instance concerns the formation of the state in the modern sense of the word. If I make this historical connection, it is obviously not in order to suggest that the aspect of pastoral power disappeared during the ten great centuries of Christian Europe, Catholic and Roman, but it seems to me that this period, contrary to what one might expect, has not been that of the triumphant pastorate. And that is true for several reasons: some are of an economic nature—the pastorate of souls is an especially urban experience, difficult to reconcile with the poor and extensive rural economy at the beginning of the Middle Ages. The other reasons are of a cultural nature: the pastorate is a complicated technique that demands a certain level of culture, not only on the part of the pastor but also among his flock. Other reasons relate to the sociopolitical structure. Feudality developed between individuals a tissue of personal bonds of an altogether different type than the pastorate.

I do not wish to say that the idea of a pastoral government of men disappeared entirely in the medieval Church. It has, indeed, remained and one can even say that it has shown great vitality. Two series of facts tend to prove this. First, the reforms that had been made in the Church itself, especially in the monastic orders—the different reforms operating successively inside existing monasteries—had the goal of restoring the rigor of pastoral order among the monks themselves. As for the newly created orders—Dominican and Franciscan—essentially they proposed to perform pastoral work among the faithful. The Church tried ceaselessly during successive crises to regain its pastoral functions. But there is more. In the population itself one sees all during the Middle Ages the development of a long series of struggles whose object was pastoral power. Critics of the Church that fails in its obligations reject its hierarchical structure, look for the more or less spontaneous forms of community in which the flock could find the shepherd it needed. This search for pastoral expression took on numerous aspects, at times extremely violent struggles, as was the case for the Vaudois, sometimes peaceful quests as among the Frères de la Vie community. Sometimes it stirred very extensive movements such as the Hussites, sometimes it fermented limited groups like the Amis de Dieu de l'Oberland. Some of these movements were close to heresy, as among the Beghards; others were at times stirring orthodox movements that dwelled within the bosom of the Church (like that of the Italian Oratorians in the fifteenth century).

I raise all of this in a very allusive manner in order to emphasize that if the pastorate was not instituted as an effective, practical government of men during the Middle Ages, it has been a permanent concern and a stake in constant struggles. There was, across the entire period of the Middle Ages, a yearning to arrange pastoral relations among men, and this aspiration affected both the mystical tide and the great millenarian dreams.

Of course, I don't intend to treat here the problem of how states are formed. Nor do I intend to go into the different economic, social, and political processes from which they stem. Neither do I want to analyze the different institutions or mechanisms with which states equipped themselves in order to ensure their survival. I'd just like to give some fragmentary indications as to something midway between the state as a type of political organization and its mechanisms, namely, the type of rationality implemented in the exercise of state power.

I mentioned this in my first lecture. Rather than wonder whether aberrant state power is due to excessive rationalism or irrationalism, I think it would be more appropriate to pin down the specific type of political rationality the state produced.

After all, at least in this respect, political practices resemble scientific ones: it's not "reason in general" that is implemented but always a very specific type of rationality.

The striking thing is that the rationality of state power was reflective and perfectly aware of its specificity. It was not tucked away in spontaneous, blind practices. It was not brought to light by some retrospective analysis. It was formulated especially in two sets of doctrine: the *reason of state* and the *theory of police*. These two phrases soon acquired narrow and pejorative meanings, I know. But for the 150 or 200 years during which modern states were formed, their meaning was much broader than now.

The doctrine of reason of state attempted to define how the principles and methods of state government differed, say, from the way God governed the world, the father his family, or a superior his community.

The doctrine of the police defines the nature of the objects of the state's rational activity; it defines the nature of the aims it pursues, the general form of the instruments involved.

So, what I'd like to speak about today is the system of rationality. But first, there are two preliminaries: First, Friedrich Meinecke having published a most important book on reason of state, I'll speak mainly of the policing theory. Second, Germany and Italy underwent the greatest difficulties in getting established as states, and they produced the greatest number of reflections on reason of state and the police. I'll often refer to the Italian and German texts.

Let's begin with *reason of state*. Here are a few definitions:

Botero: "A perfect knowledge of the means through which states form, strengthen themselves, endure, and grow."

Palazzo (*Discourse on Government and True Reason of State*, 1606): "A rule or art enabling us to discover how to establish peace and order within the Republic."

Chemnitz (*De Ratione status*, 1647): "A certain political consideration required for all public matters, councils, and projects, whose only aim is the state's preservation, expansion, and felicity; to which end, the easiest and promptest means are to be employed."

Let me consider certain features these definitions have in common.

1. Reason of state is regarded as an "art," that is, a technique conforming to certain rules. These rules do not simply pertain to customs or traditions, but to knowledge—rational knowledge. Nowadays, the expression "reason of state" evokes "arbitrariness" or "violence." But at the time, what people had in mind was a rationality specific to the art of governing states.

2. From where does this specific art of government draw its rationale? The answer to this question provokes the scandal of nascent political thought. And yet it's very simple: the art of governing is rational, if reflection causes it to observe the nature of what is governed—here, the *state*.

Now, to state such a platitude is to break with a simultaneously Christian and judiciary tradition, a tradition that claimed that government was essentially just. It respected a whole system of laws: human laws, the law of nature, divine law.

There is a quite significant text by Aquinas on these points. He recalls that "art, in its field, must imitate what nature carries out in its own"; it is only reasonable under that condition. The king's government of his kingdom must imitate God's government of nature or, again, the soul's government of the body. The king must found cities just as God created the world, just as the soul gives form to the body. The king must also lead men toward their finality, just as God does for natural beings, or as the soul does when directing the body. And what is man's finality? What's good for the body? No; he'd need only a physician, not a king. Wealth? No; a steward would suffice. Truth? Not even that, for only a teacher would be needed. Man needs someone capable of opening up the way to heavenly bliss through his conformity, here on earth, to what is *honestum*.

As we can see, the model for the art of government is that of God imposing his laws upon his creatures. Aquinas's model for rational government is not a political one, whereas what the sixteenth and seventeenth centuries seek under the denomination "reason of state" are principles capable of guiding an actual government. They aren't concerned with nature and its laws in general—they're concerned with what the state is; what its exigencies are.

And so we can understand the religious scandal aroused by such a type of research. It explains why reason of state was assimilated to atheism. In France, in particular, the expression generated in a political context was commonly associated with "atheist."

3. Reason of state is also opposed to another tradition. In *The Prince*, Machiavelli's problem is to decide how a province or territory acquired through inheritance or by conquest can be held against its internal or external rivals. Machiavelli's entire analysis is aimed at defining what keeps up or reinforces the link between prince and state, whereas the problem posed by reason of state is that of the very existence and nature of the state itself. This is why the theoreticians of reason of state tried to stay aloof from Machiavelli; he had a bad reputation, and they couldn't recognize their own problem in his. Conversely, those opposed to reason of state tried to impair this new art of governing, denouncing it as Machiavelli's legacy. However, despite these confused quarrels a century after *The Prince* had been written, *reason of state* marks the emergence of an extremely—albeit only partly—different type of rationality from Machiavelli's.

The aim of such an art of governing is precisely not to reinforce the power a prince can wield over his domain: its aim is to reinforce the state itself. This is one of the most characteristic features of all the definitions that the sixteenth and seventeenth centuries put forward. Rational government is this, so to speak: given the nature of the state, it can hold down its enemies for an indeterminate length of time. It can do so only if it increases its own strength. And its enemies do likewise. The state whose only concern would be to hold out would most certainly come to disaster. This idea is a very important one. It is bound up with a new historical outlook; indeed, it implies that states are realities that must hold out for an indefinite length of historical time—and in a disputed geographical area.

4. Finally, we can see that reason of state, understood as rational government able to increase the state's strength in accordance with itself, presupposes the constitution of a certain type of knowledge. Government is only possible if the strength of the state is known; it can thus be sustained. The state's capacity, and the means to enlarge it, must be known. The strength and capacities of the other states must also be known. Indeed, the governed state must hold out against the others. Government

therefore entails more than just implementing general principles of reason, wisdom, and prudence. Knowledge is necessary—concrete, precise, and measured knowledge as to the state's strength. The art of governing, characteristic of reason of state, is intimately bound up with the development of what was then called either political "statistics" or "arithmetic," that is, the knowledge of different states' respective forces. Such knowledge was indispensable for correct government.

Briefly speaking, then: reason of state is not an art of government according to divine, natural, or human laws. It doesn't have to respect the general order of the world. It's government in accordance with the state's strength. It's government whose aim is to increase this strength within an extensive and competitive framework.

So what the seventeenth- and eighteenth-century authors understand by "the police" is very different from what we put under the term. It would be worth studying why these authors are mostly Italians and Germans, but whatever! What they understand by "police" is not an institution or mechanism functioning within the state but a governmental technology peculiar to the state—domains, techniques, targets where the state intervenes.

To be clear and simple, I will exemplify what I'm saying with a text that is both utopian and a project. It's one of the first utopia programs for a policed state. Louis Turquet de Mayerne drew it up and presented it in 1611 to the Dutch States General. In his book *Science and Rationalism in the Government of Louis XIV*, J. King draws attention to the importance of this strange work. Its title is *Aristo-democratic Monarchy*. That's enough to show what is important in the author's eyes—not so much choosing between these different types of constitution as their mixture in view to a vital end, namely, the state. Turquet also calls it the City, the Republic, or yet again, the Police.

Here is the organization Turquet proposes. Four grand officials rank beside the king. One is in charge of Justice; another, of the Army; the third, of the Exchequer, that is, the king's taxes and revenues; the fourth is in charge of the *police*. It seems that this officer's role was to have been mainly a moral one. According to Turquet, he was to foster among the people "modesty, charity, loyalty, industriousness, friendly cooperation, honesty." We recognize the traditional idea that the subject's virtue ensures the kingdom's good management. But, when we come down to the details, the outlook is somewhat different.

Turquet suggests that in each province, there should be boards keeping law and order. There should be two that see to people; the other two see to things. The first board pertaining to people was to see to the positive, active, productive aspects of life. In other words, it was concerned with education; determining each one's tastes and aptitudes; the choosing of occupations—useful ones (each person over the age of twenty-five had to be enrolled on a register noting his occupation). Those not usefully employed were regarded as the dregs of society.

The second board was to see to the negative aspects of life: the poor (widows, orphans, the aged) requiring help; the unemployed; those whose activities required financial aid (no interest was to be charged); public health (disease, epidemics); and accidents such as fire and flood.

One of the boards concerned with things was to specialize in commodities and manufactured goods. It was to indicate what was to be produced and how; it was also to control markets and trading. The fourth board would see to the "demesne," that is, the territory, space: private property, legacies, donations, sales were to be controlled; manorial rights were to be reformed; roads, rivers, public buildings, and forests would also be seen to.

In many features, the text is akin to the political utopias that were so numerous at the time. But it is also contemporary with the great theoretical discussions on reason of state and the administrative organization of monarchies. It is highly representative of what the epoch considered a traditionally governed state's tasks to be.

What does this text demonstrate?

1. The "police" appears as an administration heading the state, together with the judiciary, the army, and the exchequer. True. Yet in fact, it embraces everything else. Turquet says so: "It branches out into all of the people's conditions, everything they do or undertake. Its field comprises justice, finance, and the army."

2. The *police* includes everything. But from an extremely particular point of view. Men and things are envisioned as to their
   relationships: men's coexistence on a territory; their relationships as to property; what they produce; what is exchanged on
   the market. It also considers how they live, the diseases and
   accidents that can befall them. What the police sees to is a
   live, active, productive man. Turquet employs a remarkable
   expression: "The police's true object is man."

3. Such intervention in men's activities could well be qualified
   as totalitarian. What are the aims pursued? They fall into two
   categories. First, the police has to do with everything providing the city with adornment, form, and splendor. Splendor denotes not only the beauty of a state ordered to perfection but
   also its strength, its vigor. The police therefore ensures and
   highlights the state's vigor. Second, the police's other purpose
   is to foster working and trading relations between men, as
   well as aid and mutual help. There again, the word Turquet
   uses is important: the police must ensure "communication"
   among men, in the broad sense of the word—otherwise, men
   wouldn't be able to live, or their lives would be precarious,
   poverty-stricken, and perpetually threatened.
   And here, we can make out what is, I think, an important
   idea. As a form of rational intervention wielding political
   power over men, the role of the police is to supply them with
   a little extra life—and, by so doing, supply the state with a little
   extra strength. This is done by controlling "communication,"
   that is, the common activities of individuals (work, production,
   exchange, accommodation).

You'll object: "But that's only the utopia of some obscure author.
You can hardly deduce any significant consequences from it!" But
I say: Turquet's book is but one example of a huge literature circulating in most European countries of the day. The fact that it is
over-simple and yet very detailed brings out all the better the
characteristics that could be recognized elsewhere. Above all, I'd
say that such ideas were not stillborn. They spread all through the
seventeenth and eighteenth centuries, either as applied policies

(such as Cameralism or mercantilism), or as subjects to be taught (the German *Polizeiwissenschaft*; let us not forget that this was the title under which the science of administration was taught in Germany).

These are the two perspectives that I'd like, not to study, but at least to suggest. First I'll refer to a French administrative compendium, then to a German textbook.

1. Every historian knows N. De Lamare's compendium, *Treaty on the Police*. At the beginning of the eighteenth century, this administrator undertook the compilation of the whole kingdom's police regulations. It's an infinite source of very valuable information. The general conception of the police that such a quantity of rules and regulations could convey to an administrator like De Lamare is what I'd like to emphasize.

De Lamare says that the police must see to eleven things within the state: (1) religion; (2) morals; (3) health; (4) supplies; (5) roads, highways, town buildings; (6) public safety; (7) the liberal arts (roughly speaking, arts and science); (8) trade; (9) factories; (10) manservants and laborers; (11) the poor.

The same classification features in every treatise concerning the police. As in Turquet's utopia program, apart from the army, justice properly speaking, and direct taxes, the police apparently sees to everything. The same thing can be said differently: royal power had asserted itself against feudalism, thanks to the support of an armed force and by developing a judicial system and establishing a tax system. These were the ways in which royal power was traditionally wielded. Now, "the police" is the term covering the whole new field in which centralized political and administrative power can intervene.

Now, what is the logic behind intervention in cultural rites, small-scale production techniques, intellectual life, and the road network?

De Lamare's answer seems a bit hesitant. Here he says, "The police sees to everything pertaining to men's *happiness*"; there he says, "The police sees to everything regulating '*society*' (social relations) carried on between men"; elsewhere he says that the police sees to *living*. This is the definition I will dwell upon. It's the most original and it clarifies the other two, and De Lamare himself dwells upon it. He makes the following remarks as to the police's eleven objects. The police deals with religion, not, of course, from the viewpoint of dogmatic truth but from that of the moral quality of life. In seeing to health and supplies, it deals with the preservation of life; concerning trade, factories, workers, the poor, and public order—it deals with the conveniences of life. In seeing to the theater, literature, entertainment, its object is life's pleasures. In short, life is the object of the police: the indispensable, the useful, and the superfluous. That people survive, live, and even do better than just that: this is what the police has to ensure.

And so we link up with the other definitions De Lamare proposes: "The sole purpose of the police is to lead man to the utmost happiness to be enjoyed in this life." Or, again, the police cares for the good of the soul (thanks to religion and morality), the good of the body (food, health, clothing, housing), wealth (industry, trade, labor). Or, again, the police sees to the benefits that can be derived only from living in society.

2. Now let us have a look at the German textbooks. They were used to teach the science of administration somewhat later on. It was taught in various universities, especially in Göttingen, and was extremely important for continental Europe. Here it was that the Prussian, Austrian, and Russian civil servants— those who were to carry out Joseph II's and Catherine the Great's reforms—were trained. Certain Frenchmen, especially in Napoleon's entourage, knew the teachings of *Polizeiwissenschaft* very well.

What was to be found in these textbooks?

Huhenthal's *Liber de politia* featured the following items: the number of citizens; religion and morals; health; food; the safety of persons and of goods (particularly in reference to fires and floods); the administration of justice; citizens' conveniences and pleasures (how to obtain them, how to restrict them). Then comes a series of chapters about rivers, forests, mines, brine pits, housing, and, finally, several chapters on how to acquire goods either through farming, industry, or trade.

In his *Précis for the Police*, J. P. Willebrand speaks successively of morals, trades and crafts, health, safety, and last of all, town building and planning. Considering the subjects at least, there isn't a great deal of difference from De Lamare's.

But the most important of these texts is Johann Heinrich Gottlob von Justi's *Elements of Police*. The police's specific purpose is still defined as live individuals living in society. Nevertheless, the way von Justi organizes his book is somewhat different. He studies first what he calls the "state's landed property," that is, its territory. He considers it in two different aspects: how it is inhabited (town versus country), and then who inhabit these territories (the number of people, their growth, health, mortality, immigration). Von Justi then analyzes the "goods and chattels," that is, the commodities, manufactured goods, and their circulation, which involve problems pertaining to cost, credit, and currency. Finally, the last part is devoted to the conduct of individuals: their morals, their occupational capabilities, their honesty, and how they respect the law.

In my opinion, von Justi's work is a much more advanced demonstration of how the police problem evolved than De Lamare's introduction to his compendium of statutes. There are four reasons for this.

First, von Justi defines much more clearly what the central paradox of *police* is. The police, he says, is what enables the state to increase its power and exert its strength to the full. On the other hand, the police has to keep the citizens happy— happiness being understood as survival, life, and improved living. He perfectly defines what I feel to be the aim of the modern art of government, or state rationality, namely, to develop those elements constitutive of individuals' lives in such a way that their development also fosters the strength of the state.

Von Justi then draws a distinction between this task, which he calls *Polizei*, as do his contemporaries, and *Politik, Die Politik. Die Politik* is basically a negative task: it consists in the state's fighting against its internal and external enemies. *Pol-*

izei, however, is a positive task: it has to foster both citizens' lives *and* the state's strength.

And here is the important point: von Justi insists much more than does De Lamare on a notion that became increasingly important during the eighteenth century—population. Population was understood as a group of live individuals. Their characteristics were those of all the individuals belonging to the same species, living side by side. (Thus, they presented mortality and fecundity rates; they were subject to epidemics, overpopulation; they presented a certain type of territorial distribution.) True, De Lamare did use the term "life" to characterize the concern of the police, but the emphasis he gave it wasn't very pronounced. Proceeding through the eighteenth century, and especially in Germany, we see that what is defined as the object of the police is population, that is, a group of beings living in a given area.

And last, one only has to read von Justi to see that it is not only a utopia, as with Turquet, or a compendium of systematically filed regulations. Von Justi claims to draw up a *Polizeiwissenschaft*. His book isn't simply a list of prescriptions: it's also a grid through which the state—that is, territory, resources, population, towns, and so on—can be observed. Von Justi combines "statistics" (the description of states) with the art of government. *Polizeiwissenschaft* is at once an art of government and a method for the analysis of a population living on a territory.

Such historical considerations must appear to be very remote; they must seem useless in regard to present-day concerns. I wouldn't go as far as Hermann Hesse, who says that only the "constant reference to history, the past, and antiquity" is fecund. But experience has taught me that the history of various forms of rationality is sometimes more effective in unsettling our certitudes and dogmatism than is abstract criticism. For centuries, religion couldn't bear having its history told. Today, our schools of rationality balk at having their history written, which is no doubt significant.

What I've wanted to show is a direction for research. These are only the rudiments of something I've been working at for the last two years. It's the historical analysis of what we could call, using an obsolete term, the "art of government."

This study rests upon several basic assumptions. I'd sum them up like this:

1. Power is not a substance. Neither is it a mysterious property whose origin must be delved into. Power is only a certain type of relation between individuals. Such relations are specific, that is, they have nothing to do with exchange, production, communication, even though they combine with them. The characteristic feature of power is that some men can more or less entirely determine other men's conduct—but never exhaustively or coercively. A man who is chained up and beaten is subject to force being exerted over him, not power. But if he can be induced to speak, when his ultimate recourse could have been to hold his tongue, preferring death, then he has been caused to behave in a certain way. His freedom has been subjected to power. He has been submitted to government. If an individual can remain free, however little his freedom may be, power can subject him to government. There is no power without potential refusal or revolt.

2. As for all relations among men, many factors determine power. Yet rationalization is also constantly working away at it. There are specific forms to such rationalization. It differs from the rationalization peculiar to economic processes, or to production and communication techniques; it differs from that of scientific discourse. The government of men by men— whether they form small or large groups, whether it is power exerted by men over women, or by adults over children, or by one class over another, or by a bureaucracy over a population—involves a certain type of rationality. It doesn't involve instrumental violence.

3. Consequently, those who resist or rebel against a form of power cannot merely be content to denounce violence or criticize an institution. Nor is it enough to cast the blame on reason in general. What has to be questioned is the form of rationality at stake. The criticism of power wielded over the

mentally sick or mad cannot be restricted to psychiatric institutions; nor can those questioning the power to punish be content with denouncing prisons as total institutions. The question is: How are such relations of power rationalized? Asking it is the only way to avoid other institutions, with the same objectives and the same effects, from taking their stead.

4. For several centuries, the state has been one of the most remarkable, one of the most redoubtable, forms of human government.

Very significantly, political criticism has reproached the state with being simultaneously a factor for individualization and a totalitarian principle. Just to look at nascent state rationality, just to see what its first policing project was, makes it clear that, right from the start, the state is both individualizing and totalitarian. Opposing the individual and his interests to it is just as hazardous as opposing it with the community and its requirements.

Political rationality has grown and imposed itself all throughout the history of Western societies. It first took its stand on the idea of pastoral power, then on that of reason of state. Its inevitable effects are both individualization and totalization. Liberation can come only from attacking not just one of these two effects but political rationality's very roots.

NOTE

* This is the text of the two Tanner lectures that Foucault delivered at Stanford University on October 10 and 16, 1979. [eds.]

1 J. King, *Science and Rationalism in the Government of Louis XIV* (Baltimore: Johns Hopkins, 1949).

THE SUBJECT AND POWER*

WHY STUDY POWER:
THE QUESTION OF THE SUBJECT

The ideas I would like to discuss here represent neither a theory nor a methodology.

I would like to say, first of all, what has been the goal of my work during the last twenty years. It has not been to analyze the phenomena of power, nor to elaborate the foundations of such an analysis.

My objective, instead, has been to create a history of the different modes by which, in our culture, human beings are made subjects. My work has dealt with three modes of objectification that transform human beings into subjects.

The first is the modes of inquiry that try to give themselves the status of sciences; for example, the objectivizing of the speaking subject in *grammaire générale*, philology, and linguistics. Or again, in this first mode, the objectivizing of the productive subject, the subject who labors, in the analysis of wealth and of economics. Or, a third example, the objectivizing of the sheer fact of being alive in natural history or biology.

In the second part of my work, I have studied the objectivizing of the subject in what I shall call "dividing practices." The subject is either divided inside himself or divided from others. This process objectivizes him. Examples are the mad and the sane, the sick and the healthy, the criminals and the "good boys."

Finally, I have sought to study—it is my current work—the way a human being turns him- or herself into a subject. For example, I have chosen the domain of sexuality—how men have learned to recognize themselves as subjects of "sexuality."

Thus, it is not power, but the subject, that is the general theme of my research.

It is true that I became quite involved with the question of power. It soon appeared to me that, while the human subject is placed in relations of production and of signification, he is equally placed in power relations that are very complex. Now, it seemed to me that economic history and theory provided a good instrument for relations of production, and that linguistics and semiotics offered instruments for studying relations of signification—but for power relations we had no tools of study. We had recourse only to ways of thinking about power based on legal models, that is: What legitimates power? Or we had recourse to ways of thinking about power based on institutional models, that is: What is the state?

It was therefore necessary to expand the dimensions of a definition of power if one wanted to use this definition in studying the objectivizing of the subject.

Do we need a theory of power? Since a theory assumes a prior objectification, it cannot be asserted as a basis for analytical work. But this analytical work cannot proceed without an ongoing conceptualization. And this conceptualization implies critical thought—a constant checking.

The first thing to check is what I should call the "conceptual needs." I mean that the conceptualization should not be founded on a theory of the object—the conceptualized object is not the single criterion of a good conceptualization. We have to know the historical conditions that motivate our conceptualization. We need a historical awareness of our present circumstance.

The second thing to check is the type of reality with which we are dealing.

A writer in a well-known French newspaper once expressed his surprise: "Why is the notion of power raised by so many people today? Is it such an important subject? Is it so independent that it can be discussed without taking into account other problems?"

This writer's surprise amazes me. I feel skeptical about the assumption that this question has been raised for the first time in the twentieth century. Anyway, for us it is not only a theoretical question but a part of our experience. I'd like to mention only two "pathological forms"—those two "diseases of power"—fascism and Stalinism. One of the numerous reasons why they are so puzzling for us is that, in spite of their historical uniqueness, they are not quite original. They used and extended mechanisms already present in most other societies. More than that: in spite of their own internal madness, they used, to a large extent, the ideas and the devices of our political rationality.

What we need is a new economy of power relations—the word "economy" being used in its theoretical and practical sense. To put it in other words: since Kant, the role of philosophy is to prevent reason from going beyond the limits of what is given in experience. But from the same moment—that is, since the development of the modern state and the political management of society—the role of philosophy is also to keep watch over the excessive powers of political rationality. This is a rather high expectation.

Everybody is aware of such banal facts. But the fact that they're banal does not mean they don't exist. What we have to do with banal facts is to discover—or try to discover—which specific and perhaps original problem is connected with them.

The relationship between rationalization and excesses of political power is evident. And we should not need to wait for bureaucracy or concentration camps to recognize the existence of such relations. But the problem is: What to do with such an evident fact?

Shall we try reason? To my mind, nothing would be more sterile. First, because the field has nothing to do with guilt or innocence. Second, because it is senseless to refer to reason as the contrary entity to nonreason. Lastly, because such a trial would trap us into playing the arbitrary and boring part of either the rationalist or the irrationalist.

Shall we investigate this kind of rationalism which seems to be specific to our modern culture and which originates in Enlightenment? I think that was the approach of some of the members of the Frankfurt School. My purpose, however, is not to start a discussion of their works, although they are most important and valuable. Rather, I would suggest another way of investigating the links between rationalization and power.

It may be wise not to take as a whole the rationalization of society or of culture but to analyze such a process in several fields, each with reference to a fundamental experience: madness, illness, death, crime, sexuality, and so forth.

I think that the word "rationalization" is dangerous. What we have to do is analyze specific rationalities rather than always invoking the progress of rationalization in general.

Even if the Enlightenment has been a very important phase in our history and in the development of political technology, I think we have to refer to much more remote processes if we want to understand how we have been trapped in our own history.

I would like to suggest another way to go further toward a new economy of power relations, a way that is more empirical, more directly related to our present situation, and one that implies more relations between theory and practice. It consists in taking the forms of resistance against different forms of power as a starting point. To use another metaphor, it consists in using this resistance as a chemical catalyst so as to bring to light power relations, locate their position, find out their point of application and the methods used. Rather than analyzing power from the point of view of its internal rationality, it consists of analyzing power relations through the antagonism of strategies.

For example, to find out what our society means by "sanity," perhaps we should investigate what is happening in the field of insanity.

And what we mean by "legality" in the field of illegality.

And, in order to understand what power relations are about, perhaps we should investigate the forms of resistance and attempts made to dissociate these relations.

As a starting point, let us take a series of oppositions that have developed over the last few years: opposition to the power of men over women, of parents over children, of psychiatry over the mentally ill, of medicine over the population, of administration over the ways people live.

It is not enough to say that these are anti-authority struggles; we must try to define more precisely what they have in common.

1. They are "transversal" struggles, that is, they are not limited to one country. Of course, they develop more easily and to a

greater extent in certain countries, but they are not confined
to a particular political or economic form of government.

2. The target of these struggles is power effects as such. For example, the medical profession is criticized not primarily because it is a profit-making concern but because it exercises an
uncontrolled power over people's bodies, their health and
their life and death.

3. These are "immediate" struggles for two reasons. In such
struggles, people criticize instances of power that are the closest to them, those which exercise their action on individuals.
They look not for the "chief enemy" but for the immediate
enemy. Nor do they expect to find a solution to their problem
at a future date (that is, liberations, revolutions, end of class
struggle). In comparison with a theoretical scale of explanations or a revolutionary order that polarizes the historian, they
are anarchistic struggles.

    But these are not their most original points. The following
seem to me to be more specific.

4. They are struggles that question the status of the individual.
On the one hand, they assert the right to be different and underline everything that makes individuals truly individual. On
the other hand, they attack everything that separates the individual, breaks his links with others, splits up community life,
forces the individual back on himself, and ties him to his own
identity in a constraining way.

    These struggles are not exactly for or against the "individ-
ual"; rather, they are struggles against the "government of individualization."

5. They are an opposition to the effects of power linked with
knowledge, competence, and qualification—struggles against
the privileges of knowledge. But they are also an opposition
against secrecy, deformation, and mystifying representations
imposed on people.

    There is nothing "scientistic" in this (that is, a dogmatic be-
lief in the value of scientific knowledge), but neither is it a
skeptical or relativistic refusal of all verified truth. What is

questioned is the way in which knowledge circulates and functions, its relations to power. In short, the regime of knowledge [*savoir*].

6. Finally, all these present struggles revolve around the question: Who are we? They are a refusal of these abstractions, of economic and ideological state violence, which ignore who we are individually, and also a refusal of a scientific or administrative inquisition that determines who one is.

To sum up, the main objective of these struggles is to attack not so much such-or-such institution of power, or group, or elite, or class but, rather, a technique, a form of power.

This form of power that applies itself to immediate everyday life categorizes the individual, marks him by his own individuality, attaches him to his own identity, imposes a law of truth on him that he must recognize and others have to recognize in him. It is a form of power that makes individuals subjects. There are two meanings of the word "subject": subject to someone else by control and dependence, and tied to his own identity by a conscience or self-knowledge. Both meanings suggest a form of power that subjugates and makes subject to.

Generally, it can be said that there are three types of struggles: against forms of domination (ethnic, social, and religious); against forms of exploitation that separate individuals from what they produce; or against that which ties the individual to himself and submits him to others in this way (struggles against subjection [*assujettissement*], against forms of subjectivity and submission).

I think that in history you can find a lot of examples of these three kinds of social struggles, either isolated from each other, or mixed together. But even when they are mixed, one of them, most of the time, prevails. For instance, in feudal societies, the struggles against the forms of ethnic or social domination were prevalent, even though economic exploitation could have been very important among the causes of revolt.

In the nineteenth century, the struggle against exploitation came into the foreground.

And nowadays, the struggle against the forms of subjection—

against the submission of subjectivity—is becoming more and more important, even though the struggles against forms of domination and exploitation have not disappeared. Quite the contrary.

I suspect that it is not the first time that our society has been confronted with this kind of struggle. All those movements that took place in the fifteenth and sixteenth centuries, which had the Reformation as their main expression and result, should be analyzed as a great crisis of the Western experience of subjectivity and a revolt against the kind of religious and moral power that gave form, during the Middle Ages, to this subjectivity. The need to take a direct part in spiritual life, in the work of salvation, in the truth that lies in the Book—all that was a struggle for a new subjectivity.

I know what objections can be made. We can say that all types of subjection are derived phenomena, that they are merely the consequences of other economic and social processes: forces of production, class struggle, and ideological structures that determine the form of subjectivity.

It is certain that the mechanisms of subjection cannot be studied outside their relation to the mechanisms of exploitation and domination. But they do not merely constitute the "terminal" of more fundamental mechanisms. They entertain complex and circular relations with other forms.

The reason this kind of struggle tends to prevail in our society is due to the fact that, since the sixteenth century, a new political form of power has been continuously developing. This new political structure, as everybody knows, is the state. But most of the time, the state is envisioned as a kind of political power that ignores individuals, looking only at the interests of the totality or, I should say, of a class or a group among the citizens.

That's quite true. But I'd like to underline the fact that the state's power (and that's one of the reasons for its strength) is both an individualizing and a totalizing form of power. Never, I think, in the history of human societies—even in the old Chinese society—has there been such a tricky combination in the same political structures of individualization techniques and of totalization procedures.

This is due to the fact that the modern Western state has integrated into a new political shape an old power technique that originated in Christian institutions. We can call this power technique "pastoral power."

First of all, a few words about this pastoral power.

It has often been said that Christianity brought into being a code of ethics fundamentally different from that of the ancient world. Less emphasis is usually placed on the fact that it proposed and spread new power relations throughout the ancient world.

Christianity is the only religion that has organized itself as a Church. As such, it postulates in principle that certain individuals can, by their religious quality, serve others not as princes, magistrates, prophets, fortune-tellers, benefactors, educationalists, and so on, but as pastors. However, this word designates a very special form of power.

1. It is a form of power whose ultimate aim is to assure individual salvation in the next world.

2. Pastoral power is not merely a form of power that commands; it must also be prepared to sacrifice itself for the life and salvation of the flock. Therefore, it is different from royal power, which demands a sacrifice from its subjects to save the throne.

3. It is a form of power that looks after not just the whole community but each individual in particular, during his entire life.

4. Finally, this form of power cannot be exercised without knowing the inside of people's minds, without exploring their souls, without making them reveal their innermost secrets. It implies a knowledge of the conscience and an ability to direct it.

This form of power is salvation-oriented (as opposed to political power). It is oblative (as opposed to the principle of sovereignty); it is individualizing (as opposed to legal power); it is coextensive and continuous with life; it is linked with a production of truth—the truth of the individual himself.

But all this is part of history, you will say; the pastorate has, if not disappeared, at least lost the main part of its efficacy.

This is true, but I think we should distinguish between two aspects of pastoral power—between the ecclesiastical institutionalization that has ceased or at least lost its vitality since the eighteenth century, and its function, which has spread and multiplied outside the ecclesiastical institution.

An important phenomenon took place around the eighteenth century—it was a new distribution, a new organization of this kind of individualizing power.

I don't think that we should consider the "modern state" as an entity that was developed above individuals, ignoring what they are and even their very existence, but, on the contrary, as a very sophisticated structure in which individuals can be integrated, under one condition: that this individuality would be shaped in a new form, and submitted to a set of very specific patterns.

In a way, we can see the state as a modern matrix of individualization, or a new form of pastoral power.

A few more words about this new pastoral power.

1. We may observe a change in its objective. It was a question no longer of leading people to their salvation in the next world but, rather, ensuring it in this world. And in this context, the word "salvation" takes on different meanings: health, well-being (that is, sufficient wealth, standard of living), security, protection against accidents. A series of "worldly" aims took the place of the religious aims of the traditional pastorate, all the more easily because the latter, for various reasons, had followed in an accessory way a certain number of these aims; we only have to think of the role of medicine and its welfare function assured for a long time by the Catholic and Protestant churches.

2. Concurrently, the officials of pastoral power increased. Sometimes this form of power was exerted by state apparatus or, in any case, by a public institution such as the police. (We should not forget that in the eighteenth century the police force was invented not only for maintaining law and order, nor for assisting governments in their struggle against their enemies, but also for assuring urban supplies, hygiene, health and standards considered necessary for handicrafts and commerce.) Sometimes the power was exercised by private ventures, welfare societies, benefactors, and generally by philanthropists. But ancient institutions, for example the family, were also mobilized at this time to take on pastoral functions. It was also exercised by complex structures such as medicine, which in-

cluded private initiatives with the sale of services on market economy principles but also included public institutions such as hospitals.

3. Finally, the multiplication of the aims and agents of pastoral power focused the development of knowledge of man around two roles: one, globalizing and quantitative, concerning the population; the other, analytical, concerning the individual.

And this implies that power of a pastoral type, which over centuries—for more than a millennium—had been linked to a defined religious institution, suddenly spread out into the whole social body. It found support in a multitude of institutions. And, instead of a pastoral power and a political power, more or less linked to each other, more or less in rivalry, there was an individualizing "tactic" that characterized a series of powers: those of the family, medicine, psychiatry, education, and employers.

At the end of the eighteenth century, Kant wrote in a German newspaper—the *Berliner Monatschrift*—a short text. The title was *Was heisst Aufklärung?* [*What is Enlightenment?*]. It was for a long time, and it is still, considered a work of relatively little importance.

But I can't help finding it very interesting and puzzling because it was the first time a philosopher proposed as a philosophical task to investigate not only the metaphysical system or the foundations of scientific knowledge but a historical event—a recent, even a contemporary event.

When in 1784 Kant asked "What is Enlightenment?" he meant, "What's going on just now? What's happening to us? What is this world, this period, this precise moment in which we are living?"

Or in other words: What are we, as *Aufklärer*, as part of the Enlightenment? Compare this with the Cartesian question: Who am I? I, as a unique but universal and unhistorical subject? I, for Descartes, is everyone, anywhere at any moment.

But Kant asks something else: What are we? in a very precise moment of history. Kant's question appears as an analysis of both us and our present.

I think that this aspect of philosophy took on more and more importance. Hegel, Nietzsche . . .

The other aspect of "universal philosophy" didn't disappear. But the task of philosophy as a critical analysis of our world is something that is more and more important. Maybe the most certain of all philosophical problems is the problem of the present time, and of what we are, in this very moment.

Maybe the target nowadays is not to discover what we are but to refuse what we are. We have to imagine and to build up what we could be to get rid of this kind of political "double bind," which is the simultaneous individualization and totalization of modern power structures.

The conclusion would be that the political, ethical, social, philosophical problem of our days is not to try to liberate the individual from the state, and from the state's institutions, but to liberate us both from the state and from the type of individualization linked to the state. We have to promote new forms of subjectivity through the refusal of this kind of individuality that has been imposed on us for several centuries.

HOW IS POWER EXERCISED?

For some people, asking questions about the "how" of power means limiting oneself to describing its effects without ever relating those effects either to causes or to a basic nature. It would make this power a mysterious substance that one avoids interrogating in itself, no doubt because one prefers *not* to call it into question. By proceeding this way, which is never explicitly justified, these people seem to suspect the presence of a kind of fatalism. But does not their very distrust indicate a presupposition that power is something that exists with its own distinct origin, basic nature, and manifestations?

If, for the time being, I grant a certain privileged position to the question of "how," it is not because I would wish to eliminate the questions of "what" and "why." Rather, it is that I wish to present these questions in a different way—better still, to know if it is legitimate to imagine a power that unites in itself a what, a why, and a how. To put it bluntly, I would say that to begin the analysis with a "how" is to introduce the suspicion that power as such does not exist. It is, in any case, to ask oneself what contents one has in mind when using this grand, all-embracing, and reifying term; it is to suspect that an extremely complex configuration of realities is allowed to escape while one endlessly marks time before the double question: what is power, and where does power come from? The flat and empirical little question, "What happens?" is not designed to introduce by stealth a metaphysics or an ontology of power but, rather, to undertake a critical investigation of the thematics of power.

"How?" not in the sense of "How does it manifest itself?" but "How is it exercised?" and "What happens when individuals exert (as we say) power over others?"

As far as this power is concerned, it is first necessary to distinguish that which is exerted over things and gives the ability to modify, use, consume, or destroy them—a power that stems from aptitudes directly inherent in the body or relayed by external instruments. Let us say that here it is a question of "capacity." On the other hand, what characterizes the power we are analyzing is that it brings into play relations between individuals (or between groups). For let us not deceive ourselves: if we speak of the power of laws, institutions, and ideologies, if we speak of structures or mechanisms of power, it is only insofar as we suppose that certain persons exercise power over others. The term "power" designates relationships between "partners" (and by that I am not thinking of a game with fixed rules but simply, and for the moment staying in the most general terms, of an ensemble of actions that induce others and follow from one another).

It is necessary also to distinguish power relations from relationships of communication that transmit information by means of a language, a system of signs, or any other symbolic medium. No doubt, communicating is always a certain way of acting upon another person or persons. But the production and circulation of elements of meaning can have as their objective or as their consequence certain results in the realm of power; the latter are not simply an aspect of the former. Whether or not they pass through systems of communication, power relations have a specific nature.

Power relations, relationships of communication, objective capacities should not therefore be confused. This is not to say that there is a question of three separate domains. Nor that there is, on the one hand, the field of things, of perfected technique, work, and the transformation of the real, and, on the other, that of signs, communication, reciprocity, and the production of meaning; finally that of the domination of the means of constraint, of inequality and the action of men upon other men.[1] It is a question of three types of relationships that in fact always overlap one another, support one another reciprocally, and use each other mutually as means to an end. The application of objective capacities in their most elementary forms implies relationships of communication (whether in the form of previously acquired information or of shared work); it is tied also to power relations (whether they consist of obligatory tasks, of gestures imposed by tradition or apprenticeship, of subdivisions or the more or less obligatory distribution of labor). Relationships of communication imply goal-directed activities (even if only the correct putting into operation of directed elements of meaning) and, by modifying the field of information between partners, produce effects of power. Power relations are exercised, to an exceedingly important extent, through the production and exchange of signs; and they are scarcely separable from goal-directed activities that permit the exercise of a power (such as training techniques, processes of domination, the means by which obedience is obtained), or that, to enable them to operate, call on relations of power (the division of labor and the hierarchy of tasks).

Of course, the coordination between these three types of relationships is neither uniform nor constant. In a given society, there is no general type of equilibrium between goal-directed activities, systems of communication, and power relations; rather, there are diverse forms, diverse places, diverse circumstances or occasions in which these interrelationships establish themselves according to a specific model. But there are also "blocks" in which the adjustment of abilities, the resources of communication, and power relations constitute regulated and concerted systems. Take, for example, an educational institution: the disposal of its space, the meticulous regulations that govern its internal life, the different activities that are organized there, the diverse persons who live there or meet one another, each with his own function, his well-defined character—all these things constitute a block of capacity–communication–power. Activity to ensure learning and the acquisition of aptitudes or types of behavior works via a whole ensemble of regulated communications (lessons, questions and answers, orders, exhortations, coded signs of obedience, differential marks of the "value" of each person and of the levels of knowledge) and by means of a whole series of power processes (enclosure, surveillance, reward and punishment, the pyramidal hierarchy).

These blocks, in which the deployment of technical capacities, the game of communications, and the relationships of power are adjusted to one another according to considered formulae, constitute what one might call, enlarging a little the sense of the word, "disciplines." The empirical analysis of certain disciplines as they have been historically constituted presents for this very reason a certain interest. This is so because the disciplines show, first, according to artificially clear and decanted systems, the way in which systems of objective finality and systems of communication and power can be welded together. They also display different models of articulation, sometimes giving preeminence to power relations and obedience (as in those disciplines of a monastic or penitential type), sometimes to goal-directed activities (as in the disciplines of workshops or hospitals), sometimes to relationships of communication (as in the disciplines of apprenticeship), sometimes also to a saturation of the three types of relationship (as perhaps in military discipline, where a plethora of signs indicates, to the point of redundancy, tightly knit power relations calculated with care to produce a certain number of technical effects).

What is to be understood by the disciplining of societies in Europe since the eighteenth century is not, of course, that the individuals who are part of them become more and more obedient, nor that all societies become like barracks, schools, or prisons; rather, it is that an increasingly controlled, more rational, and economic process of adjustment has been sought between productive activities, communications networks, and the play of power relations.

To approach the theme of power by an analysis of "how" is therefore to introduce several critical shifts in relation to the supposition of a fundamental power. It is to give oneself as the object of analysis *power relations* and not power itself—power relations that are distinct from objective capacities as well as from relations of communication, power relations that can be grasped in the diversity of their linkages to these capacities and relations.

WHAT CONSTITUTES THE SPECIFICITY
OF POWER RELATIONS?

The exercise of power is not simply a relationship between "part-ners," individual or collective; it is a way in which some act on others. Which is to say, of course, that there is no such entity as power, with or without a capital letter; global, massive, or diffused; concentrated or distributed. Power exists only as exercised by some on others, only when it is put into action, even though, of course, it is inscribed in a field of sparse available possibilities underpinned by permanent structures. This also means that power is not a mat-ter of consent. In itself, it is not the renunciation of freedom, a transfer of rights, or power of each and all delegated to a few (which does not prevent the possibility that consent may be a con-dition for the existence or the maintenance of a power relation); the relationship of power may be an effect of a prior or permanent consent, but it is not by nature the manifestation of a consensus.

Is this to say that one must seek the character proper to power relations in the violence that must have been its primitive form, its permanent secret, and last resort, that which in the final analysis appears as its real nature when it is forced to throw aside its mask and to show itself as it really is? In effect, what defines a relation-ship of power is that it is a mode of action that does not act directly and immediately on others. Instead, it acts upon their actions: an action upon an action, on possible or actual future or present ac-tions. A relationship of violence acts upon a body or upon things; it forces, it bends, it breaks, it destroys, or it closes off all possibilities. Its opposite pole can only be passivity, and if it comes up against any resistance it has no other option but to try to break it down. A power relationship, on the other hand, can only be articulated on the basis of two elements that are indispensable if it is really to be a power relationship: that "the other" (the one over whom power is exercised) is recognized and maintained to the very end as a subject who acts; and that, faced with a relationship of power, a whole field of responses, reactions, results, and possible inventions may open up.

Obviously the establishing of power relations does not exclude the use of violence any more than it does the obtaining of consent; no doubt, the exercise of power can never do without one or the other, often both at the same time. But even though consent and violence are instruments or results, they do not constitute the principle or basic nature of power. The exercise of power can produce as much acceptance as may be wished for: it can pile up the dead and shelter itself behind whatever threats it can imagine. In itself, the exercise of power is not a violence that sometimes hides, or an implicitly renewed consent. It operates on the field of possibilities in which the behavior of active subjects is able to inscribe itself. It is a set of actions on possible actions; it incites, it induces, it seduces, it makes easier or more difficult; it releases or contrives, makes more probable or less; in the extreme, it constrains or forbids absolutely, but it is always a way of acting upon one or more acting subjects by virtue of their acting or being capable of action. A set of actions upon other actions.

Perhaps the equivocal nature of the term "conduct" is one of the best aids for coming to terms with the specificity of power relations. To "conduct" is at the same time to "lead" others (according to mechanisms of coercion that are, to varying degrees, strict) and a way of behaving within a more or less open field of possibilities.[2] The exercise of power is a "conduct of conducts" and a management of possibilities. Basically, power is less a confrontation between two adversaries or their mutual engagement than a question of "government." This word must be allowed the very broad meaning it had in the sixteenth century. "Government" did not refer only to political structures or to the management of states; rather, it designated the way in which the conduct of individuals or of groups might be directed—the government of children, of souls, of communities, of families, of the sick. It covered not only the legitimately constituted forms of political or economic subjection but also modes of action, more or less considered and calculated, that were destined to act upon the possibilities of action of other people. To govern, in this sense, is to structure the possible field of action of others. The relationship proper to power would therefore be sought not on the side of violence or of struggle, nor on that of voluntary contracts (all of which can, at best, only be the instruments of power) but, rather, in the area of that singular mode of action, neither warlike nor juridical, which is government.

When one defines the exercise of power as a mode of action upon the actions of others, when one characterizes these actions as the government of men by other men—in the broadest sense of the term—one includes an important element: freedom. Power is exercised only over free subjects, and only insofar as they are "free." By this we mean individual or collective subjects who are faced with a field of possibilities in which several kinds of conduct, several ways of reacting and modes of behavior are available. Where the determining factors are exhaustive, there is no relationship of power: slavery is not a power relationship when a man is in chains, only when he has some possible mobility, even a chance of escape. (In this case it is a question of a physical relationship of constraint.) Consequently, there is not a face-to-face confrontation of power and freedom as mutually exclusive facts (freedom disappearing everywhere power is exercised) but a much more complicated interplay. In this game, freedom may well appear as the condition for the exercise of power (at the same time its precondition, since freedom must exist for power to be exerted, and also its permanent support, since without the possibility of recalcitrance power would be equivalent to a physical determination).

The power relationship and freedom's refusal to submit cannot therefore be separated. The crucial problem of power is not that of voluntary servitude (how could we seek to be slaves?). At the very heart of the power relationship, and constantly provoking it, are the recalcitrance of the will and the intransigence of freedom. Rather than speaking of an essential antagonism, it would be better to speak of an "agonism"[5]—of a relationship that is at the same time mutual incitement and struggle; less of a face-to-face confrontation that paralyzes both sides than a permanent provocation.

HOW IS ONE TO ANALYZE THE POWER RELATIONSHIP?

One can analyze such relationships or, rather, I should say that it is perfectly legitimate to do so by focusing on carefully defined institutions. The latter constitute a privileged point of observation, diversified, concentrated, put in order, and carried through to the highest point of their efficacy. It is here that, as a first approximation, one might expect to see the appearance of the form and logic of their elementary mechanisms. However, the analysis of power relations as one finds them in certain closed institutions presents a certain number of problems. First, the fact that an important part of the mechanisms put into operation by an institution are designed to ensure its own preservation brings with it the risk of deciphering functions that are essentially reproductive, especially in power relations within institutions. Second, in analyzing power relations from the standpoint of institutions, one lays oneself open to seeking the explanation and the origin of the former in the latter, that is to say in sum, to explain power by power. Finally, insofar as institutions act essentially by bringing into play two elements, explicit or tacit regulations and an apparatus, one risks giving to one or the other an exaggerated privilege in the relations of power and, hence, seeing in the latter only modulations of law and coercion.

This is not to deny the importance of institutions in the establishment of power relations but, rather, to suggest that one must analyze institutions from the standpoint of power relations, rather than vice versa, and that the fundamental point of anchorage of the relationships, even if they are embodied and crystallized in an institution, is to be found outside the institution.

Let us come back to the definition of the exercise of power as a way in which certain actions may structure the field of other possible actions. What would be proper to a relationship of power, then, is that it be a mode of action on actions. That is, power relations are rooted deep in the social nexus, not a supplementary structure over and above "society" whose radical effacement one could perhaps dream of. To live in society is, in any event, to live in such a way that some can act on the actions of others. A society without power relations can only be an abstraction. Which, be it said in passing, makes all the more politically necessary the analysis of power relations in a given society, their historical formation, the source of their strength or fragility, the conditions that are necessary to transform some or to abolish others. For to say that there cannot be a society without power relations is not to say either that those which are established are necessary, or that power in any event, constitutes an inescapable fatality at the heart of societies, such that it cannot be undermined. Instead, I would say that the analysis, elaboration, and bringing into question of power relations and the "agonism" between power relations and the intransitivity of freedom is an increasingly political task—even, the political task that is inherent in all social existence.

Concretely, the analysis of power relations demands that a certain number of points be established:

1. *The system of differentiations* that permits one to act upon the actions of others: juridical and traditional differences of status or privilege; economic differences in the appropriation of wealth and goods, differing positions within the processes of production, linguistic or cultural differences, differences in know-how and competence, and so forth. Every relationship of power puts into operation differences that are, at the same time, its conditions and its results.

2. *The types of objectives* pursued by those who act upon the actions of others: maintenance of privileges, accumulation of profits, the exercise of statutory authority, the exercise of a function or a trade.

3. *Instrumental modes:* whether power is exercised by the threat of arms, by the effects of speech, through economic disparities, by more or less complex means of control, by systems of surveillance, with or without archives, by rules, explicit or not, fixed or modifiable, with or without the material means of enforcement.

4. *Forms of institutionalization:* these may mix traditional conditions, legal structures, matters of habit or fashion (such as one sees in the institution of the family); they can also take the form of an apparatus closed in upon itself, with its specific loci, its own regulations, its hierarchical structures that are carefully defined, a relative autonomy in its functioning (such as scholastic or military institutions); they can also form very complex systems endowed with multiple apparatuses, as in the case of the state, whose function is the taking of everything under its wing, to be the global overseer, the principle of regulation and, to a certain extent also, the distributor of all power relations in a given social ensemble.

5. *The degrees of rationalization:* the bringing into play of power relations as action in a field of possibilities may be more or less elaborate in terms of the effectiveness of its instruments

and the certainty of its results (greater or lesser technological refinements employed in the exercise of power) or, again, in proportion to the possible cost (economic cost of the means used, or the cost in terms of the resistance encountered). The exercise of power is not a naked fact, an institutional given, nor is it a structure that holds out or is smashed: it is something that is elaborated, transformed, organized; it endows itself with processes that are more or less adjusted to the situation.

One sees why the analysis of power relations within a society cannot be reduced to the study of a series of institutions or even to the study of all those institutions that would merit the name "political." Power relations are rooted in the whole network of the social. This is not to say, however, that there is a primary and fundamental principle of power which dominates society down to the smallest detail; but, based on this possibility of action on the action of others that is coextensive with every social relationship, various kinds of individual disparity, of objectives, of the given application of power over ourselves or others, of more or less partial or universal institutionalization and more or less deliberate organization, will define different forms of power. The forms and the specific situations of the government of some by others in a given society are multiple; they are superimposed, they cross over, limit and in some cases annul, in others reinforce, one another. It is certain that, in contemporary societies, the state is not simply one of the forms of specific situations of the exercise of power—even if it is the most important—but that, in a certain way, all other forms of power relation must refer to it. But this is not because they are derived from it; rather, it is because power relations have come more and more under state control (although this state control has not taken the same form in pedagogical, judicial, economic, or family systems). Using here the restricted meaning of the word "government," one could say that power relations have been progressively governmentalized, that is to say, elaborated, rationalized, and centralized in the form of, or under the auspices of, state institutions.

RELATIONS OF POWER AND RELATIONS OF STRATEGY

The word "strategy" is currently employed in three ways. First, to designate the means employed to attain a certain end; it is a question of rationality functioning to arrive at an objective. Second, to designate the way in which a partner in a certain game acts with regard to what he thinks should be the action of the others and what he considers the others think to be his own; it is the way in which one seeks to have the advantage over others. Third, to designate the procedures used in a situation of confrontation to deprive the opponent of his means of combat and to reduce him to giving up the struggle; it is a question, therefore, of the means destined to obtain victory. These three meanings come together in situations of confrontation—war or games—where the objective is to act on an adversary in such a way as to render the struggle impossible for him. So strategy is defined by the choice of winning solutions. But it must be borne in mind that this is a very special type of situation, and that there are others in which the distinctions between the different senses of the word "strategy" must be maintained.

Referring to the first sense I have indicated, one may call some systems of power strategy the totality of the means put into operation to implement power effectively or to maintain it. One may also speak of a strategy proper to power relations insofar as they constitute modes of action on possible action, the action of others. Thus, one can interpret the mechanisms brought into play in power relations in terms of strategies. Obviously, though, most important is the relationship between power relations and confrontation strategies. For, if it is true that at the heart of power relations and as a permanent condition of their existence there is an insubordination and a certain essential obstinacy on the part of the principles of freedom, then there is no relationship of power without the means of escape or possible flight. Every power relationship implies, at least in potentia, a strategy of struggle, in which the two forces are not superimposed, do not lose their specific nature, or do not finally become confused. Each constitutes for the other a kind of permanent limit, a point of possible reversal. A relationship of confrontation reaches its term, its final moment (and the victory of one of the two adversaries) when stable mechanisms replace the free play of antagonistic reactions. Through such mechanisms one can direct, in a fairly constant manner and with reasonable certainty, the conduct of others. For a relationship of confrontation, from the moment it is not a struggle to the death, the fixing of a power relationship becomes a target—at one and the same time its fulfillment and its suspension. And, in return, the strategy of struggle also constitutes a frontier for the relationship of power, the line at which, instead of manipulating and inducing actions in a calculated manner, one must be content with reacting to them after the event. It would not be possible for power relations to exist without points of insubordination that, by definition, are means of escape. Accordingly, every intensification or extension of power relations intended to wholly suppress these points of insubordination can only bring the exercise of power up against its outer limits. It reaches its final term either in a type of action that reduces the other to total impotence (in which case victory over the adversary replaces the exercise of power) or by a confrontation with those whom one governs and their transformation into adversaries. Which is to say, that every strategy of confrontation dreams of becoming a relationship of power and every relationship of power tends, both through its intrinsic course of development and when frontally encountering resistances, to become a winning strategy.

In fact, between a relationship of power and a strategy of struggle there is a reciprocal appeal, a perpetual linking and a perpetual reversal. At every moment, the relationship of power may become a confrontation between two adversaries. Equally, the relationship between adversaries in society may, at every moment, give place to the putting into operation of mechanisms of power. The consequence of this instability is the ability to decipher the same events and the same transformations either from inside the history of struggle or from the standpoint of the power relationships. The resulting interpretations will not consist of the same elements of meaning or the same links or the same types of intelligibility, though they refer to the same historical fabric, and each of the two analyses must have reference to the other. In fact, it is precisely the disparities between the two readings that make visible those fundamental phenomena of "domination" that are present in a large number of human societies.

Domination is, in fact, a general structure of power whose ramifications and consequences can sometimes be found reaching down into the fine fabric of society. But, at the same time, it is a strategic situation, more or less taken for granted and consolidated, within a long-term confrontation between adversaries. It can certainly happen that the fact of domination may only be the transcription of a mechanism of power resulting from confrontation and its consequences (a political structure stemming from invasion); it may also be that a relationship of struggle between two adversaries is the result of power relations with the conflicts and cleavages they engender. But what makes the domination of a group, a caste, or a class, together with the resistance and revolts that domination comes up against, a central phenomenon in the history of societies is that they manifest in a massive and global form, at the level of the whole social body, the locking-together of power relations with relations of strategy and the results proceeding from their interaction.

NOTES

* This text first appeared in English in 1982 as an appendix to Hubert Dryfus and Paul Rabinow's *Michel Foucault: Beyond Structuralism and Hermeneutics*. [eds.]

1 When Jürgen Habermas distinguishes between domination, communication, and finalized activity, I think that he sees in them not three separate domains but, rather, three "transcendentals."

2 Foucault is playing on the double meaning in French of the verb *conduire* (to lead or to drive) and *se conduire* (to behave or conduct oneself)—whence *la conduite*, conduct or behavior—TRANS.

3 Foucault's neologism is based on the Greek agōnisma meaning "a combat." The term would hence imply a physical contest in which the opponents develop a strategy of reaction and of mutual taunting, as in a wrestling match—TRANS.

———

Q: *In your interview with geographers at* Herodote,[1] *you said that architecture becomes political at the end of the eighteenth century.[2] Obviously, it was political in earlier periods, too, such as during the Roman Empire. What is particular about the eighteenth century?*

A: My statement was awkward in that form. Of course I did not mean to say that architecture was not political before, becoming so only at that time. I meant only to say that in the eighteenth century one sees the development of reflection upon architecture as a function of the aims and techniques of the government of societies. One begins to see a form of political literature that addresses what the order of a society should be, what a city should be, given the requirements of the maintenance of order; given that one should avoid epidemics, avoid revolts, permit a decent and moral family life, and so on. In terms of these objectives, how is one to conceive of both the organization of a city and the construction of a collective infrastructure? And how should houses be built? I am saying not that this sort of reflection appears only in the eighteenth century, but only that in the eighteenth century a very broad and general reflection on these questions takes place. If one opens a police report of the times—the treatises that are devoted to the techniques of government—one finds that architecture and urbanism occupy a place of considerable importance. That is what I meant to say.

Q: *Among the ancients, in Rome or Greece, what was the difference?*

A: In discussing Rome, one sees that the problem revolves around

Vitruvius. Vitruvius was reinterpreted from the sixteenth century on, but one can find in the sixteenth century—and no doubt in the Middle Ages as well—many considerations of the same order as Vitruvius; if you consider them as "reflections upon." The treatises on politics, on the art of government, on the manner of good government, did not generally include chapters or analyses devoted to the organization of cities or to architecture. The *Republic* of Jean Bodin does not contain extended discussions of the role of architecture, whereas the police treatises of the eighteenth century are full of them.[3]

Q: *Do you mean there were techniques and practices, but the discourse did not exist?*
A: I did not say that discourses upon architecture did not exist before the eighteenth century. Nor do I mean to say that the discussions of architecture before the eighteenth century lacked any political dimension or significance. What I wish to point out is that from the eighteenth century on, every discussion of politics as the art of the government of men necessarily includes a chapter or a series of chapters on urbanism, on collective facilities, on hygiene, and on private architecture. Such chapters are not found in the discussions of the art of government of the sixteenth century. This change is perhaps not in the reflections of architects upon architecture, but it is quite clearly seen in the reflections of political men.

Q: *So it was not necessarily a change within the theory of architecture itself?*
A: That's right. It was not necessarily a change in the minds of architects, or in their techniques—although that remains to be seen—but in the minds of political men in the choice and the form of attention that they bring to bear upon the objects that are of concern to them. Architecture became one of these during the seventeenth and eighteenth centuries.

Q: *Could you tell us why?*
A: Well, I think that it was linked to a number of phenomena, such as the question of the city and the idea that was clearly formulated at the beginning of the seventeenth century that the government of a large state such as France should ultimately think of its territory on the model of the city. The city was no longer perceived as a

place of privilege, as an exception in a territory of fields, forests, and roads. The cities were no longer islands beyond the common law. Instead, the cities, with the problems that they raised, and the particular forms that they took, served as the models for the governmental rationality that was to apply to the whole of the territory.

There is an entire series of utopias or projects for governing territory that developed on the premise that a state is like a large city; the capital is like its main square; the roads are like its streets. A state will be well organized when a system of policing as tight and efficient as that of the cities extends over the entire territory. At the outset, the notion of police applied only to the set of regulations that were to assure the tranquillity of a city, but at that moment the police become the very *type* of rationality for the government of the whole territory. The model of the city became the matrix for the regulations that apply to a whole state.

The notion of police, even in France today, is frequently misunderstood. When one speaks to a Frenchman about police, he can only think of people in uniform or in the secret service. In the seventeenth and eighteenth centuries, "police" signified a program of governmental rationality. This can be characterized as a project to create a system of regulation of the general conduct of individuals whereby everything would be controlled to the point of self-sustenance, without the need for intervention. This is the rather typically French effort of policing. The English, for a number of reasons, did not develop a comparable system, mainly because of the parliamentary tradition on the one hand, and the tradition of local, communal autonomy, on the other, not to mention the religious system.

One can place Napoleon almost exactly at the break between the old organization of the eighteenth-century police state (understood, of course, in the sense we have been discussing, not in the sense of the "police state" as we have come to know it) and the forms of the modern state, which he invented. At any rate, it seems that, during the eighteenth and nineteenth centuries, there appeared— rather quickly in the case of commerce, more slowly in all the other domains—this idea of a police that would manage to penetrate, to stimulate, to regulate, and to render almost automatic all the mechanisms of society.

This idea has since been abandoned. The question has been

turned around. No longer do we ask: What is the form of governmental rationality that will be able to penetrate the body politic to
its most fundamental elements? Rather: How is government possible? That is, what is the principle of limitation that applies to governmental actions such that things will occur for the best, in
conformity with the rationality of government, and without intervention?

It is here that the question of liberalism comes up. It seems to
me that at that very moment it became apparent that if one governed too much, one did not govern at all—that one provoked results contrary to those one desired. What was discovered at that
time—and this was one of the great discoveries of political thought
at the end of the eighteenth century—was the idea of *society*. That
is to say, that government not only has to deal with a territory, with
a domain, and with its subjects, but that it also has to deal with a
complex and independent reality that has its own laws and mechanisms of reaction, its regulations as well as its possibilities of disturbance. This new reality is society. From the moment that one is
to manipulate a society, one cannot consider it completely penetra-
ble by police. One must take into account what it is. It becomes
necessary to reflect upon it, upon its specific characteristics, its constants and its variables . . .

Q: *So there is a change in the importance of space. In the eighteenth
century there was a territory and the problem of governing people in
this territory: one can choose as an example* La Métropolite (1682) *of
Alexandre LeMaitre—a utopian treatise on how to build a capital
city—or one can understand a city as a metaphor or symbol for the
territory and how to govern it. All of this is quite spatial, whereas after
Napoleon, society is not necessarily so* spatialized . . .
A: That's right. On the one hand, it is not so spatialized, yet at the
same time a certain number of problems that are properly seen as
spatial emerged. Urban space has its own dangers: disease, such
as the epidemics of cholera in Europe from 1830 to about 1880; and
revolution, such as the series of urban revolts that shook all of Europe during the same period. These spatial problems, which were
perhaps not new, took on a new importance.

Second, a new aspect of the relations of space and power was
the railroads. These were to establish a network of communication

no longer corresponding necessarily to the traditional network of roads, but they nonetheless had to take into account the nature of society and its history. In addition, there are all the social phenomena that railroads gave rise to, be they the resistances they provoked, the transformations of population, or changes in the behavior of people. Europe was immediately sensitive to the changes in behavior that the railroads entailed. What was going to happen, for example, if it was possible to get married between Bordeaux and Nantes? Something that was not possible before. What was going to happen when people in Germany and France might get to know one another? Would war still be possible once there were railroads? In France, a theory developed that the railroads would increase familiarity among people, and that the new forms of human universality made possible would render war impossible. But what the people did not foresee—although the German military command was fully aware of it, since they were much cleverer than their French counterpart—was that, on the contrary, the railroads rendered war far easier to wage. The third development, which came later, was electricity.

So there were problems in the links between the exercise of political power and the space of a territory, or the space of cities—links that were completely new.

Q: *So it was less a matter of architecture than before. These are sorts of technics of space . . .*

A: The major problems of space, from the nineteenth century on, were indeed of a different type. Which is not to say that problems of an architectural nature were forgotten. In terms of the first ones I referred to—disease and the political problems—architecture has a very important role to play. The reflections on urbanism and on the design of workers' housing—all of these questions—are an area of reflection upon architecture.

Q: *But architecture itself, the Ecole des Beaux-Arts, belongs to a completely different set of spatial issues.*

A: That's right. With the birth of these new technologies and these new economic processes, one sees the birth of a sort of thinking about space that is no longer modeled on the police state of the urbanization of the territory but extends far beyond the limits of urbanism and architecture.

Q: *Consequently, the Ecole des Ponts et Chaussées . . .*

A: That's right. The Ecole des Ponts et Chaussées and its capital importance in political rationality in France are part of this. It was not architects but engineers and builders of bridges, roads, viaducts, railways, as well as the polytechnicians (who practically controlled the French railroads)—those are the people who thought out space.

Q: *Has this situation continued up to the present, or are we witnessing a change in relations between the technicians of space?*

A: We may well witness some changes, but I think that we have until now remained with the developers of the territory, the people of the Ponts et Chaussées, etc.

Q: *So architects are not necessarily the masters of space that they once were, or believe themselves to be.*

A: That's right. They are not the technicians or engineers of the three great variables—territory, communication, and speed. These escape the domain of architects.

Q: *Do you see any particular architectural projects, either in the past or the present, as forces of liberation or resistance?*

A: I do not think that it is possible to say that one thing is of the order of "liberation" and another is of the order of "oppression." There are a certain number of things that one can say with some certainty about a concentration camp, to the effect that it is not an instrument of liberation, but one should still take into account—and this is not generally acknowledged—that, aside from torture and execution which preclude any resistance, no matter how terrifying a given system may be, there always remain the possibilities of resistance, disobedience, and oppositional groupings.

On the other hand, I do not think that there is anything that is functionally—by its very nature—absolutely liberating. Liberty is a *practice*. So there may, in fact, always be a certain number of projects whose aim is to modify some constraints, to loosen, or even to break them, but none of these projects can, simply by its nature, assure that people will have liberty automatically, that it will be established by the project itself. The liberty of men is never assured by the institutions and laws intended to guarantee them. This is why almost all of these laws and institutions are quite capable of being turned around—not because they are ambiguous, but simply because "liberty" is what must be exercised.

q: *Are there urban examples of this? Or examples where architects succeeded?*

a: Well, up to a point there is Le Corbusier, who is described to-day—with a sort of cruelty that I find perfectly useless—as a sort of crypto-Stalinist. He was, I am sure, someone full of good intentions, and what he did was in fact dedicated to liberating effects. Perhaps the means that he proposed were in the end less liberating than he thought; but, once again, I think that it can never be inherent in the structure of things to guarantee the exercise of freedom. The guarantee of freedom is freedom.

q: *So you do not think of Le Corbusier as an example of success. You are simply saying that his intention was liberating. Can you give us a successful example?*

a: No. It *cannot* succeed. If one were to find a place, and perhaps there are some, where liberty is effectively exercised, one would find that this is not owing to the order of objects, but, once again, owing to the practice of liberty. Which is not to say that, after all, one may as well leave people in slums, thinking that they can simply exercise their rights there.

q: *Meaning that architecture in itself cannot resolve social problems?*

a: I think that it can and does produce positive effects when the liberating intentions of the architect coincide with the real practice of people in the exercise of their freedom.

q: *But the same architecture can serve other ends?*

a: Absolutely. Let me bring up another example: the *Familistère* of Jean-Baptiste Godin at Guise (1859). The architecture of Godin was clearly intended for the freedom of people. Here was something that manifested the power of ordinary workers to participate in the exercise of their trade. It was a rather important sign and instrument of autonomy for a group of workers. Yet no one could enter or leave the place without being seen by everyone—an aspect of the architecture that could be totally oppressive. But it could only be oppressive if people were prepared to use their own presence in order to watch over others. Let's imagine a community of unlimited sexual practices that might be established there. It would once again become a place of freedom. I think it is somewhat arbitrary to try to dissociate the effective practice of freedom by people, the practice of social relations, and the spatial distributions in which they find themselves. If they are separated, they become impossible to understand. Each can only be understood through the other.

Q: *Yet people have often attempted to find utopian schemes to liberate people, or to oppress them.*

A: Men have dreamed of liberating machines. But there are no machines of freedom, by definition. This is not to say that the exercise of freedom is completely indifferent to spatial distribution, but it can only function when there is a certain convergence; in the case of divergence or distortion, it immediately becomes the opposite of that which had been intended. The panoptic qualities of Guise could perfectly well have allowed it to be used as a prison. Nothing could be simpler. It is clear that, in fact, the *Familistère* may well have served as an instrument for discipline and a rather unbearable group pressure.

Q: *So, once again, the intention of the architect is not the fundamental determining factor.*

A: Nothing is fundamental. That is what is interesting in the analysis of society. That is why nothing irritates me as much as these inquiries—which are by definition metaphysical—on the foundations of power in a society or the self-institution of a society, and so on. These are not fundamental phenomena. There are only reciprocal relations, and the perpetual gaps between intentions in relation to one another.

Q: *You have singled out doctors, prison wardens, priests, judges, and psychiatrists as key figures in the political configurations that involve domination. Would you put architects on this list?*

A: You know, I was not really attempting to describe figures of domination when I referred to doctors and people like that but, rather, to describe people through whom power passed or who are important in the fields of power relations. A patient in a mental institution is placed within a field of fairly complicated power relations, which Erving Goffman analyzed very well. The pastor in a Christian or Catholic church (in Protestant churches it is somewhat different) is an important link in a set of power relations. The architect is not an individual of that sort.

After all, the architect has no power over me. If I want to tear down or change a house he built for me, put up new partitions, add a chimney, the architect has no control. So the architect should be placed in another category—which is not to say that he is not totally foreign to the organization, the implementation, and all the techniques of power that are exercised in a society. I would say that one must take *him*—his mentality, his attitude—into account as well as his projects, in order to understand a certain number of the techniques of power that are invested in architecture, but he is not comparable to a doctor, a priest, a psychiatrist, or a prison warden.

Q: *"Postmodernism" has received a great deal of attention recently in architectural circles. It is also being talked about in philosophy, notably by Jean-François Lyotard and Jürgen Habermas. Clearly, historical reference and language play an important role in the modern episteme. How do you see postmodernism, both as architecture and in terms of the historical and philosophical questions that are posed by it?*

A: I think that there is a widespread and facile tendency, which one should combat, to designate that which has just occurred as the primary enemy, as if this were always the principal form of oppression from which one had to liberate oneself. Now, this simple attitude entails a number of dangerous consequences: first, an inclination to seek out some cheap form of archaism or some imaginary past forms of happiness that people did not, in fact, have at all. For instance, in the areas that interest me, it is very amusing to see how contemporary sexuality is described as something absolutely terrible. To think that it is only possible now to make love after turning off the television! and in mass-produced beds! "Not like that wonderful time when . . ." Well, what about those wonderful times when people worked eighteen hours a day and there were six people in a bed, if one was lucky enough to have a bed! There is in this hatred of the present or the immediate past a dangerous tendency to invoke a completely mythical past. Second, there is the problem raised by Habermas: if one abandons the work of Kant or Weber, for example, one runs the risk of lapsing into irrationality.

I am completely in agreement with this, but at the same time, our question is quite different: I think that the central issue of philosophy and critical thought since the eighteenth century has always been, still is, and will, I hope, remain the question: *What* is this Reason that we use? What are its historical effects? What are its limits, and what are its dangers? How can we exist as rational beings, fortunately committed to practicing a rationality that is unfortunately crisscrossed by intrinsic dangers? One should remain as close to this question as possible, keeping in mind that it is both central and extremely difficult to resolve. In addition, if it is extremely dangerous to say that reason is the enemy that should be eliminated, it is just as dangerous to say that any critical questioning of this rationality risks sending us into irrationality. One should not forget—and I'm saying this not in order to criticize rationality but to show how ambiguous things are—it was on the basis of the flamboyant rationality of social Darwinism that racism was formulated, becoming one of the most enduring and powerful ingredients of Nazism. This was, of course, an irrationality, but an irrationality that was at the same time, after all, a certain form of rationality . . .

This is the situation we are in and must combat. If intellectuals in general are to have a function, if critical thought itself has a function—and, even more specifically, if philosophy has a function within critical thought—it is precisely to accept this sort of spiral, this sort of revolving door of rationality that refers us to its necessity, to its indispensability, and, at the same time, to its intrinsic dangers.

Q: *All that being said, it would be fair to say that you are much less afraid of historicism and the play of historical references than someone like Habermas is; also, that this issue has been posed in architecture as almost a crisis of civilization by the defenders of modernism, who contend that if we abandon modern architecture for a frivolous return to decoration and motifs, we are somehow abandoning civilization. On the other hand, some postmodernists have claimed that historical references per se are somehow meaningful and are going to protect us from the dangers of an overly rationalized world.*

A: Although it may not answer your question, I would say this: one should totally and absolutely suspect anything that claims to be a return. One reason is a logical one: there is, in fact, no such thing as a return. History, and the meticulous interest applied to history, is certainly one of the best defenses against this theme of the return. For me, the history of madness or the studies of the prison . . . were done in that precise manner because I knew full well—this is in fact what aggravated many people—that I was carrying out a historical analysis in such a manner that people *could* criticize the present; but it was impossible for them to say, "Let's go back to the good old days when madmen in the eighteenth century . . ." or, "Let's go back to the days when the prison was not one of the principal instruments . . ." No; I think that history preserves us from that sort of ideology of the return.

Q: *Hence, the simple opposition between reason and history is rather silly . . . choosing sides between the two . . .*
A: Yes. Well, the problem for Habermas is, after all, to make a transcendental mode of thought spring forth against any historicism. I am, indeed, far more historicist and Nietzschean. I do not think that there is a proper usage of history or a proper usage of intrahistorical analysis—which is fairly lucid, by the way—that works precisely against this ideology of the return. A good study of peasant architecture in Europe, for example, would show the utter vanity of wanting to return to the little individual house with its thatched roof. History protects us from historicism—from a historicism that calls on the past to resolve the questions of the present.

Q: *It also reminds us that there is always a history; that those modernists who wanted to suppress any reference to the past were making a mistake.*
A: Of course.

Q: *Your next two books deal with sexuality among the Greeks and the early Christians. Are there any particular architectural dimensions to the issues you discuss?*
A: I didn't find any, absolutely none. But what is interesting is that in imperial Rome there were, in fact, brothels, pleasure quarters, criminal areas, and so on, and there was also one sort of quasi-public place of pleasure—the baths, the *thermes*. The baths were a

very important place of pleasure and encounter, which slowly disappeared in Europe. In the Middle Ages, the baths were still a place of encounter between men and women as well as of men with men and women with women, although that is rarely talked about. What were referred to and condemned, as well as practiced, were the encounters between men and women, which disappeared over the course of the sixteenth and seventeenth centuries.

Q: *In the Arab world it continues.*
A: Yes; but in France it has largely ceased. It still existed in the nineteenth century. One sees it in *Les Enfants du paradis*, and it is historically exact. One of the characters, Lacenaire, was—no one mentions it—a swine and a pimp who used young boys to attract older men and then blackmailed them; there is a scene that refers to this. It required all the naiveté and antihomosexuality of the Surrealists to overlook that fact. So the baths continued to exist, as a place of sexual encounters. The bath was a sort of cathedral of pleasure at the heart of the city, where people could go as often as they wanted, where they walked about, picked each other up, met each other, took their pleasure, ate, drank, discussed . . .

Q: *So sex was not separated from the other pleasures. It was inscribed in the center of the cities. It was public; it served a purpose . . .*
A: That's right. Sexuality was obviously considered a social pleasure for the Greeks and the Romans. What is interesting about male homosexuality today—this has apparently been the case of female homosexuals for some time—is that their sexual relations are immediately translated into social relations, and the social relations are understood as sexual relations. For the Greeks and the Romans, in a different fashion, sexual relations were located within social relations in the widest sense of the term. The baths were a place of sociality that included sexual relations.

One can directly compare the bath and the brothel. The brothel is in fact a place, and an architecture, of pleasure. There is, in fact, a very interesting form of sociality that was studied by Alain Corbin in *Les Filles de noces*.[4] The men of the city met at the brothel; they were tied to one another by the fact that the same women passed through their hands, that the same diseases and infections were communicated to them. There was a sociality of the brothel, but the sociality of the baths as it existed among the ancients—a new version of which could perhaps exist again—was completely different from the sociality of the brothel.

Q: *We now know a great deal about disciplinary architecture. What about confessional architecture—the kind of architecture that would be associated with a confessional technology?*
A: You mean religious architecture? I think that it has been studied. There is the whole problem of a monastery as xenophobic. There one finds precise regulations concerning life in common; affecting sleeping, eating, prayer, the place of each individual in all of that, the cells. All of this was programmed from very early on.

Q: *In a technology of power, of confession as opposed to discipline, space seems to play a central role as well.*
A: Yes. Space is fundamental in any form of communal life; space is fundamental in any exercise of power. To make a parenthetical remark, I recall having been invited, in 1966, by a group of architects to do a study of space, of something that I called at that time "heterotopias," those singular spaces to be found in some given social spaces whose functions are different or even the opposite of others. The architects worked on this, and at the end of the study someone spoke up—a Sartrean psychologist—who firebombed me, saying that *space* is reactionary and capitalist, but *history* and *becoming* are revolutionary. This absurd discourse was not at all unusual at the time. Today everyone would be convulsed with laughter at such a pronouncement, but not then.

Q: *Architects in particular, if they do choose to analyze an institutional building such as a hospital or a school in terms of its disciplinary function, would tend to focus primarily on the walls. After all, that is what they design. Your approach is perhaps more concerned with space, rather than architecture, in that the physical walls are only one aspect of the institution. How would you characterize the difference between these two approaches, between the building itself and space?*
A: I think there is a difference in method and approach. It is true that for me, architecture, in the very vague analyses of it that I have been able to conduct, is only taken as an element of support, to ensure a certain allocation of people in space, a *canalization* of their circulation, as well as the coding of their reciprocal relations.

So it is not only considered as an element in space, but is especially thought of as a plunge into a field of social relations in which it brings about some specific effects.

For example, I know that there is a historian who is carrying out some interesting studies of the archaeology of the Middle Ages, in which he takes up the problem of architecture, of houses in the Middle Ages, in terms of the problem of the chimney. I think that he is in the process of showing that beginning at a certain moment it was possible to build a chimney inside the house—a chimney with a hearth, not simply an open room or a chimney outside the house; that at that moment all sorts of things changed and relations between individuals became possible. All of this seems very interesting to me, but the conclusion that he presented in an article was that the history of ideas and thoughts is useless.

What is, in fact, interesting is that the two are rigorously indivisible. Why did people struggle to find the way to put a chimney inside the house? Or why did they put their techniques to this use? So often in the history of techniques it takes years or even centuries to implement them. It is certain, and of capital importance, that this technique was a formative influence on new human relations, but it is impossible to think that it would have been developed and adapted had there not been in the play and strategy of human relations something which tended in that direction. What is interesting is always interconnection, not the primacy of this over that, which never has any meaning.

Q: *In your book* The Order of Things *you constructed certain vivid spatial metaphors to describe structures of thought. Why do you think spatial images are so evocative for these references? What is the relationship between these spatial metaphors describing disciplines and more concrete descriptions of institutional spaces?*

A: It is quite possible that since I was interested in the problems of space, I used quite a number of spatial metaphors in *The Order of Things*, but usually these metaphors were not ones that I advanced but ones I was studying as objects. What is striking in the epistemological mutations and transformations of the seventeenth century is to see how the spatialization of knowledge was one of the factors in the constitution of this knowledge as a science. If the natural history and the classifications if Linnaeus were possible, it is for a certain number of reasons: on the one hand, there was literally a spatialization of the very object of their analyses, since they gave themselves the rule of studying and classifying a plant only on the basis of that which was visible. They didn't even want to use a microscope. All the traditional elements of knowledge, such as the medical functions of the plant, fell away. The object was spatialized. Subsequently, it was spatialized insofar as the principles of classification had to be found in the very structure of the plant: the number of elements, how they were arranged, their size, and so on, and certain other elements, like the height of the plant. Then there was the spatialization into illustrations within books, which was only possible with certain printing techniques. Then the spatialization of the reproduction of the plants themselves, which was represented in books. All of these are spatial techniques, not metaphors.

Q: *Is the actual plan for a building—the precise drawing that becomes walls and windows—the same form of discourse as, say, a hierarchical pyramid that describes rather precisely relations between people, not only in space but also in social life?*
A: Well, I think there are a few simple and exceptional examples in which the architectural means reproduce, with more or less emphasis, the social hierarchies. There is the model of the military camp, where the military hierarchy is to be read on the ground itself, by the place occupied by the tents and the buildings reserved for each rank. It reproduces precisely through architecture a pyramid of power; but this is an exceptional example, as is everything military—privileged in society and of an extreme simplicity.

Q: *But the plan itself is not always an account of relations of power.*
A: No. Fortunately for human imagination, things are a little more complicated than that.

Q: *Architecture is not, of course, a constant: it has a long tradition of changing preoccupations, changing systems, different rules. The knowledge [savoir] of architecture is partly the history of the profession, partly the evolution of a science of construction, and partly a rewriting of aesthetic theories. What do you think is particular about this form of knowledge [savoir]? Is it more like a natural science, or what you have called a "dubious science"?*

A: I can't exactly say that this distinction between sciences that are certain and those that are uncertain is of no interest—that would be avoiding the question—but I must say that what interests me more is to focus on what the Greeks called the *tekhnē*, that is to say, a practical rationality governed by a conscious goal. I am not even sure if it is worth constantly asking the question of whether government can be the object of an exact science. On the other hand, if architecture, like the practice of government and the practice of other forms of social organization, is considered as a *tekhnē*, possibly using elements of sciences like physics, for example, or statistics, and so on . . . , that is what is interesting. But if one wanted to do a history of architecture, I think that it should be much more along the lines of that general history of the *tekhnē* rather than the histories of either the exact sciences or the inexact ones. The disadvantage of this word *technē*, I realize, is its relation to the word "technology," which has a very specific meaning. A very narrow meaning is given to "technology": one thinks of hard technology, the technology of wood, of fire, of electricity. Whereas government is also a function of technology: the government of individuals, the government of souls, the government of the self by the self, the government of families, the government of children, and so on. I believe that if one placed the history of architecture back in this general history of *tekhnē*, in this wide sense of the word, one would have a more interesting guiding concept than by the opposition between the exact sciences and the inexact ones.

NOTES

* Conducted by Paul Rabinow, this interview first appeared in *Skyline* in 1982. [eds.]

1 Rabinow is referring to Foucault's response to a series of questions posed to him by the editors of the journal *Herodote*, and published therein as "Questions to Michel Foucault About Geography," vol. 1 (January 1976), pp. 71–85—TRANS.

2 See the article on Foucault in *Skyline* (March 1982), p. 14—TRANS.

3 Jean Bodin, *Republic* (Paris, 1577).

4 Alain Corbin, *Les Filles de noces* (Paris: Aubier, 1978).

THE RISKS OF SECURITY*

SECURITY AND DEPENDENCY:
A DIABOLICAL PAIR?

Q: *Traditionally, social security protects individuals against a certain number of risks in connection with sickness, family structure, and old age. Clearly, it must continue to fulfill this function.*

However, between 1946 and today, things have changed. New needs have appeared. Thus we are witnessing a growing desire for independence among individuals and groups: the aspirations of children vis-à-vis their parents, of women vis-à-vis men, of the sick vis-à-vis doctors, and of the handicapped vis-à-vis all sorts of institutions. It is becoming equally clear that we need to put an end to the phenomenon of marginalization, attributable in large part to unemployment, but also, in certain cases, to the deficiencies of our system of social protection.

We believe that at least these two needs must be taken into account by the next social security administration, in order that the system take on newly defined functions that entail a remodeling of its system of allocations. Do you believe that these needs really exist in our society? Would you call attention to others? And how, in your opinion, can social security respond to them?

A: I believe that it is necessary to emphasize three things right at the beginning.

First of all, our system of social guarantees, as it was established in 1946, has now reached its economic limits.

Second, this system, elaborated during the interwar years—that is, during a period when one of the goals was to attenuate or to minimize a certain number of social conflicts, and when the conceptual model was informed by a rationality born around World War I—today reaches its limits as it stumbles against the political, economic, and social rationality of modern societies.

Third, social security, whatever its positive effects, has also had some "perverse effects": the growing rigidity of certain mechanisms and the creation of situations of dependency. This is inherent in the functioning of the system: on the one hand, we give people greater security and, on the other, we increase their dependency. Instead, we should expect our system of social security to free us from dangers and from situations that tend to debase or to subjugate us.

Q: *If indeed people seem willing to give up some liberty and independence provided that the system extend and reinforce their security, how can we manage this "diabolical pair" of security and dependency?*

A: We have before us a problem the terms of which are negotiable. We must try to appreciate the capacity of people who undertake such negotiation and the level of compromise they are able to attain.

The way in which we look at these things has changed. In the thirties and after the war, the problem of security was so acute and so immediate that the question of dependency was practically ignored. From the fifties on, in contrast, and even more from the sixties on, the notion of security began to be associated with the question of independence. This inflection was an extremely important cultural, political, and social phenomenon. We cannot ignore it.

It seems to me that certain proponents of antisecurity arguments reject, in a somewhat simplistic manner, everything that might be dangerous in "security and liberty" law. We must be more prudent in considering this opposition.

There is indeed a positive demand: a demand for a security that opens the way to richer, more numerous, more diverse, and more flexible relationships with ourselves and others, all the while assuring each of us real autonomy. This is a new fact that should weigh on present-day conceptions of social protection.

Very schematically, that is how I would situate the question of the demand for independence.

Q: *The negotiation of which you speak can be conducted only along a narrow line. On one side we can see that certain rigidities in our apparatus of social protection, combined with its interventionist nature, threaten the independence of groups and individuals, enclosing them in an administrative yoke that (if one goes by the Swedish experience) becomes intolerable in the end. On the other side, the form of liberalism described by Jules Guesde when he spoke of "free foxes in free chicken coups" is no more desirable—one has only to look at the United States to be convinced of this.*

A: It is precisely the difficulty of establishing a compromise along this narrow line that calls for as subtle an analysis as possible of the actual situation. By "actual situation" I do not mean the system of economic and social mechanisms, which others describe better than I could. Rather, I speak of this interface between, on the one hand, people's sensibilities, their moral choices, their relations to themselves and, on the other, the institutions that surround them. It is here that dysfunctions, malaise, and, perhaps, crises arise in the social system.

Considering what one might call the "negative effects" of the system, it is necessary, it seems to me, to distinguish two tendencies. We can see that dependency results not only from integration, but also from marginalization and exclusion. We need to respond to both threats.

I believe that there are instances when it is necessary to resist the phenomenon of integration. An entire mechanism of social protection, in fact, does not fully benefit the individual unless he finds himself integrated into a family milieu, a work milieu, or a geographic milieu.

Q: *Could we also pose the question of integration in the context of the relationship of the individual to the state?*

A: In this regard, too, we are witnessing an important phenomenon: before the "crisis," or more precisely, before the emergence of the problems that we now encounter, it is my impression that the individual never questioned his relationship to the state, insofar as this relationship (keeping in mind the way in which the great centralizing institutions worked) was based on an "input"—the dues he paid—and an "output"—the benefits that accrued to him.

Today a problem of limits intervenes. What is at stake is no longer the equal access of all to security but, rather, the infinite access of each to a certain number of possible benefits. We tell people: "You cannot consume indefinitely." And when the authorities claim, "You no longer have a right to that," or "You will no longer be covered for such operations," or yet again, "You will pay a part of the hospital fees," or in the extreme case, "It would be useless to prolong your life by three months, we are going to let you die"—then the individual begins to question the nature of his relationship to the state and starts to feel his dependency on institutions whose power of decision he had heretofore misapprehended.

Q: *Doesn't this problem of dependency perpetuate the ambivalence that reigned, even before the establishment of a mechanism of social protection, at the creation of the first health institutions? Was it not the objective of the Hôtel-Dieu both to relieve misery and to withdraw the poor and the sick from society's view, at the same time reducing their threat to the public order?*

And can we not, in the twentieth century, leave behind a logic that links charity to isolation in order to conceive of less alienating systems, which the people could — let us use the word — "appropriate"?

A: It is true, in a sense, that in the long run certain problems manifest themselves as permanent.

That said, I am very suspicious of two intellectual attitudes, the persistence of which over the last two decades is to be deplored. One consists in presupposing the repetition and extension of the same mechanisms throughout the history of our societies. From this, one derives the notion of a kind of cancer that spreads in the social body. It is an unacceptable theory. The way in which we used to confine certain segments of the population in the seventeenth century, to return to this example, is very different from the hospitalization we know from the nineteenth century, and even more from the security mechanisms of the present.

Another attitude, every bit as frequent, maintains the fiction of "the good old days" when the social body was alive and warm, when families were united, and individuals independent. This happy interlude was cut short by the advent of capitalism, the bourgeoisie, and industrialization. Here we have a historical absurdity.

The linear reading of history as well as the nostalgic reference to a golden age of social life still haunts a great deal of thinking, and informs a number of political and sociological analyses. We must flush these attitudes out.

Q: *With this remark, we come perhaps to the question of marginality. It seems that our society is divided into a "protected" sector and an exposed or precarious sector. Even though social security alone cannot remedy this situation, it remains the case that a system of social protection can contribute to a decline in marginalization and segregation through adequate measures directed toward the handicapped, immigrants, and all categories of precarious status. At least this is our analysis. Is it also yours?*

A: No doubt, we can say that certain phenomena of marginalization are linked to factors of separation between an "insured" population and an "exposed" population. Moreover, this sort of cleavage was foreseen explicitly by a certain number of economists during the seventies, who thought that in postindustrial societies the exposed sector would, on the whole, have to grow considerably. Such "programming" of society, however, was not often realized, and we cannot accept this as the sole explanation of the process of marginalization.

There are in certain forms of marginalization what I would call another aspect of the phenomenon of dependency. Our systems of social coverage impose a determined way of life that subjugates [*assujettit*] individuals. As a result, all persons or groups who, for one reason or another, cannot or do not want to accede to this way of life find themselves marginalized by the very game of the institutions.

Q: *There is a difference between marginality which one chooses and marginality to which one is subjected.*

A: True, and it would be necessary to distinguish them in a more detailed analysis. In any case, it is important to shed light on the relationship between the working of social security and ways of life, the ways of life that we began to observe about ten years ago. But this is a study that demands more thorough investigation, at the same time that it needs to be disengaged from a too strict "sociologism" that neglects ethical problems of paramount importance.

A CERTAIN CONCEPTUAL DEFICIENCY

Q: *Our goal is to give people security as well as autonomy. Perhaps we can come closer to this goal by two means: on the one hand, by rejecting the absurd juridicism of which we are so fond in France, which raises mountains of paperwork in everyone's way (so as to discriminate yet a bit more against the marginals) in favor of an experiment with a posteriori legislation that would facilitate access to social benefits and amenities; and, on the other hand, by achieving real decentralization with a staff and appropriate places for welcoming people.*

What do you think? Do you subscribe to the objectives I just stated?
A: Yes, certainly. And the objective of an optimal social coverage joined to a maximum of independence is clear enough. As for reaching this goal . . .

I think that such an aim requires two kinds of means. On the one hand, it requires a certain empiricism. We must transform the field of social institutions into a field of experimentation, in order to determine which levers to turn and which bolts to loosen in order to bring about the desired effects. It is indeed important to undertake a campaign of decentralization, for example, in order to bring the users closer to the decision-making centers on which they depend, and to tie them into the decision-making process, avoiding the type of great, globalizing integration that leaves people in complete ignorance about the conditions of particular judgments. We must then multiply these experiments wherever possible on the particularly important and interesting terrain of the social, considering that an entire institutional system, now fragile, will probably undergo a restructuring from top to bottom.

On the other hand—and it is a nodal point—there would be a considerable amount of work to do in order to renovate the conceptual categories that inspire our way of approaching all of these problems of social guarantees and of security. We are still thinking inside a mental framework formed between 1920 and 1940, essentially under the influence of Beveridge,[1] a man who would be over one hundred years old today.

For the moment, we lack completely the intellectual instruments to envisage in new terms the framework within which we could achieve our goals.

Q: *To illustrate the obsolescence of the mental frameworks of which you speak, don't we need a linguistic study of the sense of the word "subject" in the language of social security?*

A: Absolutely! And the question is what to do so that the person would no longer be a "subject" in the sense of subjugation.

As for the intellectual deficiency that I have just outlined, one may well wonder from where new forms of analysis, new conceptual frameworks, will spring.

What stands out in my mind, to be schematic, is that at the end of the eighteenth century in England, and in the nineteenth century in certain European countries, the parliamentary life was able to constitute a place to work out and discuss new projects (such as the fiscal and customs laws in Great Britain). That is where great campaigns of reflection and exchange were ignited. In the second half of the nineteenth century, many problems, many projects, were born from what was then a new associative life, that of labor unions, of political parties, of various associations. In the first half of the twentieth century, a very important task—a conceptual effort— was carried out in the political, economic, and social domains by people such as Keynes or Beveridge, as well as by a certain number of intellectuals, academics, and administrators.

But let us admit, the crisis that we are undergoing, which soon will be ten years old, has not elicited anything interesting or new from these intellectual milieus. It seems that in those quarters there has been a sort of sterilization: one cannot find any significant innovation there.

Q: *Can the unions be those "loci of illumination"?*

A: If it is true that the current malaise brings into question everything on the side of state institutional authority, it is a fact that the answers will not come from those who exercise this authority: rather, they should be raised by those who intend to counterbalance the state prerogative and to constitute counterpowers. What comes out of union activity might then eventually, in fact, open up a space for innovation.

Q: *Does this need to renovate the conceptual framework of social protection give a chance to "civil society"—of which the unions are a part—in relation to the state?*

A: If this opposition between civil society and the state could, with

good reason, be used at the end of the eighteenth century and in
the nineteenth century, I am not sure that it is still operative today.
The Polish example in this case is very interesting: when one likens
the powerful social movement that has swept across that country
to a revolt of civil society against the state, one underestimates the
complexity and the multiplicity of confrontations. It was not only
against the state that the Solidarity movement had to fight.

The relationship between the political power, the systems of dependency that it generates, and individuals is too complex to be
captured by this schema. In fact, the idea of an opposition between
civil society and the state was formulated in a given context in response to a precise intention: some liberal economists proposed it
at the end of the eighteenth century to limit the sphere of action of
the state, civil society being conceived of as the locus of an autonomous economic process. This was a quasi-polemical concept, opposed to administrative options of states of that era, so that a certain
liberalism could flourish.

But something bothers me even more: the reference to this antagonistic pair is never exempt from a sort of Manicheism, afflicting
the notion of state with a pejorative connotation at the same time
as it idealizes society as something good, lively, and warm.

What I am attentive to is the fact that all human relationships
are to a certain degree relationships of power. We evolve in a world
of perpetual strategic relations. All power relations are not bad in
and of themselves, but it is a fact that they always entail certain
risks.

Let's take the example of penal justice, which is more familiar
to me than that of social security. An entire movement is now developing in Europe and in the United States in favor of an "informal
justice," or even of certain forms of arbitration conducted by the
groups themselves. It requires a very optimistic view of society to
think it capable, by simple internal regulation, of resolving the
problems it faces.

In short, returning to our topic, I remain quite circumspect about
playing with the opposition between state and civil society. As for
the project of transferring to civil society a power of initiative and
action annexed by the state and exercised in an authoritarian manner: whatever the scenario, a relationship of power would be op-

erating and the question would be to know how to limit the effects of this relationship, this relationship being in itself neither good nor bad but dangerous, so that it would be necessary to think, on all levels, about the way in which to channel its efficacy in the best possible direction.

Q: *What we have very much on our minds at this time is the fact that social security, in its present form, is perceived as a remote institution, with a statist character—even if this is not the case—because it is a big centralized machine. Our problem, then, is the following: in order to open up the channel of participation to the users, it is necessary to bring them closer to the centers of decision. How?*

A: This problem is empirical more than a matter of the opposition between civil society and the state: it is what I would call a matter of "decisional distance." In other words, the problem is to estimate an optimal distance between a decision taken and the individual concerned, so that the individual has a voice in the matter and so that the decision is intelligible to him. At the same time, it is important to be able to adapt to his situation without having to pass through an inextricable maze of regulations.

WHAT RIGHT TO HEALTH?

Q: *What is your position regarding the idea of the "right to health," which plays a part in the claims of the CFDT²?*

A: Here we find ourselves at the heart of an extremely interesting problem.

When the system of social security that we know today was put in place on a large scale, there was a more or less explicit consensus on what could be called "the needs of health." It was, in sum, the need to deal with "accidents"—that is, with invalidating deviations linked to sickness and to congenital or acquired handicaps.

From that point on, two processes unfolded. On the one hand, there was a technical acceleration of medicine that increased its therapeutic power but increased many times faster its capacity for examination and analysis. On the other hand, there was a growth in the demand for health, which demonstrates that the need for health (at least as far as it is felt) has no internal principle of limitation.

Consequently, it is not possible to set objectively a theoretical and practical threshold, valid for all, from which one could say that the needs of health are entirely and definitively satisfied.

The question of rights appears particularly thorny in this context. I would like to make a few simple remarks.

It is clear that there is no sense in talking about a "right to health." Health—good health—cannot arise from a right. Good and bad health, however rough or fine the criteria used, are facts— states of things and also states of consciousness. And even if we correct for this by pointing out that the border separating health from sickness is in part defined by the capacity of doctors to diagnose a sickness, by the sort of life or activity of the subject, and by what in a given culture is recognized as health or sickness, this relativity does not preclude the fact that there is no right to be on this side or that of the dividing line.

On the other hand, one can have a right to working conditions that do not increase in a significant manner the risk of sickness or various handicaps. One can also have a right to compensation, care, and damages when a health accident is, in one way or another, the responsibility of an authority.

But that is not the current problem. It is, I believe, this: must a society endeavor to satisfy by collective means the need for health of individuals? And can individuals legitimately demand satisfaction of health needs?

It appears—if these needs are liable to grow indefinitely—that an affirmative answer to this question would be without an acceptable or even conceivable translation into practice. On the other hand, one can speak of "means of health"—and by that I mean not just hospital installations and medications but everything that is at society's disposal at a given moment for effecting those corrections and adjustments of health that are technically possible. These means of health define a mobile line—which results from the technical capacity of medicine, from the economic capacity of the collectivity, and from what society wishes to devote as resources and means to health. And we can define the right to have access to these means of health, a right that presents itself under different aspects. There is the problem of equality of access—a problem that is easy to answer in principle, though it is not always easy to assure this access in practice. There is the problem of indefinite access to the means of health; here we must not delude ourselves: the problem undoubtedly does not have a theoretical solution. The important thing is to know by what arbitration, always flexible, always provisional, the limits of access will be defined. It is necessary to keep in mind the fact that these limits cannot be established once and for all by a medical definition of health, nor by the idea of "needs of health" expressed as an absolute.

Q: *That poses a certain number of problems, among which is this, a rather mundane problem of inequality: the life expectancy of a manual laborer is much lower than that of an ecclesiastic or a teacher; how would we proceed so that the arbitration from which a "norm of health" will result takes this situation into account?*

Besides, the expenditures on health care today represent 8.6 percent of the gross national product. That was not planned. The cost of health—this is the tragedy—is fed by a multiplicity of individual decisions and by a process of renewal of those decisions. Are we not, therefore, even while we demand equality of access to health, in a situation of "rationed" health?

A: I believe that our concern is the same: it is a question of knowing, and this is a formidable political, economic, as well as cultural problem, how to select the criteria according to which we could establish a norm which would serve to define, at any given moment, the right to health.

The question of costs, which intrudes in a familiar manner, adds a new dimension to this interrogation.

I do not see, and nobody can explain to me, how technically it would be possible to satisfy all the needs of health along the infinite line on which they develop. And even though I do not know what would limit them, it would be impossible in any case to let expenditures grow under this rubric at the pace of recent years.

An apparatus made to assure the security of people in the domain of health has thus reached the point in its development at which it will be necessary to decide that such an illness, such a suffering, will no longer benefit from any coverage—a point at which even life, in certain cases, will no longer enjoy any protection. And that poses a political and moral problem somewhat related, observing due proportion, to the question of the right of the state to ask an individual to die in a war. This question, without having lost any of its acuteness, has been integrated perfectly, through long historical developments, into the consciousness of people, so that soldiers have in effect agreed to be killed—thus placing their lives outside of protection. The question today is to know how the people will accept being exposed to certain risks without preserving the benefit of coverage by the welfare state.

Q: *Does this mean that we will call into question incubators, consider euthanasia, and thus return to what social security fought, namely certain forms of eliminating the most biologically fragile individuals? Will the prevailing word of order be: "It is necessary to choose; let us choose the strongest"? Who will choose among unrelenting therapy, development of neonatal medicine, and the improvement of working conditions (every year, in French companies, twenty out of every one hundred women suffer nervous breakdowns)?*

A: Such choices are being made at every instant, even if left unsaid. They are made according to the logic of a certain rationality which certain discourses are made to justify.

The question that I pose is to know whether a "strategy of health"—this problematic of choice—must remain mute. Here we touch upon a paradox: this strategy is acceptable, in the current state of things, insofar as it is left unsaid. If it is explicit, even in the form of a more or less acceptable rationality, it becomes morally intolerable. Take the example of dialysis: how many patients are undergoing dialysis, how many others are unable to benefit from it? Suppose we expose the choices that culminated in this sort of inequality of treatment—this would bring to light scandalous rules! It is here that a certain rationality itself becomes a scandal.

I have no solution to propose. But I believe that it is futile to cover our eyes—we must try to go to the bottom of things and to face up to them.

Q: *Would there not be room, moreover, to do a fairly detailed analysis of costs in order to pinpoint some possibilities of economizing before making more painful and indeed "scandalous" choices? I am thinking in particular of iatrogenic ailments, which currently represent (if one believes certain figures) 8 percent of all health problems. Is this not an example of a "perverse effect" precisely attributable to some defect in rationality?*

A: To reexamine the rationality that presides over our choices in the matter of health—this is indeed a task to which we should apply ourselves resolutely.

Thus we can point out that certain troubles like dyslexia, because we view them as benign, are but minimally covered by social security, whereas their social cost can be tremendous. For example, have we evaluated all that dyslexia can entail in educational investment beyond simply considering the treatments available? This is the type of situation to be reconsidered when we reexamine what could be called "normality" in matters of health. There is an enormous amount of work in the way of investigation, experimentation, measure-taking, and intellectual and moral reformulation to be done on this score.

Clearly, we have come upon a turning point that must be negotiated.

A MATTER OF CONSCIENCE AND CULTURE

Q: *The definition of a norm in health, and the search for a consensus about a certain level of expenditure or about the modes of allocation of these expenditures, constitute an extraordinary opportunity for people to take responsibility for matters that concern them fundamentally, matters of life and well-being. But it is also a task of such magnitude as to inspire some hesitation, is it not?*

How can we bring the debate to all levels of public opinion?

A: It is true that certain contributions to this debate have aroused an outcry.[5] What is significant is that the protests address proposals that touch on matters that are by nature controversial: life and death. By evoking these health problems, we enter into a system of values that allows for an absolute and infinite demand. The problem raised is therefore that of reconciling an infinite demand with a finite system.

This is not the first time that mankind has encountered this problem. After all, was religion not made to solve it? But today, we must find a solution to it in technical terms.

Q: *Does the proposal to make the individual responsible for his or her own choices contain an element of the answer? When we ask a smoker to pay a surcharge, for example, does this not amount to obliging him financially to assume the risk that he runs? Can we not, in the same way, bring home to people the meaning and implication of*

their individual decisions instead of marking out boundaries beyond
which life would no longer have the same price?

A: I totally agree. When I speak of arbitration and normativity, I
do not have in mind a sort of committee of wise men who can
proclaim each year: "Given the circumstances and state of our fi-
nances, such a risk will be covered and such another will not." I
picture, in a more global sense, something like a cloud of decisions
arranging themselves around an axis that would roughly define the
retained norm. It remains to be seen how to ensure that this normative axis is as representative as possible of a certain state of
consciousness of the people—that is, of the nature of their demand
and of that which can be the object of consent on their part. I believe that results of arbitration should be the effect of a kind of
ethical consensus, so that the individual can recognize himself in
the decisions made and in the values behind the decisions. It is
under this condition that the decisions will be acceptable, even if
someone protests and rebels.

Given this, if it is true that people who smoke and those who
drink must know that they are running a risk, it is also true that to
have a salty diet when one has arteriosclerosis is dangerous, just
as it is dangerous to have a sugar-laden diet when one is diabetic.
I point this out to indicate just how complex the problems are, and
to suggest that arbitration, or a "decisional cloud," should never
assume the form of a univocal rule. All uniform, rational models
arrive very quickly at paradoxes!

It is quite obvious, for all that, that the cost of diabetes and of
arteriosclerosis are minuscule compared to the expenses incurred
by tobacco addiction and alcoholism.

Q: *Which rank as veritable plagues, and the cost of which is also a*
social cost. I am thinking of a certain delinquency, of martyred chil-
dren, of battered wives . . .

A: Let us also remember that alcoholism was literally implanted
in the French working-class, in the nineteenth century, by the authority's opening of bars. Let us also remember that neither the
problem of home distillers nor that of viticulture have ever been
solved. One can speak of a veritable politics of organized alcoholism in France. Perhaps we are at a point at which it becomes pos-

sible to take the bull by the horns and to move toward a reduced coverage of the risks linked to alcoholism.

Whatever the case, it goes without saying that I do not advocate that savage liberalism that would lead to individual coverage for those who have the means to pay for it, and to a lack of coverage for the others.

I am merely emphasizing that the fact of "health" is a cultural fact in the broadest sense of the word, a fact that is political, economic, and social as well, a fact that is tied to a certain state of individual and collective consciousness. Every era outlines a "normal" profile of health. Perhaps we should direct ourselves toward a system that defines, in the domain of the *abnormal*, the pathological, the sicknesses *normally* covered by society.

Q: *Do you not think, in order to clarify the debate, it would also behoove us to distinguish, in attempting to define a norm of health, between that which arises from the medical sphere and that which arises from social relationships? Have we not witnessed, in the last thirty years, a kind of "medicalization" of what could be called society's problems? We have, for example, brought a type of medical response to the problem of absenteeism on the job, when we should have instead improved working conditions. This type of "displacement" puts a strain on the health budget.*

A: A thousand things, in fact, have been "medicalized" or even "over-medicalized," things that arise from phenomena other than medicine. It so happened that, faced with certain problems, we judged the medical solution to be the most useful and the most economical. This was the case for certain scholastic problems, for sexual problems, for detention problems . . . Clearly, we should revise many of the options of this kind.

A HAPPIER OLD AGE—UNTIL THE NON-EVENT?

Q: *We have not touched upon the problem of old age. Doesn't our society tend to relegate its old people to rest homes, as if to forget about them?*
A: I confess that I am somewhat reserved and taken aback by all that is being said about older people, about their isolation and misery in our society.

It's true that the rest homes of Nanterre and of Ivry offer a rather sordid image. But the fact that we are scandalized by this sordidness is indicative of a new sensibility, which is itself linked to a new situation. Before the war, families shoved the elderly into a corner of the house, complaining of the burden they placed on them, making them pay for their presence in the household with a thousand humiliations, a thousand hatreds. Today, the older people receive a pension on which they can live, and in cities all over France there are "senior citizens' clubs" frequented by people who meet each other, who travel, who shop, and who constitute an increasingly important sector of the population. Even if a certain number of individuals are still marginalized, the overall condition of the senior citizen has improved considerably within a few decades. That is why we are so sensitive—and it is an excellent thing—to what is still happening in certain establishments.

Q: *How, when all is said and done, can social security contribute to an ethic of the human person?*

A: Without recounting all of the elements of the answer to this question brought out in the course of this interview, I would say that social security contributes to an ethic of the human person at least by posing a certain number of problems, and especially by posing the question about the value of life and the way in which we face up to death.

The idea of bringing individuals and decision centers closer together should imply, at least as a consequence, the recognized right of each individual to kill himself when he wants to under decent conditions . . . If I won a few billion in the lottery, I would create an institute where people who would like to die would come spend a weekend, a week, or a month in pleasure, under drugs perhaps, in order to disappear afterward, as if erased.

Q: *A right to suicide?*

A: Yes.

Q: *What is there to say about the way in which we die today? What are we to think of this sterilized death, often in a hospital, without the company of family?*

A: Death becomes a non-event. Most of the time, people die in a cloud of medication, if it is not by accident, so that they entirely lose consciousness in a few hours, a few days, or a few weeks: they fade away. We live in a world in which the medical and pharmaceutical accompaniment to death removes much of the suffering and drama.

I do not really subscribe to all that is being said about the "sterilization" of death, which makes reference to something like a great integrative and dramatic ritual. Loud crying around the coffin was not always exempt from a certain cynicism: the joy of inheritance could be mixed in. I prefer the quiet sadness of disappearance to this sort of ceremony.

The way we die now seems to me indicative of a sensibility, of a system of values, which prevails today. There would be something chimerical in wanting to reinstate, in a fit of nostalgia, practices that no longer make any sense.

Let us, rather, try to give sense and beauty to an effacing death.

NOTES

* This interview, conducted by Robert Bono, first appeared in *Sécurité sociale: l'enjeu* (Paris: Syros, 1983) under the title "Un Systèmè fini face à une demande infinie." The English translation has been edited slightly—CG.

1 Lord William Henry Beveridge (1879–1963), English economist and administrator, author of a social security plan in 1942.

2 CFDT: Confédération Française du Travail. With Pierre Bourdieu, Foucault published a protest against the French Minister of Foreign Affairs' classification of the establishment of a military dictatorship in Poland as "a matter of Poland's internal politics." The protest won the support of some hundred or so intellectuals, whom the CFDT invited to participate in a common appeal "in the spirit of the Solidarity movement" (in Poland). The CFDT subsequently organized a committee of support for the Solidarity movement, in which Foucault took an active and, indeed, actively bureaucratic part. (See vol. 1 of *Dits et écrits*, "Chronologie," compiled by Daniel Defert, pp. 59–60.)—CG

3 Foucault refers here to the polemics following the publication of *L'Ordre cannibale: vie et mort de la médecine* by Jacques Attali (Paris: B. Grasset, 1979).—CG

WHAT IS CALLED "PUNISHING"?*

Q: *Your book* Discipline and Punish, *published in 1974, fell like a meteorite on the terrain of the penal specialists and criminologists. Presenting an analysis of the penal system which focused on political tactics and the technology of power, that work upset the established ideas concerning delinquency and the social function of punishment. It disturbed the penal judges, at least those who reflected on the meaning of their work; it vexed a number of criminologists who were hardly pleased, moreover, to see their discourse called "chatter." Nowadays, criminology books that don't refer to* Discipline and Punish *as a work to be reckoned with are more and more rare. Yet the penal system doesn't change, and the criminological chatter goes on as before. It's as if people were paying homage to the theorist of juridico-penal epistemology without being able to make any use of his teaching, as if a complete imperviousness existed between theory and practice. Of course, it wasn't your intention to do the work of a reformer, but couldn't one imagine a criminal justice policy that would take support from your analyses and would try to draw certain lessons from them?*

A: Perhaps I should start by explaining what I intended to do in that book. I didn't aim to do a work of criticism, at least not directly, if what is meant by criticism in this case is denunciation of the negative aspects of the current penal system. And I didn't aim to do the sort of job that a historian of institutions might do, either, in the sense that I didn't mean to recount how the penal and carceral institution had functioned in the course of the nineteenth century.

I attempted to define another problem. I wanted to uncover the system of thought, the form of rationality that, since the end of the eighteenth century, has supported the notion that prison is really the best means, or one of the most effective and rational means, of punishing offenses in a society. It's quite obvious that in doing this I had certain ideas concerning what was possible at the present time. Indeed, it has often appeared to me that by setting reformism against revolution, as is usually done, one doesn't provide oneself with the means for imagining what might bring about a real, profound, and radical transformation. It seems to me that when it was a question of reforming the penal system the reformers very often accepted, implicitly and sometimes even explicitly, the system of rationality that had been defined and put in place long before, and that they were simply trying to discover what the institutions and practices might be that would enable them to realize that system's scheme and achieve its ends. In bringing out the system of rationality underlying punitive practices, I wanted to indicate what the postulates of thought were that needed to be reexamined if one intended to transform the penal system. I'm not saying that they would necessarily have to be discarded; but I think that when one engages in a project of transformation and renovation, it's very important to know not only what the institutions and their real effects are, but also what type of thought sustains them: What elements of that system of rationality can still be accepted? What is the part, on the other hand, that deserves to be cast aside, abandoned, transformed, and so on? It's the same thing that I had tried to do with respect to the history of psychiatric institutions. It's true that I was a bit surprised, and fairly disappointed, to see that all this didn't lead to any endeavor of reflection and thought that might have brought people together around the same problem—very different people such as magistrates, penal law theorists, penitentiary practitioners, lawyers, social workers, and persons who have experienced prison. It's true that, for cultural or social reasons no doubt, the seventies were extremely disappointing in that regard. Many critiques were leveled more or less in every direction. Often, these ideas had a certain dissemination, and at times they exerted a certain influence; but the questions that were raised rarely crystallized into a collective initiative to determine in any case what transformations would need to be carried out. At any rate, for my part and

in spite of my desire, I certainly never had any opportunity to have
working contact with any magistrate or any political party. Thus,
the Socialist Party, founded in 1972, which spent nine years preparing for its coming to power, and which to a certain extent echoed in its speeches several themes that were developed during the
years 1960–70, never made a serious attempt to define beforehand
what its real practice might be when it was in power. It seems that
the institutions, groups, and political parties that might have facil-
itated a work of reflection didn't do anything . . .

Q: *One does have the impression that the conceptual system hasn't
evolved at all. Although the jurists and the psychiatrists recognize the
relevance and the freshness of your analyses, they seem to find it impossible to put them into practice, to employ them in the search for
what is called, ambiguously, a "policy concerning criminals."*
A: You've just formulated a problem that is, in fact, very important
and difficult. You know, I belong to a generation of people who
witnessed the collapse, one after another, of most of the utopias
that had been constructed in the nineteenth and at the beginning
of the twentieth century, and who also saw the perverse and sometimes disastrous results that could ensue from projects that were
extremely generous in their intentions. I've always made a point of
not playing the role of the prophetic intellectual, who tells people
what they ought to do ahead of time and prescribes conceptual
frameworks for them, objectives and means that he has drawn out
of his own brain, by working among his books in the confines of
his study. It has seemed to me that the work of an intellectual—
what I call a "specific intellectual"—is to try and isolate in their
power of constraint, but also in the contingency of their historical
formation, the systems of thought that have become familiar to us,
that appear self-evident and are integral with our perceptions, our
attitudes, our behaviors. One would then need to collaborate with
practitioners—not only to modify the institutions and practices but
to reshape the forms of thought.

Q: *What you have called "criminological chatter"—a phrase that's
been misunderstood, no doubt—is precisely the fact of not calling back
in question the system of thought in which all those analyses were
conducted for a century and a half. Is that what you meant?*
A: Yes, that's right. The phrase was a bit careless perhaps, so let's

retract it. But I do have the impression that the difficulties and contradictions that penal practice has encountered over the last two centuries have never been reexamined in a thorough fashion. And for a hundred and fifty years now, exactly the same notions, the same themes, the same reproaches, the same critical observations, the same demands have been repeated, as if nothing has changed—and, in a sense, nothing *has* changed. In a situation where an institution presenting so many disadvantages and provoking so much criticism gives rise only to an endless repetition of the same discourses, "chatter" is a serious symptom.

Q: *In* Discipline and Punish, *you analyze the "strategy" that consists in transforming certain illegalities into delinquency, turning the apparent failure of prison into a success. It's as if a certain "group" were more or less deliberately using this means to achieve results that are not declared. One has the impression, perhaps a false one, that this amounts to a ruse of power that subverts the projects and spoils the discourses of the humanist reformers. From this viewpoint, there would appear to be a resemblance between your analysis and the Marxist interpretation of history (I'm thinking of the pages in which you show that a certain type of illegality is singled out for punishment while others are tolerated). But, in contrast to Marxism, it's not clear what "group" or what "class," what interests are at work in this strategy.*

A: One has to distinguish among different things in the analysis of an institution. First, there is what can be called its *rationality*, or its *aim*, that is, the ends it has in view and the means it possesses for attaining those ends. In short, this is the institution's program as it has been defined—for example, Jeremy Bentham's ideas about prison. Second, there is the question of *results*. Obviously, the results very rarely coincide with the aim; thus, the objective of the correctional prison, of imprisonment as a means of improving the individual, has not been achieved. The result has been the opposite on the whole, and prison has tended to give a new impetus to delinquent behaviors. Now, when the result doesn't coincide with the aim, there are several possibilities: either one implements reforms, or one uses those results for something that wasn't envisaged at the start but can very well have a direction and a utility. This is what can be called the *use*. Thus prison, which did not result in any improvement, served instead as a mechanism of elimination. The fourth level of analysis is what can be called the "strategic configurations"; that is, on the basis of these unexpected uses, so to speak—which were new, but in spite of everything were deliberate to a certain extent—one can construct new rational courses of action that are different from the initial program but also correspond to its objectives, and in which the interactions among the different social groups can find their place.

Q: *Results that transform themselves into ends . . .*
A: That's right. They are results that are adapted to different uses, and these uses are rationalized—organized, in any case—in terms of new ends.

Q: *But that is not thought out in advance, of course—there's no hidden Machiavellian scheme underneath . . .*
A: Not at all. There isn't someone or some group that is controlling this strategy; but, on the basis of different results of the first aims and the usability of those results, a certain number of strategies are constructed.

Q: *Strategies whose finality once again partly eludes those who conceive them.*
A: Yes. Sometimes these strategies are entirely conscious; it can be said that the way in which the police use prison is more or less conscious. It's just that, as a rule, the strategies are not formulated. Unlike what occurs with the program. The institution's first program, the initial finality, is posted in black and white and serves as a justification, whereas the strategic configurations are often not clear even to those who occupy a place and play a role in them. But this game is quite capable of solidifying an institution, and I think that prison has been solidified, in spite of all the criticism that was made, because several strategies belonging to different groups have converged on that particular site.

Q: *You explain very clearly how the penalty of imprisonment was denounced, from the beginning of the twentieth century, as the great failure of the penal justice system, and it is denounced in the same terms as today. There isn't a single penal specialist who believes that prison achieves the goals assigned to it. The crime rate doesn't go down, and far from "rehabilitating" delinquents, prison manufactures them; it increases the repetition of offenses, and it doesn't make society any safer. The penitentiary establishments are always full, and one doesn't see the beginning of a change in this respect under the Socialist government in France.*

At the same time, though, you've turned the question around. Instead of looking for the reasons for a perpetually renewed failure, you ask yourself what purpose is served by that failure and who benefits from it. You discover that prison is an instrument for the differential management and control of illegalities. In that sense, far from constituting a failure, prison has succeeded very well in specifying a certain delinquency, that of the popular strata, in producing a particular category of delinquents, in drawing a line around them the better to dissociate them from other categories of offenders, especially those arising from the bourgeoisie.

Finally, you note that the carceral system manages to give a natural and legitimate stamp to the legal authority to punish, that it "naturalizes" the latter. This idea is connected with the old question of legitimacy and the justification for punishment, because the exercise of disciplinary power does not exhaust the power of punishing, even if that's its major function, as you have shown.

A: Let's clear up some misunderstandings, if you don't mind. First of all, in this book about prison, it's obvious that I didn't mean to raise the question of the basis of the right to punish. What I tried to show is the fact that, starting from a certain conception of the basis of the right to punish which can be found in the penal theorists or the philosophers of the eighteenth century, different means of punishment were perfectly conceivable. Indeed, in the reform movement of the second half of the eighteenth century, one finds a whole range of means of punishing that are suggested, and it turns out finally that prison was the one that was privileged, so to speak. It wasn't the only means of punishing, but it nevertheless became one of the principal means. My problem was to find out why this means was chosen, and how this means of punishment modified not only judicial practice but even a certain number of rather fundamental problems in penal law. Thus, the importance given to the psychological, or psychopathological, aspects of the criminal personality—an importance that is affirmed throughout the nineteenth century—was, to a certain extent, induced by a punitive practice whose declared aim was correction, and which only ran up against the impossibility of correcting. So I left aside the problem of the basis of the right to punish in order to foreground another problem that was, I believe, more often overlooked by historians—the means of punishing and their rationality. But that doesn't mean the question of the justification for punishment is not important. On that point I think one must be modest and radical at once, radically modest, recalling what Nietzsche said more than a century ago, namely, that in our contemporary societies we don't know any longer exactly what is being done when one punishes or what can justify punishment, truly and fundamentally. It's as if we were applying a punishment while basing ourselves on a certain number of heterogeneous ideas that were deposited on top of one another to an extent, ideas that derive from different histories, separate time periods, divergent rationalities.

Thus, if I didn't speak of this basis of the right to punish, it's not because I consider it unimportant; I think it would definitely be one of the most fundamental tasks to reconsider the meaning that can be given to legal punishment, in light of the connection between law, ethics, and the institution.

Q: *The problem of defining punishment is all the more complex because not only do we not really know what it means to punish, but it seems there is a reluctance to punish. Indeed, judges increasingly refrain from punishment: they intend to treat, to reeducate, to cure, almost as if they were trying to exonerate themselves of administering repression. Further, you write in* Discipline and Punish: *"Penal discourse and psychiatric discourse cross each other's frontiers" (p. 256). And: "With the multiplicity of scientific discourses, a difficult, infinite relation was forged that penal justice is still unable to control. The master of justice is no longer the master of its truth" (p. 98). Nowadays, recourse to the psychiatrist, the psychologist, the social worker, is a matter of judicial routine, penal as much as civil. You've analyzed this phenomenon, which no doubt indicates an epistemological change in the juridico-penal sphere. Penal justice seems to have changed directions. The judge applies the penal code to the author of an infraction less and less; more and more, he treats pathologies and disturbances of the personality.*

A: I think you're completely right. Why did penal justice establish these relations with psychiatry, relations that should be very cumbersome to it? Because, obviously, between the problematic of psychiatry and what is required by the very practice of penal law in view of the responsibility it has, I wouldn't say there is a contradiction—there's a heterogeneity. They are two forms of thought that aren't on the same plane, and so one doesn't see according to what rule they might use one another. But it's certain—and this has been a striking phenomenon since the nineteenth century—that penal justice seems to have been fascinated by that psychiatric, psychological, or medical thought, whereas one would have imagined on the contrary that it would be extremely wary of it.

There were resistances, of course; there were conflicts, and these shouldn't be underestimated. But again, when one looks at a longer time period, a century and half, it does appear that penal justice was very hospitable, and increasingly so, to those forms of thought. It may be true that the psychiatric problematic sometimes got in the way of penal practice, but these days it seems to facilitate the latter by allowing it to leave vague the question of what one does when one punishes.

Q: *In the last pages of* Discipline and Punish, *you point out that disciplinary technics have become one of the major functions of our society, a power that reaches its greatest intensity in the penitentiary institution. You say, further, that prison doesn't necessarily remain indispensable to a society like ours because it loses much of its reason for being in the midst of a growing number of mechanisms of normalization. Does this mean that a prisonless society is conceivable, then? That utopia is beginning to be taken seriously by certain criminologists. For example, Louk Hulsman, a professor of criminal law at the University of Rotterdam and an adviser to the United Nations, argues for the abolition of the penal system.¹ The reasoning that supports his theory ties in with parts of your analysis: the penal system creates the delinquent; it shows itself to be fundamentally incapable of realizing the social ends it's supposed to pursue; all reform is illusory; the only coherent solution is its abolition. Hulsman notes that a majority of violations escape the penal system without imperiling society. So he proposes that we systematically decriminalize most acts and behaviors that the law transmutes into crimes or offenses, and replace the concept of crime with that of "problem situations." Instead of punishing and stigmatizing, we should try to settle conflicts through non-*

judicial arbitration and reconciliation procedures. We should regard violations as social risks, the main concern being the indemnification of victims. Intervention by the judicial apparatus would be reserved for serious cases or, as a last resort, for failures of attempts at reconciliation or at reaching civil law solutions. Hulsman's theory is one that assumes a cultural revolution.

What do you think of this abolitionist idea as I have outlined it? Can it be seen as containing some of the possible developments that would derive from Discipline and Punish*?*

A: I think there are many interesting things in Hulsman's argument. The challenge he poses concerning the right to punish, saying there is no longer any justification for punishment, is striking in itself.

I also find it very interesting that he raises the question of the basis for punishment while, at the same time, considering the means by which the system responds to something regarded as an offense. That is, the question of means is not just a consequence of what might be presented with respect to the basis of the right to punish, but, in Hulsman's view, reflection on the basis of the right to punish must be done in conjunction with reflection on the ways of reacting to an offense. All that is very refreshing, very important, in my opinion. Perhaps I'm not well enough acquainted with his work, but I wonder about the following points. Won't the notion of "problem situations" lead to a psychologizing of both the question and the reaction? Doesn't such a practice run the risk, even if this is not what he wishes to see happen, of bringing about a kind of dissociation between, on the one hand, the social, collective, institutional reactions to the crime, which will be regarded as an accident and will need to be dealt with in the same way, and, on the other, a hyperpsychologization around the criminal himself that will constitute him as an object of psychiatric or medical interventions, with therapeutic aims?

Q: *And won't this conception of crime lead, moreover, to the abolition of the notions of responsibility and culpability? Given that evil exists in our societies, doesn't the awareness of culpability—which, according to Paul Ricoeur, originated in ancient Greece—perform a necessary social function? Can we imagine a society that would be relieved of any sense of guilt?*

A: I think it's not a question of determining whether a society can function without guilt but whether society can make guilt function as an organizing principle and a basis for law. And that is where the question becomes difficult.

Ricoeur is perfectly justified in posing the problem of moral conscience; he poses it as a philosopher or a historian of philosophy. It's completely legitimate to say that culpability exists, that is has existed for a certain time. It's debatable whether the sense of guilt comes from the Greeks or has another origin. In any case, it exists and it's hard to see how a society like ours, still firmly rooted in a tradition which is also that of the Greeks, could do without guilt. For a long time, people were able to believe that a system of law and a judicial institution could be directly linked together by a notion like that of culpability. But for us the question is open.

Q: *Currently, when an individual appears before some penal justice authority, he has to account not only for the prohibited act he has committed but also for his very life.*

A: That's true. For example, in the United States there has been a lot of discussion about indeterminate sentences. I think the practice has been abandoned almost everywhere, but it involved a certain tendency, a certain temptation, that seems not to have disappeared: a tendency to bring penal judgment to bear much more on a qualitative ensemble characterizing an existence, a way of being, than on a specific act. There's also the measure that was taken recently in France concerning sentencing judges. The idea—and it's a good one—was to strengthen the power and control of the judicial apparatus over the punishment process. Which is a good way of diminishing the de facto independence of the penitentiary institution. But there is a problem: now there will be a tribunal, composed of three judges, I believe, who will decide whether or not a prisoner can be granted parole; and this decision will be made by considering various factors, the first being the original violation, which will be reactualized in effect, since the plaintiff claiming damages and the victim's representatives will be present and able to intervene. And then factors having to do with the individual's conduct in his prison, as it was observed, evaluated, interpreted, and judged by the guards, by administrators, by psychologists, and by doctors. It is this magma of unrelated elements that will be grappled with in order to make a judicial type of decision. Even if this is juridically acceptable, one still needs to know what actual consequences it will produce. And, at the same time, what dangerous model it may present for criminal justice in its ordinary application, if in fact we make a habit of making penal decisions on the basis of good or bad conduct.

Q: *The medicalization of justice is leading to a gradual expulsion of penal law from judicial practices. The legal subject is giving way to the neurotic or psychopath who is not responsible, or not fully so, and whose behavior would be determined by psychobiological factors. Reacting against this conception, certain penalists envisage a return to the idea of a punishment that is more consonant with respect for the freedom and dignity of the individual. It's not a matter of going back to a system of brutal and mechanical punishment that would bear no relation to the socio-economic regime in which it functions, that would disregard the social and political dimension of justice, but, rather, of regaining a conceptual coherence and of differentiating between the province of law and that of medicine. One thinks of Hegel's statement: "In so far as the punishment is seen as embodying the criminal's own right, the criminal is honored as a rational being."*[2]

A: I do think that penal law is part of the social game in a society like ours, and this fact shouldn't be concealed. This means that the individuals belonging to this society need to acknowledge themselves as being legal subjects who, as such, are liable to punishment if they violate this or that rule. There is nothing shocking in that, I believe. But it is society's duty to make it possible for concrete individuals to acknowledge themselves as being legal subjects. That is difficult when the penal system employed is archaic, arbitrary, and incapable of dealing with the problems that confront a society. Just consider, for example, the area of economic delinquency. The real groundwork to be done is not to inject more and more medicine or psychiatry in order to modulate that system and make it more acceptable; what's needed is to rethink the penal system in itself. I'm not suggesting that we return to the severity of the Penal Code of 1810; I *am* suggesting that we return to the serious idea of a penal law that would clearly define what can be considered, in a society like ours, as requiring punishment or as not requiring it. Let's return to the very idea of a system's defining the rules of the social game. I'm distrustful of those who would return to the system of 1810 on the pretext that medicine and psychiatry are eroding the meaning of penal justice; but I'm equally distrustful of people who basically accept that system of 1810, and who would merely adjust it, improve it, soften it through psychiatric and psychological modulations.

NOTES

* Conducted by F. Ringelheim in 1983, this interview was published in the *University of Brussels Review* in 1984. [eds.]

1 L. Hulsman, *Le Système pénal en question* (Paris: Centurion, 1982).

2 G. W. F. Hegel, *Elements of the Philosophy of Right*, trans. H. B. Nisbet (Cambridge, Eng.: Cambridge University Press, 1991), p. 126.

Q: *In your opinion, why weren't the questions that were raised through the Groupe d' Information sur les Prisons (GIP), created in 1971, not taken up again later?*

A: The questions have remained raised, but the relay that one might have expected from certain movements didn't function. That didn't happen—which doesn't mean that it can't happen.

What we were struck by was the fact that while the justice system in France, since the end of the eighteenth century, has adhered to the principle of public debate, the penitentiary system, on the other hand, depends on another practice that remains in darkness. Of course, there were many discussions about the penal system during the nineteenth century, and there still are in the twentieth, but prison, as it actually functions day-to-day, largely escapes the control of the judicial apparatus—from which, moreover, it is administratively separate. It also escapes the control of public opinion, and finally it often escapes the rules of law.

The GIP, I believe, was a "problematizing" venture, an effort to make problematic, to call into question, presumptions, practices, rules, institutions, and habits that had lain undisturbed for many decades. This effort targeted the prison itself, but through it, also penal justice, the law, and punishment in general.

I am aware that some people were surprised by the fact that this reflection on prison did not immediately take the form of proposals to improve the way it functioned, but I think there are moments when it is not enough to measure practices against their traditional objectives and try to achieve a better fit between them. It is necessary at the same time to question the practices, their professed purpose, the means they employ, and the intended or unintended results these means may have. And, from this viewpoint, it seems to me that the work undertaken at the beginning of the seventies did frame the problem in its essential dimensions: what to make of legal punishment practices in a society such as ours.

This problem cannot be solved by a few theoretical proposals. It requires many debates, many experiments, many hesitations, attempts, and reconsiderations. It's true that very few groups, very few institutions have taken up what was begun. And, of course, no political party has.

Q: *As a matter of fact, there doesn't seem to be much happening between the current government and intellectuals. Who is distrustful of whom?*
A: When the SFIO, which represented French socialism, was dying, it had nothing left to say. Who finally spoke up toward the end of the sixties? Who raised the fundamental questions about society and the economy if it wasn't the nonorganized left, the women's movement, the movements of reflection on pyschiatric institutions, movements of reflection on self-management? Who spoke? It wasn't the SFIO, whose encephalogram was completely flat. It was that left that was called, in polemical tones, the little left, the extreme left, the "California left," and so on. There were a lot of silly things said about it—and I contributed to that, moreover. But basic problems were formulated then. It is those same problems that still appear fundamental today.

When the Socialist Party was formed in 1972, it was clearly attentive to these questions. If it hadn't echoed them in one way or another it probably wouldn't have gained the acceptance it did, including from the intellectual left. But it must be emphasized that, while it was receptive to those ideas, it never initiated the least dialogue with the intellectuals—never. Intellectuals were there to supply their names and lend support at election time, and they were not asked for anything else; to be exact, they were asked not to say anything else.

The serious point is that the Socialist Party produced a slew of programs, texts, and projects, but none of them represented an effort of reflection that might have suggested a coherent new political thought. It was a rhapsody of promises and dreams mixed with ideological items from the back of the drawer. We live in a society of political thought. There was no general reflection that would make it possible to articulate projects dealing with the penal system, medicine, or social security. People needed a framework for thinking about such matters. Of course, the intellectuals were not capable of coming up with readymade solutions; but it is likely that, if there had been enough exchanges, some basic reflection could have taken place and something might have resulted from it.

Q: *Is it too late?*

A: I don't know . . . But when the Socialists speak of the silence of the intellectuals, they are really speaking of their own silence and their regret at not having a political thought-process or rationality at their disposal. If the Socialists missed that rendezvous with the research movements that existed before and around them, there are two reasons why. One is internal: they were afraid of the Rocardians. They suspected that the intellectuals were closer to Rocard than to Jospin, for example, and there was a blockage in that area. They were obsessed with their internal struggles. And then there was a second reason, the P.C. (Parti Communiste). They needed the P.C., and the CGT (Confédération Générale du Travail): they were not going to get entangled with those blessed intellectuals, some of whom had been communists, had broken with the P.C., and were pushing anticommunism rather far—no thank you!

For these internal and external reasons, the Socialist Party preferred not to have working relationships with the intellectuals.

Q: *But on the part of the intellectuals, isn't there also a big distrust of the old-style politics of the politicians?*

A: Yes, but isn't that distrust justified? I don't have the impression that the political parties have produced anything at all interesting in the way of the problematization of social life. One may wonder whether the political parties are not the most stultifying political inventions since the nineteenth century. Intellectual political sterility appears to me to be one of the salient facts of our time.

Q: *You seem to think that a different view of things might have been possible.*

A: Yes, I thought so. Situations can always give rise to strategies. I don't believe we are locked into a history; on the contrary, all my work consists in showing that history is traversed by strategic relations that are necessarily unstable and subject to change. Provided, of course, that the agents of those processes have the political courage to change things.

Q: *You would have been ready to work with some of the people in the current government?*
A: If one of them had picked up his telephone one day and asked me if we might discuss the prison system, for example, or psychiatric hospitals, I wouldn't have hesitated for a second.

Q: *But even someone like Mr. Badinter, who doesn't wish to be seen as a politician, only refers to you in order to attribute something to you which you never said.*
A: I don't want to be drawn into that polemic. Without any question, Badinter is the best Justice Minister we have had for decades . . .

Q: *Let me just quote what he said, in* L'Âne, *about what he terms his "theory of punishment":* ¹ *"Prohibitions are necessary. . . . Certain individuals need to transgress the prohibition. . . . I'm saying that there have to be prohibitions and sanctions, and that the sanctions—the Code—must serve to internalize the prohibitions as much as to express them. . . . What is the real problem for the justice system? To express good and evil, what is permitted and what is forbidden." And to the question, "Can prohibitions be maintained without punishment?" he replies: "For those who haven't adequately internalized the prohibition, clearly not. . . . The real problem is to manage to protect the prohibitions by means of sanctions while preventing the system of sanctions from negatively affecting the essential values, such as respect for human dignity. . . ."*
Here Badinter places himself squarely within the "humanization of penality" you studied in Discipline and Punish. *But could one expect anything different?*
A: For my part, I would be very timid and would recall what Nietzsche said: "Our societies no longer know what it is to punish." He says that we give a certain number of meanings to punishment which seem to have been deposited in layers, meanings such as the

law of retaliation, retribution, revenge, therapy, purification, and a few others that are actually present in the very practice of punishment—but without our societies being capable of choosing an interpretation or of replacing it with another or of rationally basing the act of punishing on one of these interpretations. And I think we are still in the same impasse. What we need to do now is precisely to reflect on all this.

If I have tried to draw attention to the *techniques* of punishment, it is for a certain number of reasons. The first is that people have often overlooked the implicit meaning that the techniques of punishment may convey, apart from general theories that were able to justify them at the outset. The very logic of these punishment techniques entailed consequences that were neither foreseen nor intended; but, being what they were, they were used again in other tactics, other strategies. Finally, there was a whole very complicated nexus that developed around these very techniques of punishment. I thought it was important to bring this to light. But that doesn't mean we should only be interested in the technology of punishment or tell ourselves, "When all is said and done, no technique is worth anything, so there shouldn't be any punishment." On the contrary, we need to reflect on what a penal system, a penal code, and punitive practices can be in a society such as ours, traversed as it is by processes whose outlines are visible to us.

We don't have any solution. We are in a big quandary. Nevertheless, certain possible modifications of the punishment procedures have been considered: for example, how could confinement be replaced with much more intelligent forms? But all that is not enough, and, while I'm in favor of a certain radicalism, it's not a matter of saying: "In any case, every system of punishment will be catastrophic; nothing can be done; whatever you do, it will be bad." It's more a matter of saying that, in view of the problems that have arisen and continue to rise out of punitive practices that have been ours for more than a century, how is one to conceive a possible punishment today? A collaborative effort would be required for that.

The work I have done on the historical relativity of the "prison form" was an incitement to try to think of other forms of punishment. I have stayed clear of everything that wasn't an effort to find a few replacements here and there. What needs radical reexamination is what it means to punish, what is being punished, why there is punishment, and, finally, how punishment should be carried out. What was conceived in a clear and rational way in the seventeenth century has grown dim with the passage of time. The Enlightenment is not evil incarnate, far from it; but it isn't the absolute good, either, and certainly not the definitive good.

Q: *So you place yourself exactly opposite to what many of your adversaries call your determinism [*fixisme*] or even your nihilism . . .*

A: I find that amusing . . . On the contrary, I meant to show that the systematic use of imprisonment as the main form of punishment constituted only a historical episode, and therefore other systems of punishment could be envisaged. What I tried to analyze were the practices, the immanent logic of the practices, the strategies that supported the logic of these practices, and, consequently, the way in which individuals, in their struggles, in their confrontations, in their projects, freely constitute themselves as subjects of their practices or, on the contrary, reject the practices in which they are expected to participate. I firmly believe in human freedom. In questioning psychiatric and penal institutions, did I not presuppose and affirm that one could get out of the impasse they represented by showing that it was a matter of forms that were historically constituted at a particular time and in a particular context, and wasn't this a way of showing that these practices, in a different context, could be dismantled because they had become arbitrary and ineffective?

That type of analysis reveals the precariousness, the nonnecessity, and the instability of things. All this is absolutely linked to a practice and to strategies that are themselves unstable and changing. I am flabbergasted that people are able to see in my historical studies the affirmation of a determinism from which one cannot escape.

Q: *In your work you have repeatedly stressed the role of penal practices in managing illegalities and controlling their general economy. If prison were replaced by a very broad system of restoration [*amende*] (the Swedish tendency), would delinquency reproduce itself in the same way?*

A: I think that a certain number of effects characteristic of prison—such as alienation from ordinary social life, dislocation from the family environment or from the group in the midst of

which one lives, the fact of not working any longer, the fact that in
prison the convict lives with people who will become the only resort
once he has gotten out of prison—in short, everything that is directly connected with prison, may not be present in the case of
another generalized system of punishment such as restoration. Not,
at any rate, on the same scale and to the same serious degree.

But one must keep in mind that eventually a system of restoration
will reveal its flaws, and society will have to make an effort to reconsider that particular penal system. Nothing is ever stable. Whenever an institution of power in a society is involved, everything is
dangerous. Power is neither good nor bad in itself. It is something
perilous. It is not evil one has to do with in exercising power but
an extremely dangerous material, that is, something that can always be misused, with relatively serious negative consequences.

Q: *Today's criminologists are trying to come up with what they call
"replacement penalties." In France, it seems that the trend is toward
community service, which is certainly not a very new idea in the ar-
senal of old formulas based on rehabilitation.*
A: We are currently facing that very important choice. (I would
like to undertake a thorough review of these theoretical questions
with a group of people interested in reflecting on them.)

On the one hand, there is the possibility of psychologizing penalties to the maximum degree, that is, making them tilt toward "rehabilitation" and "betterment"—which, in a society like ours,
means individual psychological therapy or group therapy. Penalties
would essentially have the function and objective of altering the
economic, social, and psychological conditions thought to have produced the offense. Its general aim, then, would be to restore the
delinquent to such conditions that his chances of committing an
offense are substantially reduced.

There is another direction I believe one can go: it's the idea that
punishment and rehabilitation should be completely separated
from each other.

Since Plato, it has always been said that the penalty served both
to punish and to restore. But can we not imagine a system in which
the two functions that are now superimposed would be handled by
different authorities? One of the functions would be to apply a sanction defined by the code—obviously this would imply a revision of

the codes, a redefinition of what is punishable in a society like ours. And then there would be another entirely different function that would be the responsibility for restoring the individual to such conditions that his chances of delinquency would be diminished as much as possible.

When one moves toward a generalization of judicial amends, as in Sweden, one approaches the crux of this dissociation between punishment and restoration, because if there is one thing that doesn't amend, it's judicial amends. It has no therapeutic value, in contradistinction to the prison theorists' idea of cutting people off from their delinquent milieu, of isolating them, and subjecting them to a certain discipline with the object of doing them some good.

Q: *And it's that same idea that is revived with community service . . .*
A: One mustn't have an a priori response. Yet when things like that are done, aren't they done with the aim of merging punishment and restoration once again? Wouldn't it be better—this is a question I'm raising—to try and clarify the difficulties and thoroughly examine the possibilities we have at our disposal?

Q: *When they imagine the "ideal" prison, reformers see an arena for psychologists who would understand what went on and what goes on in the delinquent's head and would lead him "gently" to see himself and society in a different light. Prison thus becomes a place of treatment. With this idea of treatment, which is defended by many people, isn't the question of a dissociation between punishment and restoration obscured at the same time?*
A: It seems to me, in fact, that not only that fundamental question but also this rather well-known fact is obscured—namely, that whatever its forms may have been for nearly two hundred years, prison has only been a failure. It's not that I have a hostility against reformism, but it seems completely futile to go on raising this question of the "good prison" that would finally serve the two functions of punishment and restoration which it has not been able to perform up until now.

Q: *If punishment and restoration were actually separated, wouldn't the judges feel frustrated?*

A: The judiciary is fascinated by its therapeutic function. That is one of the dominant traits characterizing the evolution of the judicial system since the end of the nineteenth century. If one said to a judge, "Your job is to state what the law is, and if necessary to determine a penalty, but the rest is not your concern," he would feel very frustrated. Because he finds his therapeutic role very gratifying; it's a moral and theoretical justification for him. Since that exists, it does have to be taken into account, but the question arises: Is it really healthy? After all, don't the judges have an obligation to see themselves for what they are? The one who punishes should not regard himself as being invested with the supplementary charge of restoring or healing.

Q: *Some people advocate neighborhood peacemaker committees as an alternative to trial. What do think of that idea?*
A: Isn't it just a new expression of that theme of "people's justice" which I've always considered to be dangerous? I think that people's justice is a somewhat lyrical and utopian form in which one tries to combine some elements of the judicial system with some other elements of what is called popular consciousness, which is more a war consciousness than a justice consciousness.

Q: *But what if one tried to imagine an authority really concerned with "peacemaking"?*
A: Before all else, whatever the institution claiming to "do justice" may be, what is it referring to? That is what interests me. Will the system of rules to which these people refer be based, in their conceptual scheme, on punishment or on restoration or on both? It seems to me that that is what needs to be defined.

Q: *Looking at all these solutions aimed at replacing incarceration, you seem to have a slight preference for the system of restoration . . .*
A: Everything really must be examined. As things stand, we are in too much of a bind to allow ourselves not to consider everything; the problems are too serious . . .

NOTES

*   Conducted by C. Baker, this interview appeared in *Actes* in June 1984. [eds.]

1   R. Badinter, "Entretien avec," *L'Âne: le Magazine freudien* 13 (Nov.–Dec. 1983), pp. I–IV.

———

The general framework of what I call the "technologies of the self" is a question that appeared at the end of the eighteenth century. It was to become one of the poles of modern philosophy. This question is very different from what we call the traditional philosophical questions: What is the world? What is man? What is truth? What is knowledge? How can we know something? And so on. The question that arises at the end of the eighteenth century, I think, is: What are we in our actuality? You will find the formulation of this question in a text written by Kant. I don't pretend that the previous questions about truth, knowledge, and so on have to be put aside; on the contrary, they constitute a very strong and consistent field of analysis, what I would like to call the formal ontology of truth. But I think that a new pole has been constituted for the activity of philosophizing, and this pole is characterized by the question, the permanent and ever-changing question, "What are we today?" And that is, I think, the field of the historical reflection on ourselves. Kant, Fichte, Hegel, Nietzsche, Max Weber, Husserl, Heidegger, the Frankfurt School, have tried to answer this question. What I am trying to do, referring to this tradition, is to give very partial and provisional answers to this question through the history of thought or, more precisely, through the historical analysis of the relationships between our thought and our practices in Western society.

Let's say very briefly that, through studying madness and psychiatry, crime and punishment, I have tried to show how we have indirectly constituted ourselves through the exclusion of some others: criminals, mad people, and so on. And now my present work deals with the question: How did we directly constitute our identity through certain ethical techniques of the self that developed through Antiquity down to now? That was what we were studying in the seminar.

There now is another field of questions I would like to study: the way by which, through some political technology of individuals, we have been led to recognize ourselves as a society, as a part of a social entity, as a part of a nation or of a state. I would like now to give you an aperçu not of the technologies of the self but of the political technology of individuals.

Of course, I am afraid that the material I have to deal with could be a little too technical and historical for a so-called public lecture. I am not a public lecturer, and I know this material would be much more convenient for a seminar. But I have two good reasons to present it to you in spite of the fact it may be too technical. First, I think it is always a little pretentious to present in a more or less prophetic way what people have to think. I prefer to let them draw their own conclusions or infer general ideas from the interrogations I try to raise in analyzing historical and specific material. I think it's much more respectful for everyone's freedom, and that's my manner. The second reason why I will present rather technical materials to you is that I don't know why people in a public lecture would be less clever, less smart, or less well read than in a classroom. Let us then begin with this problem of the political technology of individuals.

In 1779, the first volume of a book entitled *System einer vollständigen Medicinische Polizei* by the German author J. P. Frank was published, to be followed by five other volumes. And when the last volume was published in 1790, the French Revolution had already begun. Why do I bring together this celebrated event of the French Revolution and this obscure book? The reason is simple: Frank's work is the first great systematic program of public health for the modern state. It indicates with a lot of detail what an administration has to do to insure the wholesome food, good housing, health care, and medical institutions the population needs to remain healthy, in short, to foster the life of individuals. Through this book we can see that the care for individual life is becoming at this moment a duty for the state.

At the same moment the French Revolution gives the signal for the great national wars of our days, involving national armies and meeting their conclusion or their climax in huge mass slaughters. I think that you can see a similar phenomenon during World War II. In all history, it would be hard to find such butchery as in World War II, and it is precisely this period, this moment, when the great welfare, public health, and medical assistance programs were instigated. The Beveridge Plan had been, if not conceived, at least published at this very moment. One could symbolize such a coincidence by a slogan: Go get slaughtered and we promise you a long and pleasant life. Life insurance is connected with a death command.

The coexistence in political structures of large destructive mechanisms and institutions oriented toward the care of individual life is something puzzling and needs some investigation. It is one of the central antinomies of our political reason. It is this antinomy of our political rationality which I'd like to consider. I don't mean that mass slaughters are the effect, the result, the logical consequence of our rationality; nor do I mean that the state has the obligation of taking care of individuals since it has the right to kill millions of people. Neither do I want to deny that mass slaughters or social care have their economic explanations or their emotional motivations.

Excuse me if I go back to the same point: we are thinking beings. That means that even when we kill or when we are killed, even when we make war or when we ask for support as unemployed, even when we vote for or against a government that cuts social security expenses and increases defense spending, even in these cases, we are thinking beings, and we do these things not only on the ground of universal rules of behavior but also on the specific ground of a historical rationality. It is this rationality, and the life and death game that takes place in it, that I'd like to investigate from a historical point of view. This type of rationality, which is one of the main features of modern political rationality, developed in the seventeenth and eighteenth centuries through the general idea of the "reason of state" and also through a very specific set of techniques of government that were called at this moment, and with a very special meaning, the police.

Let's begin with the "reason of state." I'll recall briefly a few definitions borrowed from Italian and German authors. An Italian jurist, Giovanni Botero, at the end of the sixteenth century, gives this definition of the reason of state: "A perfect knowledge of the means through which states form, strengthen themselves, endure and grow." Another Italian author, Palazzo, writes in the beginning of the seventeenth century in his *Discourse on Government and True Reason of State* (1606): "A reason of state is a rule or an art enabling us to discover how to establish peace and order within the republic." And Chemnitz, a German author in the middle of the seventeenth century, in *De Ratione status* (1647) gives this definition: "A certain political consideration required for all public matters, councils, and projects, whose only aim is the state's preservation, expansion, and felicity." Note those words: the state's preservation, the state's expansion, and the state's felicity—"to which end, the easiest and the promptest means are to be employed."

Let's consider certain features those definitions have in common. Reason of state, first, is regarded as an "art," that is, as a technique conforming to certain rules. These rules pertain not simply to customs and traditions but to a certain rational knowledge. Nowadays, the expression "reason of state," as you know, evokes much more arbitrariness or violence; but, at the time, what people had in mind was a rationality specific to the art of governing states. From where does this specific art of government draw its rationale? The answer to this question, provoked at the beginning of the seventeenth century, is the scandal of the nascent political thought, and yet the answer, following the authors I have quoted, was very simple. The art of governing people is rational on the condition that it observes the nature of what is governed, that is, the state itself. Now, to formulate such an obvious fact, such a platitude, was in fact to break simultaneously with two opposite traditions, the Christian tradition and Machiavelli's theory. The Christian tradition claimed that if government was to be essentially just, it had to respect a whole system of laws—human, natural, and divine.

There is a significant text written by Aquinas on this point, where he explains that the king's government must imitate God's government of nature: The king must found cities just as God has created the world; he must lead man toward his finality just as God does for natural beings. And what is man's finality? Is it physical health? No, answers Aquinas. If physical health were the finality of man, then we would need not a king but a physician. Is it wealth? No, because in this case a steward and not a king would suffice. Is it truth? No, answers Aquinas, because to attain truth we don't need a king, we need only a teacher. Man needs someone capable of opening up the way to heavenly bliss through his conformity on earth to what is *honestum*. A king has to lead man toward *honestum* as his natural and divine finality.

Aquinas's model for rational government is not at all a political one, whereas in the sixteenth and seventeenth centuries people are seeking for other denominations of reason of state, principles capable of guiding an actual government. They are concerned with what the state is and not with the divine or the natural finalities of man.

Reason of state is also opposed to another kind of analysis. In *The Prince*, Machiavelli's problem is to decide how a province or a territory acquired through inheritance or by conquest can be held against its internal and external rivals. Machiavelli's entire analysis is aimed at defining what reinforces the link between prince and state, whereas the problem posed in the beginning of the seventeenth century by the notion of reason of state is that of the very existence and nature of this new entity which is the state itself. The theoreticians of reason of state tried to keep aloof from Machiavelli both because he had at this moment a very bad reputation and because they couldn't recognize their own problem in his problem, which was not the problem of the state but the problem of the relationships between the prince—the king—his territory and his people. Despite all the quarrels about the prince and Machiavelli's work, reason of state is a milestone in the emergence of an extremely different type of rationality from that of the conception of Machiavelli. The aim of this new art of governing is precisely not to reinforce the power of the prince. Its aim is to reinforce the state itself.

In a few words, reason of state refers neither to the wisdom of God nor to the reason or the strategies of the prince: it refers to the state, to its nature, and to its own rationality. This thesis that the aim of a government is to strengthen the state itself implies several ideas which I think are important to touch upon to follow the rise and development of our modern political rationality.

The first of those ideas is the new relation between politics as a practice and as knowledge. It concerns the possibility of a specific political knowledge. Following Aquinas, the king had only to be virtuous. The leader of the city in the Platonic republic had to be a philosopher. For the first time, the one who has to rule others in the framework of the state has to be a politician, has to attain a specific political competence and knowledge.

The state is something that exists per se. It is a kind of natural object, even if the jurists try to know how it can be constituted in a legitimate way. The state is by itself an order of things, and political knowledge separates it from juridical reflections. Political knowledge deals not with the rights of people or with human or divine laws but with the nature of the state which has to be governed. Government is possible only when the strength of the state is known: it is by this knowledge that it can be sustained. The state's capacity and the means to enlarge it must be known. The strength and the capacity of other states, rivals of my own state, must also be known. The governed state must hold out against the others. A government, therefore, entails more than just implementing general principles of reason, wisdom, and prudence. A certain specific knowledge is necessary: concrete, precise, and measured knowledge as to the state's strength. The art of governing characteristic of the reason of state is intimately bound up with the development of what was called, at this moment, political "arithmetic." Political arithmetic was the knowledge implied by political competence, and you know very well that the other name of this political arithmetic was statistics, a statistics related not at all to probability but to the knowledge of state, the knowledge of different states' respective forces.

The second important point derived from this idea of reason of state is the rise of new relationships between politics and history. The true nature of the state in this perspective is not conceived anymore as an equilibrium between several elements that only a good law could bring and maintain together. It is conceived as a set of forces and strengths that could be increased or weakened according to the politics followed by the governments. These forces have to be increased, since each state is in a permanent competition with other countries, other nations, and other states, so that each state has nothing before it other than an indefinite future of struggles, or at least of competitions, with similar states. The idea that had been predominant throughout the Middle Ages was that all the kingdoms on the earth would be one day be unified in one last empire just before Christ's return to earth. From the beginning of the seventeenth century, this familiar idea is nothing more than a dream, which was also one of the main features of political thought, or of historico-political thought, during the Middle Ages. This project of reconstituting the Roman empire vanishes forever. Politics has now to deal with an irreducible multiplicity of states struggling and competing in a limited history.

The third idea we can derive from this notion of reason of state is this: since the state is its own finality, and since the governments must have for an exclusive aim not only the conservation but also the permanent reinforcement and development of the state's strengths, it is clear that the governments don't have to worry about individuals—or have to worry about them only insofar as they are somehow relevant for the reinforcement of the state's strength (what they do, their life, their death, their activity, their individual behavior, their work, and so on). I would say that in this kind of analysis of the relationships between the individual and the state, the individual becomes pertinent for the state insofar as he can do something for the strength of the state. But there is in this perspective something we could call a kind of political marginalism, since what is in question here is only political utility. From the state's point of view, the individual exists insofar as what he does is able to introduce even a minimal change in the strength of the state, either in a positive or in a negative direction. It is only insofar as an individual is able to introduce this change that the state has to do with him. And sometimes what he has to do for the state is to live, to work, to produce, to consume; and sometimes what he has to do is to die.

Apparently, those ideas are similar to a lot of ideas we can find in Greek philosophy. And, indeed, reference to Greek cities is very current in this political literature of the beginning of the seventeenth century. But I think that under a few similar themes something quite different is going on in this new political theory. The marginalistic integration of individuals in the state's utility is not obtained in the modern state by the form of the ethical community characteristic of the Greek city. It is obtained in this new political rationality by a certain specific technique called then, and at this moment, the "police."

Here we meet the problem I would like to analyze in some future work. The problem is this: What kind of political techniques, what technology of government, has been put to work and used and developed in the general framework of the reason of state in order to make of the individual a significant element for the state? Most of the time, when one analyzes the role of the state in our society, either one focuses attention on institutions—armies, civil service, bureaucracy, and so on—and on the kind of people who rule them, or one analyzes the theories or the ideologies developed in order to justify or to legitimate the existence of the state.

What I am looking for, on the contrary, are the techniques, the practices, that give a concrete form to this new political rationality and to this new kind of relationship between the social entity and the individual. And, surprisingly enough, people—at least in countries like Germany and France, where for different reasons the problem of state was considered a major issue—recognized the necessity of defining, describing, and organizing very explicitly this new technology of power, the new techniques by which the individual could be integrated into the social entity. They recognized its necessity, and they gave it a name. This name in French is *police*, and in German, *Polizei*. (I think the meaning of the English word "police" is something very different.) We must precisely try to give better definitions of what was understood by those French and German words *police* and *Polizei*.

The meaning of these German and French words is puzzling since they have been used at least from the nineteenth century until now to designate something else, a very specific institution that, at least in France and Germany—I don't know about the United States—didn't always have a very good reputation. But, from the end of the sixteenth century to the end of the eighteenth century, the words *police* and *Polizei* had a very broad and, at the same time, also a very precise meaning. When people spoke about police at this moment, they spoke about the specific techniques by which a government in the framework of the state was able to govern people as individuals significantly useful for the world.

In order to analyze a little more precisely this new technology of government, I think that it is best to catch it in the three major forms that any technology is able to take in its development and its history: as a dream or, better, as a utopia; then as a practice or as rules for real institutions; and then as an academic discipline.

Louis Turquet de Mayerne provides a good example at the beginning of the seventeenth century of contemporary opinion concerning the utopian or universal technique of government. His book

Aristo-democratic Monarchy (1611) proposed the specialization of executive power and of police powers. The task of the police was to foster civil respect and public morality.

Turquet proposed that there should be in each province four boards of police to keep law and order, two of which had to see to the people and two others of which had to see to things. The first board was to look after the positive, active, productive aspects of life. In other words, this board was concerned with education, with determining very precisely each individual's aptitudes and tastes. It had to test the aptitude of the children from the very beginning of their lives. Each person over the age of twenty-five had to be enrolled on a register noting his aptitudes and his occupation; the rest were regarded as the dregs of society.

The second board was to see to the negative aspects of life, that is, the poor, widows, orphans, the aged, who required help. It had to be concerned also with people who had to be put to work and who could be reluctant to go to work, those whose activities required financial aid, and it had to run a kind of bank for the giving or lending of funds to people in need. It also had to take care of public health, diseases, epidemics, and accidents such as fire and floods, and it had to manage a kind of insurance for people to be protected against all such accidents.

The third board was to specialize in commodities and manufacturers' goods: it indicated what was to be produced and how. It also controlled markets and trading, which was a very traditional function of police. The fourth board was to see to the "demesne," that is, to territory, space, private property, legacies, donations, sales, and also to manorial rights, roads, rivers, public buildings, and so on.

Many features of this text are akin to the political utopias that were so frequent at the time, and even from the sixteenth century. But it is also contemporary with the great theoretical discussions about the reason of state and about the administrative organization of monarchies. It is highly representative of what the epoch considered a well-governed state.

What does this text demonstrate? It demonstrates first that "the police" appears as an administration heading the state together with the judiciary, the army, and the exchequer. But in fact it embraces all those other administrations, and, as Turquet says, "it branches out into all of the people's conditions, everything they do or undertake. Its fields comprise justice, finance, and the army."

So, as you see, the police in this utopia include everything, but from a very particular point of view. Men and things are envisioned in this utopia in their relationships. What the police are concerned with is men's coexistence in a territory, their relationships to property, what they produce, what is exchanged in the market, and so on. It also considers how they live, the diseases and accidents that can befall them. In a word, what the police see to is a live, active, and productive man. Turquet employs a very remarkable expression. He says, "The police's true object is man."

Of course, I am a little afraid that you imagine that I have forged this expression in order to find one of those provocative aphorisms that I am supposed to be unable to resist, but it's a real quotation. Don't imagine that I am saying that man is only a by-product of police; what's important in this idea of man as the true object of police is a historical change in the relations between power and individuals. To put it roughly, I would say that feudal power consisted in relations between juridical subjects insofar as they were engaged in juridical relations by birth, status, or personal engagement, but with this new police state the government begins to deal with individuals, not only according to their juridical status but as men, as working, trading, living beings.

Now let's turn from the dream to the reality and to administrative practices. We have a compendium written in France in the beginning of the eighteenth century which gives us in systematic order the major police regulations of the French kingdom. It is a kind of manual or systematic encyclopedia for the use of the civil servants. The author of this manual was N. De Lamare, and he organizes this encyclopedia of police, *Traité de la police* (1705), under eleven chapters. The first one is religion; the second is morals; the third, health; the fourth, supplies; the fifth, roads, highways, and town buildings; the sixth, public safety; the seventh, the liberal arts (roughly speaking, the arts and sciences); the eighth, trade; the ninth, factories; the tenth, manservants and factory workers; and the eleventh, the poor. That, for De Lamare and those following, was the administrative practice of France. That was the domain of police, from religion to poor people, through morals, health, liberal arts, and so on and so on. You'll find the same classification in most of the treatises or compendiums concerning the police. As you see, as in Turquet's utopia, apart from the army and justice, properly speaking, and direct taxes, the police apparently see to everything.

Now what, from this point of view, was the real administrative French practice? What was the logic of intervening in religious rites or in small-scale production techniques, in intellectual life or in the road network? De Lamare seems to be a little hesitant trying to answer this question. Sometimes he says, "The police must see to everything pertaining to men's happiness." In other places he says, "The police see to everything regulating society," and he means by "society" social relations "carried on between men." And sometimes, again, he says that the police see to living. This is the definition I'd like to retain because it is the most original. I think that this definition clarifies the two other definitions, and it is on this definition of police as taking care of living that De Lamare insists. He makes the following remarks as to the police's eleven objects. The police deal with religion, not, of course, from the viewpoint of dogmatic orthodoxy but from the viewpoint of the moral quality of life. In seeing to health and supplies, the police deal with the preservation of life. Concerning trade, factories, workers, the poor, and public order, the police deal with the conveniences of life. In seeing to the theater, literature, and entertainment, their object is life's pleasure. In short, life is the object of the police. The indispensable, the useful, and the superfluous: those are the three types of things that we need, or that we can use in our lives. That people survive, that people live, that people do even better than just survive or live: that is exactly what the police have to ensure.

This systematization of the French administrative practice seems to me important for several reasons. First, as you see, it attempts to classify needs, which is, of course, an old philosophical tradition, but with the technical project of determining the correlation between the utility scale for individuals and the utility scale for the state. The thesis in De Lamare's book is that what is superfluous for individuals can be indispensable for the state, and vice versa. The second important thing is that De Lamare makes a political object of human happiness. I know very well that from the beginnings of political philosophy in Western countries everybody knew and said that the happiness of people had to be the permanent goal of governments, but then happiness was conceived as the result or the effect of a really good government. Now happiness is not only a simple effect. Happiness of individuals is a requirement for the survival and development of the state. It is a condition, it is an instrument, and not simply a consequence. People's happiness becomes an element of state strength. And, third, De Lamare says that the state has to deal not only with men, or with a lot of men living together, but with society. Society and men as social beings, individuals with all their social relations, are now the true object of the police.

And hence, last but not least, "police" became a discipline. It was not only a real administrative practice, it was not only a dream, it was a discipline in the academic meaning of the word. It was taught under the name of *Polizeiwissenschaft* in various universities in Germany, especially in Göttingen. The University of Göttingen has been extremely important for the political history of Europe, since it was at Göttingen that Prussian, Austrian, and Russian civil servants were trained, precisely those who were to carry out Joseph II's or Catherine the Great's reforms. And several Frenchmen, especially in Napoleon's entourage, knew the teaching of this *Polizeiwissenschaft*.

The most important testimony we have about the teaching of police is a kind of manual for the students of *Polizeiwissenschaft*, written by von Justi, with the title *Elements of Police*. In this book, in this manual for students, the purpose of the police is still defined, as in De Lamare, as taking care of individuals living in society. Nevertheless, the way von Justi organizes his book is quite different from De Lamare's book. He studies first what he called the "state's landed property," that is, its territory. He considers it under two different aspects: how it is inhabited (town versus country), and then who inhabits these territories (the number of people, their growth, their health, their mortality, immigration, and so on). Then, von Justi analyzes the "goods and chattels," that is, the commodities, manufacture of goods, and their circulation, which involved problems pertaining to cost, credit, and currency. And, finally, the last part of his study is devoted to the conduct of individuals, their morals, their occupational capabilities, their honesty, and how they are able to respect the law.

In my opinion, von Justi's work is a much more advanced demonstration of how the police evolved than De Lamare's introduction to his compendium, and there are several reasons for that. The first is that von Justi draws an important distinction between what he calls police (*die Polizei*) and what he calls politics (*die Politik*). *Die Politik* is basically for him the negative task of the state. It consists in the state's fighting against its internal and external enemies, using the law against the internal enemies and the army against the external ones. von Justi explains that the police (*Polizei*), on the contrary, have a positive task. Their instruments are neither weapons nor laws, defense nor interdiction. The aim of the police is the permanently increasing production of something new, which is supposed to foster the citizens' life and the state's strength. The police govern not by the law but by a specific, a permanent, and a positive intervention in the behavior of individuals. Even if the semantic distinction between *Politik* endorsing negative tasks and *Polizei* endorsing positive tasks soon disappeared from political discourse and from the political vocabulary, the problem of a permanent intervention of the state in social processes, even without the form of the law, is, as you know, characteristic of our modern politics and of political problematics. The discussion from the end of the eighteenth century till now about liberalism, *Polizeistaat*, *Rechtsstaat* of law, and so on, originates in this problem of the positive and the negative tasks of the state, in the possibility that the state may have only negative tasks and not positive ones and may have no power of intervention in the behavior of people.

There is another important point in this conception of von Justi that has been very influential with all the political and administrative personnel of the European countries at the end of the eighteenth century and the beginning of the nineteenth. One of the major concepts of von Justi's book is that of population, and I do not think this notion is found in any other treatise on police. I know very well that von Justi didn't invent the notion or the word, but it is worthwhile to note that, under the name "population," he takes into account what demographers were discovering at the same moment. He sees all the physical or economic elements of the state as constituting an environment on which population depends and which, conversely, depends on population. Of course, Turquet and utopianists like Turquet also spoke about the rivers, forests, fields, and so on, but essentially as elements capable of producing taxes and incomes. For von Justi, the population and environment are in a perpetual living interrelation, and the state has to manage those living interrelations between those two types of living beings. We can say now that the true object of the police becomes, at the end of the eighteenth century, the population; or, in other words, the state has essentially to take care of men as a population. It wields its power over living beings as living beings, and its politics, therefore, has to be a biopolitics. Since the population is nothing more than what the state takes care of for its own sake, of course, the state is entitled to slaughter it, if necessary. So the reverse of biopolitics is thanatopolitics.

Well, I know very well that these are only proposed sketches and guidemarks. From Botero to von Justi, from the end of the sixteenth century to the end of the eighteenth century, we can at least guess at the development of a political rationality linked to a political technology. From the idea that the state has its own nature and its own finality to the idea of man as living individual or man as a part of a population in relation to an environment, we can see the increasing intervention of the state in the life of individuals, the increasing importance of life problems for political power, and the development of possible fields for social and human sciences insofar as they take into account those problems of individual behavior inside the population and the relations between a living population and its environment.

Let me now summarize very briefly what I have been trying to say. First, it is possible to analyze political rationality, as it is possible to analyze any scientific rationality. Of course, this political rationality is linked with other forms of rationality. Its development in large part is dependent upon economical, social, cultural, and technical processes. It is always embodied in institutions and strategies and has its own specificity. Since political rationality is the root of a great number of postulates, commonplaces of all sorts, institutions and ideas we take for granted, it is both theoretically and practically important to go on with this historical criticism, this historical analysis of our political rationality, which is something different from the discussion about political theories and which is different also from divergences between different political choices. The failure of the major political theories nowadays must lead not to a nonpolitical way of thinking but rather to an investigation of what has been our political way of thinking during this century.

I should say that in everyday political rationality the failure of political theories is probably due neither to politics nor to theories but to the type of rationality in which they are rooted. The main characteristic of our modern rationality in this perspective is neither the constitution of the state, the coldest of all cold monsters, nor the rise of bourgeois individualism. I won't even say that it is a constant effort to integrate individuals into the political totality. I think that the main characteristic of our political rationality is the fact that this integration of the individuals in a community or in a totality results from a constant correlation between an increasing individualization and the reinforcement of this totality. From this point of view, we can understand why modern political rationality is permitted by the antinomy between law and order.

Law, by definition, is always referred to a juridical system, and order is referred to an administrative system, to a state's specific order, which was exactly the idea of all those utopians of the beginning of the seventeenth century and was also the idea of those very real administrators of the eighteenth century. I think that the conciliation between law and order, which has been the dream of those men, must remain a dream. It's impossible to reconcile law and order because when you try to do so it is only in the form of an integration of law into the state's order.

My last point will be this: the emergence of social science cannot, as you see, be isolated from the rise of this new political rationality and from this new political technology. Everybody knows that ethnology arose from the process of colonization (which does not mean that it is an imperialistic science). I think in the same way that, if man—if we, as living, speaking, working beings—became an object for several different sciences, the reason has to be sought not in an ideology but in the existence of this political technology which we have formed in our own societies.

NOTES

* Foucault presented this lecture at the University of Vermont in 1982; it was first published in 1988. [eds.]

POMPIDOU'S TWO DEATHS

---

*O*n September 21, 1971, Buffet and Bontems, incarcerated at
*Clairvaux Prison for a bloody crime, killed a nurse and an officer
taken hostage during an escape attempt. To calm the anger of the
prison guards, the Interior Minister disallowed, for all prisons, the
one package that the prisoners were authorized to receive each year
for Christmas. This was the spark that inflamed the penitentiary system in the winter of 1971. Subsequently, prison reform and keeping
or abolishing the death penalty became political questions pitting the
Left against the Right, while the Groupe d'Information sur les Prisons
(GIP) distributed information about the real situation in the prisons.
In June of 1972, the celebrities of the bar clashed with one another
during Buffet's and Bontems's trial, which was becoming a trial about
the death penalty itself. In December, President Pompidou refused their
appeal for mercy and they were guillotined in the courtyard of the
Santé.*[1]

There is a man living in Auteuil who, during the night of last Monday to Tuesday, earned 1,200,000 francs. Mr. Obrecht pulled on the
cord twice: 600,000 old francs for a head falling in a basket.

That still exists, forms part of our institutions, convokes around
its ceremony the magistracy, the Church, the armed police, and, in
the shadows, the president of the republic—in short, all the powers
that be. There is something about it that is physically and politically
intolerable.

But the guillotine is really just the visible and triumphant apex, the red and black tip, of a tall pyramid. The whole penal system is essentially pointed toward and governed by death. A verdict of conviction does not lead, as people think, to a sentence of prison *or* death; if it prescribes prison, this is always with a possible added bonus: death. An eighteen-year-old-boy gets six months for one or two stolen cars. He's sent to Fleury-Mérogis, with isolation, idleness, a megaphone as his only interlocutor. It suffices for him to receive no visits or for his fiancée to stop writing to him; then his only recourse will be to beat his head against the walls or twist his shirt into a rope and try to hang himself.

So begins, already, the risk, the possibility, worse, the temptation, the desire for death, the fascination with death. When a prisoner is released, there will be the police record, unemployment, the relapse, the indefinite repetition until the end, until death. Let us say, in any case, until the twenty-year sentence or confinement in perpetuity—"for life," as they say. "For life," or "for death," the two expressions mean the same thing. When a person is sure that he will never get out, what is there left to do? What else but to risk death to save one's life, to risk one's very life at the possible cost of death. That is what Buffet and Bontems did.

Prison is not the alternative to death: it carries death along with it. The same red thread runs through the whole length of that penal institution which is supposed to apply the law but which, in reality, suspends it: once through the prison gates, one is in the realm of the arbitrary, of threats, of blackmail, of blows. Against the violence of the penitentiary personnel, the convicts no longer have anything but their bodies as a means for defending themselves and nothing but their bodies to defend. It is life or death, not "correction," that prisons are about.

Let us give this some thought: one is punished in prison when one has tried to kill himself; and when the prison is tired of punishing you, it kills you.

Prison is a death machine that has produced, with the Clairvaux affair, two times two deaths. And one must bear in mind that, in the past, Buffet had gone through the Foreign Legion, that other machine in which one also learns the dreadful equivalence of life and death.

People told themselves: Pompidou is going to kill Buffet—harsh profile—and he will pardon Bontems—gentle profile. But he had both men executed, and why was that?

An electoral scaffold? No doubt. But maybe not because 63 percent of French people, according to the IFOP, are in favor of keeping the death penalty and the right of pardon. It's probably more serious than that; if the numbers were reversed, I think he would have done the same thing. He wanted to show that he was a tough, uncompromising man, that if necessary he would resort to extreme measures—that, if the circumstances required, he was prepared to rely on the most violent and reactionary elements. The sign of a possible orientation, the sign of a course of action already decided upon rather than a faithfulness to the nation's majority impulse. "I will go that far when I need to."

To that first calculation another was added. Here it is, summed up in three propositions:

1. If Buffet alone had been executed, he would have appeared to be the last person guillotined. With him, after him, no one else. From that point on, the machine would have been blocked. And by the same token, Pompidou would have been the last to operate it. Bontems enables it to go on indefinitely; his execution generalizes the guillotine all over again.

2. Bontems was not convicted for murder but for complicity. His execution is actually addressed to all prisoners: "If you undertake, together with an accomplice, any action whatsoever against the penitentiary administration, you will be held responsible for anything that may happen, even if you didn't do it." A collective responsibility. Here the refusal of mercy is in the spirit of the antivandalism law.

3. It is undeniable that Buffet helped a good deal to get Bontems convicted. So it may look as if he shared the responsibility for his execution—at least that's the official calculation. "You shouldn't get worked up about this Buffet; he lured his accomplice into death; the nasty world of crooks, with its hatreds and its betrayals, is manifested again in this double execution." Pompidou is not alone in having killed Bontems.

Such was the calculation, no doubt. Let us hope that it will be foiled and that it will have to be paid for.

But I'm speaking as if the two condemned men and the president were the only ones on stage, as if it were only a question of the legal machinery. Actually, there is a third element to consider, the penitentiary system and the battle that is now under way in the prisons.

We know about the pressures that were applied by the unions of prison guards in order to obtain this double execution. An official of the CGT spoke of a plan that was ready in case their desire for revenge was not satisfied. One has to know what the atmosphere was at the Santé Prison last Monday: Pompidou had just come back from Africa. Now, executions traditionally take place on Tuesday, a day when there are no visits. So everyone knew it would be that night. A young guard said before witnesses: "Tomorrow we'll have a head with vinaigrette sauce for dinner." But well before them, Bonaldi (F.O.) and Pastre (CGT) had made imperative and inflammatory statements without being called to order.[2]

Once again, the penitentiary administration overstepped the legal system. Before the trial and before the appeal for mercy it demanded, and imposed, its own brand of "justice." It loudly claimed and was granted the right to punish, this administration that should only have the obligation to calmly apply penalties whose principle, measure, and control belong to others. It established itself as a power, and the chief of state has just given his assent.

Is he unaware that this power which he has just sanctioned is being combated today, everywhere, by prisoners struggling to gain respect for the rights they still have; by magistrates who insist on controlling the application of penalties they have prescribed; by all those who no longer accept either the machinations or the abuse of the repressive system?

It's true there is nothing in common between Buffet and Bontems and a mother who lets a bill go unpaid.[3] And yet, "our" repressive system imposed a common "measure" on them: prison. And so, once again, death came for some men and for a child.

We accuse the prisons of murder.

NOTES

1 Extracted from the editors' prologue in *Dits et écrits*, volume 2, p. 386. Foucault's commentary appeared in *Le Nouvel Observateur* in December 1972. [eds.]

2 Bonaldi and Pastre were officers of the two big unions of prison guards, regarded as the real leaders of the penitentiary administration.

3 Yvonne Huriez, mother of eight children, sentenced to four months in prison with no possibility of remission for having failed to respond to a court that ordered her to pay a bill of 75 francs for the rental of a television set. Her fourteen-year-old son, Thierry, who couldn't stand hearing his mother called a thief by his school buddies, committed suicide.

———

The Groupe d'Information sur la Santé (Group for Information about Health [GIS]) regularly holds its meetings: industrial medicine, health of immigrants, abortion, medical power. Just as regularly, a police spy hangs out near the entrance, seeing who comes. With the GIS having published, at the beginning of this year, a collective brochure, *Oui, nous avortons* [*Yes, we do abortions*], Judge Roussel has just ordered a summons of three "presumed authors." "Serious circumstantial evidence" against them, said the police agent: they were seen at meetings of the GIS.

Let us leave the narc business out of this for now; it is ludicrous and odious. And so that Judge Roussel will no longer have to stoop so low, the three of us, Alain Landau, Jean-Yves Petit, and Michel Foucault, "presumed authors" because we were "seen," hereby affirm that we belong to the GIS, that we wrote and distributed the brochure, and we participated in and lent our support to the Mouvement pour la Liberté de l'Avortement (Movement for Freedom of Abortion). Go ahead and indict us.

But there are questions to be raised. After the trial of Marie-Claire at Bobigny, after the physicians' manifesto that appeared in 1973, after the Grenoble movement supporting Dr. Anne Ferray-Martin, and after the seven Saint-Etienne doctors and their four hundred abortions, why this threat against the authors of a brochure? *Why*, and why *now?*

Every year, hundreds of thousands of women could take up the affirmation "Yes, we have abortions" on their own account. But up to now, it is done—and often under the worst conditions—but it isn't talked about. The brochure is aimed at creating a situation in which it can be talked about, and in which, once they have come out of the shameful secrecy where some people seek to keep them, women can finally have free access to information on abortion and contraception: a situation in which they are no longer at the mercy of greedy and hypocritical doctors or left to themselves, forced to resort to maneuvers that are dangerous for their lives. Now, it is precisely this information which the government wishes to deprive women of, and that is the meaning of the legal investigation under way. For, if women learn that it is possible to have an abortion in a simple and risk-free way (using the suction method under the best sterile conditions) and without charge; if they learn that it isn't necessary to do seven years of study in order to practice this method, they risk deserting the commercial circuits of abortion and denouncing the collusion of doctors, police, and the courts, which makes them pay dearly, in every sense of the term, for the liberty they take in refusing a pregnancy.

It may be recalled that in 1967 the Neuwirth Law authorized effective contraceptive measures. But it wasn't until 1972 that a course of instruction in that area appeared at the School of Medicine. And this instruction is restricted to gynecologists: a general practitioner won't hear the pill mentioned at the school. With such ignorance on the part of doctors, they easily become the victims and agents of a mendacious propaganda. How many women want to abort because a doctor forbade them to use the pill for pseudo-scientific reasons? It is they, those dishonest propagandists, those doctors imbued with their "science," who induce women to have abortions.

A bill is being drafted that is supposed to liberalize abortion. One only has to look at its provisions.

When will a woman be able to abort? In the event of rape, incest, a definite abnormality in the embryo, and when the birth would risk provoking "psychic disturbances" in the mother. Hence, in a number of strictly limited cases.

Who will make the abortion decision? Two doctors. So there will be a strengthening of a medical power that is already great, too great, but that becomes intolerable when it is coupled with a "psychological" power that has earned a reputation for incompetence and abuse in its application to internments, medico-legal evaluations, "children at risk," and "predelinquent" young people.

Where will a woman be able to abort? In a hospital setting, which is to say, in hospitals and no doubt in private clinics. So there will be two abortion circuits: one, a restrictive hospital experience for the poor; the other, private, liberal—and expensive. In this way, the time-honored profits of the old abortion will not be lost.

Now, on these three points, the GIS takes issue with the government: it insists on the right to abortion; it does not want doctors to be the only ones to decide; it does not want abortions for the double benefit of those who stand to profit from them.

Why does the government seek to charge several members of the GIS, and, significantly, a nondoctor among them? It is because it wishes to set at odds—no doubt before the bill is passed and in order to bring right-thinking people over to its side—on the one hand, the "good doctors," to whom it will give complete authority and every benefit, and, on the other, those who would establish abortion, contraception, and the free use of one's body as rights.

NOTES

* The French editors provide the following contextualization of this statement, signed by Foucault, A. Landau, and J.-Y. Petit, and published in *Le Nouvel Observateur* in November 1973:

> Foucault participated in many of the works of the Information Group concerning Health (GIS), created by doctors on the model of the GIP. The struggle in favor of the legalization of abortion initiated by the Women's Liberation Movement profoundly divided the medical world. On 11 October 1972, seventeen-year-old Marie-Claire appeared before the Bobigny juvenile court for having had an abortion, a crime punishable under article 137 of the Penal Code. Because the accused was a minor, the proceedings were closed to the public. In fact, a public debate ensued, and the abortion law itself was put on trial. Four hundred women, with the comedienne Delphine Seyrig at their head, signed their names to a testament of their having had an abortion. The GIS published a practical manual on the demedicalization of abortion through the aspiration method, known as the "Karman method." The government undertook to expand the number of indications that would allow for a therapeutic abortion, even as the association Choose, inspired by Gisèle Halimi, the defense lawyer at the Bobigny trial, and by Simone de Beauvoir, was drafting another proposal calling for the legalization and free provision of abortion, acknowledging that the woman concerned had the right of choice. Abortion was legalized in 1975, under medical control, with a conscience clause for the doctors (*Dits et écrits*, vol. 2, p. 445). [eds.]

————

After Croissant[1] was extradited, you were good enough to say you were indignant: the right of asylum was flouted; the process of legal appeal was circumvented; a political refugee was handed over. Some will say that you might have made your thoughts known earlier . . . Many people who are not usually petitioners had suggested a way for you to avoid being completely alone or too obviously ahead.[2]

Fortunately, in a manner of speaking, it is still not too late. The Croissant affair is not finished in Germany. In France, either, as you may know. Two women, Marie-Josèphe Sina and Hélène Châtelain, indicted for "harboring a criminal," are risking six months to two years in prison.

The reason? They are said to have helped Croissant in his "clandestinity"—a word that is quite exaggerated, moreover; just ask the gentlemen of the judicial police—after he had come to France to formally request asylum, a petition provided for by the Constitution and one to which our government never responded.

I don't know how one can speak of "harboring a criminal" in this case, since Croissant was extradited not for belonging to an association of criminals, as the German government insisted, but for helping his clients to correspond with each other.

What I do know is that these women are being prosecuted for having done what you reproach the state for not having done. You know the state too well not to know that it rarely sets a good example for individuals to follow; and that the latter have always felt honor-bound to do on their own and sometimes alone that which the authorities were incapable of doing—through calculation, inertia, coldness, or blindness. In matters of political morality—excuse this juxtaposition of words, there are cases where it has a meaning—the lesson usually comes from below.

The same government that has refused to recognize asylum—that generosity which goes back to a time beyond memory—as a right is hounding two women for having made it their duty. What do you think about this situation?

You don't wish to "interfere with the course of justice," as the phrase goes? But you are not in the government! And if you came to be, you would stay mindful of your rash predecessors; you would remember that Justice Minister who called for the death penalty the day after an arrest was made; or that other one who justified an extradition not yet ordered; you would recall the criticism you directed against them. For the present, you are citizens like the rest of us. A good thing? In this affair it is, since it leaves you free to say what you think.

Are you not willing to do so on your own behalf—and if need be with us in this case? My question isn't rhetorical, because it's a concrete, specific, and urgent case. It isn't a snare, because the matter is simple: for thousands of years, the private practice of asylum has been one of those lessons that individual hearts have given to states. Even when they don't heed the lesson, it would be iniquitous for those states to penalize the ones who give it. Don't you agree?

I don't want to be hypocritical. You aspire to govern us, and that is another reason why we appeal to you. You know that in the future you may have to deal with an important problem: governing one of these modern states that prides itself on offering populations not so much territorial integrity, victory over the enemy, or even general enrichment as "security": a staving-off and repair of risks, accidents, dangers, contingencies, diseases, and so on. This security pact entails dangerous extensions of power and distortions in the area of recognized rights. And it leads to reactions aimed at contesting this "securizing" function of the state. In short, we risk entering a regime in which security and fear will challenge and reinforce one another.

It is important for us to know how you react to an affair such as this one. Because they allegedly "harbored" the legal defender of "terrorists," the state is prosecuting two women who did nothing else—even if the allegations were proven—but one of the oldest acts of comfort that time has bequeathed to us. Doesn't the public zeal with which they are being prosecuted signify the desire to kindle and stoke that fear, and that fear of fear, which is one of the conditions for security states to function? What do you think about the timeliness of prosecutions carried out in the name of society, our own in this case? Do you approve?

NOTES

*   This statement appeared in *Le Nouvel Observateur* in December 1977.

1   Klaus Croissant was the attorney for a German terrorist group, the Red Army Faction, and was widely suspected of abetting its actions. He was stripped of his professional license in West Germany in 1977, and subsequently sought political asylum in France. He was instead arrested and incarcerated and ultimately extradited back to West Germany to face trial.

2   I'm not talking about Mr. Marchais. How could he have known that so many people were protesting, since *L'Humanité* of November 15 only cited four names among all those who might have attracted his attention? Was it a matter of indifference for French public opinion, and German opinion as well, that the protesters against the potential extradition of Croissant included Jean-Louis Barrault, Roland Barthes, Pierre Boulez, César, Patrice Chéreau, Maurice Clavel, Georges Conchon, Jean-Loup Dabadie, Jean-Marie Domenach, André Glucksmann, Max Gallo, Costa-Gavras, Michel Guy, Jacques Julliard, Claude Manceron, Chris Marker, Yves Montand, Claude Mauriac, François Perier, Anne Philipe, Emmanuel Roblès, Claude Sautet, Simone Signoret, and Pierre Vidal-Naquet?

THE PROPER USE OF CRIMINALS

F or a justice system to be unjust, it doesn't need to convict the wrong individual; it only needs to judge in the wrong way.

Was Ranucci, guillotined on July 28, innocent of the murder of a little girl two years earlier?[1] We still don't know. We may never know. But we do know, irrefutably, that the justice system is guilty. Guilty of having, after five sessions of inquiry, two days of trial, a denied appeal, and a refused petition for mercy, led him without further ado to the scaffold.

Gilles Perrault[2] has reexamined the case. Given the subject, I hesitate to evoke the talent of his account, its clarity, its power. A single phrase seems decent to me: it's a good piece of work. I don't know how many months of patience it took him, together with that impatience that refuses to accept the easiest explanation. But once you've closed the book, you wonder what went wrong with that machine that should have halted at every moment or, rather, what kept it going: the bias of the police, a judge's hostility, the sensationalism of the press? Yes, those things were a factor, but at bottom, and holding it all "on track," there was something simple and monstrous—laziness. The laziness of the investigators, the judges, the lawyers, of the whole legal apparatus. A justice system is ludicrous when it is so indolent that it doesn't manage to deliver a verdict. But one that deals out a death sentence with an almost sleepy gesture . . .

Perrault's book is a shocking treatise on judicial laziness. The major form of that laziness is the cult of the confession.

It is toward the confession that all the proceedings lead, from the first interrogation to the final hearing. People are content, the secret is revealed, the fundamental truth uncovered; you said it yourself. The prestige of the confession in Catholic countries? The desire, according to Rousseau, for the culprit to endorse his own conviction? No doubt, but who does not see the "economy" that makes the confession possible? For the investigators who only have to model their inquiry on what was admitted, for the examining magistrate who only has to tie up his case around the confession, for the presiding judge who, in the rush of the debates, can refer the accused back to himself, for the jurors who, lacking knowledge of the documents, have before them an accused who acknowledges his guilt; for the defense attorneys, because, all things considered, it is easier to resort in their argumentation to the standard rhetoric of attenuating circumstances, the unhappy childhood, the moment of insanity, than to fight, step by step, at each stage of the inquiry and to investigate, dig, suspect, verify—the confession is a locus of gentle complicity for all the functionaries of penal justice.

On June 3, 1974, the horribly wounded corpse of Marie-Dolorès Rambla was discovered. She had been kidnapped by a man who had asked her to help him find a lost dog. There are signs and tracks around this crime: a Simca 1100, which the little girl had gotten into; a man in a red sweater who had already asked some children to find his dog. Moreover, we learn that not far from the place where the body was discovered, a motorist had a slight accident, that he ran away, he was chased, he hid. The vehicle's number was traced. It was that of Christian Ranucci, who was arrested.

A coincidence of places, an approximate overlapping of times: and what if the two series, that of the crime and that of the accident, were only one? It's true that Ranucci didn't have a Simca but a Peugeot; true that he wasn't recognized by the only two witnesses of the kidnapping; true that only one person was seen in the accident-involved vehicle; but there *was* a pair of pants spotted with blood in his vehicle, and why did he hide before calmly going home?

Eleven hours of interrogation, and he confesses. He confesses again twice in the following moments. An impressive confession, Gilles Perrault admits. But the investigators had many other possible leads near at hand; they had facts available showing that certain details of the confession were not correct; and that on many, seemingly false points, Ranucci had told the truth. They had enough to know that this decisive piece of evidence was dubious, and that, far from being proof positive, it needed to be proved in turn.

But it's just the opposite that occurred. The confession deployed its magical powers. The kidnap vehicle changed from a Simca to a Peugeot. A man running with a package became a man pulling a little girl by the hand. The hesitant witnesses were forgotten, and the red sweater, which could not be Ranucci's, was abandoned in a corner of the inquiry. The confession that was obtained and the facts that were established could not be part of the same diagram. It would be necessary either to break down the confession and re-examine it point by point, or sort through the facts and pick those that would enable one to cement the confession. You can guess which solution was decided upon.

People often reproach the police for the manner in which they induce confessions. And they are right. But if the justice system, from top to bottom, were not such a consumer of confessions, the police would be less apt to produce them, and by every means. In order to obtain Ranucci's confessions, the Marseilles police doubt-less did not just employ the insidious words of persuasion; but, be that as it may, was there anyone in the chamber of inquiry, the prosecutor's room, or the court to point out that a confession, any confession, is not a solution, it is a problem? You have to establish the truth about a crime whose unfolding, whose motives, whose partners elude you. You must never substitute a criminal who de-clares himself guilty and stands in lieu of the certainties you lack.

A manifest criminal has therefore taken the place of an obscure crime. But it is still necessary for his criminality to be anchored more solidly than in a confession that is always revocable. After handing the case over to the suspect himself, the inquiry will now appeal to the psychiatrist to set things in order. The latter must answer two types of question: Was the accused in a state of de-mentia when the events occurred? If so, it will be considered that no crime was committed and the prosecution will cease. It is logical that the psychiatrist should answer this question as soon as possi-ble.

But he will also be asked whether he does not see some connec-tions between the crime and the psychic anomalies of the subject, whether the latter is dangerous, and whether he is amenable to rehabilitation—questions that have a meaning only if the subject is indeed the author of the crime in question and if the doctor has the task of situating that crime in the life of its author.

So the psychiatrist had before him a Ranucci, who already had a crime attached to his person, since he confessed to it; all that was left to do was to construct a criminal personality. Let's see, then. A divorced mother: she is possessive, therefore. Her son lives with her: obviously he's never left her (it matters little that he has long worked elsewhere). He takes her car for the weekend: this must be the first time he's slept away from home (let's not count a year of military service in Germany). And if he's had mistresses over a period of seven years, this shows that he is emotionally "immature" and his sexuality is "misdirected."

I don't know if it makes much sense to say of someone who is the established killer of a little girl that he was babied too long by his mother. But, in a legal document submitted to judges who will have to decide whether the accused is guilty, I can see the effect quite clearly: lacking the elements of the crime, the report traces a profile of the criminal for you. The crime may remain to be proven, but one understands the criminal, one has him "cold." The crime will easily be deduced from that psychology as a necessary consequence.

And then, what can really be done with this crime, this obscure, idiotic, horrible act, this absurdity that will fade away with the passing of time (even if there are sorrows that will never be forgotten), what can be done on the day of the trial? What would it mean to react against something irreversible? One doesn't punish an act, one has to punish a man. And so, once again, a crime one can no longer do anything about will be dropped in order to deal with the criminal.

It is the criminal, in fact, that is needed by the press and public opinion. It is he who will be hated, against whom all the passions will be directed, and for whom the penalty and oblivion will be demanded.

It is the criminal that is needed by the jurors and the court as well. For the fact of the crime is buried in enormous records; the jurors are not familiar with it, and the presiding judge would have a hard time explaining it. In theory, the hearing can and must review everything; the truth must be produced in its entirety for all to see and hear. But, concretely, how does one proceed? A division is established: on the one hand, in the dust of the records, with their complicated filing system, the facts, the traces, the pieces of evidence, the countless elements that the mind connects only with difficulty and where the attention wanders. But what does it matter? For, on the other hand, there is, in flesh and blood, alive, incontestable, the criminal. His face, his expressions, his toughness, his smile, his panics—all that which "doesn't mislead." So let us rely on the skillful technicians of the inquiry for the crime and stay focused on the criminal himself.

It is also that criminal, not the crime, that is needed for determining the sentence. To be lenient, to understand and excuse. But to be severe as well. And to kill. I think it won't offend anyone's sorrow to say that the people responsible for the Morhange talcum powder did at least as much harm as the murderer of a little girl.[5] And the facts were there, absolutely. There was never any question of sentencing them to death, and that's all to the good. But why do we so easily accept such a difference of fates? The reason is that, on the one hand, we had unscrupulous manufacturers, greedy or cynical businessmen, or incompetent engineers, as one prefers, anything but "criminals"; on the other, we had a poorly elucidated crime, but in the light of day, a very real criminal. And while we might have qualms about answering one death with another, one slaughter with another, how can anyone not want to get rid, and by means without appeal, of someone who is fundamentally a "criminal," essentially a "danger," and naturally a "monster." The safety of all of us is at stake.

A paradoxical fact: today one of the most solid roots of the death penalty is the modern, humanitarian, scientific principle that one must judge not crimes but criminals. It is economically less costly, intellectually less demanding, more gratifying for the judges, more reasonable in the view of the sober-minded, and more satisfying for those keen on "understanding a man" than it is to establish the facts. And so we see a justice system that one morning, with a facile, routine, barely awake gesture, cut in two a twenty-two-year-old "criminal" whose crime had not been proven.

I haven't spoken of the exceptional and harsh aspects of this affair: why an execution was needed just then and how the petition for mercy, recommended by the commission, was rejected. I have only alluded to what made it resemble so many others.

The Penal Code is being reformed. A fervent campaign is being conducted against the death penalty. And certain magistrates are well aware of the danger of relics like the cult of the confession, or of modern phenomena such as the immoderate intervention of the psychiatrist. More generally still, there needs to be a thorough review of the way in which we punish.

The way in which punishment is meted out has always been one of the most fundamental traits of every society. No important mutation is produced in a society without an alteration taking place in that domain. The current system of penality is worn beyond repair. The "human sciences" must not try to put a new shine on it. It will take years, and many groping efforts, many disruptions, to determine what should be punished, and how, and whether punishing has a meaning and whether punishing is possible.

NOTES

1   "Ranucci" is a certain C. Ranucci, who was executed in July of 1976 for the murder of a young girl, which he may or may not have committed.

2   Gilles Perrault is the author of *Le Pull-over rouge*, an investigative report of the Ranucci case and the possible miscarriage of justice it may have entailed. "The Proper Use of Criminals" is Foucault's review of Perrault's book.

3   In 1972, a defect in the manufacture of Morhange brand talcum powder had caused the death of several children and inflicted serious injuries on many others.

LEMON AND MILK*

Among all the things that one learns in the book by Philippe Boucher, there is this one: the pleasure of doing business is only half-fulfilled by working at the Department of Justice. A matter of little consequence. But it matters a good deal, on the other hand, that the function of justice is no longer so essential and imposing that it can serve, as it once did, as the model for the exercise of civil power: the original form of the state, historians tell us, was a state that dispensed justice.

Nowadays, the legal system is a bit like the penalties it inflicts: it doesn't much like to display itself. Its rituals no longer serve to impress the parties to a dispute [*justiciables*] but to give a little comfort to the justiciaries; the blustering litigants having disappeared, it is no longer the grand social theater that it was for centuries.

Enveloped first in the dull business of an administration more and more like the others, it then underwent a double decline: it lost its grip on a whole, ever-widening domain of transactions that were concluded behind its back (its hold on financial dealings became fragmentary or symbolic); and it increasingly found itself reduced to the meager, humdrum, and thankless tasks of social control.

This decline doubtless explains why the judicial system no longer interests the public except in its acute form: where there are crimes, trials, the game of life and death. The judges are visible only in red. (Another point that makes it so difficult to eradicate the death penalty: without the right to kill, would the judicial system be anything more than a public utility a bit less efficient than the post office and certainly less useful than social security? The right to kill is the last emblem of its supremacy. It enables it to stand *a head above* all the other administrations.)

What I've always liked about Philippe Boucher's articles, here too, is that he has tried to get hold of the legal apparatus where it was beginning to become invisible: he has been the opposite of a legal affairs reporter. For him, the "affair" was never the singular case that stood in sharp contrast to the everyday but, rather, that which reveals or foreshadows it. It offered an angle for grasping a silent operation being put in place. Philippe Boucher sees things as a jurist rather than as a juror.

If his book were ironic only toward others, it would only interest me half as much. Fortunately, it is ironic toward itself. It says the opposite of what its title implies. All its analyses emphasize that the judicial system is neither a ghetto nor a fortress; it is fragile, permeable, and transparent, in spite of its fogs. It is "as flexible as one pleases."

You say that and people immediately translate: the judicial system is "subject to orders." Philippe Boucher would say, rather, that it is "subject to disorders." And these "disorders," the "orders" of the government, or its justice department, are only one aspect, and doubtless not the most important one. As a matter of fact, these disorders are neither accidents nor obstacles nor limits of the judicial apparatus. They are not even disturbances, but operational mechanisms. The law is applied by and through the incompetence of a minister, the requirements of an interest, the aberrations of an ambition.

Philippe Boucher draws many descriptive sketches. They don't call to mind Saint-Simon (obviously), but Tinguely: you think you are seeing one of those enormous contraptions, full of impossible cog wheels, of conveyor belts that don't convey anything and of grimacing gears: all these things that "don't work" end up making "it" work.

But in this game of disorders, the judges' moods are not the essential matter. Around or within the judicial apparatus, there are whole areas that are so arranged that the disorder will produce its useful effects. And *Le Ghetto judiciare* [*The Judiciary Ghetto*] shows, in a remarkable way, I believe, that these are not instances of tolerance or laxity but parts of the mechanism. Thus, the principle of the timeliness of prosecutions, which grants the amazing right to open or shut one's eyes according to circumstances that have nothing to do with the law. Thus, the well-known autonomy of the police, which selects out beforehand what will constitute the object of judicial intervention—that is, when it doesn't fashion that object. Thus, the measures of expulsion and blockage brought to bear on that substantial fringe segment of the population, the immigrants— a kind of parallel judicial system (which even has its parallel prison, at Arenc).

You will tell me that there's nothing extraordinary about all this. What private or public organization doesn't operate in this manner? What rule could survive if it did not breathe irregularity on a daily basis? Our judicial system is not put to shame by that of the Ancien Régime, or by that nineteenth-century apparatus that judged the strikers and communards.

Philippe Boucher says it very well: the issue is not in the smaller or larger quantity of disorder but in the nature of the effects that it produces. Now, the fact is, in the judicial apparatus that watches over us, the disorder produces "order." And in three ways. It produces "acceptable irregularities" under the cover of which (assisted by habit and convenience) we find ourselves in a state of tolerance assented to by just about everyone. It produces "usable asymmetries" providing benefits to a few at the cost of the others who either don't know it's happening or are too dumbstruck to protest. But finally, and above all, it produces what has the highest value in civilizations like ours: social order.

Our judicial system, at least since the nineteenth century, is supposed to have no other role than to apply the law. Something that it does in a very lame way if you consider all the exceptions that it tolerates, all the legal distortions it inflicts. But if you look at the apparatus in motion, with its ins and outs, you notice that the violence done to the law obeys the principle of protection of order. As Philippe Boucher puts it, "The judicial system doesn't concern itself with injury, it apprehends disturbances." It is for the sake of order that the decision is made to prosecute or not to prosecute; for the sake of order that the police are given free rein; for the sake of order that those who aren't perfectly "desirable" are expelled.

This primacy of order has at least two important consequences: the judicial system increasingly substitutes concern for the norm for respect for the law; and it tends less to punish offenses than to penalize behaviors. Thinking of another fine book, but in which it is a question of love, I would have liked Philippe Boucher's to be called *The New Judicial Disorder*.

Philippe Boucher's book cannot be dissociated from a recent phenomenon, whose importance the author himself underscores: for the first time since the high courts of the Ancien Régime were dissolved, the judges joined together in 1968 to found the Syndicat de la magistrature. And this "*réunion*" had as both its origin and its consequence an awakening in the form of a question: "What are we, then, and what are we made to do, we who on principle are supposed to apply the law while being insidiously pressured and even asked in so many words to produce social order?" It has often been said that the Syndicat de la magistrature wanted to "politicize" the administration of justice. I would be inclined to think rather the opposite: it wanted to bring the question of law to bear on a certain "policy" of justice which was that of order. "Law and Order" is not simply the motto of American conservatism, it is a hybridized monster. Those who fight for human rights are well aware of this. As for those who have forgotten that fact, Philippe Boucher's book will remind them of it. Just as people say milk or lemon, we should say law *or* order. It is up to us to draw lessons for the future from that incompatibility.

NOTES

*   "Lemon and Milk" is Foucault's commentary on Boucher's *Le Ghetto judiciare* (Paris: Grasset, 1978). Boucher is a journalist, and a frequent contributor to *Le Monde*. The commentary appeared in the same newspaper in October 1978. [eds.]

Dear Mr. Prime Minister,

In September of last year—several thousand men and women had just been machine-gunned in the streets of Tehran—you granted me an interview. It was in Qom, at the residence of the Ayatollah Chariat Madari. Ten or twelve human rights activists had taken refuge there and soldiers carrying machine pistols kept watch on the entrance to the little street.

At the time, you were chairman of the Association for the Defense of Human Rights in Iran. It took courage on your part. Physical courage: prison lay in wait for you, and you were already familiar with it. Political courage: the American president had recently included the Shah among the defenders of human rights.[1] Many Iranians are irritated that they are now the object of vociferous lectures. They have shown that they know how to go about asserting their rights. And they refuse to think that the conviction of a young black in racist South Africa is equivalent to the conviction in Tehran of a Savak torturer. Who can blame them?

A few weeks ago, you put a stop to summary trials and hasty executions. Justice and injustice are the sensitive point of every revolution: that is where they are born, and often it is also where they lose their way and die. And since you saw fit to allude to this subject in public, I feel the need to remind you of our conversation about it.

We spoke of all the regimes that oppressed people while invoking human rights. You expressed a hope: that in the will, so generally affirmed then by Iranians, for an Islamic government, those rights would find a real guarantee. You gave three reasons for the hope. A spiritual dimension, you said, would traverse a people's revolt in which each individual, for the sake of a completely different world, would risk everything (and, for many, this "everything" was neither more nor less than themselves): it was not the desire to be ruled by a "government of mullahs"—you employed that expression, I believe. What I saw, from Tehran to Abadan, did not contradict your views, far from it.

You also said that Islam, with its historical depth and its present-day dynamism, was capable of facing, on this issue of rights, the formidable challenge that socialism had not met any better—to say the least—than capitalism. "Impossible," some are saying—individuals who think they know a lot about Islamic societies or about the nature of any religion. I would be much more modest than they, not seeing in the name of what universality Muslims should be prevented from seeking their future in an Islam whose new face they will have to shape with their own hands. In the expression "Islamic government," why cast suspicion immediately on the adjective "Islamic"? The word "government" by itself is enough to awaken one's vigilance. No adjective—democratic, socialist, liberal, popular—frees a government from its obligations.

You said that a government deriving its authority from Islam would limit the considerable rights of ordinary civil sovereignty by obligations based on religion. Being Islamic, such a government would be bound by a supplement of "duties." And it would respect these ties, because the people could turn this shared religion back against it. The idea seemed important to me. Personally, I am a bit skeptical about the voluntary respect that governments are apt to give to their own obligations. However, it is good for the governed to be able to stand up and point out that they did not simply grant rights to those who govern them but, rather, that they intend to impose duties as well. No government can escape from those fundamental duties. And from that viewpoint, the trials that are now taking place in Iran are nothing short of alarming.

Nothing is more important in the history of a people than the rare moments when it rises up as a body to strike down a regime it can no longer tolerate. Nothing is more important for its everyday life than the moments, quite frequent on the other hand, when public authority turns against an individual, proclaims him its enemy, and decides to strike him down: never does it have more, or more essential, duties to respect. Political trials are always touchstones. Not because the accused are never criminals but because public authority shows itself without a mask, and it presents itself for judgment in judging its enemies.

It always claims that it must make itself respected. But, in fact, it is precisely there that it must be utterly respectful. The right that it exercises to defend the people itself burdens it with very heavy responsibilities.

It is necessary—imperatively so—to give the person being prosecuted every means of defense and every possible right. Is he "manifestly guilty"? Does he have public opinion completely against him? Is he hated by the people? That, precisely, bestows rights on him, though rights that must be all that much more intangible; it is the duty of the governing authority to grant and guarantee them. For a government, there cannot be any "least deserving of men."

It is also a duty for each government to show everyone—and I mean the lowliest, the most pigheaded, the blindest of those it governs—under what conditions, in what way, on what principle, the authority can claim the right to punish in its name. A punishment that goes unaccounted for may well be justified; it will still be an injustice. Toward the condemned, and also toward all those under the authority's jurisdiction.

And I believe this duty to submit to judgment when one intends to pass judgment must be accepted by a government with respect to all men throughout the world. I imagine you don't grant the principle of a sovereignty that would only have to answer to itself, any more than I do. Governing does not go without saying, any more than condemning, or killing, does. It is good when a person, no matter who, even someone at the other end of the world, can speak up because he or she cannot bear to see another person tortured or condemned. It does not constitute interference with a state's internal affairs. Those who protested on behalf of a single Iranian tortured in the depths of a Savak prison were interfering in the most universal affair that exists.

Perhaps it will be said that the majority of Iranians have demonstrated their trust in the regime that is installing itself, and so they must approve of its judicial practices. The fact of being accepted, wished for, and voted for does not lessen the obligations of governments—it imposes stricter ones.

Of course, I do not have any authority to address you in this way, Mr. Prime Minister—just the permission to do so, in being given to understand, during our first encounter, that in your view governing is not a coveted right but an extremely difficult duty. You are called upon to make sure that this people never has to regret the unyielding force with which it has just liberated itself.

NOTES

* This letter to then Iranian Prime Minister Bazargan appeared in *Le Nouvel Observateur* in April 1979. [eds.]

1 In 1978, President Jimmy Carter had hailed the Shah as a human rights defender.

FOR AN ETHIC OF DISCOMFORT

————

It was toward the end of the Age of Enlightenment, in 1784. A Berlin journal asked a few worthy thinkers the question, "What is enlightenment?" Immanuel Kant answered, after Moses Mendelssohn.[1]

I find the question more noteworthy than the answers. Because enlightenment, at the end of the eighteenth century, was not news, was not an invention, a revolution, or a party. It was something familiar and diffuse, something that was going on—and fading out. The Prussian newspaper was basically asking: "What is it that has happened to us? What is this event that is nothing else but what we have just said, thought, and done—nothing else but ourselves, nothing but that something which we have been and still are?"

Should this singular inquiry be placed in the history of journalism or of philosophy? I only know that, since that time, there have not been many philosophies that don't revolve around the question: "What are we now? What is this ever so fragile moment from which we cannot detach our identity and which will carry that identity away with it?" But I believe this question is also the basis of the journalist's occupation. The concern to say what is happening—will Jean Daniel contradict me?—is not so much prompted by the desire to know always and everywhere what makes this happening possible but, rather, by the desire to make out what is concealed under that precise, floating, mysterious, utterly simple word "today."[2]

Jean Daniel wrote *L'Ere des ruptures* [*The Age of Ruptures*] from a vertical viewpoint on his journalist's trade—looking at things from above and also from underneath. It is the opposite of "The Time that Remains." There are people for whom time is destined to pass away and thought is bound to stop. Jean Daniel is one of those for whom time stands still and thought moves. Not because it is always thinking something new but because it never stops thinking the same things differently. And because this makes it live and breathe. This is a treatise on movable thought.

Everyone has their own way of changing, or, what amounts to the same thing, of perceiving that everything changes. In this matter, nothing is more arrogant than to try to dictate to others. My way of being no longer the same is, by definition, the most singular part of what I am. Yet God knows that there are ideological traffic police around, and we can hear their whistles blast: go left, go right, here, later, get moving, not now . . . The insistence on identity and the injunction to make a break both feel like impositions, and in the same way.

Periods overshadowed by great pasts—wars, resistances, revolutions—call for fidelity. Today, people tend to favor ruptures. I can't help but think there is a kind of smile in the title that Jean Daniel chose. What he talks about instead are the imperceptible moments of modification: shifts, slides, cracks, moving viewpoints, increasing and decreasing distances, roads that stretch out, bend sharply, and suddenly turn back. In the fifteen years since the founding of *Le Nouvel Observateur*, Jean Daniel has changed, things have changed around him, the journal has changed, along with its contributors, its friends, and its adversaries too. Each and all, and each in relation to all.

It took political courage, it took self-discipline and a control of language, to dive into that general mobility. Not to yield to the temptation to say that nothing much has changed in spite of appearances. Not to say either, "That is what happened, that is the tidal wave and the force that swept everything along with it." And, above all, not to pose it as a fixed point, and say, "I saw it coming, I always told you it would happen."

The "day" that has changed? That of the Left. The Left: not a coalition of parties on the political chessboard but an adherence that many felt without being able and without wanting to give it a very clear definition. A kind of "essential" Left, a blend of things held self-evident or obligatory: "A home rather than a concept." A

Left whose existence Jean Daniel had contributed to more than anyone else.

In the immediate postwar period, this idea of a Left constituted by a free moral affiliation had a difficult time existing. Credentialed by the Resistance, supported by the USSR and the "socialist camp," and wielding its doctrine, the Communist Party exerted a triple legitimacy, historical, political, and theoretical. It laid down the law to everything that claimed to be of the Left, either subjecting it to its own law or outlawing it. The Party magnetized the political field, orienting the filings located in its neighborhood, imposing a direction on them; one was for or against, an ally or an adversary.

Khrushchev, Budapest: the political justifications crumbled. De-Stalinization, the "crisis of Marxism": the theoretical legitimation became blurred. And the opposition to the Algerian War formed a historical meeting point from which, in contrast to the Resistance, the Party would be strikingly absent. No more law on the Left: the Left could emerge. And the question asked by the brave anti-Stalinists, "We know who we are, but how do we manage to exist in reality?" could be turned around: "We exist; now it is time to know who we are." A question that was the founding charter and compact of *Le Nouvel Observateur*. Out of this felt adherence it was a matter of forming not a party, not even an opinion, but a certain self-consciousness. *L'Ere des ruptures* tells how the work, the determined effort to sharpen a fuzzy consciousness ended by undoing the shared assumptions that had given rise to it.

This search for an identity was indeed carried out in a very strange way. Jean Daniel is right to be retrospectively surprised and not to find "all that obvious" all those initiatives that seemed at a given moment to "go without saying."

First surprise: People sought less and less to situate themselves in relation to the great geodesics of history: capitalism, bourgeoisie, imperialism, socialism, proletariat. They gradually gave up following the "logical" and "historical" consequences of choices to the limits of the inadmissible or the unbearable. The heroism of political identity has had its day. One asks what one is, moment by moment, of the problems with which one grapples: how to take part and take sides without letting oneself be taken in. Experience with, rather than engagement in.

Second surprise: It was not the socialist-communist Union of the

Left or its Common Program, nor the abandonment of the dictatorship of the proletariat by the "party of the revolution," which exercised the conscience of the Left in France. It was a small piece
of territory in the Middle East. It was the bombings and camps in
an Indochina that was no longer French. The third world, with the
revolutionary movements that arose and the authoritarian states
that formed there, Palestine, the Arabs and Israel, the USSR with
its concentration camps—and perhaps Gaullism because of the de-
colonization it brought about in spite of the blind soothsayers; that
is what troubled the mind of the Left.

Third surprise: At the end of all these experiences or all these
dreams, there was neither unanimity nor reward. No sooner had a
consensus formed (as against the American presence in Vietnam)
than it came apart. Worse, it became harder and harder for an individual to stay in line with himself; rare were those who could say
without hesitation, "This is something I had wanted." Identities got
defined by trajectories.

Fourth surprise: From these scattered experiences, which
seemed to occur in the name of ideals held more or less in common, working through similar kinds of organization and in a vocabulary that could be shared across cultures, no universal way of
thought took shape. We are witnessing a globalization of the economy? For certain. A globalization of political calculations? Without
a doubt. But a universalization of political consciousness—certainly
not.

Jean Daniel tells the tale of these surprises: his own, those of
others, his surprise at seeing that others still let themselves be surprised, the surprise of others who are astonished or indignant that
he no longer lets himself be surprised. And, as this subtle story
unfolds, he reveals what constitutes for him the great "self-
evidence" that had structured the whole consciousness of the Left—
namely, that history is dominated by revolution. Many on the Left
had given up the idea. But this was on condition of finding something to take its place. And of being able to say: "I can do as well,
but more tidily and surely." And thus, from the third world where
it had not taken place, it was necessary for this revolution to come
back to us in the emaciated form of pure violence, in order for it
to lose the mute self-evidence that always placed it over and above
history.

This is what the book brings into focus, it seems to me: thirty years' worth of experiences led us "not to put trust in any revolution," even if one can "understand every revolt." Now, what can such a conclusion have for a people—and a Left—whose taste for "revolution later and eventually" was probably due simply to a deep-seated immediate conservatism? Abandoning the empty form of a world revolution must, if one is to avoid a total immobilization, be accompanied by a breaking-free from conservatism. And such an effort is especially urgent when the very existence of this society is threatened by that conservatism, that is, by the inertia inherent in its development.

Jean Daniel's book proposes replacing that old question of the Left, "We exist, but who are we?"—that old question to which the Left owes its existence without ever having given it an answer—with this other question, "What about those who understand the need to tear themselves free from conservatism, if only in order to *exist*, and for the long term to keep from all being dead? What do they need to be, or rather to do?"

Jean Daniel has not attempted to reconstruct those moments, which happen in life, when what one was most sure of is suddenly revealed to be a mistake. His whole book is a quest for those subtler, more secret, and more decisive moments when things begin to lose their self-evidence. Such moments are difficult to grasp, not only because they never have a precise date but because they are always long past when one finally becomes aware of them.

Of course, new experiences and sudden upheavals in the world order have a part to play in these changes. But not the main part. As a reflection on manifest truths that blur, *L'Ere des ruptures* shows two things very clearly. First, a manifest truth disappearing not when it is replaced by another one that is fresher or sharper but when one begins to detect the very conditions that made it seem manifest: the familiarities that served as its support, the darknesses that brought about its clarity, and all those far-away things that secretly sustained it and made it "go without saying."

And then, the new manifest truth is always a bit of an idea from the back of your mind. It allows you to see again something you had never completely lost sight of; it gives the strange impression that you had always sort of thought what you had never completely said, and already said in a thousand ways what you had never before thought out. Read, in the chapter "La Terre à tous promise" ["The Land Promised to Everybody"], the pages on the rights of the Palestinians and the fact of Israel: all the changes of lighting that are triggered by new events or vicissitudes happen through resurgences of former lights and shades: those of long-gone Blida and Algeria.

Impossible, as one turns these pages, not to think of Maurice Merleau-Ponty's teaching and of what was for him the essential philosophical task: never to consent to being completely comfortable with one's own presuppositions. Never to let them fall peacefully asleep, but also never to believe that a new fact will suffice to overturn them; never to imagine that one can change them like arbitrary axioms, remembering that in order to give them the necessary mobility one must have a distant view, but also look at what is nearby and all around oneself. To be very mindful that everything one perceives is evident only against a familiar and little-known horizon, that every certainty is sure only through the support of a ground that is always unexplored. The most fragile instant has its roots. In that lesson, there is a whole ethic of sleepless evidence that does not rule out, far from it, a rigorous economy of the True and the False; but that is not the whole story.

NOTES

1 Moses Mendelssohn, "Über die Frage: Was ist Aufklären?" *Berlinsche Monatsshrift*, 4.3 (Sept. 1784), pp. 193–200. Immanuel Kant, "Beantwortung der Frage: Was ist Aufklärung?" *Berlinsche Monatsshrift*, 4.6 (Dec. 1784), pp. 491–94.

2 This review of Jean Daniel's *Ere des ruptures* (Paris: Grasset, 1979) appeared in *Le Nouvel Observateur* in April 1979. [eds.]

W e are ready to die in thousands to make the shah leave," Iranians were saying last year. And the Ayatollah these days: "Let Iran bleed so the revolution will be strong."

There is a strange echo between these phrases that seem connected. Does the horror of the second condemn the intoxication of the first?

Revolts belong to history. But, in a certain way, they escape from it. The impulse by which a single individual, a group, a minority, or an entire people says, "I will no longer obey," and throws the risk of their life in the face of an authority they consider unjust seems to me to be something irreducible. Because no authority is capable of making it utterly impossible: Warsaw will always have its ghetto in revolt and its sewers crowded with rebels. And because the man who rebels is finally inexplicable; it takes a wrenching-away that interrupts the flow of history, and its long chains of reasons, for a man to be able, "really," to prefer the risk of death to the certainty of having to obey.

All the forms of established or demanded freedom, all the rights that one asserts, even in regard to the seemingly least important things, no doubt have a last anchor point there, one more solid and closer to experience than "natural rights." If societies persist and live, that is, if the powers that be are not "utterly absolute," it is because, behind all the submissions and coercions, beyond the threats, the violence, and the intimidations, there is the possibility of that moment when life can no longer be bought, when the authorities can no longer do anything, and when, facing the gallows and the machine guns, people revolt.

Because they are thus "outside history" and in history, because everyone stakes his life, and his death, on their possibility, one understands why uprisings have so easily found their expression and their drama in religious forms. Promises of the afterlife, time's renewal, anticipation of the savior or the empire of the last days, a reign of pure goodness—for centuries all this constituted, where the religious form allowed, not an ideological costume but the very way of experiencing revolts.

Then came the age of "revolution." For two hundred years this idea overshadowed history, organized our perception of time, and polarized people's hopes. It constituted a gigantic effort to domesticate revolts within a rational and controllable history: it gave them a legitimacy, separated their good forms from their bad, and defined the laws of their unfolding; it set their prior conditions, objectives, and ways of being carried to completion. Even a status of the professional revolutionary was defined: By thus repatriating revolt, people have aspired to make its truth manifest and to bring it to its real end. A marvelous and formidable promise. Some will say that the revolt was colonized in Realpolitik. Others that the dimension of a rational history has been opened to it. I prefer the naive and rather feverish question that Max Horkheimer once posed: "But is this revolution really such a desirable thing?"

The enigma of revolts. For anyone who did not look for the "underlying reasons" for the movement in Iran was but attentive to the way in which it was experienced, for anyone who tried to understand what was going on in the heads of these men and women when they were risking their lives, one thing was striking. They inscribed their humiliations, their hatred for the regime, and their resolve to overthrow it at the bounds of heaven and earth, in an envisioned history that was religious just as much as it was political. They confronted the Pahlavis, in a contest where everyone's life was on the line, but where it was also a question of millennial sacrifices and promises. So that the famous demonstrations, which played such an important role, could at the same time respond in an effective way to the threat from the army (to the extent of paralyzing it), follow the rhythm of religious ceremonies, and appeal to a timeless drama in which the secular power is always accused.

This startling superimposition produced, in the middle of the twentieth century, a movement strong enough to overthrow an apparently well-armed regime while being close to old dreams that the West had known in times past, when people attempted to inscribe the figures of spirituality on political ground.

Years of censorship and persecution, a political class kept under tutelage, parties outlawed, revolutionary groups decimated: where else but in religion could support be found for the disarray, then the rebellion, of a population traumatized by "development," "reform," "urbanization," and all the other failures of the regime? True. But should one have expected the religious element to quickly move aside in favor of forces that were more real and ideologies that were less "archaic"? Undoubtedly not, and for several reasons.

First there was the rapid success of the movement, reconfirming it in the form it had just taken. There was the institutional solidity of a clergy whose sway over the population was strong, and whose political ambitions were vigorous. There was the whole context of the Islamic movement: with the strategic positions it occupies, the economic keys which Muslim countries hold, and its own expansionary force over two continents, it constitutes an intense and complex reality all around Iran. With the result that the imaginary contents of the revolt did not dissipate in the broad daylight of the revolution. They were immediately transposed to a political scene that seemed fully prepared to receive them but was actually of a completely different nature. This scene contained a blend of the most important and the most atrocious elements: the formidable hope of making Islam into a great civilization once again, and forms of virulent xenophobia; global stakes and regional rivalries. Along with the problem of imperialisms and the subjugation of women, and so on.

The Iranian movement did not come under that "law" of revolutions which brings to visibility, so it would seem, the tyranny lurking within them, beneath the blind enthusiasm. What constituted the most internal and the most intensely experienced part of the uprising bore directly on an overloaded political chessboard. But this contact was not an identity. The spirituality which had meaning for those who went to their deaths has no common measure with the bloody government of an integrist clergy. The Iranian clerics want to authenticate their regime by using the significations that the uprising had. People here reason no differently when they discredit the fact of the uprising because today there is a government of mullahs. In both cases, there is "fear." Fear of what happened in Iran last autumn, something the world had not produced an example of for a long time.

Hence, precisely, the need to grasp what is irreducible in such a movement—and deeply threatening for any despotism, whether that of yesterday or that of today.

To be sure, there is no shame in changing one's opinion; but there is no reason to say one has changed it when today one is against severed hands, having yesterday been against the tortures of the Savak.

No one has the right to say, "Revolt for me; the final liberation of all men depends on it." But I am not in agreement with anyone who would say, "It is useless for you to revolt; it is always going to be the same thing." One does not dictate to those who risk their lives facing a power. Is one right to revolt, or not? Let us leave the question open. People do revolt; that is a fact. And that is how subjectivity (not that of great men, but that of anyone) is brought into history, breathing life into it. A convict risks his life to protest unjust punishments; a madman can no longer bear being confined and humiliated; a people refuses the regime that oppresses it. That doesn't make the first innocent, doesn't cure the second, and doesn't ensure for the third the tomorrow it was promised. Moreover, no one is obliged to support them. No one is obliged to find that these confused voices sing better than the others and speak the truth itself. It is enough that they exist and that they have against them everything that is dead set on shutting them up for there to be a sense in listening to them and in seeing what they mean to say. A question of ethics? Perhaps. A question of reality, without a doubt. All the disenchantments of history won't alter the fact of the matter: it is because there are such voices that the time of human beings does not have the form of evolution but that of "history," precisely.

This is inseparable from another principle: the power that one man exerts over another is always perilous. I am not saying that power, by nature, is evil; I am saying that power, with its mechanisms, is infinite (which does not mean that it is omnipotent, quite the contrary). The rules that exist to limit it can never be stringent enough; the universal principles for dispossessing it of all the occasions it seizes are never sufficiently rigorous. Against power one must always set inviolable laws and unrestricted rights.

These days, intellectuals don't have a very good "press." I believe I can employ that word in a rather precise sense. This is not the moment to say that one is not an intellectual; besides, I would just provoke a smile. I am an intellectual. If I were asked for my conception of what I do, the strategist being the man who says, "What difference does a particular death, a particular cry, a particular revolt make compared to the great general necessity, and, on the other hand, what difference does a general principle make in the particular situation where we are?", well, I would have to say that it is immaterial to me whether the strategist is a politician, a historian, a revolutionary, a follower of the shah or of the ayatollah; my theoretical ethic is opposite to theirs. It is "antistrategic": to be respectful when a singularity revolts, intransigent as soon as power violates the universal. A simple choice, a difficult job: for one must at the same time look closely, a bit beneath history, at what cleaves it and stirs it, and keep watch, a bit behind politics, over what must unconditionally limit it. After all, that is my work; I am not the first or the only one to do it. But that is what I chose.

NOTES

* This statement appeared in *Le Monde* in May 1979. [eds.]

SO IS IT IMPORTANT TO THINK?

———

Q: *The evening of the elections,[1] we asked you what your first reactions were, and you didn't wish to say. But today you feel more comfortable talking . . .*
A: Yes, I was thinking that voting was itself a way of acting, and it was up to the government to act in turn. Now the time has come to react to what is beginning to be done.

In any case, I believe we have to consider that people are mature enough to make their own decisions in the voting booth, and to be glad about the result if that's what's called for. Moreover, it seems to me that they managed very well in this instance.

Q: *So what are your reactions today?*
A: I'm struck by three things. For a good twenty years, a series of questions have been raised in society itself. And, for a long time, these questions weren't accepted in "serious," institutional politics. The Socialists seem to have been the only ones to grasp the reality of these problems, to echo them back—which no doubt had something to do with their victory.

Second, with respect to these problems (I'm thinking in particular of the judicial system or the question of immigrants), the first measures or the first statements are completely consistent with what might be called a "logic of the Left," the one for which Mitterrand was elected.

Third, the most remarkable thing is that the measures don't follow the majority opinion. On both the death penalty issue and the question of immigrants, the choices don't go along with the most common opinion.

This is something that gives the lie to what was said about the inanity of all these questions raised in the course of the past ten or fifteen years: what was said about the nonexistence of a logic of the Left in the manner of governing; what was said about the demagogic facility of the first measures that would be taken. On the nuclear question, immigrants, the judicial system, the government has anchored its decisions in actual problems that have been raised, by referring to a logic that did not accord with the majority opinion. And I am sure that the majority approves of this way of doing things, if not with the measures themselves. In saying that, I'm not saying that it's taken care of and we can go take a rest. These measures are not a charter, but they *are* more than symbolic gestures.

Compare with what Giscard did right after his election: a handshake with prisoners. That was a purely symbolic gesture directed to an electorate that wasn't his. Today we have a first set of real measures that may not suit a portion of the electorate, but that mark a style of government.

Q: *It does seem to be a completely different way of governing that is being set in place.*

A: Yes, that's an important point and one that appeared as soon as Mitterrand's electoral victory was declared. It seems to me that this election was experienced by many people as a kind of victory event—that is, a modification of the relation between governors and governed. After all, it involved a shift in the political class. France is entering a party government with all the dangers that entails, and one mustn't ever forget the fact.

But what is at stake with this modification is the possibility of establishing a relation between governor and governed that is not a relation of obedience but a relation in which work will have an important role.

Q: *Are you saying that it is going to be possible to work with this government?*

A: We need to escape the dilemma of being either for or against. One can, after all, be face to face, and upright. Working with a government doesn't imply either a subjection or a blanket acceptance. One can work and be intransigent at the same time. I would even say that the two things go together.

Q: *After Michel Foucault the critic, are we going to see Michel Foucault the reformist? All the same, this was a reproach that was often made: the criticism carried out by intellectuals doesn't lead to anything.*

A: I'll reply first to the point about not having "produced any results." There are hundreds and thousands of people who have worked for the emergence of a certain number of problems that are now actually before us. Saying that such efforts have not produced any results is completely false. Do you think that twenty years ago the problems of the relation between mental illness and psychological normality, the problem of imprisonment, the problem of the relation between the sexes, and so on, were raised as they are today?

Furthermore, there are no reforms in themselves. Reforms do not come about in empty space, independently of those who make them. One cannot avoid considering those who will have to administer this transformation.

And then, above all, I don't think that criticism can be set against transformation, "ideal" criticism against "real" transformation.

A critique does not consist in saying that things aren't good the way they are. It consists in seeing on what type of assumptions, of familiar notions, of established, unexamined ways of thinking the accepted practices are based.

We need to free ourselves of the sacralization of the social as the only instance of the real and stop regarding that essential element in human life and human relations—I mean thought—as so much wind. Thought does exist, both beyond and before systems and edifices of discourse. It is something that is often hidden but always drives everyday behaviors. There is always a little thought occurring even in the most stupid institutions; there is always thought even in silent habits.

Criticism consists in uncovering that thought and trying to change it: showing that things are not as obvious as people believe, making it so that what is taken for granted is no longer taken for granted. To do criticism is to make harder those acts which are now too easy.

Understood in these terms, criticism (and radical criticism) is utterly indispensable for any transformation. For a transformation that would remain within the same mode of thought, a transformation that would only be a certain way of better adjusting the same thought to the reality of things, would only be a superficial transformation.

On the other hand, as soon as people begin to have trouble thinking things the way they have been thought, transformation becomes at the same time very urgent, very difficult, and entirely possible.

So there is not a time for criticism and a time for transformation; there are not those who have to do criticism and those who have to transform, those who are confined within an inaccessible radicality and those who are obliged to make the necessary concessions to reality. As a matter of fact, I believe that the work of deep transformation can be done in the open and always turbulent atmosphere of a continuous criticism.

Q: *But do you think that the intellectual should have a programming role in such a transformation?*
A: A reform is never anything but the outcome of a process in which there is conflict, confrontation, struggle, resistance . . .

To say to oneself from the start, "What is the reform that I will be able to make?"—that's not a goal for the intellectual to pursue, I think. His role, since he works precisely in the sphere of thought, is to see how far the liberation of thought can go toward making these transformations urgent enough for people to want to carry them out, and sufficiently difficult to carry out for them to be deeply inscribed in reality.

It is a matter of making conflicts more visible, of making them more essential than mere clashes of interest or mere institutional blockages. From these conflicts and clashes a new relation of forces must emerge whose temporary profile will be a reform.

Whatever the project of reform, if its basis has not been thought working in itself; and if ways of thinking—which is to say, ways of acting—have not actually been modified, we know that it will be phagocyted and digested by behavioral and institutional modes that will always be the same.

Q: *After having participated in numerous movements, you have placed yourself a bit in retreat. Are you going to enter into such movements once again?*

A: Every time I have tried to do a piece of theoretical work it has been on the basis of elements of my own experience: always in connection with processes I saw unfolding around me. It was always because I thought I identified cracks, silent tremors, and dysfunctions in things I saw, institutions I was dealing with, or my relations with others, that I set out to do a piece of work, and each time was partly a fragment of autobiography.

I am not a retired activist who would now like to go back on duty. My way of working hasn't changed much; but what I expect from it is that it will continue to change me.

Q: *You are said to be rather pessimistic. Listening to you, though, I get the impression that you are something of an optimist instead.*

A: There is an optimism that consists in saying, "In any case, it couldn't be any better." My optimism would consist rather in saying, "So many things can be changed, being as fragile as they are, tied more to contingencies than to necessities, more to what is arbitrary than to what is rationally established, more to complex but transitory historical contingencies than to inevitable anthropological constants . . ." You know, to say that we are more recent than we thought is not a way of bringing the whole weight of our history down on our shoulders. Rather, it is to make available for the work that we can do on ourselves the largest possible share of what is presented to us as inaccessible.

NOTES

1 The elections in question brought the left to power, with François Mitterrand winning the presidency. This interview, conducted by Didier Eribon, appeared several weeks later in *Libération* (30–31 May 1981). [eds.]

T he oldest penalty in the world is in the process of dying in France. This is a cause for rejoicing, but not for self-congratulation. It is a catching-up. Unlike the large majority of Western European countries, France has not lived on the Left for a single moment over the past twenty-five years. This fact accounts for some surprising lags in many areas. We are now trying to conform ourselves to the average profile. Our penal system, I dare say, was taller by a head(sman). We're doing away with him. Fine.

But, here and elsewhere, the way in which the death penalty is done away with is at least as important as the doing-away. The roots are deep. And many things will depend on how they are cleared out.

If death figured at the apex of the criminal justice system for so many centuries, this was not because the lawmakers and judges were especially sanguine people. The reason was that justice was the exercise of a sovereignty. That sovereignty had to be an independence in regard to all other power: little practiced, it was spoken of a good deal. It also had to be the exercise of a right of life and death over individuals: it was more apt to be passed over in silence insofar as it was regularly manifested.

Giving up the habit of lopping off a few heads because blood spurts, because it is something no longer done among civilized people, and because there is sometimes a risk of decapitating an innocent person is relatively easy. But giving up the death penalty while citing the principle that no public authority has the right to take anyone's life (any more than any individual does) is to engage an important and difficult debate. The question of war, the army, compulsory military service, and so on, immediately takes shape.

Do we want the debate on the death penalty to be anything other than a discussion on the best punitive techniques? Do we want it to be the occasion for and beginning of a new political reflection? Then it must take up the problem of the right to kill at its root, as the state exercises that right in various forms. The question of more adequately defining the relations of individual freedom and the death of individuals must be taken up anew, with all its political and ethical implications.

Another reason acclimatized the death penalty and ensured its long survival in the modern codes—I mean in the penal systems—that have claimed, since the nineteenth century, both to correct and to punish. In point of fact, these systems always assumed that there were not two kinds of crimes but two kinds of criminals: those who can be corrected by punishment, and those who could never be corrected even if they were punished indefinitely. The death penalty was the definitive punishment for the incorrigibles, and in a form so much shorter and surer than perpetual imprisonment . . .

The real dividing line, among the penal systems, does not pass between those which include the death penalty and the others; it passes between those which allow definitive penalties and those which exclude them. This is doubtless where the true debate in the legislative assembly, in the coming days, will be situated. The abolition of the death penalty will probably be easily approved. But will there be a radical departure from a penal practice that asserts that it is for the purpose of correction but maintains that certain individuals cannot be corrected, ever, because of their nature, their character, or a bio-psychological defect, or because they are, in sum, intrinsically dangerous?

Safety will serve as an argument in both camps. Some will point out that certain prisoners will constitute a danger for society once they are freed. Others will submit that certain prisoners with life sentences will be a continuous danger in the penitentiary institutions. But there is a danger that will perhaps not be evoked—that of a society that will not be constantly be concerned about its code and its laws, its penal institutions and its punitive practices. By maintaining, in one form or another, the category of individuals to be definitively eliminated (through death or imprisonment), one easily gives oneself the illusion of solving the most difficult problems: correct if one can; if not, no need to worry, no need to ask oneself whether it might be necessary to reconsider all the ways of punishing: the trap door through which the "incorrigible" will disappear is ready.

To proceed on the assumption that every penalty whatsoever will have a term is to go down a path of anxiety—there's no denying it. But it is also to commit oneself not to leave all the penal institutions in a state of immobility and sclerosis, as has been done for so many years. It is to pledge onself to remain on the alert. It is to make penal practice a locus of constant reflection, research, and experience, of transformation. A penal system that claims to exert an effect on individuals and their lives cannot avoid perpetually transforming itself.

It is good, for ethical and political reasons, that the authority that exercises the right to punish should always be uneasy about that strange power and never feel too sure of itself.

NOTES

* This statement appeared in *Liberation* in September 1981. [eds.]

TO PUNISH IS THE MOST DIFFICULT THING THERE IS*

Q: *The abolition of capital punishment is a considerable step forward! Yet you prefer to speak of a "catching-up," while emphasizing the problem that is more important, in your view: the scandal of definitive sentences, which dispose of the guilty individual's case once and for all.*

You are of the opinion that no one is dangerous by nature and no one deserves to be labeled guilty for life. But in order to protect itself, doesn't society need a sentence that is sufficiently extended in time?

A: Let's draw a distinction. To condemn someone to a perpetual prison term is to transpose a medical or psychological diagnosis onto the judicial sentence; it is to say, "He is irredeemable." To impose a determinate sentence on someone is to ask a medical, psychological, or pedagogical practice to give a content to the judicial decision that punishes. In the first case, a (very uncertain) knowledge of the man serves as the basis for an act of justice, which is unacceptable; in the other, justice resorts, in its implementation, to "anthropological" techniques.

Q: *If we deny psychology's right to deliver a definitive diagnosis, on what basis can we decide that an individual, at the end of a sentence, is ready to reintegrate into society?*

A: We have to get out of the current situation, which is not satisfactory; but it cannot be superseded from one day to the next. For nearly two centuries our penal system has been "mixed." It aims to punish and it means to correct. So it mingles juridical practices and anthropological practices. No society like ours would accept a return to the pure "juridical" (which would penalize an act, without taking its author into account)—or a slide into the pure anthropological, where only the criminal (or even the potential criminal) would be considered, independently of his act.

An effort is called for, of course, to determine whether another system might be possible. An urgent effort, but long-term. For now, we must avoid the easy slippages. The slippages toward the pure juridical—the fixed-term sentence, as opposed to the self-defense groups. Or the slippage toward the pure anthropological: the indeterminate sentence (the Prisons Administration, the doctor, the psychologist deciding, as they see fit, the length of sentence served).

We must work inside this bifurcation, at least for the short term. A sentence is always a wager, a challenge addressed by judicial authority to the penitentiary institution: can you, in a given time, and with the means you possess, make it possible for the delinquent to reenter collective life without again resorting to illegality?

Q: *I would like to go back to the question of imprisonment, whose effectiveness you dispute. What type of penalty do you suggest then?*

A: Let us recognize that the criminal laws only penalize a few of the behaviors that can be harmful to others (look at industrial accidents, for example): there we have a first set of distinctions whose arbitrariness one may question. Then, among all the offenses actually committed, only a few are prosecuted (look at tax evasion): a second set of discriminations.

And among all the possible constraints by which a delinquent can be punished, our penal system has made use of very few—fines and imprisonment. There could be many others, appealing to other variables: public service, extra work, privation of certain rights. The constraint itself could be modulated by systems of obligation or contracts that would bind the individual's will other than by confining him.

I pity the current penitentiary administration more than I blame it: it is expected to "rehabilitate" a prisoner by "debilitating" him through imprisonment.

Q: *What you are proposing doesn't just assume a recasting of the penal system. It would be necessary for society to look at the convicted offender in a different way.*

A: To punish is the most difficult thing there is. A society such as ours needs to question every aspect of punishment as it is practiced everywhere: in the army, the schools, the factories (fortunately, on this last point, the amnesty law has lifted a corner of the veil).

That certain of our great moral problems—such is this one—are reappearing in the political domain, that in our day there is a new and serious challenge directed at politics by morality is a counter to all the cynicisms; this I find encouraging. I think it's good that these questions (we have seen this in regard to prisons, immigrants, and relations between the sexes) are being raised in a continual interplay between intellectual work and collective movements. Never mind all those who complain of seeing nothing around them worth seeing; they are blind. Many things have changed over the past twenty years, and there where it is essential for things to change: in thought, which is the way in which humans face reality.

NOTES

* Conducted by A. Spire, this interview appeared in *Témoignage chrétien* in September 1981. [eds.]

––––––––––

Q: *You have just returned from Poland. What can the Poles be feeling after the banning of Solidarity?*

A: I imagine that every French person—unless he is a French Communist Party official—was stunned when he read about the provisions approved the other day by the parliament. Before the Gdansk agreements in August of 1980, all independent labor unions were forbidden. According to the new legislation, "free" union activity is circumscribed in such a way that it will continually give rise to condemnations, interdictions, imprisonments. Yes, all that may well astonish us. But it hardly surprises the Poles, who know their socialism from experience.

Last week there was a good deal of tension. But what is remarkable about this whole history of the Solidarity movement is that people have not only struggled for freedom, democracy, and the exercise of basic rights but they have done so by exercising rights, freedom, and democracy. The movement's form and its purpose coincide. Look at what's happening right now: the workshops of Gdansk reply to the antistrike law by staging a strike.

The problem or, rather, one of the problems is to know whether and for how long it will be possible to maintain, in spite of the new legislation, this identity of objective and process.

Q: *While you were there, did you experience the reality of that Polish schizophrenia? On one side, the nation, on the other, the state, which of course have not spoken the same language for a long time, but are condemned to live together?*

A: I lived for more than a year in Poland, twenty years ago. Two things made a strong impression on me then. The first was that, for the Poles, the regime was something external that had been imposed on them following a war, an occupation, and as the result of the state of military and diplomatic forces in Europe. The Communist Party, the government (and the Russians behind them), constituted a foreign bloc to which they were obliged to submit. So I'm not sure that the analysis in terms of a totalitarian state is the right one for understanding what was occurring then and what is occurring today in Poland. Further, at that time the situation was still perceived—although fifteen years had gone by between the end of the war and the sixties—as a painful, persistent aftermath of the war. Because of that, an atmosphere of temporariness still bathed everything. In 1960, Warsaw was still in ruins. All the traces of the war were still visible. The war lingered on the horizon. That gave the Poles a historical perception very different from ours, because at that time the aftereffects of war were ten years behind us. Twenty years later, I found Warsaw completely rebuilt. The war's aftermath was forgotten. The gates of that great, savage, and terrible historical period are now closed and a new generation has appeared. But, at the same time, the situation they are in (the communist regime and the Soviet domination) look like a historical destiny to the Poles. Worse—like a future. The same state of affairs that, in 1958–60, recalled their worst fears now defines their future. This accounts for a historical sadness that exists in Poland.

Q: *Isn't there also the unreal feeling of belonging to a political past and a political camp to which they do not wish to belong?*

A: The Poles undoubtedly have, more than in the past, the feeling that their destiny is tied to a geopolitical and strategic situation that is what it is only because of what happened during the war, but that has become completely frozen now. The fact that the West perceives its own history as if the partition of Europe were now something definitively established—as definitive as the sinking of Atlantis or the separation of the continents—accentuates their anguish. We need to take this suffering into consideration, for we are ourselves implicated in their justifiable rancor.

Q: *And yet there were, after August 1980, several euphoric, almost miraculous months when the Poles saw authority recoil from their virtually unanimous rebellion.*
A: That's true. There were two extraordinary months of hope. Better still, of gaiety. For once, politics, while being upsetting, could also be joyful. There aren't so many countries in which politics can be a positive, lively, and intense experience for everyone. The Poles glimpsed an unblocking of their history. They were finally engaged in inventing a future for themselves, while never losing sight of the perilous and fragile character of their experience. There was such an intensity in the movement that no one could think in his heart, in his body and his everyday life that such a movement could be met by a total refusal, a state of war, and an emergency legislation. That being said, there is no way that what is currently happening can bring to heel twenty or thirty million Poles who reject the order that is imposed on them.

Q: *Is what we are seeing in Poland today a Pyrrhic "normalization"?*
A: One mustn't delude oneself or indulge in empty prophesying. We don't really know what will happen. But a certain number of things are already accomplished. When I speak of accomplishments, I'm not talking about freedoms and rights that may have been won at a given moment and most of which one may fear, in the current state of things, will be quashed. But in the behavior of the Poles there was an experience that can no longer be obliterated. What am I referring to? First, the consciousness they had of all being together. That is paramount. Thirty-five years of the previous regime had convinced them, finally, that the invention of new social relations was impossible. In a state like that one, each individual can be consumed by the difficulties of his own existence. One is, in every sense of the word, "occupied." This "occupation" is also the solitude, the dislocation of a society . . . So the Poles discovered something they knew but had never been able to bring fully into the light of day—their shared hatred of the regime. That hatred was inside each one of them, to be sure, but now surfaced and was clearly formulated in words, discourses, and texts, and it was

converted into the creation of something new and shared in common.

Q: *So what was involved was the moral awakening of a whole society?*
A: Yes. And that's very important. One often imagines that the socialist countries function on the basis of fear, terror, and repression. But they are also countries that run on schemes, favors, and rewards. After all, when five people live in two rooms, obtaining a third is a primary concern. In Poland, one can wait twelve years for an apartment. The thirteenth year, how does one resist a little concession, an indulgence, an arrangement? In these regimes that function as much on the basis of reward as on the basis of punishment, the reward is even more humiliating than the punishment, because it makes one an accomplice. Now, after Solidarity, after the collective formulation of all these individual hatreds, I believe that a certain number of these obliging or weary behaviors will become much more difficult. People are going to be much stronger in resisting all these petty mechanisms by which they were made, if not to sanction, at least to accept the worst. This moralization seems to me to be, in fact, a process that has been incorporated into people's behavior and will not be obliterated any time soon.

Q: *Are the Poles disappointed by the softness of the Western reactions after the coup of December 13?*
A: The Poles expect a lot from us personally. For isolated individuals or private groups such as Médecins du Monde to do something for them, go see them, talk with them, is actually very important to them. That can and should continue, unless the country again becomes a closed place one can neither enter nor leave. As long as one can get in, one must go there as often as possible. It is absolutely necessary to maintain contact. There is a real political effort and an effort of thought to be carried out with the Poles. As far as the political problems from state to state, it must be said that France's position was one of the firmest with respect to what happened on December 13. On the other hand, since January, the cultural, scientific, economic, and political cooperation between the East and the West was hard for Polish opinion to swallow. The restructuring of the debt, the gas pipeline, the French cosmonauts in Moscow—all that provoked a great resentment and a good deal of anger.

Q: *Would you say that in France one form of political and intellectual work concerning the Poles that should have priority would consist in doing some deep reflecting on this division of Europe in two, which is declared to be irreversible?*

A: I believe this is something that the Poles feel: there has been an abundance of reflection on Europe over the past thirty-five years—whether one thinks of the creation of a free exchange zone, the Atlantic Alliance, a more or less developed political integration ... But there was an impasse over the division of Europe in two, by a line that was not imaginary. It's a state of affairs that everyone is aware of, but it's still a political blank insofar as it isn't thought about and no longer causes a problem. It has become a familiar image, endlessly repeated stories—in short, a de facto situation. Neither those who govern, nor the political parties, nor the theorists, nor the Europeans themselves raise as a present, distressing, and intolerable problem the fact that in Europe there are two existing regimes. Two historical time frames. Two political forms that are not only incompatible but one of which is utterly intolerable. There are hundreds of millions of Europeans separated from us by a line that is both arbitrary in its reason for being and uncrossable in its reality: they are living in a regime of totally restricted freedoms, in a state of subright. This historical fracture of Europe is something that we must not resign ourselves to.

Q: *Is it also the role of intellectuals to face this problem?*

A: I was very struck, last December, by the insistence of some people on saying that this was not the time to raise this problem of Europe because in France there is a socialist experiment in which the communists are taking part and that would risk compromising it. Others were also able to say, "In any case, we don't have the means to raise this question in strategic and diplomatic terms, because today everything is controlled by the equilibrium of the two blocs." To the first objection, one can easily reply by saying, "On the contrary, it's because there is a socialist experiment in France that this question must be raised." All the more so, after all, because the form of collaboration between socialists and communists is not so clear and, concerning a problem as important as this one—namely, the partition of Europe, trade union freedoms in socialist countries—it is essential to know to what point the socialists and

the communists who govern us can act in concert. This would be
an excellent test. Their pact was wrapped in too much obscurity,
too many things unsaid for us not to seize every occasion to raise
these questions clearly and force them to answer clearly. As for the
strategic objection, it doesn't really hold up any better. We are told
that the situation of tension between the two blocs, the problem of
energy resources prevents us from raising those question in a re-
alistic way. That won't do. We know very well that in history it is
the unspoken problems that one day explode with the most violence. All the same, we do have to recall that Europe is currently
in a state of permanent imbalance. We also know perfectly well in
what state of economic fragility, of political distress the satellite
countries of the Soviet Union are immersed. So the immobility of
the past thirty-five years cannot in any way be mistaken for stability.
That is why we must no longer bury the global problem of Europe
in a political silence that will one day bring about a historical explosion.

Q: *But in regard to this European question, many people are paralyzed by a feeling of impotence and tell themselves: the Russians will
never let go of a single piece of their empire.*
A: The Russian empire, like all empires, is destined not to live on
indefinitely. The political, economic, and social successes of socialism in the Soviet style are not such that one cannot foresee serious difficulties, at least in the not-so-distant future. Why, then,
should we endow such a flagrant failure with the status of a historical destiny? It is extraordinary, really, that certain individuals
always recommend not to raise the problems that stem from that
glaring failure.

Q: *But there is a real problem caused by the alternating interest in
the hot points of the planet. One day it's Iran, another it's Lebanon, El
Salvador, Afghanistan, or Poland. Doesn't this form of jerky, inter-
mittent vigilance prohibit a sustained reflection and a sustained support for these countries that are always in a state of crisis or war?*
A: The fact that there is this succession of passions is often connected to the events themselves. It wasn't French intellectuals who
invented the siege of Beirut or the outlawing of Solidarity. Yet, a
continuity is created that is connected to the interests of each individual. As for the emotional aspect, it is, after all, the role of the

governed to take offense and put passion into their reactions. I do believe in the importance of political affect.

Q: *But how can an authentic human rights policy be developed on the basis of these political affects, these personal interests?*
A: If governments make human rights the structure and the very framework of their political action, that is well and good. But human rights are, above all, that which one confronts governments with. They are the limits that one places on all possible governments.

Q: *Can't one imagine that every political situation might be subjected to a human rights screening, so that no one could compromise those rights?*
A: There you have a wonderfully eighteenth-century perspective in which the recognition of a certain form of juridical rationality would make it possible to define good and evil in every possible situation. It is certain, for example, that in a situation as incredibly confused as the Lebanese affair, people did not perceive things in the same way. But after the Sabra and Shatila massacres, apart from a few extremist speeches, the most compelling part of the debate centered around the absolutely unacceptable character of the massacre of the Palestinians. I find that, on the whole, the debate was extremely interesting, from that standpoint. On the part of the friends of Israel, but also on the part of the pro-Palestinians, there was a kind of symmetrical anguish and concern. There was no attempt to dodge the issues. Let's leave aside, of course, the statements of the officials, which are not the ones that interest us. Neither Begin nor Arafat are people to whom we refer in order to think. Generally speaking, there was a rather extraordinary moral reflection in the face of that intolerable core that the massacres constituted. Many good people lament because nowadays there is no longer any dominant thought. Thank heaven! There is a labor of thought, a moral labor being carried out. There is a certain moralization of politics and a politicization of existence that are developing not through the obligatory reference to an ideology or to membership in a party but through a more direct contact of people with events and with their own choices of existence.

Q: *So thought concerning human rights should not be put in terms of a hegemonic [dominante] thought?*

A: Precisely. One must guard against reintroducing a hegemonic thought on the pretext of presenting a human rights theory or policy. After all, Leninism was presented as a human rights policy . . .

Q: *How did you react to the irritation manifested by the French socialists over the rapprochement that occurred between the CFDT and many intellectuals, including yourself, on the occasion of the Polish crisis?*

A: The anxiety of certain political officials with regard to this rapprochement is, in the end, very encouraging. That proves that politicians are always anxious about any kind of politico-intellectual work. They don't like that. And it's just as well that they don't. As for us, we are made for that. If I were a politician, I would make it a point to ask myself this essential question: what judgment will history pronounce on these heads of the greatest nations who, for thirty-five years, have not managed to solve any of the major political, diplomatic, and strategic problems that were raised by the war itself? Neither the problems of Korea, Indochina, the Middle East, nor of Europe were solved. There is a definitively negative judgment to be pronounced on that colossal incapacity. Those responsible for world politics have not been capable of solving a single one of the major problems that were raised by the last war. It's staggering.

Q: *So what can be done in the face of such situations of political and intellectual blockage?*

A: One has to react and avoid the mechanisms of obstruction that cause one to forget a reality, so that one gives it a status of non-existence because one hasn't been able to consider it.

Q: *So we mustn't "forget" the communist presence in the government?*

A: When one hears, for example, Mr. Gremetz say that a trade union in Poland must be prohibited in order to avoid civil war, I don't see how anyone could fail to register what he's saying! And keep from jumping out of their chairs!

Q: *Their socialist partners may be subject to distraction . . .*

A: If they are hard of hearing, their ears must be unblocked. By being pulled!

Q: *Unblocking ears is one of the tasks of intellectuals?*

A: Rather than saying what lesson intellectuals should give to others, I would prefer to give you the one I try to give myself. I don't really know what they mean by "intellectuals," all the people who describe, denounce, or scold them. I do know, on the other hand, what I have committed myself to, as an intellectual, which is to say, after all, a cerebro-spinal individual: to having a brain as supple as possible and a spinal column that's as straight as necessary.

NOTES

* Conducted by G. Anquetil, this interview appeared in *Les Nouvelle Littéraires* in October 1982. [eds.]

CONFRONTING GOVERNMENTS:
HUMAN RIGHTS*

————

W e are just private individuals here, with no other grounds for speaking, or for speaking together, than a certain shared difficulty in enduring what is taking place.

Of course, we accept the obvious fact that there's not much that we can do about the reasons why some men and women would rather leave their country than live in it. The fact is beyond our reach.

Who appointed us, then? No one. And that is precisely what constitutes our right. It seems to me that we need to bear in mind three principles that, I believe, guide this initiative, and many others that have preceded it: the *Île-de-Lumière*, Cape Anamour, the Airplane for El Salvador, Terre des Hommes, Amnesty International.

1. There exists an international citizenship that has its rights and its duties, and that obliges one to speak out against every abuse of power, whoever its author, whoever its victims. After all, we are all members of the community of the governed, and thereby obliged to show mutual solidarity.

2. Because they claim to be concerned with the welfare of societies, governments arrogate to themselves the right to pass off as profit or loss the human unhappiness that their decisions provoke or their negligence permits. It is a duty of this international citizenship to always bring the testimony of people's suffering to the eyes and ears of governments, sufferings for

which it's untrue that they are not responsible. The suffering of men must never be a silent residue of policy. It grounds an absolute right to stand up and speak to those who hold power.

3. We must reject the division of labor so often proposed to us: individuals can get indignant and talk; governments will reflect and act. It's true that good governments appreciate the holy indignation of the governed, provided it remains lyrical. I think we need to be aware that very often it is those who govern who talk, are capable only of talking, and want only to talk. Experience shows that one can and must refuse the theatrical role of pure and simple indignation that is proposed to us. Amnesty International, Terre des Hommes, and Médecins du monde are initiatives that have created this new right— that of private individuals to effectively intervene in the sphere of international policy and strategy. The will of individuals must make a place for itself in a reality of which governments have attempted to reserve a monopoly for themselves, that monopoly which we need to wrest from them little by little and day by day.

NOTES

* The occasion for this statment, published in *Libération* in June 1984, was the announcement in Geneva of the creation of an International Committee against Piracy. [eds.]

INDEX

abortion rights, xiii, 423–25

Actes, 394–402

Algerian War, 258, 271, 278–79, 444

Althusser, Louis, 250, 252, 265, 274

Amnesty International, xxxviii, 474–75

L'Ane: le Magazine freudien, 397, 402n1

Annales d'hygiène publique et de médecine légale, 151

Anti-Machiavel (Frederick II), 209–10

Anti-Oedipus (Deleuze, Guattari), 16–17, 106–10

Aquinas. *See* Thomas Aquinas

The Archaeology of Knowledge (Foucault), 240, 272

architecture, 349–59

Association for the Defense of Human Rights, 439

asylum, political, xiii, xxxvii, 426–28

Badinter, Robert, xxxii, 397

Bataille, Georges, 241, 246–49, 251–53, 257

Bazargan, Mehdi, xxviii, 439–42

Beccaria, Cesare de, 53–56, 60, 67, 70, 85, 186, 199

Bentham, Jeremy, xiv, 53–55, 58, 70–72, 186, 385; *Panopticon*, 232–33

Der Berlinsche Monatsshrift, xxxiv, 335, 443, 448n1

Bettelheim, Bruno, 225, 228n1

Beveridge, William Henry, 156, 156n8, 370–71, 381n1, 405

Bichat, Xavier, 136, 141

The Birth of the Clinic (Foucault), xvi, 111, 117, 240, 266, 281, 283

Blanchot, Maurice, 241, 243, 246–47, 251–53, 258

Botero, Giovanni, 314, 405–6, 416

Boucher, Philippe, 435–38; *Le Ghetto judiciare*, 438

Bulletin of the History of Medicine, 142

Bullough, Varn L.: *The Development of Medicine as a Profession . . .* , 136

Canguilhem, Georges, xvii, 255–56, 267

capitalism, 75–76, 86–87, 136–37, 255

Catholicism, 203, 334, 356–57

CFDT, 373, 381n2, 472

CGT, 396, 421, 422n2

Chemnitz, Bogislaw Philipp von: *De Ratione status*, 314, 406

Code of Criminal Procedure, 72–73

Collège de France, 135, 282, 289

Comit de mendicité, 102

communications, 337–39, 348n1

Communist Party, 269, 286, 444, 466

Confédération Française du Travail (CFDT), 373, 381n2, 472

Confédération Générale du Travail (CGT), 396, 421, 422n2

Corbin, Alain: *Les Filles de noces*, 360–61

crimes. *See* juridicial forms, infractions

Croissant, Klaus, xiii, xxxvii, 426, 428nn 1–2

"dangerous individual" concept, 176–200; accused, 176–79; civil law, 195–98; Criminal

"dangerous individual"
(*continued*)
Anthropology (Italian
School), 190, 193–95,
197–98; criminology,
176–79, 194–95, 198,
432–34; degeneration,
178–82, 189–95, 197,
199; demand for
repression, 192–93, 460–
61; *dementia or furor*,
180, 186–90, 200;
homocidal monomania,
182–85, 189–91;
individual judged by
what he is, 176–79, 197–
200; insanity, 182, 185,
189–91, 195–98; legalist
theory, xxix, 70–71,
85, 178–79, 193–94,
199–200, 432–34,
436–37; mitigating
circumstances, 56, 178–
79, 199; psychiatry,
criminal, 179–82;
responsibility, 176–79,
190–94, 289–90; risk,
185, 189, 195–200. *See
also* juridicial forms;
penal system
Daniel, Jean, 444, 446–47;
L'Ere des ruptures,
443
death penalty, xiii, 53, 55,
62–63, 66–67, 418–21,
427, 429, 434–36, 441,
454, 459–61
De Lamare, N.: *Treaty on
the Police*, 94, 320–23,
412–14
Deleuze, Gilles: *Anti-
Oedipus*, 16–17, 106–10
demography, 95–96, 101,
124–25, 139
Descartes, René, 10, 251,
335
Discipline and Punish
(Foucault), xiv–xvii,
xxvi, xxix, xxxv, 119–
20, 124, 240, 243, 291,
382–93, 397; anesthetic
effect, 234–38, 245–46
discontinuity, 248, 255
"dividing practices," xv,
326, 460–61

Dumézil, Georges, xxvi,
31, 262

Ecole des Beaux-Arts,
353
Ecole des Ponts et
Chaussées, 354
Les Enfants du paradis,
360
Enlightenment, xxxiv,
xxxix, 273, 298–300,
328–29, 335, 399, 443
L'Ere des ruptures, 443,
445, 447
Esquirol, Etienne, 180,
243
ethics, xxxiii–xxxix, 108–
10, 443–48
existentialism, 246–48,
257–58
extradition, political, xiii,
xxxvii, 426–28

families, 96–98, 101–2,
105, 206–8, 215–16, 218,
334
fascism, 108–10, 328
fiction, 172–74, 242–43
Foucault, Michel (on
his work), 239–97;
existentialism, 257–58;
experience and work,
240, 243–46; foreign
experiences, 258, 264;
history of sciences,
252–57; intellectual
formation of, 241–42,
246–59; intellectualism
in France, 246–49, 269–
72, 278–82; method,
xxiv–xxv, xxviii, 226–
38, 245–46; political
experience, 249–50,
278–84, 455–58;
structuralism, 113, 115,
250–51, 272. *See under*
individual titles for
works
"Foucault révolutionne
l'histoire," xxvi
Fourcroy, Antoine-
François de, 147, 149–
50
Frank, J. P.: *System einer
vollständigen

Medizinische Polizei,
404
Frankfurt School, 224,
272–78, 291, 299, 328,
403
French Communist Party
(PCF), 112–13, 249–50,
269, 271
Freud, Sigmund, 106–7,
118–19

Garafalo, B. R., 176–79;
Criminology, 192
"Garafalo principle," 176–
79
Le Ghetto judiciare, 435–
38
GIP, 281, 394, 418
GIS, 423, 425
Godin, Jean-Baptiste:
Familistère, 355–56
government, art of:
debate, 201–4; family
model of economy,
206–8, 215–16, 218;
individuals and things,
208–10; internal forms
governing, 201, 205–8;
obstacles to
development, 212–15;
population, xxiv, 215–
20; *The Prince*, 202–12;
sovereignty, xii, xxiii,
xxix–xxxiii, 122–23,
163, 168–69, 203–5, 210–
11, 214–15, 218–19;
statistics, 137–39, 151,
212, 215–16, 335, 408.
See also police
governmentality, xxiii–
xxix, 201–22;
appropriation of justice,
xxix–xxxiii, 459–61;
appropriation of social
control groups, xl, 62–
68, 71; civil society *vs*
state authority, xxviii–
xxix, 371–73, 378,
381n2; competition
among states, 408–9;
emphasis on, 218–22;
limits on, xxvii–xxviii,
351–52, 440; rights,
xxix–xxxiii, xxxvi,
xxxvii–xl, 426–28, 439–

42, 449–53, 465, 471–75; states, 201–2, 220–22, 408–9. *See also* political rationality; power relations; power techniques

Groupe d'Information sur la Santé (GIS), 423, 425

Groupe d'Information sur les Prisons (GIP), 281, 394, 418

Guattari, Félix: *Anti-Oedipus*, 16–17, 106–10

Habermas, Jürgan, 348n1, 357–59

health: children, 95–98; city, medical control of, 99, 105; collective control of, 91–101; costs, 424–25; dispensaries, 91, 102–3; doctors, 98–100, 102, 104–5, 136, 140–41, 423–25; education, 93, 96–99, 425; family role, 96–98, 101–2, 105; hospitals, 57, 72, 75–76, 78–79, 92–93, 99, 101–5; hygiene regime, 94, 98–105; individuals, 98, 105, 135–37, 155–56, 404–5; innoculation/ vacination, 98, 103; labor force maintenance, 93, 95; medical staff distribution, 102–5; medicine, 91, 100–101, 104–5; noso-politics, 91–92, 95–98; population (social body), 91–93, 95–96, 98, 101–2, 105; private medicine, 90–91, 98; social control groups, 91–93, 100. *See also* medicine, social; police; security, risks of

Health Service (England), 154

Hegel, Georg Wilhelm Friedrich, 58, 86, 116, 241, 246–49, 335, 392, 403

Heidegger, Martin, 257, 403

Herodote, 349, 364n1

historians, 226, 228, 236–38

history, 233, 276–78, 357–59, 368–69

The History of Sexuality (Foucault), xvi, xxiv–xxv, xxix, xxxv, 239–40, 284

Hitler, Adolf, 235, 238n2

Homer: *Iliad*, 17–18, 32–33, 304; *Odyssey*, 304

L'Homme, 115

Horkheimer, Max, 272–73, 450

Hulsman, Louk, 389–90

L'Humanité, 428

human rights, xxix–xxxiii, xxxvi, xxxvii–xl, 426–28, 439–42, 449–53, 465, 471–75

"human sciences," 59, 83–84, 86–87, 326–27

Husserl, Edmund, 112, 252, 403

ideology, 15, 87, 111, 116, 118–19, 132–33, 269

Île-de-Lumière, 474

imprisonment, 56, 65–67, 77, 85; abolishment of, 389–91; acceptance of, xxvii, 85–86, 225–27; correction by, 67, 385–89, 460 (*see also* normalization); effects of, 225, 385–86, 399–401, 418–21, 463; prisoners' rights, 419, 421; release conditions, 391–92; selection of, 384, 387–88, 394–95, 398; strategy of, 385–86; suspending law, xxix, 419, 421. *See also* juridicial forms; penalties; prisons; punishment

individuals: bodies, control of, 81–82, 125; decisionmaking, xxxiii, 294, 367–68, 405, 474–75; de-individualization,

109; discourse with power, 164–72; focus of pastoral power, xii, 300, 335; government focus, 208–10; government of oneself, 201–2; individualization, xxiv–xxv, 120, 300–3, 307–12, 325, 328–36, 356–57, 417; knowledge of self, 403–4; life and death, 404–5, 409; marginalization, 365, 367, 369, 380; medicalization, 98, 105, 135–37, 155–56, 404–5; normalization of, 57–59, 67, 71, 78–79, 87, 117, 255, 259, 385–89, 460; reason of state, xxiii, 405–9; totalization, xxiii–xxvii, 318–20, 325, 332, 334–36, 417

institutional sequestration, 73–87

intellectuals, role of, xii, xxxv–xxxix, 126–33, 285–91, 294, 297, 358–59, 384, 395–99, 453–58, 469–73. *See also* philosophy

internment, 111–13, 115, 117, 145–46, 167, 169, 181, 189, 227

Introduction to the Nonfascist Life, 108

Iran, xxxvi, 442, 449–51

Isocrates: *Areopagiticus*, 304

Julius, Nicolaus Heinrich: *Lessons on the Prisons*, 71–72

juridicial forms, 1–89; Ancient Germanic law, 34–37, 44; appropriation by state, 45, 52, 60; attorneys, 37–38; Carolingian Empire, 36, 42, 44–47; confession, 46, 430–31, 433; "discourse analysis," 2–3; evidence

juridicial forms
(*continued*)
and truth, 20–21, 23, 29–
30, 32–33; *examination*,
5, 19–20, 26, 58–59, 87;
feudal society, 37–42,
44, 80, 87; flagrant
offense, 44, 47; in
France, 53–55, 64–67;
games, 2–4, 17–19, 34–
38; goods, 40–42, 68–70;
Greek law, 32–34;
infractions, 36, 42–44,
47–49, 53, 55, 70–71,
73, 179–82, 192;
infrapower *[sous-
pouvoir]*, 86–87;
inquiry, 4–5, 16–32, 34,
44–52, 58–59, 87, 167;
interrogation, 45–47;
judgment *[sentence]*, 39,
43–52; laws, 35, 42–53,
55–56, 63–64, 69;
legalist theory, xxix, 70–
71, 85, 178–79, 193–94,
199–200, 432–34, 436–
37; *lettres de cachet*, 65–
67, 164, 167–72; in
Middle Ages, late, 42–
52; monarchical, 23–24,
32, 42–43, 45–46, 64–67;
normalization, 55, 57–
59, 67, 70–71, 78–79, 87;
penal law, 4, 53, 55–56;
penal system control,
xxix–xxxiii, 57, 391–95,
421, 435–38; political
power, 15–17, 31–32,
83, 86; prosecutors, 42–
47, 72–73; psychiatry/
psychology, 57, 84, 431–
34; punishment by
law, 66, 70, 82;
responsibility, legal,
176–79, 190–94, 289–90;
rights of accused, 439–
42; Roman Law, 36–37;
"rule of halves," 19–22;
society, injury to, 35, 53–
54, 56; *sumbolon*, 22,
24; tests, 5, 17–19, 31–
39, 44, 46–48, 50–51;
transgression and
lawbreaking, 48–49, 53,
63–64; used by social

control groups, 64–68;
violation and
knowledge, 9–10;
witnesses, 17–18, 26, 29–
30, 33, 39, 47, 51. *See
also* "dangerous
individual" concept;
penal system; truth

Kanapa, Jean, 235, 238n2
Kant, Emmanuel, 9–10,
13, 58; role of
philosophy, 298, 328–
29, 335–36, 358; "What
is Enlightenment,"
xxxiii–xxxv, xxxviii–
xxxix, 335–36, 403, 443
King, J.: *Science and
Rationalism in the
Government of Louis
XIV*, 317–19
Kirscheimer, Otto, 224,
273
knowledge, 13–15;
connaissance, 6, 10, 28–
32, 49, 256–57;
knowledge-power, xiv–
xix, 11–15, 32, 49–52,
59, 83–87, 283–86;
savoir, 6, 10, 17, 87,
255–57, 330–31
Koyré, Alexandre, 112, 252

labor, 66, 76–82, 86, 93,
95, 151–55, 465–69, 472.
See also institutional
sequestration
Lacan, Jacques, 151,
258
La Légende dorée, 162,
175n1
Landau, Alain:
*Mouvement pour la
Liberté de l'Avortement*,
423
La Perrièrre, Guillaume
de: *Miror Politique*,
203, 205–12
"law of the third
element." *See* "Garafalo
principle"
Left, xxxii, 113, 271, 444–
48, 454–55, 459;
nonorganized
movements, 395

LeMaitre, Alexandre: *La
Métropolite*, 352
Lessons on the Prisons
(Julius), 71–72
Lévi-Strauss, Claude, 250–
51, 274
liberalism, xxvii–xxviii,
352, 415
Liber de politia
(Huhenthal), 321–22
limit-experience, 241–46,
248, 251, 253, 256–57
Linnaeus, 362–63
literary forms, 172–75
Lyotard, Jean-François,
17, 357

Machiavelli, Nicollò: *The
Prince*, 202–12, 316,
406–7
madness, 182, 185, 189–
91, 195–98, 254–55, 259
Madness and Civilization
(Foucault), xvi, 111,
115, 117, 119–20, 239–
40, 243, 254, 258–61,
265–66, 268, 281, 283
Manon Lescaut, 174–75n
Maoists, 269–72
Marcuse, Herbert, 272–
73, 278
Marx, Karl, 137, 269, 274–
75
Marxism, 248–53, 257,
270, 274, 276, 279–82;
French neo-Marxists,
269–72; and intellectual
discourse, 106–7; on
structuralism, 262–65
Marxist-Leninists, 269
May '68, 270, 278–84
Médecins du Monde,
xxxviii, 468, 475
medicine, social, 90–91,
134–35, 155–56;
collective controls, 153–
56; disease control, 134–
35, 145–46, 149, 152,
154; doctors, 136, 140–
41; in England, 151–56;
in Germany, 137–42,
156; individuals,
medicalization of, 98,
105, 135–37, 155–56,
404–5; labor force

medicine, 151–55; medical police *[Medizinischepolizei]*, 140–42; medicine, 137, 141–42, 149–50; private medicine, 136, 156; private property, control of, 152–53; quarantine, 144–45; recordkeeping, 139–41, 145–46, 154; religious groups, 154–55; state medicine, 137–42; urban medicine, 142–51; welfare system, 153–54. *See also* health

Mémoires de deaux jeunes mariées, 168–69, 175n3

mercantilism, 139, 212–14, 320

Merleau-Ponty, Maurice, 247, 252, 448

Millot, J. A.: *Le Nestor français*, 97

Miror Politique (La Perrièrre), 203, 205–12

Mitterrand, François, xiii, 454–55, 458n1

Morgagni, Giambattista, 136, 141

Mouvement pour la Liberté de l'Avortement: (Foucault, Landau, Petit), 423

Nietzsche, Friedrich, 5–15, 251, 253, 256, 335, 359; discontinuity, 248–49; knowledge, xxvi, 10–15, 83, 241, 247; punishment, 388, 397, 403; *The Gay Science*, 6–7, 9–12; *On the Genealogy of Morals*, 7, 13; *The Will to Power*, 13

normalization, 57–59, 67, 71–71, 78–79, 87, 117, 255, 259, 385–89, 460

Le Nouvel Observateur, 428, 444–45

objective capacity, 337–39

Oedipal triangle, 16–32; power in, 19–22, 24–28

order, law and, xxii, xxvii, xxviii–xxxiii, 61–63, 435–38

The Order of Things (Foucault), 113–15, 261, 265–72, 275, 362–63

L'Ordre du discours, 282

Oui, nous avortons, 423

Palazzo, 314; *Discourse on Government and True Reason of State*, 314, 406

panopticism, 58–59, 71–87

Panopticon, 58–59, 72

PCF (French Communist Party), 112–13, 249–50, 269, 271, 279, 287, 396

pedagogical institutions, 57, 72, 75–76, 78–80, 83–84

Penal Code, 425, 434

penal system, 67, 83, 130; abolishment of, 389–91; architecture, 58, 71–72; asylums, 57, 75–76, 84; criminal as internal enemy, 54, 441; criminology, 57, 67, 84, 176–79, 192, 194–95, 198, 432–34; in England, 52–53; judiciary, separation from, 57, 391–95, 421, 435–38; in law, 4, 53–56, 70–71; psychiatry/psychology, 57, 84, 387–92, 431–34; theory, 111–13; therapeutic functions , 402. *See also* "dangerous individual" concept; imprisonment; juridicial forms; punishment

penalties, 35–36, 43, 54–56, 65–67, 70, 82; "dangerous individual," 193–95, 197–200; death, xiii, 53, 55, 62–63, 66–67, 418–21, 427, 429, 434–36, 441, 454, 459–61; "replacement penalties,"400–401,459–61

Perrault, Gilles, 429–30,

434n2; *Le Pull-over rouge*, 434

Petit, Jean-Yves: *Mouvement pour la Liberté de l'Avortement*, 423

Petit Larousse, 113

phenomenology, 116–18, 226, 241, 246–47, 251–53, 257–58

philosophy, xxxiv, xxxvi, 240, 246, 298, 328–29, 335–36, 358, 443–48. *See also* intellectuals, role of

Plato, 30–32, 116; *Critias*, 304; *Laws*, 304–5; *The Republic*, 30–31, 304–5, 407; *The Statesman*, xxvi, 304–7

Poland, 279, 283, 465

police, 167, 169, 318–23, 409–17; in art of government, 207, 212, 220; control of individuals, 318–19, 322, 351–52; "disciplinary society," xxvii, 56–70, 77–80, 83–84, 389; in France, 64–66, 320–21, 410–14; in Germany *[Polizeiwissenschaft]*, xxvii, 322–23, 414–16; health functions, 94–95; life in society as object of, 412–14; man as object of, 410–12; medical police *[Medizinischepolizei]*, 140–42; panopticism, 58–59, 71–87; population as object, xxiv, 215–20, 414–16; social control groups, xl, 60–66, 69, 77, 91–93, 100; supervision *[surveillance]*, 57–64, 71–73, 77–79, 91–92, 94–95, 99, 101–2; urbanism, focus on, 349–53. *See also* imprisonment; penal system; political reason

political parties, 288–89, 395–96, 455. *See also* individual parties political reason, 298–325; "crisis of governability," xxiii; excessive power of, xix, 298–99, 358, 440; freedom to resist, xiii, xxxvii–xl, 324, 449–53, 465–75; individualization of power, xxiv–xxvii, 120, 300–303, 307–12, 325, 328–36, 356–57, 417; intellectuals, role of, 358–59; pastoral themes, xii, xxvi–xxvii, xxvii, xxix, 300, 303–13, 315, 335, 356–57; philosophy, role of, 298–99, 358–59; questioning method, 298–300, 323–25; reason of state, 317–20; totalization, 318–20, 325

Pompidou, Georges-Jean-Raymond, 418–21

Poor Law, 153–54, 156n6

popular uprisings, 61–62, 143–44, 152, 449–52. *See also* revolution

power relations, 40–45, 47–49, 51–52, 83–87, 94, 106–10, 400; below state level ("microphysics"), xxiv–xxv, xxvii, 123–24; disalignment, 232–33

power techniques, xiv–xix, 116–25, 291–96, 331–35

Prinz, A.: *Social Defense*, 190, 198

prisons, 65, 83, 99, 111–13, 130, 224–26; architecture, 71–72, 77, 356–57; prison factories, 73–76, 80; union, 421, 422n2

psychiatry/psychology, 3, 16, 57, 84, 107–8, 184, 257, 259–60, 387–92, 400–402, 431–34, 462; reaction to Foucault, 234–35, 243, 260–61. *See also* "dangerous individual" concept

Public Law, 154

Le Pull-over rouge, 434

punishment, 122, 382–93, 395–96; definitive sentences, 460–64; determinism, 395–96; differentiating illegalities, 385–87, 436, 463; of individual potentiality, 391–92; infractions, 389–90; intellectuals, role of, 384, 395–99; judicial system role, 387–93, 402, 419, 421; means, rationality of, 382–88, 459–61; means, selection of, 394–95, 398–402, 462–64; moral conscience, 390–91; "people's justice," 402; prisoners' rights, 419, 421; and psychiatry, 387–92, 462; rationality of, 397–99; restoration as means of, 399–402; right to punish, 387–88, 390, 441, 459–61; in Sweden, 399–401; therapeutic functions, 402. *See also* imprisonment; penalties

Pythagoreans, 304–5, 310

Quesnay, François, 207–8

Rais, Gilles de, 163, 175n2

Ranucci, Christian, 429–34

Reading Capital, 265

recordkeeping, 139–41, 145–46, 154, 166, 169, 171–72

religion, 6–7, 46–47, 154–55, 203, 334, 440, 449–51; pastoral themes, xii, xxvii, xxix, 300, 303, 307–13, 315, 335, 356–57; social control groups, 60–64, 77, 91–93; transgression and lawbreaking, 48–49, 63–64

revolution, xxxiv, 123, 439, 446–47, 449–53

Revolutionary Penal Code, 55

rhetorical forms, 33–34

Ricoeur, Paul, 390–91

Rosen, George: "Cameralism and the Concept of Medical Police," 142; *A History of Public Health*, 142

Rousseau, Jean-Jacques, 54, 430; "Political Economy," 207, 218; *The Social Contract*, 218

Rumsay, T.K.: *Health and Sickness of Town Populations*, 153

Sade, Donatien-Alphonse-François de, 163, 175n2

Sade, Donatien Alphonse FranMarquis de, 163, 175n2

Saleilles, Raymond, 197–98

salubrity, 150–51

Sartre, Jean-Paul, 247–48, 251, 257, 261, 276, 281

School of Medicine, 105, 424

sciences, life, 255–56

security, risks of (social security), 153–54; arbitration, 372, 378; civil society *vs* state authority, xxviii, 371–73, 378, 381n2; conceptual basis, 370–73; conscience, xxxiii, 377–79; criteria for limits to access, 374–76; death, 380–81; decentralization, xxxiii, 370–73; dependency, 365–70; integration, 367, 370; marginalization, 365, 367, 369, 380; norms in health, 374–79; old age, 379–80; "right to health," 373–77; Solidarity movement,

371, 381n2; suicide, xxxiii, 380

Security, Territory, and Population (Foucault), 219

self-evidence, 226–29, 234, 238, 384, 443–48, 456–57

sexuality, 118–21, 125; control of, 35, 66, 81–82; self-subjectification, 327; space and, 357, 359–61

SFIO (Section Française d'internationale ouvrière), 247, 395

Simon, John, 154–55

Socialist Party, 286, 454

Socialist Party (France), xxxii, 384, 387, 395–96, 454–55, 469–70, 472

social security. *See* security, risks of

solidarity. *See* rights

Solidarity movement, 371, 381n2, 465–75

Solon, 27–28

Sophocles, 19–20, 26; *Antigone*, 33; *Electra*, 33; *Oedipus, the King*, xxvi, 17–33

sovereign, control in individual lives, 163, 168–69

Soviet Union, 260, 262, 265, 271, 274, 444, 470

space and power relations, 349–65; architecture, 349–57; city model, 349–52; communications technologies, 352–54; and exercise of freedom, 354–57; knowledge, spatialization of, 362–63; and sexuality, 357, 359–61; as technique of government, 349–53; urban environment, control for health, 146–51; urbanism, police focus on, 349–53

Spinoza: "The Meaning of Knowing," 11–12

Stalinism, 112, 250, 262–63, 271, 328

structuralism, 26, 113–16, 223, 241, 265

subject, 10–11, 241, 247, 331–32; "agonism," 342–43, 346–48, 348n3; excessive power, 327–29; freedom of subjects in, xxviii–ix, 340–43, 346–48, 348n2, 449–53; humans as, xv–xviii, 241–46, 326–27, 331; individualization techniques, 328–36; power, techniques of, 294–95, 331–35; rationalities of, 327–29; resistance, types of, xiii, xix–xxiii, xxxvii–xl, 295, 329–32, 449–553; strategies and, 329, 346–48; totalization procedures, 332, 334–36; types of relationships, 336–39, 341, 343, 348n1–348n2. *See also* governmentality; political reason; power relations

Sweden, 279, 283

Syndicate de la Magistrature, xxix, 438

"La Terre à tous promise," 448

La Terre des Homes, xxxviii, 474–75

Thomas Aquinas, Saint, 315, 406–7

Traum und Existenz (Binswanger), 257

Treaty on the Police (De Lamare), 94, 320–23, 412–14

Treilhard, Jean-Baptiste: *Code of Criminal Procedure*, 72–73

truth (and power), 126–33; discourse, 106, 116–18; ideology, 15, 87, 111, 116, 118–19, 132–33, 269; intellectuals'

role, 112–13, 126–33; normalization, xxix, 117–19, 122; power, negative functions of, 121–23; power, products of, xxi–xxiii, 118–21, 125; power, techniques of, 116–25; regimes, 237–38, 242; repression, 118–21; sciences, 111–15, 132–33; sexuality, 118–21, 125; sovereignty, xii, 122–23; structuralism, 113–16; subject constraining discourse, xxi–xxii, 116–18; truth regimes, xvi–xviii, xxxix–xl, 131–33, 237–38, 242. *See also* political rationality

truth (juridicial), 17–19; disclosure of, 18–20, 23–24, 30, 32–33; establishment mechanisms, 43–52; games, 2–4, 17–19, 34–38; gaze (sight), 20, 23–24, 29–30, 32, 47, 72–73; gods and disclosure of, 18–20, 23–24, 31–32; history of, 2, 4, 15; and limit-experience, 256–57; limits in intellectual discourse, 106; models, 15–16; philosophical forms, 33–34; power relations, 40–42; "rule of halves," 19–22; *sumbolon*, 22, 24; tests, 5, 17–19, 31–39, 44, 46–48, 50–51; verification and fabrication, 243–46

Tunisia, 279–83

Turquet de Mayerne, Louis: *Aristo-democratic Monarchy*, 317–20, 323, 410–13, 415

tyrants, 27–31

Union of the Left, 445–46

Veyne, Paul: *Le Pain dt le Cirque*, xxii–xxiv, 238

von Justi, Johann
Heinrich Gottlob:
Elements of Police, 322–
23, 414–16

war, xxi–xxii, 12, 35–36,
38–40, 116, 123–24, 466–
70

wealth, 41–42, 62–64, 68–
70, 76, 80–81, 87, 94
Weber, Max, xxix, 229–
31, 358, 403
welfare state. *See*
security, risks of
Wesley, John, 60–61

Willebrand, J. P.: *Précise
for the Police*, 322
Women's Liberation
Movement, 425
writers, as intellectuals,
127–29
writing, 239–42